IDEAS IN CONFLICT

Other Books by Edward McNall Burns

JAMES MADISON:
Philosopher of the Constitution   (1938)

WESTERN CIVILIZATIONS:
Their History and Their Culture
Sixth Edition (1963)

DAVID STARR JORDAN:
Prophet of Freedom   (1953)

WORLD CIVILIZATIONS
(with Philip L. Ralph) Third Edition (1964)

THE AMERICAN IDEA OF MISSION   (1957)

Ideas
IN CONFLICT

THE POLITICAL THEORIES OF
THE CONTEMPORARY WORLD

EDWARD McNALL BURNS, 1897—

NEW YORK
W · W · NORTON & COMPANY · INC ·

JA
83
B85
c.2

Library of Congress Catalog Card No. 60-7571

PRINTED IN THE UNITED STATES OF AMERICA
FOR THE PUBLISHERS BY THE VAIL-BALLOU PRESS

56789

To those graduate students whom
it has been my privilege to guide and instruct
in completing the requirements for the doctor's degree
in political philosophy:

DANIEL M. BERMAN
MARTIN BIRNBACH
JULES COHN
HARRIS I. EFFROSS
JOSEPH B. HAMPTON
DAVID MARS
WALTER E. VOLKOMER
NORMAN L. ZUCKER

Contents

Preface

The purpose of this book is to summarize and interpret the leading political theories and ideological movements from about 1900 to the present. Forays have had to be conducted into the nineteenth and preceding centuries for the sake of comparison or analysis or to gain perspective, but the span of the book is essentially that of the twentieth century. So brief a period may seem like a tiny segment of intellectual history, but this is largely because we are still in the midst of it. We do not think of our own time as history, nor do we stop to consider that our century is already well past its meridian, with a record of accomplishments that merits attention. Obviously, not every half-century period has been fertile enough in political thinking to justify a volume of exposition and analysis, but several have met that test. The period of Plato and Aristotle was one example. The age of Hobbes, Harrington, Sydney, and Locke was another. William A. Dunning devoted the third volume of his famous trilogy on political thought since the Greeks to the less-than-a-century period from Rousseau to Spencer. William L. Davidson considered the period from Bentham to John Stuart Mill to be sufficient to justify a sizable volume.

In all probability, historians of the future will look back upon the twentieth century as one of the most crucial in the records of mankind. They will doubtless invent neat characterizations for it, calling it perhaps the Age of World Conflict, the Age of Revolution and Counter-revolution, the Age of Competing Ideologies, or, more simply, the Age of Agony. It can certainly be described as all of these things, and a great many more besides. As a time of troubles, it may be supposed to have been unusually productive of political ideas. Most political theory has been born of turmoil and conflict. By way of example, we could cite the achievements of the Age of Contending States in ancient China, the period of the collapse of the city-states in ancient Greece, the seventeenth and eighteenth centuries of the modern era, and the so-called Critical Period of American history. It is a mistake, however, to suppose that every age of crisis gives rise to a high level of political thinking. Few such accomplishments grew out of the declining centuries of the Roman Empire. Evidently the time of troubles must not be an age of hopelessness, of despondency, or of escape from the problems of the practical world into some realm of passivity and otherworldliness. The fact that our century thus far has participated so actively in a clash of ideologies and has encouraged new viewpoints and new approaches to political problems may actually be a sign of basic intellectual health. Despite the clouds of pessimism that seem to encompass us, most of us apparently still have a great deal of confidence that remedies and solutions will ultimately be found. Such confidence, grounded upon knowledge and understanding, is the first prerequisite for distinguished achievement.

A substantial part of the political theory of the twentieth century has not been the work of political scientists. Much of it has emerged from the policies of men in power, whether statesmen or mountebanks. Some of it has been developed by philosophers like John Dewey and Bertrand Russell; by economists like J. A. Hobson and Friedrich Hayek; by sociologists like Max Weber and Émile Durkheim; by psychologists like Sigmund Freud and Erich Fromm; by literary men like T. S. Eliot and Aldous Huxley; and even by engineers like Vilfredo Pareto and Georges Sorel. But the situation described has not been peculiar to the twentieth century. Political theory has always sprung from heterogeneous sources. Aristotle was a biologist as well as a philosopher. John Locke was a physician. Montesquieu was a judge. Rousseau was an essayist and novelist. Herbert Spencer was an engineer and inventor. John Stuart Mill was a high official of the British East India Company.

Political theory has always been seeded and nourished by other branches of knowledge. This condition has become increasingly true in the twentieth century as boundary lines between disciplines have grown less distinct. It seems now almost as logical for an anthropologist or an economist to formulate theoretical judgments about politics as it is for a political scientist.

This book is not written in defense of any thesis or political doctrine. Nevertheless, it would be foolish to pretend that the author does not have a point of view. He sees the contemporary world as torn by philosophical conflict which seems to grow sharper with each passing year. This conflict has no necessary connection with the familiar polarity of democracy and totalitarianism but grows out of a cleavage along broader lines. On the one side are those philosophies which take an optimistic view of human nature, recognize the *possibility* of progress, accept the universality of change, welcome inquiry and experiment as sources of knowledge, and emphasize the values of tolerance and freedom. On the other side are those philosophies of pessimism which disparage human nature, reject the possibility of progress by human effort, deprecate science as a false messiah, glorify tradition and authority, and applaud coercion as an indispensable means of social control. The author does not hesitate to take his stand on the side of the first of these groups of philosophies.

The completion of this book would not have been possible without the assistance and counsel of numerous individuals whose services no words of appreciation can adequately measure. The author is indebted, most of all, to his colleague, Dr. Eugene J. Meehan, who has read every word of the manuscript and contributed enormously to its improvement by his discerning criticisms. The author is grateful also to Professor Neil A. McDonald of Douglass College and to Dr. Alfred deGrazia, formerly of Stanford University and subsequently Director of the Center for Applied Social Research at New York University, who have each read about a third of the chapters and offered valuable suggestions for their improvement. Others who have read portions of the manuscript or given thoughtful advice in connection with it include Professors Benjamin Baker, Sidney Ratner, Norman L. Stamps, and Henry R. Winkler of Rutgers University and Philip L. Ralph of Lake Erie College. Professor Edward R. Tannenbaum of Douglass College has supplied useful information on Integral Nationalism in France. Special gratitude is due to the Rutgers University Research Council for providing the funds to employ, in successive years, two research assistants, Mrs. Sunok Pai and Mr. Knud Rasmussen, to help with the collection of factual and bibliographical data and with the checking of references. The author is especially indebted to the second of these assistants, Mr. Rasmussen, for his interest and zeal in performing duties beyond the responsibilities of his assignment. Other graduate students have made more contributions than they may have realized, especially those who have participated in, or read papers for, the author's seminars. In this connection he would like to acknowledge his debt to Mrs. Charlotte N. Wehrfritz for material on Existentialism and to Drs. Martin Birnbach and Joseph B. Hampton for their contributions to an understanding of the political philosophies of the Neo-Freudians and Jean-Paul Sartre, respectively. Acknowledgment should be made also of the services of the Rutgers Library staff, particularly the members of the Reference Department, in responding so faithfully and efficiently to demands for checking data and answering questions. Finally, the author would be remiss if he failed to acknowledge his debt to his wife for her arduous labors of typing the manuscript, reading proof, checking references, and preparing the index—and for her loyalty, patience, and self-sacrifice. Without her contributions, this book would not have been possible.

EDWARD MCNALL BURNS

New Brunswick, New Jersey

PART ONE

Liberal and Democratic Theories

CHAPTER

I

The High Tide of Democracy

At the beginning of the twentieth century no political ideal seemed more solidly entrenched than that of democracy. Among most bourgeois liberals, intellectuals, and socialists it was esteemed as gospel. Only a few die-hard conservatives, disgruntled cynics, and hard-bitten defenders of direct action appeared to hold out against it. From the great revolutions of the seventeenth and eighteenth centuries it had been handed down as a shibboleth to nearly all who were dissatisfied with the relics of despotism and feudalism that still remained as encumbrances to progress in many countries. So strong was the faith in democracy that it made some headway even in such backward nations as Spain, Russia, and Turkey. France went through one revolution after another during the nineteenth century, each of them followed by constitutional changes designed to maximize popular rule. Though Britain accomplished her revolutions "by consent" instead of by violence, they were nonetheless effective in advancing the cause of democracy. The movement in the United States reached the farthest extremes of all, with its opening-up of the bulk of offices to popular election, with its policy of rotation in office, and its adoption about the turn of the century of such devices of direct democracy as the initiative, the referendum, and the recall.

3

1. Prophets of the Golden Age

Few words have been more loosely and variously defined than democracy. It has almost literally meant all things to all men. A story is told of the difficulties encountered by a diplomat from Paraguay newly arrived in the United States. Observing conditions in the country to which he was accredited and hearing democracy acclaimed as their source and inspiration, he was deeply troubled; for he had been led to believe that democracy was "what we have in Paraguay." Actually, political democracy has acquired throughout history two principal meanings. On the one hand, it has meant primarily a system of government based upon the principle of majority rule. In this sense it has been synonymous with the idea that the voice of the people is the voice of God. In expressing that voice the will of the majority is sovereign and is the supreme judge of what is right politically. The minority is always wrong, and can never claim any right against the majority except the right to exist and to strive to become the majority. This was the conception of democracy developed by Rousseau. It was basically the theory also of the Jacksonian Democrats and of many of their followers in the United States.

But democracy has had another and broader meaning given to it originally by the Stoics and made more precise and specific by the teachings of John Locke. In this broader sense democracy has been almost identical with what some writers refer to as liberalism. That is, it has been founded upon the conviction that all power is dangerous, and that therefore the only just government is a government of limited authority. The absolute sovereignty of the majority is no more to be trusted than the absolute power of an autocrat or an aristocracy. All governments must be surrounded by checks and limitations for the protection both of minorities and individuals. In part these restrictions take the form of mechanical devices to prevent the abuse of power, but in the main they consist of guaranties of civil and personal rights. John Locke considered these rights as basic ingredients of the law of nature. John Stuart Mill regarded them as privileges absolutely essential to the progress of civilization. Still others have conceived them as indispensable to human dignity or as qualities appertaining to man by virtue of the fact that he is a human being and not an animal. In all cases democracy of this type has been concerned more with freedom than with order, and at least as much with the sanctity of the individual as with the good of society.

During its Golden Age, which we may consider as the period from about 1900 to 1918, democracy was generally conceived from the first of the viewpoints described above. Rule by the majority was popularly regarded as the most salutary form of political system ever devised. If democracy had any defects, they could be cured, not by introducing elements from some opposite system, but by more democracy. Such was the approach predominantly expressed in the writings of such notables as James Bryce (1838–1922), A. Lawrence Lowell (1856–1943), and A. V. Dicey (1835–1922). In his time the most revered of Britons in the hearts of American citizens, Bryce climaxed a long career in Parliament and as a professor of civil law at Oxford by serving as ambassador to the United States from 1907 to 1912. In 1888 he published *The American Commonwealth* and in 1921 his more searching *Modern Democracies*. He defined democracy as "a government in which the will of the majority of qualified citizens rules . . ."[1] Hardly anywhere did he concern himself with the fundamental rights of individuals. Though he admonished democracies to cherish liberty, which he held to be "a life-giving spirit," he said nothing about it as an automatic limitation upon the powers of government. In *The American Commonwealth* he devoted a chapter to "The Tyranny of the Majority," but mostly for the purpose of rebuking the disciples of Alexis de Tocqueville for seeing dragons where none existed. According to Bryce, majority sovereignty was not a blemish upon the United States. Even her Western towns were havens of liberty. Taking the country all in all, it was hard to imagine more complete freedom to express one's views or to act as one pleased within the broad limits of the law.[2]

[1] *Modern Democracies*. New York, Macmillan, 1921, I, 22.
[2] *The American Commonwealth*. New York, Macmillan, 1922, II, 342–43.

In the philosophy of Lord Bryce, the all-important consideration was how to make the rule of the people more complete and
effective. He believed this despite a seemingly contradictory
tendency to depreciate the human race. He regarded the masses
as lazy and stated, "They willingly accept what is given them because they have nothing to do further than to receive it." [3] He
recognized a kind of iron law of oligarchy which would forever
stand in the way of actual government by the many. Yet in a
democratic framework this rule of the few would never be the
domination of an oligarchy of birth or of wealth but of those to
whom Nature has given qualities or opportunities she has
denied to the rest. Moreover, three vital and essential functions
will always remain in the hands of the people: They can prescribe the ends of government. They can choose their leaders.
And they can oppose and defeat a policy which their governors
may plan to adopt. At times they can even suggest an alternative
policy and procure its adoption. Thus, although government
may not be "by the people," it can always be "for the people." [4]

As for methods of bringing the sovereignty of the people as
close to reality as possible, Bryce had only a limited number of
suggestions to offer. One was better education of the masses.
Instruction must be provided, he asserted, for every man must
have his chance of using for the best whatever endowment Nature has given him. Yet mere knowledge is not sufficient. People
whose minds have been crammed with facts and have not been
taught to judge and reflect are little better qualified for the
duties of citizenship than those who have received no instruction
at all. From such a conclusion the distinguished Briton moved
logically to his second concrete proposal: for a revival of something akin to the New England town meeting. This institution,
he claimed, had the great merit of encouraging citizens to become interested in the business of the community, to acquire
familiarity with its needs by constant discussion, and to learn
to know and judge men.

Lord Bryce did not hesitate to recommend certain democratic

[3] *Studies in History and Jurisprudence.* New York, Oxford University
Press, 1901, II, 469.
[4] *Modern Democracies,* II, 550.

devices which many of his associates scarcely considered respectable. Pre-eminent among them was a frank recognition of party government. To be sure, he hoped there would be no degeneration into a multi-party system, and he deplored the growth of "Labour" parties, which, he naively supposed, appealed more to a class interest than did their older and more orthodox rivals. Nevertheless, he maintained that parties are inevitable, and that no one has shown how representative government can operate without them. So few people think seriously about any subject beyond their personal interests that public opinion would be vague and useless if parties did not operate to bring issues to the front, to stimulate discussion of them, and to marshal sentiment for or against them. Political parties keep a nation's mind alive and bring order out of chaos. In the parliamentary system of government, which he generally favored, they are especially needed. Otherwise, cabinet ministers would not know from one hour to the next whether they had a chance of getting their proposals through the legislative body. Without the support of disciplined, cohesive parties, cabinets would have no assurance of remaining in office more than a few days.

Not only party government but even some forms of direct democracy attracted Bryce's support. He disliked the initiative because the proposals initiated were often carelessly drafted and therefore confusing, and because they frequently embodied freakish or frivolous ideas. He did maintain, however, that the initiative could be made reasonably successful if those sponsoring a measure were required to obtain the services of an expert legal draftsman. Bryce had much to say in defense of the referendum. He applauded it especially as an unparalleled instrument of practical education in politics. It forced the citizen to think, to analyze an issue, to ask himself, Is this proposal sound in principle? Will it work? It seemed not to occur to him that few voters would indulge in such extensive reasoning. Many when confronted by any but the simplest legislative proposals would vote just as blindly for or against as they would for party labels or for unknown candidates for obscure offices.

It would be too much to expect that an observer with the

acumen of Viscount Bryce would accept democracy uncritically. In the first place, he held that it was not a government suited to all peoples. It was not appropriate for Russia or Turkey or China, and of course not for India. The natives of these countries, he argued, do not even want self-government; they merely resent the real or fancied oppression of those who rule over them. But democracy has fallen short of perfection even in the most politically advanced countries. It has failed to establish a sense of brotherhood among the peoples of the world and to abate the evils of nationalism. It has not exorcised the specter of class war or eliminated the danger of revolution. It has not purified or dignified politics or eradicated corruption. It has not enlisted in the service of the state the highest quality of leadership or a sufficient quantity of the best intellectual talent. Yet with all these deficiencies, government based upon the will of the majority must somehow prevail, "for the acceptance of its decision is the only alternative to force." "However grave the indictment that may be brought against democracy, its friends can answer, 'What better alternative do you offer?' " [5]

Second in the triumvirate of early prophets of the Golden Age of democracy was A. Lawrence Lowell. Born soon after the middle of the nineteenth century, he spent all his life among the Boston Brahmins. Following his graduation from Harvard he gave twenty years to the study and practice of law and then returned to his alma mater in 1897 as a lecturer in government. In 1900 he became professor and in 1909 President of the University. He served in the latter capacity twenty-four years. He published his first book, *Essays on Government,* in 1889 and his more famous *Public Opinion and Popular Government* in 1913.

At first glance, Lowell may appear to be a dubious champion of democracy. In his *Essays on Government* he wrote as if the functions of government should consist primarily of acts of negation. There were too many laws, too many political interferences with the enterprise and initiative of the people. He admired the Constitution of the United States, with all its restraints upon legislative power. He lauded especially the authority of the

[5] *Modern Democracies,* II, 390, 608.

Supreme Court to prevent inroads by the majority upon the sacred rights of minorities. He deplored the growth of socialism and of paternalism manifested in the tendency to regulate even the private morality of individuals. He considered a monarch less likely than the majority to inflict an absolute tyranny upon a nation. A monarch, he avowed, is restrained by public opinion as well as by fear of revolt, "Whereas a popular majority, or a representative assembly possessed of absolute power, being itself the organ of public opinion, has little except the votes of its own members to reckon with." [6]

Yet there can be little doubt that Lowell, after his fashion, was one of democracy's foremost prophets. He drew a distinction between democracy and the sacredness of private rights, considering them independent if not inconsistent principles. The former he defined, in its political aspect, as "popular government, the exercise of power by the mass of the people." [7] In his later work he did not condemn majority sovereignty, but described it in such a way as to divest it of much of its ordinary meaning. When he spoke of the sovereignty of the majority, he meant, not the numerical, but the *effective* majority. The latter he conceived as a body of men agreed upon the ends and aims of government and united by the conviction that their views ought to prevail. In order to make their will effective, they must constitute the great bulk of the citizens. But numbers do not confer authority to rule. A mere mass of citizens, with no interests or aims in common, do not have the right to control a government simply because of some passing allegiance to a victorious party. For this reason Lowell advocated restrictions on immigration in order to exclude elements that could not be readily assimilated into a homogeneous nation. He thought it desirable that the whole population should be capable of common aims and aspirations, and should have a common stock of political traditions. "Without homogeneity," he declared, "a nation may be great, but it can hardly be a successful democracy." [8]

[6] *Essays on Government.* Boston, Houghton Mifflin, 1889, p. 66.
[7] *Public Opinion and Popular Government.* New York, Longmans, 1913, p. 57.
[8] *Ibid.*, p. 36.

The two most important contributions of Lowell to democratic theory were undoubtedly his insistence upon the importance of experts in government and his vision of the role of political parties. He contended that the extensive use of trained officials by ancient Rome was the principal factor in preserving the long life of the Roman Empire and extending its influence. But he considered the need much greater in modern governments. We no longer assume, he pointed out, that a man who has been successful as a farmer or manufacturer is thereby qualified to manage a bank or operate a railroad. What better warrant do we have for the assumption that an untrained politician has the capacity to manage the finances, direct the education, or purify the water supply of a large city? This does not mean, he explained, that chief executives and heads of departments must be experts. But it does mean their principal subordinates should be drawn from a body of educated civil servants. He thought it regrettable that the United States should be the only great nation with a popular government that does not have permanent undersecretaries professionally trained for their jobs. Lowell agreed with Bryce on the importance of political parties as instruments for framing issues and directing and marshaling public opinion. In addition, he conceived of them as stabilizing influences. Parties, he held, are essentially conservative, operating to check political vagaries and to hold a balance between extremes. The division of an assembly into organized parties makes it less susceptible to the emotional appeals of demagogues. In like manner, the continued presence of an organized opposition is a restraint upon despotism.

Lowell was as keenly aware as Bryce of the shortcomings of democracy, and he was equally optimistic that remedies could be successfully applied. He thought the proponents of democracy habitually attempted too much, expecting to achieve the millennium by the extension of popular rule. This was particularly evident in their advocacy of direct legislation, rotation in office, and the direct primary. To Lowell, such devices seemed to be based upon the assumption that the multitude is omniscient. Lowell also singled out aspects of representative government in his time that left much to be desired. He recognized a growing distrust of legislatures and attributed it to the tendency of their members to subordinate community interests to local politics. The results were logrolling and pork-barrel legislation. Each member conceived it to be his function to serve as a messenger-boy for his district and to obtain for his constituents as many dams and post offices as he could wheedle out of the public treasury. Lowell believed that the best remedy for this would be to abolish private bills. America, he said, is the only country where questions that affect only particular localities are thrown into the vortex of national legislation. On the Continent of Europe they are regarded as administrative matters and are decided by the executive branch. In England they are subjected to a special procedure entirely different from that employed for public bills. Although Lowell did not mention the short ballot by name, he certainly approved of its objective. He believed that the quality of all public officials would be improved if the people were not called upon to choose so many by popular vote. His attitude was summed up in the motto: "Where you want skill, appoint; where you want representation, elect." [9]

The third of the noted early prophets of twentieth-century democracy, Albert Venn Dicey, was less prolific in original contributions to democratic theory than either Bryce or Lowell. He was also the most legalistic of the three. A graduate of Balliol College, Oxford, Dicey was admitted to the Inner Temple in London in 1863 and devoted nearly sixty years to the practice and teaching of law. He was the first legal scholar to clarify the significance of the "conventions" of the British Constitution, especially those upon which the cabinet system depends. A curious perversity, however, characterized most of his life. He was generally unsympathetic toward the new tendencies of British politics, and he regarded human nature with a jaundiced eye. Men, he asserted, are imitative creatures, indifferent to the detection of error and too indolent to expend their energies in the attainment of truth. Inventiveness and originality are "the rarest of all gifts." [10] In addition, he interlarded his observations on constitutional government with dogmas essentially incom-

[9] *Ibid.*, pp. 260–61.
[10] *Law and Opinion in England.* London, Macmillan, 1905, p. 436.

patible with democratic ideals. In the first place, he was a historical determinist. According to his view, the great reforms of the nineteenth century were not the result of increasing enlightenment or of deepening sympathy with the plight of the masses but of changing historical conditions. Secondly, he espoused a thesis of "cultural lag." Law-makers, he said, retain the prejudices and habits of thinking which they acquired in their youth. Consequently, when they legislate, they give effect to the ideas that were suitable to a period twenty or thirty years in the past. For this reason it often happens that an ideal or opinion will find its way into law when its force is already spent and it has become socially obsolete.

It should be noted, finally, that Dicey gave a prominent place in his writings to the irrational element in politics. He emphasized what he called the "apotheosis of instinct" or the "apotheosis of sentiment." This expressed itself, he maintained, in the sense of imperial greatness which the British people acquired at the turn of the century. This sentiment carried them through the Boer War and imbued them with a new spirit which could not be explained in rationalist terms. It made possible a ready acceptance of the doctrine that the day of small states is past, and that great empires are necessary for the preservation of free society.

It would be a mistake, however, to assume that Dicey was in any important degree antidemocratic. No one could have written more cogently on the power of public opinion. In fact, he went almost to the extreme of describing every government as in essence democratic, for he insisted that the authority of every ruler, no matter how seemingly powerful, depends in the final analysis upon the support of the people. He agreed with David Hume that "force is always on the side of the governed." Moreover, he had nothing but praise for the British parliamentary system. To his way of thinking, it combined perfectly the implementation of the will of the majority with protection for the rights of individuals under the supremacy of established laws. The reason for this he found in the fact that "Parliament speaks only through an Act of Parliament," which immediately becomes subject to judicial interpretation. And, trained as they are, the judges render their interpretations in accordance with the great traditions of liberty which have come down from the past.[11] Perhaps, above all, he admired democracy for its conservative influence. Though its mechanisms facilitated rapid change, the masses, he believed, were suspicious of radical innovations. He thought it a significant fact that the Established Church in England occupied a stronger position in 1904 than it had a hundred years earlier, and that aristocratic traditions generally continued to be firmly entrenched.

2. Progressive Democracy

If there was any one movement that epitomized democracy in its Golden Age, it was the Progressive movement which flourished in the United States from about 1905 to 1924. To be sure, it was not wholly new or original. Some of its thunder had reverberated from the Populists of the 1890's, with their advocacy of direct election of United States Senators; the initiative, referendum, and recall; direct primaries; graduated income taxes; and government ownership of railroads and telegraph and telephone lines. Their peerless spokesman, William Jennings Bryan, developed a concept of democracy virtually synonymous with the divine right of the majority. Whatever the masses wanted was, to him, the unimpeachable standard of political and moral right. Later, at the Scopes evolution trial in 1926, he extended his belief in the sovereignty of the masses to include the realm of science.

With the exception of the free-coinage-of-silver doctrine, the Progressives adopted nearly everything that the Populists had advocated. But the character of the two movements was radically different. Whereas Populism was confined primarily to the Middle West and the South, Progressivism appealed to almost every section except the South. The class basis of Populism was agrarian; that of Progressivism was much broader. It crystallized the discontent not only of farmers but of a motley collection of Brahmins, small-townsmen, lawyers, clergymen, and intellectuals who felt themselves deprived of status by the power

[11] *The Law of the Constitution.* London, Macmillan, 1893, p. 335.

and wealth of vulgar pork-packers, railroad magnates, and the barons of coal, oil, and steel. The Progressives added significant new doctrines of their own to those they had inherited from the Populists. They favored a much stronger element of Hamiltonianism than had been suggested by the Populists. For the Progressives, the state was not a necessary evil, but a powerful instrument for the general welfare in promoting prosperity, improving standards of living, and fostering the good life. More specifically, they demanded regulation of monopolies; prohibition of child labor; insurance against sickness, unemployment, and industrial accidents; pensions for the aged; corrupt-practices acts; reduction of the power of the courts as a means of strengthening representative government; and home rule for cities as a device to free them from the clutches of venal state legislatures. Quite a few of the leaders were enamored of Henry George's idea for a single tax on the unearned increment of land values. Numerous others advocated the short ballot and proportional representation. They lauded the former as a device for relieving the burden of choice on the voter and thereby enabling him to express his preferences more intelligently. They cherished proportional representation in the hope that it would weaken the old-line parties and give intelligent Mugwumps like themselves a voice in the government relative to their actual voting strength.

The list of outstanding Progressives ran the gamut of American public life: Senators like Robert M. La Follette, George W. Norris, William E. Borah, and Hiram W. Johnson; Governors like Joseph Folk and Charles Evans Hughes; civic reformers like Tom L. Johnson, Frederic C. Howe, and Lincoln Steffens; educators like Charles Van Hise of Wisconsin and David Starr Jordan of Stanford; and intellectual crusaders like the philosopher John Dewey and the *New Republic* editors Herbert Croly and Walter Weyl; and President Woodrow Wilson. Theodore Roosevelt must also be mentioned, not only because he was the Progressive nominee for President when the movement was at its peak, but also because he contributed the idea of the recall of judicial decisions to the Progressive body of doctrine. The two leaders, however, who deserve credit for developing most of the Progressive doctrine were probably La Follette and Woodrow Wilson.

Born in 1855 in a log cabin in Dane County, Wisconsin, Robert M. La Follette worked his way up from pioneer poverty to the governorship of his state in 1901. Four years later he was chosen to the United States Senate and was honored thrice by re-election. Shunted aside for the benefit of Theodore Roosevelt as Progressive candidate for President in 1912, he was finally made the standard-bearer of a resuscitated Progressive party in 1924. Though he waged a vigorous campaign and polled one-sixth of the total vote, his health was unequal to the strain, and he died the following year.

La Follette's democracy was based upon a sublime confidence in the wisdom and virtue of the people. Sometimes he spoke as if the common sense of the plain people was equal to all the exigencies of government; yet in his program known as the Wisconsin Idea he seemed to contradict this, for he insisted that the resources of the State University be made available to the legislature and to the various agencies of administration. It was the people, however, who must rescue the government from the corrupt bosses and from the wicked party machines. In his view, the paramount objective of all reform was the restoration to the voters of complete control over public officials. To achieve this, numerous measures were necessary. First, all offices must be made elective, including Federal judgeships. Second, the power of judicial review must be abolished, or at least severely curtailed. Third, the initiative, referendum, and recall must be applied not merely in the state and local spheres but in the Federal as well. And fourth, unlimited freedom must be granted for the discussion and propagation of ideas, no matter how radical or unconventional. He urged this last not as a natural right of the citizen but as an indispensable safety valve to prevent explosions. Bad ideas, he argued, "cannot live in the open air and under the sunlight of free, liberal discussion. But if you seek to repress them, if you force them into underground channels, if you get them where they cannot be answered, then they may do harm." [12]

Though La Follette accepted the support of the Socialists in the campaign of 1924, he did not subscribe to their basic prem-

[12] *Congressional Record*, Vol. 59, pp. 506–507, 1920.

ises. He believed in a substantial measure of collectivism, not as a good in itself but rather as a corrective of the defects of private ownership. About 1920 he declared himself willing to give the old theory of individual initiative a fair chance, but if the experiment failed he would then advocate government operation of all essential industries. In the meantime, he would urge government control and operation of facilities of transportation and communication. He maintained that public ownership of utilities had been successful every place in the world where it had been given a fair opportunity. At the same time, he never recommended collectivization of the land or such fundamental dogmas of the Marxist program as socialization of all means of production, the dictatorship of the proletariat, and the ultimate achievement of a classless society.

One year younger than La Follette, Woodrow Wilson was born in a Presbyterian parsonage in Staunton, Virginia, in 1856. His early years were spent amid the horrors of Reconstruction in the Carolinas and Georgia. Failing as a lawyer following his graduation from Princeton and the University of Virginia Law School, he entered Johns Hopkins to prepare himself for college teaching. He was awarded the Ph.D. in 1886 and taught successively at Bryn Mawr, Wesleyan, and Princeton. The last institution made him its president in 1902. Eight years later the old-guard Democratic politicians of New Jersey allowed themselves to be persuaded that Wilson would make an "ideal candidate" for Governor. Elected after a strenuous campaign, he achieved such success in combating the bosses and in pushing through a program of impressive reforms that he made himself a logical contender for the Presidential nomination in 1912. The Baltimore convention accorded him the honor on the forty-sixth ballot, and the split in the Republican party guaranteed his election. As President, Wilson devoted his first term to the realization of Progressive principles. He procured the enactment of a child-labor law, an eight-hour law on interstate railways, the Clayton Anti-Trust Act for the curbing of monopolies, and the establishment of the Federal Farm Loan system, the Federal Trade Commission, and the Federal Reserve system. The entire program he proudly named the New Freedom. It came to an untimely end, however, in 1916, as threats of a war with Germany darkened the skies. From that point on, political idealism for Woodrow Wilson was identical with the self-determination of nations protected by an international association pledged to maintain the *status quo* and to enforce the principle of collective security. To this ideal he virtually sacrificed his life, suffering a stroke in 1919 brought on by exhaustion from his crusade in behalf of the League of Nations. He died a broken and disillusioned man in 1924.

Wilson's democracy was in some ways quite different from that of La Follette. To begin with, he envisaged a much more limited role for the state. His economic theory was derived from the individualism of Louis D. Brandeis rather than from any collectivist sources. Though he accepted the graduated income tax and justified it as a means of leveling down large fortunes, he never advocated any form of government ownership. The Federal Trade Commission and the Federal Reserve system were essentially regulatory instruments. With respect to purely political reforms he was also more conservative. He supported the direct primary, but he had little interest in the initiative, referendum, and recall, and he was by no means as sharply critical of the power of the courts. More significant was the contrast with regard to popular election. Whereas La Follette urged election by direct vote of the people of as many officials as possible, Wilson endorsed the short ballot, complaining that he himself, in his own little borough of Princeton, was unable to make intelligent choices from the large number of names appearing on the ballot. It may be pertinent to add that Wilson was a late convert to the cause of reform. In his doctoral thesis, *Congressional Government,* published in 1886, he pilloried the evils resulting from the separation of the legislative and executive branches of the government, and arraigned the powers of Congressional committees. But from then on until his nomination for Governor of New Jersey he had been largely indifferent to proposals for political change. On at least one occasion he had expressed contempt for the "heresies" of Bryan.

That Wilson's general conception of democracy would be simple or even consistent would be almost too much to expect, in view of the shifting patterns of his active career. In his early life he placed so much stress upon habit, tradition, and use and wont as to give the impression of being a disciple of Sir Henry Maine or even of Edmund Burke. He contended that only "highly developed, self-conscious communities" were capable of self-government. They must have attained a sense of "common interests and of common standards of life and happiness" acquired through a long period of evolving tradition.[13] From all indications he had a low opinion of man's ability to improve society by devising new forms of political organization. "Constitutions are not inventions," he wrote. "They do not create our liberty. They are rooted in life, in fact, in circumstance, in environment." They are not the source of our liberty, but its expression. The fact of democracy comes first; institutions are merely its embodiment.[14] In some measure he was affected even by the blandishments of the Nordicists and of other exponents of the racial *mystique*. He thought it a deeply significant fact that "only in the United States, in a few other governments begotten of the English race, and in Switzerland, where old Teutonic habit has had the same persistency as in England" had democracy come to successful fruition.[15] This was because the Teutonic race had approached political institutions through habit. All other races had rushed prematurely into them. They had adopted democracy instead of cultivating it.

But Wilson said many other things which indicated a devotion to democracy in nearly all of its aspects. In an article written in 1901 he described it as "the most wholesome and livable kind of government the world had yet tried." [16] As he advanced toward the goals of the New Freedom, he abandoned the racist doctrine and gave increasing attention to ideals of equality, popular sovereignty, and the enhancement of the general welfare. He began to eulogize the common man, arguing

[13] *Constitutional Government in the United States.* New York, Columbia University Press, 1908, pp. 26, 51–52.

[14] R. S. Baker and W. E. Dodd, eds., *The Public Papers of Woodrow Wilson: College and State.* New York, Harper, 1925, II, 428–29.

[15] *An Old Master and Other Political Essays.* New York, Scribner, 1893, p. 118.

[16] S. K. Padover, ed., *Wilson's Ideals.* Washington, American Council on Public Affairs, 1942, p. 16.

that the genius which springs up from the ranks of ordinary people is the spirit which renews the youth and energies of a nation. He identified representative government with government by partisan majorities and described it as "the only known means of self-government." He disparaged the ideal of government as a mere policeman restraining individuals from doing each other injury. Calling attention to the growing complexity of society, he warned that it was not sufficient to deal merely with old conditions but that the law must step in and create new conditions designed to make life more livable and tolerable. These efforts, however, must spring not from charity but from justice. Benevolence never developed a strong man or a free nation. Schemes for social uplift must be based "upon the right of free men to breathe pure air, to live; upon the right of women to bear children, and not to be overburdened so that disease and breakdown will come upon them; upon the right of children to thrive and grow up and be strong." [17] At the same time, he did not neglect the libertarian aspect of democracy. Suppression, he argued in line with the views of many of his contemporaries, is dangerous. The wisest thing to do with a charlatan or rabble-rouser is to encourage him to hire a hall and display his folly to his fellow citizens. "Nothing chills nonsense like exposure to the air." And nothing gives pent-up feelings so good a chance to warp and poison people's minds as an attempt to hem them in and prevent them from finding an outlet.[18] Unfortunately, he seems to have forgotten these counsels of wisdom in dealing with the Debs case and the Bolshevik and syndicalist agitators of 1919–1920.

3. Latter-Day Champions

During the 1920's democracy went through a Gethsemane of doubt and disparagement stemming from various sources. Conservatism and the quest for normalcy made anything but dyed-in-the-wool reaction seem almost dangerously radical. Cynicism, prohibition, and the revolt of youth fanned the flames of an

[17] *The New Freedom.* New York, Doubleday, 1913, pp. 19–20, 218–19.
[18] *Constitutional Government*, p. 38.

anarchic individualism and made democratic idealism appear old-fashioned. New psychological discoveries which brought to the fore the irrational elements in human nature cast doubts upon the ability of men to govern themselves. At the end of the period the downward plunge of the economy through the spiral of depression led frightened and impatient folk to lose their faith in democracy and to demand authoritarian measures or government by specialists. Some pinned their hopes on Technocracy, while others cast longing eyes in the direction of socialism or to assorted forms of planning and share-the-wealth movements that bore an unsavory resemblance to fascism. However, as the initial shocks of the economic earthquake subsided, Western Europeans and Americans generally abandoned their fears and made efforts to salvage time-honored traditions. As a result, democracy was revived and rehabilitated in accordance with modern needs. It was even strengthened as fascism flung its brutal challenge to a free society and eventually engulfed the world in war.

Pre-eminent among the champions of democracy in the depression years was Franklin D. Roosevelt (1882–1945). As architect of the New Deal he affirmed the strength and adequacy of democratic government to provide for the needs of the hour. No matter what storms assailed, he never wavered in his robust optimism. In his Third Inaugural he hailed democracy as "the most humane, the most advanced, and in the end the most unconquerable of all forms of human society." He acclaimed the power of the people "expressed through the free ballot" as the surest protection against alien movements that sap at the foundations of the Republic.[19]

But democracy for Roosevelt was not a mere matter of universal suffrage and unhampered expression of the popular will. It must be a positive and constructive force in the daily lives of the people, and provide not merely for political but for economic needs. If men are forced to choose between liberty and bread, he asserted, they will choose bread. The real reason why democracy collapsed in a number of European countries was

[19] Samuel Rosenman, ed., *Public Papers and Addresses of Franklin D. Roosevelt*. New York, Random House, 1938–1950, XIII, 322.

not because the people disliked it but because they had "grown tired of unemployment and insecurity and of seeing their children hungry." [20] Although Roosevelt maintained that democratic government could accomplish everything necessary to restore economic justice without violating any of the liberties guaranteed by the Constitution, he showed little interest in mechanical restrictions upon the sovereignty of the majority. He revered the safeguards of personal rights in the First Ten Amendments, but he was not impressed by the sanctity of private property or the inviolability of the separation of powers. No President went farther in justifying experiment and expediency as cardinal political policies.

The function of interpreting democracy during the crisis of World War II was also performed by Roosevelt's Vice President, Henry A. Wallace (1888–). Wallace conceived of democracy partly in terms of social welfare and partly as a defense of the dignity and rights of the individual. Under the former he included economic democracy, which he defined as the "promotion of a stable but ascending general welfare by increasing the productivity of the people and distributing the income as evenly as possible without destroying incentives." Concern for the social welfare also necessitated ethnic democracy, or equality of opportunity for different races and minority groups. He thought the record of Britons and Americans particularly shameful in this regard. In fact, he believed that all Western nations might profit by the example of the Russians in moderating their attitude of superiority toward the colored races. A final ingredient of democracy, as Wallace conceived it, was education. He accepted the principle of majority rule, but only on condition that the people should have full opportunity to gain information concerning the problems needing solution. [21]

For Wallace, quite as much as for Roosevelt, democracy was inseparable from guaranties of personal rights and the sacredness of the individual. He insisted that the democratic body of faith must honor the right of the individual to use his talents

[20] Fireside Chat, April 14, 1940.
[21] *The Price of Freedom.* Washington, National Home Library Foundation, 1940, pp. 31–32; *The Century of the Common Man.* New York, Reynal and Hitchcock, 1944, pp. 37–39.

and abilities for the full attainment of whatever "great and
glorious conception" his mind had developed. He spoke also for
"tolerance and humor in recognizing the right of all men to be
different"; for freedom of speech, press, art, science, and religion; for "stability, order, and the avoidance of violence, bloodshed, and anarchy"; and for a "joyous faith in a progressive
future based on the intelligent and constructive efforts of all
the people to serve the general welfare." He affirmed his belief
that unlimited possibilities of human progress could be realized
if those who were talented in science, art, and religion could
"approach the unknown reverentially" without being forced to
glorify some particular despot, race, or nation.[22] Unfortunately,
he sullied many of his lofty professions by failing to perceive
any distinction between the liberal democracy of Western nations and the pseudo-democracy of Soviet Russia. Perhaps he
was deceived by the propaganda of the Soviets or the paper
guaranties in their constitution. Possibly he assumed that the
Communist dictatorship was a mere excrescence that would be
eliminated with the passage of time and the achievement of a
more prosperous economy.

It would be a mistake, of course, to suppose that the theory
of democracy in recent times has been developed only by oc-
cupants of the seats of the mighty. Important additions have
also been made by academicians. One of the most renowned was
Charles E. Merriam, born in 1874, who taught political science
at the University of Chicago from 1902 until his death in 1953.
He also found time to serve as Alderman of the City of Chicago,
to run for Mayor, to act as adviser to Presidents Theodore and
Franklin D. Roosevelt, and to apply his talents to membership
on the United States Loyalty Review Board, the Hoover Commission, and the National Resources Planning Board. He wrote
voluminously on almost every aspect of political science, from
political theory to political parties and public administration.
Merriam defined democracy as "not merely a form . . . but a
means through which the highest ideals of mankind may be
achieved." He scorned the theory that democratic government
is synonymous with inefficiency. Bourbon kings and tsars of

---

[22] *The Price of Freedom,* pp. 31–32.

Russia were guilty of far more egregious blundering than can commonly be found in democratic states. Even the dictators of the twentieth century, with all the advantages of science and technology at their disposal, were not able to avoid catastrophic errors. But Merriam believed that if democracy were to be made fully effective, it must be "streamlined." He saw nothing incompatible between the democratic system and the highest standards of scientific management now being applied in business and industry. "Freedom and efficiency are not opposites," he wrote, "but complementary one to the other." [23] Expedients he suggested for improving democracy included reducing the powers of the legislative branch to the decision of broad issues and the determination of policy, a centralized budget with provision for an item veto by the President, and a much greater use of skilled personnel by the executive branch of the government.

In defending democracy, Merriam wrote with evangelical zeal. Transformed in accordance with modern intellectual discoveries, the ideal, he maintained, would have virtually limitless possibilities for leading mankind into a Promised Land of freedom and abundance. Under the aegis of democracy, science would have the power to lift the burdens of war, famine, poverty, and disease from the brows of men. The attainment of such ends Merriam conceived to be one of the primary functions of democracy. Prosperity in his judgment had a vital importance which no spiritual satisfactions could fully replace. In fact, the former was to a large extent the key to the latter. For prosperity meant not simply more comforts and conveniences but better education, more cultural opportunities, and freedom from individual and social frustration. Squalor, filth, and ignorance never enhanced the dignity of man, but were always the fertile breeding grounds of superstition, fanaticism, race hatred, and injustice. Merriam did not hesitate to identify democracy with equality—not an equality of leveling-down but of building-up. He aspired to no Marxist aim of transforming the whole population into proletarians; instead, he looked forward to the *extinction* of the proletariat. Rather than crushing talent, democracy

[23] *On the Agenda of Democracy.* Cambridge, Harvard University Press, 1941, p. 5.

properly interpreted would make necessary the highest premium upon the utilization of talent and remove barriers against its realization. By its nature the democratic system must be predicated upon the assumption that "the gains of commonwealths are essentially mass gains and should be diffused through the mass by whom they were created as rapidly as possible." [24]

A more restrained philosophy of democracy is expounded by the Columbia University sociologist and professor of political theory, Robert M. MacIver (1882–). Educated at the University of Edinburgh and at Oriel College, Oxford, he was appointed Professor of Political Science at the University of Toronto in 1915. In 1927 he became Professor of Sociology at Barnard College and two years later Lieber Professor of Political Philosophy at Columbia. MacIver views democracy as essentially a means for consulting the wishes of the majority and at the same time protecting the rights of the minority. It does not mean the rule of the majority or the rule of the masses, since despots and dictators have undoubtedly had, in some cases, the support of a majority of their subjects. It is not a way of governing, regardless of how large the majority, but is "primarily a way of determining who shall govern and, broadly, to what ends." [25] Democracy requires fundamentally three things: universal suffrage, free discussion of political issues, and full opportunity for political parties to campaign for the votes of the people. Under no other system can the citizens be masters of their government, for under no other system is it possible to determine what the citizens want. Where there is no free exercise of opinion on questions of policy, nor any legal means whereby changing currents of opinion can find expression, it is the sheerest confusion to classify a system as democratic.

Like Viscount Bryce and Woodrow Wilson, MacIver does not regard democracy as suited to all peoples. He is more liberal than either in the exceptions he allows. Democracy cannot flourish where the people are sharply divided by racial or ethnic differences, or where the masses, through ignorance or poverty, are

[24] *The New Democracy and the New Despotism.* New York, Whittlesey House, 1939, p. 37.
[25] *The Web of Government.* New York, Macmillan, 1947, p. 198.

unable to participate in community life. It cannot be successful, either, under conditions of crisis or continued unsettlement. When men are disillusioned, bewildered, and beset by fears, they are almost certain to fall a prey to the first wily demagogue who promises them deliverance from their misery. In contrast with Merriam, he refuses to assign to democracy any direct connection with economic reform. It is of the essence of democracy that it be not tied to any program or creed. The people under a democratic system may approve a collectivist economy or reject it. Whatever their choice, they do not cease to be democratic. For democracy itself is a form of government, not an economic system. The "economic democracy" commonly identified with collectivism is a misnomer. Properly defined, it would mean that the workers in particular establishments or industries would elect the managers and boards of directors and participate in the decision of business issues.

In insisting thus upon democracy as a form of government with no necessary relation to programs or ideologies, MacIver seems to strike at least a minor note of inconsistency. He maintains that a democratic state is always a limited state, and then seeks to locate the limitations. In nations with written constitutions the problem is simple, but what of a country like Britain? Here he can only say that the protection of minorities depends upon an unwritten law or hallowed tradition that "certain principles, whether embodied in the ordinary laws or in the clauses of a constitution, are binding on the government, beyond its power to revoke." [26] Certainly such principles can scarcely be regarded as elements in a *form of government*.

One of the most profound and discerning democratic philosophers of recent times was the noted scholar and pillar of the British Labour party, A. D. Lindsay. Born in 1879, he joined the Fabian Society as an undergraduate. In 1906 he became a tutor in the classics at Oxford, in 1911 Jowett Lecturer in Philosophy, and in 1924 Master of Balliol College. He was subsequently appointed Vice-Chancellor of Oxford and was elevated to a peerage as Lord Lindsay of Birker a few years before his death in 1952. Lindsay's political philosophy was founded primarily upon

[26] *Ibid.*, pp. 203–204.

Aristotle and Rousseau. In common with the former he held the chief function of the state to be "to serve the community and in that service to make it more of a community." [27] Again, like Aristotle, he taught that this object could be attained primarily by education. The state, therefore, should operate largely as an educational institution, not only for the instruction of the young but of adults also. Lindsay believed that Rousseau had provided the clue to a correct understanding of the true nature of democracy. Democratic society cannot function on the basis of a mere counting of ballots. According to both Rousseau and Lindsay, when a man votes he does either one of two things: he casts his ballot for the advancement of his own particular interest, or else he votes for what he thinks is the common good. Only when he makes the latter choice is he expressing the general will, which is the essence of democracy. Just how the citizens were to be persuaded to subordinate their private interests to the common good, Lindsay did not explain. Probably he meant that this would be one of the functions of education.

Many other things than mere voting, even for the common good, would be necessary, in Lindsay's judgment, to constitute a real democracy. There must be full liberty of opinion and discussion. Democratic rule cannot be carried on unless the citizens can be kept constantly informed as to what is happening and given ample opportunities for questioning, criticism, and protest. As a second requirement, there must be a government of law. The constitution must be sovereign—instead of the commands of men, based upon crises or needs of the moment. A democratic society must also be cosmopolitan. It can recognize no distinctions of race, creed, or class. It must believe in not simply the rights of Englishmen or Americans, but the rights of man. More than this, it must be international. The nation, insofar as it unites men by emotion instead of by education and discussion, is the antithesis of democracy. Hitler was right when he said that democracy and internationalism go together. Finally, according to Lindsay, the democratic system must make ample provision for government by experts. It is no longer possible for a modern

[27] *The Modern Democratic State.* New York, Oxford University Press, 1947, I, 245.

government to conduct its business by simple rules of thumb or ordinary commonsense. But this does not mean that the average citizen is to play no significant role in political affairs. After all, he is the one who must bear the brunt of governmental policies. He knows when the shoe pinches, and, better than anyone else, he knows where it pinches. To devise means to correct the pinching, the trained specialist is necessary. Still, a definite place remains for the wisdom and sound judgment of the plain man. Such qualities are derived not from books or technical study, but from experience, from facing responsibilities, and from deep knowledge of the realities of life. People possessing these qualities should be vested with the final control over government. Nevertheless, they should not do the actual work of governing. That is a function to be performed only by experts.

Though Lindsay was a socialist, he was one of the least dogmatic and opinionated writers who ever professed that doctrine. He accepted the idea that the Industrial Revolution produced class divisions and intensified the antagonism between them. He even admitted the partial truth of the accusation that the state is an instrument of class domination. But he would have no truck with the Marxist theories of revolution, the dictatorship of the proletariat, or the inevitability of communism. He would not even agree that public ownership would be the panacea for economic ills. He spurned even more emphatically all suggestions of totalitarianism. The ideal state he envisaged would be a limited state, with an authority that would fall far short of directing the whole life of the community. Instead of enforcing the good life, its function would be to maintain such conditions as would enable its citizens to *lead* the good life. While Lindsay did not approve of weak government, he nevertheless insisted that the main reliance should not be force but consent, based upon understanding and intelligence. He conceded that under special and crucial circumstances there may even be a duty to disobey and resist the state. As for specific proposals to change the character of social democracy, he showed little enthusiasm for anything more than two favorite projects of liberal socialists in Britain. One was the extension of trade-union branches, cooperative guild meetings, workers' education classes, and discussion groups of all kinds that might serve to transform the mob into responsible citizens. The other was the establishment of a guaranteed national minimum to eliminate unemployment and starvation wages, and to prevent any industry from being carried on under conditions inimical to the public welfare.

4. Contemporary Critics

The period before and after World War I spawned a multitude of theorists who weighed democracy in the balance and found it wanting. Their popularity was due largely to the cynicism and disillusionment bred by imperialist rivalries, by the war itself, and by the peace conferences that followed. It was a consequence also of disclosures resulting from the intelligence tests given by the United States Army during the conflict—for example, that about half the people of the United States had a mental age not greater than that of a normal fourteen-year-old child. How, it was asked, could democracy succeed under such conditions?

Some of the new critics of democracy were belated followers of Social Darwinism, disciples in some cases of Friedrich Nietzsche, who looked upon the democratic system as an expression of misguided sympathy for weaklings and degenerates who would always be obstacles to the evolution of a superior humanity. Others were admirers of the hero worship and élitism of Thomas Carlyle. To such thinkers, only the select few who had distinguished themselves by beating down their fellows or by climbing to the highest rungs of the success-ladder were fit to rule. Still other critics were biologists or pseudo-biologists who found the facts of heredity so overwhelming as to make man the helpless victim of a ruthless ancestry. The most notorious exponent of this view was probably Albert E. Wiggam, popular-science writer and columnist for the Hearst newspapers. In his *New Decalogue of Science* he pontificated: "Biology warns us that nearly all the happiness and nearly all the misery of the world are due, not to environment, but to heredity; that the differences among men are, in the main, due to differences in the germ cells from which they are born." He then drew the convenient conclusion that aristocracy and inequality are "ordained by nature" and cannot be abolished by law.

The most radical opponents of democracy in the twentieth century have been élitists and authoritarians who have found little, if anything, good to say about popular government. Their ideas will be discussed in later chapters. But there have been other more moderate theorists who have discovered serious flaws in democracy without condemning it entirely. Notable among them are William McDougall (1871–1938), Graham Wallas (1858–1932), and Walter Lippmann (1889–   ). Born and educated in England, McDougall taught at Oxford and served in the British Medical Corps during World War I before being invited to Harvard to head its Department of Psychology. In 1927 he became Professor of Psychology at Duke University. McDougall's objections to democracy were founded upon his theory of human nature. He considered the nature of man to be predominantly non-rational. The behavior of human beings is motivated primarily by instincts, of which he discovered no fewer than eleven. Examples include pugnacity, flight, curiosity, sex, self-assertion, acquisition, and gregariousness. Each of the major instincts, he maintained, is accompanied by a related emotion. Thus pugnacity is accompanied by anger, flight by fear, curiosity by wonder, self-assertion by elation, and so forth. These instincts and their accompanying emotions are the very substance of human nature. As a consequence, "mankind is only a little bit reasonable, and to a great extent very unintelligently moved in quite unreasonable ways." [28] It should be noted that McDougall did not regard human nature as depraved. Animal-like it might be, but it had definite inherent tendencies for good. Numbered among the eleven instincts was an instinct of construction, and the instinct of mother-love was the source of benevolence and altruism. To this latter instinct McDougall traced such achievements as the abolition of slavery, and the adoption of social-welfare legislation for the benefit of the aged and the unfortunate. He insisted, nonetheless, that civilization was in danger from the inherited defects of human beings, and expressed his particular concern for the United

[28] *An Introduction to Social Psychology*. Boston, J. W. Luce, 1921, p. 11.

States in a book which he published in 1921, *Is America Safe for Democracy?* He denied that any nation could safely entrust control over its public affairs to hordes of undiscerning citizens dominated for the most part by instincts and feelings. He seemed to regard human nature as predetermined by heredity and recognized few possibilities for intellectual growth through education or environmental improvement.

More erudite and less extreme than McDougall was the noted British political scientist and Fabian socialist, Graham Wallas. Educated at Oxford, he gained experience in practical politics as a member of the London School Board and the London County Council. In 1914 he became a professor in the University of London. Two of his books, *Human Nature in Politics* and *The Great Society*, are virtually classics of political theory. Wallas conceived of human nature as made up of both rational and irrational elements. The latter, he said, offer no basis for social improvement. The only hope for civilization lies in securing the triumph of human reason. Unfortunately, the ordinary forms of democracy provide but little support for such a triumph. Candidates for office find it to their advantage to prey upon the gullibility of the masses. Capturing votes becomes largely an affair of manipulating subconscious minds. Words and images laden with emotional content are shrewdly exploited by political orators. The process of voting is seldom governed by an objective weighing of facts and issues. Instead, the voter is swayed by the emotional impulses aroused by clever slogans or by particularly appealing posters. The effects of non-rational factors are only slightly less evident in legislative assemblies, particularly those of sufficient size to reduce the role of the ordinary member to one of little consequence.

The solution to the problems raised by the dominance of the irrational in politics lay, according to Wallas, in two directions. First, he suggested that some gain might result from substituting more desirable slogans and images for the tawdry ones now in vogue, and suffusing them with emotional power. He was more deeply concerned with modifications of the political and social structure. He would extend education so as to raise the level of the voters' intelligence and make possible the management of political parties by men with a high degree of civic consciousness. He would do everything practicable to stimulate on election day a sense of responsibility and the seriousness of the occasion. He would have the citizens instructed to employ as much weighing and sifting of evidence before casting their votes as they would do if they were members of a jury. He would relieve the burden on the voters and enable them to make more intelligent judgments by diminishing the number of elective offices. To encourage more discussion and deliberation, legislative bodies would be reduced in size, and more of their work would be turned over to committees. The English House of Lords he would transform into something like a Royal Commission, or board of inquiry, to conduct investigations and collect information. By these means he hoped to give democracy a chance to succeed despite the deficiencies of human nature.

The third of the judicious and discriminating critics is the American journalist and philosopher Walter Lippmann. Receiving his bachelor's degree at Harvard in 1908, Lippmann stayed on for an extra year to pursue graduate study in philosophy. He became an assistant to the Secretary of War in 1917 and served as adviser to the American delegation to the Peace Conference in 1919. For many years he was an associate editor of the *New Republic* and editor of the *New York World*. His books are legion, ranging in scope and in time from *A Preface to Politics* (1913) to *Essays in the Public Philosophy* (1955). Instead of being interested primarily in psychology, Lippmann is a latter-day Platonist yearning for government by an informed élite devoted to the great ideals that have lifted man to a civilized level. In his early career he had occasionally paid homage to democracy. He referred to it at least once as "an enlightened form of government," providing not merely "a safeguard against ignorant tyrants" but "an insurance against benevolent despots as well." Its paramount value was educational, to convey wisdom about the people to their leaders and to force the leaders to learn to consult the people's interests.[29] In *Public Opinion* (1922) and *The Good Society* (1937), however, he was much less optimistic. Democracy now appeared as suited only to small

[29] *A Preface to Politics.* New York, Mitchell Kennerley, 1914, pp. 115–16.

and simple communities. The knowledge possessed by the majority of citizens was totally inadequate for the successful administration of complex modern states. In the main, it consisted of little but stereotypes, or "pictures in our heads." The ideal society would not be one ruled by "the sovereign but incompetent people," nor by despots enforcing an arbitrary will. Instead, it would have a government of limited authority, with the role of the people confined largely to giving consent and the power of the governors restrained by fundamental law descending from custom or embalmed in a constitution. It will be necessary to examine this conception at greater length in a succeeding chapter because of the relation it bears to the conservative movement of our own day.[30]

The decline of democracy since 1918 as the reigning political ideal must be assigned to a number of causes. Foremost among them was World War I and its legacy of disillusionment, resentment, frustration, and depression. When these eventuated in dictatorship and World War II, the cycle was complete. But all of these factors were to a large extent the product of an anterior influence. That influence was nationalism. Nationalism inspired the fears and jealousies which were largely responsible for the outbreak of war in 1914. The end of World War I brought no abatement of these emotions but fanned them more violently than ever. Democracy could hardly have been expected to flourish in such an environment, especially when suspicion and rivalry led to the development of trade wars and a mania for economic nationalism. These last two factors combined with the devastation and disruption of war to produce an economic catastrophe which seemed to demand authoritarian rule as the only remedy.

But part of the responsibility for the decline of democracy must be laid at the door of its major prophets. Many of them expected it to accomplish too much. This attitude was especially characteristic of such men as William Jennings Bryan, Robert M. La Follette, and Viscount Bryce. For the most part, all of them accepted what is sometimes called Jacobin, or ma-

[30] See Chapter Ten.

joritarian, democracy. Though several of them had qualms about the wisdom of ordinary citizens, they believed in the *right* of the masses to govern themselves and to pass judgment on the most complicated public issues. Bryan and La Follette, in particular, assumed a level of intelligence and of civic-mindedness beyond the capacity of the average person. They would have done well to have taken a leaf from the writings of Jefferson, who taught that the function of the masses is not to govern but to select those who are to do the governing. Some of democracy's later apostles have offered at least promising suggestions for averting its further decline. They would streamline it by making more effective use of government by experts. They would reduce the burden on the voters by limiting popular election to legislative and top-ranking executive officers. Above all, they would seek to prevent disillusionment with democracy by utilizing the government as a positive agency for advancing the general welfare. They would give to democracy not merely the character of a political ideal embodying constitutional rights and privileges; they would endow it also with such elements as equality of opportunity, the right to employment, and a fair return for one's labor. In short, they would make economic democracy of equal importance with political democracy.

ADDITIONAL READINGS *

Babbitt, Irving. *Democracy and Leadership.* Boston, Houghton Mifflin, 1924.

Barker, Ernest. *The Citizen's Choice.* Cambridge, England, Cambridge University Press, 1937.

————. *Reflections on Government.* London, Oxford University Press, 1948.

Becker, Carl. *Modern Democracy.* New Haven, Yale University Press, 1941.

Brown, Ivor. *The Meaning of Democracy.* London, Cobden-Sanderson, 1950.

* Reading lists at the end of chapters do not generally include works referred to in the footnotes to the chapters.

Commager, Henry Steele. *Majority Rule and Minority Rights.* New York, Oxford University Press, 1943.

Cram, Ralph Adams. *The End of Democracy.* Boston, Marshall Jones, 1937.

Edman, Irwin. *Fountainheads of Freedom.* New York, Reynal and Hitchcock, 1941.

Friedrich, Carl J. *Constitutional Government and Democracy.* Boston, Ginn, 1950.

———. *The New Belief in the Common Man.* Boston, Little, Brown, 1942.

Hofstadter, Richard. *The Age of Reform.* New York, Knopf, 1955.

Ickes, Harold L. *The New Democracy.* New York, Norton, 1934.

Krabbe, Hugo. *The Modern Idea of the State.* New York, D. Appleton, 1922.

Laski, Harold J. *Democracy in Crisis.* Chapel Hill, N. C., University of North Carolina Press, 1933.

Lerner, Max. *Ideas for the Ice Age.* New York, Viking, 1941.

———. *It Is Later Than You Think.* New York, Viking, 1939.

Lindsay, A. D. *The Essentials of Democracy.* Philadelphia, University of Pennsylvania Press, 1929.

MacIver, Robert M. *Leviathan and the People.* Baton Rouge, La., Louisiana State University Press, 1939.

———. *The Modern State.* New York, Oxford University Press, 1926.

McKeon, Richard, ed. *Democracy in a World of Tensions.* Chicago, University of Chicago Press, 1951.

Marriott, Sir J. A. R. *Dictatorship and Democracy.* Oxford, Clarendon Press, 1935.

Merriam, Charles E. *The New Democracy and the New Despotism.* New York, McGraw-Hill, 1939.

———. *What Is Democracy?* Chicago, University of Chicago Press, 1941.

Mims, Edwin, Jr. *The Majority of the People.* New York, Modern Age, 1941.

Noble, David W. *The Paradox of Progressive Thought.* Minneapolis, University of Minnesota Press, 1958.

Perry, Ralph Barton. *Shall Not Perish from the Earth.* New York, Vanguard, 1940.

THE HIGH TIDE OF DEMOCRACY

Reves, Emery. *A Democratic Manifesto*. New York, Random House, 1942.

Spitz, David. *Democracy and the Challenge of Power*. New York, Columbia University Press, 1958.

Stace, W. T. *The Destiny of Western Man*. New York, Reynal and Hitchcock, 1942.

Stapleton, Lawrence. *The Design of Democracy*. New York, Oxford University Press, 1949.

Tead, Ordway. *The Case for Democracy and Its Meaning for Modern Life*. New York, Association, 1938.

Trueblood, David E. *The Life We Prize*. New York, Harper, 1951.

Tugwell, Rexford G. *The Battle for Democracy*. New York, Columbia University Press, 1935.

CHAPTER

II

Contemporary Ideals
of Liberty

That liberty ought to have a close association with democracy seems almost self-evident. The relationship was recognized in Athens as early as the fifth century B.C. In his celebrated Funeral Oration, Pericles idealized the democracy of his countrymen in such a way as to include tolerance, the honoring of talent in every branch of achievement, and understanding of varying modes of behavior indulged in for mere pleasure. In like manner he portrayed liberty in terms of reverence, self-discipline, and "obedience to whosoever is set in authority, and to the laws, more especially to those which offer protection to the oppressed and those unwritten ordinances whose transgression brings admitted shame." The Fathers of the American Constitution affirmed with equal clarity the ideal relationship of self-government and liberty. They wanted liberty protected because they considered it indispensable to the conduct of representative government. After the beginning of the nineteenth century, however, the assumption that liberty should be allied with democracy became the target of a formidable attack. The Hegelians elevated the state to an object of worship, the instrument of God upon earth, and identified liberty with complete if voluntary subjection of the individual to the state's authority. At the other extreme, those who hated and feared the state, notably the anarchists, repudiated all coercive government and

made the will of the individual the supreme determinant of social action. The dichotomy of democracy and liberty persists to
our own time, and perhaps has grown wider as government
tends to be associated more and more with authority, and considerations of national security overshadow the sphere of freedom. Yet traditional liberty still has its defenders who, if not
so numerous, are just as zealous as those of earlier periods.

1. The Anarchist Thesis

Correctly defined, anarchism means opposition to government
based upon force. No anarchist with pretensions to philosophical understanding has ever proposed to dispense entirely with
government. He condemns the state, conceived as an agency of
coercion with armies, jails, and police, but he regards government as at least potentially a beneficent institution. He recognizes that every society must have some agency to pave streets,
maintain schools, and safeguard and promote sanitation and
health. But such agencies must be purely voluntary, with no
authority to use physical force against any citizen. An individual
refusing to conform or obey might be subjected to the pressure
of public opinion or invited to leave the community, but no
further punishment would be applied. Most anarchists assume
that human nature is inherently good, that men have a fundamental sense of decency that will cause them to comply voluntarily with all reasonable requests, and that agencies of coercion
pervert or destroy these noble impulses. Though some antisocial
offenses will continue to occur, they will be neither frequent
nor particularly serious. According to the anarchist, the elimination of the state will actually reduce crime, for the state itself
commits the greatest crimes through wars and the exploitation of
its members. Moreover, penitentiaries, jails, and so-called reform
schools serve largely to convert their inmates into more hardened criminals and to imbue them with a desire to get even
with society.

Anarchists of modern times fall for the most part into two
schools. The early proponents were generally economic individualists. William Godwin (1756–1836), for instance, urged the

possessors of property to give it away but espoused no theory of collective ownership of wealth. Although Pierre Proudhon (1809–1865) answered his own question, "What is property?" by calling it "theft," he limited his proposals for economic reorganization to advocating free credit and equitable exchange. The German anarchists Max Stirner (1806–1856) and Friedrich Nietzsche (1844–1900) were even more indifferent to schemes for economic reform.

The other and more important school of contemporary anarchists is what may be termed the collectivist school. With the outstanding exception of Count Leo Tolstoi, whose philosophy will be discussed in another connection, most of its members have also been revolutionists. The founder of collectivist anarchism was Mikhail Bakunin (1814–1876). Born a member of the Russian aristocracy, Bakunin dedicated his life to the cause of revolutionary anarchism, spent twelve years in prison, and was twice sentenced to death. For a time he was associated with Karl Marx in the propagation of socialism through the First International (International Workingmen's Association), but Marx repudiated him when he realized the significance of Bakunin's belief that the state could be abolished overnight. Bakunin condemned the state and its related institutions of religion and private property on the dual ground that they were unscientific and incompatible with true morality. The evolution of man, he contended, is from a primitive stage of animal impulses restrained by physical force to a higher stage in which ideal aims and self-discipline predominate. Coercive government, private property, and religion were natural institutions in this earlier stage, but the progress of mankind has left them outmoded. Not only is this true, but they have become immoral. True morality consists in doing good for its own sake, without fear of punishment or hope of reward. An act done under compulsion or for the sake of some prize or benefit is not a moral act. To the extent that the state imposes its will upon its subjects, and gives to the few exalted privileges over the many, it degrades and corrupts man's nature. Religion is no better. It sanctions evil institutions and blesses the possessors of power and privilege in their enjoyment of unmerited superiority. It diverts man's interest from the improvement of society and promotes superstition and credulity. The time has come in the evolution of humanity when religion should be displaced by science and other forms of useful knowledge.

According to Bakunin, the objectives of anarchism would be attained by a combination of evolution and revolution. Its followers would work to overcome ignorance of natural laws of social evolution and at the same time demolish where necessary the institutions standing in the way of that evolution. The anarchist revolution would involve the complete destruction of the churches and the coercive machinery of the state. In addition, all titles to private property would be obliterated. Inevitably, some bloodshed would occur, both because of counter-revolutionary activities by supporters of the old regime and because of acts of vengeance by the masses against their former oppressors. Although Bakunin did not welcome such acts of violence, he considered it impossible to prevent them. After the revolution the anarchist leaders would proceed to reorganize society on the basis of voluntary collaboration. The society would take possession of the land and all the materials and instruments of production. These would then be leased to individuals and associations, under contract to use them productively. Local associations would gradually merge into larger associations, until eventually they would cover all of Europe and ultimately the whole world.

Bakunin left a number of disciples. One was the Italian Enrico Malatesta (1853–1932). Expelled from medical school for participating in a student demonstration, Malatesta learned the trade of electrician. For a time he was a follower of Garibaldi and then joined the Italian section of the First International. In this affiliation he came under the influence of Bakunin. After Bakunin's death he turned to the career of an agitator and conspirator, participating in two bloody uprisings. His life thereafter was an alternation of wanderings and prison sentences in various countries of the Western world. As a revolutionist, Malatesta developed a scheme for a kind of united front of all parties opposed to the existing system. He advocated a combined effort of anarchists, socialists, and syndicalists to overthrow capitalism and the capitalist state, and then hoped to convert all of them to anarchism once the revolution had succeeded. The influence of this program in Latin countries was seen during the Spanish Civil War of 1936–1939. A more important contribution of Malatesta was his development of a theory of communism to complement the philosophy of anarchism. This theory received its clearest exposition in the writings of the most noted of Bakunin's disciples, Prince Peter Kropotkin (1842–1919).

Prince Kropotkin was a scientist as well as a political philosopher. One of his first books bore the title, *Mutual Aid a Factor of Evolution*. In it he attempted to show, by copious examples chosen from his own research, that the Darwinian principle of natural selection had frequently been misunderstood. Nature, he pointed out, is not red in tooth and claw nor is the race always to the swift or the battle to the strong. Instead, an ability to cooperate with other members of the species often confers survival powers superior to those of ruthless competition. With many organisms, mutual aid rather than a struggle for existence is actually the law of life. Kropotkin attempted to apply this principle to the human species. He believed that the effects of struggle, war, and savage competition had been grossly exaggerated as factors in the improvement of the human race. Instead of preserving the fittest and best, they often destroyed these very types. Moreover, they put a premium on selfishness and brutality which it would be hard to reconcile with civilized standards. Like the *philosophes* of the eighteenth-century Enlightenment, Kropotkin maintained that human beings, freed from tyranny and exploitation, would live peaceably together, respecting each other's rights, and cooperating for mutual advantage without being forced to do so.

Kropotkin condemned the whole system of political and economic arrangements in modern society. He divided existing laws into three classes—laws for the protection of property, laws for the protection of government, and laws for the protection of persons. Those in the first category, he said, rob the producer of a portion of what he has created, and protect the privileged few in the enjoyment of what they have stolen either from the producer himself or from society as a whole. Laws for the protection of government serve essentially the same purpose, since the mission of all governments is to maintain by force the privileges and position of the possessing classes. Laws for the protection of persons are equally useless and vicious. The abolition of private property will eliminate the motive for most crimes, which is the desire to gain as much wealth as possible in the quickest and easiest way. As for crimes resulting from passion or hatred, nothing can be done to prevent them. The most drastic penalties imaginable will not serve as deterrents against them. Therefore, if all punishments were abolished, there would be no increase in the number of crimes. In all probability they would decrease, since there would no longer be prisons to brutalize men or to school them in the commission of greater crimes.

With the overthrow of the state, Kropotkin would set up an association of free communes composed of individuals banded together for a definite economic purpose. The original communes, in turn, would federate with others in neighboring localities until eventually a large area would be covered by voluntary organizations seeking mutual advantages. Thus a foundation would be laid for an entire social structure resting upon consent instead of establishment by force. Perhaps more important would be the provisions for the economic system. Kropotkin embraced the principle of complete communism. Everyone would work in accordance with his talent or ability and be entitled to draw from the common fund of wealth produced in accordance with his needs. Even the demands of the sluggard would not be denied. As a human being he could not be refused his right to subsistence. But no one would need to work very hard. If the profit system were abolished, labor requirements could be reduced to less than half their present minimum. The result would be increased opportunities for all members of the population for cultural and social pursuits. On the basis of his private researches Kropotkin estimated that 300 half-days of five hours each would be sufficient to provide for all the material needs of a family of five for a year. Furthermore, the working life of any citizen need not extend beyond the age of forty-five or fifty.

Under Kropotkin's anarchism most of the conditions now obtaining in the economic sphere would cease to exist. Production would be decentralized, so that men would work partly in the factories and partly in the fields. Manual work would no longer be performed by a degraded class, nor would intellectual labors be the monopoly of a privileged few. Instead, both types would be shared by all to the extent of their abilities. Payment would be exclusively on the basis of need. Kropotkin denied the justice of any other system. It is impossible, he argued, to discriminate among workers as to the relative merits of their positions. Is the job of the electrician in a coal mine more important, he asked, than that of the miners who dig the coal? Does the superintendent in his office make a more valuable contribution than those of his subordinates who go down into the pit and risk their lives every minute? Or is the farmer who feeds the miners of less consequence than they? There is manifestly no justice, according to Kropotkin, in rewarding workers on the basis of their abilities or talents or the supposed value of their contributions to society. The logical alternative is to pay them in proportion to need. The man with a large family should be entitled to draw more from the common fund than the man with few children or no family at all. The man in delicate health would have greater needs and therefore should receive more generous allowances than his more robust comrade, even though the amount of work he performed might be considerably less. After the elemental needs of all members of the community had been provided for, any surplus remaining would be divided equally.

The last of the anarchist theorists who requires a brief word of comment was Johann Most (1846–1906). Most was born in Germany of parents so poor that the father could not find the money to pay for a marriage license until two years after the birth of his son. Young Most struggled against hardships and misfortune—brutal employers, a cruel stepmother, and an accident which disfigured him for the rest of his life. Though he was imprisoned for two years in Austria and three in Germany, he was elected twice to the Reichstag as a representative of the

Socialist party. Gradually his ideas veered more and more in the direction of extremism, and he became an anarchist. Following his expulsion from Germany, he established himself in London as editor of a weekly organ, *Die Freiheit*, transferring in 1882 to the United States. He soon gained an unenviable reputation as the foremost exponent of terroristic anarchism. He formulated the idea that especially obnoxious public officials should be singled out and assassinated as a means of striking terror into the hearts of all members of the governing classes. Designated "propaganda by the deed," such measures were supposed to attract attention to the anarchist movement and give proof that it could not be ignored. Most was accused of having been partly responsible for much of the violence occurring in the United States between 1882 and 1906, including the Haymarket Square riots and the assassination of President McKinley. Though sentenced for three terms in prison, he was never convicted of a terroristic act. His punishments were always for what he said, never for what he did.

Since the early 1920's, anarchism as an organized political movement has been practically defunct. In scarcely any country of the world at the present time would its supporters equal a corporal's guard. The reasons for the swift decline are not far to seek. The rise of communism and its apparent success in Russia seemed to offer to extremists of the left their brightest ray of hope. To almost everyone the economic disasters of 1929 and the years following magnified the need for the state and made its services appear indispensable. Its erstwhile enemies dreamed no longer of absolute liberty; what they wanted now was the image of a benevolent father who would take their hand in his and guide them across the darkling plain. Finally, the emergence of fascism emphasized for many people the idea that strong government was the one best means of saving a nation from being engulfed by a devastating flood.

2. The Sovereign Individual

In a different category from the anarchists have been those theorists who have placed the individual upon so exalted a pedestal as to make the defense of his freedom the prime consideration of political policy. They have not despised the state as an unnecessary evil, or even as a necessary one. On the contrary, they have generally regarded it as a positive good, or at least as an essential regulatory instrument to safeguard liberty. In no sense is it an end in itself, but a mere means to an end. Nevertheless, all power is dangerous. Whether exercised by government or by economic associations, it must be surrounded by safeguards. The one effective way to curb it is to set power as a check on power. Without such controls, no group or individual, either public or private, is to be trusted.

The views described above were exemplified especially by two Americans of widely different political interests. The first was Louis D. Brandeis (1856–1941), and the second was H. L. Mencken (1880–1956). Brandeis, the son of Jewish immigrants from Bohemia, graduated from Harvard Law School with the highest average in the records of the institution. He became an eminently successful corporation lawyer (dealing, however, only with the heads of corporations as his personal clients, not with the companies themselves) and left a fortune when he died of over $3,000,000. He was a staunch defender also of the rights of labor and of the interests of the public against monopolies. When in 1916 he was appointed by President Wilson to the Supreme Court he already had acquired so fearsome a reputation for unorthodox opinions that his nomination was only reluctantly confirmed by the Senate. Brandeis was, first of all, an ardent champion of political liberty. The right of the citizen to take part in government, he argued, necessarily includes the right to discuss political issues, to express any opinion about them, and to attempt to persuade others that his views are correct. Interference with this right cannot be reconciled with the operation of democracy. According to Brandeis, the Fathers of our government recognized this. They believed that freedom is indispensable to the discovery and spread of political truth, that public discussion is a political duty, and that "the greatest menace to freedom is an inert people." They realized that order cannot be maintained by force alone or by fear of punishment. They knew that "fear breeds repression; that repression breeds hate; that hate menaces stable government."[1] The path of safety lies in providing full opportunity to discuss grievances and to propose remedies. The appropriate medicine for evil counsels is good ones.

Nevertheless, freedom of expression, as Brandeis conceived it, is not absolute. Its exercise is subject to restriction, if necessary, in order to protect the state from destruction, or even from serious injury. But the situation must be one of crisis, fraught with the threat that dire consequences will occur before there is opportunity for full discussion. If there is time to refute the falsehood or fallacies by argument, or to combat the evil by education, the remedy to be applied is more discussion, not enforced silence. Only an emergency, Brandeis believed, can justify a policy of repression. No minor danger or fears of harm will suffice. In the days of our ancestors men feared witches and burned them. When such irrational fears prevail, it is the function of free discussion to combat them. To justify restriction of such discussion, there must be reasonable ground to believe that a serious evil is actually imminent and that it will befall if freedom of expression is permitted. What the eminent jurist seems to have meant was that plotting or planning to commit an overt act against the state must actually be under way before suppression of freedom of speech or of press would be justified.

Brandeis attached so much importance to liberty that he demanded it not only for individuals but for nations as well. He was one of the originators of the doctrine of self-determination of nations and seems to have been largely responsible for influencing President Wilson to espouse that principle. Unlike Wilson, however, he seemed to have little interest in internationalism. According to Brandeis, history has proved that peoples have individuality no less conspicuous than that of single persons, and that the "misnamed internationalism" which seeks to blot out nationalities or peoples is an impossibility. Each "race" or nation, like each individual, has the right and the duty to develop in accordance with its peculiar character, and only as a consequence of such development can a high civilization be achieved. Faith in nationality has inspired whole peoples

[1] *Gilbert v. Minnesota*, 254 U.S. 325.

with hope, confidence, and self-respect. It has ennobled them, offered them a future, and infused their lives with purpose. The assertion of nationality lifted the Irish from a fatal despondency. It roused the Greeks and Serbs to throw off their oppressors. It unified Italy. That it also fired some other peoples with beliefs in manifest destiny, in "sacred egoism," in irredentism, in race superiority, and in revenge movements he failed to mention.

The great jurist's primary interest in self-determination was to further the aims of Zionism. He regarded the Jews as not simply a nationality but a "race." He admitted that during the 3,000 years of the Jews' historic period, some intermarriage with non-Jews had taken place. But he thought the chief result had been a series of subtractions from the Jewish community. Few additions had ever been made. As a consequence, the Jews were probably the purest "important race" in Europe. Through Zionism alone the spirit of this pure race could reach its full and natural development. To be sure, not all of the world's Jews could find homes in Palestine. The land was not large enough to accommodate more than three million of them. But to believe that Palestine is doomed to remain sterile and treeless is patently absurd. The country was made sterile and treeless by man's mismanagement. With intelligent care it would be capable of becoming again "a land flowing with milk and honey." It has the climate, topography, and agricultural possibilities of a "miniature California." But it is not necessary that more than a small percentage of the Jews should actually live there. That those who wished to go there could do so would fill the hearts of all the others with hope and pride. From a homeland in Palestine the Jewish spirit would radiate and spread the inspiration which comes from memories of a glorious past and confidence in a splendid future. In fact, Brandeis maintained that the best interests of America, and presumably of other lands, demanded that every Jew become a Zionist. For only through the ennobling effect of Zionism's strivings could the son of Israel develop the best that was in him and give to his country the full benefit of Judaism's great inheritance.[2]

[2] O. K. Fraenkel, ed., *The Curse of Bigness*. New York, Viking, 1934, pp. 209–28.

In the opinion of Justice Brandeis political liberty is not by itself a guaranty of complete freedom. The individual can never be entirely free as a result of serving on juries or exercising an unrestricted right to vote as he pleases and to run for office. Not even full enjoyment of all the privileges of the Bill of Rights would give him the ultimate liberty that he ought to enjoy as a human being. The difficulty springs from the fact that the individual is not free economically. So long as the citizen has no voice in the determination of matters that vitally affect his livelihood, but must accept the bidding of a master who pays him a wage, such privileges as the right to keep and bear arms or to assemble peaceably and petition for a redress of grievances are woefully inadequate. And Brandeis believed that this was the fate that was rapidly overtaking a large proportion of industrial workers. He saw the growth of giant corporations destroying the independence of the individual enterprises and creating for the worker an existence so inhuman as to "make our former Negro slavery infinitely preferable." The master, at least, owned the slave and therefore had an incentive to provide him with decent care. The new monopolies considered their employees as creatures to be worked to the point of exhaustion and then thrown aside. The result was physical and moral degeneracy and the divesting of human beings of every quality that raised them above the level of animals. The reason for this exploitation, according to Brandeis, was not the inherent depravity of the employers, but the fact that excessive power corrupts those who wield it. The very size of a great corporation deprives its managers of a sense of responsibility for their workers. They are the agents of a multitude of absentee owners, the stockholders, who care for nothing but increased dividends. Such a system, Brandeis believed, made economic democracy impossible and industrial oligarchy inevitable. He wondered how long, under the circumstances, political democracy could actually endure. He argued, moreover, that the excesses of big business were the chief factors paving the way for communism or socialism. He scolded socialistic thinkers for laughing up their sleeves at the operations of Morgan and Rockefeller. "They see approaching the glad day when monopoly shall have brought all industry and finance under a single head, so that with the cutting of a single neck, as Nero vainly wished for his Christian subjects, destruction of the enemy may be accomplished." [3]

Brandeis suggested numerous reforms to preserve the sovereignty of the individual he prized so highly. To begin with, he would abolish all forms of corporate giantism that fostered monopoly and irresponsibility. He admitted that competition involves waste, but so, he contended, does democracy. The gains in both cases counterbalance the losses. He recommended, in addition, positive measures for preserving the freedom and self-reliance of the individual. One would be the maintenance of private property and private enterprise. He opposed all forms of government ownership, and he doubted that any man can be really free unless he has a substantial measure of economic independence. He proposed further that labor unions be fully protected in their right to use collective bargaining as a check on capitalist tyranny. He believed that power must always be set to curb power, and that bringing representatives of capital and labor together in direct negotiation would force each side to see the other's point of view. Though he emphasized the importance of shorter working hours and regular periods of rest, he was just as deeply concerned with a higher standard of living. To this end he recommended a guaranteed annual wage, which would be a fixed charge upon the operations of industry, in the same class with interest on bonds or other indebtedness. In his judgment, irregularity of employment was one of the worst features of the industrial system. The time had come, he maintained, when society and labor should demand continuity of employment. The best way to ensure it was to insist that workingmen be paid throughout the year, in the same manner as the officers of the corporation. If the employees had to be paid at regular intervals whether they worked or not, they would undoubtedly be kept working. The results would be improved morale, greater productivity, and more wealth for distribution among all the citizens.

[3] A. T. Mason, *The Brandeis Way*. Princeton, Princeton University Press, 1938, p. 68.

As a final recourse for strengthening the sovereignty of the individual, Brandeis presented a strong case for industrial democracy. He argued that the position of the average worker, so far as his livelihood is concerned, is that of a mere subject bound to the will of an oligarchy. He has no control whatever over company policy and little or no voice in determining his economic fate. But democracy in the industrial sphere is just as important as in the political. It is essential for the proper education and development of the individual and for giving him the status of a free man instead of a human tool. The solution is to be found in participation by labor representatives in all important company decisions. Competent representatives of the workers should sit on the board of directors and grapple with problems of profit and loss, hiring and firing, and creating and supplying markets. They would acquire in this way a sense of dignity and a knowledge of how difficult it is to run a business. It would be an expedient better than profit-sharing, for it would give to its beneficiaries a consciousness of responsibility and make them citizens of the realm most vital to them—that which provides their livelihood. In no other way can the destiny of the great mass of our people be fulfilled. Democracy must be concerned not merely with the provision of social justice but with the perfection of manhood. The basis of democracy, Brandeis insisted, is the free individual. Its success, therefore, is possible only where the process of perfecting the individual is zealously pursued.

Except for their fervid defense of the individual, Brandeis and H. L. Mencken had so little in common that it would hardly be justifiable to refer to them in the same breath. Whereas Brandeis was a democrat, Mencken was an aristocrat and even an admirer of enlightened monarchy. The jurist extolled the common man and believed him capable of almost infinite improvement. The Baltimore editor and critic despised the multitude, regarding its members as unspeakably swinish and utterly beyond redemption. While Brandeis looked to the state as the instrument whereby reformers might make their dreams a reality, Mencken distrusted the state as a mere agency of police tyranny and looked upon reformers as meddlers and visionaries more likely to do harm than good. Even their doctrines of individualism differed widely. For Brandeis, individual fulfillment meant freedom from political and economic tyranny. For Mencken, it meant freedom from the tyranny of the mob, with opportunities for the enlightened few to pursue their cultural interests unhindered by Puritans and charlatans.

Henry Louis Mencken began his career as a journalist. For years he wrote for the Baltimore *Herald* and for the famous Sunpapers of his native city. In 1908 he became literary critic of the *Smart Set* and subsequently editor. From 1924 to 1933 he was editor of *The American Mercury*. In addition he found time to write such pungent and challenging books as *Prejudices, Notes on Democracy, The American Language,* and *Minority Report*. Mencken conceived of the superior individual as a solitary, isolated figure, as lonely as Prometheus on his rock. Though the storms of passion and barbarism might rage around him, his duty was to remain steadfast and unflinching. He could do this, however, only if the howling dervishes of mob resentment were kept in their place. For, according to Mencken, the masses are the great enemy of civilization. Everything of value that has ever been accomplished has been the work of talented individuals, striving alone or with the help and encouragement of a very small number of kindred spirits. The multitude sometimes accepts these accomplishments and makes them its own; more often it denounces them and attempts to prevent their use or adoption. The dominating passion of the mob is envy. Its members hate what they cannot understand, and tend to be jealous of every individual who rises above their intellectual level. Behind all the great tyrants and butchers of history they have marched "with loud hosannas." They chose Nero and Torquemada by instinct, and condemned Socrates and Galileo by the same instinct. They seldom recognize either their own interest or the interest of civilization. They encumber the statute books with anti-evolution, anti-vivisection, and anti-vaccination laws. They authorize the licensing of chiropractors, naturopaths, and "other such frauds." They have no more regard for liberty than Wat Tyler had for learning, when he justified the hanging of everyone who confessed to being able to read and write.

They do not even want liberty; they merely want to be safe.

In the light of the foregoing it should not be surprising that Mencken condemned democracy as the worst form of government on earth. Though he conceded that it had a few merits which he never got around to describing, he regarded it as fundamentally out of line with scientific discoveries as to the nature of man. Science, or at any rate *his* "science," had shown that the lower orders have almost no capacity to use or understand abstractions. Their minds cannot grasp even the simplest ideas. All their thinking is done on the level of appetites and emotions. "It is thus a sheer impossibility to educate them, as much so as it would be if they were devoid of the five senses." [4] Man has changed but little since the earliest dawn of history, and that change has been for the worse quite as often as for the better. He is still ignorant, superstitious, lazy, shiftless, and unclean. Whenever he is confronted by a choice between two ideas, one true and the other false, he chooses almost invariably, and by a sort of perverse compulsion, the one that is false. To make matters worse, according to Mencken, a kind of animal depravity has dogged man's footsteps ever since he descended from the tree-top homes of his arboreal ancestors. He is rapacious, slavish, stubborn, envious, and spiteful. For example, there is nothing to equal the wolfishness of peasants, who still constitute the majority of inhabitants of most countries. They may be thought of as the "sediment remaining in the filter after the stream of progress has gone through." A shade superior is the proletariat, but only because it includes the "more intelligent yokels who have had the wit to escape from the dreadful drudgery of the dunghill." [5]

Mencken also blasted democracy for what he considered its association with Puritanism. The two, he contended, are but different sides of the same coin. Both derive their basic substance from the inferior man's envy and hatred of his betters. He sees the superior man having an easier time going through this tragic world than he has. Therefore, he must seek to hold him back, to hamstring him, or to push him down. Hence ascetic laws

[4] *Notes on Democracy.* New York, Knopf, 1926, p. 21.
[5] *Ibid.*, p. 33.

like prohibition that impose restrictions upon liberty, and egalitarian measures to force the competent and frugal to take care
of the slothful and improvident. It is not strange, according to
Mencken, that "witch-hunting," "priestcraft," and persecution of
minorities should flourish in the very country which prides itself most upon its democracy. For these are the virtues of
Puritanism, and he who fails to understand Puritanism will
never understand democracy.

The political philosophy of H. L. Mencken was almost entirely a negative one. It was alien to his nature to do much
dreaming about the future or to formulate plans for an ideal
society. In so far as he had any program at all, it was a suggestion for a state ruled by an easy-going autocrat or a council of
enlightened oligarchs. But the only reason for his preference
for either of these forms was the protection it would give to the
individual. Uppermost in Mencken's mind was the idea that the
superior individual must be allowed as large a sphere of independence as possible in which to exercise his cultural sovereignty. He praised the government of Frederick the Great for
permitting and even encouraging "gross dissents." Free speech,
he contended, was actually given its first support in law by this
most absolute of Prussian kings. In other cases ideals of freedom were formulated by intelligent country gentlemen, with
some aid from poets and philosophers, but usually the courage
of some wise old monarch was necessary to give them effect.
They never spring from the loins of the common man, to whom
liberty is meaningless; he feels uncomfortable with it, a bit
frightened, and unbearably lonely. "He longs for the warm, re-
assuring smell of the herd, and is willing to take the herdsman
with it." [6]

3. Liberty and the Law

Whether the state is considered as the source, the enemy, or
the protector of liberty, no subject in political theory is more
important than the relationship of liberty and law. Few theorists of the twentieth century with the exception of the anarchists

[6] *Ibid.*, p. 147.

have thought of the state as the enemy of liberty. The great majority have assumed that in some measure, at least, the state is both the source and the protector of liberty. The real questions, of course, are how to reconcile liberty with authority, and how much liberty to allow in the face of the crises plaguing modern society. The answers given occupy a central place in the political theories of some of the most distinguished jurists of the twentieth century.

It is commonly believed that the man who did most to define and uphold the juristic conception of liberty in modern times was Oliver Wendell Holmes, Jr., Associate Justice of the United States Supreme Court from 1902 to 1932. Born when the nineteenth century had run less than half its course, he was the son of the famous physician, poet, and "Autocrat of the Breakfast Table." His education at Harvard was interrupted by service as an officer in the Union Army during the Civil War. He was thrice wounded, at Ball's Bluff, at Antietam, and at Fredericksburg. In the fall of 1864 he entered Harvard Law School and was admitted to the bar three years later. He became a professor of law at Harvard in 1882, but after only one term was appointed to the Supreme Judicial Court of Massachusetts. In 1902 President Theodore Roosevelt named him an Associate Justice of the Supreme Court of the United States. Few judges, the most notable exception being John Marshall, exerted a greater influence upon the development of American law than did Holmes in his fifty years on the highest courts of Massachusetts and the United States.

Americans of liberal inclinations have long revered Justice Holmes as one of the great prophets of freedom. Actually, he was a man of complex mind who believed in liberty only as a kind of necessary condition to the proper functioning of the cosmic order. The basic tenets of his philosophy were derived from Social Darwinism. He considered the law of the universe to be competition and conflict, a struggle for existence resulting in the survival of the fittest. Since ideas as well as institutions should be regarded as subject to this law, there should be as little interference as possible by government agents with their free expression. Those which emerged victorious in the struggle would be the ones best adapted to a particular time and condition. The others should suffer elimination as ruthless as the destruction of summer insects by an autumn frost. This same principle Holmes extended to human relations. He glorified war as something romantic, with a message divine, and a necessary medicine for the heedlessness, irresponsibility, and sybaritic tendencies of modern youth. He thought that faith "true and adorable" which leads a soldier to throw away his life in a cause which he little understands and for purposes that appear to him useless.[7] He believed that every society is founded upon the death of men. With a cynic's view of human nature, he taught that morality is merely a check on the ultimate domination of force, just as politeness is a device to prevent the pigs from putting their feet in the trough. He had almost no sympathy with reform and none at all with panaceas or nostrums. He scoffed at proposals for tinkering with the economic system, and doubted that the condition of the lower classes could be much improved by either governmental or social action. In his view, one of the highest embodiments of social wisdom was the Malthusian law, combined apparently with sterilization of the "unfit." The misery of the poorer classes was primarily a matter of reckless spawning and the preservation by society of weak and incompetent offspring who ought to be allowed to die. Not until these conditions were corrected would there be any hope for a better world.

Holmes' reputation as a champion of freedom stems almost entirely from the opinions he rendered in a series of civil-liberties cases which came before the Supreme Court between 1919 and 1925. The first and most notable was the case of *Schenck v. United States*. Schenck was a Socialist agitator convicted of distributing leaflets condemning the Conscription Act during World War I. The leaflets arraigned conscription as despotism in its worst form, a monstrous wrong against humanity in the interest of Wall Street. Holmes made use of this case to develop his renowned "clear and present danger" doctrine. He admitted that under ordinary circumstances the propa-

---

[7] Max Lerner, ed., *The Mind and Faith of Justice Holmes*. Boston, Little, Brown, 1946, p. 20.

gation of the opinions contained in the leaflets would not have
been a crime. But the significance of every act depends upon
the circumstances under which it is done. Holmes chose an unfortunate example by alleging that there is no freedom to shout
"Fire!" in a crowded theater. He failed to perceive that the
commission of such a harebrained act could hardly be compared with the expression of unorthodox opinion. Freedom of
speech, the justice continued, is not absolute but relative. "The
question in every case is whether the words used are used in
such circumstances and are of such a nature as to create a clear
and present danger that they will bring about the substantive
evils that Congress has a right to prevent. It is a question of
proximity and degree." When a nation is at war, many things
that might be said in calmer times will be regarded as so dangerous to the nation's safety that their utterance will not be
tolerated.

Although Holmes disappointed many of his liberal friends by
upholding the decision that led to the imprisonment of the
Socialist leader Eugene V. Debs, the principle on which the
decision rested was essentially the same as that in the Schenck
case. Debs had been convicted of violating the Espionage Act of
1917 and was sentenced to ten years in prison. His specific offense consisted in making a speech in Canton, Ohio, in which
he proclaimed himself a pacifist and expressed sympathy for
some other Socialists who, he alleged, had been unfairly convicted of obstructing the draft. He declared his opposition to
America's war against Germany because he abhorred *all war*,
and argued that the master class had always exploited the common people by forcing them to fight its battles. In upholding
the decision against Debs, Holmes said nothing about the "clear
and present danger" test, but he made emphatic his belief that
Debs' speech had a natural and probable tendency to obstruct
recruiting and therefore to interfere with the war effort. In
short, it was not just the words themselves but the circumstances under which they were uttered that determined a
speaker's guilt or innocence.

Holmes added new laurels to his brow in the estimation of
liberals by his opinions in the Abrams and Gitlow cases. In the

former, decided in 1919, the majority of the court affirmed the
conviction of Jacob Abrams, who had been sentenced to twenty
years' imprisonment for throwing around the streets of New
York some leaflets denouncing American intervention in Russia.
The leaflets reminded American workers that in producing
bullets, bayonets, and guns they were conspiring to murder not
only their German enemies but also their comrades in Russia
who were fighting for freedom. Holmes dissented from the will
of the majority and incorporated in his opinion a mellow,
philosophical discourse on the virtue of tolerating unorthodox
doctrines. He admonished all dogmatists that time had upset
many fighting faiths, that "the ultimate good desired is better
reached by free trade in ideas," and that "the best test of truth
is the power of the thought to get itself accepted in the competition of the market." [8] Why this test could not have been
applied to the Debs speech is far from clear. Apparently in
Holmes' mind there were two distinctions between the cases.
First, whereas Debs was a prominent Socialist leader, Abrams
was unknown. Second, the intent of Debs' speech was directly
related to its probable result of hindering the war effort by
obstructing the draft. The possible result of Abrams' leaflet—
hampering the prosecution of the war—bore only a secondary
and indirect relation to his real intent of aiding the revolutionists in Russia.

In the Gitlow case in 1925, Holmes again found himself in
disagreement with the majority of the brethren on the Supreme
Bench. Benjamin Gitlow, a former member of the New York
Assembly and one of the leaders of the left wing of the Socialist party, had been convicted in 1919 of writing a pamphlet
condemning the right-wing Socialists for moderation and urging all members of the proletariat to join in the struggle for
world revolution. His conviction was appealed to the Supreme
Court of the United States and upheld by a majority decision.
Holmes wrote a dissenting opinion. In it he admitted that Gitlow's manifesto was more than a theory, and that it was an
incitement. But he contended that every idea is an incitement,

[8] *Abrams v. U.S.,* 250 U.S. 616.

and if believed firmly enough will somewhere be acted upon. The vital question was whether the action would constitute a real and immediate threat to the peace and safety of the United States. The incitement contained in the Gitlow manifesto posed no such threat. It had not the remotest chance of "starting a present conflagration." Holmes reiterated the clear and present danger doctrine he had enunciated in the Schenck case and contended that the court had endorsed it. He then set forth more boldly than he had done before his pragmatic, Darwinian conception of the role of free speech in social evolution. "If in the long run," he said, "the beliefs expressed in proletarian dictatorship are destined to be accepted by the dominant forces of the community, the only meaning of free speech is that they should be given their chance and have their way." [9] In other words, liberty of expression has nothing to do with fundamental rights. It is merely a convenient instrument of the evolutionary process. Conceptions of truth and right are purely relative. The survival of an idea is no test of its truth, nor is the truth of an idea a guaranty of its survival. Instead, the ability of an idea to gain acceptance simply means that the dominant classes of a particular time and place regard that idea as favorable to their interests. Society merely evolves; it does not necessarily improve or progress.

The Holmes doctrines in regard to liberty would seem to have diluted the conceptions generally held by the authors of the American Bill of Rights. Not once did he assert that liberty is essential to the dignity of man, that it is as important as life itself if the individual is to preserve his self-respect and be able to develop his capacities. He did not even concede that it is necessary to the success of democracy, though he certainly believed in such democratic doctrines as legislative supremacy, judicial continence, and experience as the foundation of law. To Holmes, freedom was merely the lubricant which would enable the wheels of the cosmic process to run smoothly. It had no relevance either to right or to truth. Like some of the ancient Sophists, he seemed to regard right as fundamentally the will

[9] *Gitlow v. N.Y.*, 268 U.S. 652.

of the strongest. Truth, as he once expressed it, is "the majority vote of that nation that can lick all the others." [10]

As already indicated, the clear and present danger doctrine of Holmes was modified and given a more precise formulation by Justice Brandeis. In a concurring opinion written in 1927 he avowed that it is not sufficient that fear or expectation of some possible evil should prevail. The evil must be a serious one, and the danger of its occurrence must be imminent. In fact, to justify interference with freedom of speech, the danger must be so imminent that it may actually befall before there is a chance for full discussion. "If there be time to expose through discussion the falsehood and fallacies, to avert the evil by the processes of education, the remedy to be applied is more speech, not enforced silence." [11] Brandeis also made clear his contention that even advocacy of criminal action, however reprehensible morally, is not in itself a justification for denying free speech. There must be evidence of incitement, and there must also be evidence that the advocacy will immediately bear fruit in action. What form this evidence would take he did not make clear, but he seems to have had in mind not mere intent or encouragement but overt acts of the nature of attempts or plots or conspiracies. He spoke of the fundamental difference between advocacy and incitement, between preparation and attempt, and between assembling and conspiracy.

The meaning of liberty under the First Amendment faced a new test during the Cold War between the United States and Russia. In 1951 the case of eleven Communist leaders, convicted and sentenced to long terms, reached the Supreme Court. They had been indicted for violating the Smith Act, which Congress had passed in 1940, making it a crime to advocate, advise, or teach the overthrow of any government in the United States by force or violence; or to organize or become a member of any society, group, or assembly of persons that teaches, advocates, or encourages the overthrow of any government in the United States by force or violence. By a vote of six to two, the Supreme Court, speaking through Chief Justice Vinson, upheld

[10] Lerner, *op. cit.*, p. 306.
[11] *Whitney v. California*, 274 U.S. 357.

the conviction. The Chief Justice began his evaluation of the case by drawing a distinction between advocacy and discussion. He agreed with the trial judge that the defendants would not have been guilty if they had done no more than pursue peaceful study and discussion of the theories of Marx, Lenin, and other revolutionaries. Constitutional freedom of speech permitted this, but apparently nothing beyond it. The Chief Justice acknowledged the importance of the clear and present danger doctrine, but he denied that its formulators had ever intended that "a shorthand phrase" should be crystallized into a universal rule to be applied rigidly to every case. The conspiracy of the eleven accused leaders to teach and advocate Communism was not an academic exercise in peaceful persuasion. It was a revolutionary act committed with the full intent of contributing to the destruction of our political institutions. Though the actual launching of the revolution might never occur, the government must be enabled to protect itself. It must not be required to wait "until the putsch is about to be executed, the plans have been laid, and the signal is awaited." [12] In thus repudiating the connection between speech and its consequences, and in making advocacy itself a crime, the Chief Justice practically nullified the clear and present danger doctrine. For both Holmes and Brandeis the directness and immediacy of the connection had been the very heart of the doctrine.[13]

How far certain judges were willing to go under the stress of the Cold War in limiting the realm of free expression is illustrated by the opinion in which Justice Robert H. Jackson concurred with the sentiments of Chief Justice Vinson. In an earlier case Jackson had espoused the noble principle that "If there is any fixed star in our constitutional constellation, it is that no official, high or petty, can prescribe what shall be orthodox in politics, nationalism, religion, or other matters of

[12] *Dennis et al. v. U.S.*, 341 U.S. 494.
[13] In the opinion of some authorities, the Supreme Court revived the clear and present danger doctrine in 1957, in the case of *Yates v. U. S.* (354 U. S. 298). Actually, it was only a partial revival, since the Court insisted merely that the danger be real, but not necessarily imminent.

opinion or force citizens to confess by word or act their faith therein." He had asserted also that "freedom to differ is not limited to things that do not matter much. . . . The test of its substance is the right to differ as to things that touch the heart of the existing order." [14] In the Dennis case, however, he flatly repudiated both of these principles. Though he centered attention upon the defendants' indictment for conspiracy, he denied that even an individual has the right to teach or advocate the overthrow of government by force or violence. The clear and present danger test he described as an "innovation" introduced before the era of revolutionary techniques made infamous by totalitarians. If applied to such a case as that in which the defendants were involved, it would mean that Communist plotting would be protected during its period of incubation. The government would not be able to move until the danger of imminent action was clearly evident, and then it would be too late. The real innovation would seem to have been the wide departure of the Justice's doctrine from the original meaning of the First Amendment. Those who sponsored the Bill of Rights agreed with Jefferson that it is time enough for the officers of government to intervene "when principles break out into overt acts against peace and good order."

The principal dissenting opinion in the Dennis case was written by Justice William O. Douglas, regarded by many as the most eloquent judicial defender of individual rights since Brandeis retired from the Court. In fact, Douglas reaffirmed the Brandeis position. Free speech, he insisted, is the rule, not the exception. Restriction to be justifiable must be based upon more than fear, or extreme contempt, dislike, or revulsion. Serious danger to society must actually impend. Conditions must be so critical that there will be no chance of avoiding the injury if the exercise of free speech is continued. No such critical danger, according to Douglas, was presented by the Communist movement. As a political party in the United States it was of little consequence, the "most beset and least thriving of any fifth column in history." Its members were so well known to the FBI that in case of war with Russia they would be picked up over-

[14] *West Virginia State Board of Education v. Barnette,* 319 U.S. 624.

night. Its leaders were "miserable merchants of unwanted ideas." He doubted that they could carry a single village in an election, let alone a city or county or state. He admitted the reality of the Communist menace on the world scene, but he contended that it had been crippled as a political force in the United States, and that it was free speech that had done it. No more than Holmes or Brandeis was Douglas willing to regard liberty of expression as an absolute right. It was a privilege granted by a free society for its own benefit and a necessary bulwark of democracy. It was so essential to the health of democracy, however, that the burden of proof must always rest upon those who would propose limitations. Nothing but the most crucial and immediate danger could justify restrictions or interference.

4. Liberty under Democracy

The early pages of this chapter referred to the close relationship that would seem to subsist between liberty and democracy. It was also observed that recognition of this relationship has grown more and more difficult as the demands of nationalism and power politics have become more imperious, and as revolutionary threats from both the right and the left have underlined the need for security. As early as 1901 William James, distinguished philosopher of Pragmatism, declared that liberalism in America, founded upon the rights of man and the sanctity of the free individual, was dead. Addressing the Anti-Imperialist League of which he was one of the leaders, he advised the organization to disband. We have been fighting, he said in effect, to preserve a national way of life based upon values and traditions inconsistent with imperialism. We have lost. The appetite for empire will now sweep everything before it. We shall build great armies and fleets. We shall send our goods and capital abroad. We shall enter into the arena of power squabbles with other nations. We shall be like unto them in our disregard for the fundamental rights of alien peoples under our rule. It was useless, he thought, to make any effort to stem the tide. The old era of freedom and isolation that had provided the milieu for democratic progress in the nineteenth century had come to an end.

Many of the philosophers of the twentieth century have doubtless shared James's disillusionment, but few have accepted his defeatism. To the majority the cause of liberty has appeared by no means hopeless. Though they recognize the obstacles and dangers, they refuse to believe that the battle has ended or that victory may not some day be possible. Exemplifying this attitude with force and clarity have been the British philosophers L. T. Hobhouse (1864–1929) and Ernest Barker (1874–   ), the American philosopher Morris R. Cohen (1880–1947), and also the American statesman Franklin D. Roosevelt. After graduating from Oxford and teaching there for a season, Leonard T. Hobhouse devoted himself to a brief career in journalism before settling down to his major undertaking as Professor of Sociology at the University of London. His political philosophy owed inspiration to a number of sources: the evolutionism of Herbert Spencer, the positivism and humanitarianism of Auguste Comte, and the social and libertarian theories of John Stuart Mill. For Hobhouse the central purpose and justification of democracy was the preservation of liberty. He saw its vindication in the opportunity it gives for the perfection of individual personality. He acknowledged that democracy is no more efficient than some other forms of government, but he held that it is the only government embodying "the idea of Right." Democracy, he argued, should be extended into every sphere of group activity, for it is the supreme instrument whereby Right or justice can be made to displace degrading or dehumanizing social conditions. This should not mean the deification of either the state or the government. In Hobhouse's view the government was a mere agent of the state, and the state itself was an association of individuals. It had no existence apart from or superior to that of its members. The good of the whole was simply the combined and coordinated good of its component parts.

Although Hobhouse stressed the importance of the individual, he had traveled far from the Spencerian conception of man and the state as enemies. He taught that both the community and the individual have rights, and that the rights of neither are absolute. All are derived from the moral order which underlies social relations, and the criterion by which every right must be measured is whether it promotes the principle of harmony in society. From such reasoning it followed that the sovereignty of the state must be considered as limited. As a matter of fact, Hobhouse deprecated the use of the term sovereignty. All authority, he contended, is pluralistic. The state itself owes allegiance to the civilized order of the world and is subject to the ethical community of mankind. This was simply a way of restating the old doctrine derived originally from the Stoics that a higher law of right and justice overrides the decrees and enactments of rulers and renders them null and void if they conflict with its principles. Hobhouse agreed that the state may coerce, but that it must not violate the consciences of its subjects. The individual must take into account the limitations of his own intelligence and the possible evils of dissent, but if, having done so, he is still firmly convinced of the rightness of his judgment, disobedience becomes a moral duty. Hobhouse placed so great a premium upon social harmony that he seems to have envisioned the state as operating somewhat after the fashion of a Quaker meeting. Just as the Quakers defer action on any proposal until the "sense of the meeting" tells them that agreement is practically unanimous, so the state would presumably refrain from enforcing any measure that violated the conscientious scruples of any citizen. Hobhouse considered as practically sacred the reflective moral judgments of the individual.

In Hobhouse's philosophy, rights and liberties went hand in hand. Liberties were simply privileges of exercising rights. Liberty, properly speaking, was therefore an aggregate of liberties. All liberties, he asserted, rest "on the spiritual nature of the social bond, and on the rational character of the Common Good." [15] In the main, Hobhouse advocated a wide sphere of freedom for the individual, exempt from interference by the state. He would tolerate no curbs on expression of opinion or on conduct relating exclusively to personal concerns. The economic sphere, however, he regarded as open to exceptions. In this area restrictions of liberty were justifiable in order to secure

[15] *The Elements of Social Justice.* New York, Holt, 1922, p. 67.

more valuable personal rights and for the purpose of maintaining social harmony. He therefore recommended the abolition of inheritance and of private property in land and other natural resources. He urged also a restriction on the accumulation of private wealth, a guaranteed minimum income for all citizens, participation of workers in the management of industry, and provision for sickness, old-age, and unemployment insurance. At the same time he rejected complete collectivism lest it magnify the importance of the state to proportions that would threaten individual liberty. He feared that the administration of large industries by the central government would result in the development of bureaucratic control unanswerable to public opinion. As a substitute he proposed the operation of monopolistic enterprises by tripartite boards of control representing the three basic interests of management, workers, and consumers. What he sought was a halfway house between the statism of Marx and the economic anarchy of the free-enterprise system. He believed that individual liberty without economic justice has little meaning. Nevertheless, he was unwilling to throw out the baby with the bath water by sacrificing liberty in order to be assured of justice.

To students of both ancient and modern political theory few names are more familiar than that of Sir Ernest Barker. Educated in the classics and in modern history at Oxford, Barker devoted his entire active life to teaching and writing. For twenty years he taught in various colleges of Oxford University and then was made Principal of Kings College in the University of London. In 1927 he became the first holder of the chair of political science in Cambridge University. He retired in 1939 and was knighted five years later. The major assumptions of Barker were almost identical with those of Hobhouse. Both recognized the value of democracy and glorified liberty as its soul and purpose. For Barker as much as for Hobhouse, a higher law of justice and right was the test supreme which determined the validity of decrees and statutes. Barker recognized more clearly, however, the dilemma which arises from having two laws, one the law of the state and the other the law of Right. His solution attempted to show that the higher law is really the work of the people themselves as expressed in a constitution. But the people who make this accomplishment are not the voters of any one day or generation, as Rousseau assumed. Barker turned to the theory of Burke for a more satisfactory explanation. Both the individual and the multitude of a particular moment, the great Whig had taught, are foolish. Only the species is wise. Barker adopted this argument, substituting merely the word "society" for "species." He sought to emphasize the point that a constitution emerges only as the result of a cumulative process, to which many generations contribute.

There were other contrasts with Hobhouse of greater significance. Barker drew a distinction between the legal and moral obligations of the citizen. The citizen has a *legal* obligation to obey any law that is declared, recognized, and enforced as law by the constituted agents of the state. This obligation is absolute and admits of no exceptions. The citizen has not only a legal but a *moral* obligation to obey a law if it possesses the inherent quality of justice. In contrast with Hobhouse, Barker gave no clear indication that he recognized for the individual a moral *duty* of *dis*obedience. But he did recognize such a duty for groups. Each social group, he taught, has a contribution to make to the total process of social development. In some cases the contribution must be made in the form of a protest or even rebellion. "A group which feels its idea to be a vital element in any just order of relations will then feel bound to stake itself upon that idea: it will disobey, or even resist, any law to the contrary: it will seek by the visible testimony of its disobedience and its acceptance of the legal consequences, to impress the value of its idea on others, to get it incorporated in social thought . . . and ultimately to secure its adoption as part of the law of the State." [16] He cited the Abolitionist crusade in the United States and the Suffragette campaign in England as examples of group defiance that had troubled the waters of social sentiment and ultimately gained their objectives.

The whole subject of rights, as Barker viewed it, had a strangely enigmatic character. Though he wrote as an opponent of the

[16] *Principles of Social and Political Theory.* Oxford, Clarendon Press, 1951, p. 223.

omnipotent state, he seemed never quite able to divorce himself
from the collectivist influences of Plato and Aristotle. He admitted that, ideally, rights are derived from two sources: the
individual personality and the authority of the state. He contended, however, that, in actuality, the state is the immediate
source of rights, and that rights in the full sense of the word
are not rights at all unless they proceed immediately from that
source. He recognized what he called quasi-rights, such as the
right of a slave to personal liberty in a state whose laws sanctioned the institution of slavery. Though founded upon justice,
such rights in actual life would fall short of validity. Further,
according to Barker, all rights, even those pertaining to the individual personality, exist in a social context. The right to liberty,
for example, is not absolute or unconditioned. Liberty for any
one individual is necessarily limited by the requirement of liberty
for all. Because the liberty of each is relative to that of others,
it must always be regulated. In fact, without regulation liberty
would not exist. Barker distinguished three kinds of liberty:
civil liberty, political liberty, and economic liberty. The first he
described as physical freedom, intellectual freedom, and freedom
of choice in the general field of contractual and social relations.
The second he defined as the liberty to constitute and control
government through the processes of voting and representation.
As to economic liberty, he had little to say. In discussing its
importance in the modern world about all he could come up
with was the dusty answer that it is related to both civil and
political liberty.

Among contemporary American philosophers none produced
a more incisive statement of the significance of liberty under
democracy than did Morris R. Cohen. Born in Minsk, Russia,
he was brought to the United States at the age of twelve, and
was educated at the College of the City of New York (CCNY)
and at Harvard. From 1902 to 1912 he taught mathematics at
CCNY, and from 1912 to 1938 he was Professor of Philosophy.
In addition, he lectured from time to time at Harvard, Yale,
Columbia, Johns Hopkins, Stanford, and the New School for
Social Research. His views had such clarity and penetration
that, according to Felix Frankfurter, every judge and lawyer in

the United States has been influenced by them. Harold J. Laski described him as the "most creative U. S. philosopher since William James."

Even though the judgments of Frankfurter and Laski may be somewhat exaggerated, Morris R. Cohen stands as one of the great American liberals. His liberalism, however, was not the traditional variety. Though he possessed an abiding faith in reason, he did not consider it an infallible guide. Man is an emotional as well as a thinking creature, he asserted, and passion at times may reduce reason to a subordinate place. If reason is to achieve its full value, it must be supplemented and fortified by the findings of science. Nor did Cohen accept the optimism of the eighteenth-century *philosophes*. His study of history taught him that there is no ground for their belief that progress is certain. Instead of assuming the *inevitability* of progress, the liberal should confine himself to a faith in the *possibility* of progress. Just as in life there is growth and decay, so in history there are periods of flowering and periods of decline. No one phase continues forever.

For Cohen, liberalism meant "a pride in human achievement, a faith in human effort, a conviction that the proper function of government is to remove the restraints upon human activity." [17] It was synonymous with toleration, a determination to suspend judgment until all the facts are in, the use of principles as hypotheses subject to verification, and a willingness to experiment and to look upon life as an adventure, in which risks must be taken in the face of new conditions. Viewed negatively, liberalism meant opposition to fanaticism and intolerance, repudiation of dogmatism, and rejection of omniscience and the assumption that the whole of virtue is in one's own possession. Cohen maintained that a degree of skepticism is absolutely essential to tolerance, since anyone who believes in final answers is not likely to be solicitous of the opinions of others. At one point, he summed up liberalism as "free inquiry, free discussion, and accommodation." [18]

Liberalism, for Cohen, also included opposition to revolution

[17] *The Faith of a Liberal.* New York, Holt, 1946, p. 449.
[18] *Ibid.*, p. 117.

and to all short-cut methods, such as force and violence, to
achieve social change. He condemned Communism, not because
of its economic goals but because of its program for seizure of
power by armed force and the establishment of a dictatorship of
the proletariat. He recognized the possibility of good in some
social upheavals, notably those such as the American and French
Revolutions, which were national movements involving the
cooperation of many elements; but he denied that any single
class had ever gained security and freedom through bloody rebellion. Moreover, the establishment of a class dictatorship
would not bring in a new dawn of peace and plenty, but would
simply rivet the chains of tyranny more firmly than ever. The
whole idea of forced change through revolution offended his
taste for progress through reason and science. He preferred the
middle road of compromise, experiment, and adjustment.

Morris R. Cohen's philosophy of liberalism logically prescribed
a maximum of liberty of expression and action. He did not attempt to justify liberty as a natural right, nor did he defend it by
arguing that suppression defeats its own purpose by making
martyrs of heretics or rendering them even more dangerous
by driving them underground. He preferred to stake his defense
of liberty upon the social importance of full examination and
discussion of alternative proposals. Just as mathematics proceeds
by tracing the results of erroneous propositions, so enlightenment must grow by the analysis and discussion of conflicting
opinions. It was essentially the Socratic method of discovering
truth by examining alternative opinions and knocking them
down one by one until a kernel of accurate knowledge was all
that remained. To guarantee the success of the method, no
muzzles whatever should be placed upon freedom of expression.
Cohen went back to the Jeffersonian idea that no limits should
be imposed upon the preaching of doctrines, no matter how
dangerous, until attempts were made to carry the doctrines into
overt acts. Writing on the eve of World War II, he took note of
the argument that liberty must be restricted in order to prevent
the greater evil of totalitarian conquest; but he pronounced this
a fallacy. "If it is an evil to lose our liberty in a war," he said,

"it is much worse to sacrifice it ourselves on the altar of fear." [19]
To the end of his life he refused to believe that liberalism was
dead or had become a vestigial remnant of a venerable past. And
the essence of liberalism, as he saw it, was freedom.

It seems appropriate to end this section with a discussion of
the ideas of a contemporary statesman who was concerned not
only with the preservation of liberty but with its reinterpretation
and extension into new areas of social purpose. Such were the
aims of Franklin D. Roosevelt, especially during the long period
when the forces of fascism threatened to overwhelm liberal and
democratic civilization. The first hint of his objectives was presented in his Commonwealth Club speech of 1932, when he
credited Jefferson with teaching the necessity of government
intervention when the exercise of property rights threatens to
interfere with rights of the person.[20] His most famous reinter-
pretations came later. One was the renowned Four Freedoms
speech of 1941. In it he championed the cause of liberty not only
in America but "everywhere in the world." The four essential
freedoms he declared to be: freedom of speech and expression,
freedom of religion, freedom from want, and freedom from fear.
Freedom from want was to be attained by economic agreements
which would secure to every nation a "healthy peacetime life
for its inhabitants." Freedom from fear meant "a world-wide
reduction of armaments to such a point and in such a thorough
fashion" that no nation would be able to commit aggression
against its neighbors.

Three years after the Four Freedoms were proclaimed, America was engaged in a death grapple with the Axis powers over
a major portion of the globe. Though victory was uncertain,
the war had entered its decisive phase. President Roosevelt now
went before Congress to emphasize the duty of laying plans for
a lasting peace and "the establishment of an American standard

[19] *Ibid.*, p. 129.
[20] It is commonly recognized, of course, that many of Roosevelt's political
theories were products of expediency. Most of his more radical and provocative doctrines were developed for him by his subordinates or by those who
surrounded him as a "brain trust." Nevertheless, it was Roosevelt himself
who made the selection from various theories submitted to him.

of living higher than ever before known." Declaring that as the
nation had grown in size and stature, the old guaranties of life
and liberty in the first Ten Amendments had proved inadequate,
he called for a new Bill of Rights "to assure us equality in the
pursuit of happiness." Genuine freedom, he said, cannot exist
without economic security and independence. "People who are
hungry and out of a job are the stuff of which dictatorships are
made." Accordingly, he appealed for a supplementary Charter
of Rights, which would include the following:

The right to a useful and remunerative job.
The right to earn enough to provide adequate food and clothing
and recreation.
The right of every farmer to raise and sell his products at a
return sufficient for a decent living for himself and his family.
The right of every businessman to trade under conditions of free
competition and without domination by monopolies, domestic or
foreign.
The right of every family to a decent home.
The right to adequate medical care and the opportunity to achieve
and enjoy good health.
The right to adequate protection from the economic hazards of
old age, sickness, disability, and unemployment.
The right to a good education.[21]

It is significant that Roosevelt regarded this new Bill of Rights
as necessary to prevent history from repeating itself. He avowed
that a return to the normalcy of the 1920's would be tantamount
to throwing away the victory on the battlefields and surrendering
to the spirit of fascism within our own borders.

The liberals of the twentieth century have not been a particularly happy group. Perhaps liberals have never been. They
have always occupied a difficult middle ground between extremes. They have been subject to attacks from the Right as
traitors to stability and order who would open the gates to
dangerous radicals. They have been maligned from the Left
as amiable do-gooders who think they can make omelettes without breaking eggs. Because of their general disposition to believe
in progress and in the basic decency of human nature, they have

[21] *The Public Papers and Addresses of Franklin D. Roosevelt*, XVIII, 41.

suffered from the pessimistic deductions drawn from Darwinism and especially from Freudian psychology. The effect of the wars and revolutions of the twentieth century in creating a climate inhospitable to liberalism seems almost too obvious for assertion. Finally, liberalism has suffered from internal disagreements and controversies to a greater extent than most other political movements. In recent history there have been nearly as many brands of liberals as of Christians or socialists. The multiplication and division have gone so far that one can hardly determine what a liberal is. Does he believe in natural rights, in inflexible natural laws, in *laissez faire,* in the diminishing state? If he believes in natural rights, does he include among them the right to property? Or is a liberal one who considers economic justice more important than the right to trial by jury and would therefore tincture his concern for the dignity of man with enough collectivism to make possible the welfare state?

Despite all this confusion of definition, liberalism still has a fundamental meaning which leaves little room for challenge. Few would deny, for example, that it falls somewhere between conservatism, on the one hand, and radicalism, on the other. The liberal cannot be an opponent of change, for he believes in at least the possibility of progress, and he must therefore welcome . experiments as means of finding the best road to the future. The liberal refuses to subscribe to the dictum that the end justifies the means. He believes, rather, that the two are interdependent, that the choice of means may condition the end, at least to the extent of perverting it and possibly to the extent of destroying it.

Perhaps, above all, liberalism should be defined in terms of freedom. Both historically and etymologically that has been the substance of its meaning. It seems utterly inconceivable that liberals at any time or under any conditions could refer to liberty as a "treacherous phantom," as John Ruskin described it, or as the "putrefying corpse" of Mussolini's trenchant language. Alike as an ideal and as a practical program, liberalism has been inseparable from freedom from authoritarianism, from arbitrary arrest and punishment, from fear and privation, and from enslavement, whether of the body, the conscience, or the mind.

It is the antithesis of concentration camps, of secret police, of censorship, of the monolithic state, of the blood purge, and of the bullet in the back of the neck. It comprehends nearly everything included in the modern ideal of democracy; yet it is not the same, for democracy is more directly concerned with expression of the popular will.

ADDITIONAL READINGS

Acton, Lord. *The History of Freedom and Other Essays*. London, Macmillan, 1907.

Adler, Mortimer J. *The Idea of Freedom*. Garden City, Doubleday, 1958.

Anshen, Ruth, ed. *Freedom: Its Meaning*. New York, Harcourt, 1940.

Barth, Alan. *The Loyalty of Free Men*. New York, Viking, 1951.

Benda, Julien. *The Treason of the Intellectuals*. New York, Morrow, 1928.

Chafee, Zechariah. *The Blessings of Liberty*. Philadelphia, Lippincott, 1956.

Cranston, Maurice. *Freedom: A New Analysis*. New York, Longmans, 1953.

Dewey, John. *Liberalism and Social Action*. New York, G. P. Putnam, 1935.

――――. *The Problems of Men*. New York, Philosophical Library, 1946.

Guerard, Albert L. *Testament of a Liberal*. Cambridge, Mass., Harvard University Press, 1956.

Hartz, Louis. *The Liberal Tradition in America*. New York, Harcourt, 1955.

Hocking, William E. *The Lasting Elements of Individualism*. New Haven, Yale University Press, 1937.

Kallen, Horace M. *The Liberal Spirit*. Ithaca, N. Y., Cornell University Press, 1948.

Laski, Harold J. *The Dangers of Obedience and Other Essays*. New York, Harper, 1930.

Leacock, Stephen B. *Our Heritage of Liberty*. New York, Dodd, 1942.

Lippmann, Walter. *The Method of Freedom*. New York, Macmillan, 1934.

Orton, William A. *The Liberal Tradition*. New Haven, Yale University Press, 1945.

Pennock, J. Roland. *Liberal Democracy*. New York, Rinehart, 1950.

Popper, Karl R. *The Open Society and Its Enemies*. Princeton, Princeton University Press, 1950.

Russell, Bertrand. *Power*. New York, Norton, 1938.

————. *Unpopular Essays*. New York, Simon and Schuster, 1950.

Salvadori, Massimo. *Liberal Democracy*. London, Pall Mall, 1958.

Shklar, Judith. *After Utopia*. Princeton, Princeton University Press, 1957.

Ward, Barbara. *Faith and Freedom*. New York, Norton, 1954.

Weldon, T. D. *States and Morals*. New York, Whittlesey House, 1947.

C H A P T E R

I I I

Positivists, Relativists, and Realists

Several times in human history an age of faith has been followed by a new era in which science takes the place of religion, skepticism supplants belief, and materialism and cynicism largely supersede hopes and ideals. One such new era was the Renaissance, substituting the humanist's delight in the earthly and natural for the otherworldliness and supernaturalism of the Christian Middle Ages. Another was the period after 1880. By that year the victory of the greatest scientific revolution in the history of the world was complete, or so it seemed. Evolutionists had almost a clear field against the champions of Biblical literalism and special creation. Theologians were forced to cover their retreat by centering attention more and more upon a Social Gospel, which emphasized human rather than spiritual values. Materialism flourished as the burgeoning industrial system provided increasingly for the satisfaction of physical needs and stimulated new cravings for both comforts and luxuries. As in the age of the Renaissance, the growth of science and the change in philosophical and religious attitudes were accompanied by similar developments in political theory. Ideals and absolutes were thrown aside. The rigorous objectivity of the natural sciences was proclaimed as the goal of political research, and the relativist approach took the place of the quest for final answers. Underlying many of these attitudes was a cynical contempt for human nature, a denial that mortals are ever prompted by noble impulses, and a belief, as Machiavelli expressed it, that "whoever desires to found a state and give it laws, must start with assuming that all men are bad and ever ready to display their vicious nature, whenever they may find occasion for it."

The founding of Positivism in modern philosophy is generally credited to Auguste Comte (1798–1857). It was based upon his cardinal doctrine that the only knowledge of any value is *positive* knowledge, or knowledge gained by objective research. He rejected metaphysics as utterly futile; no man can discover the hidden essences of things—why events happen as they do, or what is the ultimate meaning and goal of existence. All we know is *how* things happen, the laws which control their occurrence, and the relations existing between them. Such knowledge may not answer all the questions that trouble our dreams, but it is the limit of which the human mind is capable. Comte conceived of universal history as progressing through a series of stages, each superior to the one that preceded. The first was the theological stage, in which the control of events was ascribed to animistic forces or anthropomorphic beings. The second was the metaphysical stage, in which ideas or philosophic principles took the place of supernatural powers. Finally would come the positive or industrial stage, when science would rule supreme and men would devote their efforts exclusively to the cultivation of useful and practical knowledge for the benefit of society. In general, Comte was more optimistic than most of his later disciples. Instead of assuming human beings to be wholly selfish, he taught that men are also influenced by impulses of altruism, or feeling for others. The paramount object of all social teaching, he maintained, should be to promote the supremacy of altruism over egoism.

1. Pareto, Mosca, and Michels

Positivism in the twentieth century has received its most forceful exposition from certain Italian and German philosophers who have probably been even better known as critics of democracy and exponents of sundry theories of minority rule. The most prolific of them, as well as the first in chronological order, was Vilfredo Pareto. Born in Paris in 1848 of Genoese parents, he achieved a brilliant record as a student of mathematics, history, and the classics. In choosing a career he followed the footsteps of his father and became an engineer. He was employed for a few years by the Italian railways, but left his job to prepare himself for a professorship in economics. After twelve years of seeking, he finally obtained an appointment as Professor of Political Economy at the University of Lausanne. In 1917 he completed his four-volume work, translated into English as *The Mind and Society*. Shortly before his death in 1923 he accepted a royal appointment to membership in the Italian Senate.

Pareto insisted upon a rigorous application of the scientific method to all branches of knowledge. To him a fact was a fact, no matter the realm in which it was found. It was as much the business of the sociologist or economist as it was of the physicist or chemist to discover facts and the relations between them. So-called laws are simply another name for "experimental uniformities," and there is not the slightest difference between the laws of political economy or sociology and the laws of other sciences. The apparent differences spring from the fact that most professors of political economy and sociology still cling too fondly to metaphysical and religious presuppositions. Pareto would have no truck with the *a priori* thinking that commonly passes for philosophy. He castigated unmercifully the theorizers about natural law, the social contract, justice, and right reason. Sheer laziness and superstition, he alleged, blind such men to the realities of knowledge. It is much easier, he suggested, to speculate about natural law than to dig out the legal codes of various countries in different periods and see what they really contain. Prattling about the will of God and what it imports for the ways of men is also a very comfortable pursuit. But what God? The God of the Christians? The God of the Moslems? Or the God of the Hindus? Pareto would accept as true only such principles and propositions as could be fully tested, measured, and verified. All others would be relegated to the status of fables, possibilities, or probabilities, depending upon the evidence or lack of evidence to support them. The famed syllogism of the textbooks on logic: "All men are mortal; Socrates is a man; therefore Socrates is mortal" would be restated thus: "All men of whom we have had any knowledge have died; what we know of Socrates induces us to classify him with such men; therefore it is very probable that Socrates is mortal." [1]

If Pareto had shown greater consistency in adhering to his own preachments, it would doubtless be possible to take him more seriously. In his desire to be tough-minded he sometimes displayed prejudices that had little more evidence behind them than did other men's beliefs in natural law or the social contract. He regarded democracy as impossible, socialism as a fraud, and humanitarianism as a snare and a delusion. He considered the vast majority of human beings to be weak and depraved creatures with neither the skill to govern themselves nor the wit to control the destinies of others. Practically all human behavior he divided into what he called *residues* and *derivations*. By residues he meant the manifestations of sentiments and instincts. For example, asceticism would be a manifestation of an instinct or urge for self-punishment. Derivations are the rationalizations of residues. To illustrate: the Crusades as organized military expeditions were manifestations of a primitive migration or wandering urge. But they were rationalized as noble enterprises to rescue the holy places of Palestine from desecration by the Turks. The vast bulk of man's reasoning, as Pareto conceived it, is made up of these rationalizations, or "nonlogical" behavior. Except in the minds of the talented few, enlightenment does not increase. Among the masses, prejudice and superstition do not diminish; they merely change their forms. But creeds, ideologies, and metaphysical philosophies also belong in the category of the non-logical. Science alone gives us truth.

Aside from his insistence upon the application of the scientific method to all branches of knowledge, Pareto's main contribution lay in his elaborate theory of the structure and mobility of classes. Every society, he taught, is composed of two types of individuals: the foxes and the lions. The foxes are bold and

[1] *The Mind and Society.* New York, Harcourt, 1935, I, 5.

adventurous; they throw caution to the winds, and live by cunning and cleverness. In the economic sphere, they are speculators; they welcome risks for the sake of maximum profits and indulge in promotion schemes. The lions are solid, conservative, cherishing tradition and ancient custom, loyal to family, church, and nation, and preferring to rely upon force rather than cleverness. In their economic life they are *rentiers*—cautious, thrifty, content with small returns on "safe" investments, and unwilling to gamble. Either of these types of individuals may gain the ascendancy, depending upon the sort of residues that happen to prevail. When Class I residues are dominant, the foxes will rule; for these are the "Residues of Combinations," representing tendencies to originate, manipulate, and combine institutions and ideas. On the other hand, the dominance of Class II residues brings the lions to the fore. These are the "Residues of the Persistence of Aggregates," or the expressions of urges to worship, protect, and defend the established order. Civilizations retrogress under a heavy preponderance of Class II residues. But unless these same residues are sufficiently intensified, the nation may be too weak to defend itself. What is needed is a proper balance between the residues that encourage originality and those that favor loyalty and stability. But such a balance is seldom maintained for more than a brief period.

According to Pareto, every society is also composed of two main classes or groups, the élite and the non-élite. The élite, in turn, is subdivided into the governing and the non-governing élites. The latter consists simply of the successful ones who rise to the top in every occupation and stratum of society. Thus there is an élite of lawyers, an élite of mechanics, and even an élite of thieves and an élite of prostitutes. These élites are not stationary but undergo an almost constant circulation. In every society there is an unceasing movement of individuals from lower to higher levels, so that every élite is doomed ultimately to extinction. "History is a graveyard of aristocracies." [2] Nevertheless, attempts are sometimes made to slow down or even to prevent the circulation of élites. The result is stagnation and ossification, followed eventually by inevitable ruin. Rome went through such

---

[2] *Ibid.*, III, 1430.

a period after the time of Hadrian. The second, third, and fourth centuries saw deliberate efforts to transform Roman society from a regime of individual initiative to a regime of hereditary status. Peasants were bound to the soil. The son of the artisan or tradesman was forced to follow in his father's footsteps.

Pareto professed to discover similar tendencies in modern society. Trade unions, he maintained, are becoming more restrictive. The movement of immigrants into new countries like America and Australia is drastically limited. Nearly everywhere governments are extending their control over economic matters and strangling private initiative. Majorities impose increasing tax burdens on the wealthy few with the effect of destroying incentive and causing capital to flow out of the country. Since Pareto believed that the circulation of élites was directly proportional to the ease with which men might accumulate wealth, he considered a free-enterprise capitalist system to be the most conducive to the good of society.

The élite in which Pareto was most vitally interested was, of course, the governing élite. Even this he divided into two parts: an inner group which wields power and an outer group which possesses authority. As examples of the power-wielders, he mentioned the Ephors of Sparta, the Council of Ten in Venice, the favorite ministers of absolute monarchs, and the political bosses in modern democracies. All governing cliques rule by a mixture of force and consent, but it is force, he contended, that must predominate. Because of the nature of the subject masses, their consent will almost certainly be procured by bribery, deceit, or chicanery. The governors will be tempted to purchase obedience by appeasing discordant minorities. Success may crown such practices at first, but the long-term results are disastrous. When governments abdicate their proper function of maintaining social order by force, the subjects themselves, in one way or another, usually fill the vacuum. It is a familiar historical fact that the private vendetta languishes or flourishes as governmental power to enforce the law waxes or wanes. Feudalism or some other form of private exercise of public authority invariably crops out as the power of a central government shrinks toward nullity. Little states grow up within the larger state, and society is fragmented into smaller societies. Pareto was therefore ready to say that when a governing class becomes recreant to its obligation to rule effectively by the use of coercion, it should be overthrown and replaced by another that is willing and able to use force. In not only overthrowing the old élite of degenerate weaklings, but in killing a large number of them, the new class is "performing a useful public service, something like ridding the country of a baneful animal pest." [3] Pareto was so convinced of the justifiability of resorting to violence under certain circumstances that he was willing to approve its use, also, by workingmen in connection with strikes. He could see no difference between the acts of a government in shooting down smugglers to enable the beneficiaries of protective tariffs to collect their profits, and the acts of workers in taking up arms to defend a union wage scale.

Pareto played such a splendid role in combating superstition, hypocrisy, and prejudice and in extolling objectivity in the social sciences that it is regrettable that he came to be considered one of the forerunners of fascism. That he was not a fascist can be seen from his defense of the right to strike and his insistence upon freedom of expression as essential to the discovery of truth. It can be seen even more clearly in his sardonic references to imperialism, including that of the Italians. "If an Englishman, a German, a Frenchman, a Belgian, an Italian," he wrote, "fights and dies for his country, he is a hero; but if an African dares defend his homeland against any one of those nations, he is a contemptible rebel and traitor." Europeans profess to be performing a sacred mission by carrying civilization to benighted peoples. With a hypocrisy truly remarkable, they claim to be acting for the good of their subjects by oppressing or exterminating them. They have freed the poor savages from native tyranny; and to make them freer still, have killed quite a few of them and reduced the rest to a condition approaching slavery. "The cat catches the mouse and eats it; but it does not pretend to be doing so for the good of the mouse. It does not proclaim any dogma that all animals are equal, nor lift its eyes hypocritically to heaven in worship of the Father of us all." [4]

³ *Ibid.*, IV, 1532.
⁴ *Ibid.*, II, 626–27.

Yet Pareto did lay himself open to misunderstanding in a democratic age by his contempt for the intellectual abilities of all but a small minority, by his justification of violence, by his defense of capital punishment (because it rids society of murderers), by his hatred of socialism, pacifism, and humanitarianism, and by his scorn for democracy as inseparable from corruption, machine politics, and gangsterism. In addition, he took a wholly negative view in regard to progress. One of his characteristic axioms was: "Whenever war is declared on Cythera, Sodom, Lesbos, and Onan gain in vogue." [5] But most of these attitudes were probably motivated by a desire to avoid sentimentality. He appears to have believed that objective realism can best be achieved by avoiding softness and all womanish sympathy. Subconsciously he seems to have associated pacifism, socialism, humanitarianism, and democracy with idealism, and idealism was but another name for hypocrisy. Besides, the growth of strong nationalism in Italy made such concepts all but untenable. Instead of a totalitarian, Pareto should probably be classified as a positivist and a realist, who leaned so far backward to avoid their opposites that he became a cynic.[6]

In the opinion of some authorities Pareto adapted a number of his ideas from the teachings of his compatriot, Gaetano Mosca. Although Mosca was ten years younger than Pareto, his *magnum opus, The Ruling Class,* preceded Pareto's *Mind and Society* by more than two decades. The possibility, therefore, cannot be dismissed that the older man may have sat, figuratively speaking, at the feet of the younger. Mosca was born in Sicily in 1858, and was educated at the University of Palermo. Subsequently he taught constitutional law and political theory at the universities of Palermo, Turin, and Rome. From 1908 to 1919 he served in the Chamber of Deputies as a representative of the Conservative party. In the latter year he was appointed a Senator and held this position throughout the era of Fascism until his death in 1941.

The philosophy of Gaetano Mosca bore many resemblances to that of Pareto. There was the same insistence upon the merits

[5] *Ibid.*, III, 1282.
[6] Pareto actually condemned what he thought of as positivism because of the large element of humanitarianism in the philosophy of Auguste Comte.

of the scientific method, though Mosca limited his efforts to applying it to politics, whereas Pareto extended it to the whole range of social issues. There was the same opposition to democracy and a similar conception of the division of society into a minority of rulers and a vast majority of those who are ruled. Both men emphasized the irrational character of political behavior, and in general taught that intellectual activity is the monopoly of a small élite. Both justified war and considered revolutions inevitable. Both stressed the importance of a fluidity of classes and an alternation of ruling groups. Although Mosca as much as Pareto had his remedies to prevent the dissolution of the state, both were about equally pessimistic as to the chances of their being adopted.

But here all significant resemblance between the two theorists ends. Mosca was a political scientist almost exclusively. Pareto was a sociologist and psychologist, with elaborate explanations of the instinctual and pseudo-logical processes of human behavior. Mosca did not share Pareto's abhorrence of idealism and humanitarianism, nor was he especially opposed to imperialism. An even more striking contrast appears with respect to their attitudes toward force. Pareto considered force as the indispensable instrument of efficient rule. In his judgment, any political class that shrank from using it was decrepit and no longer entitled to govern. Mosca emphasized the more subtle influences of habits of obedience, religion, and patriotism. Any of these, he contended, might evoke in the individual a spirit of loyalty or even of sacrifice for the common good. The effectiveness of religion, however, would depend upon the degree to which the society was religiously oriented.

Like many of his contemporaries, especially in Continental Europe, Mosca repudiated the traditional methods of political classification stemming from Plato and from Aristotle. He thought it ridiculous to fit all governments into a Procrustean pattern of monarchy, aristocracy, and democracy. Only one type of government has ever existed, and that is oligarchy. "In all societies— from societies that are very meagerly developed and have barely attained the dawnings of civilization, down to the most advanced and powerful societies—two classes of people appear—

a class that rules and a class that is ruled." [7] The first class, which is always a minority, monopolizes power and enjoys the perquisites that power brings. The second class, which comprises the majority, is directed and dominated by the first, in a manner either legal or arbitrary, and supplies the rulers with the means of subsistence and with the instrumentalities necessary to the maintenance of the state. The percentage of the citizens constituting the ruling class is quite variable. In general, it is inversely proportional to the number of inhabitants. States with huge populations have small ruling classes, and *vice versa*. But even the smallest governing clique is no absolute sovereign. It is under the constant necessity of taking some account of the desires of the majority. No matter what the form of political organization, the masses always exert an upward pressure, which rarely fails to exert some influence upon the will of the rulers. Despite Mosca's theory of minority rule, the omnipresence of oligarchy was perhaps, after all, largely a matter of form. True, the oligarchs ruled, but in accordance with pressures exerted upon them from below. Did this make the majority, in the final analysis, sovereign?

The position of the ruling class, or political class, as Mosca called it, is never permanent. And this in spite of its constant attempt to make its power hereditary. Even in democracies, Mosca maintained, the elected officials are usually the relatives of other elected officials. In addition, hereditary relationships may be supplemented by appeals to supernatural sanctions or to high-sounding philosophical principles. In the long run, however, failure is the portion of all these devices. The old ruling class is ultimately deposed and is replaced by a new one to suffer the same fate in its turn. The causes, according to Mosca, are not far to seek. The governors fail to provide the necessary services, or the services they do provide lose their value because of an increase in knowledge, the spread of a new religion, or some similar change in the great social forces pervading a given society. In the midst of such changes, the political class undergoes an alteration in structure. Resourceful, ambitious, and unscrupulous men push themselves up from below and usurp

[7] *The Ruling Class.* New York, McGraw-Hill, 1939, p. 50.

the places of the old leaders. Once this revolutionary movement has begun, it is impossible to stop it. It must continue until a new set of rulers is firmly entrenched in the government and has developed the arts of ruling and of holding power. The great class of the governed will then gradually resign themselves to their place at the bottom of the political hierarchy. The conservative power of habit will slowly envelop the whole society and solidify the new order.

But there is one more element necessary to the effective rule of any political class. This, he contended, is the political formula. In every society above a modest level of civilization, the governors do not justify their holding power by the mere fact of possession, "but try to find a moral and legal basis for it, representing it as the logical and necessary consequence of doctrines and beliefs that are generally recognized and accepted." [8] The political formula does not necessarily embody absolute truth. It may just as well be merely a plausible myth which is accepted by the people. Even so, it should not be regarded as a fraud, cleverly contrived by the ruling class to dupe the masses into subjection. On the contrary, it ministers to a definite social need. It gratifies a deeply felt human requirement that man should be governed on the basis of some moral principle and not by mere physical force. Besides, the political formula has fundamental value in unifying political institutions, peoples, and civilizations. Mosca had grave doubts that, without such a factor of moral cohesion, societies had much chance of holding together.

Although nothing was more evident to Mosca than the certainty that every political regime will ultimately be overthrown by either gradual or violent revolution, he nevertheless believed that stability ought to be preserved for as long a time as possible. To stave off violent revolution he recommended gradual alterations in the political system to comport with changes in public opinion. He thought it essential also that the governing class should admit to its ranks from time to time the best elements from among the masses. The ruling hierarchy in England had taken these lessons to heart and had survived into the twentieth century. The *ancien régime* in France had refused to

[8] *Ibid.*, p. 70.

heed them and had gone down to destruction in the Revolution of 1789. To prevent slow erosion of the power of a political class, Mosca urged what he called a balance of social forces. By a social force he meant any activity or influence that has social significance—money, land, military prowess, religion, education, science. The more of these forces a regime is able to represent, the stronger it is. If it could represent all of them, its position would be virtually impregnable. But since such a consummation is practically impossible, the necessary compromise is a balance of forces. To achieve this it is essential, above all, that no single social force be allowed to predominate. In addition, religion and the state must be kept separate, lest governmental acts become immune from questioning. Finally, steps must be taken to promote a wide distribution of property. The concentration of wealth in an advanced society is a sure road to the worst form of tyranny.

Though Mosca's philosophy was saturated with anti-democratic prejudice, he was certainly no more fascistic than was Pareto. True, he justified war, but not for purposes of conquest. He feared that without armed conflict, or at least preparation therefor, nations would stagnate and become soft. They would no longer have the patriotism, the desire, or the ability to defend themselves. Moreover, the elimination of standing armies would result in the weakening of central government, the re-emergence of private armies, and the return of Western civilization to feudal warfare. The form of rule which Mosca really desired was constitutional government, a form under which the actual work of governing was performed by cabinet ministers responsible to the head of the state. The latter appointed and dismissed them and retained the ultimate authority to determine policy. The model of this form of government was Imperial Germany. Such a system, Mosca contended, fostered the maximum of liberty, because it made possible the most perfect balance of social forces. Democracy pandered to only one social interest, that of the propertyless majority. It was therefore inimical to liberty. The conclusion seems obvious that Mosca belonged to the conservative school of Cavour, Bismarck, and Hegel rather than to that of the totalitarians, and that the democracy he was fighting was the absolutist democracy of Rousseau rather than the liberal democracy already in existence in Switzerland, England, and the United States.

Similar in underlying philosophy to both Pareto and Mosca was Roberto Michels. Born in Cologne in 1876, he attended the universities of Paris, Munich, Leipzig, Halle, and Turin. He left Germany as a young man, traveled widely, and conceived an ardent affection for Italian culture. His first teaching position was at the University of Turin. From 1914 to 1927 he was Professor of Political Economy at the University of Basel. In 1927 he was a visiting professor at the University of Chicago, and the following year was called by Mussolini to the chair of Political Sociology at the University of Perugia. He died in 1936. Although Michels pronounced Pareto's doctrine of circulation of élites "one of the most remarkable theories of the philosophy of history of recent times," he nevertheless modified it to fit his own conclusions. He held that the circulation was not so much an absolute exchange or displacement of one class by another as it was a perennial amalgamation of new elements with the old. Instead of disappearing or becoming proletarianized, old aristocracies are forced to share their power with ambitious upstarts from the lower orders. He observed a constant infiltration of merchants, bankers, intellectuals, and bureaucrats into the ancient feudal aristocracy. The latter, however, continued in many cases to hold its nominal authority, suffering merely a dilution of power from outside its ranks. Even when members of a former ruling class fall upon evil days, they seldom sink to the bottom. Instead, their descent is halted at some intermediary level. They go "underground" for a time until they can recoup their fortunes, and then work their way back to their former status. Michels had such high regard for the talents of the upper classes, and so low an opinion of the masses, that he could hardly entertain the thought of an aristocrat giving way to a proletarian.

The doctrine upon which the fame of Michels chiefly rests is his Iron Law of Oligarchy. This he declared to be "one of the iron laws of history, from which the most democratic modern societies and, within those societies, the most advanced parties, have been unable to escape." [9] The primary factor supporting this law he found to be the element of organization. Under the conditions of modern society no movement or party can hope to succeed without organization. But "organization" is simply another way of spelling "oligarchy." As a movement or party grows in size, more and more functions must necessarily be delegated to an inner circle of officers and leaders. Simultaneously, the members themselves become less and less able to direct and control their chosen officials. As a consequence, the latter acquire freedom of action and a vested interest in their position. They hold on to their new perquisites and privileges desperately and become almost irremovable. Particularly is this true of working-class parties and proletarian movements. Their leaders exhibit a rapidly diminishing interest in returning to manual labor or to the unadorned life of the rank-and-file member. They learn to revel in the sumptuous banquets and the committee meetings and congresses in expensive hotels. Their salaries often exceed those of the most highly skilled workers and in some cases approximate those of business executives.

Of almost equal influence in the growth of oligarchy are the peculiar qualities of the mass mind. The majority of human beings, according to Michels, are apathetic, indolent, and slavish. They are permanently incapable of self-government and must always be guided and led. They tend to be gullible, susceptible to flattery, timid and obsequious in the presence of strength, and willing to lick the boots even of their oppressors. Leaders find it easy to take advantage of these qualities to perpetuate themselves in power. They employ all the wiles of oratory to inflame the passions of their followers. They cultivate the arts of the parliamentarian to suppress and outwit their opponents. They play upon the sympathies of the multitude by posing as martyrs who must suffer persecution, defamation, and sometimes imprisonment. Because of these factors enhancing the strength of oligarchy, the progress of social reform movements becomes almost a mockery. "If laws are passed to control

[9] Alfred deGrazia, trans., *Roberto Michels' First Lectures in Political Sociology.* Minneapolis, University of Minnesota Press, 1949, p. 142.

the dominion of the leaders, it is the laws which gradually weaken, and not the leaders." [10] The state can never be anything other than the organization of a minority. Crusaders may strive for some exalted program of social amelioration, but long before they attain their goal, the vices common to all leadership groups will overtake and conquer them. They will become *professional* leaders, jealous of their power and privileges, and eager to retain and enlarge them. Thus it is that socialists may triumph, but socialism never. The latter "would perish in the moment of its adherents' triumph." [11] Revolutions do indeed occur, and tyrants are sometimes deposed; but new tyrannies spring up, often in alliance with remnants of the old, and the world goes on as before. "The democratic currents of history resemble successive waves. They break ever on the same shoal." [12] They are repeatedly renewed in a cruel game that will doubtless continue forever.

Notwithstanding his conviction that it had no chance of really succeeding, Michels acknowledged the merits of democracy. We must choose it, he said, as the least of evils. It is infinitely preferable to hereditary monarchy, which is "inferior even to the most revolting of demagogic dictatorships." He admitted that doubtless the ideal government would be an aristocracy of virtue and wisdom. But where, he asked, can such an aristocracy be found? Certainly not in any class of hereditary nobles. The only way out, he thought, is to correct, as far as possible, the defects of democracy. The chief difficulty lies in the fact that the masses are so ignorant and helpless. Their intellectual inferiority makes it impossible for them to appraise the significance of their leaders' actions. As a result, they are trapped before they realize what is happening. Their educational level must be raised to enable them to understand, and to some extent control, the oligarchic tendencies within their own ranks. Neither of these objectives can be fully realized, but there is hope for modest success. In the judgment of some authorities,

---

[10] *Political Parties: A Sociological Study of the Oligarchical Tendencies of Modern Democracy.* Glencoe, Ill., Free Press, 1949, p. 406.
[11] *Ibid.*, p. 391.
[12] *Ibid.*, p. 408.

Michels deserves criticism for not having recognized the substantial success of democracy in Switzerland, where he spent so many years of his professional life. It seems probable, however, that the example of Switzerland was very much in his mind when he stressed the importance of a superior educational level as a necessary condition for popular rule.

2. The Pragmatists

As the title of this chapter implies, Positivism in modern philosophy was frequently allied with a relativist approach. In rejecting metaphysics and enthroning science, the Positivist himself was often led to the conclusion that there is no final truth. Even the so-called laws of science are mere estimates of what we assume to be universally and completely true. But science changes as new discoveries bring out facts hitherto ignored or underemphasized. The Positivist, therefore, was forced to admit that the truths he possessed are mostly expressions of appearances or probabilities. So long as conditions remain the same, they are valid for practical purposes and as operational programs for further research. But they are not absolute or final truths. Should conditions change or new knowledge be discovered, the conclusions formerly assumed to be valid will have to be modified or abandoned. Instead of being fixed and eternal verities, they are relative to the conditions of the moment and to the stage of advancement of human knowledge.

The relativists of major importance in the twentieth century have generally marched under the banner of Pragmatism. Pragmatism takes its name from its central teaching that any idea which gives practical results must be accepted as true; provided, of course, it does not conflict with experience. In other words, if a belief in natural law or in the divine ordination of government gives ethical or spiritual satisfaction to any individual, that belief is true for him. The Pragmatists scoff at all efforts to discover absolute truth or to determine the ultimate nature of reality. They reject metaphysics as futile and teach that knowledge should be sought after, not as an end in itself, but as a means for improving conditions on earth. It should be noted also that

Pragmatists repudiate all forms of determinism, whether conceived in spiritual or materialistic terms. They spurn interpretations of the universe which reduce man to a slave of some rigid
principle or place him at the mercy of an all-powerful Fate.
They will have neither a "block universe" nor a blind cosmic
machine.

Founded in the United States about 1875 by Charles Peirce,
Pragmatism was propagated in England by F. C. S. Schiller and
in Germany by Hans Vaihinger. It was given its most popular
and comprehensive expression, however, by the renowned Americans William James (1842–1910) and John Dewey (1859–1952).
The education of William James was desultory and erratic. A
delicate and imaginative youth, he was deeply influenced by
the utopianism and mysticism of his father, who was a Sweden-
borgian. After pursuing varied studies in European and American schools, young James obtained an M.D. degree from Harvard Medical School at the age of twenty-seven but was too ill
to practice. In 1872 he began a teaching career as an instructor
in anatomy and physiology at Harvard. Years later he transferred
his interest to psychology, and in 1889 was made Professor of
Philosophy. His best-known writings are *Pragmatism, The Will
to Believe, Varieties of Religious Experience,* and *The Meaning of
Truth.*

For William James, philosophy was so much a matter of
sentiment and feeling that he might almost be considered anti-
intellectual. He advised his followers to give up logic, "fairly,
squarely, and irrevocably," and to substitute "reality, life, experience, concreteness, immediacy." Ideas, he said, take on the
character of truth in so far as they bear a direct relation to the
facts and experiences of daily living. Truth is not some stagnant
quality that dwells within an idea. Instead, ideas *become* true;
they are made true by events. Truth is constantly changing.
What "works" or gives practical results in one period may be
altogether worthless in another. For this reason we must be
ready to "live today by what truth we can get today, and be
ready tomorrow to call it falsehood." [13] James considered this
essential just as much in the political as in any other branch of

[13] *Pragmatism.* New York, Longmans, 1928, p. 223.

philosophy. He refused to regard any form of government as ideal for all men under all conditions or any social issue as finally settled. He had no sympathy for the idea of the state as the unfoldment of the divine in history or as the embodiment or source of right. Notions of absolute sovereignty and unlimited authority were no less repugnant to him than were other absolutes.

It was the pluralism of James that dominated his political philosophy. He denounced both unity and uniformity. For him, the very idea of a *universe* was shocking. He preferred to think of a *pluriverse*. Variation, diversity, is the spice of life and the matrix in which freedom is formed. James applied this idea especially to his conception of society. For all practical purposes he was the founder of cultural pluralism, or the doctrine that a nation's progress in civilization is furthered best by a policy of tolerating and even encouraging diversity. Such a policy James believed in with evangelical fervor. He would have tolerated anarchists, nihilists, free-lovers, single-taxers, socialists, prohibitionists, and antivivisectionists—to name but a few. All would compete with one another and help to decide by actual experiment what kind of policies would be most beneficial to the whole society. In the competition the freakish ideas would generally be weeded out. But once in a while some genius would bring forth a conception that would revolutionize the world of knowledge. Nothing short of complete toleration of all ideas, no matter how radical or eccentric, could ensure this result. So convinced was James of the importance of free trade in ideas that he opposed the compulsory licensing of physicians lest it produce a rigid orthodoxy maintained by the mandarins of the profession. He had no confidence in the faith-healers and naturopaths who would be debarred by such licensing, but he deplored the shutting-down of the "extremely important experiences" which "these peculiar creatures" were rolling up.[14]

Individualism followed as a necessary corollary to cultural pluralism and the rejection of absolutes. In the judgment of

[14] *The Will to Believe.* New York, Longmans, 1897, pp. 207–8; Henry James, ed., *The Letters of William James.* Boston, The Atlantic Monthly Press, 1920, II, 67.

James, society was completely atomistic, and nothing was of much consequence except the welfare of its members. Mankind makes no progress, he taught, except through the initiative of individuals. But those of the ordinary sort must be guided and led by their intellectual superiors. The masses accomplish nothing except as they are inspired and stimulated by men of genius. Some Rembrandt must be there to show them the struggle of light with darkness, some Wagner to teach them to enjoy the dramatic in music, some Emerson to kindle a moral fire within them. What would have been the future development of the British Empire, James asked, if Robert Clive had shot himself, as he tried to do at Madras? If Bismarck had died in his cradle, "the Germans would still be satisfied with appearing to themselves as a race of spectacled *Gelehrten* and political herbivora." [15] If shown a particular way by its leaders, a nation may follow it; if not, it will never find it. The more rapid advancement of some nations than others is attributable solely to genius. Great epochs of civilization can be accounted for by an exceptional concourse of brilliant leaders within a limited time. James was not discriminating in the types of leaders he chose to approve. A Napoleon or a Garibaldi seemed to him as worthy of admiration as a Charles Darwin or a John Stuart Mill.

In line with his belief in the maximum of freedom for individuals and nations, James had no stomach for either imperialism or war. He hated bigness in all its forms and sympathized with the struggles of small nations to retain their independence. At the turn of the century he criticized American imperialism in the Philippines and hoped that the Boers would "give fits" to the British. In his celebrated argument for a "moral equivalent of war" he attempted to put pacifism on a sound psychological basis. War he regarded as an outgrowth of subliminal instincts of pugnacity and love of glory and excitement. Behind the façade of civilized human nature lurked a savage beast, ready to break through at the first opportunity. Our ancestors bred pugnacity into our very bones, and a hundred generations of peace would not be sufficient to get rid of it. The people want war, and would be bored by the dullness and insipidity of per-

[15] *The Will to Believe*, pp. 227–30.

petual peace. Unless some substitute is found which will provide the thrills and excitement and the appeals to heroism and self-sacrifice that are the fruits of military conflict, pacifism will rest upon flimsy foundations. It will fail and will deserve to fail. For, according to James, the virtues of militarism must be preserved to prevent the evolution of a nation of mollycoddles. With this end in view he urged the adoption of the "moral equivalent of war" in the form of a universal conscription of the whole youthful population to wage war against evil and hardship. Some "gilded youths" would be drafted to work in the coal mines; others would engage in dishwashing, road-building, or tunnel-making; still others would go into foundries and stoke-holes, to freight yards, or to fishing fleets in the dead of winter. All would "get the childishness knocked out of them," and would "come back into society with healthier sympathies and soberer ideas." [16] By such methods James believed that the benefits of war and the military life could be gained without the blood-letting. But he was enough of a sentimentalist to romanticize wars of the past. Clashes at arms had been "the gory nurse" that had sustained and nourished some of the greatest blessings of civilization. The God of Battles had been no less important than the Prince of Peace in hammering nations into cohesiveness and in determining the triumph of noble ideals.

The philosophy of Pragmatism, so sharply delineated by William James, was carried forward by John Dewey. A New England Yankee, educated at the University of Vermont and at Johns Hopkins, Dewey devoted his entire life to teaching and writing, with brief excursions into public affairs. He taught philosophy at the universities of Michigan, Minnesota, and Chicago before coming to Columbia, where he served for more than forty years. Well known as a philosopher and psychologist, he gained fame (and in some quarters infamy) as the Father of Progressive Education. Dewey revealed some significant disagreements with his great predecessor in the Pragmatist school. Whereas James was accused of "turning the lights down low in order to give the spirits a chance," Dewey believed that man, making use of his resources of reason and experience, could

[16] *Memories and Studies.* New York, Longmans, 1912, pp. 276–92.

solve his own problems without any assistance from the supernatural. Dewey rejected or at least ignored the elements of savagery which James professed to discover in human nature. Dewey also emphasized more strongly than James the practical objectives of philosophy. Indeed, his particular gospel of Pragmatism came to be called *Instrumentalism,* because of his insistence that philosophy be employed as an instrument, partly for the improvement of man himself, but mainly for the improvement of society.

The political philosophy of Dewey differed even more sharply from that of James. In the first place, Dewey was a democrat, not an exponent of intellectual aristocracy. He conceived democracy as almost synonymous with equality. While he did not for a minute maintain that the human race includes neither geniuses nor morons, he held it to be part of the democratic creed that intelligence is sufficiently general to enable each individual to contribute something of value. He asserted that democratic ends could only be achieved by democratic means— such means as universal suffrage, recurring elections, and responsibility to constituents. These elements of democracy, he maintained, rest upon the conviction that "no man or limited set of men is wise enough or good enough to rule others without their consent." [17] They are important, moreover, for their educative value. They involve consultation and discussion, which generally contribute to enlargement of views and to clarification of issues. Finally, according to Dewey, democracy embodies the idea of experiment. Its meaning must be continually explored afresh. "It has to be constantly discovered and rediscovered, remade and reorganized." [18] And the institutions in which it is embodied have to be rebuilt to meet the changes that are taking place in the development of new needs of the citizens.

Both Dewey and James were individualists, but the individualism of the former was so different from that of the latter that it is hardly possible to think of them under the same name. At

---

[17] Joseph Ratner, ed., *Intelligence in the Modern World; John Dewey's Philosophy.* New York, Modern Library, 1939, p. 401.
[18] *The Public and Its Problems.* New York, Holt, 1927, pp. 206–207.

the beginning of the depression of the 1930's, when waves of radical discontent were lapping at the foundations of the capitalist economy, Dewey published his *Individualism, Old and New.* In it he celebrated the obsequies of the *laissez-faire* individualism of the nineteenth century. He called attention to the growth of a corporate society, destroying initiative and independence. The emergence of vast combinations of capital, the mechanization of industry, and the integration of economic activities of every kind were reducing the individual to a cog in a machine. Even crime, he pointed out, was becoming organized and syndicated. In the face of such changes, the old idea of a sovereign individual making his way to the top by sheer initiative, industry, and ability under a regime of free competition had lost its meaning. It was time for individualism to take into account the demands of life in a revolutionized society. The citizen could no longer be left to wander by himself, confused and helpless in an alien world. He must be freed from anxiety and insecurity by the collective intelligence of the group. Only by this means could he be saved from the powerful pressures destroying his independence and be set once more on the road to an equal chance with his fellows.

The so-called individualism of Dewey implied a considerable degree of regimentation; for what it actually involved was the relegation of freedom to a secondary place in order to give primacy to security and to equality of economic opportunity. He emphasized what he called *positive* freedom in place of the older negative freedom that grants an individual the right to do as he pleases, so long as he does not interfere with the equal right of other individuals to do the same. Dewey's concept of positive freedom embraced those forms of liberty needed by the citizen to enable him to develop his potentialities and make his contribution to society. In no sense was this freedom to be regarded as absolute. It could not be claimed by the individual as a right; it was a right only to the extent that it was useful for the good of society. Freedom of expression, for example, could be regarded as a positive freedom, for without it the citizen had no chance of developing his intelligence to the maximum and thereby rendering a social service to the limit of his capacity.

Most of the regimentation regarded by Dewey as essential to individualism would take the form of what is commonly designated social engineering. The origins of this doctrine are somewhat obscure. It was foreshadowed in the teachings of Auguste Comte in his description of the positive stage of society controlled by the methods of objective research. It was developed much further by the American sociologist Lester Frank Ward (1841–1913). The deity of the social engineers was science and their gospel the scientific method. They argued that nature is one, and that the entire universe is governed by identical laws. The principles that guide the astronomer, physicist, or chemist in his researches are fully applicable to the social, political, and economic realms. It was not enough, however, that knowledge should be discovered by the scientific method. It must also be applied through continuous planning for the public good.

Dewey accepted the foregoing theses with an alacrity born of conviction. He contended that free enterprise had failed, and that collective control was already upon us. The only choice that remained was whether we should accept the capitalistic control that already exists or establish a new one that would operate in the public interest. Although Dewey at one time looked hopefully toward Soviet Russia as the nation that would provide the clue for saving the world from collapse, he eventually decided that neither communism nor fascism had anything to offer as models of social engineering. Both claimed to be planned societies; but Dewey argued that a tremendous difference exists between a *planned* society and a *continuously planning* society. The former requires fixed blueprints handed down from above. The latter involves continuous inquiry and investigation to discover the best methods of solving present and future problems. The former makes use of the frozen intelligence of some past thinker, sect, or cult. The latter regards all theories and accumulations of knowledge as tentative until verified by scientific investigation.

Unlike most of his predecessors among the social engineers, Dewey made no suggestion of a newfangled political system to carry on the work of continuous planning. On the contrary, he considered democracy to be admirably suited to that end. Democratic procedure, he contended, necessarily involves experimentation, investigation, analysis, and testing of results—in other words, a close approximation of the scientific method. Determination of policies arbitrarily or in accordance with some gospel or tradition of the past is not democracy but authoritarianism. Dewey maintained that adequate knowledge already exists for dealing scientifically with such problems as crime and war. But most people persist in thinking of these problems in "prescientific moral terms." They categorize both nations and individuals as "good" or "evil" and hope to win over the good to their side and to punish the bad. Punishment, revenge, retribution, however, are antiquated concepts with no foundation in science. The urgent need, according to Dewey, is for training the citizens of a democracy in an appreciation and understanding of the scientific attitude. Then only will the scientific revolution which began three hundred years ago be brought to fulfillment. Great as have been the social transformations of the past, "they are not to be compared with those which will emerge when our faith in scientific method is made manifest in social works." [19]

3. Contemporary Realists

Closely allied with both Positivism and Pragmatism is a contemporary philosophy known as Realism, or sometimes called the New Realism to distinguish it from ancient and medieval Realism. Actually, contemporary Realism bears so many similarities to Positivism and Pragmatism that it is not easy to keep them separate. All three recognize the importance of science. All three are anti-metaphysical. All three acknowledge the limited character of human knowledge. Yet there are differences. Though the Realist emphasizes the primacy of science, he admits the possible validity also of knowledge derived from reason. What is more, he is not a relativist. He believes in objective truth, no matter how incomplete and unsatisfying it may be. He would never dream of saying as did William James, that an

[19] *Philosophy and Civilization.* New York, Minton, Balch, 1931, p. 330.

idea is true which has "cash value" for him who holds it. He rejects everything that smacks of mysticism or of reliance upon
the supernatural. Finally, the Realist differs from the Positivist
and the Pragmatist in the extent of his pessimism and in the
depth of his sense of the tragic. He conceives of science as confronting human beings with a cold and alien universe, and as
portraying man himself as merely a bundle of atoms whose gift
of immortality is probably no more than the privilege of mingling
with the dust of centuries. Yet in the face of such hopelessness,
the attitude called for is not one of despair or repining but of
stoical dedication. Man can still live nobly and wage a good
fight to overcome such evils as are within his power. He can at
least preserve his self-respect by striving to direct the forces of
nature to the good of his fellows and himself, by avoiding any
action which may be the cause of suffering to others, and by
cherishing "the lofty thoughts that ennoble his little day; dis-
daining the coward terrors of the slave of Fate to worship at the
shrine that his own hands have built." [20]

The political and social attitudes of the New Realism are
best personified by two eminent citizens of the contemporary
world. One is an Englishman, Bertrand Russell (1872–   ),
and the other is an Indian, Jawaharlal Nehru (1889–   ).
Bertrand Russell is the grandson of the famous Lord John
Russell who fathered the Reform Act of 1832. In 1931 he himself inherited the title. Educated at Trinity College, Cambridge,
he has been a lecturer and professor at various institutions in
Britain and the United States during most of his life, except for
a brief period at the University of Peking. Though long recognized as one of the foremost logicians and mathematicians of
modern times, he has several times had to face the intolerance
of those who disliked his social views. During World War I he
was deprived of his lectureship at Trinity College, refused a
passport by the British government to allow him to leave the
country in order to lecture at Harvard, and ultimately imprisoned for six months as a result of his pacifist activities. As late

[20] Bertrand Russell, *Mysticism and Logic.* New York, Longmans, 1918, p. 57.

as 1940 his appointment to teach at the College of the City of New York (CCNY) aroused a furor of opposition in America on account of his unorthodox opinions on marriage and religion.

As a political philosopher, Bertrand Russell brings to a focus nearly all the liberal and radical intellectual currents of the eighteenth and nineteenth centuries. He personifies the rationalism of the Enlightenment, the practicality of the Utilitarians, the materialism and scientism of the Positivists, the collectivism and economic determinism of the socialists, and the skepticism and anti-metaphysical attitude of the Pragmatists. Yet all of these movements combined do not represent the totality of his thinking. For one thing, he is a confirmed exponent of democracy, though his opinions at times have been erratic. No government of the few, he contends, can ensure to all its citizens the rights and privileges essential to their happiness or provide the organization and management of economic resources necessary to maintain security. "The good life," he insists, "is one inspired by love and guided by knowledge." [21] No aristocratic society will be interested in such an ideal. Gentlemen of wealth and leisure, who regard themselves as superior by birth, look down upon the mass of human beings and consider no status too degrading for them. Such an attitude is the very antithesis of love and benevolence. It must be noted, however, that Russell's conception of democracy bears a closer resemblance to that of Jefferson than to that of Rousseau. He believes in government of and for the people, but not by the people. He applauds popular sovereignty but not popular rule. At the same time, there is at least one respect in which he deviates from the Jeffersonian ideal. Jefferson had faith in the capacity of the common people to select the men of wisdom and virtue, the *aristoi*, who would run the government. Russell postulates the ability of the masses themselves to *judge* and *appraise* the actions of their rulers and to criticize and call them to account. The only essentials for these purposes, he believes, are a modicum of education and full liberty of thought and discussion. He would set no limits whatever to the latter. Freedom

[21] *What I Believe*. New York, Dutton, 1925, p. 20.

of speech and the right to organize propaganda, "even if it brings incitement to assassination or violent revolution," are essential for the preservation of democracy.[22]

Along with his espousal of democracy, Russell advocates a substantial collectivism. The belief in private property he holds to be one of the greatest obstacles to human progress, and he urges its destruction as a condition precedent to a better world. All property, he argues, had its origin in violence and theft, as illustrated by the events surrounding the opening of gold and diamond mines in the Boer republics of South Africa. Despite such beliefs, he rejects the theories of both Marx and Lenin. For his skeptical mind, they are too thoroughly saturated with dogma. They are absolutist systems, which would set up a new despotism in place of the old. He prefers the indeterminism (tychism) of William James to the mechanical, deterministic logic of Marx and his followers. He repudiates also the Marxist theory of the state as an agency of class domination, a state which must ultimately wither away when the whole population has been transformed into a single class of workers. To Russell the state is a useful and necessary institution for regulatory purposes essential to the interests of all classes. It can never be dispensed with so long as the community has need for an organized life. He rejects, finally, the Marxist doctrines of class war, surplus value, and the excessive Marxist glorification of manual labor.

At one time, Russell's fears of tyranny led him to endorse the doctrines of the Pluralists, who proclaimed that the state is only one of a number of sovereign agencies prescribing rules for the governance of society. In this stage he seemed to regard all law and government as evils, which could be justified only for the purpose of preventing greater evils. All forms of coercion, he has stated, are hindrances to freedom and individual vitality. They therefore inhibit creativeness, which is the paramount source of human happiness. The type of collectivism which makes the strongest appeal to Russell is that advocated by the Guild Socialists during the 1920's. They proposed a system un-

---

[22] "Freedom and Government," in Ruth Nanda Anshen, ed., *Freedom: Its Meaning*. New York, Harcourt, 1940, p. 254.

der which the state would own the means of production and represent the interests of consumers, while management and operation of the factories, mines, railways, stores, etc. would be conducted by guilds, or associations of workers. By this means they hoped to prevent the growth of an oppressive bureaucracy, under which the workers would simply have exchanged one set of masters for another. Like the Guild Socialists, Russell considers power to be a kind of poison. He mistrusts every form of it, except that which derives from wisdom and consent. He sees every official caste as bound to include a set of men "whose whole instincts will drive them toward tyranny." [23] Largely for this reason, he condemns revolution, which he feels is almost certain to bring into power a dictatorial minority dominated by fear and determined to protect its supremacy by whatever ruthlessness appears to be necessary. He recognizes a right of revolution only when the government is so oppressive that laws cannot be repealed or revised through constitutional procedure and public opinion. What Russell really yearns for is socialism restrained by democracy. But if asked to accept the one without the other, he would choose democracy even when associated with a defective economy.

Enthusiasm for democracy and collectivism does not exhaust the ideals and objectives of Bertrand Russell. Like John Dewey he is a firm believer in the efficacy of education to liberate man from the weaknesses of his own nature and to correct the evils of an unfortunate environment. He contends that fear is the primary cause of hatred and envy and of man's inhumanity to his fellow men. Education in the understanding of self and environment is the only specific that can eradicate fear. A more obvious cause of human misery than fear is an excessive birthrate. For all practical purposes Russell is a Neo-Malthusian, who sees in birth control a sovereign remedy for a majority of the ills that trouble this tortured planet. Limitation of births would help to alleviate poverty, relieve nations of insecurity, and contribute toward allaying the specter of war. So great is his zeal for this remedy that he would not only have the state provide universal instruction in birth control, but impose penal-

[23] *Proposed Roads to Freedom.* New York, Holt, 1919, p. 128.

ties upon "those who have too many children." [24]

Russell stands out as an ardent proponent of international security. Though he supported the cause of the Allies in World War II, because of his belief that nothing could be worse than a fascist victory, he abhors war as totally evil. Nations attack one another when they become fearful of a loss of advantage or an impairment of national security. Wars will continue to occur until an international government is set up with an armed force strong enough to defeat any probable combination of states. The League of Nations did not provide for such a force. Neither does the charter of the United Nations. Escape from the evil of war, Russell contends, will not be found short of the establishment of a World Federation representing the *people* of the world instead of the governments of sovereign states.

Similar in interests and principles to Bertrand Russell is the Indian philosopher and statesman, Jawaharlal Nehru. Though the latter has a vast country to administer and powerful competing groups to conciliate, he continues to adhere closely to the doctrines of agnosticism, materialism, and socialism that have been the guiding stars of his life for nearly fifty years. The son of a wealthy Kashmir Brahman, Nehru was educated in England at Harrow and at Cambridge. In 1912 he was admitted to the bar but practiced for only a few years. After World War I he devoted his talents almost exclusively to the Indian Nationalist movement, in association with his father and with Gandhi. In 1929 he was elected president of the Indian National Congress (in reality the political party in India dedicated to the winning of independence) and was re-elected three times thereafter. Sentenced by the British on several occasions to long terms in prison, he utilized his enforced leisure in acquiring a familiarity with Marxist theory and in developing his own philosophy. When India gained her independence in 1947, Nehru, quite appropriately, became her first Prime Minister. Despite turmoil and disillusionment in some parts of the country, he still seems (after more than a decade of rule) to be the only statesman with sufficient prestige to keep the

[24] *New Hopes for a Changing World.* New York, Simon and Schuster, 1951, p. 40.

golden cord of national unity from being broken. Indeed, one of his major concerns seems to be the prevention of excessive adulation on the part of his people. He rebukes them sharply when they seek to deify him as a national savior. Some years ago he went so far as to warn them anonymously in an article in a Calcutta newspaper of the danger of his becoming a dictator. "Men like Jawaharlal," he wrote, "with all their capacity for great and good work, are unsafe in a democracy. He calls himself a democrat and a socialist, and no doubt he does so in all earnestness . . . but a little twist and he might turn into a dictator." [25]

Three main influences have shaped the development of Nehru's mind. The first was his Western education; the second was the philosophy of Gandhi; and the third was Marxian socialism. As a student at Harrow and Cambridge, Nehru was brought into contact with Western traditions of democracy, industrialism, and science. As a result, he turned his back upon everything Indian—rejecting the traditional Hindu religious pattern of mysticism, pessimism, denial of life. The Indian preoccupation with the spiritual and metaphysical and contempt for the worldly and material failed to attract Nehru. He became a rationalist, a humanist, an enthusiastic devotee of science, and a firm believer in the value of industrial and technological progress. "It is folly," he says, "to talk of God when human beings starve and die." [26] He contends that industrialization, combined with birth control, offers to India's teeming millions their only possible way of escape from their age-old burden of poverty, ignorance, and filth. His determination to raise the Indian standard of living is one of the prime explanations of his so-called neutralism in foreign policy. He feels strongly that he must not imperil his major objective by becoming entangled in the web of international power rivalries.

Nehru became a follower of Gandhi in 1919 after the infamous Amritsar Massacre in which 400 Indians were mowed down by the rifle fire of a regiment of soldiers commanded by a Brit-

[25] *Toward Freedom*. New York, John Day, 1942, p. 437.
[26] *Jawaharlal Nehru's Speeches, 1949–1953*. Government of India, Ministry of Information and Broadcasting, 1954, p. 361.

ish general. The future Prime Minister thereby deserted the moderate elements of the Congress party and identified himself with the radical wing demanding complete independence. Nevertheless, Nehru shrank from adopting the Gandhian philosophy in its entirety. He had no use for the otherworldliness, pietism, and asceticism of his master. He detested also Gandhi's primitivism, which would have led India back to a self-sufficient village economy, with no technology more intricate than the use of the spinning wheel and the hand loom. He disliked even more Gandhi's contempt for science, his willingness to eradicate all modern improvements in transportation and communication and even in medicine and sanitation in order to express his antagonism toward Western culture. On the other hand, the two men agreed in their defense of nationalism, in their opposition to imperialism, and in their devotion to the principle of non-violent resistance. Nehru, however, justified the use of force when necessary for the defense of liberty, and he criticized Gandhi during World War II for insisting that even a Japanese invasion must not be met with violent opposition.

The Marxist influence upon Nehru has been in some respects the most penetrating of all. To a large extent it has been the source of his opposition to imperialism and his antipathy to authoritarian rule. It has not only colored his philosophy of the past but has given him a "spectrum analysis" for the present and the future. He sees all history as a record unfolding with order and purpose. The clue to its understanding is the dialectical process in which the forces of production determine in each successive stage the political and social pattern. "The triumph of the machine and of industrialism meant the triumph of classes that controlled the machine . . . the class that controls the means of production is the class that rules." [27] Though he refuses in theory to accept absolute determinism, he admits that his own principles have been molded by the events of his life, and he persists in believing in the inevitability of a brighter future.

In recent years Nehru has modified his collectivist theory to the extent at least of preferring the socialism of the British Labour party to that of the strict Marxists or Communists. In

---

[27] *Glimpses of World History*. New York, John Day, 1942, p. 347.

other words, he advocates democratic planning, with government ownership of only the basic industries, instead of the revolutionary destruction of all private enterprise as it has been carried out in Russia. He still believes, however, that capitalism is the cause of many of the evils of the world—of greed and injustice, of depressions, wars, and grinding poverty in the midst of plenty. He thinks that imperialism would never have developed except as it was nourished by capitalism, and he considers fascism to be the noxious but inevitable fruit of imperialism. There is only one difference, he argues, between them. Whereas imperialism functions as a form of tyranny in colonies and dependencies, fascism operates in the same way in the home country also. To establish freedom in the world it is therefore not sufficient to destroy fascism; imperialism must be liquidated as well. He seems to think, however, that the complete elimination of capitalism can be postponed until some time in the future. It is significant that after eight years of Nehru's rule, all of the land and most of the industry remain in private hands. More and more he talks of a utopia, in which India will lead the world toward some vague ideal of equality, where no country or class can practice exploitation. But he dreams also of India at the head of a bloc of neutrals maintaining a balance of power in a bipolar world. Perhaps he feels that to play this role successfully his country should avoid committing herself too strongly to the ideology of either side.

Of all the political philosophies of the modern world, Relativism and Realism seem to reflect most accurately contemporary attitudes and ideals. They fit in neatly with the humanism, scientism, skepticism, materialism, and secularism which have grown increasingly prevalent with the spread of industrialization and urbanization. Positivism, also, has a close consistency with most of these ideals and attitudes. But Positivism is too directly associated with a discredited authoritarianism to appeal to many Western peoples. It is also too deeply impregnated with a fatalistic pessimism. Realism also has its pessimistic quality, but this quality is not a degrading hopelessness. It is a perception of the tragedy of life rather than a confession of defeat. Though man as the Realist sees him may be fated for oblivion, he does not surrender his pride or dignity.

It would, of course, be foolish to assume that Positivism, Relativism, or Realism, or any combination thereof, will ever enjoy universal sway over the minds of men. No matter how brilliant the triumphs of science, some people will not be satisfied with positivist or materialist answers to political and social questions. They will refuse to consider the state a secular institution. They will demand a source of law in the will of God or in the moral teachings of religion. They will yearn for eternal standards of justice and right, not subject to change with each passing era or dying culture. Representatives of these points of view are legion today as in many eras in the past. They range all the way from secular conservatives like Lewis Mumford to religious idealists like Reinhold Niebuhr, John H. Hallowell, Christopher Dawson, and Jacques Maritain. Whatever the differences in their premises, they share common beliefs in rationalism, humanitarianism, and ethical absolutism. They contend that positivism, skepticism, and scientism undermine the conception of man as a moral being endowed by God with a conscience and an ability to reason, and reduce him to a mere creature of his environment; in their opinion, these philosophies thereby detract from the nobility of man and make democracy impossible.

ADDITIONAL READINGS

Burnham, James. *The Machiavellians: Defenders of Freedom.* New York, John Day, 1943.

Dewey, John. *Characters and Events.* New York, Holt, 1929.

——. *Freedom and Culture.* New York, Putnam, 1939.

——. *Human Nature and Conduct.* New York, Holt, 1922.

——. *Individualism, Old and New.* New York, Minton, Balch, 1930.

——. *Liberalism and Social Action.* New York, Putnam, 1935.

——. *Philosophy and Civilization.* New York, Minton, Balch, 1931.

——. *Problems of Men.* New York, Philosophical Library, 1946.

————. *Reconstruction in Philosophy*. New York, Holt, 1920.

Elliott, William Y. *The Pragmatic Revolt in Politics*. New York, Macmillan, 1928.

Frankel, Charles. *The Case for Modern Man*. New York, Harper, 1956.

Henderson, Lawrence J. *Pareto's General Sociology*. Cambridge, Mass., Harvard University Press, 1935.

Homans, George C., and Curtis, Charles P., Jr. *An Introduction to Pareto*. New York, Knopf, 1934.

James, William. *Memories and Studies*. New York, Longmans, 1912.

————. *The Philosophy of William James*. New York, Modern Library (no date).

————. *Selected Papers on Philosophy*. New York, Dutton, 1917.

————. *The Will to Believe, and Other Essays in Popular Philosophy*. New York, Longmans, 1897.

Russell, Bertrand. *Authority and the Individual*. New York, Simon and Schuster, 1949.

————. *Human Society in Ethics and Politics*. New York, Simon and Schuster, 1955.

————. *New Hopes for a Changing World*. New York, Simon and Schuster, 1951.

————. *Philosophy and Politics*. Cambridge, England, Cambridge University Press, 1947.

Smith, Donald E. *Nehru and Democracy*. Bombay, Orient Longmans, 1958.

Spitz, David. *Patterns of Anti-Democratic Thought*. New York, Macmillan, 1949.

I V

Changing Conceptions
of Law

To speak of changing conceptions of law in the twentieth century may seem almost like carrying coals to Newcastle or adding gold to the sunset. Concepts of law have always been changing. Indeed, they have done little else. Aristotle defined law as "reason unaffected by desire." In writing thus he appears to have had the notion of a metaphysical embodiment of absolute justice superior to the wills of individual men; for he said "He who bids the law rule, may be deemed to bid God and Reason alone rule, but he who bids man rule adds an element of the beast." Apparently this law found its best expression in the customary law, since Aristotle considered the latter the safest of all rules for men to follow. It was left for Cicero and the Stoics to broaden and make more explicit Aristotle's conception of law as the embodiment of reason and justice. What they did was to formulate the theory of a higher law of nature, a product of the order of the universe and discoverable by human reason. As Cicero defined it, "True law is right reason consonant with nature, diffused among all men, constant, eternal. . . . To make enactments infringing this law, religion forbids, neither may it be repealed even in part, nor have we power through Senate or people to free ourselves from it."

The doctrine of a higher law formulated by the Stoics has

had a longer survival than any other legal theory of the Western world. It was adopted by Christian philosophers of the early Middle Ages and identified with the law of God. It was revived by St. Thomas Aquinas in the thirteenth century when he defined law as an "ordinance of reason for the common good promulgated by him who has the care of the community." From medieval sources it found its way, through the medium of Richard Hooker, into the teachings of the natural-rights philosophers of the seventeenth and eighteenth centuries. For John Locke and his followers the higher law was the law which had governed and guided men in the state of nature preceding the establishment of government. As such, it contained the fundamental rights which belong to all men under the order of nature. When governments are formed, these rights, so essential to the life of man as a reasoning creature, are not transferred but remain as an automatic limitation upon the acts of rulers. This was the theory which underlay the French Declaration of the Rights of Man and of the Citizen, the English Bill of Rights, and both the American Declaration of Independence and the American Constitution. It is still invoked occasionally by the Supreme Court of the United States in overruling laws of Congress or state legislatures alleged to conflict with some basic principle of justice or right. Chief Justice Marshall set the precedent in *Fletcher v. Peck* by overruling an act of the legislature of Georgia on the ground that it conflicted with "general principles which are common to our free institutions." As late as 1935 Chief Justice Hughes, in *Perry v. United States,* declared that when a government makes a contract, it incurs responsibilities similar to those of individuals who are parties to such instruments. Although the plaintiffs against the government have in such cases no legal remedy, Hughes asserted that the obligation remains "binding on the conscience of the sovereign."

Long before the twentieth century the theory of true law as the embodiment of justice and right was forced to compete with an altogether different conception. This was the conception of positive law, or law as a command of the state or an expression of the will of the sovereign. Lawyers in ancient Rome developed the idea of an omnipotent state, to which the people by a kind of irrevocable contract had delegated their power. By so doing they had authorized the organs of government to issue commands with the force and effect of laws. Under the Byzantine Empire this theory was used as a justification of autocracy. The *Corpus Juris* of Justinian declared that what pleases the prince has the force of law, since the people have delegated all power to him. With the revival of the study of the Roman law in the twelfth and thirteenth centuries, it was inevitable that this doctrine should win support. To combat the papal claims to temporal authority, if for no other reason, it was expedient to assert that what the Emperor willed had the force of law. By the sixteenth century it was possible for Machiavelli to take virtually for granted the idea that law is the command of any ruler who has the power to enforce it. A similar view was propounded by Thomas Hobbes in the seventeenth century. For more than a hundred years thereafter the opposing theory of law as a product of nature, discoverable by reason, held sway. But in 1762 Rousseau ridiculed the idea of universal justice and proclaimed law to be an expression of the general will, or in other words a command of the sovereign people.

The most definitive exposition of positive law in modern times came from the pen of an English Utilitarian by the name of John Austin (1790–1859). Though in many ways a follower of Jeremy Bentham, he studied for some years in Germany and was strongly influenced by the authoritarian theories of German jurists. Austin's legal conceptions were limited exclusively to the category of *positive* law. He defined law as a command given by a superior to an inferior, and binding by virtue of the power of the superior to enforce penalties. All other rules he relegated to the outer limbo of positive morality. These included so-called international law, the principles and precedents of English constitutional law, and even to a great extent customary law as represented by the common law of England. International law was not law, because there was no sovereign to enforce it. The principles and precedents of the British constitution suffered from a similar disadvantage—that they had never been enacted by a determinate sovereign. The English common law was recognized by Austin as law only to the extent that some of it had been accepted and given the force of law by enactment of parliament. As Austin saw it, law can proceed only from the express or implied commands of some definite person or persons, whom the rest of the people habitually obey because of the fear of penalties, and who render no obedience to any superior. Though it was a narrow, authoritarian conception, incompatible with the ideals of liberal democracy, to say nothing of most plans for international government, the Austinian theory was extensively adopted in nearly all countries of the civilized world. To this day it is the sheet anchor of those who call themselves legal positivists as distinct from the naturalists, who cling to the ideal of absolute justice which the reason of man can discover and apply for the good of society.

1. Pluralism

Theories of the nature and sources of law almost inevitably involve theories of the organization and authority of the state. For example, the positivist who insists upon thinking of law as the command of a sovereign enforced by a sanction is very likely to hold to a *monistic* conception of the state. In other words, since the state in modern times is the only institution equipped with police, jails, executioners, and soldiers, he may be tempted to classify the state as the one institution that can really be the source of law. But this is not a necessary deduction. If the positivist is willing to think of sanctions or penalties in something other than physical terms, he may readily adopt a *pluralistic* conception of the state. That is, he may recognize not only the state but other organizations within the state as sources of law. In this view, the rule of a medical association prohibiting advertising on the part of its members would be just as much of a law as any decree of a government. It would be backed, not by the threat of fine or imprisonment, but by the powerful sanction of moral pressure and even by the threat of expulsion.

With regard particularly to the *character* of law, the term pluralist may well be synonymous with naturalist. That is, the pluralist may think of the statutes and decrees of governments as only one classification of laws. He may believe in a higher law emanating from God and made manifest, perhaps, in the decrees of the Church. Or he may consider long-standing custom as a basis of law when it is adopted and applied by some social or professional organization. He may even think of abstractions such as justice, ideas of right, or beneficent social purpose as essential foundations of law. In fine, the pluralist, in his attitude toward law, may be either a positivist or a naturalist. The monist, who believes in an omnipotent state, recognizes only one sovereign, and therefore is invariably a positivist.

Pluralism, which regards the state as only one of a number of sovereign agencies to which the members of a modern community render allegiance, flourished during the first quarter of the twentieth century. Its origins, however, went back to the theories of Otto von Gierke and F. W. Maitland in the late nineteenth century. Briefly summarized, the doctrines of Gierke and Maitland attributed real personalities to those enduring associations which arise within any society. Each has a collective consciousness and a will independent of the minds and wills of its several members. Each, moreover, is an originating agency in the development of law. That is, without any prior authorization from the state, each functions as an organ through which common beliefs of a legal character find their way into rules of law. The state plays a primary part in this process, but its role is far from exclusive. In writing as they did, Gierke and Maitland were motivated chiefly by a desire to gain for the major social organizations recognition of their corporate privileges, obligations, and rights. They held that individuals are not the only units of which society is composed. They contended that fraternal, religious, and professional associations also have personalities and should be accorded a like status as citizens.

In denying the omnipotence and omnicompetence of the state, most pluralists centered their attention upon the sovereignty and rights of professional and economic associations. Such was notably true of Joseph Paul-Boncour (1873–   ) and Harold J. Laski (1893–1950). The former, in his active years, was one of France's most distinguished statesmen. In 1932, in 1933–1934, and again in 1938 he was Minister of Foreign Affairs. In 1932 he held also the position of Premier, in a Cabinet that lasted six weeks. He assisted in the establishment of both the League of Nations and the United Nations and was one of the most ardent advocates of an international police to curb aggression. Paul-Boncour attributed great importance to occupational and professional associations such as medical societies, learned societies, and trade associations. He contended that they arise spontaneously in all countries and that they develop rapidly to a stage in which they impose rules upon their own members and dictate conditions to the rest of society. Though originally contractual, their relations with their members and in some cases with elements outside their ranks tend to become compulsory. He hoped not merely to gain legal recognition for economic organizations, but to win for them an important role in the democratic process. The system of popular sovereignty, he argued, rests upon the assumption that the majority recognizes and understands the common interest of all the citizens and is capable of acting in that interest. But this assumption, he contended, is contrary to the facts. The majority of a nation does not have the knowledge and ability to perceive and provide for the interests of the whole population, for the simple reason that those interests are not common in all respects. There is danger, therefore, that the majority will bestow its favors on special groups. To prevent this, there should be particular sovereigns to decide issues of vital concern to special economic groups, leaving to the general sovereign, or the state, the function only of resolving issues that are really of common interest. For example, the question whether labor-union funds should be contributed for the support of a political party is really of most vital concern to the union itself. But it is also a matter of public concern, and neither Paul-Boncour nor any other pluralist ever devised a satisfactory means of distinguishing sharply between areas of jurisdiction.

Similar arguments, in somewhat more pointed form, were adduced by Harold J. Laski. During his pluralist period, Laski emphasized not merely the normative aspects of sovereignty in modern society but the actualities as well. That is, he denied that the monistic theory corresponds to reality. To believe in the omnipotence and omnicompetence of the modern state is to pin one's faith to a myth. He cited the reluctance of the British government, during World War I, to enforce the anti-strike provisions of the Munitions Act against Welsh miners and the threat of a nationwide strike by the railroad brotherhoods that forced the American Congress to enact the Adamson law in 1916. How can it be true, he asked, that the state is the only sovereign when it is compelled by powerful groups of a non-political nature to acquiesce in policies to which it is opposed? Society, he concluded, is essentially federal in character. The state must compete for the allegiance of the citizens with churches, trade unions, employers' associations, chambers of commerce, bar associations, and medical associations. In comparison with these others, the state itself has no peculiar merit. When a conflict arises, the question whether the state shall be accorded pre-eminence depends entirely upon the moral superiority it can demonstrate in that instance. "The only state to which I owe allegiance," he wrote, "is the state in which I discover moral adequacy. . . . Our first duty is to be true to our conscience." [1] But what he granted with one hand he almost took away with the other. He spoke of "the ultimate reserve power of the state"; recognized that the state, because of its compulsory membership, is distinct from other associations; and admitted that, in order to satisfy common needs, the state "must control other associations to the degree that it secures from them the service such needs require." [2]

Because Christianity from its very inception laid claim to a position independent of the state, it was inevitable that some pluralist should expound the theory that the Church is a sovereign body with an authority superior in some instances to that of the state and with the right to share the loyalties of citizens. This role was essayed particularly by J. Neville Figgis (1866–1919), an English clergyman, famous for his study of *The Divine Right of Kings*. After serving as curate of a number

---

[1] *A Grammar of Politics*. New Haven, Yale University Press, 1925, pp. 249, 289.
[2] *Ibid.*, pp. 62, 69–70.

of Anglican parishes, Figgis became a lecturer in various institutions in Britain and America, including Cambridge University, Harvard University, and the General Theological Seminary. He spent the last ten years of his life as a member of the Anglo-Catholic Community of the Resurrection.

Although Figgis insisted upon an inviolable sphere for all important social groups, such as trade unions, colleges, and families, he was interested primarily in the independence of the Church. Religion he held to be anterior to the state and for that reason alone entitled to an exalted status. But more than this, he set forth the idea of the Church as a corporate association with a distinct personality. It must be recognized, he said, "as a social union with an inherent original power of self-development, acting as a person with a mind and will of its own." [3] As a corporate person it has the same rights and privileges as an individual. It exists for purposes as vital as those of the state itself and should have full control over matters of concern to its own members. Such secular movements to control the Church as Bismarck's *Kulturkampf* were ethically and spiritually wrong, said Figgis, for they were founded upon the assumption that the state is entitled to a monopoly of the loyalty of its citizens. But neither Figgis nor any other of the pluralists appeared to be more than dimly conscious of the fact that the line between secular and ecclesiastical functions is difficult to draw. Even in the Middle Ages, when the Church was much stronger than it is now, it ran into conflict with one secular ruler after another and eventually went down to defeat. Perhaps Figgis would have argued that it was the kings and emperors who overstepped the bounds of their rightful authority; but who can be sure that such matters of social concern as contracts, marriages and divorces, and exemption of Church property from taxation belong exclusively in the ecclesiastical sphere?

We come finally to a group of pluralists who were interested chiefly in the juristic implications of their theory. Foremost among them were Léon Duguit (1859–1928) and Hugo Krabbe (1857–1936). Duguit was a professor of law in the University of Bordeaux for forty-two years. He lectured also from time to

[3] *Churches in the Modern State.* London, Longmans, 1913, p. 99.

time in the United States, in Argentina, in Egypt, and in various European countries. Though he is sometimes classified as a positivist, this was true only in the philosophical sense. His theory of the source of law was not that of either a positivist or a naturalist. As a philosopher he sought to develop a theory of the state based solely upon objective data and excluding all metaphysical ideas. He refused, however, to consider the state as the fountain of law. The state is not even entitled to sovereignty, since it is composed merely of a group of governors, who are themselves limited by law. Historical evidence shows, he contended, that law is anterior and external to the state. It comes into existence as a body of rules arising from social relationships among men. These rules become laws when certain leaders decide that in order to guarantee their observance, it is expedient to support them with sanctions. The leaders themselves are not necessarily rulers; they are more commonly medicine men, priests, or elders. And the sanctions they originally invent are more likely to resemble taboos than threats of physical coercion.

According to Duguit, the state has no necessary relation to law. To be sure, it issues commands and makes decisions which are normally obeyed by the great majority of its citizens. But whether these are actually laws depends, he said, not upon the fact that they emanate from the state but upon their intrinsic character and the purpose they serve. Fundamentally, laws are the rules of conduct that must be observed if society is to be held together. Long ago men discovered that they could not live as isolated individuals. Even to survive they were forced to band together in clans and tribes. As their knowledge and experience increased, they came to the conclusion that they could live still better in larger groups. Thus states were formed, composed of governors and subjects. The rule of the former was based in some cases upon physical strength, in others upon wealth or intellectual superiority. But laws continued to exist wholly independent of states and their rulers. Most of them had their origin in social objectives prior to the evolution of the state. Others represented customary rules endorsed and supported by governments. But in order to possess the quality of laws, all such regulations, whether in unwritten or statutory form, must promote the end of social solidarity. To Duguit this was all-important, since neither society nor the individual could exist without it. The conclusion followed that any so-called law which ignored or hindered this aim was not law at all, no matter how much organized coercion there might be behind it or how many people faithfully obeyed it. The validity of a law depends not upon its source or origin but upon the purpose it serves. A state that violates the object of social solidarity, whether through legislative enactments, judicial decisions, or administrative decrees, operates unlawfully.

In one important particular Duguit's conception of law was different from that of most naturalists. He professed no belief in a higher law of nature inherent in the order of the universe and embodying the indefeasible rights of the individual. He was not concerned with the rationality of the laws or the quality of justice they might reflect. The only question that needed to be asked to determine a law's validity was whether or not it was consistent with the aim of social solidarity. Such a test would bear little or no relation to justice or reason. It tended also to make the theory of Duguit more compatible with collectivism than it was with individualism. Though law in his judgment was superior to the state, it was superior also to the individual. He recognized no body of sacred rights appertaining to the individual because of his membership in the human race or his dignity and worth as a person. If freedom of speech, assembly, or press conflicted with the goal of social solidarity, these specific freedoms would have to give way to the social good. The same principle would hold true in the event of a conflict between the needs of society and individual citizens' ownership and use of property.

Hugo Krabbe, Professor of Public Law in the University of Leyden, and author of *The Modern Idea of the State*, was as deeply concerned as Duguit with upholding the superiority of the law. Like his French contemporary, he regarded law as anterior to the state and as dependent in no sense upon the will or commands of a sovereign. But he did not agree that the purpose of a law is the exclusive criterion of its validity.

Instead, he defined law as "every general or special rule, whether written or unwritten, which springs from men's feeling or sense of right." [4] The function of the state is to discover which rules of society correspond to the people's ideals of right and to give them effect as statutes. As such, they become binding not merely upon the citizens but upon the government as well. Neither the rulers nor anyone else can be above the law, for the law is simply the concrete expression of right which has an objective and eternal existence independent of human will or command. Krabbe rejected completely the Austinian idea that the state makes or originates laws. The state performs no function whatever except to approve and to aid in the enforcement of what is already law because it is the embodiment of right. He rejected also the theory that the authority of the state depends upon its power to impose its will upon its subjects. The authority of the state resides in the authority of the law, and only to the extent that its actions comport with the law does it have any rightful claim to the people's allegiance.

Krabbe assigned to the state a much more restricted sphere than that envisaged by Duguit. Both philosophers believed in limited government, but Duguit conceived of the public authority as extending in almost any direction consistent with the general good. His only demand was that political action be consonant with the aim of social solidarity. He would apparently have welcomed the development of the state into a gigantic social-service agency. Krabbe, on the other hand, insisted upon limiting the acts of the state to the narrow sphere of discovering and maintaining law. The implications of his theory were democratic, for he held that no autocrat or oligarchs could discover the community sense of right. Only the community itself or its authorized representatives, he argued, can accurately determine this. In case of difference of opinion, the convictions of the majority would normally be decisive, though he admitted they might be modified in some instances by the trained and experienced judgment of courts acting in the community interest. He still contended, however, that the province of the state does

[4] G. H. Sabine and W. J. Shepard, trans., *The Modern Idea of the State.* New York, D. Appleton, 1922, p. 39.

not extend beyond the domain of law. Its true character does not manifest itself in delivering telegrams, in building railroads and canals, or in paying pensions to the unemployed or to the aged and infirm. To whom he would delegate these functions remains somewhat obscure. But he seems to have thought very highly of the public corporation as a device for such purposes. Many organizations answering to this description, he argued, already exist. Postal-savings banks, telephone and telegraph systems, state universities, and public insurance authorities in various countries have developed into public corporations more or less independent of governments. The system needs only to be extended, Krabbe maintained, to fulfill all of the essential demands of modern society.

Pluralism has now been virtually extinct for twenty years. Perhaps it left too many questions unanswered and permitted an excess of loopholes through which the absolute sovereignty of the state could regain its vitality. Doubtless it alarmed some people as a near approach to anarchism or as so great a threat to the integrity of the state as to cause it to collapse. Nationalism, patriotism, fear of aggression, and the demand for a universal welfare agency combined to relegate pluralism to the past. That it will ever be revived as long as men feel the need of an omnipotent state to protect a way of life against the hostile designs of foreigners seems out of the question. Yet pluralism made a number of contributions which deserved a better hearing than they generally received. It exposed the absurdity of the old legalist doctrine that the sovereign makes the law and at the same time is bound by the law. It revealed the barbarity of the assumption that the essence of the state is power, and that all of its commands, no matter how brutal or irrational, have an equal claim to validity. By establishing reason, justice, right, or benevolent social purpose as the basis of law, it provided a means of safeguarding the consciences of individuals without inviting insubordination or revolution. As developed by Krabbe, in particular, it offered a logical foundation for a world republic and the only one with more than a scanty prospect of being accepted. What Krabbe proposed was that international government be restricted to the single function of ratifying and giving effect to the world community's sense of right. Had he lived until 1948, he would have been pleased by the adoption by the United Nations of a Universal Declaration of Human Rights embodying civilized man's conceptions of equity and justice. The great step that remains to fulfill Krabbe's ideal is for a world government to give these conceptions the effect of laws.

2. Positivist Jurisprudence

In the first section of this chapter we noted that the legal positivist is one who believes that law is made by the state, and that it acquires its validity from the power of the sovereign to inflict penalties for infractions of it. The legal positivist stands at the opposite pole from the naturalist, who teaches that law expresses ideals of right and justice, and that it derives its validity from the extent to which it is an actual embodiment of those ideals. Legal positivism is sometimes referred to as legal realism, especially when its exponents deny the existence of any other law than that which has the form of commands of the state.

Although positivist jurisprudence, or the science of law conceived from the positivist viewpoint, dates back at least to John Austin, it attained no major importance except in Germany until the twentieth century. Among its German defenders were Karl Gerber (1823–1891), Georg Jellinek (1851–1911), and Paul Laband (1838–1918). Their cardinal purpose was the development of the theme of the *Rechtstaat*, or the state which functions under the rule of law. They emphasized adherence to legal form and juridical procedure as the best safeguards of the welfare of the citizens. Though they conceded that the state alone can make law, and that every one of its sovereign commands is *ipso facto* valid, they characterized the state as only potentially omnipotent. While its sovereignty is unlimited, there are some things it will refrain from doing because of its nature as the supreme incarnation of the social objectives of man. For instance, it will not deprive an individual of his property without compensation. Moreover, the sovereignty of the state does not extend to its rulers. They are its servants, not its masters, and are bound by the laws that control the ordinary citizen. The whole conception of the *Rechtstaat* was founded upon the assumption of a government of laws and not of men. Under the restraint of its own purposes, the state would enact and develop codes which would control the acts of its officials. The rights and privileges of the citizens would also be clearly defined. The process of governing would be largely a matter of administration, with professional bureaucrats issuing decrees and making decisions in strict accordance with the content and procedures of the official codes.

In the twentieth century, legal positivism and its derivative, legal realism, have been especially important in the United States. Its original prophet in America was John Chipman Gray (1839–1915). For more than forty years a teacher of law at Harvard, he became the foremost authority of his time on property. In 1909, at the age of seventy, he expounded his views on jurisprudence in *The Nature and Sources of Law*. His major thesis was that the real creators of law are the judges. They draw their opinions from many sources, from tradition, precedent, the teachings of philosophers and jurists, but especially from the moral convictions that are part of their own emotional make-up. None of these sources are laws until incorporated in official opinions of judges. Even statutes and constitutional amendments are not really laws until judges have determined their validity or interpreted their meaning. In effect, Gray was saying that the constitution is what the judges say it is, and laws are what the courts will enforce. How much influence Gray may have had in shaping the convictions of some of his later contemporaries is unknown, but it must have been considerable. There is at least a close resemblance between several of his ideas and those of Justice Holmes.

We have already examined Justice Holmes as a Pragmatist, a Social Darwinist, and a romanticist. The boundaries of his philosophy took in an even larger territory. Despite his belief that under the cutthroat competition of capitalism, the masses got all they deserved, he was nevertheless a social collectivist or societarian. That is, he exalted society above the individual. For him, society was the end, and the individual an instrument for the attainment of that end. He declared himself in emphatic rebellion against "the Kantian injunction to regard every human being as an end in himself and not as a means." [5] In the opinion of Holmes, the universe was a blind machine, indifferent to the fate of men. The law of life was struggle, and the victory went to the strongest and the most ruthless. Idealism and pity for the weak were unreal and useless. "If a man is on a plank in the deep sea which will only float one, and a stranger lays hold on it, he will thrust him off if he can. When the state finds itself in a similar position, it does the same thing." [6]

As a legal philosopher and jurist Holmes clung to his Social Darwinist concepts by striving to eliminate from the law all traces of moral and sentimental idealism. He thought it would be a gain if every word of moral significance could be banished from the law and absolutely nothing left which was external to the statutes, precedents, and constitutional provisions. All of our conclusions about morality and truth, he contended, are arbitrary anyway, and in the last analysis the only factor to re- solve deep-seated differences is force. Men fight for what they believe to be their rights as animals fight over scraps of food. But these rights have no existence except as the state creates and grants them. Holmes dismissed the doctrines of natural rights and natural law as amiable fictions and insisted that no state had ever hesitated to sacrifice the welfare of individuals for the sake of preserving its own existence.

The actual meaning of law, to Holmes, was disarmingly sim- ple. As he approached the zenith of his career, he defined law as "The prophecies of what the courts will do in fact, and noth- ing more pretentious." [7] To the end of his life he remained firmly convinced that the judges were not the discoverers of law, but its creators. In a very real sense, therefore, the law was what the courts would enforce. It was not "a brooding omni- presence in the sky" which learned men of the law could pull down and apply to concrete cases. Instead, it was a product of the minds and emotions of the judges themselves. With such an

[5] Max Lerner, ed., *The Mind and Faith of Justice Holmes*, p. 392.
[6] *Ibid.*, p. 59.
[7] *Ibid.*, p. 75.

interpretation in view, it was idle to dream of absolutes like justice and right. There could be no such thing as an unjust decision, though there might be incompetent or erroneous decisions. The test, however, was not conformity to a metaphysical or theological standard of justice or goodness, but compliance with the will of the community. It was the duty of the jurist to take the rules and precedents which had come down from the past and shape them in accordance with the needs of the present. "The first requirement of a sound body of law is, that it should correspond with the actual feelings and demands of the community, whether right or wrong." [8] Determination of the feelings and demands of the community rested, in the first instance, with the legislature; and Holmes believed that the wise judge would exercise continence in reviewing the actions of the people's representatives. Nonetheless, he never abandoned his assumption that the ultimate power reposed in the courts.

In assuming that the needs and demands of the community are the supreme justification of laws, Holmes did not mean that they could be interpreted frivolously or unreasonably. He did agree, however, that they could be construed broadly. His doctrine of judicial continence meant that judges should take it for granted that legislators have the wisdom and experience to understand community problems, and that they generally act reasonably in attempting to solve them. Unless there is evidence of arbitrary or unreasonable action, the courts should not interfere. It was premises of this kind which enabled Holmes to arrive at the conclusions he did in *Commonwealth v. Davis*, in which he upheld a Boston ordinance forbidding anyone to make a speech on the Boston Common without a permit from the mayor; in *Coppage v. Kansas*, in which he dissented from the opinion of the majority of the Supreme Court invalidating a Kansas statute which outlawed "yellow dog" contracts; in *Debs v. United States*, in which he affirmed the conviction of the famous Socialist leader for making anti-war and anti-militarist speeches during World War I; in *Buck v. Bell*, in which he endorsed a Virginia statute permitting sterilization of inmates of institutions for the feeble-minded; and in various other cases.

[8] *The Common Law*. Boston, Little, Brown, 1881, p. 41.

of equal significance. In essence his philosophy held that the state may do almost anything it considers necessary for the defense of its own existence and for promotion of the health, safety, good morals, and general welfare of its citizens, provided it does not act arbitrarily or beyond reason. Moreover, any threat to its existence or its objects must be direct and immediate; otherwise the threat should go unpunished in order to foster that free exchange and competition of ideas which is necessary for social progress.

The thesis of the legal realists that judges are the creators of law has received support in various quarters. Charles Evans Hughes once declared "Judges must and do make laws." The distinguished English jurist Sir Frederick Pollock exclaimed that "No intelligent lawyer would in this day pretend that the decisions of the courts do not add to and alter the law." Another British legalist, A. V. Dicey, asserted that "Judge-made law is real law." The American philosopher Morris R. Cohen ridiculed what he called the "phonograph theory of law," which regards judges as mere spokesmen or mouthpieces of a rigid, mechanical body of principles handed down through the ages. But the most radical exponent of legal realism in our time was Jerome Frank (1889–1957). Educated at the University of Chicago, Frank began the practice of law in Chicago in 1912, transferring later to New York. When the New Deal was launched in 1933 he was appointed General Counsel of the AAA. In 1937 he became a member of the SEC, and two years later its chairman. From 1941 till his death he was a judge of the United States Court of Appeals for the Second Circuit. He was the author of such provocative books as *Law and the Modern Mind, If Men Were Angels, Fate and Freedom,* and *Courts on Trial.*

Judge Frank gave the impression of being a devout admirer of Justice Holmes, whom he lauded as "the completely adult jurist." He seemed, however, to overlook most of the weaknesses of the Supreme Court Justice. He ignored Holmes' exaltation of the "divine message" of war, his uncritical Social Darwinism, his contempt for reformers, and his prejudices against socialism and the strivings of the masses to throw off the shackles of poverty and hardship. Frank retained the relativism and skepticism of Holmes but did not accept his fatalistic belief in change as the sole law of the universe. Frank had an abiding confidence in the power of man to take a firm hold upon this raw and defective world and reshape it in accordance with what science has taught him the world should be like. Finally, it should be noted that whereas Holmes was essentially a deductive philosopher with little conception of the scientific method, Frank regarded the determination of the scientist to discover the truth regardless of its consequences for hoary tradition as the one best hope for a better society. Though both men admired William James, Frank approached more closely the ideal of Dewey.

To explain the real nature of law, Frank submitted the following: "For any particular lay person, the law, with respect to any particular set of facts, is a decision of a court with respect to those facts. . . . Until a court has passed on those facts no law on that subject is yet in existence." [9] He admitted that this was not the definition of the majority of the members of the bench and the bar. The majority regarded law as a fixed and immutable body of principles which the courts applied to individual cases; somewhere at the end of a rainbow there was a golden pot of law which judges and lawyers could find if they searched diligently for it. But all this certainty and immutability is a myth, according to Frank. Law, like every other social phenomenon, is in constant flux. The courts make it and unmake it with almost as much abandon as characterizes the work of legislatures in revising and repealing statutes. But instead of admitting this fact, judges resort to evasions and circumlocutions. The result is to delude the public into believing that there is much more precision about rights, entitlements, obligations, and penalties than actually exists. This deception, however, has nothing sinister or diabolical about it. The judges deceive others because they are themselves deceived. They have come to accept myths as truths without investigating them or thinking very much about them.

But why this harboring and dissemination of myths? According to Frank, the explanation lies deeply buried in psycho-

[9] *Law and the Modern Mind.* New York, Brentano's, 1930, p. 46.

logical truth. It results from the fact that human beings carry over into their adult lives the dreams and wish-fulfillments of childhood. The child craves security. He finds it in dependence upon his parents, who provide for his needs, answer his questions, and furnish an anchor of safety to which he can cling. The father, in particular, becomes a symbol of strength, authority, and infallibility. With increasing age and experience, the child discovers that his father is not a paragon of strength and wisdom who can command the sun to stand still or halt the stars in their courses. But this does not diminish his craving for security. He invents a substitute, a father-image, and turns to the worship of a king or dictator or to the veneration of some abstraction which seems to provide a haven amid the fears and anxieties of a troubled world. The law, as Frank saw it, is admirably fitted to become this father-image. It is a body of rules apparently devised for determining positively and infallibly what is right and what is wrong and for imposing penalties upon willful violators—in other words, the precise functions commonly attributed to the father. The law therefore becomes personified as a father-substitute in the minds of people who yearn for security and certitude. This sets up an emotional block which befuddles the thinking of lawyers and judges as well as laymen, and prevents them from viewing the problems that come within the legal sphere with realism and objectivity.

The remedy for this disease of apotheosizing the law as a father-image Frank found in science. The study of the law, he taught, must be infused with the scientific spirit, "which yearns not for safety but risk, not for certainty but adventure, which thrives on experimentation, invention and novelty and not on nostalgia for the absolute." [10] Above all, it is imperative that lawyers and judges be trained in psychological understanding of themselves and others in order that they may be made keenly aware of the roots of their own prejudices, biases, and antipathies. The vital need, in a field so important as the law, is emotional maturity. Modern civilization requires a mind free of father-dominance. "Until we become thoroughly cognizant of, and cease to be controlled by, the image of the father hidden

[10] *Ibid.*, p. 98.

away in the authority of the law, we shall not reach that first step in the civilized administration of justice, the recognition that man is not made for the law, but that the law is made by and for men." [11]

Juristic positivists and legal realists are sometimes accused of opening the gates for arbitrary government and the rule of force. By teaching that law is man-made and by denying the reality of absolutes like reason and right, they are supposed to be saying in effect that fallible human beings can usurp the role of God and decide for themselves what constitutes morality and justice. From this it is alleged that it is only a step to the imposition by force of the beliefs of some dominant group or class upon the rest of mankind. Such, however, is a distortion of the theories of most positivists and realists. In particular, those who take their cue from John Dewey do not agree that law should be nothing more than the commands and decrees of men in power. On the contrary, they emphasize the importance of knowledge, training, perspective, and insight. While the judges would not be restrained by an imaginary law of nature, they would be held in check just as effectively by their allegiance to the scientific attitude, by their training in objectivity and the understanding of human nature, and by their devotion to the principle that law is an instrument of the general good.

3. Sociological Jurisprudence

A number of jurists properly classified as positivists or realists are commonly regarded as exponents of sociological jurisprudence. This is notably true of Justice Holmes, despite his impatience with social science and with fact-gathering in general. Actually, about all he had in common with the sociological jurists was his belief in evolutionary change and his tolerance for social experiment. Sociological jurisprudence may, indeed, bear some resemblance to juristic positivism. Both recognize the value of the scientific approach and urge the adaptation of law and of legal institutions to changing social conditions. Both teach that law is functional, that it is something to be explained

[11] *Ibid.*, p. 252.

in terms of ends rather than origins, and that its operation and effects are more important than its abstract legal content. On the other hand, the sociological jurists do not necessarily agree with the positivists that law is created by judges or by any other agents of a sovereign authority. They may look for at least a part of the law in philosophical principles that bear no relation to the will or desires of any one generation.

To pinpoint the origins of sociological jurisprudence or to assign credit to any one individual as its founder would be impossible. It was foreshadowed extensively in the theories of Rudolf von Jhering (1818–1892) and Ludwig Gumplowicz (1838–1909). The former, a professor in the universities of Basel, Rostock, Kiel, Giessen, Vienna, and Göttingen, is renowned as the most encyclopedic of the German jurists of the nineteenth century. His celebrated work, *The Struggle for Law*, was translated into twenty languages. Prior to Jhering's time most legal theories were individualist. Law was conceived as something which the individual invoked against society for the protection of rights carried over from the state of nature. Jhering set forth a social theory of law. Law, he maintained, is created by society. Its purpose is not so much to protect rights as to enable the citizen to secure his interests, to the extent that society recognizes them. Gumplowicz, a Polish sociologist who taught at the University of Graz, produced the doctrine that the behavior of human beings has significance only in relation to groups. He saw the history of civilization as an unending struggle, first between primitive races, then between states after one race has conquered the others, and finally between classes within each state. Law he conceived as the result of a struggle among social groups. He relegated the individual so far to the background as to reduce him almost to a nonentity.

Sociological jurisprudence has been said to have been born in the United States when Louis D. Brandeis submitted his brief to the Supreme Court in the case of *Muller v. Oregon* in 1908. Studded with facts garnered by painstaking research, it was a brilliant example of the use of the data of the social sciences to buttress a legal argument. In his crusades against bigness, in his defense of free competition and the right of collective bargaining, in his advocacy of the guaranteed annual wage, Brandeis marshaled facts and figures in a fashion more suggestive of the social reformer or statistician than the old-time lawyer appealing to Blackstone or to Coke on Littleton. Appointed to the Supreme Bench in 1916, he continued his sociological approach and eventually found valiant allies in Chief Justice Stone and Associate Justices Benjamin Cardozo and Felix Frankfurter.

The most systematic exponent of sociological jurisprudence, however, has not been a judge but a law-school dean and a voluminous writer on juristic philosophy. His name is Roscoe Pound (1870–), and his influence has probably surpassed that of any other recent commentator on the theory and practice of law, with the possible exception of Holmes. Growing up in Nebraska in the turbulent days of the Granger and Greenback movements, Pound majored in botany at the State University in Lincoln before going to Harvard Law School for his LL.B. Even after that he returned to Nebraska for a Ph.D. A teacher of law at Northwestern University and the University of Chicago, he became Story Professor at Harvard in 1910 and Dean of the Law School in 1916. His twenty years as Dean were the most productive of his life. A profusion of books issued from his pen, explaining the origins and nature of the law and seeking to give it new life and meaning in terms of the realities of modern life. Among his best-known titles are *The Spirit of the Common Law, Introduction to the Philosophy of Law, Interpretations of Legal History,* and *Criminal Justice in America.*

Pound defined sociological jurisprudence as a movement for the adoption of pragmatism as a philosophy; "for the adjustment of principles and doctrines to the human conditions they are to govern rather than to assume first principles; for putting the human factor in the central place and relegating logic to its true position as an instrument." [12] He drew sharp contrasts between the new jurisprudence and the old. The jurists of the nineteenth century, he explained, sought to deduce fundamental principles

[12] "Liberty of Contract," *Yale Law Journal*, XVIII (1909), 454.

from metaphysics and from history. The new jurisprudence seeks to persuade those responsible for making and applying legal rules "to take more account and more intelligent account of the social facts upon which law must proceed and to which it is to be applied." The jurists of the past studied law in the abstract; those of the new era insist upon studying the actual social effects of institutions and doctrines. Where the jurists of the nineteenth century held comparative law to be the best foundation for wise legislation, those of the twentieth century believe that it is not enough to compare the laws but that it is even more important to examine and understand their social operation. The jurists of the past century were interested primarily in the making of law; those of the new day consider it more valuable to concentrate on means of giving effect to the legal rules. These basic differences, according to Pound, constitute the spirit of twentieth-century jurisprudence. "Such is the spirit in which legal reason is to be employed upon our received jural materials in order to make of them instruments for realizing justice in the world of today." [13]

Dean Pound has been especially critical of the American system of law as it has developed since the seventeenth century. He admits that it has one great element of strength in its common-law background, which gives it flexibility and the advantage of dealing with concrete controversies. In these respects, it is superior to what he calls Byzantine law, founded upon the idea of a fixed body of rules embalmed in a code, which the courts must apply mechanically.

Allowing for these merits, he still regards the American system as seriously defective. It has too little concern with social righteousness and too much with individual rights. It tries questions of the greatest social consequence as mere private litigation between John Doe and Richard Roe. In addition, it is too deeply involved in metaphysical conceptions of natural law. According to Pound, these have worked incalculable mischief in limiting the power of the state to effectuate measures for the general good. They have substituted doctrines drawn from a world of

[13] *The Spirit of the Common Law.* Boston, Marshall Jones, 1921, pp. 212–13.

unreality for the pragmatic elements of the common law evolved through centuries of adaptation to changing conditions.

Further, as Pound conceives it, American law suffers from the lengthy shadow of Puritan influence. With his predominant middle-class interests, the Puritan exalted individual independence, especially in the form of conducting economic affairs without interference from the state. Partly, no doubt, on account of this, the Puritan also emphasized the moral independence of the true believer. The right of a stiff-necked member of God's elect to follow the dictates of his conscience was the most sacred of rights. Since obedience to conscience frequently involved clashes with governments, Puritanism tended to become an anti-state religion. Finally, to the Puritan influence must be placed the discredit, in Pound's opinion, of suffusing American criminal law with dogmas of vengeance and retribution.

In addition to the blight of Puritanism, Pound discovers various factors responsible for the defects in American law. One, he contends, is the substratum of Germanic institutions and legal doctrines. Pound believes that our law at present is more Germanic than the law of Germany itself. Germanic ideas placed a heavy premium on strict adherence to the letter of the law. The result was to treat litigation as a kind of game in which woe betide the player who made the slightest deviation from the rules. There was no allowance for accident and no mercy for the defaulter or even for the victim of coercion or fraud. Every human being was supposed to be a mature and rational creature who entered into bargains with his eyes open and therefore must assume all risks.

Another of the formative influences, according to Pound, was seventeenth-century political theory, which had a stronger impact on American thinking than any ideas of later vintage. Most Americans living when the foundations of our system of law were laid were the immediate descendants of forebears who had come to this continent in the seventeenth century. The England they knew was the England of Milton, Sydney, Harrington, and Locke. The result was to impress indelibly upon American thinking the validity of a higher law of nature which automatically restricted the powers of governments.

The last of the chief factors molding the development of our legal system was the pioneer condition of a large segment of American agricultural life in the first half of the nineteenth century. On the lonely frontier the individual was king. Though he might suffer from the pressure for social conformity, he enjoyed a freedom from the restraints of law unequaled since the Dark Ages. He was, in fact, often a law unto himself.

The net effect of these various factors, in the judgment of Pound, was to endow American law with an almost anarchic quality and to cover it over with a metaphysical artificiality quite out of keeping with the basic requirements of modern society. As remedies, Pound proposes both mechanical and theoretical reforms. He would abolish elective judgeships, which he believes to be responsible for the bulk of incompetent decisions of American courts. He would provide the judiciary with reference bureaus and laboratories staffed by research scholars, sociologists, psychologists, and economists. These would furnish the factual background necessary for wise decisions. He would make judicial organization more flexible by abolishing the hard-and-fast distinction between judging and administering. He would give the courts the power to organize administrative agencies, some of them to gather the facts for the support of intelligent judgments, and others to apply the judgments once they had been handed down. Thus every court would become a *bureau of justice,* not simply a machine for grinding out opinions. Most important of all, perhaps, he would consign to the junk heap both the absolute theory of law and the absolute theory of politics. The former assumes that certain legal principles are eternal and unchangeable regardless of modifications of social conditions. The latter holds that the sovereign political authority may act without any restrictions except such as are self-imposed. Neither, in Pound's estimation, can be reconciled with the realities of the modern world.

It remains to place the sociological school of jurisprudence in the spectrum of legal philosophies. As noted, it has something in common with the positivist school in its concern with the accumulation of facts and its emphasis on the purposes of law rather than on its origin or nature. It has a point of resemblance with the historical school to the extent that it regards the development of law in the past as a guide of some significance to its application in the present. It has nothing in common with the analytical school founded by John Austin, which limits law to the commands of a sovereign, enforced by a sanction. Despite their opposition to absolute legal principles, the sociological jurists are not completely at odds with the metaphysical school. Though they reject both natural law and natural rights, they nevertheless attach a high premium to the normative element in law. To Roscoe Pound, for example, the "ought" in law is just as important as the "is." In other words, jurisprudence should consider "not merely how judges decide but how they ought to decide" in order that the legal system and society itself may go forward.[14]

It must be recognized, however, that this normative element, in Pound's philosophy, does not proceed from the law of God or from any higher law of eternal justice and absolute right. Instead, it is a product of a general recognition of the needs of society. Reasonable men soon come to realize that an orderly society cannot be maintained simply on a basis of force. Life would hardly be worth living without protection from the arbitrary acts of willful rulers. There is a need for some system of social control that will make it possible to do the most good for the greatest number of people. Conflicts are bound to occur; no one can have all he wants. A regime of law is therefore necessary to provide "such an adjustment of relations and ordering of conduct as will make the goods of existence, the means of satisfying human claims to have things and do things, go round as far as possible with the least friction and waste."[15]

The conception of law described above is not tantamount to justice in any ideal or absolute sense, but it is what the sociological jurists mean by justice. At the same time, it is poles apart from the doctrine that law is anything the courts will enforce. Dean Pound and his followers regard international law as a kind of model for all law. Though it is not enforceable by

[14] "Jurisprudence," *Encyclopedia of the Social Sciences*, VIII, 485.
[15] *Social Control through Law*. New Haven, Yale University Press, 1942, p. 65.

sanctions, it nevertheless embodies the will of the community as to what is reasonable and appropriate. It is often flouted and seems at times to be in a state of eclipse, but it still has value as an expression of what the civilized world thinks *ought* to be the rules governing the conduct of nations. For a long time domestic law went through similar tribulations until it evolved into its present effective form. The development of more adequate machinery for applying the rules will complete this evolution on a world scale.

4. The "Pure" Theory of Law

Related, superficially at least, to both sociological jurisprudence and positivist jurisprudence is the so-called "pure" theory of law. It derives its name from the desire of its sponsors to eliminate from the law everything of a "non-law" character, including ethics, religion, and metaphysics. In this respect it resembles positivism, which would reduce law to the decrees and enactments expressing the will of a sovereign. But the "pure" theory also has its relation to sociological jurisprudence. Both straddle the fence between absolutism and relativism. The "pure" theorists posit a basic form or pattern of law which they assume to be comparatively static. At the same time, they admit that specific law is constantly changing. Dean Pound and his followers take a similar position. They recognize what virtually amounts to absolute standards of justice and right for short periods of a generation or so. For epochs of longer duration, however, nothing can be considered immutable. Ideals and standards originate, vary, and die in accordance with slowly evolving patterns of social conditions.

As suggested already, the "pure" theory of law is founded on the thesis that there is an original pattern or archetype which underlies all law and determines its character. Comparable to the Platonic Idea, the archetype is not the law but rather the form which makes the law what it is, in the same way that man as a physical being is a copy of and is created by the Idea, "Man." The archetype is at least semi-eternal, though law in its concrete manifestations is forever changing. It is futile, according to the "pure" theorists, to try to discover absolutes in any law that comes within the range of human experience. No law of nature or universal law of justice and right can be eternally valid for all men under all conditions. Such laws are merely expressions of the hopes of different peoples in different ages, and therefore must vary as time and circumstance alter men's interests. Only the transcendent archetype, which of course no one ever sees, remains durable and beyond influence. Just why this archetype is necessary, and what valuable purpose it serves, is not always clearly apparent.

The principal forerunner of the "pure" theory of law was Rudolph Stammler (1856–1938). A doctor both of theology and jurisprudence, he was a professor for many years at the universities of Marburg, Giessen, Halle, and Berlin. In addition to anticipating many of the doctrines of the "pure" theory of law, he was the most significant legal philosopher of the Neo-Kantian movement.

Kant had postulated a universe divided into two worlds. One, the realm of physical nature, or the world of *phenomena,* was discoverable by the methods of science and reason; the other, the realm of ultimate reality, or the world of *noumena,* could alone be perceived through faith, intuition, and spiritual conviction. Stammler and other Neo-Kantians translated this dichotomy of worlds and theories of knowledge into the realm of law. They hypothesized a transcendent "idea of law" which they held to possess an absolute validity. According to Stammler, "There are certainly pure forms of juristic thought which are unconditionally necessary as ordering principles for any content of law whatsoever." [16]

Stammler was not satisfied merely to postulate an ideal pattern of law remote somewhere in the heavens. He taught that in some limited sense, at least, the idea of law becomes immanent in the minds of men. When the members of a community submit to a regulation for the purpose of achieving ends common to them all, they may be said to have attained the "notion of law." Actually, as Stammler conceived it, a regulation or statute

[16] Quoted by J. H. Hallowell, *Main Currents in Modern Political Thought.* New York, Holt, 1950, p. 345.

is not law at all unless it accords with such a purpose. He thought of justice as a harmony of wills, and defined any aspiration as fundamentally right which fits harmoniously into the combined aims of the entire community. He was much less interested, however, in the content of laws than he was in their adherence to form. His idea of justice was a purely formal idea devoid of specific content. In other words, it included no guaranties or rights but required simply that those accepting the laws should act in accordance with a collective will. The ingredients or purposes of that will made no difference. He believed the substance of the law to be much less important than its efficient and equitable carrying-out. Procedure was almost everything, content little or nothing. Furthermore, his idea of justice, even in this narrow sense, was not eternal. It was the "ideal of an epoch," restricted mainly as to time, but also as to place and people.

By general acknowledgment, the major living exponent of the "pure" theory of law is Hans Kelsen. Born in Prague in 1881, he received his education at the universities of Vienna, Heidelberg, Cologne, Prague, and Geneva. Prior to World War II he served as professor at the universities of Vienna and Cologne and in the Institute of Advanced International Studies at Geneva. Meanwhile, he found time to collaborate on the Constitution of the Republic of Austria, and to serve as a member of the Constitutional Court of Justice and as editor of *Zeitschrift für Öffentliches Recht*. Since 1940 he has lived in the United States, most of the time as Professor of Law at Harvard and at the University of California. His principal writings include *Law and Peace in International Relations* (1942), *Peace through Law* (1944), and *General Theory of Law and State* (1945).

Kelsen seeks to interpret law from an exclusively scientific approach. He therefore eliminates all moral and spiritual considerations. He will not even admit that justice is an essential characteristic of law, for he contends that no one can produce a scientific definition of justice. He has no interest in a law of nature or in any other higher law of abstract right. For him, law is a matter of legitimacy. That is, to be valid it must have been issued by an authorized agency. Not every command is a law, regardless of the force that may stand behind it to compel obedience. No jurist would admit that the command of a highwayman to surrender a purse at the point of a gun fulfills the requirements of legality. The same view would have to be taken of the decrees of a tyrant who rules arbitrarily by sheer force or intimidation. To achieve the status of laws, statutes and decrees must be products of a "legal order." This means that they must have their derivation from an established reign of law accepted, supported, and recognized as a valid instrument of social unity. As Kelsen conceives it, the legal order is a hierarchy of norms. Every ordinance and decree must derive its validity from conformity with a statute. A statute, in turn, depends for its validity upon correspondence with the constitution. And the constitution must comply with the "basic norm" which stands at the apex of the legal order. What is this basic norm? It certainly does not permeate the universe or dwell in the mind of God, like the natural law of the medievalists. For the most part, it is a presupposition that makes possible the rest of the legal order. As Kelsen has stated, all the lesser norms are valid "because and insofar as, they have been created in the way prescribed by the basic norm." [17]

To comprehend the nature of the basic norm, it is necessary to understand Kelsen's conception of constitutions and revolutions. Every state, he claims, has a constitution of some kind. It may be written or unwritten, brief or detailed, flexible or rigid. Whatever its character, it is an organic law and has its origin in a recognized need for a legal order. This need finds expression in the acts and opinions of the "founding fathers." Insofar as their will is the establishment of a legal order, these acts and opinions become the basic norm. That is, they constitute, in a broad and general way, a set of standards commonly accepted at the time as a desirable basis of national laws and national institutions. But suppose that, later on, a revolution occurs. What becomes of this basic norm? A revolution, if genuine and not just an exchange of one set of rulers for another, brings into existence a new type of political system and new

[17] "Centralization and Decentralization," in *Authority and the Individual*. Cambridge, Harvard University Press, 1937, p. 213.

conceptions of law as an instrument of social policy. Perhaps a monarchical regime gives way to a republic, or a bourgeois republic is displaced by a socialist democracy. In either case, an entirely different pattern of presuppositions comes into vogue. The ideas and acts of the original founding fathers are repudiated, and altogether different acts and conceptions take their place. The result is to supplant the old basic norm by a new one. But neither the new basic norm nor any other derives its validity from its content. "It is valid because it is presupposed to be valid because without this presupposition no human act could be interpreted as a legal act." [18]

Kelsen's theory of the state is also somewhat formalistic. In his view the state has no relevance to anything other than legal objects. It is neither a social-service agency nor an instrumentality for promoting national prosperity. Its sole function is governing in accordance with law, for the purpose of maintaining order and peace. On the other hand, it is not to be considered as a mere instrument of force. Tolstoi was wrong when he described it as "Genghis Khan with the telegraph." "Even the sociologist," Kelsen remarks, "recognizes the difference between a State and a robber gang." [19] In actuality, the state is the personification of the legal order. It cannot be accurately designated as the power behind the law, for this suggests the existence of two separate entities where really there is only one. Law and the state are but different manifestations of the legal order. It follows that the essential quality of the state is legitimacy. It does not create the legal order, as the positivists maintain, but operates within it. For all practical purposes it is the effectuating mechanism of that order. Its authority is legitimate and binding only to the extent that it complies with the norms which constitute the legal order.

According to Kelsen, the traditional classification of states as monarchies, aristocracies, and democracies has no scientific justification. The number of persons with whom the sovereign power rests is a superficial standard of classification. The fun-

[18] *General Theory of Law and State.* Cambridge, Harvard University Press, 1945, p. 116.
[19] *Ibid.*, p. 187.

damental distinction between states grows out of the relation which the citizen bears to the legal order. If he participates in the creation of that order, the state is a democracy. If he merely accepts and supports the legal order and has no right of participation, the state is an autocracy. These are the extremes, and do not exist in their pure form. But every state is a mixture, to a greater or less extent, of these two types. Its ultimate classification as either a democracy or an autocracy depends on which element predominates. Along with his repudiation of the classical triad of states (monarchy, aristocracy, and democracy), Kelsen also rejects the traditional separation of powers. He regards the division into legislative, executive, and judicial branches as artificial and inaccurate; for he considers the judicial as a subdivision of the executive. In common with most other legalists, he attaches little importance to administration, despite its emergence in most modern states as the major function of government. For Kelsen, administration is a mere aspect of the executive power.

When Kelsen discusses freedom, he deals with it almost exclusively in a Rousseauist sense. Rousseau in the *Social Contract* referred to two kinds of liberty: natural liberty which men enjoyed in the state of nature, and civil liberty which men acquire from membership in the state. The former is a mere animal liberty to follow the promptings of instinct. The latter is true liberty, for by entering into political society and accepting its obligations, man obtains security and the privilege of obeying laws which he himself has made. Like Rousseau, Kelsen has no sympathy for the old idea of freedom against the state. Such freedom, he teaches, is anarchy. Society means order, and order involves restrictions. The fundamental issue is the source of these restrictions. If imposed by the will of another, they spell tyranny. But if imposed by the will of all for the common good, they are the essence of freedom. In practice, the will of all must mean the will of the majority, since otherwise a lone individual might veto the interests of the bulk of the citizens. Nevertheless, the rule of the majority does not mean a majority dictatorship over the minority. The very principle of majority rule implies the existence of a minority and the right of that minority to influence public opinion and to win enough converts to enable it to become the majority. To ensure such rights there must be intellectual freedom and freedom of speech, press, and religion. It should be added that Kelsen thinks so highly of modern liberal democracy that he would safeguard it by the recall and by at least a limited use of the initiative and referendum. He would also protect the rights of minorities by assuring them a voice in legislative bodies through proportional representation.

Everything that has been said thus far in connection with Kelsen's political theory pertains to the domestic or national sphere. He is almost as well known as a philosopher of the international realm. In fact, he sees the differences between the two as less than fundamental. He regards the international community as a true community and international law as real law. The international community is decentralized. There is no single state to personify a legal order as is true on the national scene. As a consequence, the will of the international community must generally be enforced by the separate units or states of which it is composed. This gives it a character in many ways suggestive of primitive society, where private vengeance takes the place of state administration of justice. Nevertheless, according to Kelsen, an international legal order exists. It has its norms, or generally accepted tenets of what ought to be, analogous to those of national communities. True, they often go by the board in time of war; yet they are commonly invoked even by the most ruthless and irresponsible governments. Examples are the rule against piracy and the prohibition of acts of war by persons not enrolled in the armed forces. Since appeals of this kind are usually judged and remedied by the very parties claiming to have been wronged, the international community is still essentially primitive. It is not a state but a union of states. That it will become a state in the foreseeable future Kelsen does not seem to think probable. Evidently he does not even consider it desirable, for he looks forward merely to the development of an agency or organization with a degree of centralization that "does not exceed that compatible with the nature of international law." [20]

[20] *Law and Peace in International Relations.* Cambridge, Harvard University Press, 1942, p. 28.

Although the "pure" theory is often associated with legal positivism and legal realism, in reality it is quite different. It does have the aim of scientific objectivity, and for that reason excludes ideas of justice and absolute right as not being scientifically knowable. It also exhibits a certain indifference to the content of laws and emphasizes the importance of authority and legitimacy. In other words, a law is to be considered valid not because of its intrinsic merit but because it has been issued under the proper authority. Nevertheless, it is a mistake to classify the "pure" theorists as mere formalists. True, Kelsen does say that every act of state is a legal act; but it is necessary to remember what he means by the state. He defines the state as the personification of the legal order, which is made up of norms. These, and especially the basic norm, imply a sense of obligation and regard for the public welfare far removed from technical adherence to legal forms. In addition, Kelsen's concern for liberal democracy and for international law and order gives further evidence of an idealism at variance with a servile allegiance to procedural formalities.

ADDITIONAL READINGS

Cohen, Felix S. *Ethical Systems and Legal Ideals.* New York, Falcon Press, 1933.

Cohen, Morris R. *Law and the Social Order.* New York, Harcourt, 1933.
———. *Reason and Law.* Glencoe, Ill., Free Press, 1950.

Duguit, Léon. *Law in the Modern State.* New York, Huebsch, 1919.

Follett, M. P. *The New State.* New York, Longmans, 1918.

Friedrich, Carl J. *The Philosophy of Law in Historical Perspective.* Chicago, University of Chicago Press, 1958.

Gray, John Chipman. *The Nature and Sources of the Law.* New York, Macmillan, 1927.

Hocking, William E. *Man and the State.* New Haven, Yale University Press, 1926.

Holmes, Oliver Wendell, Jr. *The Common Law.* Boston, Little, Brown, 1938.
———. *Collected Legal Papers.* New York, Harcourt, 1920.

Hsiao, Jung-Chuan. *Political Pluralism.* New York, Harcourt, 1927.

Jouvenel, Bertrand de. *Sovereignty; an Inquiry into the Political Good.* Chicago, University of Chicago Press, 1957.

Kelsen, Hans. *General Theory of Law and State.* Cambridge, Mass., Harvard University Press, 1945.

————. *What Is Justice?* Berkeley, University of California Press, 1957.

Laski, Harold J. *Authority in the Modern State.* New Haven, Yale University Press, 1919.

————. *A Grammar of Politics.* New Haven, Yale University Press, 1925.

————. *The Problem of Sovereignty.* New Haven, Yale University Press, 1917.

Morris, Clarence. *The Great Legal Philosophers.* Philadelphia, University of Pennsylvania Press, 1959.

Pound, Roscoe. *Contemporary Juristic Theory.* Claremont, Calif., Claremont Colleges, 1940.

————. *The Formative Era of American Law.* Boston, Little, Brown, 1938.

————. *Interpretations of Legal History.* Cambridge, Mass., Harvard University Press, 1923.

————. *An Introduction to the Philosophy of Law.* New Haven, Yale University Press, 1925.

————. *Justice According to Law.* New Haven, Yale University Press, 1951.

————. *Social Control through Law.* New Haven, Yale University Press, 1942.

Seagle, William. *The Quest for Law.* New York, Knopf, 1941.

PART
TWO

Theories of Collectivism

CHAPTER
V

Offshoots and Allies of Marxism

About 1934 a distinguished Hungarian-American scholar wrote that "however great the difficulties and logical contradictions in Bolshevism may be, the colossal attraction of its ultimate vision, combined with a heroic activism, will continue for mankind with the growth of intelligence and moral freedom." [1] Superficially, this prophecy may seem to be bearing fruit, since more than three times as many people now live in the shadow of the Kremlin than was true in 1934. But such evidence is far from conclusive. A large proportion of the hundreds of millions in Communist countries would probably submit to any regime backed by sufficient force or holding out promise of definite improvement in material conditions. Furthermore, experts are no longer sure that the systems operating in Russia and China are actually socialist in the sense in which Marx and Engels used the term. Perhaps they never were, or possibly they have undergone changes imposed by their own basic defects or by unanticipated developments within and without the countries. Certainly it can be argued that Russia during the Stalin era pursued policies quite different from those propounded by Lenin. The establishment of glaring wage differentials, the encouragement of bureaucracy, the revival of militarism, the cultivation of national patriotism, and the dis-

[1] Oscar Jaszi, "Socialism," *Encyclopedia of the Social Sciences*, XIV, 210.

couragement of divorce and small families were only a few of
them. Nor did the death of Stalin substantially alter the picture.
More and more it has become evident that Russia—and, apparently, China—is an example of political and economic regimentation dictated by national crisis and the necessity of meeting the demands of an industrialized age. Though the methods
vary, the basic objectives do not differ greatly from those of
other regimented states of the twentieth century.

If we could discover the truth we should probably find that
the Marxist program had already become obsolete by the beginning of the twentieth century. True, the movement itself had
plenty of vitality and gained converts steadily until the eve of
World War II. Political and economic conditions, however, had
changed so radically since Marx wrote that the remedies he proposed no longer conformed to the disease. When the *Communist Manifesto* was published, the Industrial Revolution had
hardly emerged from its swaddling clothes. Capitalism truly
appeared to be a system of ruthless exploitation, with the worker
inexorably doomed to a fate of increasing misery. Capitalism,
Marx argued, would thereby create its own gravediggers, who
had only to become fully conscious of the wretched plight of
their class to rise up against their oppressors and overthrow them.
By 1900, however, the evils of the capitalist system had begun
to fade into the background. Wages were increasing faster than
the cost of living. Comforts and even some luxuries formerly a
monopoly of the rich were becoming available to the masses.
Most important of all, the application of science to industry and
the expansion of economic services were bringing into existence
a vast army of technicians, clerical workers, salesmen, and advertising and public-relations employees who took their places
as a "white-collared salariat" between the capitalist owners and
the grimy serfs in the mills. Although most of them were hire-
lings, who sold their labor power for a wage, and were therefore
proletarians in the Marxist sense, their interests and sympathies
were altogether different from those of the industrial workers.
Most of them thought of themselves as members of the middle
class and even as potential capitalists. As their numbers increased, the chances of a successful socialist revolution in the

prosperous Western countries receded farther and farther into the shadows of history.

1. The Marxist System

The philosophy of Karl Marx (1818–1883) is unquestionably one of the most important bodies of doctrine of modern times. It has occupied a place in the second half of the nineteenth century and the first part of the twentieth at least equal to the teachings of Rousseau and Adam Smith a hundred years earlier. Marx's theory was both political and economic. In fact, he could never countenance a separation of the two, since, for him, politics, like religion, philosophy, law, ethics, and even aesthetics, was simply an expression of man's age-old struggle for material possessions. The state he regarded as an executive committee of the dominant economic class. No matter how cleverly concealed by ideological veils, its real purpose was to keep in power the men who controlled the forces of production. Its character was exclusively coercive. It was in no sense a social-welfare agency or an instrument for maintaining and promoting general prosperity. It existed to provide the armies, courts, police, and jails which enabled the owning classes to exploit those who must work for a living. In the Marxist conception, the state and the government were radically different. The state was a police agency, an organization of force to maintain the supremacy of a dominant class. The government was an agency for management and administration and had nothing to do with exploitation. There never had been and never would be a free and democratic society under the control of a state. Government, however, was perfectly consistent with a maximum of liberty and democracy.

The Marxist system rested on several broad theories. Among them the following are fundamental:

1. Historical materialism. The first important contribution of Marx, according to his faithful collaborator and admirer, Friedrich Engels, was the observation that human beings must eat and drink and obtain shelter and clothing before they can pursue politics, science, religion, and art. Thus the stage of advancement of the production, distribution, and exchange of goods, and the organization of society resulting therefrom, determine in the final analysis the political, social, and cultural developments. For Marx, the ultimate cause of all growth and change in society was to be sought not in the increasing knowledge and wisdom of man but in alterations in the modes of producing and exchanging goods. Every society is an integrated cultural whole, and the cement which gives it unity is the economy. The ruling ideas of every great epoch are simply the ideas of its dominant class. Marx did not insist that the economic motive is the sole explanation of human behavior, but he did maintain that every fundamental historical development, regardless of its character on the surface, is the result of changes in methods of production and the property relations of the particular time. Thus the Protestant Revolution was fundamentally an economic movement. The disagreements over religious doctrine were mere ideological "fig-leaves" concealing the naked and actual causes.

2. *Dialectical materialism.* In addition to his theory of the economic causation of specific developments in history, Marx had a conception of progressive evolution or historical dynamics operating in response to economic forces. This he derived from the German idealist Hegel, who conceived of history as a dialectical process, or struggle of opposites, in which the dominant "idea" of each age assumed the role of a "thesis." The thesis was soon confronted and eventually defeated by an "antithesis," or opposite. This contest finally resulted in the production of a "synthesis," which incorporated the more valuable elements of both thesis and antithesis. Each synthesis in turn became a new thesis, to be confronted soon by its antithesis, and the process would continue until the "perfect state" had been realized. This Hegel defined as the ultimate fulfillment of the Divine Idea on earth or, more precisely, as a community in which every citizen had merged his individual interests with the interests of society as a whole. It was the proud boast of Marx that he took this dialectical theory of Hegel and stood it right-side-up. What he did was to substitute economic systems for the "ideas" of Hegel.

More specifically, he taught that every distinct system of production, with its accompanying property relations, grows to a point of maximum efficiency, then develops contradictions within it which produce its rapid decay. Meanwhile, the foundations of an opposing system are being laid, and out of the conflict between these a new system emerges which absorbs their most valuable elements. This dynamic process will continue, by a series of victories of the new over the old, until the perfect goal of "communism" has been attained. After that there will doubtless still be change, but it will be change within the limits of communism itself.

3. *The theory of the class struggle.* History has not only its major theme of a war between opposing economic systems but includes also the minor theme of a struggle between classes. By classes Marx meant economic classes, that is, groups having distinct roles in the production, distribution, or exchange of goods. For example, men who supplied either capital or labor were classes in the Marxist sense, but educated men or illiterates as such were not. In ancient times class struggles took place between masters and slaves and between patricians and plebeians. During the Middle Ages the conflict raged between guild-masters and journeymen and between lords and serfs. During the modern epoch it has been narrowed down to a struggle between the class of capitalists and the proletariat. The former includes those who derive their chief income from *owning* the means of production. The proletariat consists of those who must sell their labor power in order to exist.

4. *The theory of revolution.* A belief in the necessity of revolution was almost inseparable from the Marxist system. To be sure, Marx did say, in his Amsterdam speech in 1872, that "there are certain countries, such as the United States and England in which the workers may hope to secure their ends by peaceful means." [2] But in everything else he wrote or said he left no doubt that he regarded revolution as at once inevitable and indispensable. It is necessary to understand, however, what he meant by revolution. He expressly disavowed the conspiratorial

[2] Quoted by Sidney Hook, *Towards the Understanding of Karl Marx.* New York, John Day, 1933, p. 291.

coup d'état conception known as Blanquism (from Louis Auguste Blanqui, 1805–1881), and warned his followers that they would have to go through "15, 20, 50 years of civil war and national struggles," not only to change conditions but to change themselves. A revolution, he taught, is not created by any party or band of men, no matter how zealous or determined. Instead, it is the product of a *revolutionary situation.* The latter is the result of many factors: chronic discontent; dissension among the members of the ruling class, with the breaking-away of important segments; the recurrence of crises and depressions with increasing frequency; strikes, riots, and mass demonstrations; and the ultimate breakdown of the old order. The revolution itself cannot succeed until the masses become convinced that they do not want the old regime, and the rulers have demonstrated their inability to govern. When the revolution does come it will be forceful and violent, but the role of force is merely to eliminate the rubbish of an already decrepit system and to prepare the way for its successor. As Marx expressed it, "Force is the midwife of every old society pregnant with a new one." [3]

5. *The doctrine of surplus value.* According to Engels, the second most important contribution of Marx was the doctrine of surplus value. This doctrine is based upon the premise that all wealth in terms of exchange value is created by the worker. True, the wood in a tree, created by nature, has value, but this is not exchange value and does not become such until labor power has been expended upon it to convert it into objects which can be bought and sold in the market. The value of all marketable commodities is determined by the quantity of labor power necessary to produce them. Capital creates nothing, but is itself created by labor. However, the worker does not receive a just share of the value his drudgery or skill creates. Instead, he receives a wage, which ordinarily is just enough to enable him to subsist and reproduce his kind. The remainder is divided in several ways. Some of it must be set aside to provide for depreciation, expansion, or replacement of plant equipment. Another portion must go to pay taxes, insurance premiums, etc. But the bulk of it flows into the pockets of the capitalist in the form

[3] Karl Marx, *Capital.* New York, Modern Library, 1906, p. 824.

of interest, rent, and profits. Properly speaking, it is these three elements which constitute *surplus value*. Since the capitalist creates none of them, it follows that he is a thief who confiscates the fruits of the laborer's toil. The exploitation of the worker is measured by the amount of this surplus value. That is, it is determined not by what he actually receives but by what part he fails to receive of that which is justly his.

6. *The theory of socialist evolution.* In no sense did Marx regard the destruction of capitalism as the end and goal of the workers' efforts. Instead, it would be the prelude to other developments of greater importance. Of itself it would merely establish the *political* supremacy of the proletariat, who must then, by degrees, wrest all capital from the bourgeoisie, centralize all instruments of production in the hands of the state, and increase the total productive forces as rapidly as possible. To accomplish these aims, it would be necessary to establish a temporary despotism or *dictatorship of the proletariat*. This would be the first stage of socialism and would be characterized by payment in accordance with work performed; ownership and operation by the state of the means of production, distribution, and exchange; and an iron rule by the working class over all other elements of the population. Within the ranks of the proletariat, however, certain democratic forms would prevail: universal suffrage, rotation in office, the recall, and limitation of officials' salaries to the wages of ordinary laborers. In time the first stage of socialism would fulfill its purpose. It would gradually abolish the distinction between manual and intellectual labor. It would greatly increase the productive forces and cause the "springs of cooperative wealth" to flow abundantly. It would transform work "from a mere means of life to a prime necessity of life." [4] Having accomplished these ends, it would give way to communism, the perfect goal of historical evolution. Communism would mean, first of all, the classless society. No one would live by owning, but all men solely by working. The state would wither away; it would be relegated to the museum of antiquities, "along with the bronze ax and the spinning wheel."

[4] Marx, *Critique of the Gotha Program*. New York, International Publishers, 1938, p. 10.

Nothing would replace it except voluntary government to operate the means of production and provide for social necessities. But the essence of communism would be payment in accordance with needs. The wage system would be completely abolished. Each citizen would be expected to work in accordance with his faculties and would be entitled to receive from the total fund of wealth produced an amount in proportion to his needs. This would be the acme of justice according to the Marxist conception.

Though Marx left many of the details of his economic and political system undescribed, there can be little doubt that he meant it to be taken as an architectonic pattern for the future. He lived in a predominately optimistic age when men believed that history was on their side, and that Fate would bring better and brighter things. Was not the modern age infinitely superior to the darkness of the Middle Ages, and, for the common man, at least, decidedly more comfortable than the slavery of Greece and Rome? All that modern man needed to do was to discover the proper formula and pattern to be put into effect when the tides of history should have brought the old order to a stage of decay. Ridicule as he might the Utopian Socialists as authors of "duodecimo editions of the New Jerusalem," Marx was just as utopian as they. His final goal of a communist, classless society presented an apocalyptic vision of a heaven on earth for the toiling masses. The time of its arrival was even more definite than that of the Christian millennium. When the first stage of socialism had fulfilled its purpose it would be superseded by the final stage, or communism, with the same inevitability that socialism itself would supplant a defunct capitalism. This assumption of historical inevitability was probably Marxism's major weakness. As it became more and more patently untrue, the entire system incurred the risks of ridicule and discredit.

2. The Persistence of Orthodoxy

Even before Marx died in 1883, dissension and disagreement had developed among his followers. So great was the confusion and so bitter the acrimony that Marx himself was led to declare that he was "not a Marxist." Gradually the contenders began to divide into two groups or sects: a sect of orthodox or Strict Marxists and a sect of Revisionists. The former embraced the teachings of Marx as an absolute gospel and refused to admit that one jot or one tittle of it should be changed. The Revisionists maintained that in some respects Marx had fallen into error, that he had failed to foresee certain developments, and that therefore his teachings should be "revised" in order to bring them into harmony with changing conditions.

For almost half a century the most important of Marx's orthodox followers was his co-author, Friedrich Engels (1820–1895). He collaborated with Marx in issuing the *Communist Manifesto* in 1848 and edited the second and third volumes of *Capital* from notes left by Marx after his death. In addition, he was the author of *The Peasant War in Germany* and *The Origin of the Family, Private Property and the State*. No partnership was more strange than that of the two most famous exponents of "scientific" socialism. In contrast with the brooding, ascetic Marx, Engels was gay and almost bohemian. Whereas Marx was totally devoid of business sense and practically indigent, living for days on bread and potatoes and pawning his coat and even his children's shoes, Engels was a successful manufacturer until his retirement at the age of forty-nine and possessed enough wealth to enable him to come to the rescue of his impractical friend on several occasions. Despite these sharp contrasts, ideological differences seem never to have troubled their weird partnership. Engels appears always to have worshiped the superior genius of Marx and to have accepted his teachings as final truth.

The death of Engels in 1895 brought new theorists to the fore as leaders of the orthodox sect. Foremost among them were August Bebel, Wilhelm Liebknecht, Jules Guesde, Karl Kautsky (for a time), and Vladimir Lenin. In general, they agreed on the major issues agitating socialists before World War I. They condemned reformism and insisted upon the inevitability of revolution. In their view, acceptance of concessions like minimum-wage laws and maximum-hours laws from capitalist governments would destroy the unity of the working class, blunt the edge of the class struggle, and postpone indefinitely the achievement of socialism. For similar reasons the orthodox leaders denounced association with bourgeois political movements, no matter how liberal or democratic. They would not approve acceptance of positions by socialists in bourgeois cabinets or the formation of parliamentary alliances with bourgeois parties. They would have no truck with government ownership provided by the capitalist state. Such schemes, they contended, are merely offers of a tub to the socialist whale. They are not socialism, for they involve no substantial change in the relation of the workers to the instruments and materials of production. The state simply steps into the role of the private capitalist, and the workers remain proletarians, subject to the same old methods of exploitation.

On a few great issues, orthodox Marxists failed to see eye to eye. Examples were the issues of internationalism, militarism, and war. Marx and Engels were internationalists in a special sense. They declared in the *Communist Manifesto* that "The proletariat has no country," and called upon the working men of all nations to unite. Marx himself, however, contradicted this doctrine when it came to support of the military ventures of his own country. He approved participation by his followers in the early stages of the Franco-Prussian War, in the belief that it was a war of defense against Napoleon III. So long as the actions of Napoleon threatened Prussia, he said, it was the duty of every citizen to defend the Fatherland. And he made it clear that, in his judgment, a defensive war did not exclude offensive methods.

Even more ambivalent were the attitudes of his orthodox disciples. Gustave Hervé proclaimed the idea of a Fatherland to be of no concern to the proletariat, and asserted that it should be a matter of indifference to the workers whether France belonged to Germany or Germany belonged to France. This doctrine, however, was too extreme for the majority of orthodox Marxists. During the war of 1870 August Bebel, as a member of the Reichstag, abstained from voting when requests for military appropriations were made by Bismarck. But in 1896 he condemned a French proposal for an international general strike and mass uprising in the event of outbreak of war and spoke approvingly of defensive wars. Time after time, at international socialist congresses, a minority of Marxists attempted to get a resolution adopted providing for the thwarting of military hostilities by an international general strike. The scheme was successively defeated, though in 1907 by a narrow margin. The vote cut across sectarian lines. Some members of the orthodox sect were ardently in favor, while others were fanatically opposed.

A similar division occurred among Revisionists. The most that could be obtained was the adoption at Stuttgart in 1907 of a resolution deploring war as the chief obstacle to the highest aim of socialism and advising the working classes of the various nations that each must work out its own methods of preventing the occurrence or continuation of war. Thus the Marxists of Europe and the United States came to the great holocaust of 1914 without any uniform policy as to a course of action. It is not surprising that the majority in each country followed the path of national interest defined by its own government and bolstered by the pressure of popular hysteria. Few factors contributed more to the decline of the socialist movement than this failure to adopt a consistent policy toward militarism and war that would accord with the basic internationalism of the Marxist philosophy.

Of the several disciples of Marx who are commonly considered orthodox, two stand out and require more than passing attention. One was Karl Kautsky; the other was Vladimir Lenin. Kautsky was born in Prague in 1854 but was taken to Vienna at the age of nine and spent most of his life in Austria and Germany. He sat at the feet of both Marx and Engels and, after the latter's death, quickly emerged as the leader of German socialism. He dominated the Second International, founded in Amsterdam in 1889, as Marx had dominated the First. With the outbreak of war in 1914, Kautsky became the leader of a small faction of German socialists who refused to accept the military propaganda of the Kaiser's government. Though he took no prominent part in the revolution of 1918, probably because its leaders were Revisionists working in close collaboration with Catholics and Democrats, he eventually accepted an appointment as Assistant Secretary for Foreign Affairs under the Weimar Republic. He died in 1938 in the Netherlands as a refugee from Nazism.

Kautsky not only affirmed but cogently defended most of the fundamental tenets of Marxism—the materialistic interpretation of history, the exploitive nature of capital, the universality and intensity of the class struggle, the increasing misery of the proletariat, the concentration of capital, and the inevitable downfall of the capitalist system. With the passage of time, however, he moderated more and more the revolutionary doctrines of Marx. He taught that the proletarian revolution need not always be violent. "There are instances in history," he wrote in 1910, "when the ruling classes were either so exceptionally clear-sighted or so particularly weak and cowardly that they submitted to the inevitable and voluntarily abdicated." [5] Nor is it necessary, he continued, that the revolution be accomplished at a single blow. The making of a revolution may extend over years or even decades. The tides of the struggle may ebb and flow, with periods of success interrupted by extended intervals of reaction. When Bolshevism triumphed in Russia, Kautsky became one of its bitterest critics. He condemned Lenin and his associates not merely for the bloody violence of their accession to power but for the brutal tyranny they proceeded to establish. In a series of essays written a few years before his death he renounced force entirely. Though continuing to affirm his adherence to the principle of revolution, he maintained that the only proper means for attaining the Marxist goal is democracy. "Democracy is the shortest, surest, and least costly road to Socialism," he wrote, "just as it is the best instrument for the development of the political and social prerequisites for socialism. Democracy and socialism are inextricably entwined." [6]

The leading theoretician and promulgator of orthodox Marxism in Eastern Europe was Vladimir Ilyich Lenin (1870–1924). Originally named Vladimir Ulianov, he was the son of an enterprising Russian who had raised himself from penury to Director of Schools for the province of Simbirsk. By virtue of his position

[5] *The Class Struggle,* trans. William E. Bohn. Chicago, Charles H. Kerr, 1910, pp. 90–91.
[6] *Social Democracy versus Communism.* New York, The Rand School Press, 1946, p. 119.

the elder Ulianov was entitled to the rank of Councillor of State and membership in the petty nobility. But tragedy stalked his family. In 1881 Tsar Alexander II was assassinated. His successor, Alexander III, regarded education as a source of godlessness and rebellion. Director Ulianov was deprived of his position, and his achievements in twenty-five years of service were largely destroyed. The reactionary policies of the new Tsar inspired so much bitterness that movements were launched to assassinate him. In 1887 Alexander Ulianov, Vladimir's older brother, was arrested for participating in one of these movements. He was convicted and sentenced, without right of appeal, for preparing a dynamite bomb. His mother made valiant efforts to have his sentence commuted, but learned one day from a newspaper she had bought in the street that her son had been hanged.

Vladimir Lenin was then seventeen years old. According to his sister, the execution of Alexander "hardened" his younger brother and started him thinking seriously about the problems of revolution. Admitted to the University of Kazan for the study of law, he was soon afterward expelled for participating in a student revolt. He finally obtained permission to complete the requirements by examination at the University of St. Petersburg. He worked up the four-year course in a year and a half and passed the examination first on a list of 124. But he never succeeded as a lawyer and after a short time ceased to practice. In 1895 he was imprisoned for fourteen months and then was exiled to Siberia. He emerged after three years in Siberia with a resolve to devote the remainder of his life to the cause of revolution. He spent the next sixteen years abroad, principally as editor of *Iskra* (The Spark). Like most of the Russian revolutionists, he wrote under a pseudonym, signing his articles N. Lenin. When the Tsar was overthrown by the March Revolution of 1917, Lenin was living in Switzerland. By arrangement with the Germans, who hoped that he would foment chaos behind the lines, he was permitted to re-enter Russia. By a *coup d'état* during the night of November 6 and morning of Nov. 7, he and a little band of associates overthrew the government of Alexander Kerensky, which in July had succeeded the bourgeois regime that had deposed the Tsar.

Lenin was not the creative philosopher he is frequently represented as being. His original contributions were few—so few, in fact, that one prominent student of Marxism goes so far as to say that "Lenin never challenged a single word in Marx or Engels." [7] Possibly Trotsky's judgment of him was just as accurate. Trotsky predicted in 1904 that if Lenin ever took power "the bovine head of Marx would be the first to fall under the guillotine." [8] Lenin developed a theory of imperialism which in some ways amplified Marx, but most of it duplicated teachings advanced some fifteen years earlier by the British economist John A. Hobson. [9] Lenin conceived of imperialism as the last stage of capitalism. Capitalist economy, he averred, evolves through a series of stages. Ordinary capitalism develops in time into monopoly capitalism. Monopolies pass under the control of banks and other institutions of an investment oligarchy, and finance capitalism begins its history. The chief product of finance capitalism is excess capital, which must be exported in order to bring a larger return. The result is the formation of international capitalist monopolies which seek to gain economic control over undeveloped countries and demand the support of their own governments to protect their investments. The final stage is "the territorial division of the whole earth completed by the greatest capitalist powers." [10]

Most of the remainder of Lenin's theory was founded directly upon Marx. He gave it, however, a conspiratorial and élitist emphasis which Marx had never suggested. Perhaps this development was inevitable, since Tsarist tyranny encouraged intrigue and violence as methods of opposition, and since the illiteracy of the Russian masses made socialism on a democratic basis practically impossible. Whatever the reasons, Lenin insisted first and foremost upon violent revolution as an absolutely necessary means of smashing the capitalist state and estab-

[7] Sidney Hook, *Towards the Understanding of Karl Marx*, p. 292.
[8] Quoted by William Ebenstein, *Great Political Thinkers*. New York, Rinehart, 1956, p. 662.
[9] Chapter XV, pp. 513–14.
[10] Lenin, *Imperialism—The State and Revolution*. New York, Vanguard, 1926, p. 72.

lishing proletarian rule. He recognized that Marx had singled out certain countries such as England and the United States in which the workers might be able to secure their ends by peaceful means. But he contended that times had changed since Marx had made that statement. England and the United States now had bureaucracies, whose members would fight to the last ditch against any displacement from power. He argued, moreover, that both the achievement of the revolution and the construction of the new society must depend upon a small minority of the working class. Not the entire proletariat, but a vanguard, a disciplined élite, trained in the methods of conspiracy and ready to sacrifice their lives for the cause, would be the essential instrument for achieving the new order. Lenin conceived of this vanguard as a small but highly organized political party in which membership would be a privilege, difficult to gain and easy to lose.

Lenin modified a number of other Marxian teachings or at least assumptions. Whereas Marx believed that each economic system was a kind of preparation for the one that was to follow and must therefore grow to maturity and then disintegrate because of contradictions developing within it, Lenin maintained that Russia could skip the stage of bourgeois capitalism and leap directly from a semi-feudal to a socialist economy. This argument had been the basic issue of the famous split in the Russian Social Democratic party in 1903. A faction of Mensheviks under the leadership of Julius Martov believed in postponing the revolution in Russia until a stage of industrial capitalism under the guidance of the bourgeoisie had been completed. The Bolsheviks, under Lenin's leadership, insisted that the party should be ready to take advantage of any crisis or breakdown to precipitate a revolution, regardless of the economic development of the country. Lenin seemed to believe that capitalism would never be destroyed, or even seriously weakened, by factors inherent within it. Instead, its breakdown would occur primarily as a result of the demoralizing effects of war, which the workers must then use to deal it the final blow.

Lenin was more of an internationalist than Marx. Whereas the chief author of the *Communist Manifesto* thought of the socialist revolution occurring in separate countries, one after another, with the proletariat in each constituting itself the nation, Lenin conceived of the revolution in Russia as in no sense a national movement but simply the opening stage of an upheaval that would quickly engulf all civilized countries. It would not be the result of separate causes in individual nations but would be a product of the universal crisis precipitated by World War I. Just as soon as the workers everywhere became fully aware of the corruption and the monstrous inequities of the capitalist system, with its wars, depressions, and enslavement of innocent peoples, they would join in mass uprisings and raze it to the ground. When Lenin arrived in Russia in April, 1917, he was already convinced that the proletarians in all of Europe were on the verge of turning their weapons against their capitalist exploiters. Any day now, he told his followers, "may see the general collapse of European capitalism. The Russian revolution you have accomplished has dealt it the first blow and has opened a new epoch. . . . Long live the International Social Revolution!" [11] In later years, when he had become disillusioned over the prospects of a world revolution in his lifetime, he divided the globe into the Soviet republic, on the one side, and the imperialist states on the other. The two, he said, could not live indefinitely side by side. Eventually, one or the other must triumph. It is significant that when the first constitution of a united socialist Russia was adopted in 1923, it made no reference to Russia as a nation. The new state was called the Union of Soviet Socialist Republics and was so organized as to make possible the admission to it of any or all of the states of the world as they adopted socialism of the Leninist variety.

Though Lenin's contributions to Marxist theory are not particularly profound or original, his career is of tremendous importance. He provided the groundwork for a fateful cleavage in the ranks of Marxists which went far toward weakening the movement. Previous to the Bolshevik Revolution of 1917, Marxists of both orthodox and Revisionist varieties had generally

[11] Quoted by Edmund Wilson, *To the Finland Station.* Garden City, Doubleday, 1955, p. 469.

been included in the same political party. In most countries it was called the Social Democratic party. The Bolshevik Revolution resulted in a secession of the orthodox faction from most of these parties. Henceforth the name Communist came generally to be applied to persons who subscribed to the theories of Lenin and his colleagues. The roster of Communist leaders of more recent times has included such well-known figures as Nikolai Bukharin, Joseph Stalin, and Nikita Khrushchev, whose doctrines will be discussed in later chapters. Josip Broz (Tito) in Yugoslavia and Mao Tse-tung in China also profess to be following in the footsteps of Lenin, but with sufficient deviation from orthodoxy to make definite characterization difficult. The term *socialist,* since 1918, has come to be reserved almost exclusively for reformist, nonrevolutionary advocates of collective ownership and operation of the means of production, distribution, and exchange. It describes, of course, the Revisionists who still survive in such countries as West Germany, Austria, Italy, Scandinavia, Belgium, and the Netherlands. It is used to designate also the Fabian Socialists of Great Britain and, less accurately, such moderate, non-Marxian advocates of mixed collectivization as Norman Thomas in the United States.

3. Revisionism

As has been indicated already, disagreements among Marx's followers began to develop even before his death. A faction of orthodox adherents believed in preserving the pristine purity of the master's teachings. Others of less dogmatic conviction argued that Marx's theories needed "revision" to bring them up to date and to correct certain errors and fallacious assumptions. But Revisionism was not formally launched until 1896–1898, when Eduard Bernstein published a series of articles in *Die Neue Zeit* entitled "The Problem of Socialism." In these articles and in a subsequent book Bernstein criticized some of the major conclusions set forth by Marx. He denied, first of all, the validity of the doctrine of surplus value. Marx had used this doctrine as a principal justification of the collectivization of the means of production. In his judgment capitalism was evil largely because it cheated the worker out of wealth his own labor had created. Bernstein repudiated this view. He pointed out that the most prosperous and best-treated workers were often to be found in those industries with the highest rate of surplus value, while those with the lowest pay and the poorest working conditions were frequently the employees of enterprises with a low rate of surplus value.

Bernstein was especially critical of Marx as a prophet. He denied that the proletariat was becoming more miserable, that it was increasing in numbers because of the elimination of small business by the growth of monopolies and chain enterprises, and that it was waxing in unity and class-consciousness. He cited statistics to prove the persistence of small business and the emergence of new, intermediate classes between the capitalists, on the one side, and the proletarians on the other. He rejected also the Marxian thesis of the increasing concentration of capital. Not only did he contend that small-scale industries were not disappearing, but he argued that the evolution of large corporations tended to diffuse rather than concentrate the ownership of wealth. The number of owners of shares of stock was larger than ever, and to the extent that they received dividends they were participating in the collection of surplus value. He ignored the fact that the number of shares in the possession of these owners was small, and that the dividends most of them received were insignificant in comparison with the total.

Bernstein had the assistance of able collaborators in propagating the theories of Revisionism. Among them were Jean Jaurès in France, Karl Branting in Sweden, and Émile Vandervelde in Belgium. In general, they agreed on fundamental doctrines. Though professing to be revolutionists in principle, the Revisionists pushed the idea of staging a revolution so far into the future that they practically reduced it to a fiction. They became gradualists, or evolutionists, adhering to a program of reform rather than a policy of all-or-nothing to be achieved by a class upheaval. They adopted the slogan, "less for the better future, and more for the better present." True, they allowed some exceptions. Bernstein admitted that in despotically governed countries or in countries where wealth was heavily concentrated and where the masses were impoverished, revolution might be the only means at the disposal of the oppressed majority. Jaurès approved of a violent general strike as a last desperate recourse of the workers when nothing else would suffice. But these exceptions were sharply at variance with the tactics commonly advocated by the Revisionist leaders. They condoned participation by their own followers in governments dominated by "liberal" bourgeois politicians. They sponsored or supported sweeping programs of reform, which orthodox Marxists insisted could have no other effect than to wean the proletariat away from the vital objective of achieving socialism. Such programs included minimum-wage laws, social insurance, progressive income and inheritance taxes, municipal ownership of public utilities, and assistance to trade unions in establishing cooperative stores. Even such purely political reforms as universal suffrage, proportional representation, and the initiative, referendum, and recall were often demanded. Bernstein urged the German Social Democrats to stand before the nation for what they really were: "a democratic, socialistic party of reform." [12]

On one subject the Revisionists did not agree. That subject was war. They were probably much closer to a harmony of views, however, than were their orthodox opponents. When World War I loomed on the horizon, the vast majority of reformist socialists rallied with enthusiasm to the support of their governments. A few held out. Jean Jaurès in France denounced the policies which seemed to him to make war inevitable and called for a general strike as a gesture of protest. Two days before the storm burst over Europe he was assassinated by a fanatical patriot. The Social Democratic party of Germany, controlled by the Revisionists, endorsed the war almost unanimously. Some of the leaders justified their position on grounds of expediency: they would support the government in order to gain control of it later and divert the war to socialist purposes. Others maintained that Germany, encircled as she was by a ring of steel, must fight for survival, and that it was the duty

[12] *Evolutionary Socialism*, trans. Edith C. Harvey. London, Independent Labour Party, 1909, p. 197.

of every German to subordinate his party interests to his obligations as a citizen. Overriding nearly everything else were considerations of nationalism. Revisionists, in common with many orthodox Marxists, had been unable to resist the prevailing appeals to patriotic pride and national glory. Bernstein argued that socialists should work for popular control of foreign policy and for peaceful settlement of international disputes. But he also insisted upon the propriety of their defending national rights and even supporting colonial expansion, on the ground that it was better for backward peoples to be governed by an enlightened nation than by some half-barbarian autocracy. Even the pacifist Jaurès, on occasions before the war, delighted in the loyalty of socialists to the French Republic and acclaimed French democracy as the best vehicle for the achievement of socialism.

4. Non-Marxian Socialism

By no means can all socialists of the contemporary world be classified as either moderate or orthodox disciples of Karl Marx. Some have owed their inspiration primarily to one of Marx's chief rivals—Ferdinand Lassalle (1825–1864), who was the son of a well-to-do silk merchant of Breslau. In his youth he admired Marx and aspired to become one of his followers. But he was vain, egotistical, overbearing, and unstable. He spent much of his time in philandering and in reckless speculation. At the age of twenty-two he contracted syphilis. His life was brought to an end before he was fifty by a rival in a love affair whom he had challenged to a duel. Marx developed such a hatred for him that he could scarcely conceal his satisfaction over his death. During his lifetime he berated Lassalle for his "Jewish aggressiveness" and darkly hinted that he must have Negro blood. The German workers, however, idolized him, and there can be no denying his competence. He founded the General Association of German Workers, which became the German Social Democratic party, though it passed eventually under Marxist control. His philosophy presented a simple program of state socialism. Unlike the Marxists, he had no plans for destroying the bourgeois state, but hoped to gain control of it and to use it for putting socialism into effect. Like a good Hegelian, he glorified the state as eternal and unchanging, an end in itself. He had no vision of a communist millennium or classless society but contented himself with such reforms as universal suffrage, religious toleration, prohibition of child labor, state factory inspection, regulation of prison labor, abolition of the wage system, and the formation of producers' cooperatives.

Among other socialists of a distinctly non-Marxian origin are the Christian socialists. Christian socialism, properly speaking, is scarcely socialism at all, for it involves no drastic reorganization of the economic system. The essential aim of its votaries is to introduce palliatives to correct the most glaring injustices and to make the production and distribution of goods satisfy the demands of a Christian conscience. The origins of this so-called socialism go back to the early nineteenth century. Its founder was Robert de Lamennais (1782–1854), a French Catholic priest who sought to infuse new life into the Christian religion by making it an aid to reform and social justice. From France the movement spread to England and was adopted by a number of Protestant intellectuals, especially by the novelist Charles Kingsley (1819–1875). The English Christian socialists viewed with consternation the widening gulf between rich and poor and the threats of revolution that lurked within it. They upbraided the clergy for their indifference to the plight of the masses, and for wasting time on fruitless theological disputes. They deplored the practice of using the Bible for keeping the poor in subjection and promising them the joys of heaven to compensate for their hell on earth. They denounced the economics of the Manchester school, with its rigorous doctrine of *laissez faire* and its theory of poverty as the deserved fate of the shiftless and improvident, as "narrow, hypocritical, anarchic, and atheist." [13] It seems obvious that what they had in mind was the transformation of society into a kind of Christian brotherhood whose members would assume obligations of charity and helpfulness toward one another in accordance with the teach-

[13] Charles Kingsley, *His Letters and Memories of His Life*. London, Macmillan, 1901, II, 57.

ings of the New Testament.

Christian socialism took on a more tangible character toward the end of the nineteenth century. An encyclical issued in 1891 by Pope Leo XIII under the title *Rerum Novarum* brought Catholics to a keener awareness of the economic disabilities of the working classes. Though the encyclical expressly recognized private property as a natural right and vigorously repudiated the Marxist doctrines of class conflict, revolution, and the dictatorship of the proletariat, it may be considered as socialistic in tone as most other important pronouncements attempting to provide a religious foundation for economic reform. It appealed to employers to respect the dignity of their workers as men and not to treat them as "chattels to make money by, or to look upon them merely as so much muscle or physical power." By way of specific proposals to mitigate the harshness of the industrial regime, it recommended factory legislation, the formation of labor unions, an increase in the number of small landowners, limitation of hours of employment, and a minimum wage that would be "enough to support the wage earner in reasonable and frugal comfort." The Pope urged that men should not consider their possessions as exclusively their own, "but as common to all, so as to share them without difficulty when others are in need." [14]

The issuance of Pope Leo's encyclical gave a mighty impulse to the growth of Christian socialism among liberal Catholics. In European countries before World War I, Catholic parties frequently played an active role, sometimes in combination with the moderate Marxists, in furthering movements for social reform. This was especially true of the Center party in Germany, the Christian Socialist party in Austria, and the Liberal Action party in France. Since World War II the Catholic Christian Socialist movement has been more or less faithfully represented by the Christian Democratic parties in West Germany and Italy and by the Popular Republican Movement in France.[15]

[14] The substance of Pope Leo's encyclical was reaffirmed in 1931 by Pope Pius XI in a new encyclical, *Quadragesimo Anno*.

[15] For further discussion of the politico-economic ideas of contemporary Popes, see Chapter Eleven.

Perhaps the most important variety of contemporary socialism which does not trace the paternity of its doctrines to Marx is Fabian socialism. It derives its name, of course, from the Fabian Society, organized in 1884. The Fabians chose for their motto a statement intended to make crystal clear the gradualist nature of their program:

For the right moment you must wait, as Fabius did, most patiently, when warring against Hannibal, though many censured his delays; but when the time comes you must strike hard, as Fabius did, or your waiting will be in vain and fruitless.[16]

It seems pertinent to remark that only the first part of this motto received much emphasis. The Fabians never "struck hard," and perhaps never intended to. They have been intellectuals and men of ideas rather than men of revolutionary action. Nevertheless, their ranks have included some of the most gifted and brilliant individuals England has produced in recent decades. Numbered among them were George Bernard Shaw, H. G. Wells, Graham Wallas, G. D. H. Cole, Sidney and Beatrice Webb, and Ramsay MacDonald.

The principal sources of Fabian socialism were British and American. They included the writings of David Ricardo, John Stuart Mill, and Henry George. The dominant idea derived from these sources was the premise that most forms of unearned wealth are created by society. A cardinal example, of course, is the unearned increment of land. A tract of land at one time of very little worth will undergo a marked increase in value if the population expands in the area or if new schools, sewers, or streets are constructed. The Fabians extended this concept to many other forms of property. The prosperity of a steel company, for example, depends also upon growth of population and a general expansion of business activity. The profits of a bank depend upon the demand for loans, which, in turn, is determined by the growth and prosperity of the entire economy. Only to a very limited extent can the owners and managers of such enterprises claim that the wealth which flows into their coffers is a product of their own skill and initiative. The whole character

[16] H. W. Laidler, *History of Socialist Thought.* New York, Crowell, 1933, pp. 234–35.

of the economic system, the Fabians maintained, has undergone a fundamental change. The great fortunes of modern times have not been built up, to any important degree, by hard work and frugality. Instead, they have grown through appreciation in the value of land and of the stocks of corporations. And most of this appreciation has been the contribution of society. For all practical purposes, the owners have been able to sit with folded hands, or to devote their lives to golf and fox-hunting, and the rise in values has occurred just the same. The great majority of modern capitalists, the Fabians argued, are no longer entrepreneurs; they have degenerated into "interest and rent receivers."

Obviously, the Fabians rejected the Marxian theory of value. Value, they said, is not created primarily by the expenditure of labor power upon the raw materials of nature. Instead, it is the product, chiefly, of the growth of society and the progress of civilization. It belongs, therefore, not to the workers or to any other segment of society but to society as a whole. Though the Fabians accepted the Marxist thesis that ownership of capital creates no title to wealth, they rejected the doctrine of an irrepressible conflict between capital and labor. The real conflict in the modern world is not a conflict between wage-earners and employers but a conflict between the community as a whole and those who grow rich from investment. As a consequence, the Fabians opposed the idea of giving to the worker the full product of his toil. This would not be justice, they argued, but a travesty on justice. Their real objective was to effect such a redistribution of wealth as to make possible a sharing by all members of the community in the benefits society has created. To achieve this objective they proposed a gradual transfer of ownership of the land and of all industrial, commercial, and financial properties to the community, or to the government representing the community. The transfer would be made without any attempt to give full compensation to the former owners. Relief might be provided, however, where necessary, to expropriated individuals in accordance with the judgment of the community's representatives in the political parliament.

Though Fabians, in accordance with their name and their

motto, might logically espouse a doctrine of ultimate revolution, they have never done so. When Sidney Webb wrote about "the inevitability of gradualness," he set the tone for the Fabian emphasis upon peaceful, evolutionary change. As Shaw expressed it, the Fabians long ago "agreed to give up the delightful ease of revolutionary heroics and to take to the hard work of practical reform on ordinary parliamentary lines." [17] In 1912 they established the Fabian Research Department to conduct investigations into diverse experiments in collectivism and to make data available for guiding the planners of the future. Fabian leaders have nearly always written in laudatory terms of the modern democratic state. They conceive it as an ideal instrument for establishing socialism in the first place and for operating a collectivized economy as trustee for the people. Of course, a few changes will be necessary: a widening of the suffrage, a more enlightened civil service, improved educational opportunities, and a more effective representation of talent and intelligence in the offices of government. But such reforms are designed for the perfection of democracy, not for its transformation into something else.

On subjects relating to international politics, the Fabians tended to be just as parochial as the Revisionists. Few indeed have shown much interest until recent years in a world community. It has been one of the Society's major tenets that the nation is the logical unit for promoting human welfare. In the heyday of the British Empire the majority of Fabians defended imperialism almost as ardently as did Winston Churchill or Joseph Chamberlain. During the Boer War, Sidney Webb urged the necessity of "virility in government" to the end that the nation might raise "an Imperial race." [18] Webb and other leaders implored the Society to "accept the Empire," recognize its merits and its promise, and show how it could be made more humane and efficient. They begged the Society to champion an enlightened policy in India, for example, urging the government to pro-

[17] Quoted by F. W. Coker, *Recent Political Thought*. New York, Appleton-Century, 1934, p. 102.
[18] "Lord Rosebery's Escape from Houndsditch," *The Nineteenth Century*, L (Sept., 1901), p. 377.

vide a Western education for natives capable of benefiting from it, to develop the germs of democracy in the country, and to expend funds generously on the study and correction of economic and social maladies. But the Fabian prophets repudiated the Liberal assumption that each people has some "inherent right to have its own government and work out its own policy, unfettered by any consideration of the effect of their independence on other races, or on the world at large." [19] In their devotion to the public welfare, the Fabians were willing to include the welfare of subject peoples. But it was a welfare that could best be secured through a benevolent, efficient, and firm-handed control by the Mother Country.

Some of the Fabian leaders, however, were rank nonconformists and propagated ideas markedly at variance with those of their colleagues. The most celebrated of these prima donnas was George Bernard Shaw (1856–1950), the dramatist, who wrote many of the early Fabian tracts but subsequently resigned from the Society. Shaw was born in Dublin, the son of a furtive and hypocritical drunkard, whose generally impecunious condition belied his pretensions to bourgeois respectability. The future playwright never could remember a time when the printed page was not intelligible to him and therefore concluded that he must have been born literate. He received almost no formal education, satiating his intellectual appetite by omnivorous reading of everything that appealed to his interests. After working for five years in Dublin as a clerk and cashier, he gambled everything on the conviction that he was a genius and went to London to devote the rest of his life to writing fiction and plays. He achieved no distinction as a novelist, but before he died at the age of ninety-four he had written more than sixty plays (most of which were popular and successful); a large proportion of these plays were vehicles for political and social satire.

Shaw drew the inspiration for his political philosophy from many sources. He was intoxicated by the ideas of Henry George and Karl Marx, but he also drank copiously from the fountains of Schopenhauer, Nietzsche, Pierre Proudhon, Edward Bellamy,

[19] *Ibid.*, p. 367.

and Henri Bergson. In addition, he was essentially a Puritan, interpreting political and social issues from an ethical viewpoint. He condemned capitalism not because of its economic injustice but primarily because he considered it immoral; it made money the most important thing in the world and poverty the worst of crimes. To solve this problem of immorality, socialism was not enough. There must also be absolute equality of income, irrespective of age, sex, occupation, beliefs, or ability. Shaw's attitude toward government was a strange farrago of élitism, aristocracy, Machiavellianism, and worship of efficiency and getting things done. He defined democracy as "a big balloon, filled with gas or hot air, and sent up so that you shall be kept looking at the sky whilst other people are picking your pockets." [20] He thought it a misfortune that Guy Fawkes did not succeed in blowing up Parliament, and described the modern electoral system with its political parties and moronic campaign appeals as a ghastly and disastrous fraud. He proposed to replace these obsolete institutions with a government of wisdom and talent, made up of persons selected by scientific tests for their knowledge of statecraft.

But Shaw also had a lurking admiration for contemporary dictators who had cleaned things up, made the trains run on time, and "solved" the problem of unemployment. He saluted Mussolini at the peak of *Il Duce*'s power, acclaimed Stalin as the greatest man in Europe, and praised Hitler for infusing hope and confidence in the German nation after the disasters of defeat, inflation, and depression. Perhaps some of this was mere impish perversity, but there can be little question that Shaw had a considerable regard for almost anyone who could relegate democracy to the scrap heap and rule with efficiency, order, and power; especially if that person called himself a socialist. Like Fabians in general, Shaw professed a philosophy of gradualism. He admitted that he had no zest for revolution and confessed that if an outbreak occurred he would be found hiding under the bed. Yet he had a curious addiction to the Machiavellian

---

[20] Radio Broadcast, October, 1929; quoted by Archibald Henderson, *George Bernard Shaw: Man of the Century*. New York, Appleton-Century-Crofts, 1956, p. 630.

doctrine that the end justifies the means. He seemed willing to tolerate almost any extreme of brutality or tyranny if it would contribute to the attainment of some shining utopia—or even some tawdry dream of national destiny. He defended the strong-arm techniques of Mussolini, the murder of Matteotti, and the banishment of hundreds of intellectuals and democrats. He justified some of the unspeakable atrocities of Hitler, to say nothing of the mass murders, purges, and persecutions committed by Stalin.[21] Apparently, in his judgment, the sins of capitalist, bourgeois society were so heinous that to look askance at ruthlessness as a means of wiping them out was a kind of old-maidish squeamishness.

Almost equally famous as a literary proponent of a New Jerusalem tinged with Fabian idealism was Herbert George Wells (1866–1946). His life was virtually a blueprint for the kind of doctrines he preached. The son of a professional cricket-player, he was born under squalid conditions over a china shop in Kent, England. After pitifully inadequate schooling, he was apprenticed to a draper, for whom he worked from half past seven in the morning until eight in the evening. Later he became a student assistant in a Church of England school and finally was awarded a scholarship in the Normal School of Science, in London. The last was a glorious opportunity, for it brought him into contact with T. H. Huxley and gave him a penchant for science which pervaded the rest of his life. But science did not exhaust his interests. By temperament he was a rebel and a crusader. The poverty and hardship of his early career imbued him with a sense of injustice and a hatred of sham and servility. He longed to wreck the "sorry scheme of things entire" and rebuild it in accordance with a nobler ideal. He became a militant atheist at an early age and, throughout his life, flouted the conventions of Christian morality. His defiance of respectability aroused the enmity of some of the pillars of British socialism, who feared that he would bring their movement into disrepute. Though he remained a socialist to the end of his life, he resigned from the Fabian Society after only a few years and never again became closely identified with any particular faction or sect.

[21] Henderson, *op. cit.*, pp. 638–39.

Despite the brevity of his membership in the Fabian Society, Wells' ideas bore a substantial impress of Fabian influence. In fact, his philosophy was in many ways similar to that of Shaw, the founder of the Society. Both men were champions of equal rights for the sexes, of the prerogative of the state to be the ultimate guardian of all children, and of the paramount importance of order and efficiency. Both men made science their god, though the scientism of Shaw was diluted with a mystical element of creative evolution taken over from the philosophy of Bergson. Wells, quite as much as Shaw, rejected the democratic dogma that the people are capable of self-government and proposed an élite, with special training in administration and in the philosophy of government, to rule the state. Yet there were outstanding differences in the political attitudes of the two. Wells never expressed admiration for the personal dictatorships of Mussolini, Hitler, and Stalin nor justified their savagery in disposing of their opponents. He seems to have paid deference to the Machiavellian principle of the end justifying the means only in connection with World War I. He regarded that war as a "war to end war" and therefore in an altogether different class from previous conflicts. No weapon, regardless of its brutality, was to be excluded if it would contribute to winning the war. And after the victory, if Wells had had his way, Berlin would have been looted and a special tax of two marks would have been added to every German railway ticket to pay for war damage in Belgium.[22]

In a much more comprehensive way than Shaw, Wells was a utopian. Whereas Shaw's ideas for a heavenly city were derived largely from Nietzsche and Bellamy, Wells went back to Plato. In *A Modern Utopia*, published in 1905, he envisaged a model society comprising four classes. At the top would be the "Samurai," or ruling class, composed of men completely devoid of personal interest, ambition, or passion. Second in rank would be the "Poietic," or creative class, capable of constantly exploring new areas. Next would be the "Kinetic," or ordinary intelligentsia, able to work within the formulas discovered by

[22] For material on Wells' propaganda for a "war to end war," see I. C. Willis, *England's Holy War*. New York, Knopf, 1928.

their creative superiors. Finally would come the "Dull and the Base," or persons with an "anti-social disposition," who would remain permanently at the bottom of the economic scale. But for almost all of its inhabitants a Modern Utopia would be a scented, sun-kissed paradise. Even the factories would be beautiful, and work in them would terminate around midday or soon afterward. Everyone would have a job and prosperity would reign uninterruptedly. Marvels of comfort and convenience would banish drudgery, while laws would mitigate such pain and hardship as could not be prevented. Mothers, for example, would be paid for having children. Only the Samurai would be required to follow a regime of austerity, somewhat after the fashion of Plato's philosopher-rulers. They would live together in group marriage, abstain from wine, tobacco, and meat, and devote all their energies to serving the state.

Everyone familiar with the works of H. G. Wells knows that on occasion he produced glowing portrayals of the future of mankind. Some bordered on the fantastic, as illustrated by his romance *In the Days of the Comet,* in which he imagined a human species exalted intellectually and morally by the brush of a comet's tail. Through much of his life he seems to have dreamed of a race perfected by education, science, and law, who would "stand upon the earth as one stands upon a footstool and laugh and reach out their hands amidst the stars." [23] Six years before his death, however, he wrote a discerning and realistic appraisal of the contemporary world that would have done honor to the sternest of his critics. The title of the book was *The New World Order,* and the date was 1940, which he described as the end of an era. Gone were the days of free communication, trade, and exchange among nations. Sovereignty had become a fetish, nationalism a festering sore, and competition in armaments a nightmare that made peaceful relations among peoples impossible. The individual worker, he admitted, was better off than his forebears, but his prosperity was artificial and could not last. It was a result of increased productivity very largely for military purposes, and it meant the wholesale destruction of natural resources. The final consequence, unless some corrective were

[23] *New Worlds for Old.* New York, Macmillan, 1913, p. 241.

speedily applied, would be the impoverishment and collapse of the Western nations.

Wells maintained that nothing short of a revolution would remedy the ills of the modern world. But the revolution he advocated would bear little resemblance to the Marxist victory of the proletariat over the bourgeoisie. It would be neither a bloody nor a violent revolution. No workers would mount the barricades or storm the palaces of kings and grand dukes. Instead, it would be a peaceful upheaval accomplished by men of intelligence and good will for the purpose of eliminating chaos and waste and the inhumanities of the existing system. It would owe nothing to the Soviet revolution, for its aim would be to protect and enlarge freedom, not to degrade or enslave. Its principal objectives would be the following:

1. The vitalization of education, especially through the promotion of research.
2. Insistence upon the reign of law and the rights of man.
3. Complete freedom of expression.
4. Extinction of party politics through proportional representation.
5. World socialism, to eliminate exploitation of subject peoples and to provide for a more efficient and equitable use of the world's resources.
6. The abolition of national sovereignty through the merging of all peoples into a world federal republic.[24]

In this concept of social revolution, Wells perhaps moved closer than ever before to the tenets of orthodox Fabianism.

Similar in many respects to Fabian socialism was another socialist movement which flourished in Great Britain during the 1920's. It was called Guild Socialism, and many of its prominent leaders had formerly been or continued to be members of the Fabian Society. Among them were G. D. H. Cole, R. H. Tawney, S. G. Hobson, and Bertrand Russell. Guild Socialism was inspired in part by the teachings of William Morris, a medievalist poet and artist of the nineteenth century, who condemned mod-

---

[24] For a full discussion of Wells' ideas on world federation, see Chapter Fourteen.

ern industrialism because of its ugliness and its destruction of individual craftsmanship. The essence of Guild Socialism was the transfer of ownership of the means of production to the state, with the management and operation of factories, mines, railroads, etc., to be vested in guilds of workers. Each guild would have complete jurisdiction over the interests of its members as producers. It would determine their compensation, hours of labor, and conditions of employment. The interests of persons as consumers and as citizens would be taken care of by the state. With regard to the possibility of a conflict of jurisdictions, the Guild Socialists disagreed. Some would have made the state the final arbiter over all issues. Others would have left the state with nothing more than a coordinate rank with the congress of guilds. Disputes between them would have to be settled by negotiation. Whatever the solution to this problem, the Guild Socialists agreed that the state under the new order must not become a huge bureaucratic machine with power to hold its citizens in a subjection little better than slavery. They believed that if the workers should set up the proletarian state envisaged by the Marxists, they would simply be exchanging one master for another. They repudiated the revolutionary doctrines of the Marxists and adopted the gradualism of the Fabians, hoping to achieve their ends by evolution and the granting of "compassionate allowances" to the dispossessed capitalists.

A cardinal concern of the Guild Socialists was the preservation of democracy. They not only disliked the dictatorship of the proletariat, but they contended that democracy, to be more than a sham, must involve participation by the citizen in affairs immediately affecting his welfare, especially affairs pertaining to his income and conditions of employment. They believed also that decentralization of the economic system into guilds would prevent the growth of industrial giantism with its assembly lines and automatic machinery, and thereby help to preserve individual craftsmanship. But the tides of economic development were running heavily against them. The exigencies of World War I produced a scarcity of workers and accented the demand for labor-saving machinery. The depressed conditions of the postwar era intensified competition for limited markets and forced small enterprisers to sell out to their powerful rivals. When times were good the workers grew indifferent to the "movers and shakers" who wanted to remake the world. In lean years they lost courage and became fearful that association with radicals might blast all their hopes of economic advancement. Long before the depression of 1929 had reached its nadir, Guild Socialism had passed into oblivion. Its chief prophet, G. D. H. Cole, eventually emerged as an advocate of a generalized socialism resembling the Revisionism of Continental Europeans. Alarmed by the menace of fascism, he abandoned all faith in the inevitability of the socialist commonwealth and pinned his hopes on a Popular Front to save the world from eclipse.[25]

By the middle decades of the twentieth century, socialism, correctly defined, appeared to be passing into the limbo of history. In its Marxist form, especially, it was out of harmony with the trends of the new era. With its assumptions of the fundamental goodness of the common man, the certainty of progress, the perfectibility of human institutions, and the ultimate triumph of freedom and justice it epitomized the dreams of the eighteenth-century philosophers of the Enlightenment and the nineteenth-century romanticists. But both of these movements had been corroded by the acids of irrationalism and pessimism. Strong currents of these corrosives flowed from the pens of Schopenhauer, Nietzsche, Kierkegaard, Freud, Sorel, Pareto, and Spengler. Even more disastrous were the effects of the two world wars, the growth of fascism, and the most devastating depression in history. Confronted by such tragedies, few people had the courage to dream of a paradise of justice and freedom even in the distant future. Finally, socialism declined in appeal because of the failure of Marx to appraise accurately the trends of the times. He anchored his hopes too firmly to the increasing wretchedness of the lower classes and the concentration of wealth in the hands of the few. He failed to perceive the significance of the growth of intermediate classes engaged in new occupations and the wide diffusion of corporate wealth into

[25] G. D. H. Cole, "Can Capitalism Survive?" in G. D. H. Cole, Sir Arthur Salter and Others, *What Is Ahead of Us?* New York, 1937, pp. 9–47.

the possession of insurance companies, pension funds, investment trusts, and the public at large. He closed his eyes to the substantial increase in real wages, even in his own lifetime. Though some of his followers attempted to show that it is not what the worker receives but what he fails to receive that is the measure of his exploitation, few people found this argument convincing in the face of a rising standard of living.

The decline of socialism has been accompanied by the rise of democratic collectivism. In some measure, the latter has been a cause of the former, for it is notorious that democratic collectivists have stolen a great deal of the socialists' thunder. But democratic collectivists, as we shall presently see, are not socialists. They do not desire to destroy the present economic system but to shore it up to make it work more successfully. At the same time they have adopted many of their ideas from the reformist branch of Marxism. And it is in this manner that socialism may be considered to have made its main contribution. It has exposed the defects of a *laissez-faire* economy and has shown the need for regulation and planning under democratic control to mitigate the most flagrant injustices of a system which creaks and groans and occasionally almost breaks down, but which seems to provide more generously for the mass of humanity than any other system the world has known.

ADDITIONAL READINGS

Boudin, Louis B. *The Theoretical System of Karl Marx*. Chicago, C. H. Kerr, 1907.

Brailsford, H. N. *Socialism for Today*. London, Independent Labour Party, Publication Dept., 1925.

Bukharin, Nikolai. *Historical Materialism*. New York, International Publishers, 1925.

Bukharin, N., and Preobraschensky, E. *The ABC of Communism*. New York, Century Press, 1952.

Chang, Sherman H. *The Marxian Theory of the State*. Philadelphia, University of Pennsylvania Press, 1931.

Cole, G. D. H. *Guild Socialism Restated*. London, L. Parsons, 1920.

————. *The Intelligent Man's Guide to the Post-War World.* London, V. Gollancz, 1947.

————. *What Marx Really Meant.* New York, Knopf, 1934.

Engels, Friedrich. *Socialism, Utopian and Scientific.* New York, International Publishers, 1935.

Eucken, Rudolf. *Socialism: An Analysis.* New York, Scribner, 1922.

Gurian, Waldemar. *Bolshevism: Theory and Practice.* London, Sheed and Ward, 1932.

Hillquit, Morris. *From Marx to Lenin.* New York, Hanford Press, 1921.

Hook, Sidney. *Towards the Understanding of Karl Marx.* New York, John Day, 1933.

Laidler, Harry W. *Socialism in Thought and Action.* New York, Macmillan, 1920.

Lenin, Vladimir. *The State and Revolution.* New York, International Publishers, 1932.

Kautsky, Karl. *The Road to Power.* Chicago, S. A. Bloch, 1909.

————. *The Social Revolution.* Chicago, C. H. Kerr, 1908.

Marx, Karl. *Capital.* New York, Modern Library, 1936.

————. *The Civil War in France.* New York, International Publishers, 1940.

————. *Critique of the Gotha Program.* New York, International Publishers, 1938.

Overstreet, Harry and Bonaro. *What We Must Know about Communism.* New York, Norton, 1958.

Rühle, Otto. *Karl Marx: His Life and Work.* New York, Viking, 1929.

Russell, Bertrand. *The Practice and Theory of Bolshevism.* London, Allen and Unwin, 1954.

————. *Proposed Roads to Freedom.* New York, Holt, 1919.

Shaw, G. B., and Others. *Fabian Essays in Socialism.* London, Allen and Unwin, 1948.

Tawney, R. H. *The Sickness of an Acquisitive Society.* London, Allen and Unwin, 1920.

Trotsky, Leon. *The Defence of Terrorism.* London, Labour Publishing Co., 1921.

————. *History of the Russian Revolution.* Ann Arbor, University of Michigan Press, 1957.

————. *The Permanent Revolution*. New York, Pioneer Publishers, 1931.

Webb, Sydney. *The Decay of Capitalist Civilization*. New York, Harcourt, 1923.

Wilson, Edmund. *To the Finland Station*. Garden City, Doubleday, 1955.

CHAPTER
VI

Democratic Collectivism

A Tory statesman in Britain about the turn of the century is reported to have said: "We are all socialists now." What he meant was the fact that almost everybody took for granted the desirability of municipally owned gas and water works, laws for regulating the labor of women and children, and such measures as factory inspection and old-age pensions. But these things are not socialism. Even when extended to provide for government ownership of railroads and public utilities, graduated income and inheritance taxes, and social insurance, they do not necessarily make any fundamental change in the economic and social system. If they did, we should have to classify Germany in the time of Bismarck as a socialist state. Socialism is not synonymous with government ownership of the principal industries, nor is it the equivalent of the "Middle Way" in Sweden, the mixed economy of Nehru's India, or the welfare state in the United States. Accurately defined, socialism means the abolition of private enterprise and the substitution of collective ownership and control, for the benefit of the whole society, of at least the principal instruments of production, distribution, and exchange. It involves the destruction of private investment and the profit system and the adoption of an entirely new standard for the distribution of wealth. Society itself, through its governmental agencies, must provide the capital; and the total return on that capital, after the necessary deductions for maintenance and plant expansion, sanitation, education, etc., must be devoted to the remuneration of labor.

1. "Democratic Socialism"

With the foregoing definition as a touchstone, it seems obvious that various movements commonly classified as socialist do not belong in that category. We have seen that this is true of so-called Christian socialism, in its most common forms at least. It is equally true of the New Deal and of the "creeping socialism" of the TVA. The same judgment can be applied, though less emphatically, to much of what passes for "democratic socialism." The name of this movement is almost a contradiction in terms. It is possible to achieve either democracy or socialism separately, but difficult to have both in combination. Socialism entails such a drastic transformation of the lives and habits of individuals that dictatorial measures may be necessary to ensure its success and to repress the opposition it would be bound to arouse. There is the danger also that it may call into existence a bureaucracy so vast and complicated that popular control would be out of the question. In addition, democracy requires, as one of its essential features, freedom of the citizen to choose between rival political groups. But the succession of a socialist party by an antisocialist one would scarcely be conducive to the smooth operation of a socialist system. It might easily happen that the antisocialists, upon regaining power, would proceed to undo a great many of their rivals' accomplishments. Or a socialist government, determined to perpetuate the results of its victory, might succumb to the temptation to outlaw opposition parties or at least to limit drastically the voters' choice.

One of the most typical "democratic socialists" of recent times was the British Labourite politician and professor, Evan F. M. Durbin. He was one of the few who did not take democracy for granted but sought to explain his conception of it and to show how it could be brought into harmony with a socialist economy. Born in 1906, the son of a Baptist minister, he was educated at Oxford, winning first-class honors in philosophy, politics, and economics. He became a lecturer at the University of London, wrote several books on economic theory and national policy, and was co-author of a treatise on *Personal Aggressiveness and War*.[1] His career was brought to an untimely end in 1948 when he was drowned while bathing off the coast of Cornwall. At the time of his death he was a member of Parliament and a junior minister in the Labour Government of Clement Attlee.

E. F. M. Durbin's political theory is summarized chiefly in his *Politics of Democratic Socialism*. He looked upon the dominant trends of economic and social reform in the contemporary world and found them much less than satisfactory. The planning programs of the welfare state, he contended, were leading directly toward organized monopoly and restricted production. They benefited both labor and certain owners of property at the expense of the community. The taxation policies of America's New Deal and of similar movements were destroying initiative and enterprise and draining away the capital needed for expansion if the economic system was to continue to prosper. At the same time, the extension of social services augmented the fiscal burdens of governments and magnified the requirement for additional revenue. The result was the growth of "an ever thickening jungle of uncoordinated government control, whose main purpose is restriction, and whose chief fruit is the substitution of monopoly for competition."[2] But Durbin recognized that programs of this kind were bound to be popular. They gave short-run benefits to large segments of the population. They provided employment, stabilized prices, and stimulated an apparent prosperity. No party in power would be likely to hazard its fortunes by taking an adverse stand on such issues. Nevertheless, Durbin regarded these trends as "diseases of the body economic" which would continue unfailingly to weaken the patient.

As Durbin saw it, socialism was vastly different from a program of reforms or ameliorative measures. It would include these, but they must come *after* and not before the socialization of industry. The latter would be the prime necessity in order to give the state

[1] E. F. M. Durbin and John Bowlby, *Personal Aggressiveness and War.* Columbia University Press, 1940.
[2] *The Politics of Democratic Socialism.* London, Routledge and Paul, 1940, p. 136.

the power it would need to organize and control the national economy for the good of all. The strategy of socialism would include the nationalization as rapidly as possible, with full compensation to the owners, of the factories, mines, stores, banks, public utilities, and transportation. In a few cases control might be secured without compulsory purchase, but the important consideration would be the transfer of power, which would then be available to the state for any other purpose affecting the national welfare.

Socialism would not be complete, according to Durbin, without "egalitarian measures," or measures to accomplish the withering-away of large incomes. The devices he recommended for this purpose were capital levies and inheritance taxes. He delighted in a special form of inheritance tax, graduated not only in accordance with the size of the estate, but also in proportion to the number of times the property had been transmitted since the tax was first imposed. He thought that by this means society would "rid itself of large fortunes" and reduce unearned income to the vanishing point "without at any time bearing harshly upon particular persons or generations." [3]

No words could be more emphatic than Durbin's insistence upon a close alliance between socialism and democracy. In fact, he affirmed that "the democratic method is an inherent part of socialism, and cannot be separated from it." [4] He was just as emphatic in defining his conception of democracy. It is distinguished, he said, by three characteristic habits or institutions. The first and most typical is the right of the people to choose a government. This does not mean some original right of a sovereign to decide whether the state shall be a republic or a monarchy, but a continuing prerogative of the sovereign people to choose their governors and to keep those governors in office as long as, and only as long as, they pursue policies satisfactory to the majority of the voters. In this sense, democracy is synonymous with what the British mean by "responsible" government. Secondly, democracy, according to Durbin, implies existence of the party system. If responsible government is to be more than a

[3] *Ibid.*, p. 297.
[4] *Ibid.*, p. 235.

fiction, there must always be genuine choice before the voters. Unless the electorate is confronted by at least two opposing political groups, either of which is ready to assume the reins of governing, there is no real choice before the voters. Each party must be free to criticize and denounce its rival, with the understanding that, no matter who wins, the defeated party will not hinder the peaceful transition of its rival to power. Finally, democracy means that there must be an implicit agreement between the parties contending for power that they will not persecute each other. The very suspicion that one or another of the parties intended to violate this agreement would result in the utter breakdown of democratic government. Democracy means, above everything else, the toleration of opposition.

Yet when it came to application of this philosophy to specific questions, Durbin wavered and was not a little ambiguous. Should Communists and Fascists be tolerated? Should they be denied freedom of speech as well as the right of association? There seemed to be no doubt in Durbin's mind that the latter right should be forbidden. "We should continuously remind ourselves," he wrote, "that the enemies of democracy have no moral right to the privileges of democracy; and that a time may come when, to defend ourselves, it will be necessary to suppress their political organizations." The reader may wonder what would then become of the requirement that the voters be confronted with a real choice, particularly when the author went on to suggest that "it might easily be the duty of Socialists and Conservatives to combine against Communists and Fascists for the protection and the preservation of democracy amongst themselves." But the question of freedom of speech for extremist dissenters is even more pertinent. Would Durbin have denied anti-democrats the right to make speeches in Hyde Park? He did not say so categorically. Nevertheless, he bracketed the rights of free speech and free association together and condemned both Communists and Fascists for not accepting the obligations by which those rights were created. They were not "parties to the contract that alone creates political liberty." "Why then," he asked, "should they enjoy it?" [5] This contradictory position illustrates the difficulty

[5] *Ibid.*, pp. 275–76, 278.

that might easily occur in any persistent attempt to combine socialism with democracy.

Probably the outstanding collectivist philosopher of recent times in the English-speaking world was Harold J. Laski. Though he almost defies classification, it would seem as logical to place him in the category of democratic socialists as anywhere else. During most of his life he was quite as much of a democrat as he was a socialist. True, for a period during the 1930's he practically despaired of the achievement of socialism by other than violent measures. In *The State in Theory and Practice,* for example, he spoke of "the inevitability of revolution as the midwife of social change." [6] But in 1941 he abandoned this position and advanced the idea of a "revolution by consent." He thought that it might be possible to form a "partnership between privilege and the masses" in England that could well be permanent.[7] His attitudes evoked so much controversy that Right-wing socialists in Britain denounced him as a Communist while Communists condemned him as a Social Democrat.

Laski was born in Manchester in 1893 and was brought up in an Orthodox Jewish household. He abandoned the family traditions at an early age, married a Gentile girl when he was eighteen, and turned almost all his attention to science and to problems of social injustice. Competing successfully for honors at Oxford, he nevertheless found time to join the Fabian Society and to participate in its activities. Following his graduation he was employed for a time as an editorial writer for the *Daily Herald,* national organ of the Labour party. He was still thus engaged when war clouds loomed on the horizon in 1914. Though he advocated a general strike to stop the warmakers, at the outbreak of hostilities he volunteered for enlistment. Rejected on account of a weak heart, he went to Canada to accept a lectureship in McGill University. Two years later he joined the faculty of Harvard. In 1919–1920 he incurred the displeasure of the Harvard authorities and some Jew-baiting students for his defense of the Boston police strike and of persecuted radicals. Soon afterward he resigned, and returned to England to accept a professorship

---

[6] *The State in Theory and Practice.* New York, Viking, 1935, p. 119.
[7] *Where Do We Go from Here?* New York, Viking, 1940, p. 132.

at the London School of Economics and Political Science. For thirty years his wit and unfailing brilliance graced the lecture halls of this famous institution. But he varied his academic duties with a prodigious activity in public affairs. He campaigned for the Labour party, wrote speeches for politicians less articulate than he, championed the trade unions in the great strike of 1926, lectured in Moscow, Geneva, and Paris and at numerous universities in the United States. In 1940 he became a member of the National Executive, the policy-determining agency of the Labour party. In 1945 he was made Chairman of the National Executive. Always in fragile health, he suffered from chronic bronchitis, occasional fainting spells, and a weak heart. The combined effects of overwork, bronchitis, and an abscessed lung terminated his life in 1950.

The clue to an understanding of Laski's philosophy would seem to lie in his rebellion against every obstacle which stood in the way of justice and freedom of economic opportunity for any individual. He wanted to see ignorance, poverty, and suffering obliterated, and he fervently believed that radical changes in social institutions would be an all-sufficient remedy. From his years of adolescence when he informed his father: "I am an agnostic, not a Jew. I cannot reconcile Maimonides with Mill nor *Ann Veronica* with the Mosaic Law," [8] he was a rebel against everything which savored of darkness, superstition, or bondage to an outworn past.[9] He made liberty almost a fetish and abhorred the Leviathan state as a chief enemy of man. This attitude was exemplified, as we have seen, in his philosophy of pluralism. But even his allegiance to Marxism was predicated in part upon the assumption that it would lead to a classless utopia with no coercive state. Equality and fraternity also bulked very large in his catalogue of ideals. Religion, for instance, he regarded as the "search for a fraternal relation with all who suffer and all who are broken by the tragedy of a pain they cannot face." [10]

The evolution of Laski's political philosophy may be divided

[8] *Ann Veronica*, a novel of social protest by H. G. Wells.
[9] Kingsley Martin, *Harold Laski, A Biographical Memoir*. New York, Viking, 1953, p. 3.
[10] *The American Democracy*. New York, Viking, 1948, p. 320.

roughly into three periods. The first was the period of pluralism, from about 1916 to about 1930. The year 1930 marks a transition from individualist, anti-state theories to dogmas of revolutionary Marxism. In that year Laski published *Liberty in the Modern State*. In it he espoused a conception of liberty almost wholly negative. He defined it as the absence of restraint. He declared himself totally unable to understand how a man could be more free by subordinating his right to act in accordance with his own judgment to some body of men who would directly proceed to negate that judgment. In essence, he made liberty the right of the individual to obey his own conscience. He admitted that conscience "for most of us is a poor guide. It is perverse, it is foolish, the little knowledge it has is small alongside the worth of the social tradition. But perverse, foolish, ignorant, it is the only guide we have." [11] Those who accept commands they know to be wrong, he argued, make it easier for wrong commands to be issued. He insisted that no penalties should be imposed for the expression of any opinion, no matter how incendiary, heretical, or obscene. If governments are to be permitted to punish one man for preaching revolution against an established system, they can just as easily punish another for saying that that system was not divinely ordained. He wanted to make it possible for issues like birth control, extra-marital love, and companionate marriage to be considered in scientific fashion, and he denied that this could be done within a legal framework derived from the standards "of a nomadic Eastern people which drew up its rules more than two thousand years ago." [12] The only limitation he would consider upon utterance of any kind was the clear-and-present-danger test of Justice Holmes. But even this test he thought inferior to the Jeffersonian canon that opinion should be left completely untrammeled except when it breaks over into criminal action. And then it would be the action that would be punished and not the opinion. He did not exclude conditions of wartime or other emergencies. In a period of crisis, he contended, it is all the more important that the citizens should hear both sides of troublesome issues.

[11] *Liberty in the Modern State*. New York, Harper, 1930, p. 76.
[12] *Ibid.*, p. 92.

Notwithstanding his stalwart defense of individual freedom, Laski introduced into *Liberty in the Modern State* a number of conceptions which foreshadowed his emergence as a revolutionary Marxist. He began by asserting that "without economic security, liberty is not worth having." He broadened this to say that any society in which the fruits of economic operations are unequally distributed "will be compelled to deny freedom as the law of its being." And he declared that he knew of no instance in history in which a class in possession of power had "voluntarily abdicated its privileges." [13] He had the discernment to recognize that revolutionists in process of making a forcible change from one way of life to another would also maintain a monopoly of privileges and throw liberty away. Such had happened in Cromwellian England, Revolutionary France, and Communist Russia. Whether he believed that when the revolutionists had finally triumphed, they would recover liberty from the discard, he did not make clear.

The second period in the development of Laski's theory was the period of revolutionary Marxism, from 1931 to 1940. As has been noted previously, he now came to believe that the establishment of socialism was impossible except by violent means. The events which brought him to this conclusion were probably the great depression and the humiliating defeat of Labour in the election of 1931. The most typical of his writings in this period was *The State in Theory and Practice.* In it he expounded a theory of the state and its functions almost exclusively Marxist. Like Marx, he defined the state as an instrument of class domination. He insisted that in the so-called democracies of the contemporary world the state is an agency for protecting and enhancing the interests of the capitalist class. The state is never neutral; it does not stand over and above competing classes. Instead, "it is simply coercive power used to protect the system of rights and duties of one process of economic relationships from invasion by another class which seeks to change them in the interests of another process." [14] The capitalist class, in command of the power of the modern state, will resort to any means to maintain its supremacy.

[13] *Ibid.,* pp. 4, 220–21.
[14] *The State in Theory and Practice,* p. 100.

It will make war when necessary to prevent collapse at home or to protect investments abroad. World War I was simply a struggle of competing imperialisms, and America's entrance into that war resulted from the fact that her capitalists had committed themselves so heavily by loans and credits to the Allies that they could not afford to see them lose. Pacifists who think that war can be prevented by disarmament and international agreements must recognize that while capitalists do not necessarily want war, they insist upon pursuing objectives which, in the long run, cannot be secured without war.

But war is not the only desperate expedient resulting from the determination of the capitalist class to protect its interests. Another is fascism. Laski conceded that the supremacy of the bourgeoisie has been accompanied by a luxuriant growth of democracy. He insisted, however, that such things as universal suffrage, ministerial responsibility, and bills of rights are mere sops to the masses to keep them contented while their masters revel in the privileges and the reality of power. But whenever it becomes evident that the masses are about to make a serious attempt to change the bases of political and economic power, their rulers respond by abrogating democracy. This is what happened in Italy and Germany. For, according to Laski, fascism is nothing more than an attempt by ruthless capitalists to safeguard their dying system from being overthrown. The beneficiaries of the old order will never yield without a fight, and no weapons will be too barbarous to be included in their armory. It follows, according to Laski, that the masses should prepare themselves for the ultimate step of revolution. They have no other choice when their efforts to accomplish a peaceful transfer of power are frustrated by the negation of democracy. When events reach this stage, "the difference between classes can only be settled by force." [15] Though Laski at this time continued to sing the praises of conscience and to emphasize the right of private judgment in determining obedience to laws, it seems legitimate to suspect that his major concern was to justify the right of revolution.

The third phase in the development of Laski's political thought

[15] *Ibid.,* p. 123.

was the period from 1940 to 1950. He now displayed a keenness of insight and a breadth of understanding which did not always characterize his earlier stages. Though he was still a Marxist, he recognized that the maladies of the times were not simply the result of class exploitation. One of his major contributions was the description of a great revolution sweeping over the modern world—a revolution "as significant in its essentials as that which saw the fall of the Roman Empire, the birth, with the Reformation, of capitalist society, or, as in 1789, the final chapter in the dramatic rise of the middle class to power." [16] As a Marxist, he naturally saw as one of the incidents of this revolution a growing disproportion between property relationships and the forces of production. But he noted many others: the revolt of the subject peoples against imperialism; the demand, all over the world, for a standard of living sufficient to guarantee a respectable minimum of health, education, and comfort; the decline of religion, which hitherto had offered compensation in the next world for the deficiencies of the present; a widespread demand for planning and for economic expansion; and a revolt against national sovereignty, as a principal cause of war and a major obstacle to prosperity and an efficient use of the world's resources.

Laski saw the Russian Revolution as an important climax of the world revolution and also as a beacon light for the guidance of other nations. Though he deplored the brutalities of the Soviet leaders, he did not regard them as damning the movement. They were ugly excrescences, but not fundamental characteristics. The Soviet experiment was conceived on so tremendous a scale that it could never have been brought to completion without repressive measures. Furthermore, the invasions and threats of invasion from without instilled into the nation a feeling of insecurity and confronted the rulers with the danger of defeat and annihilation. It was fear which prompted the cruelties, not original sin or the defects of the system. Laski believed that other nations, unbesieged by such dangers, could safely emulate the Russian example of a social and economic revolution. Their revolutions would not

[16] *Reflections on the Revolution of Our Time.* New York, Viking, 1943, p. 1.

need to be quite so drastic, for recent experience had shown that
it is possible to accomplish a genuine transfer of power to the
masses without a root-and-branch extermination of all forms of
private production. Nevertheless, the land would have to be collectivized, and also transport, fuel, power, and import and export
trade. Equally vital would be control by the state of the supply
of capital and credit. This would necessitate nationalization of
the banks, insurance companies, and building-and-loan societies.
Even if all the remaining elements of the economy were left to
private enterprise, the fundamental bases of economic power
would be transferred to the community. This would be the prime
consideration, according to Laski.

Equally significant in the new viewpoint of Laski was his belief in the possibility of a "revolution by consent." His studies and
observations had now convinced him that there is a relationship
between ends and means. A revolution by violence, he wrote,
is bound to result in the suspension of democracy. If it succeeds,
as in 1789 in France and in 1917 in Russia, it will be followed
by an iron age. If it fails, it will usher in a black reaction of stern
repression and bloody reprisals. Much to be preferred, though
considerably slower, are the peaceful methods of political action.
Let the masses organize their own political parties, cultivate their
class-consciousness, utilize the splendid opportunities afforded
them by the scientific revolution, and take full advantage of the
difficulties of the owning classes during periods of labor scarcity,
depression, and war. Laski considered the conditions of World
War II an excellent foundation for a "revolution by consent." It
created a ferment, stirred men's feelings to the depths, and raised
many anxious inquiries regarding the future. Nearly everyone
realized that the world as he had known it was being rudely shattered, and that a new epoch was about to dawn. In many minds
there was a feeling that radical steps should be taken to ensure
that the new world would not be a pale simulacrum of the old.
Whether Laski was fully satisfied with the mild revolution that
occurred in his own country in 1945 is not clear. Certainly the
modifications that have since been made would not have met his
approval.

2. Conservative Collectivism

In certain quarters in Britain there used to be a saying that "The Left Center is always right." It would probably have been more accurate to have said, "The Right Center is never left." For no body of thinkers exerted more influence, not merely in Britain but in Western countries generally, than that group of British economists in the thirties and forties who occupied a position in the political spectrum a little to the right of Center. Rejecting *laissez faire* as outmoded and impossible, they also repudiated socialism. They believed that capitalism with all its faults was a better instrument of equity and abundance than any of the schemes of extreme collectivists. They therefore opposed the substitution of government ownership for private enterprise in any field of economic activity already occupied by individual initiative. A few of them were ready to move toward socialism if absolutely necessary, but only as a last resort. For the most part, they believed that control of investment, money, and credit would be quite sufficient to instill new life into a flagging economic system. Instead of taking as their objectives the elimination of unearned increment or the distribution to labor of the full product of its toil, they were concerned primarily with preventing a "boom and bust" economy and with achieving full employment. They were the originators and chief sponsors of the idea that the principal cause of depressions is an improper balance between saving and investment. They were also the chief architects of the governmental policy of deficit financing.

The high priest of conservative collectivism was John Maynard Keynes (1883–1946). The son of distinguished parents (his father was an eminent economist and philosopher, and his mother was Mayor of Cambridge), he was thoroughly educated in mathematics and the classics before being sent to Cambridge University. When only twenty-three he passed the British Civil Service examination with the second-best score. He would have ranked first except for a low grade in economics. He spent two years in the India Office and then returned to Cambridge as a lecturer.

At the Paris Peace Conference of 1919 he was the chief economic adviser of the British delegation. The ignorance and indifference of the most powerful members of the conference appalled him, and he blasted them in *Economic Consequences of the Peace,* a book which gained him world recognition. After the war he continued his lecturing at Cambridge but also found time for an active business career as chairman of an insurance company, manager of an investment trust, and director of the Bank of England. He amassed a large fortune, which he expended principally in promoting the arts. Though he remained a Liberal, he was elevated to a peerage by the Churchill government in 1942.

Despite his belief that capitalism, "wisely managed," could probably "be made more efficient for attaining economic ends than any alternative system yet devised," Keynes had no use for the economic theories of Adam Smith, Malthus, and Ricardo which had provided the main justification for capitalism.[17] Classical economics had assumed that the unhindered operation of natural economic laws would actually guarantee the greatest good of the greatest number. They would provide their own corrective for booms and depressions by curtailing consumption in the face of overproduction. They would then bring about a revival of demand when production had fallen below normal levels. The operation of these laws was likewise assumed to be an effective remedy for unemployment. As production declined, labor would become plentiful. Consequently, wages would fall, until they reached such a level that it would become profitable for employers to reopen their plants. Thus a balance would eventually be restored. There would be occasional periods when business was exceptionally good. There would also be occasional years when business was exceedingly poor. But the seven fat kine would never eat up the seven lean kine, as in the Pharaoh's celebrated dream. Instead, it was assumed that most of the time economic activity would be normal, employment would be good if not total, and production and consumption would be in relative equilibrium.

Keynes disputed this pleasant supposition. He substituted the

[17] *Laissez-Faire and Communism.* New York, New Republic, 1926, pp. 76–77.

contrary assumption that prosperity and full employment can only
be assured by the adoption of a deliberate public policy. This
policy would consist of several elements. It would include, first
of all, the socialization of investment. This might take the form of
a deliberate unbalancing of the national budget, a borrowing
against the future, in order to obtain funds for the construction
of public works to counterbalance a decline in private investment.
It might also take the form of differential rates of taxation on
venture and *rentier* capital, or perhaps a regulation of interest
rates in favor of venture capital. If there was any class for which
Keynes had contempt, it was the *rentier* class, whose members
refused to risk their capital in new ventures but sought a "safe"
return by investing in bonds or other securities of established
enterprises which had little need for new capital. He believed in
penalizing this class by taxing their incomes at a higher rate than
that levied on the returns from venture capital. He ridiculed the
idea that the savings of the rich provide the principal nourishment of a national economy. Saving in itself is purely negative; it
is simply the opposite of spending. Though undoubtedly desirable
for personal advantage, it adds nothing to a nation's prosperity.
This fact, he contended, is abundantly illustrated in wartime. It
is not the purchase of war bonds and war stamps that produces
tanks and planes to defeat the enemy. It is the positive act of
spending by the state. Unless either the state or private citizens
in peacetime use savings to purchase goods, to establish new
enterprises, or to repair or expand old ones, money saved performs no more useful function than the Biblical pound hidden in
a napkin.

Another element in the Keynesian policy for promoting prosperity and full employment was monetary control. He would
establish what is commonly called a managed currency, regulating its value by a policy of contraction and expansion in accordance with the needs of the economy. Prosperity would thus be
assured in terms of the conditions of the home market, and no
nation would be tempted to "beggar its neighbor" in the foolish
pursuit of a favorable balance of trade. Finally, the growth of
population would have to be brought under control; for Keynes
recognized that nothing is so destructive of a high standard of

living as population pressure upon the margin of subsistence.

The economic theory of Lord Keynes still stands in the minds of many as a symbol of almost everything that goes to make up the Western conception of the positive state. To a large extent it was the fountainhead of that conception. For example, Keynesian theory makes obsolete a hands-off policy by the state while business languishes and robust men walk the streets in a vain quest for jobs to enable them to feed their families. The great economist taught that it is better, if necessary, that a moderate number of men be put to work digging holes and filling them up again than that a large number should be unemployed.[18] Nothing could illustrate more pointedly the contrast with the old negative conception of the state, which was not only expected to follow the *laissez-faire* principle but was supposed to spend as little money as possible lest business men be frightened into a loss of confidence. A large number of the fiscal policies of post-depression governments reflected Keynesian doctrine in spite of the fact that the master, according to reports, did not have a high opinion of the economic literacy of some of his disciples. An eminent American economist has said that Keynes' chief work, *The General Theory of Employment, Interest and Money,* "has had a greater impact on economic analysis and policy . . . than any book since Ricardo's *Political Economy.*" [19]

Second only to Keynes as a significant exponent of conservative collectivism is Sir William Beveridge. He was born in India in 1879, the son of an official of the Indian Civil Service. He was educated, however, exclusively in England, initially at Charterhouse and then at Oxford. He specialized originally in mathematics and astronomy but obtained his degree in law. After graduation he shifted his interests more and more into economics and sociology. In 1908 Winston Churchill, then President of the Board of Trade, gave him a position in the government. From 1919 to 1937 he served as Director of the London School of Economics. In 1941 he was appointed Under-Secretary of Labour.

---

[18] *The General Theory of Employment, Interest and Money.* New York, Harcourt, 1936, p. 220.

[19] Seymour E. Harris, "Introduction" to Alvin H. Hansen, *A Guide to Keynes.* New York, McGraw-Hill, 1953, p. x.

His famous *Report on Social Insurance and Allied Services* which he made to His Majesty's Government in 1942 became a bestseller. Though he sympathizes with many of the principles of both Labour and the Liberals, he has never identified himself with any political party.

A number of resemblances characterize the theories of Beveridge and Keynes. Preoccupation with the importance of full employment, emphasis upon the duty of the state to take positive action for the welfare of its citizens, and insistence upon the obligation of each nation to put its own house in order before trying to remake the world—these are typical of the points of agreement. But there are numerous differences. Beveridge said little about monetary policy, perhaps for the reason that he assumed such questions had been settled. He was concerned not so much with conquering depressions as with abolishing them by a uniform policy applied continuously. More important, he seemed to place a higher premium upon the preservation of liberty and other individual values than did Keynes. He described these values "as more precious than full employment itself," and he defined them as including "freedom of worship, speech, writing, study, and teaching"; freedom of assembly and of association; "freedom of choice of occupation; and freedom in the management of a personal income." [20] Paradoxically, however, he was more tolerant of socialism than was Keynes. He held to the view that full employment could actually be achieved under private enterprise, but he admitted that if experience should subsequently reveal that this view was erroneous, he would be prepared to recommend abolition of private ownership of the means of production.

The original Beveridge Report proposed a comprehensive program of social insurance for every individual, "from the womb to the tomb"; or, as others described it, "from the sperm to the worm." He won even greater renown, though, for a sequel to that Report, which he published under the title of *Full Employment in a Free Society.* By full employment he did not mean that absolutely everyone able and willing to work should be continuously employed. He recognized that there must always be some

[20] *Full Employment in a Free Society.* New York, Norton, 1945, p. 21.

unemployment produced by seasonal or frictional factors.[21] Some industries and occupations are definitely seasonal, while in others there may be necessary variations in employment resulting from retooling operations or from the closing-down of a plant in one locality and the opening of a new one elsewhere. Beveridge defined full employment as meaning that the labor market should always be a seller's market rather than a buyer's market—that is, that the number of vacant jobs should always exceed the number of unemployed men. He considered that full employment existed if not more than three per cent of the labor force was seeking work and unable, for the time being, to find it. He thought that under such a condition the normal lag between losing one job and finding another would be very short. It could be easily covered by unemployment insurance without any risk of discouragement or demoralization for the worker.

Beveridge regarded full employment as the prime measure of the justice and efficiency of an economic order. That men should be reduced to idleness and forced into a kind of second-class citizenship because of an inability to find work he considered disgraceful. Enforced idleness corrodes the soul of man even when supported, for any length of time, by a dole. It makes men seem useless, unwanted. It causes them to live in fear, "and from fear springs hate." It is a major source of xenophobia, of anti-Semitism, and of enmity between the sexes. So long as mass unemployment exists, each man appears to every other man as a competitor in a mad scramble for jobs. And so long as there is a scramble for jobs, it is futile to deplore organized efforts by workers to limit their output, to resist technological improvements, and to set up all kinds of jealous restrictions to prevent new members from entering their crafts.[22] It was Beveridge's conviction that no malady of modern times, except war, surpasses in its corrupting and disastrous effects the evil of mass unemployment. He maintained that the most devastating effect of both was the diversion of all that is best in man's spirit into channels

---

[21] "Frictional unemployment" is unemployment that results from the lack of mobility and interchangeability in the labor supply. *Ibid.*, App. D, pp. 408–409.

[22] *Ibid.*, p. 248.

of hatred, fear, and revenge.

Though Beveridge considered full employment to be the principal aim of public policy, he did not regard it as the only one. He was also profoundly interested in a redistribution of income. Such a redistribution would contribute to full employment by encouraging more spending and less saving, but he considered it important also as a means of eliminating booms and depressions. Leveling-down large incomes in order to give greater purchasing power to the masses would provide a stable market for the output of industry instead of one in which production was constantly tending to outrun consumption. But Beveridge did not believe that a mere increase in the spending power of the majority of consumers would be a panacea. There would be no guaranty that they would spend their surplus wisely or in such a way as to benefit depressed industries. They might prefer to buy beer rather than household appliances. As a consequence, it would be necessary to endow the state with ultimate responsibility for controlling expenditure with reference to social priorities. The state "must adopt neither the consumption approach nor the investment approach exclusively, but must be free to adjust policy according to circumstances, over the whole range of possible subjects of spending." [23] What Beveridge demanded was a *total* policy of guidance, direction, and control of economic functions in the interests of the whole society, and without the sacrifice of essential freedoms.

3. The Welfare State

At first thought the conservative collectivism described in the preceding section may seem just another name for the welfare state. They do bear resemblances, exemplified especially by some of the implications of Sir William Beveridge's "total policy." But the welfare state is much broader even than anything suggested by Beveridge's program. It includes not simply a policy of guiding, directing, and controlling economic functions with a view to social objectives, but using the machinery of the state in almost any way and for almost any purpose to enhance the welfare of

[23] *Ibid.*, p. 187.

its citizens. It is founded upon the principle that the state exists for the positive promotion of the good of all. Unlike the conservative collectivists, exponents of the welfare state do not shrink from advocating government ownership, either to supplement private enterprise or to benefit the public by lower prices. They generally advocate not only steeply graduated income taxes but "death duties," which all but abolish the right of inheritance. Their program is also very likely to include economic planning, comprehensive social insurance, some form of "socialized medicine," and legislation to extend and strengthen collective bargaining and other privileges of unionized labor. At the same time, proponents of the welfare state have not hesitated to sponsor measures for restricting production of both agricultural and industrial commodities. Examples include the AAA and NIRA in the United States and the crop-control and marketing acts in France and Great Britain in the 1930's. All such schemes for achieving an "economy of scarcity" were anathema to economists like Keynes and Beveridge.

Illustrations of the welfare state can be found in almost every Western European country in the late nineteenth and early twentieth centuries. Even Bismarck's program of social insurance, maximum-hours laws, factory inspection, and old-age pensions was inspired partly by a Junker conception of *noblesse oblige* toward the weak and less fortunate. The Iron Chancellor himself expressed a desire that the humbler citizens should "not be run over and trampled under foot on the highway of life." Other European nations followed the German example. The program in Great Britain, sponsored by the rejuvenated Liberal party in the early 1900's, was the most comprehensive. It included not only sickness and old-age insurance and maximum-hours laws but unemployment insurance and minimum-wage laws for workers in depressed industries. Later examples were represented by the New Deal in the United States, the regime of the Popular Front in France (1936–1938), and the Labour Government in Great Britain (1945–1950).

The theory of the welfare state bears a closer resemblance to democratic socialism. Yet the differences here are notable and fundamental. The proponents of the former remain capitalists.

If they advocate degrees of government ownership, and some of them certainly have done so, they are not actuated by motives of destroying capitalism but rather of shoring it up and making it work more effectively for the benefit of a greater number. Their demands for other reforms may duplicate in nature and severity those of the democratic socialists; but the purpose is always different. The theorists of the welfare state conceive of reforms as expedients for improving an existing system. For the democratic socialist the existing system is an evil. He does not believe in its destruction by violent revolution, but he does insist that its eventual elimination and replacement by something better is the goal that must never be forgotten. He yields to no one in acknowledging the value of reforms, but he holds that reforms without some initial measures for socializing the means of production may do more harm than good. They may foster monopoly, stimulate an artificial prosperity, and benefit certain elements of the population at the expense of the community. For him as for the proponents of the welfare state, reforms are expedients—but expedients for the achievement in some roseate future of a completely transformed society.

In developing the *theory* of the welfare state, the United States rode in the van most of the time. It seemed much easier to evolve ideas than to put them into practice. American theories of the welfare state date back to Roger Williams and Thomas Paine. Williams, famed as a champion of religious freedom in Colonial America, also had pronounced political views. He conceived of the state as a public-service corporation, a servant of the people to provide for their needs. Accordingly, he advocated an equal division of the land among families and fixed prices for the necessaries of life in time of shortage. He believed that the government should assume responsibility not only for caring for the poor and disabled and for widows and orphans but also for procuring work for the able-bodied.

Thomas Paine, in his *Rights of Man*, advocated progressive taxes on unearned incomes and steeply graduated inheritance taxes. The revenues obtained would be used to provide subsidies for the support of children and the aged, public works for the relief of unemployment, and benefits for education. In a shorter work entitled *Agrarian Justice* he recommended a special tax on land, similar to a levy on unearned increment. He proposed that every owner of cultivated land pay to the community a *ground-rent* as his contribution to society for wealth he did not create.

Other Americans, through the nineteenth century, expounded theories equally radical if not so comprehensive. Abraham Lincoln, for example, though in most respects a staunch individualist, declared that it is the legitimate object of government "to do for a community of people whatever they need to have done, but cannot do at all, or cannot so well do, for themselves, in their separate and individual capacities." [24] The Greenback and Populist movements of the 1880's and 1890's committed themselves along several lines to a positive policy of state benevolence. Leaders of both movements agitated for income taxes, government ownership of railroads and telegraph lines, and monetary inflation for the benefit of the debtor classes. In addition, the Populists demanded arbitration of labor disputes, licensing and control of corporations, and government guaranties of bank deposits.

Inclusive theories of the welfare state were not developed until the twentieth century. The Theodore Roosevelt Progressive movement adopted the platforms of the Greenbackers and Populists, with the exception of the currency provisions, and expanded them to embrace workmen's compensation, prohibition of child labor, minimum wages for women and children, and insurance against sickness, unemployment, and old age. Woodrow Wilson and his Progressive followers were more interested in controlling monopoly and in preventing unfair business practices. Nevertheless, Wilson as President succeeded in procuring the enactment of an eight-hour law for interstate railways, a child-labor act to prevent the shipment in interstate commerce of products of child labor, a Federal Farm Loan act to provide easier credit for the farmers than they could obtain from commercial banks, and a Federal Reserve Act to stabilize the banking system and make possible a more flexible currency. Not until the advent of the New Deal, however, did "welfare state" become a household

[24] J. G. Nicolay and John Hay, eds., *The Complete Works of Abraham Lincoln.* New York, Francis D. Tandy Co., 1905, II, 186–87.

phrase and gain wide acceptance as a necessary and desirable program. And no one did more to promote such results than the great standard-bearer of the New Deal, Franklin D. Roosevelt.

For Roosevelt the welfare state was almost synonymous with security—a fact which is certainly not surprising when one takes into account the condition of the country when he became President. But he did not conceive of security in the narrow sense of old-age pensions and unemployment insurance. He identified it rather with a broad idea of confidence on the part of the masses that they would not have to worry about losing their homes, about being ill-fed or ill-clad, or becoming objects of charity. It meant also that even the poorest Americans would have full opportunity for education and for "reasonable leisure and recreation." Despite many speeches on the subject, Roosevelt never went much beyond this simple but eloquent conception. At the end of the campaign of 1940, with a second world war threatening to draw the nation into its vortex, he portrayed his ideal of the future America in terms which still revealed a deep preoccupation with social and economic security. But these were his speeches. His policies and the achievements of his administration bear witness in more tangible form to the strength of his ideals. For the Roosevelt era saw the origins of such milestones on the road to the welfare state as the FDIC, the SEC, the TVA, the AAA, the Wagner Act, the Federal Social Security Act, and the Fair Labor Standards Act.

A large part of the ideology of the welfare state propounded during the four administrations of Franklin D. Roosevelt emanated from his subordinates and even from his critics. Foremost among the latter was Charles A. Beard (who turned against Roosevelt with venomous wrath for leading the country into World War II). Born in Indiana in 1874, he received his education at DePauw, Columbia, and Oxford universities. The author of about thirty books, he won distinction as a scholar of broad perspective and was elected successively president of the American Political Science Association and the American Historical Association. His teaching career was brief, since he resigned from Columbia in 1917 because of conflict with the University administration.

It is impossible to deny Beard an eminent place among American thinkers. His concept of the welfare state gave major emphasis to the idea of planning. The basic factor in modern civilization, he contended, is technology; and he denied the possibility of taking full advantage of improvements in technology without planning. Education, research, the encouragement of the basic sciences, the use of resources—all must be planned if a nation is to reap the full reward of its technological potential.

Beard did not stop with mere advocacy of an idea. He went on to suggest means of implementation. He recommended the establishment by Congress of a National Economic Council. Represented in the Council would be all the great industries of a high degree of concentration, together with the various organizations in agriculture, labor, wholesale and retail trade. The original function of the Council would be to serve as a kind of federal convention to draw up an economic constitution for the approval of the voters. To facilitate the establishment of the program, all anti-trust laws would be repealed. Every industry of a high degree of concentration would be classified as a business "affected with a public interest" and made subject to the same extent of regulation as is already required of public utilities. Associated with the National Economic Council would be a Board of Strategy and Planning, with the primary functions of surveying the resources and capacities of the country and planning production. Each industry represented in the Council would also have its own organization, set up as a holding company for the various enterprises. Dividends would be limited, and any surpluses earned would be used to pay bonuses and to provide reserves for unemployment.

Though Beard set great store by a historical materialism quite similar to that of Karl Marx, he was no socialist. His scheme for a planned society contemplated the utilization of the existing business corporations as owners and operators of the means of production. He would simply induce or require the existing stockholders to exchange their shares for 3-per-cent bonds, and then issue new stock to the directors, managers, and employers of the several corporations. Except for the elimination of idle, absentee stockholders, the character of the economy would be essentially unchanged. Moreover, Beard had no sympathy for the kind of drastic economic and social reorganization carried out in Russia. "If capitalism," he wrote, "were cursed with all the evils ascribed to it by communists (and it has plenty to its credit), still the American people, on a fair and free count, would vote one hundred to one for keeping it rather than enslave themselves to the kind of political and economic despotism regnant in the land of the former tsars." [25]

The so-called isolationism of Beard was closely enmeshed with his schemes for national planning. He did not believe in a closed state with impenetrable barriers against foreign trade. He expected, on the contrary, that national planning would result in an even greater demand for foreign goods. The "full use of the American endowment would create a national buying power of enormous proportions and a corresponding demand for foreign commodities of peculiar distinction." [26] His objective was really Continentalism, involving a concentration of interest on the Western Hemisphere and on building here a civilization peculiar to American conditions. He did not scorn sympathetic collaboration with other countries so long as their policies were enlightened and peaceful. What he really opposed was the policy of *Machtpolitik*, under which foreign trade was cultivated and extended by force of arms, or by the politer methods of diplomacy concealing threats of force. For the American Republic he recommended a procedure of self-restraint. No participation in trade wars, no quest for empire, and no meddling in the affairs of Europe or Asia. America should have no part in the predatory activities of foreign powers. She should lend them no money in time of war and sell them no guns. She should abandon forever the "imbecilic belief" that she should defend every dollar invested abroad by Americans regardless of risk. In place of these grievous errors she should substitute the example of a "garden well tended" and thereby "teach the most effective lesson—a lesson without words." [27]

Among the subordinates of President Roosevelt advocating

[25] *America Faces the Future*. Boston, Houghton Mifflin, 1932, p. 122.
[26] *The Open Door at Home*. New York, Macmillan, 1934, p. 214.
[27] *Ibid.*, p. 319.

the welfare state, the names of two command particular attention. The most emphatic in asserting his ideas, perhaps, was
Jerome Frank, whose theories of jurisprudence have already been
discussed. Frank served the New Deal as general counsel of
the AAA from 1933 to 1935 and as chairman of the SEC from
1939 to 1941. Though an ardent admirer of President Roosevelt, he disagreed with his chief on at least one important issue.
He was staunchly opposed to redistribution of existing income
without any attempt to increase production. This method he
denominated a fascist procedure. Instead of that, he would raise
production above the 1929 level and raise it again with each
succeeding year, allocating the major portion of the increase
to those with meager incomes. Like Charles A. Beard, he would
institute an economic parliament or council through which the
necessary cooperation with business in planning production for
the future would be secured. He would supplement this by constant lowering of prices, by government construction of public
works, and by government purchases and distribution to counterbalance insufficient earnings and wages. By such expedients
he believed it would be possible to create a good life for all
Americans without undermining political democracy, without
destroying producers' property in small enterprises, and even
without affecting the property rights of "ordinary investors in
giant corporations." He contended that, by the exercise of intelligence, we could steadily reduce the working hours of the great
majority of our citizens and arrive at a goal resembling the
leisure society of which Sir Thomas More dreamed. He admitted the remote possibility that an excess of leisure might
weaken the social fabric. If it did so, he was then prepared to
advocate the conscription of young men and young women for
a battle against the evils and hardships of nature in the manner
recommended by William James.[28]

The department of the United States government most deeply
concerned with the ideas of the welfare state, during the New
Deal, was probably the Department of Agriculture. Here were

[28] *Save America First.* New York, Harper, 1938, pp. 250–51, 342–43, 357,
373–74, 401; *Fate and Freedom.* New York, Simon and Schuster, 1945, pp.
194, 201–02.

located such agencies as the AAA, the Federal Farm Loan Corporation, and the Rural Electrification Administration. Its formulators of policy included not only Jerome Frank but Mordecai Ezekiel and Rexford G. Tugwell, two noted apostles of an economy of abundance. Heading the Department was Henry A. Wallace, whose name symbolized the New Deal in the public mind almost as much as did that of Franklin D. Roosevelt.

Wallace came from a long line of agricultural specialists. His father was Secretary of Agriculture under Harding and Coolidge. His father and grandfather were founders and publishers of *Wallace's Farmer*. Before his appointment to Roosevelt's cabinet, Henry A. Wallace had devoted his life to plant-breeding and agricultural journalism. Few were more cognizant of the problems of the farmer. He had seen agriculture sink into the slough of depression even during the fat years of the 1920's. As time passed, he became more and more convinced that the problems of agriculture were inextricably linked with the problems of the economy as a whole. Though he had a high regard for the "way-of-life" farmer, and longed for some method of saving him, he considered him doomed, in the vast majority of cases. He was being "tractored" off his farm by advances in agricultural technology. Mechanized farms were rapidly increasing their percentage of the total agricultural production, leaving the acres tilled by the horde of marginal cultivators far behind. To relieve depression in agriculture, the best of all methods, Wallace argued, would be the creation of sixty million jobs in industry. Not only would this increase the demand for agricultural products, but it would entice surplus farmers away from the soil, and enhance the opportunities of those who remained. Moreover, by raising the economic status of the poorest ten million families it would ensure an annual market for fifteen billion dollars' worth of goods and services.

Wallace's association with the Communists in the Presidential campaign of 1948 must not blind one to the fact that he was about as far removed from Marxism as any American reformer who ever lived. In 1943 he avowed that "the spirit of free competition will and must continue to be one of our main driving forces." This spirit, or something closely akin to it, he identified with Horatio Alger, who "is not dead in America and never will be." [29] He recognized, however, that obstacles had arisen which stood in the way of some forms of free competition. He enumerated two of these as the closing of the frontier and the growth of monopoly. Unlike Franklin D. Roosevelt, who seemed to think that the American economy had passed its zenith and afforded little further opportunity for expansion,[30] Wallace apparently did not take much stock in the idea of a mature and stagnant economy. He seems to have been firmly convinced that sixty million jobs in industry could be created by 1950, and the results have borne out his conviction. He admitted that, to attain this goal, a considerable amount of planning and a small degree of regimentation would be necessary. But he denied that either would be sufficient to justify alarm. The important issue, he maintained, is not the fact of government control of economic affairs, but "which group will be in control of the government, and whether or not that group will have ulterior purposes to serve." [31]

Wallace never considered himself a radical, with respect to the welfare state or anything else. Though he was horrified by the unemployment of millions of good people and the waste and destruction of natural resources, he proposed no drastic correctives. He believed in the Sermon on the Mount and envisaged an America where all would be members of the middle class, and even the humblest citizen would enjoy the bourgeois benefits of central heating, electric refrigeration, vacation trips, and a college education for his children. His proposals for planning did not penetrate very far beneath the surface of the economic system, except as pertained to natural resources and a few specialized segments of the national life on an emergency basis. He would have the government manage the tariff and the money

[29] Russell Lord, ed., *The Century of the Common Man*, p. 57.

[30] Roosevelt said in his Commonwealth Club address, San Francisco, 1932, that our industrial plant was complete, and that our task in the future was "not discovery or exploitation of natural resources, or necessarily producing more goods." Instead, the government must play a major role "in the soberer, less dramatic business of administering resources and plants already in hand," of re-establishing foreign markets, of adjusting production to consumption, and of "distributing wealth and products more equitably."

[31] *Sixty Million Jobs.* New York, Reynal and Hitchcock, 1945, p. 17.

system, control railroad interest rates, and encourage price and production policies in such a way as to maintain a balanced relationship between the incomes of agriculture, industry, and labor. He would also have the government utilize its credit resources to get the economy off dead-center when necessary.

Though Wallace realized that the old regime of more or less free international trade was gone forever, and though he admitted that the United States could come close to achieving self-sufficiency—at a price—he did not advocate economic nationalism. Instead, he proposed a middle course: "a line of march along which we would lower tariffs enough to bring in another half-billion dollars worth of goods annually," and at the same time withdraw permanently from cultivation twenty-five million acres of good agricultural land.[32] Whether he ever recommended, as he was supposed to have done, that every Hottentot be provided with a quart of milk a day, he fully realized that no nation can live to itself alone, that the prosperity of the United States is inseparably linked with the prosperity of the rest of the world.

The most penetrating British apostle of the welfare state is probably Richard Henry Tawney. Though at one time he considered himself a Guild Socialist, his most original contribution has been a comprehensive theory of state intervention, rather than state ownership, for the promotion of human welfare. When he wrote *The Acquisitive Society* in 1920, he demanded a system under which no one would receive compensation except for service rendered to society. All payments of profit, interest, rent, and royalties on mineral wealth would be rigorously eliminated. The basis of remuneration would be function and not ownership. It would be a system close to the Marxist ideal of no one living by owning but all men by working. But in his later writings Tawney diluted this socialism so as to limit collectivization to industries of a monopolistic character and to those essential to the health and prosperity of the national economy. The methods he would use would not be those of confiscation, class warfare, or forced purchase but chiefly regulation, progressive taxation,

[32] *America Must Choose.* New York, Foreign Policy Association, 1934, p. 27.

and industrial democracy. In short, so far as concerned basic principles, his later proposals did not differ greatly from those of other advocates of the welfare state.

R. H. Tawney was born in Calcutta in 1880, the son of a British official. Educated at Rugby and at Oxford, he has devoted his entire career to teaching and writing. From 1931 to 1949 he was Professor of Economic History at the University of London. He won acclaim throughout the world for his three most important books, *The Acquisitive Society, Religion and the Rise of Capitalism,* and *Equality.* Though listed as a member of the Labour party, he has never stood for Parliament or taken an active part in any purely political affairs. He has served, however, on many advisory boards and commissions, and in 1942 was economic and social adviser to the British Embassy in Washington. He is credited with exerting a moderating influence upon both the Labour party and the Fabian Society. Unlike some other Fabians, he is profoundly concerned with the preservation of civil liberties.

Tawney's interest in the welfare of human beings is not limited to achieving higher incomes for the underprivileged. In fact, he maintains that no scheme devised thus far for raising the purchasing power of the masses will procure for them the measure of social well-being to which they are entitled. High incomes "will not purchase the mass of mankind immunity from cholera, typhus, and ignorance, still less secure them the positive advantages of educational opportunity and economic security." [33] Not even if he works overtime every day of his life can the ordinary worker procure these things. The reason is that society has grown immensely complex and interdependent. Civilization has become a collective product, and an enormously expensive one; and nothing less than the combined power of society can provide the health, education, recreation, security, and good living to which all of its members, and not simply the rich, are entitled. The need for hospitals, schools, libraries, research centers, parks, and highways is a constantly growing one and can never be satisfied by individual enterprise. Only the social income derived by the state through progressive taxation and the confiscation

[33] *Equality.* London, Allen and Unwin, 1952, pp. 134–35.

of inheritance will ever suffice for these purposes. And the state alone through these methods can convert the surplus personal incomes of the wealthy minority into social income. If not thus converted, these surplus incomes are almost certain to be wasted on such articles of conspicuous consumption as jewelry, expensive motor cars, country houses, and yachts.

For Tawney the welfare state was not confined to a judicious use of the social income. He believed that it should also include industrial democracy. That fundamental issues vitally affecting the employment conditions and livelihood of the workers should be settled without any pretense of consulting their wishes seemed to him a monstrous violation of human rights. He was not thinking merely of collective bargaining for the determination of wages and hours or perhaps such fringe benefits as pensions and disability insurance. These were excellent but they did not go far enough. In an argument similar to that of Justice Brandeis, he insisted that the workers be consulted also with respect to such matters as the closing of uneconomic plants, the introduction of new machines and techniques, and the disciplining of employees. Workmen have "precisely the same right," he contended, "to be satisfied that organization is efficient, and management up to date, as management has that workmen are earning their wages." [34] That a partnership between management and labor would result in utilizing minds incompetent to deal with complex questions, Tawney vigorously denied. He argued that nine-tenths of existing boards of directors are composed of laymen. They have no more specialized knowledge of intricate problems of production and factory management than does many an intelligent worker. Why not therefore accord to the representatives of labor an equal voice with management in settling issues of vital concern to the workers? Both would need to be guided by expert advice, but labor as well as management could cast its vote in line with its own considerations of desirable policy.

Democratic collectivism remains to this day the most successful movement for political and social reconstruction west of the Iron Curtain. It far surpasses, in fact, any others. Despite

[34] *Ibid.*, p. 199.

condemnations of "creeping socialism" in the United States, it appears inconceivable that in any country there will be a return, in the foreseeable future, to an unregulated, free-enterprise economy. Whether in the form of democratic socialism, conservative collectivism, or the welfare state, democratic collectivism seems permanently entrenched. To enthrone any one of its opposites would constitute an effort to turn the clock back to a simpler age when the robust health of a growing economic system could compensate readily for the greed and stupidity of individuals. But the complexities of our own era make such a reliance, in the opinion of most economists, impossible.

Notwithstanding their success, democratic collectivists can scarcely be regarded as above criticism. Whether blinded by Marxist dogma or for some other reason, the majority of them seem to have placed too much emphasis on economic determinism. Above everything else they have sought to obtain for the working class a larger share of the national wealth. And this wealth they have measured in terms of money income. They have made social justice almost synonymous with higher wages and an increased capacity to consume. If they have advocated collective bargaining, the cardinal purposes have been to enable the worker to augment his rate of pay or to reduce his hours of work. The results have been several. High wages have been translated into a higher cost of living, which affects both workers and owners, and is particularly serious for those living on fixed incomes or deficient in collective power to extort increased wages. High wages and short hours mean high production costs, and therefore constitute a kind of built-in inflationary factor which interferes with the effects of supply and demand.[35] With living equated with consuming, Western nations, and the United States in particular, almost exhaust themselves in a scramble for physical possessions, depleting their heritage of natural resources, and drawing upon the rest of the world to make up their deficits. Yet few indeed of the democratic collectivists, with the exception of R. H. Tawney, have recognized that there are other

---

[35] It must be emphasized, of course, that mounting costs of production have not been the only inflationary factors disturbing the economies of modern nations. The effects of wars have been much more disastrous.

values which the positive state can provide of at least equal importance with money income.

ADDITIONAL READINGS

Cole, G. D. H. *Socialism in Evolution*. Middlesex, England, Penguin, 1938.

Durbin, E. F. M. *Problems of Economic Planning*. London, Routledge and Paul, 1949.

Finer, Herman. *The Road to Reaction*. London, D. Dobson, 1946.

Hansen, Alvin M. *Economic Policy and Full Employment*. New York, McGraw-Hill, 1947.

————. *Full Recovery or Stagnation?* New York, Norton, 1938.

————. *A Guide to Keynes*. New York, McGraw-Hill, 1953.

Keynes, J. M. *The End of Laissez Faire*. London, L. & Virginia Woolf, 1927.

————. *Laissez-faire and Communism*. New York, New Republic, 1926.

Lilienthal, David E. *TVA: Democracy on the March*. New York, Harper, 1953.

Lippmann, Walter. *An Inquiry into the Principles of the Good Society*. Boston, Little, Brown, 1937.

Merriam, Charles E. *On the Agenda of Democracy*. Cambridge, Mass., Harvard University Press, 1941.

————. *Public and Private Government*. New York, Oxford University Press, 1944.

Pigou, A. C. *The Economics of Welfare*. London, Macmillan, 1932.

————. *Keynes' General Theory; a Retrospective View*. London, Macmillan, 1951.

————. *Socialism versus Capitalism*. New York, Macmillan, 1937.

Polanyi, Karl. *The Great Transformation*. New York, Rinehart, 1944.

Schumpeter, Joseph A. *Capitalism, Socialism and Democracy*. New York, Harper, 1950.

Slichter, Sumner H. *The American Economy*. New York, Knopf, 1948.

Soule, George. *A Planned Society*. New York, Macmillan, 1932.

Thomas, Norman. *Democratic Socialism: A New Appraisal.* New York, League for Industrial Democracy, 1953.

———. *Socialism on the Defensive.* New York, Harper, 1938.

———. *A Socialist's Faith.* New York, Norton, 1951.

———. *The Test of Freedom.* New York, Norton, 1954.

Titmuss, Richard M. *Essays on "The Welfare State."* London, Allen and Unwin, 1959.

Wootton, Barbara. *Freedom under Planning.* Chapel Hill, University of North Carolina Press, 1945.

———. *Plan or No Plan?* New York, Farrar and Rinehart, 1935.

CHAPTER
VII

The Totalitarian Reaction

Nearly everyone would agree that totalitarianism in the contemporary world has embodied itself in three principal forms: Italian Fascism, German Nazism, and Soviet Communism. The essential character of each of these forms has been reaction, culminating, of course, in brutal tyranny. Italian Fascism was a reaction against the nineteenth-century liberal regime which was condemned for its failure to gain for Italy her rightful place as a world power and successor to the greatness of ancient Rome. German Nazism was a revolt against the supposed injustices of the Treaty of Versailles, and the "weak democracy" of the Weimar Republic that had failed to bring Germany out of a severe depression. It was also a protest against the alleged treachery and disloyalty of socialists and Jews who were accused of having stabbed their nation in the back while it was fighting for its very existence. Soviet Communism began its history as a reaction against the sufferings and injustices inflicted upon the peasants and workers during World War I, and also against the efforts of the bourgeois and Kerensky regimes to force Russia to renew the struggle against the Germans.

But all of these forms of totalitarianism were a great deal more than expressions of dissatisfaction with conditions of the moment. It is almost unanimously assumed that they grew out of factors deeply embedded in the cultural, social, and economic history of the twentieth century. But what these factors were in all cases is by no means universally agreed. Experts psycho-

215

logically inclined consider totalitarianism the result of profound disturbances in the mentality of modern man. They contend that modern civilization, by virtue of its complexity and artificiality, has afflicted large numbers of people with feelings of resentment, frustration, and insecurity. The victims of these feelings attempt to get rid of them by projecting them upon others. This they seek to accomplish by aggression, domination, and the infliction of cruelty. Too cowardly to commit depredations individually, they join mobs or private armies and bully or persecute helpless minorities. Sociologists, in assessing the causes of totalitarianism, may stress what they call the *anomie* of modern life. By this concept they mean the absence of social pressures and beliefs which impel the individual to discipline himself. Freed from such restraints, he becomes the worst of all tyrants, a veritable beast who knows no law and responds to no conscience.[1]

Some economists think of totalitarianism as a product of the cataclysmic changes wrought by the rapid extension of the Industrial Revolution. These changes include the growth of monopoly, the drive for autarchy as a means of protecting national industry, the threat of chronic unemployment, the increasing severity of depressions, the reduction of the worker to insignificance as a mere bolt-tightener on an assembly line, the growth of chain enterprises threatening the existence of the independent shopkeeper, the collapse of the free market and of free international exchange. These menacing developments imbued the masses with a feeling of despair and resulted in a clamor for a strong state ruled by a class of "managers" and concerned primarily with success and efficiency rather than with the sanctity of law or with the protection of private rights.

Other observers, of a more historical bent, have emphasized purely political factors. They point to a trend over a considerable period toward the Leviathan state and toward the erosion of liberty by demands for power and security. They have seen na-

---

[1] See Harry Alpert, *Émile Durkheim and His Sociology*. New York, Columbia University Press, 1939, p. 206. See also Sebastian deGrazia, *The Political Community: a Study of Anomie*. Chicago, University of Chicago Press, 1948, pp. 3–42, 134–83.

tionalism as a liberating movement evolve into conformism and state-worship and bear fruit in chauvinism and in a quest for empire. They have found in war, militarism, and the fear of new wars sturdy support for the totalitarian forces. To these observers the emergence of totalitarianism was chiefly the culmination of a long effort to check the progress of liberal democracy. To use the words of Henry A. Wallace, it was largely a counterrevolt against the "People's Revolution" which had begun with the establishment of parliamentary supremacy in England in 1688, had been strengthened by the American and French revolutions of the eighteenth century, and had continued through the various triumphs of liberal and democratic rule down to our own era. Totalitarianism is undoubtedly all of these things, and perhaps a great many others besides. In some of its forms it may prove in the future to have elements of a progressive character. Thus far, however, the evidence of its retrograde nature seems almost overwhelming.

1. *Italian Fascism*

The original forerunners of Italian Fascist political theory were a group of intellectuals who had adopted with some weird modifications the philosophy of Hegel. Taking as their fundamental proposition the Hegelian idea that the state is the supreme manifestation of God on earth, they demanded that Italians should submerge their individual and class interests in a united endeavor to revive the greatness of their nation. Italy, they avowed, had a glorious mission to give light to the civilized world as she had done under the Roman Empire and in the age of the great Renaissance. Their slogan was "Nothing for the individual, all for Italy." An even more frenzied and irrational gospel was propagated by the Futurists. Futurism originated as a literary and artistic movement, but it soon took on political significance. Its vociferous apostles condemned every form of enslavement to the past. They denounced liberalism, democracy, pacifism, quietism, tourism, "the erotic obsession," and all other attitudes and ideals which they alleged were the special favorites of Italy's elder statesmen. In addition, they glorified war as "the world's only hygiene,"

the necessary instrument for rejuvenating the nation and for giving "a thousand flavors to life and a little genius to imbeciles." [2]

First among the prominent philosophers of Italian Fascism was
Giovanni Gentile (1875–1944). He was born in Sicily and was
educated at the University of Pisa. He was appointed Professor
of Philosophy at Pisa and eventually Professor of the Philosophy
of History at the University of Rome. In 1923 he was commis-
sioned by Mussolini to revise the educational program for the
Fascist state and a short time later was appointed Director of
the Institute of Fascist Culture. Gentile was a disciple of Hegel
who carried his master's idealism almost to the point of mysticism. His objective was to unify "the infinite variety of man
and nature in an absolute one, in which the human is divine
and the divine is human." [3] He rejected the scientific, positivist
trend of modern culture and criticized even the philosophy of
Plato as insufficiently spiritual. As for his own philosophy, he
proudly described it as anti-intellectual. Though he said little
about specific problems of government, he helped to prepare the
minds of millions of his compatriots for attitudes of unquestion-
ing submission and contempt for reason. He denied that there
was ever any basis for antagonism between the individual and
the state, and he taught that "the maximum of liberty coincides
with the maximum force of the state." [4] He praised the use of
violence, even the blackjack violence of the Fascists, when employed in the interest of the state. It is "willed by God, and by
all men who believe in God, in order, and in the law which God
certainly wills for the world." [5]

A second writer who contributed to the development of Fascist
philosophy was Giuseppe Prezzolini. Born in Perugia in 1882, he
belonged to a family of cultural and literary interests. He had apparently no zest for formal education, however, and obtained no
degrees. Though he read widely and accumulated a wealth of

[2] Quoted by H. W. Schneider, *Making the Fascist State*. New York, Oxford University Press, 1928, p. 8.
[3] *The Theory of Mind as Pure Act*, trans. H. W. Carr. London, Macmillan,
1922, p. 265.
[4] "Gentile's Version of Fascism," in Schneider, *Making the Fascist State*,
p. 347.
[5] *Ibid.*, p. 348.

knowledge, he found no purpose in life till he met Giovanni Papini, the great idealist and romantic poet, in 1903. From 1903 to 1907 he collaborated with Papini in editing *Leonardo*, a journal of literary criticism which they established in Florence. From 1908 to 1916 he was editor of *La Voce* (The Voice) and devoted his energies to stimulating Italian nationalism and, after the outbreak of World War I, to promoting Italian intervention on the side of the Allies. After the war he renounced active participation in politics. Invited by a publisher to write a biography of Mussolini, he laid down the condition that he also write a biography of Mussolini's chief opponent, Giovanni Amendola. Both books appeared in 1923. Two years later Prezzolini wrote a sympathetic account of Italian Fascism, which included a laudatory chapter on Mussolini.

Prezzolini's influence on Fascist theory followed a pattern quite similar to that of Gentile. Both men were Hegelian idealists, exalting the state above the individual, despising parliamentary institutions, and condemning the liberal-democratic tradition of the nineteenth century as a menace to the strength of the nation. Prezzolini acclaimed Fascism as "the true religion" of Italy, and the embodiment of "the most exalted conception of the patriotic spirit." [6] He regarded the March on Rome of 1922 as both inevitable and desirable. The old leaders were incompetent, corrupt, and degenerate. Moreover, in adopting liberal and democratic institutions, they were forcing the nation to sail under false colors. Italy had always been "anti-reform"— "reactionary rather than revolutionary, catholic rather than freethinking." The Italian carried "a dagger in his pocket, not a gun slung over his shoulder." Italy could never be "an industrial capitalist country with an Anglo-Saxon constitution." [7] Alien radical importations, such as socialism, trade-unionism, and Bolshevism, according to Prezzolini, were deeply resented by the Italian people. They set one class against another, incited lawlessness, and caused severe losses from riots and strikes. The cowardice and passivity of the parliamentary government in the face of these evils made a thorough house-cleaning by direct action im-

[6] *Fascism*, trans. Kathleen Macmillan. London, Methuen, 1926, pp. 34, 35.
[7] *Ibid.*, p. 90.

perative. It should be added, though, that, unlike Gentile, Prezzolini did not justify all of the castor-oil and strong-arm techniques of the Black-shirt squadrons. He granted that excesses had been committed. It was inevitable that they should be, for the movement had so broad an appeal that it attracted all types —misfits and potential criminals as well as youthful idealists and devoted patriots.

Benito Mussolini earned his niche in history as the founder and demagogic mouthpiece of the Italian *Fascisti* movement. It would be an error, however, to overlook his contribution to the political theory of Fascism. Though he did not have an originating or analytical mind, he was perceptive enough to recognize important trends in Italian thinking, and he had a flair for giving them eloquent expression. His own nature and background fitted him admirably for the role he was to play in Italian politics. He was a misfit and a rebel, embittered by poverty and by his inability to achieve for himself a satisfactory place in life. He was born in 1883, the son of a socialist blacksmith. His mother was a schoolteacher, and in deference to her wishes he entered the same profession. But he was restless and dissatisfied and soon left Italy for Switzerland. Here he gave part of his time to study and the rest of it to begging his bread and writing articles for socialist newspapers. He was finally expelled from the country for fomenting strikes in factories. Upon returning to Italy he took up journalism as a definite career and eventually became editor of *Avanti,* the leading socialist daily. When World War I broke out in August, 1914, Mussolini insisted that Italy should remain neutral. But he had scarcely adopted this position when he began urging participation on the Entente side. As early as October, 1914, he had gone over bag and baggage to the interventionist camp. Deprived of his position as editor of *Avanti,* he founded the paper *Il Popolo d'Italia,* and dedicated its columns to whipping up enthusiasm for the war. The decision of the government the following spring to go in on the side of the Entente Allies he regarded as a personal victory. He entered the army as a private in September, 1915, and eventually rose to be a corporal. In February, 1917, he was wounded by the explosion of a trench mortar and returned to his position as editor of *Il Popolo* to stimulate the flagging enthusiasm of the Italian people. From then on he worked zealously for a Fascist revolution. In October, 1922, he led his successful March on Rome. He ruled Italy as dictator until his deposition in 1943. In 1945 he was lynched, together with his mistress, by partisans shortly before the Allied victory in Italy.

Mussolini's ideas in his early life were a mixture of contradictory forms of extremist doctrines. He professed to be a Marxian socialist, but he mingled his socialism with doctrines taken from Georges Sorel, the French syndicalist. In fact, Sorel once referred to him as his most promising disciple. It seems obvious that Mussolini, during this period, was not a radical by sincere and reasoned conviction; for no man with a definite philosophy could have reversed himself so often. He not only condemned the imperialism which later he practiced so zealously, but at one time or another before 1914 he defamed the church, vilified the king, and called the Italian flag "a rag to be planted on a dung hill." [8] As he moved closer to leadership of a successful movement, however, he became increasingly conservative. Whereas the platform of the Fascist party in 1919 called for universal suffrage, abolition of the Senate, a capital levy, and a heavy tax on inheritances, the platform of 1921 omitted all reference to reform and consisted of nothing but some vague assertions about "revindicating" the principles for which the war had been fought and wholesale condemnation of "politicians'" socialism.

Mussolini's ideas after he became dictator bore witness to the reactionary character of the Fascist movement. He threw socialism overboard entirely and substituted a pattern of economic organization derived from syndicalism. This structure he called the corporate state. It was designed to eliminate all conflict between capital and labor by bringing representatives of both into syndicates and corporations under the control of the state. He openly repudiated democracy, denying that the "majority, by the simple fact that it is a majority can direct human society," and affirming "the immutable, beneficial, and fruitful inequality of

[8] For these and other contradictions between his earlier and later teachings, see Gaudens Megaro, *Mussolini in the Making*. Boston, Houghton Mifflin, 1938.

mankind." [9] He repudiated liberalism also, describing it as a passing fad of the nineteenth century. It was not born, he alleged, until 1830, and it began to decay about twenty years later with the failure of the revolutions of 1848. Consistent with his repudiation of these doctrines was his glorification of the state. He made it an absolute, in comparison with which individuals and groups were merely relative. He deified it as the embodiment of the immanent spirit of the nation, the educator of the people in wisdom and virtue, and the civilizer of mankind. Finally, he repudiated pacifism, denying both the possibility and the desirability of perpetual peace. War alone exalts and ennobles human beings. "All other trials are substitutes, which never really put men into the position where they have to make the great decision—the alternative of life or death." [10] Moreover, it is the instrumentality by which the nation grows and expands into an empire. Imperialism is an essential manifestation of vitality, and the renunciation thereof is a sign of weakness and death. For the individual, life is duty, struggle, and conquest; such conditions, he contended, are even more emphatically true for the state.

2. German Nazism

Unlike Italian Fascism, German Nazism had no direct philosophical antecedents. Whereas Mussolini was an avid reader of Machiavelli and Sorel, Hitler seems to have read little or nothing except the rantings of anti-Semites and other racists. Italian Fascism had a direct connection with Hegelian idealism, which glorified the state as the indispensable instrument of human progress. Despite the German origin of the Hegelian philosophy, its influence upon Nazism was almost negligible. Hitler had a low opinion of the state, regarding it as a mere apparatus or mechanism. Instead, he glorified the nation, or the *Volk*. As for the possibility of other philosophical antecedents, proof is difficult to obtain. Efforts have been made to discover the foundations

[9] *The Political and Social Doctrine of Fascism,* trans. Jane Soames. London, Hogarth, 1933, p. 14.
[10] *Ibid.,* p. 11.

of Nazi ideology in the philosophy of Friedrich Nietzsche. Nietzsche was undoubtedly a nihilist and a rebel against Christian morality. But he was neither a nationalist, a militarist, nor an anti-Semite. He despised the Prussians, looked down upon the clanking generals, and praised the Jews as "the toughest and strongest race in Europe." [11] He would probably have regarded with horror the primitivism and anti-intellectualism of the Nazis. Only to the extent that he was a Social Darwinist glorifying the survival of the fittest in a ruthless struggle for existence did he make any significant contribution to the brutal ideology of the Nazis.

It seems obvious that the triumph of Nazism was not the result primarily of philosophical influence. Instead, it grew out of the humiliation and despair of the German people and their feeling that almost any change would be a change for the better. As the most highly industrialized country of Europe, Germany suffered severely during the depression. Unemployment rose to a peak of 6,000,000 in 1932, wholesale prices collapsed, and trade and production slowed almost to a halt. Members of all classes groped in bewilderment and terror. Never in the history of the nation had the future appeared so dark. Although the majority were not yet Nazis, their despair was so great as to induce them to accept almost any messiah who promised to deliver them from confusion and fear. Even earlier, large numbers of the middle class had been reduced to poverty by runaway inflation. The hardships of these victims, the plight of debt-ridden farmers, the hopelessness of the unemployed seemed, in the minds of many, to be the work of mysterious demons. Gradually these demons were identified as members of two groups. The first comprised Germany's enemies among the Allies, who had inflicted upon her the cruel punishment of Versailles and were still keeping her in an iron grip to prevent her recovery. The second embraced the Jews, who were alleged to have stabbed the nation in the back in 1918, to have indulged in speculative orgies at the expense of substantial citizens during the inflation of 1923, and to have been responsible for the weaknesses and failures of the Weimar Republic. Since the Jews were already unpopular,

[11] *Beyond Good and Evil.* New York, Macmillan, 1907, p. 185.

and since they were conspicuous leaders in business and politics during the Weimar regime, it was easy to make them scapegoats for all the miseries of the German nation.

The most original ideologist of German Nazism was probably Carl Schmitt. Born in 1888, he was educated at Berlin, Munich, and Strasbourg universities. He served successively as a professor of law at Greifswald, Bonn, Cologne, and Berlin. From 1933 to 1945 he was a Prussian State Councillor. Though he made important contributions to what the Germans considered the science of politics, he was deficient in adherence to principle. His uncritical attitude toward power led him to support almost any movement that gave promise of gaining the ascendancy. In the turbulent years between the two wars he shifted political allegiances more frequently even than did Mussolini. In 1919 he was virtually a Communist. From this he changed consecutively into a Social Democrat, a Democrat, a Catholic Centrist, a Nationalist, and, finally, a full-fledged Nazi. In 1927 he published an article entitled "The Concept of 'The Political.'" Expanded later into a book, this work became a cardinal addition to the Nazi gospel. It was read and quoted widely by Hitler's minions.

Schmitt's political theory as revealed in this work was founded upon the dogma that the only important political distinction is the distinction between *friend* and *enemy*. Nations, in particular, fall into one or the other of these categories. The distinction has nothing to do with good and evil, beautiful and ugly, useful and harmful. In like manner, it bears no relation to economic rivalry. Engaging in trade with an enemy may even be advantageous. What, then, is the character of an *enemy* nation? According to Schmitt, an enemy nation in the political sense is simply one that is strange or different, in some intense or provocative way. Its strangeness "constitutes the negation of one's own kind of existence, and must therefore be repulsed or fought, in order to preserve one's own way of life." [12] The conclusion follows that struggle must be recognized as the law of life among nations. And struggle does not mean intellectual or economic competition. On the contrary, its essence is war, the physical

[12] "The Concept of 'The Political,'" *Archiv für Sozialwissenschaft und Sozialpolitik*, Vol. XXVIII (Sept., 1927). Translated by William Ebenstein.

killing of human beings. War is simply the logical extreme of enmity, and is bound to occur whenever any nation reaches the conclusion that the strangeness of a neighboring nation is no longer tolerable. The idea of world unity or international peace was to Schmitt preposterous. The world of nations, he taught, is a *pluriverse*, not a *universe*. The very nature of political organization, he declared, makes universality impossible. A world state would be a contradiction in terms.

Better known than Schmitt as a Nazi philosopher, though less discerning and creative, was Alfred Rosenberg. A native of Reval (now Tallinn), Russia, he was born in 1893, a descendant of German forebears. He was graduated from Moscow University as an architect and an engineer, though he seems to have made his living principally as a journalist. After the Bolshevik Revolution he fled to Munich and eventually offered his services to the German Workers' Party as a fighter against the Jews. Introduced to Hitler, he poured into the Fuehrer's ear glowing descriptions of a triumphant Germany where blond Nordics would honor the ways of their tribal ancestors. Hitler was entranced and gave him a preferred place in the party hierarchy. When the future dictator was imprisoned in Landsberg Fortress after the failure of the Beer-hall *Putsch* of 1923, Rosenberg visited him every day. Rosenberg soon became editor of the *Voelkischer Beobachter*, the Nazi party organ, and in 1930 was elected to the Reichstag. Hitler was said to be his only friend in all Germany; but doubtless that friend was sufficient so long as his power lasted. In 1946 Rosenberg was brought to trial before the International Military Tribunal in Nuremberg. He was convicted of responsibility "for plunder throughout invaded countries" and was hanged.

Rosenberg's philosophical education began at the age of fifteen when he read Houston Stewart Chamberlain's *Foundations of the Nineteenth Century*. He was fascinated by it and used some of it later as the basis for a work of his own, which he entitled *The Myth of the Twentieth Century*—a strange amalgam of ideas taken from Chamberlain, Gobineau, Spengler, Nietzsche, Bernhardi, and Treitschke. The core of it was Nordicism. According to Rosenberg, Nordic superiority accounted for all the great cultures of the past, including those of Greece and Rome. All decay and corruption resulted from the infusion into the superior race of blood from inferior strains. So important did Rosenberg consider this idea that he urged the German people to adopt Nordicism as a religion in place of Christianity. His fanatical Nordicist notions led to violent anti-Semitic creeds. The Jews he regarded as the incarnation of cultural decadence. Moreover, he saw them as the chief conspirators against the Nordic purity of the Germans.

From the beginning of his career as a Nazi, Rosenberg seems to have identified himself with the Rightist faction of the Party. He opposed the socialist emphasis given to the Party program by the Strasser brothers (Gregory and Otto). He considered Great Britain a natural ally of Germany, and argued that the two countries were destined to share the world, since the Nordic blood of their peoples assured their superiority. Finally, he was one of the most bitter of anti-Bolsheviks. He regarded the Soviet regime as a decrepit, barbarian system and urged that Germany should work out an accommodation with the West and direct her expansion eastward. The fertile fields of Russia would provide a much richer prize of conquest than any of the crowded areas of western Europe. Besides, Asiatic barbarians had no right to rule over a territory so badly needed by the civilized Germans. Hitler's eventual decision to launch an invasion of Russia probably represented the triumph of Rosenberg's ideas over those of Haushofer and other German generals who feared that an attack upon Russia might result in a repetition of the Napoleonic fiasco of 1812.[13]

To suggest that the most active leader of the Nazi movement

---

[13] Some authorities regard Gottfried Feder as an important source of Nazi ideas. But there is danger of exaggerating his influence. Feder was a civil engineer who was one of the original members of the little band (the German Workers' Party) that became the nucleus of the Nazi movement. His specialty was attacks on "unproductive" capitalism, which he identified with Jewish financial activity. Hitler heard him lecture several times and was deeply impressed. About 1920 Feder drafted a party platform or Program of Twenty-five Points, which demanded the nationalization of trusts, the breaking up of department stores into small shops, and the confiscation of all incomes received "without work or trouble." Although this platform was adopted by the Nazis as an "unalterable program," no attempt was ever made to give effect to its "anti-capitalist" provisions.

was a political philosopher would be to invite derision. Yet the
emotionally charged garrulities of Adolf Hitler did provide a
verbal framework for the feelings and aims of his followers. Hitler was born in 1889, the son of a petty customs official in the
Austrian civil service. His early life was unhappy and maladjusted. Rebellious and undisciplined from childhood, he seems
always to have been burdened with resentment and frustration.
He wasted his time at school and finally decided that he would
become an artist. But he failed the examinations for entrance into
the Vienna Academy, and for the next four years was compelled to
eke out a dismal existence as a casual laborer and by painting little sketches and watercolors which he sometimes managed to sell
to the humbler art shops. When World War I broke out, Hitler
was living in Munich, and, though still an Austrian citizen, he
enlisted in the Bavarian army. He served through the four years
of fighting with enough distinction to be awarded an Iron Cross
and a promotion to corporal. After the war he became leader of
the National Socialist German Workers' Party, which he helped
to organize. In 1923 he was sentenced to five years' imprisonment for participating in a *Putsch* to overthrow the government,
but was released after less than a year. He gradually attracted
a following of half-educated ruffians, augmented later by hordes
of Germany's unemployed. In January, 1933, President von
Hindenburg appointed him Chancellor of the German Reich,
upon the advice of a group of reactionaries—industrialists, bankers, and Junkers. Two months later he abolished the Weimar
Republic and proclaimed the establishment of the Third Reich,
with himself as dictator. His career in this capacity is still sufficiently familiar to require no recounting here. It was brought to
a timely end in May, 1945, when the Fuehrer of a Reich that
according to his propaganda was to last for a thousand years
committed suicide rather than allow himself to be captured by
the Russians, who had broken through the defenses of Berlin.

Nearly all of Hitler's theoretical outpourings are contained in
Mein Kampf, the bulk of which he wrote while in prison. His
doctrines were legion and many of them too trivial to be considered here. The following would seem to merit attention as
among the more significant:

(1) Nationalism. Hitler was a nationalist in the sense that he opposed internationalism and deified the nation rather than the state. He regarded the nation as a "folk" community, ethnically homogeneous, a kind of tribal brotherhood in which all the members cooperated for the achievement of a common destiny. The state he considered as primarily an instrument for the preservation of racial integrity and for instilling into the people a consciousness of their destiny. It was also an implement for promoting the victory of the superior races and for demanding the submission of the inferior.

(2) The *Fuehrerprinzip* (leadership principle). Since the state has the mission of giving the world to the best people, it must be organized on the principle of rule by natural leaders, not on the democratic principle of majority rule based on the dogma of inborn equality. The "folkish" state has no representative bodies deciding questions by majority vote. Instead it has advisory councils standing at the side of the leader or subleader, but authority always descends from above. "For humanity blessing has never lain in the masses, but in its creative heads." [14]

(3) Racism. Hitler copied his racial ideas from Austrian anti-Semites and especially from Rosenberg, but he substituted the name Aryan for Nordic. He seemed to think of the Germans, the Dutch, the Scandinavians, and the British as the only true Aryans. He classified the peoples of the earth into culture-creators, culture-bearers, and culture-destroyers. The first included the Aryans, the second such peoples as the Japanese who imitated the achievements of the Aryans, and the third the Negroid and Semitic peoples. Like Rosenberg, Hitler believed that the foundation of cultural progress was purity of race. "All the great cultures of the past," he insisted, "perished only because the original creative race died off through blood-poisoning." [15] His passionate conviction of the greatness of the Aryan peoples was bolstered by a seemingly literal belief in the Teutonic legends.

(4) Anti-Semitism. Hitler despised the Jews as the most deadly

[14] *Mein Kampf.* New York, Reynal and Hitchcock, 1940, p. 665.
[15] *Ibid.,* p. 396.

enemies of Aryan supremacy and the fulfillment of the mission of the German *Volk*. He accepted with childish credulity the infamous forgery of the Protocols of the Wise Men of Zion, which purported to be an account of a meeting of Jewish leaders in a cemetery in Prague in 1897, in which a plot was hatched to undermine society, overthrow governments, and destroy Christianity. While on the one hand he condemned the Jews as international bankers, on the other he accused them of being Bolsheviks and Socialists. In some fashion he imagined that the Russian Revolution was a scheme to harness the resources and population of Russia in a gigantic plot to conquer the world for Jewish finance. The Jew possessed no culture-creating energy whatever and could do nothing but debase and destroy.

(5) *Lebensraum*. The most important asset of any nation is living space. This must be abundant, not merely to ensure an ample food supply but to balance the urban population with a just proportion of healthy peasants. Hitler believed that a solid peasant stock of small and medium landholders was the best protection against social disturbance. He admired the peasants not only for their conservatism but also because they were the most prolific of the nation's citizens. But *Lebensraum* was necessary also for reasons of security. Hitler taught that nations crowded into small territories have always gone down to military defeat more quickly than nations occupying territories capable of defense in depth. Many peoples with such advantages do not deserve them. According to Hitler, Nature intended that the best lands of the earth should belong to those peoples with the energy to take them and the intelligence to cultivate them efficiently.

(6) Expansionism. Hitler was an expansionist but not an imperialist in the ordinary meaning of that term. He scoffed at the acquisition of colonial territories and overseas empires. He compared many European states to pyramids standing on their points, that is, their European territories were ridiculously small compared to their overseas possessions. For Germany he advocated expansion almost exclusively in Europe, the "winning of land for settlement which increases the area of the motherland itself." [16] In pursuance of this dream he thought primarily of Russia; and,

[16] *Ibid.*, p. 950.

like Rosenberg, advocated an alliance with Britain as a means of locking the back door before launching an invasion eastward. To gain Britain's favor, he argued, no sacrifice would be too great, including the renunciation of colonies and sea power and the withholding of competition with her industry.

As expressed in the doctrines of Hitler and his Nazi supporters, German fascism resembled quite closely the Italian variety. Both movements were collectivistic, authoritarian, nationalistic, militaristic, élitist, and anti-intellectual. Yet there were a number of differences. Italian Fascism never had a racial basis. True, after the formation of the Rome-Berlin Axis in 1936, Mussolini issued some anti-Jewish decrees; but most of them appear not to have been enforced very strictly. By contrast, German fascism made the factor of race a central pillar of its theory. As a second difference, Nazism had a peculiar peasant flavor which Italian Fascism did not possess. The key to an important section of Nazi theory was contained in the phrase *Blut und Boden* (blood and soil). The word *soil* typified not only a deep reverence for the beautiful homeland, but an abiding affection for the peasants, who were considered to embody the finest qualities of the German race. A final difference consisted in the fact that, under German fascism, there was no elaborate theory of the corporate state. To be sure, Hitler abolished the right to strike and subjected all economic activities to control by the state; but he had no plan for direct representation of economic interests in the government. As a consequence, members of the Reichstag continued to be chosen from geographic districts, and the state retained its exclusively political character.

3. Soviet Communism

As was noted in a previous chapter, Vladimir Lenin made numerous modifications of the original gospel of Marx. In the main, these were concerned with a stronger emphasis on the revolutionary nature of the movement and its adaptation to the special conditions of Russia. At the same time, Lenin preserved much of the original idealism of Marx. He seemed firmly to believe in the advent of the classless society and in the withering-away of the state in the not too distant future. He organized the proletarian state in accordance with a pattern of socialist democracy —with short terms for public officials, subjection of officeholders to recall, and limitation of salaries for even the highest officials to the equivalent of $1500 a year. In addition, he substituted a people's militia for the professional army, instituted penal reform, legalized abortion, and provided for almost unlimited freedom of marriage and divorce. His successors have almost completely nullified these policies. They have strengthened the element of personal dictatorship until Soviet rule is quite as autocratic as the regime of the Tsars. Short terms and the recall of public officials have been reduced to meaningless relics. Limitations on incomes have been abolished, not only for officeholders but for all kinds of privileged minions, with the result that disparity of payments is apparently as great under Soviet Communism as it is under capitalism. A professional army, commanded by marshals and colonel-generals, has been raised to a high place in the system, while the erstwhile freedom in family relations has been abolished in the interest of numerous offspring to enhance the military and political power of the state.

The two Russian theorists who remained closest to Lenin in their basic views of Soviet policy were Nikolai Bukharin and Leon Trotsky. Bukharin was born in 1888. A Bolshevik of long and orthodox standing, he rose rapidly among the leaders of the movement. For years he was president of the Comintern and editor of *Pravda*, the Party organ. Eventually, however, he ran afoul of Stalin. He opposed the ruthlessness of the latter's crusade against the kulaks and his relentless campaign of forced industrialization. Stalin denounced him for "Right deviationism" and in 1938 had him condemned to death as an enemy of the state. In many of his views Bukharin was indeed a moderate. He agreed with Lenin on the necessity, at times, of a policy of caution and even of retreat in order to prepare for greater advances in the future or to consolidate gains already achieved. In particular, he emphasized the value of economic concessions as a means of averting the surrender of political power. Throughout his writings he centered attention on the political and social and minimized the economic. The major defect in capitalism, he argued, is not inequality in the distribution of goods but inequality in power and privilege. The modern state, regardless of its form, is simply an agency for preserving the power and privileges of the capitalist class. Its laws reflect their desires, and its punishments wreak vengeance upon any who would challenge the established order. Modern justice is therefore capitalist justice, and modern culture, religion, and education are the propaganda weapons whereby the owners of wealth hoodwink the masses into believing in the righteousness of the system.

Bukharin stressed the importance of class quite as much as did Marx. But he denied that poverty of income and possessions is the distinguishing feature of the proletariat. Beggars and vagrants, he pointed out, are also impoverished, but they do not constitute true proletarians. The proletarian class, like any other class capable of taking advantage of a revolutionary situation, is characterized by a hatred of its oppressors and their system, a psychology of comradeship, habits of organized action, and constructive intentions with respect to the establishment of a new order. The class struggle itself is the matrix within which develops every alteration in the social system; and "every class struggle is a political struggle," since the dominant social and economic class is always the possessor of political power and must be divested of that power as the first step toward the creation of a new society.[17] Yet Bukharin was unwilling to gamble on the proletarian class alone as the instrument of revolution and the founder of Utopia. He was as much of an élitist as Lenin and insisted that an enlightened vanguard was necessary to "express the interests" of the class. But even this was not all. For just as the class might be torn by internal dissension and therefore unable to express its interests, so might the vanguard be rendered impotent by disagreements among its members. The solution would be found in individual leaders to "express the proper tendencies of the party."[18] Under the new dawn of socialism, consequently, the class would rule through the party, and the party through its leaders. Lenin had done everything in his power

[17] *Historical Materialism,* authorized translation from the Third Russian edition. New York, International Publishers, 1925, p. 298.
[18] *Ibid.,* p. 306.

to discourage this leader-worship. The fact of its endorsement by Bukharin did much to prepare the way for an exaggerated "cult of personality" during the regime of Stalin.

Better known, though less influential, than Bukharin was the brilliant but erratic Leon Trotsky. Originally named Lev Bronstein, he was born in 1879 of middle-class Jewish parents in Odessa. He seems to have been the stormy petrel of revolutionary politics during most of his life. Before the revolution he refused to identify himself with any particular faction, preferring to remain an independent Marxist. Though he collaborated with Lenin in editing *Iskra* (The Spark), he did not become a Bolshevik until 1917. For his part in the revolutionary movement of 1905 he was exiled to Siberia; but he escaped, and then for some years led a roving existence in various European capitals. He was expelled from Paris in 1916 for pacifist activity and took refuge in the United States. Upon learning of the overthrow of the Tsar, he attempted to return to Russia. Captured by British agents at Halifax, he was eventually released on the plea of Kerensky. He arrived in Russia in April and immediately began plotting for the overthrow of the provisional government and later of Kerensky himself. His part in the Bolshevik triumph consisted in organizing and disciplining the Red Guard and in ousting the Mensheviks and Social Revolutionaries from control of the Petrograd Soviet. He became Minister of Foreign Affairs in the government headed by Lenin and subsequently Commissar for War. For a variety of reasons Trotsky did not become Lenin's successor. He was too fiery in temperament, and some of the comrades distrusted him because he was not an Old Bolshevik. Besides, Stalin had maneuvered himself into control of the party machine. In 1927 Trotsky was banished to a remote area of the Soviet Union, and two years later he was deported from the country. In 1940 he was assassinated, allegedly by Stalinist agents, in Mexico City.

The most notable contribution of Trotsky to Communist political theory was the doctrine of permanent revolution. By this concept he meant a continuing revolution, on a national and international scale, until the entire world has been brought under the sway of socialism. A national revolution, complete and sufficient unto itself, he maintained, is unthinkable. It is merely a link in an international chain. The October revolution in Russia must therefore be considered as simply "the first stage in the world revolution, which inevitably extends over several decades." [19] The permanent revolution makes no concessions to any form of class rule; it does not stop with democracy but makes continuous progress toward socialism and wars implacably against reaction; it is a revolution "whose every next stage is anchored in the preceding one and which can only end in the complete liquidation of all class society." [20] The explanation for this, according to Trotsky, is twofold. To begin with, the world economy is not a collection of independent segments but is a single unit. It has been made thus by the international division of labor and the world market. With the growth of industrialization, the productive forces of modern society long since overleaped national frontiers. Since there is no such thing as national capitalism, socialism flourishing in a single nation is inconceivable. As a second reason, a socialist revolution is bound to have earth-shaking effects. It will arouse longings, kindle ambitions among the oppressed, and stir their governors to angry repression. It will set class against class and nation against nation around the globe, and civil conflicts and foreign wars will follow each other in bloody succession. If the leaders of the revolution in its first stage remain steadfast in their refusal to compromise with reaction, the remaining stages will follow inevitably until the whole world is rescued from tyranny.

Trotsky agreed with most of the formulations of Lenin. He seemed, however, to be more antagonistic toward the peasants. He insisted that industrialization is the only conceivable basis of socialism. In common with Lenin, he believed that a vanguard of the proletariat should be entrusted with leadership of the revolution, but he seemed determined to give to this vanguard sole responsibility for the movement, with the peasants merely providing the cannon fodder. He accused Lenin of "overestimating the independent role of the peasantry." Lenin, in turn, ac-

---

[19] *The Permanent Revolution.* New York, Pioneer Publishers, 1931, Preface, xx.
[20] *Ibid.,* Introduction, xxxii.

cused him of "underestimating the revolutionary role of the peasantry." [21] Apparently, Trotsky did not accept in its entirety Lenin's thesis that Russia could leap directly from a semi-feudal economy to the initial stage of socialism. Though he admitted that socialism might come to an undeveloped country sooner than to one in an advanced stage of industrialization, he denied, between 1905 and 1917, that Russia was ripe for a socialist revolution. He would not even recognize any definite correlation between a stage of economic development and the outbreak of revolution. "The day and hour when power passes into the hands of the proletariat," he said, "do not depend directly upon the state of the productive forces, but upon the conditions of the class struggle, upon the international situation, and, finally, upon a series of objective factors: tradition, initiative, readiness for struggle . . ." [22] It would seem justifiable to conclude that such a conception of the coming of revolution was neither good Leninism nor good Marxism. It made the triumph of the proletariat almost a fortuitous occurrence, instead of an orderly culmination of the dialectical process.

Finally, Trotsky emphasized somewhat more strongly than did Lenin the role of violence. Both men believed that the bridge to the socialist paradise could not be built except by the use of force. But Trotsky went out of his way to justify betrayals, the taking of hostages, bloody reprisals, and wholesale murder. All he required was that these acts be perpetrated in the interest of socialism. He not only believed that the socialist end justifies the means, but he almost glorified the means themselves. They unite the revolutionary proletarians, "fill their hearts with irreconcilable hostility to oppression, teach them contempt for official morality and its democratic echoers, imbue them with consciousness of their own historic mission, raise their courage and spirit of self-sacrifice in the struggle." [23] All human history prior to the classless society Trotsky regarded as a gigantic civil war. Each side in this struggle will stop at nothing to achieve victory. Under ordinary conditions the chief weapons of the bourgeoisie are lying,

[21] *Ibid.*, p. 55.
[22] *Ibid.*, p. 29.
[23] *Their Morals and Ours.* New York, Pioneer Publishers, no date, p. 45.

bribery, intimidation, and deceit. But in case of any real threat to bourgeois supremacy the more effective cudgels of imprisonment, executions, lynchings, and open warfare are taken up. The oppressed masses have no alternative but to retaliate with whatever measures seem necessary for self-protection and for the overthrow of tyranny. Idealistic moral preachments calling for generosity, humanity, and tolerance have no relevance to this struggle. They are simply glosses of deceit for gulling the masses into acquiescence and servility.

But Trotsky was no hardened moral cynic, denying all values and endorsing the law of the jungle. He did not divest human actions of moral significance or teach that executions, betrayals, assassination, and the murder of hostages are condonable so long as they serve the interests of one's own class. On the contrary, he would approve no form of human action which did not contribute to the liberation of humanity. To illustrate, mass murder of reactionaries for the sake of preventing a counter-revolution is thoroughly commendable; assassination of an employer as an act of personal vengeance is a despicable offense. The question which must always be asked is: Are the acts referred to really capable of enhancing the goal of emancipating humanity from capitalist oppression? If such be the case, they are above condemnation. If not, they are either useless, and therefore a waste of precious energy; or actual hindrances, and therefore crimes against the majority of mankind. The human race can be saved only through the triumph of the socialist revolution. "Only that which prepares the complete and final overthrow of imperialist bestiality is moral, and nothing else. The welfare of the revolution—that is the supreme law!" [24] Trotsky was as blind as every other fanatic who believed that he held in his hand the golden key to the salvation of mankind. In his view, any means was good which contributed to this end. He ignored completely the possibility that means may condition ends, that men habituated to terrorism and cruelty do not readily return to civilized methods, that violence breeds new violence, and that revolutionists nourished on a diet of conspiracy, betrayal, and assassination develop complexes of fear and suspicion that cause them to in-

[24] *Ibid.*, p. 63.

vent new enemies in unending succession after the original ones have been vanquished.

Trotsky's chief rival for the mantle of Lenin also made significant contributions to Soviet theory. Joseph Dzhugashvili, better known as Stalin, was born, in 1879, in the province of Georgia, the son of a peasant shoemaker. He received part of his education in a theological seminary. But he was expelled at the age of seventeen for "lack of religious vocation," and thereafter dedicated his career to revolutionary activity. He was exiled no fewer than six times to the frozen wastes of the north; five times he managed to escape, and on the sixth occasion he was released by the provisional government. In 1917 he became Secretary-General of the Communist Party, a position through which he was able to build a party machine. The battle between Stalin and Trotsky was not simply a struggle for personal power, but fundamental issues of political policy were also involved. The outcome of the duel was a complete triumph for Stalin, who continued as ruler of the Soviets from Lenin's death in 1924 until his own death in 1953. It is interesting to note that Lenin did not hold either of the two rivals in high esteem. In a "testament" written shortly before his death, he criticized Trotsky for "far-reaching self-confidence" and for being too much preoccupied with administrative detail. He dealt even more ungently with Stalin, condemning him as "too rough" and "capricious," and urged that the comrades "find a way" to remove him from his position at the head of the party.[25]

Although Stalin has been brought into disrepute by the denunciations of his successors, he will probably continue to occupy an important place in the history of the Communist movement. Ruthless though he certainly was, he established, through his famous Five Year Plans, a basis for the rapid economic growth of the Soviet Union. His very suspiciousness of foreign govern-

[25] The Testament of Lenin is contained in Leon Trotsky, *The Real Situation in Russia*, Supplement I. The authenticity of the document was implicitly admitted by Stalin in a session of the Party Central Committee in October, 1927. W. H. Chamberlin, *Soviet Russia: A Living Record and a History*, p. 93n. In an effort to discredit Stalin, Nikita Khrushchev distributed the full text of this Testament at the Twentieth Party Congress in February, 1956.

ments, to say nothing of his own associates, led him into a kind of opportunism which necessitated compromises with official theory. Had Trotsky emerged victorious in the battle for power, the Soviets would probably have dissipated their energies in promoting revolutions all over the world. Stalin saw to it that Russia developed into a mighty bulwark of national power. And he did not hesitate to make agreements even with fascists to achieve his objective.

The distinctive elements in Stalin's theory may be summed up as follows:

1. It is possible for socialism to be established and to flourish in a single country, even though the rest of the world may continue under bourgeois rule. But Stalin made clear that this did not mean the final stage of socialism. To attain such a stage, "the victory of the revolution, if not everywhere, at least in several countries," would be requisite. Furthermore, he regarded "socialism in one country" as merely the first step. "It must be looked upon," he said, "as a support, as a means for hastening the proletarian victory in every other land." [26] Both Stalin and Trotsky believed in world revolution. The difference in their views was largely a matter of strategy. Stalin maintained that an impregnable base must first be built in one country. After that the task of revolutionizing the world could go forward. Trotsky insisted upon a continuing effort. He regarded the proletarians of every country as members of a single class, who could never be satisfied with socialism in one nation while their brethren across the frontier suffered in bondage.

2. The U.S.S.R. is the fatherland of the world proletariat. Stalin maintained that his own country, as the first to establish a socialist state, was the hope of the world. The collapse of this bastion of the workers' freedom would be a catastrophe for the toilers of all nations. They should look, therefore, to the U.S.S.R. for guidance and leadership. They should accommodate their interests to its welfare and be ready to defend it against every enemy.

[26] *Leninism*, trans. Eden and Cedar Paul. New York, International Publishers, 1928, I, 109, 212.

3. The world revolution is a long-term process. It is scarcely conceivable except over a span of many decades. Moreover, it proceeds at an uneven rate. In the course of the decades that make up the epoch of world revolution, "there will occur, nay, must occur, ebbs and flows in the revolutionary tide." [27]

4. The ultimate stage of capitalism is fascism. The revolts that led to the establishment of Fascism in Italy and of Nazism in Germany were simply desperate attempts by financial and industrial tycoons to instill new vigor into a dying system. With the occurrence of another depression, new forms of fascism will appear, perhaps under different names, but bearing the same significance as efforts to prevent the destruction of a decadent capitalism.

5. The fatherland of socialism is encircled by a ring of enemies. So long as Russia is surrounded by capitalist states there will always be the danger of foreign attack. Some fascist state among their number will provide the spearhead. Confirmation of these evil designs of capitalism was furnished, according to Stalin, by the events leading up to World War II and by Hitler's invasion of Russia in 1941. The whole appeasement policy of the Western powers was simply a diabolical attempt to divert Nazi aggression eastward.

Since the death of Stalin, responsibility for shaping the course of political theory in the Soviet Union has rested primarily with Nikita Sergeyevich Khrushchev. Born in 1894, Khrushchev was the son of a mine worker who lived near Kursh, close to the Ukrainian border. He apparently received no education in his early life but worked as a shepherd and later as a locksmith in factories of the Ukraine. During World War I he fought in the Tsarist army until the collapse of 1917. After the Bolshevik revolution he joined the Communist Party and fought in the Red Army in defense of the new regime. At the end of the civil war he returned to the Ukraine to work in the mines. He managed to obtain a high-school education and became a local Party leader. Thereafter he rose rapidly through the various echelons of Party leadership. By 1935 he was First Secretary of the Moscow

[27] *Ibid.*, I, 220.

Regional Committee. In this capacity he was responsible for carrying out the industrialization program of the Second Five Year Plan, and for building the Moscow subway. In 1939 he became a member of the Politburo and of the Presidium of the U.S.S.R. When the Germans invaded Russia, Khrushchev was given the rank of lieutenant-general and charged with coordinating the guerrilla defense of the Ukraine. In 1944 he became chairman of the Council of Ministers of the Ukrainian Republic with responsibility for restoring order and rebuilding the shattered economy. A few months after Stalin's death in 1953, Khrushchev advanced to the most powerful position in the Soviet Union when he assumed the title of First Secretary of the All-Union Communist Party.

When Stalin succumbed to a stroke in March, 1953, he was succeeded as Premier within twenty-four hours by Georgi M. Malenkov, a dominant figure in the Party apparatus. Malenkov survived as Premier for less than two years. He was succeeded in February, 1955, by Nikolai A. Bulganin, with Nikita S. Khrushchev as First Secretary of the Communist Party. For some time the two men appeared to rule jointly, though it gradually became obvious that Khrushchev was wielding the scepter. No one, outside the country at least, was greatly surprised when, in 1958, he displaced Bulganin as Premier. On various occasions Khrushchev has affirmed the principle of the peaceful co-existence of states. He seems really alarmed by the danger of a nuclear war in which no one could be the victor. As recently as the summer of 1958, in letters to President Eisenhower, Khrushchev expressed his desire to terminate the "cold war," "to ensure conditions of peaceful co-existence of states," and to make "a good beginning which would pave the way toward solution of all major international problems." He emphatically denied the Leninist doctrine of the "fatal inevitability" of "frightful collisions" between the capitalist and Communist worlds. He seemed desirous of creating the impression that the only threat the West needed to fear from the Soviet power was cultural and economic competition. The Soviet economy was already growing at a faster rate than that of the West; it would soon overtake and surpass the achievements even of capitalist America. "We will bury you," he boasted. "Your grandchildren will live under socialism." [28]

The most spectacular of Khrushchev's disagreements with the policies of Stalin was his repudiation of the "cult of the individual." In his celebrated speech to the Twentieth Party Congress, three years after Stalin's death, he denounced the old man of steel as an autocrat and a tyrant. Stalin, he alleged, developed delusions of grandeur, exalting himself to a state of omnipotence which the most despotic of the tsars might well have envied. He made of himself "a superman possessing supernatural characteristics akin to those of a god." So indifferent was he to the rights of his colleagues that he allowed thirteen years to elapse between the eighteenth and nineteenth Party Congresses. Even after the end of the war, according to Khrushchev, a Congress was not convened for over seven years. Along with delusions of grandeur went the other characteristic symptom of a paranoid personality —delusions of persecution. These were evidenced by suspicions and morbid fears and expressed themselves in violence and brutality. Khrushchev excoriated Stalin for his purges, secret arrests, mass executions, and his attempts to liquidate prominent physicians on suspicion that they were plotting to poison him. According to Khrushchev, no fewer than seventy per cent of the 139 members and candidates elected to the seventeenth Congress were shot on Stalin's orders. Such blatant terrorism, Khrushchev maintained, was not only unnecessary; it was a violation of Leninist principles. Lenin believed in ruthlessness as a means of achieving a socialist revolution or of suppressing a counterrevolution; but once these ends had been accomplished, he argued that violence should be abandoned. Khrushchev contended that after the socialist victories of the 1920's "there was no basis for mass terror in the country." [29]

Khrushchev's demand for collective leadership and for the

[28] Department of State, *Bulletin*, Vol. XXXIX, No. 995 (July 21, 1958); Harry Schwartz, "Khrushchev: Reappraisal of a Riddle," N.Y. *Times Magazine*, Aug. 3, 1958, p. 46. See also N. S. Khrushchev, "Letters to Bertrand Russell," *The New Statesman*, Vol. LIV, No. 1397 (Dec. 21, 1957), p. 846; *ibid.*, Vol. LV, No. 1399 (March 15, 1958), p. 317.

[29] The Russian Institute, ed., *The Anti-Stalin Campaign and International Communism, a Selection of Documents*. New York, Columbia University Press, 1956, pp. 2, 21, 22–23, 27.

abolition of violent repression impressed many people in the West as singularly at variance with his official behavior. For he established himself in a dictatorial position about as "personal" as anything imaginable, and in 1956 he suppressed a revolt in Hungary with savage cruelty. Still, he indulged in no personal glorification. He did not encourage his followers to endow him with attributes of divinity, or to acclaim him as the source of the nation's life and the fountain of all sweetness and light. His use of repression was not applied, to any great extent, on the domestic scene. Except for Lavrenti Beria, the head of Stalin's secret police, Khrushchev's opponents were not liquidated. They were demoted to relatively unimportant positions, but their lives were spared, and they were not even imprisoned.

The Khrushchev regime has been marked also by a greater attention to the production of consumer's goods and a relaxation of some of the restrictions on publication and on the admission of ideas from abroad. Gone was the cultural chauvinism of Stalin's day, under which every innovation of modern history was credited to the Russians—from the discovery of America to the development of antibiotics. Finally, Khrushchev opened the door, if ever so slightly, to the doctrine of "more than one road to socialism." Early in 1955 he went, in company with Bulganin, to Yugoslavia and apologized to Marshal Tito, almost abjectly, for discriminating against his government in the past. Despite earnest entreaties and promises of political and economic advantages, he was unable to penetrate the hard shell of Tito's determination to remain independent. When, later in the year, the Poles revolted, they were treated rather leniently and allowed to establish their own brand of socialism in return for pledges to remain within the Soviet orbit. As we have noted, the Hungarian revolt of the same year received altogether different treatment; but repressive measures were justified on the ground that the Hungarians were attempting, not merely to change the economic system, but to break all ties with the Soviet Union. The importance of month-to-month or year-to-year changes in Soviet theory must not be exaggerated. The fundamental objectives will probably remain essentially the same as long as the regime continues. Changes in attitude and emphasis, however, do occur and exert some influence upon immediate policy.

According to a widespread popular belief, the day of totalitarianism has passed its zenith. The victory of the Allies in World War II is supposed to have sealed the doom of fascism. Though Soviet Communism survives, it is frequently alleged to be shot through with instability. Reports circulate every once in a while of serious dissension within the government. High officials of some capitalist governments believe these stories and lend the weight of their influence to gaining credence for them. In the case of Russia as in that of Germany under the rule of Hitler, it is commonly supposed that the people as a whole do not support their government. With a little more enlightenment and prosperity, or with the coming of a convenient opportunity, they will rise up against their dictators and destroy them.

But the current optimism regarding the decline of totalitarianism overlooks a number of realities. In the first place, it ignores the fact that fascism, or similar forms of authoritarian rule, still exist in such countries as Spain, Portugal, Indonesia, Egypt, and the Dominican Republic. This optimistic view also overlooks the fact that Communism has grown tremendously since World War II, until it now holds sway over more than a third of the population of the earth. Most serious of all, it fails to take account of the fact that totalitarianism appears to fulfill certain needs that grow out of the chaos and uncertainties of our age. Countless people feel themselves alienated and distraught by the fiercely competitive conditions of the modern world. Fearful of depression, unemployment, or loss of status, and bewildered by the rapidity of technological and organizational changes, they seek security and solace by submerging themselves in a nationalist or racist movement or in a mass party, or in worship of a charismatic leader. In short, the growth of totalitarianism is not to be interpreted as the product of human depravity, but of fear, insecurity, and anxiety. Psychologists have recognized for a long time that fear is one of the strongest of human emotions, especially when it pervades a crowd or a mob. Under its impulsion men will commit deeds of savagery which seem to refute the very existence of civilization. One has only to recall the intermittent racial disturbances in Great Britain, the barbarous treatment of natives by the descendants of the Dutch in South Africa, and the discrimination against Negroes in the United States to realize that no people can consider itself immune from mob terrorism and tyranny. Conditions of the sort described provide excellent opportunities for the authoritarian personality to emerge from the mass and direct the forces of blind hatred inspired by fear.

ADDITIONAL READINGS

Almond, Gabriel. *The Appeals of Communism.* Princeton, Princeton University Press, 1954.

Arendt, Hannah. *The Origins of Totalitarianism.* New York, Harcourt, 1951.

Borkenau, Franz. *European Communism.* New York, Harper, 1953.

Brady, Robert A. *Business as a System of Power.* New York, Columbia University Press, 1943.

————. *The Spirit and Structure of German Fascism.* New York, Viking, 1937.

Brecht, Arnold. *Prelude to Silence.* New York, Oxford University Press, 1944.

Crankshaw, Edward. *Russia without Stalin.* New York, Viking, 1956.

Crossman, Richard, ed. *The God That Failed.* New York, Harper, 1949.

Dallin, David J. *The New Soviet Empire.* New Haven, Yale University Press, 1951.

DeGrazia, Sebastian. *The Political Community: a Study of Anomie.* Chicago, University of Chicago Press, 1948.

Dennis, Lawrence. *The Coming American Fascism.* New York, Harper, 1936.

Drucker, Peter F. *The End of Economic Man.* New York, John Day, 1939.

Fainsod, Merle. *How Russia Is Ruled.* Cambridge, Mass., Harvard University Press, 1954.

Fischer, George. *Russian Liberalism.* Cambridge, Mass., Harvard University Press, 1958.

Flynn, John T. *As We Go Marching*. Garden City, Doubleday, 1944.

Fraenkel, Ernst. *The Dual State: A Contribution to the Theory of Dictatorship*. New York, Oxford University Press, 1941.

Heiden, Konrad. *Der Führer*. Boston, Houghton Mifflin, 1944.

Hoffer, Eric. *The True Believer*. New York, Harper, 1951.

Kelsen, Hans. *The Political Theory of Bolshevism*. Berkeley, University of California Press, 1948.

Kolnai, Aurel. *The War against the West*. London, V. Gollancz, 1938.

Leites, Nathan. *A Study of Bolshevism*. Glencoe, Ill., Free Press, 1953.

Mises, Ludwig von. *Omnipotent Government*. New Haven, Yale University Press, 1944.

Mumford, Lewis. *Faith for Living*. New York, Harcourt, 1940.

Neumann, Franz. *Behemoth: The Structure and Practice of National Socialism*. New York, Oxford University Press, 1944.

Neumann, Sigmund. *Permanent Revolution*. New York, Harper, 1942.

Overstreet, Harry A. and Bonaro. *What We Must Know about Communism*. New York, Norton, 1958.

Rauschning, Hermann. *The Revolution of Nihilism*. New York, Alliance Book Corp., 1939.

Seton-Watson, Hugh. *From Lenin to Malenkov*. New York, Praeger, 1953.

Stamps, Norman L. *Why Democracies Fail*. Notre Dame, University of Notre Dame Press, 1957.

Talmon, J. L. *The Rise of Totalitarian Democracy*. Boston, Beacon Press, 1952.

Viereck, Peter. *Metapolitics: From the Romantics to Hitler*. New York, Knopf, 1941.

P A R T
THREE

Theories of Conservatism

CHAPTER

VIII

Idealists and Romanticists

It seems almost a commonplace of history that ideas do not die. They are sometimes buried for a period under an avalanche of opposing ideas, but they are usually resurrected and revivified to suit the needs of some new epoch. A characteristic example is the philosophy of idealism. Originated by Plato, it was forced into an eclipse by Stoicism, Epicureanism, and Skepticism; but it was revived by Christianity and became an integral part of both Catholic and Protestant theology. It passed into eclipse again during the Intellectual Revolution of the seventeenth century, re-emerged in the eighteenth century, and, in the Age of Reaction that followed the French Revolution, blossomed in a more vigorous form than ever. It became the vehicle of protest against everything that was supposed to have inspired the Reign of Terror and the whole range of excesses that accompanied the demise of the *Ancien Régime*. Clericals embraced it in the defense of religion. Authoritarians saw in it a means of combating freedom, which they virtually identified with anarchy. Conservatives perceived it as an antidote to democracy, for through it they could glorify the state, and reduce the individual to a cog in a machine. Perhaps most important of all, it served the needs of that virulent nationalism which sprang up in the wake of Napoleon's conquests. To make up for the bitterness of defeat, nationalists demanded unity, conformity, unswerving loyalty, and subordination of the individual to the group. They exalted the state as divine, endowed it with a personality and a will of its own, or identified it with the march of God in history. For such leaders as Johann Gottlieb Fichte and Georg Wilhelm Hegel, in Prussia, worship of the state as the personification of the spirit of the nation was essential for realization of the national destiny.

Romanticism, as a philosophy of revolt against formalism and artificiality, has no ancient pedigree. Yet as an anti-intellectual movement, denying the competence of reason and demanding a reliance upon faith, intuition, sentiment, and emotion, it has roots going back to some of the early Church Fathers. The famous dictum of Tertullian (160?–230?), *Credo quia absurdum* (I believe because it is absurd), summarized a main viewpoint of romanticism. So did some of the teachings of Martin Luther when he blasted against reason as "the devil's harlot" and adjured his followers to "keep to revelation and don't try to understand." [1] Like idealism, romanticism underwent an eclipse during the Intellectual Revolution, and especially during the Enlightenment; but it was given a rebirth by Rousseau about the middle of the eighteenth century, and thenceforth it became a dominant force in the modern world. After the French Revolution it was frequently combined with idealism to war against radicalism and skepticism. It was often joined with idealism, also, in glorification of national achievements and in worship of the state as the embodiment of a people's destiny. In fact, such idealists as Fichte and Hegel were frequently called Romantic Idealists. However, it must not be supposed that all romanticists were worshipers of authority, uniformity, and submission. Some, like Lord Byron, Percy Bysshe Shelley, and William Godwin, were fiery apostles of liberty, individualism, and even anarchism. The common bond among them was allegiance to emotion rather than reason as a guide through the crises of life.

1. The New Idealism

Idealism contains so many ingredients that it almost defies a compact definition. To begin with, it is an anti-materialist philosophy. It assumes that the spiritual or ideal is the supreme

---

[1] Preserved Smith, *The Age of the Reformation.* New York, Holt, 1920, pp. 625–26.

reality and either denies the existence of the world of matter or relegates it to a place of minor importance. Secondly, idealism is a collectivist philosophy, exalting Church, state, and society above the individual and stressing the importance of duties and obligations rather than rights. The idealist usually venerates tradition and authority, repudiating revolution, and insisting that change must come about through the gradual unfolding of some spiritual Purpose in the universe. Finally, idealism is anti-empirical and anti-humanist. For its theory of knowledge it relies upon pure reason, intuition, or revelation, or some combination of them, rather than upon experience or sense perception. It conceives of man as an instrument of the divine, placed on this earth for the advancement of spiritual ends. In no sense does it recognize the right of the individual to pursue self-aggrandizement or mundane happiness after the fashion of an animal.

The idealism of the contemporary world was developed primarily, in England, by T. H. Green, F. H. Bradley, and Bernard Bosanquet. It is generally called the New Idealism, to distinguish it from the doctrines of Kant, Fichte, and Hegel, upon which it was based.

Thomas Hill Green was born in Yorkshire in 1836. His father was a clergyman of the Church of England. The future philosopher Green graduated from Oxford and spent the remainder of his life there, eventually being appointed Whyte Professor of Moral Philosophy. His chief writings were *Prolegomena to Ethics* and *Lectures on the Principles of Political Obligation*. Both of these works were published after his death in 1882 and did not attract much attention until a much later date.

Green was the most liberal of the New Idealists. In fact, he is sometimes considered the real father of the liberalism of the twentieth century. This brand of liberalism, of course, is much different from that of the nineteenth century. It is not concerned essentially with the life, liberty, and pursuit of happiness of atomistic individuals but with the welfare of the whole society and especially with the welfare of its less privileged members. Green owed almost nothing to the natural-rights, *laissez-faire* philosophy of his English predecessors. He did not recognize rights as grounded in the law of nature or belonging to the indi-

vidual by virtue of his membership in the human race. A right
he defined as a power of acting for one's own ends: "—for what
he conceives to be his good,—secured to an individual by the
community, on the supposition that its exercise contributes to the
good of the community." [2] In other words, the individual really
has no rights except those conferred upon him by the community,
to be exercised not in his own self-interest but in such a way as to
enhance the general good. True, the individual does have a claim
to seek his own ends, but it is more like a privilege than a right
and ceases to exist unless pursued in the common interest.

According to Green, the state is the highest form of community,
the embodiment and fulfillment of the idea of society. Without
the state the individual would be nothing. He can have no rights
against the state; for, "as the sustainer and harmoniser of social
relations . . . its law must be to him of absolute authority." [3]
Nor would Green concede that the state is an artificial creation,
resting upon a social compact or voluntary consent. At the same
time, he denied that it rests entirely upon force. Its real foundation, he argued, is *will*. Men acquiesce in obeying the state because of a common rational will to act together for common ends.
Only occasionally does this will need to be backed by coercive
force. When coercion is used it must be exercised in a certain
way for certain ends, i. e., "according to law, written or customary, and for the maintenance of rights." [4] The exercise of
arbitrary or despotic power would negate the true character of
the state and would perhaps absolve the citizens from obedience,
though Green did not say so.

Unlike his liberal predecessors of the seventeenth and eighteenth centuries, Green did not regard the state as a necessary
evil. He did not consider that government best which governs
least, though he seldom envisaged it as acting in a positive fashion. The great function of the state, he maintained, is the removal of obstacles which stand in the way of the equality and
harmony of social relations. He conceived of a society in which

[2] *Lectures on the Principles of Political Obligation.* London, Longmans,
1941, p. 207.
[3] *Ibid.*, pp. 148–49.
[4] *Ibid.*, p. 136.

every individual would have full opportunity, to the limit of his capacity, to enjoy and participate in the cultural benefits which that society afforded; and he was distressed by the fact that such was not true of the England of his day. "The underfed denizen of a London yard," he wrote, has hardly more share in the civilization of England than a slave had in ancient Athens. The chief obstacles to social harmony and cultural participation he enumerated as ignorance, drunkenness, and poverty. The state, he maintained, has the function of eliminating such obstacles, by legislation or by any other means that will enhance the moral freedom of the citizens. He contended that classical liberalism had gone too far in restricting the functions of the state to those of a policeman. And though he was far from specific in suggesting measures for removing the obstacles he so greatly deplored, he at least opened the door for such elements of the welfare state as old-age pensions, sickness and unemployment insurance, and progressive inheritance taxes.

Curiously, when it came to the sphere of private ownership, Green clung almost desperately to the old tenets of individualist doctrine. He recognized a virtually unlimited right of every citizen to accumulate wealth, subject only to the condition that inequality of fortunes must not result in the creation of a proletariat living in wretchedness and in constant danger of exploitation. But he did not think such a condition very likely to arise. In general, he held that unlimited freedom of one man to accumulate wealth does not interfere with the like freedom of other men, because wealth is not a fixed quantity but is constantly being augmented by the increasing productivity of labor. Besides, he insisted, there is nothing to prevent the ordinary man from accumulating wealth in considerable quantity, except possibly his own ignorance and self-indulgence. Workers have every opportunity to become small-scale capitalists if they will exercise a modicum of intelligence and avoid the more flagrant vices. Why, then, is there so much poverty? Green found the answer in the inequitable distribution of land. Property in land, he pointed out, is unique in comparison with all other forms. Whereas industrial wealth is not fixed but is constantly increasing, the supply of land is limited. No one can enlarge it by his own industry or frugality. If he wishes to acquire more he must purchase it out of hard-earned wealth from other sources. The original landlords were conquerors, and they have handed their possessions down from one generation to another as a family monopoly. In the light of these premises it would seem that Green should have advocated a heavy tax on the unearned increment, but he rejected the idea as too complicated and too liable to reduce the incentive of the individual "to make the most of the land." [5] It seems strange that for all Green's collectivist leanings, he could not even go as far as some of the Utilitarians (notably the Mills) in advocating remedies for the maldistribution of land.

The second member of the great triumvirate of New Idealists, Francis Herbert Bradley, was the least concerned with political doctrine. Born in 1846, Bradley was educated at University College, Oxford. Soon after his graduation he was elected to a fellowship at Merton College. On account of ill health he did not teach, but, as a fellow, devoted the rest of his life to meditation, research, and writing. He personified the scholarly gentleman, dedicating his energies to the pursuit of truth in monastic seclusion, supported by the burgeoning prosperity of Victorian England. He died in 1924.

Bradley's theory of the individual's place in society was summed up in an essay entitled "My Station and Its Duties." In it he repudiated the Utilitarian conception of society as a collection of self-seeking individuals. He emphasized, instead, the importance of community. An individual, he declared, "is what he is because of and by virtue of community. . . . The 'individual' apart from the community is an abstraction." Man is real only because he is social.[6] In writing of "My Station and Its Duties" Bradley was not advocating a rigidly stratified society made up of hereditary castes impenetrable from without. He did believe that there are various positions or roles in society, and that each has its duties and responsibilities. By filling one of these places and performing its duties, the individual would achieve "self-realization." But there is no single station to which a person is doomed for the entirety of his life. What Bradley seems to have meant

[5] *Ibid.*, p. 229.
[6] *Ethical Studies*, Oxford, Clarendon Press, 1927, pp. 166–74.

was that everyone is always in a particular station, and that station, whatever it is at the moment, includes obligations which must be fulfilled. The way of escape from a particular station lies in moral improvement, in striving to make oneself and one's world better. It was a conception of society almost medieval in character, with a hierarchy of status for the majority and an avenue of escape to higher levels for the saints and the mystics.

When we come to the philosophy of Bosanquet we approach the logical extreme of subordination of the individual to the interests of society or the demands of the state. Bernard Bosanquet was born in 1848, the son of an Anglican clergyman. After preparing at Harrow he entered Balliol College, Oxford, where he came under the influence of T. H. Green. For ten years after his graduation he served as a fellow and tutor at University College. From 1903 to 1908 he was Professor of Moral Philosophy at St. Andrews University in Scotland. At the age of thirty-two he inherited considerable wealth and went to live in London, where he resided until his death in 1923, except for the brief period at St. Andrews. His most important book was *The Philosophical Theory of the State,* published in 1899.

Bosanquet introduced into his philosophy so many resemblances to the idealism of Hegel that he is often referred to as a Neo-Hegelian. He recognized no rights except those conferred by the state and no freedom except that resulting from the submergence of individual interests in the larger interests of the community. Like Rousseau, he argued that individuals can be "forced to be free," in the sense that the government can compel them to be what they know in their own consciences they ought to be, in contrast with the indolence and ignorance of their "casual private selves." [7] Though he did not describe the state as divine, he defined it as the embodiment of absolute physical power, and he went far toward removing it from the sphere of morality. He denied that a state could be guilty of murder when it wages war, regardless of the purpose or cause, or of theft when it engages in confiscation or annexation. Such acts are the acts of a supreme power with "ultimate responsibility for protecting the form of life of which it is the guardian." No one has the right to

[7] *The Philosophical Theory of the State.* London, Macmillan, 1899, p. 127.

question the means it chooses to employ, or to judge its acts by
the standards applied to personal morality. Nor can a state be
held accountable for the cruelty or injustice of its agents. The
agents themselves may be blamable, but the acts of the state are
public acts, expressions of the public will, and cannot be judged
by the ordinary canons of morality. This argument came peril-
ously close to the doctrine that the state can do no wrong. If
Bosanquet were living today, he would apparently reject the
principle that armed aggression and genocide are crimes against
international law and punishable by the combined force of the
world community.[8]

On the other hand, it is clear that Bosanquet was not advocating fascism or totalitarianism. Though he criticized Green for
his "scrupulous caution" in restricting the role of the state, he
never conceded an absolute authority of rulers to direct and
control every aspect of the lives of their subjects. Like Green, he
conceived of the prerogative of the state as essentially one of
removing obstacles. The state is acting within its authority, he
said, when it "hinders hindrance" to the general welfare or the
best life. It would be amply justified in hindering illiteracy and
intemperance by making education compulsory and by regulating
the liquor traffic. He was not so sure, however, whether it should
hinder unemployment by the construction of public works, or
overcrowding under bad sanitary conditions by provision of
extensive public housing. On every such problem the question
must be asked, "Is the proposed measure *bona fide* confined to
hindering a hindrance, or is it attempting direct promotion of the
common good by force?" Every form of human behavior dictated
or imposed by force is automatically withdrawn from the higher
life. "The promotion of morality by force . . . is an absolute self-
contradiction." [9] He went on to argue that providing a good house
for a family previously occupying a dilapidated one would be
justified only in case the decrepit building interfered with "a
better life struggling to utter itself." [10] In other words, like all
idealists, he insisted upon moral, spiritual, and cultural ends to

---

[8] *Ibid.*, p. 326.
[9] *Ibid.*, pp. 191–92.
[10] *Ibid.*, p. 199.

justify state action. Mere health and happiness, employment, and economic security were not in themselves sufficient.

The only noted American, in the contemporary period, who has sought to give political philosophy an idealist interpretation was Josiah Royce (1855–1916). With its surging individualism and materialism after the Civil War, America gave poor hospitality to a philosophy that exalted the state as a god and reduced human beings to mere instruments for the achievement of state purposes. Even Royce felt obliged, in his later years, to abandon all attempts to deify the state. The future American idealist was born in the gold-mining area of California. His original ambition was to study engineering, and he enrolled in the University of California for that purpose at the age of sixteen. His interests shifted gradually to literature and philosophy, and after his graduation he went to Germany to study these subjects at Leipzig and Göttingen. He returned to Johns Hopkins as one of its first fellows in 1876 and received his Ph.D. two years later. After four years of teaching English at the University of California, he became a member of the Philosophy Department at Harvard, where he taught until his death in 1916. His political theory is contained chiefly in *The Philosophy of Loyalty; Race Questions, Provincialism and Other American Problems;* and *The Hope of the Great Community.*

Josiah Royce was one of the most atypical of American philosophers, at least for his time. He maintained that the individual can be saved only by losing himself in loyalty to the community. He had no sympathy with the cynicism and pessimism that grew out of the Social Darwinism so popular toward the end of the nineteenth century. Instead, he maintained that man is much more than an intelligent animal, and he upheld a radiant faith in the eternal verities and in a universe governed by benevolent purpose. In place of the pragmatism and experimentalism of philosophers like William James and John Dewey, Royce held fast to an absolutist metaphysics and to the importance of ideals as manifestations of the will of God. He showed little faith in machinery, in new voting arrangements, in new institutions and agencies to conquer the problems of society. He preferred to stake everything on the power of ideals to change men's attitudes toward their neighbors and gradually to imbue them with feelings of oneness toward the whole human race. Almost his only point of agreement with his leading contemporaries was his acceptance of the doctrine of a fundamental law. This law he envisaged as the underlying principle of nature and society and as an expression of the divine plan for the universe.

In contrast with European idealists, Royce did not glorify the state as the alpha and omega of man's life on this earth. He actually feared the nation-state because he thought it susceptible to mob influence and therefore likely to pass under the control of demagogues or tyrants. In place of nationalism he preferred what he called "provincialism." By a "province" he meant "any one part of a national domain, which is, geographically and socially, sufficiently unified to have a true consciousness of its own unity, to feel a pride in its own ideals and customs, and to possess a sense of its distinction from other parts of the country." [11]

The key to both the salvation of the individual and the progress of society Royce found in his principle of loyalty. Man can raise himself above the baseness of his own nature, he taught, by identifying himself with a cause, by cooperating in the relief of suffering, in the conquest of disease, or in the cultural and educational advancement of other human beings. The first loyalty is loyalty to one's family, then to one's province, to one's nation, to the whole human race. Above everything else is "loyalty to the principle of loyalty." Royce believed that this ultimate loyalty would provide a panacea for all ills—for crime, greed, and even for war. Assume, he said, that your enemy is as firmly attached to his cause as you are to yours. Give him credit for his devotion and for his willingness to sacrifice himself in what he believes to be a just cause. So far as motives are concerned, his loyalty rests upon as sound an ethical basis as your own. Respect for your enemy's loyalty is loyalty to the principle of loyalty. Diffusion and general adoption of this principle is the one best hope for peace. On no other foundation is a community of nations possible. It was typical of Royce that he should have rejected coercion as

[11] *Race Questions and Other American Problems*. New York, Macmillan, 1908, p. 61.

the basis of order on the international scale as he did on the regional and local. He had no faith in a League to Enforce Peace or in schemes for the punishment of aggressors by military and naval sanctions. Ethical voluntarism was the core of his proposals for both individual and social improvement.

2. The New Romanticism

Romanticism as it has developed in the late nineteenth and early twentieth centuries has varied considerably from its earlier forms. The romanticism which opposed the Enlightenment was largely concerned with liberty and with the rights of the individual to self-assertion and self-expression. To be sure, Rousseau and some of his disciples distinguished between what they called animal liberty and true liberty, or liberty in obedience to law. But these philosophers have been identified, in the popular mind at least, as exponents of freedom for the individual to affirm his own essence. The later romanticists tended to relegate the individual to the background, or even to subordinate him entirely, and to emphasize the power and glory of a nation, the welfare of a class, the preservation of race purity, or the production of a species of super-beings. Rousseau and his disciples were primitivists, glorifying the simple and the natural. Comparatively little of this viewpoint has survived in contemporary romanticism. The Nazis made efforts to deify the peasants, but they seem to have done so primarily because of the peasants' prolificness and because of a desire to express contempt for the proletariat. It is almost impossible to conceive of a contemporary romanticist echoing the thought of Wordsworth that

> One impulse from a vernal wood
> May teach you more of man,
> Of moral evil and of good,
> Than all the sages can.

Finally, contemporary romanticists applaud the use of force and even of violence, not simply as means but as ends. They argue that fighting back against oppression ennobles men, puts iron into their souls, and inculcates heroism and loyalty. The early romanticists approved of revolution, but they also championed democracy and the rights of man. Though they commonly assumed that blood must be shed in the cause of freedom, they never contended that butchery has a therapeutic effect upon those who practice it.

During the latter half of the nineteenth century the boldest prophet of romanticism was Friedrich Nietzsche. To this day he symbolizes, in the minds of many people, ruthlessness, contempt for morality, and all the other horrible qualities of an Antichrist. Nietzsche was born in 1844, the son of a Lutheran minister. Educated in the classics at Leipzig and Bonn, he became a professor of philosophy at the University of Basel at the age of twenty-four. Ten years later he was forced to retire on account of severe illness. He spent the next decade of his life in agony, wandering from one resort to another in a fruitless quest for relief. If we can believe his own statement, each year was made up of 200 days of pain. In 1888 he lapsed into hopeless insanity, which continued until his death in 1900.

Nietzsche's philosophy is contained in such works as *Thus Spake Zarathustra, A Genealogy of Morals, Beyond Good and Evil,* and his unfinished *magnum opus, The Will to Power.* In addition to being a romantic poet dreaming of the advent of the superman, he was also an apostle of Social Darwinism. However, he placed an unusual emphasis on the dysgenic effects of public policy in perpetuating the dull and the unworthy rather than the noble and superior beings. His prime objective was to accomplish a "transvaluation of values," to debase those qualities now commonly regarded as virtues—pity, humility, sympathy, self-denial, sacrifice—into vices, and to exalt the ancient Germanic qualities of strength, bravery, loyalty, and honor, into virtues. He defined *good* as "all that heightens in man the feeling of power, the desire for power, power itself." *Bad* he characterized as "all that comes from weakness." [12] To achieve the revolution in values he demanded it would be necessary to overturn the moral supremacy of Christianity and Judaism. Both of these religions, Nietzsche alleged, are Oriental cults glorifying the vir-

[12] Quoted by E. A. Singer, *Modern Thinkers and Present Problems.* New York, Holt, 1923, p. 204.

tues of slaves and of other downtrodden folk. They attempt to impose upon the strong and the free a slave morality fit only for the craven and the weak. By so doing they prevent the elimination of the unfit and preserve them to pour their degenerate blood into the veins of the race.

As with most romanticists, consistency was not a crowning jewel in the philosophy of Nietzsche. Though he worshiped force, his attitude toward the state was almost that of an anarchist. In *Thus Spake Zarathustra* he referred to the state as "a dissembling dog," speaking "with smoke and roaring," and seeking to make itself "the most important creature on earth." The state was devised "for the superfluous ones"; when the superman appears, it will no longer be necessary. Though he wrote admiringly of the "blond beast" who merits the privilege of riding roughshod over the weak and inferior, Nietzsche liked to think of himself as "a good European," despised the Prussians as a "race of cattle," and wished that he had been born in France. He scoffed at militarists, but sang paeans of praise to war in his great hymn to the super-race:

> You I advise not to work, but to fight. You I advise not to peace, but to victory. Let your work be a fight, let your peace be a victory. . . .
> Ye say it is the good cause which halloweth even war? I say unto you: it is the good war which halloweth every cause.[13]

Underlying Nietzsche's political theories was a vivid contempt for the society around him. He condemned all, the rulers and the ruled alike, who did not contribute to the development of a "race of men which does not yet exist . . . the lords of the earth." He repudiated with equal fervor the individualist and the collectivist because both, in his estimation, were more concerned with freedom than with power.

During the twentieth century thus far romanticism has been exemplified by various movements of a definitely political character. It was expressed, first of all, in the syndicalism of Georges Sorel (1847–1922). Sorel was originally a French engineer, who, about 1905, turned his attention to political theory and wrote

---

[13] *Thus Spake Zarathustra*. New York, Modern Library, no date, pp. 62–63.

Reflections on Violence. He acclaimed the use of violence as the one sure way to give confidence and courage to the workers and imbue them with pride in their cause. He taught the necessity of a relentless struggle until capitalism and the capitalist state should be destroyed and society reorganized into associations of producers. This struggle, he affirmed, must take the form of open warfare, waged without hatred or revenge, but with heroic resolve to conquer the enemy. Sorel was a romanticist also in his cultivation of the "myth" as a kind of substitute for reason. A Sorellian myth is an expression of a determination to act. It is not necessarily true, but it has value in giving the workers a vision of the glorious future and thereby inspiring them with fanatical zeal and a willingness to sacrifice even their lives in pursuit of a goal. It has the appeal of a paradise for devout believers.

Romanticism in our century was also exemplified by Futurism, a revolutionary movement which developed in Italy against liberal traditions and bourgeois respectability. The Futurists fulminated against reason, compromise, pacifism, democracy, and quietism. They clamored for action, heroism, and belligerency and sang hymns of praise to the beauties of violence. The doctrines of the Futurists found a natural home in fascism—especially in its Italian form. Mussolini at one time had been a follower of Sorel. Not only does fascism glorify violence and extol war as a blessing to humanity, but it repudiates the intellectual approach and demands that reason be largely supplanted by will and by mystic faith in the nation and its leader.

As has been indicated already in this chapter, romanticism bears a close relationship to idealism. Indeed, it is often difficult to draw a clear boundary between them. The idealist who supplements reason by faith, intuition, or strong conviction is verging very close upon romanticism. He has not subordinated intellect completely, for he still admits the competence of reason; nevertheless, by giving a large place to sentiment and emotion, he risks the tendency toward becoming anti-intellectual. A characteristic example of this tendency was Benedetto Croce (1866–1952), who ran the gamut from Hegelian idealism and aristocratic conservatism to veneration of Mussolini. Croce was born in the province of Aquila, the son of a prosperous landowner. Sent to a Catholic boarding school, he captured all the academic honors and also acquired a contempt for liberalism. At the age of seventeen he was seriously injured in an earthquake in which his father, mother, and sister were killed. He went to live with an uncle in Rome, and registered at the University for jurisprudence, but seldom attended classes and never sat for the examination. With the advantage of an ample inheritance, he devoted his time to reading and research. He wrote his first philosophical essay at the age of twenty-seven.

Croce divided his later career between literary pursuits and politics. In 1903 he became co-editor with Giovanni Gentile of *La Critica*, a review of literature, history, and philosophy. Between 1903 and 1917 he published his four-volume *Philosophy as the Science of Spirit*. In 1910 he was elected to the Italian Senate, the youngest member of that body, and soon emerged as a leader of the Conservatives. In 1913 he issued his *Philosophy of the Practical*, in which he upheld the Machiavellian theory of power, approved the Inquisition as a legitimate employment of force in politics, identified right with might, and justice with success. He published the same year a translation of Sorel's *Reflections on Violence* and accompanied it with a laudatory preface. In 1914 he opposed Italy's entrance into the war, and at the time of the Peace criticized the League of Nations as a relic of Freemasonry and an eighteenth-century mentality. The triumph of Fascism in 1922 inspired Croce with hope that Italy was repudiating her bourgeois-liberal past, and that the Fascisti would inject vigor and purity into the government. He broke with Mussolini, however, after the murder of Matteotti in 1924, and became even more critical in 1929 after the Concordat with the Vatican. Mussolini retaliated by depriving Croce of his chair at the University, expelling him from the learned academies, and forbidding the circulation of *La Critica* in the schools. In 1941 Croce wrote *History as the Story of Liberty*. It was a plea for a new liberalism, but it revealed little faith in the masses. Quantity, the author held, must not be substituted for quality, lest the door be opened for demagoguery, with tyranny and dictatorship as the ultimate results. After the overthrow of Mussolini in 1943, Croce joined with Count Sforza in advocating a regency under Marshal

Badoglio as the best way of saving the monarchy. He assumed the monarchy to be necessary for the return of stability and constitutional rule.

Although Croce is frequently referred to as a Neo-Hegelian, he seems to have held the great German exponent of dialectic in high esteem for only a brief period. He discovered Hegel in 1905 and declared that in plunging into the reading of Hegel, he seemed to be plunging into himself. Years later he wrote that, like Catullus in love with Lesbia, he could live neither with Hegel nor without him. The specific Hegelian element he found most unacceptable was the conception of a dialectic process representing the unfoldment of the divine in history. Progress and retrogression in the universe, according to Croce, are not the results of intervention by a power extraneous to life. Instead, "they are to be found in life itself—in fact, they are life itself . . . life is perpetually distinctive in its forms and within the circle of those forms finds its unity." [14] Though at one time Croce endorsed Hegel's conception of the amorality of power and his identification of right with might, he later criticized both of these notions as "base affections of liveried servants and courtiers." He also repudiated the Hegelian tendency to worship the state, describing it as "stupid." The great purpose of the state is to "provide the necessary condition of stability for the developing of the highest spiritual achievements." [15] It is the instrument, and to a certain extent the source, of culture and civilization, but it is not superior to them.

Yet on other subjects Croce wrote in a manner that was certainly reminiscent of Hegel or of his Romantic Idealist predecessors. He agreed with Hegel that history is the history of liberty. And just as Hegel found liberty becoming manifest in different forms in only a few peoples (in the ancient Orient, one was free; in the Classical world, some were free; in the Germanic world, all were free), so Croce discovered liberty "abiding purely and invincibly and consciously only in a few spirits." These are the great philosophers, great poets, and other great

[14] *History as the Story of Liberty,* trans. Sylvia Sprigge. New York, Norton, 1941, p. 56.
[15] *Ibid.,* p. 167.

men and the few who can understand them. Liberty is not an achievement of the masses, or of the exploited classes struggling against oppression. It has nothing to do with rebellion or revolution. The real representatives of liberty are those choice spirits who strive for "things lofty and worthy," who "carry forward mankind with their work." The same may be said of parties. Those engaged in "the creation of a new and richer form of life," and which are not mere bands or factions, are both the instruments and personifications of true liberty. Communism, for example, cannot represent true liberty, since, far from striving for "things lofty and worthy," it sets its goal as equality.[16] Finally, as an ethical ideal, liberty has no relevance to happiness or to the optimism and pessimism arising from it. It cultivates no aim of pleasure, serenity, or escape from pain, but strives for "the clear, coherent, unequivocal ideal of a creation to be achieved, in whose life alone we live." Good men sacrifice their happiness and even life itself "in reverence to duty and to human dignity." [17]

Croce's attitudes toward war and violence likewise reflected Hegelian and romanticist points of view. He declared the nature of war to be amoral and deprecated attempts to judge its methods by moral principles. "Strife knows no law but strife," he avowed; "its only arbiters are the actual results in which it will issue." [18] War, according to Croce, is simply a reflection of the suffering and tragedy that are inseparable from life itself. There can be no "life without death, beauty without ugliness, truth without error, gain without loss, good without evil, pleasure without pain." War and violence and every other form of evil are essential to human progress. To dream of perpetual peace is fatuous, for its aim is nothing less than to weaken the springs of human action, whose source is in pain and danger. Temporary peace is desirable, but it must be peace which leads eventually to war. Such is the only "practicable and real peace, the only kind which the world-spirit allows and ordains, a

[16] Ibid., pp. 61, 227–28, 242–43.
[17] My Philosophy and Other Essays on the Moral and Political Problems of Our Time, selected by R. Klibansky; trans. E. F. Carritt. London, Allen and Unwin, 1949, pp. 31, 104.
[18] Ibid., p. 237.

peace which tames war but cannot absolutely prevent it from erupting now and again in fits of its native savagery if such is God's will." [19] It was typical of the romanticism of Croce that he could justify war while voicing sharp criticisms of some of its direct consequences, especially militarism and irresponsible autocracy. The same Croce who declared that war is an essential element in historical progress could also write extensively on the ideological bases of liberalism.

A somewhat different brand of romanticism emerged from the philosophy of Henri Bergson (1859–1941). Whereas Croce considered faith and reason virtually identical, Bergson relegated reason to a distinctly subordinate place and taught that the true nature of things is apprehended by intuition. Henri Bergson was born in Paris of Anglo-Jewish parents. After a brilliant career at the Lycée Condorcet, he studied at the École Normale Supérieur. He taught philosophy at the Lycées of Angers and Clermont and then in Paris at the Lycée Henri IV, the École Normale Supérieur, and the College de France. After World War I he gave up teaching entirely, devoting himself to international affairs as head of a mission to America, and as President of the Committee on International Cooperation. In 1927 he was awarded the Nobel Prize for literature. He is supposed to have influenced Georges Sorel and Émile Durkheim as well as a host of other writers of varying beliefs. Indeed, he is more important in political theory for his influence than for any constructive contributions of his own.

Bergson's philosophy was at once a species of skepticism and an affirmation of mystical faith. He laid great store by the conclusions of various scientists that the so-called laws of physics, chemistry, astronomy, etc., are simply observed relationships among phenomena and, in essence, are nothing more than convenient postulates or assumptions. He deduced from these conclusions the doctrine that the empiricism of the sciences yields no final truth. He was just as hostile toward rationalist philosophy. Reason, he contended, is a flagrant deceiver. It may be affected by prejudice, ambition, and self-interest. The philosopher who thinks he is solving the problems of the world and of

[19] *Ibid.*, pp. 119, 124, 205–6.

society by pure reason may be blinded by some preconceived notion of what is best for himself and his class. Witness the example of Plato pleading eloquently for an intellectual aristocracy, or of Aristotle writing his cogent defense of slavery. For Bergson the path to truth lay in the adjustment of one's intelligence to the *élan vital*, or life-force, of the universe. Intelligence alone is simply a factor in biological adaptation which has a practical value for survival purposes and for control of the environment. But intelligence cooperating with the *élan vital* contributes to the fulfillment of the highest ends of the universe. Evolution is a continuously creative process. It is not simply a mechanical process of natural selection, but it is teleological or purposive, and is guided and directed by a vital force contained within the organisms themselves. Perception of this force is not possible by means of the senses. It can be apprehended only by intuition, a faculty which Bergson regarded as akin to instinct and more deeply imbedded in the human psyche than reason. By intuition we discover a more basic truth than is available to us through the instrumentalities of reason and science. Our senses reveal to us nothing but the world of matter, a static, lifeless world. To penetrate the mysteries of the real world of life, motion, and continuity it is necessary to sound the depths of the universe, to feel "the pulse of its spirit by a sort of intellectual auscultation." [20]

A mystical probing or feeling for reality pervaded all branches of Bergson's philosophy. So completely did he rely upon a nonintellectual approach that he came to believe that there was overwhelming proof of mental telepathy. In 1913 he accepted the presidency of the Society for Psychical Research. It is perhaps not surprising that some of his disciples among the syndicalists should have made the substance of their political theory "Less thought and more action." Bergson's religion was essentially the worship of the life-force. God, as he conceived Him, was virtually synonymous with life itself. He was neither omnipotent nor omniscient. He was limited by matter, struggling painfully to overcome its defects. As a Creator, He was laboring constantly toward goals of perfection, aided by individuals in

[20] *Introduction to Metaphysics.* New York, Putnam, 1912, p. 14.

their yearnings to make themselves stronger and better. Morality, for Bergson, was essentially a matter of striving by the individual for a higher and more satisfying life. Success in this endeavor he equated largely with increasing freedom. The trend of evolution, he maintained, has been in favor of the light and mobile species. The armor-plate of the dinosaur has given way to the perilous freedom of the bird. The mammoth and the mastodon, with their sluggish ways and heavy protection, have been replaced by small and sentient mammals with no defenses except their wits and their agility of movement. "In the evolution of life, just as in the evolution of human societies and of individual destinies, the greatest successes have been for those who accepted the heaviest risks." [21] With Bergson, therefore, as with other romanticists, the good life consisted not in reflection or understanding but in activity, in danger, and in the pursuit of impulse and emotion.

Contemporary romanticism in American political thought has been best represented by George Santayana (1863–1952). Born in Madrid of Spanish-American parents, he was brought to the United States at the age of nine. He received vigorous intellectual stimulation from his father, a retired civil servant and translator of Seneca into Spanish verse, and from his mother, who had a wide range of intellectual interests. His formal education was acquired mostly at Harvard, where he earned three degrees, though he also studied Greek literature at the University of Berlin. In 1889 he became an instructor in philosophy at Harvard. In 1905–1906 he published his five-volume *Life of Reason*. Having inherited a substantial legacy, he resigned from Harvard in 1911, after twenty-two years of teaching. He spent five years in writing and contemplation in England, and in 1923 migrated to Italy. For sixteen years he lived in an obscure hotel in Rome. Finally, as the burden of old age pressed upon him, and as war clouds loomed larger on the horizon, he took refuge, in 1939, in a nursing home conducted by the Blue Nuns. There he died.

Santayana was not a romanticist to the exclusion of all other persuasions. Some authorities deny that he was a philosopher at all, for his views were so varied and perverse. He attempted to

[21] *Creative Evolution.* New York, Holt, 1911, p. 132.

reconcile Catholicism and paganism, materialism and idealism, classicism and romanticism. Though he was often satirical, he had a deep sense of the tragedy and mystery of life. "Everything in nature," he wrote, "is lyrical in its ideal essence, tragic in its fate, and comic in its existence." Despite an almost brutal skepticism, he was an aesthete, delighting in whatever color and poetry this world affords. He scolded the Protestants for divesting Christianity of its beauty and especially for neglecting the warmth and humanity of the myths of the Virgin. His own view of religion has been more or less accurately described as resting on the creed: "There is no God, and Mary is His Mother." He considered happiness, perhaps mostly in the form of aesthetic enjoyment, as the chief value in life. "Where happiness fails," he declared, "existence remains a mad and lamentable experiment." [22] Unlike the general lot of romanticists, he had few strong convictions. He hated ideologists, propagandists, and fanatics. Interviewed in 1944, with World War II moving to a climax, he refused to express either approval or disapproval of fascism or communism; though he admitted that there might be some good in both.

Despite a generally skeptical and critical attitude, Santayana was not without prejudice, and on some political issues was surprisingly naive. He was both a monarchist and an aristocrat, considering royalty a logical extension of the authority of the father over the family, and aristocracy an essential antidote for the ignorance and incompetence of the masses. He thought that a court and a hierarchy, with their pomp and splendor, would "redeem human existence from pervasive vulgarity and allow somebody at least to strut proudly over the earth." [23] He had the audacity to claim that all great social and cultural regenerations were brought about by conquest, ignoring the evidence to the contrary in the barbarian conquest of Rome and in the development of Renaissance culture and the Enlightenment without any conquest whatever. He taught that in a wholly rational world an hour or two a day of manual labor would suffice

[22] *Current Biography* (April, 1944), pp. 589–94.
[23] "Reason in Society," *The Life of Reason.* New York, Scribner, 1936, Book II, pp. 73–74.

for material wants, leaving most of the remainder of the time for intellectual and aesthetic endeavors. As an interesting contrast, Sir Thomas More had supposed that six hours a day would be necessary even in Utopia.

A more glaring example of Santayana's naivete and inconsistency is to be found in his attitude toward race. Though he scoffed at venerating race for its own sake, he nevertheless insisted that "some races are obviously superior to others." He disavowed the objective of conserving race purity, but he emphasized the importance of avoiding intermarriage with inferior stocks. "Reason protests as much as instinct," he declared, "against any fusion, for instance, of white and black peoples." Attempts to achieve such fusion will speedily fail, he maintained, for the real difference in their souls will become quickly apparent, and "an irresistible impulse" will cause the groups to segregate.[24]

Santayana's conception of government was similar in some ways to that of Thomas Hobbes and in others to the patriarchal theories of Robert Filmer, a seventeenth-century advocate of the divine right of kings. Like Hobbes, he regarded human beings as helpless. Government, therefore, came into existence not because it was useful or benevolent but because it was inevitable. Men could not live in peace or security without it. In one sense, government is simply "a modification of war," or, more accurately, "potential war," in which opposition or disloyalty is the capital crime. "Every government is essentially an army carrying on a perpetual campaign in its own territory." In this sense, government is always an evil; but, like war itself, it is sometimes also a good.[25] But government does not rest exclusively upon force. The helplessness of man leads to acquiescence in the rule of a powerful individual who can preserve order and provide security, just as little children yield to domination by a strong parent. Nature therefore generates spontaneously a kind of benevolent despotism exemplified by the family and the patriarchal tribe.

[24] "Reason in Society," op. cit., pp. 167–68; Dominations and Powers. New York, Scribner, 1951, p. 357.
[25] Dominations and Powers, pp. 79–80.

The ideal government, according to Santayana, is not a democracy—most emphatically not in the sense of the absolute sovereignty of the majority. He feared what he called the vulgar passion of the mob, unrestrained by the intelligence and refinement of their betters. The mass of the people "has the mind of a worm and the claws of a dragon." Anyone would be a hero who would kill such a monster.[26] The remedy for this absolute democracy of the mob is some form of government by the best. It might be an enlightened monarchy, or preferably a kind of "timocracy." Under the latter, everyone would have equal opportunity to make the most of his talents, but only the best could rise to the top positions. The aristocracy would be an open one, instead of hereditary. Its blood would be drawn from the very best blood of the people. Even a dictatorship, according to Santayana, is preferable to "proletarian" democracy, provided that the dictator is an expert and not an adventurer. In 1950 Santayana in a letter to Corliss Lamont expressed the opinion that Italy under Mussolini was "a stronger, happier, and more united country" than it had ever been—especially better off than under the "disorderly socialism" that preceded the Fascist revolution. The ruinous fate that befell the country in the 1940's, he said, was the result of a militant foreign policy and of imperialist adventurism.[27]

Notwithstanding his tolerance for dictatorship, Santayana was a staunch defender of an individualist economy. He admitted that the first duty of a government is to see that its subjects have enough to eat, but he argued that an equally important duty is to regulate population so as to keep it within the limits of the means of subsistence. Like the classical economists, he feared all sorts of increasing misery from the tendency of all living creatures to multiply prodigiously. Like the classical economists, also, he seemed to believe in the universal beneficence of selfishness. In pursuing prizes for themselves, he contended, people benefit their fellows more than they would be likely to do in any other way. A social system offering no prizes for individual

---

[26] "Reason in Society," op. cit., pp. 127–28.
[27] Daniel Cory, ed., The Letters of George Santayana. New York, Scribner, 1955, p. 405.

achievement would rarely inspire much effort. To individualism we owe nearly everything we have derived from Greece
and Rome, from Italy and England. For these reasons Santayana
would not approve limitations on the accumulation or transmission of wealth. Under full equality of opportunity, he insisted,
any man would be extremely lucky to accumulate more than a
modest competence by a lifetime of effort. No restrictions should
therefore surround these efforts. Furthermore, he should not be
denied the right to bequeath what he had accumulated. If fortunes cannot be transmitted or used to establish great families,
they will lose their "chief imaginative charm." The transmission
of such fortunes is necessary also, Santayana maintained, for
the nourishment of aristocracy, without which there can be no
balance of refinement in society. "Everybody would take his ease
in his inn and sprawl unbuttoned without respect for any finer
judgment or performance than that which he himself was inclined to." [28] Just how equality of opportunity was to be reconciled with the inheritance of unequal fortunes the author failed
to make clear.

Santayana's romanticism was exemplified best of all, perhaps,
by his conflicting attitudes toward war. On one hand, he could
find no good word to say for war. The glories of war, he said, are
all "bloodstained, delirious, and infected with crime." War is the
source of every wrong, and to argue that we can do nothing
about it because it has always existed is the height of nonsense.
But at another time, he came to somewhat different conclusions. To fight, he avowed, is a radical instinct, a primitive necessity. "If men have nothing else to fight over, they will fight over
words, fancies, or women, or they will fight because they dislike each other's looks, or because they have met walking in opposite directions." [29] Life cannot grow or develop or take any
definite form without crowding, or crushing, or devouring some
other form of life. The only enduring peace is peace of stagnation, between two nothings. Whenever two living and growing
organisms come within range of each other, there is danger of
war. Though war wastes a nation's wealth, kills the flower of

[28] "Reason in Society," *op. cit.*, pp. 135–36.
[29] *Ibid.*, pp. 81–82.

its manhood, and leaves the future to the puny, weak, and deformed, conflict is inherent in the law of the universe, and is an agency for good as well as evil.

When Santayana consulted his innermost feelings, he saw no way of abolishing war except by the creation of a universal government capable of imposing its will upon all of the states of the earth. No League of Nations or United Nations would suffice, nor did he believe in the practicability of a world republic. What he had in mind was similar to the conquests of Cyrus the Great or a *Pax Romana*. "As the suppression of some nest of piratical tribes by a great emperor substitutes judicial for military sanctions among them, so the conquest of all warring nations by some imperial power could alone establish general peace." [30] The Romans, he noted, approached this achievement because of their vast preponderance of power. But no nation today is in any position to emulate the Roman accomplishment. The only state with even a remote chance of doing so is the Soviet Union; not merely because of its power but because it is international and shows tendencies of becoming completely neutral in matters of race, nationality, education, and religion. With all of his respect for power, however, Santayana dreaded the uniformity which might come from a peace imposed by military strength. Nevertheless, he could not escape the feeling that war is romantic, that at times it has been an instrument of progress, that it has given the breath of life to chivalry, and that it has enabled men to preserve or enhance liberty. He found himself attracted also to a kind of poetry of death. "When death is habitually defied," he wrote, "all the slavery, all the vileness of life is defied also." [31] Perhaps only a philosophical recluse could have cultivated such a *mystique*.

In our twentieth-century age of science it may seem strange that such philosophies as idealism and romanticism should still have a popular appeal. Yet science and reason have never held undisputed supremacy over the minds of men. During the first great age of science, from about 300 B.C. to 100 A.D., anti-

[30] *Ibid.*, p. 87.
[31] *Dominations and Powers*, p. 207.

rationalist philosophies like Skepticism, Philonism, and Neo-Pythagoreanism flourished side by side with the finest fruits of critical inquiry and empirical analysis. The Italian Renaissance was distinguished not only by the epochal scientific achievements of Galileo, Copernicus, and Leonardo da Vinci but by such irrational manifestations as Neo-Platonism and the Savonarola hysteria. The truth seems to be that the rationalist, scientific approach to the problems of life is one that repels many thoughtful people. Like Erasmus in the sixteenth century, they see it as destructive of humanism and spirituality. They feel that it degrades man to the level of an animal and saps the foundations of religion. For this reason, a number of eminent scientists of the contemporary world put science and religion into entirely separate compartments, assuming that the methods valid for the former have no relevance for the solution of problems of the latter.

Most of all, perhaps, critics of modern science think of it as the enemy of both ethics and aesthetics. The arts, they contend, are responses to the deepest yearnings of the soul. They can be understood and appreciated only by instinctive feeling, intuition, and emotion. Ethics, according to this viewpoint, is a matter of values, which are manifestations of conscience, of revelation, or of spiritual perception. Science cannot provide us with norms of moral behavior or tell us why we should observe them. It seems necessary, therefore, to those dissatisfied with induction and critical reasoning that they be supplemented by appeals to the "higher" faculties of man, to those not based upon sense perception. They are willing to run the risk that conclusions founded upon feelings, intuition, or "spiritual" longings may lead to justification of war, violence, fascism, or racism. Indeed, they have been especially inclined to condone violent methods because, to them, the ideals are worth achieving at any price.

ADDITIONAL READINGS

Barrett, Clifford. *Contemporary Idealism in America*. New York, Macmillan, 1932.

Barzun, Jacques. *Romanticism and the Modern Ego.* Boston, Little, Brown, 1944.

Bosanquet, Bernard. *The Philosophical Theory of the State.* New York, Macmillan, 1899.

——. *Social and International Ideals.* London, Macmillan, 1917.

——. *The Value and Destiny of the Individual.* London, Macmillan, 1923.

Bradley, F. H. *Ethical Studies.* Oxford, Clarendon Press, 1927.

Brown, Stuart G., ed. *The Social Philosophy of Josiah Royce.* Syracuse, Syracuse University Press, 1950.

Croce, Benedetto. *History as the Story of Liberty.* New York, Norton, 1941.

——. *My Philosophy.* London, Allen and Unwin, 1949.

——. *Politics and Morals.* New York, Philosophical Library, 1945.

Edman, Irwin, ed. *The Philosophy of Santayana.* New York, Scribner, 1936.

Ewing, A. C., ed. *The Idealist Tradition: from Berkeley to Blanshard.* Glencoe, Ill., Free Press, 1957.

Green, Thomas Hill. *Lectures on the Principles of Political Obligation.* London, Longmans, 1895.

——. *Prolegomena to Ethics.* Oxford, Clarendon Press, 1899.

Harris, F. P. *The Neo-Idealist Political Theory.* New York, King's Crown, 1944.

Hocking, W. E. *The Coming World Civilization.* New York, Harper, 1956.

——. *Man and the State.* New Haven, Yale University Press, 1926.

Lindsay, A. D. *The Philosophy of Bergson.* London, Dent, 1911.

Muirhead, J. H. *The Platonic Tradition in Anglo-Saxon Philosophy.* London, Allen and Unwin, 1931.

Royce, Josiah. *The Hope of the Great Community.* New York, Macmillan, 1916.

——. *Lectures on Modern Idealism.* New Haven, Yale University Press, 1919.

——. *The Philosophy of Loyalty.* New York, Macmillan, 1908.

——. *The World and the Individual.* London, Macmillan, 1916.

Santayana, George. *The Life of Reason.* One-volume edition. London, Constable, 1954.

———. *Platonism and the Spiritual Life*. London, Constable, 1927.

———. *Scepticism and Animal Faith*. New York, Scribner, 1923.

Seeley, Charles S. *Philosophy and the Ideological Conflict*. New York, Philosophical Library, 1953.

I X

The Revolt against Intellect

The denigration or repudiation of reason is no recent phenomenon. Mystics and revelationists, even before the Christian era, contended that the rational faculties must be supplemented by other methods of knowing if men were to come into possession of real truth. The ancient Gnostics denied that the truths of religion could be discovered by reason or could even be made intelligible. No one could know such truths unless he was the possessor of a secret spiritual knowledge given to him directly by God. The Neo-Platonists believed that ultimate truth could be gained only through a mystic union with the divine. To achieve this ecstatic state one must liberate himself completely from bondage to matter, through prolonged contemplation and subjugation of the flesh by self-torture. The influence of both these philosophies in promoting the development of mystical and other non-rational forms of Christianity is well known.

Christianity developed through its early history as an essentially non-rational religion, until medieval Scholasticism in the twelfth and thirteenth centuries provided it with a rationalist structure. True, it was a rationalism buttressed by the authority of Aristotle; nevertheless, its exponents firmly believed that there was no truth which could not be made to surrender to the power of reason, except possibly such recondite mysteries of theology as the doctrine of the Incarnation, which had to be taken on faith. But the proud structure of Scholasticism had only a limited supremacy. It was undermined in the fourteenth century by nominalism. The Nominalists contended that only individual things that we can see and hear and touch are real, and that all knowledge has its source in experience. Anything beyond the realm of concrete experience had to be taken on faith, if it were to be taken at all.

Nominalism paved the way for modern science. Since the scientific revolution of the seventeenth century, rationalism has had scant acceptance. It enjoyed a brief revival during the Enlightenment, but it was a rationalism that paid homage to sense perception as the original ground of all knowledge. By the end of the nineteenth century, philosophy as a form of speculative thinking unrelated to the world of nature had virtually ceased to exist. The problems of the universe, of course, had not been solved, nor had men lost the capacity for accurate deduction; but the methods of science, rather than those of pure reason, had come to be generally accepted as the only reliable guides to truth. More recent times have seen the rebirth and the increasing popularity of philosophies which repudiate both reason and science.

1. The Pattern of Anti-intellectualism

The revolt against intellect has taken a variety of forms. Some of its leaders have been mystics or transcendentalists. Others have been venerators of authority or tradition. Still others have been materialists and skeptics who have denied all or nearly all competence to human reason and have demanded that philosophy be grounded exclusively on verifiable facts and experiences. Typical of this last group are the Positivists, whose chief tenets were discussed in a previous chapter. The Positivists maintain that knowledge which comes from the sciences is the only reliable knowledge we have, and that problems lying beyond its scope must be abandoned as insoluble. Such views were especially characteristic of the celebrated Italian Positivist, Vilfredo Pareto. Yet in spite of his esteem for the sciences, Pareto had such a low opinion of man's intellect that he considered the great mass of human beings incapable of any genuine thinking. Practically all they ever do, he contended, is to "rationalize" their own instincts, prejudices, and urges. Only in the minds of the talented few is there any progress in enlightenment. Among the masses the quantity of superstition is almost constant. It never diminishes, but merely changes its form. So contemptuous of the human intellect was Pareto that he could not even conceive of science as a guide to action. "For purposes of knowing," he wrote, "logico-experimental science is the only thing of value." For purposes of doing, he averred, "it is of much greater importance to follow the lead of sentiments." [1]

The noted founder of syndicalism, Georges Sorel, was another who emphasized non-logical beliefs as guides to action. Though he developed no elaborate philosophy of truth, his theory of knowledge was similar to that of Pareto. He was a hardheaded materialist, rejecting religion and social and political idealism as the stuff of which dreams are made. As the mainspring of action, however, he glorified the "myth," which could have no real basis in fact but must rest upon hope and wish-fulfillment. He anticipated the Freudian emphasis upon instinctual behavior and the importance of the unconscious mind. He also foreshadowed Pareto's theory of "residues" and "derivations." Though he despised the average man as a mere sheep, fit only to be a follower, and professed his belief in an élite of natural leaders, he spurned the idea that its members should be intellectuals. "What more horrible government could there be," he asked, "than that of academicians?" [2] Before World War I he became associated for a time with the Action française, a little band of hate-mongering royalists. He apparently saw nothing contradictory between monarchism and his working-class philosophy of syndicalism, though he eventually repudiated the methods of his royalist allies. Later he expressed his admiration for both Mussolini and Lenin, but his death in 1922 precluded the formation of more definite attitudes toward Fascism and Communism.

The two most famous teachers who helped to shape the men-

---

[1] *The Mind and Society.* New York, Harcourt, 1935, III, 1241–42.
[2] Quoted by Richard Humphrey, *Georges Sorel: Prophet without Honor.* Cambridge, Mass., Harvard University Press, 1951, p. 125.

tality of Sorel were Henri Bergson and Émile Durkheim. Bergson was classified and discussed in the preceding chapter as a romanticist. Durkheim reflected similar attitudes, but he leaned farther in the direction of minimizing the competence of individual intellect. He was born in 1858 at Épinal, France, of Jewish parents. After completing his education at the College d'Épinal, the Lycée Louis-le-Grand in Paris, and the École Normale, he taught for five years in French lycées. In 1887 he was appointed lecturer in sociology at the University of Bordeaux, and nine years later Professor of Social Science. In 1898 he founded the *Année Sociologique* and became its editor. The last years of his life were spent as Professor of the Science of Education at the University of Paris. He vigorously supported the cause of Dreyfus during the celebrated *affaire* of the 1890's and did zealous propaganda work for the French government during World War I.

In his writings Durkheim frequently gave the impression of being a staunch defender of the intellectual approach. He regarded society as a natural phenomenon to be studied with the same objectivity that physical scientists would demonstrate in studying matter and energy. He urged his followers to eradicate from their minds "all preconceptions" and warned them of the insidious nature of prejudices, which permit only a limited vision of reality without our being aware of the restriction. He declared also that he ascribed a "considerable role" to reason and that he had a high regard for science.[3] But it is necessary to understand what he meant by these terms. He was scarcely interested in either as a function of the individual mind. "Science," he avowed, "is not an individual; it is a social thing, pre-eminently impersonal." And reason, properly understood, "is simply science, the science of morality."[4]

Durkheim's purpose in arguing thus was apparently to give to society the predominant role in cultural progress. Society, he maintained, is the source of all the innovations that have been

---

[3] *The Rules of Sociological Method,* trans. S. A. Solovay and J. H. Mueller. Glencoe, Ill., The Free Press, 1950, p. 31; *Sociology and Philosophy,* trans. D. F. Pocock. Glencoe, Ill., The Free Press, 1953, pp. 20–21, 66–67.
[4] *Sociology and Philosophy,* pp. 66–67.

produced in the course of history. He believed in a kind of social "thinking" that is much more important than the ratiocinations of the individual. Society creates "representations," which result from the action and reaction between individual minds but are not derived directly from them. Each "representation" is a synthesis of group thinking. It is the work of the group, and therefore surpasses the work of the individual as the whole surpasses the part. "No doubt each individual contains a part, but the whole is found in no one." [5] What Durkheim had in mind by "representations" was apparently the traditions, customs, and ideals of a given society. He was using the term "society" with essentially the same meaning and purpose that Edmund Burke ascribed to "species." Just as Burke maintained that the individual is foolish and only the species is wise, so Durkheim regarded the thinking of the individual as superficial and ephemeral. The traditions and regulations of society alone had the wisdom and depth to be of lasting value.

In so far as Durkheim's theory was indebted to earlier sources, it owed more to the philosophies of Rousseau and Kant than to any others. His adulation of society, for example, was as great as Rousseau's veneration of the state. Apart from society, the individual would be nothing. He derives his very existence as a civilized being from association with his fellows. Civilization is the result of cooperation of men in society through successive generations. "Society made it, preserves it, and transmits it to individuals." [6] Society has a will of its own, wholly apart from the wills of its members. Society thinks, feels, and acts quite differently from the way in which its members would do if they were isolated persons. Most important of all, society is the creator of morality. It determines the standards of right and wrong and produces the sense of duty and obligation as a sanction to enforce them. The individual has nothing to do with the creation of morality, except perhaps to help the age in which he lives "to be more aware of itself, its needs, and its sentiments." But Durkheim rejected the idea that the individual has the right to oppose his own reason or conscience to the collective will of

[5] *Ibid.*, p. 26.
[6] *Ibid.*, p. 54.

society. He had no sympathy with Thoreau's doctrine that one man in the right is worth more than a majority in error, or with the thesis of Ibsen, "A minority may be right—a majority is always wrong." He praised Socrates for expressing, "more clearly than his judges, the morality suited to his time," but he lauded him more highly for bowing in the end to the sovereign will of society.[7]

For Durkheim the function of society was of such transcendent importance that he exalted it into a religion. Society in his mind was not simply the instrument of God; it *was* God. "The believer bows before his God," he wrote, "because it is from God that he believes that he holds his being, particularly his mental being, his soul. We have the same reasons for experiencing this feeling before the collective." He saw in the Divinity "only society transfigured and symbolically expressed." And as Kant insisted that a belief in God was absolutely necessary as a foundation for the moral law, so Durkheim argued for a society "specifically distinct from individuals," since otherwise morality would have no object and duty no roots.[8] In taking this position he left little room for the exercise of either conscience or intellect. The ultimate effect was the debasement of both.

But Durkheim as a prophet of anti-intellectualism did not come within target distance of his older compatriot, Gustave Le Bon (1841–1931). Though Le Bon was trained as a physician and had read widely in theoretical physics, archaeology, and anthropology, he disparaged not only the intellectual powers of individuals but of crowds as well, and found in national and racial characteristics the keys to the progress of civilization. Born in 1841, he lived through ninety years of revolutions, crises, and wars. Perhaps such events as the Franco-Prussian War, the downfall of Napoleon III, the Paris Commune, and the Dreyfus Affair colored his perspective. Whatever the source of his prejudices, he seems never to have wanted for honors and friends. At his death he was Director of the Library of Scientific Philosophy and Professor of Psychology and Allied Sciences at the University of Paris. He numbered among his admirers President

[7] *Ibid.,* pp. 64–65.
[8] *Ibid.,* pp. 51–52, 73.

Sadi Carnot of France and Theodore Roosevelt and Charles Dawes in the United States.

Le Bon's fame derived primarily from his study of the psychology of crowds. He defined a crowd as an aggregate of people dominated by a passion for the achievement of some object. Crowds have characteristics absolutely different from those of the individuals who compose them. Le Bon believed in a crowd mentality inferior to that of the average member when acting alone. It is not a conscious mentality, but it grows out of a fusion of the subconscious minds of the various participants. It is in no sense a product of rational thinking but is a composite of primitive, subliminal urges and desires. As a consequence, crowds are capable of extremes of behavior which their members acting as individuals would scarcely dream of attempting. There is no excess of savagery or fiendishness to which men united in a crowd will not descend, even though as individuals they may be cultivated gentlemen. On the other hand, mob behavior is not always bestial and criminal; it may even be heroic. On occasions, crowds have been known to execute deeds of courage or foolhardiness which individuals would shrink from attempting. The point of significance is that men in the mass respond to blind, instinctive promptings that lie beneath the surface in every human being. When acting alone the individual keeps these urgings under restraint, for fear of social penalties. The members of a mob, however, because of numerical strength and the boldness acquired from the example of others, feel strong enough to throw off these restraints. They then act as if hypnotized and yield to any savage suggestions that may be made to them by leaders of the moment.

Though Le Bon hinted at a kind of collective sadism as a characteristic of mob behavior, he appears not to have understood the phenomenon completely. Although he pointed out, in general terms, the irrational nature of crowd responses, he failed to perceive the sexual excitement which appears to run through lynching mobs when dragging naked bodies through the streets, inflicting mutilations, etc. Crowds, he claimed, are never swayed by reason but by rumors, legends, superstitions, hatreds, and fears. The plain fact, he avowed, is that men in the mass never shape their conduct on the basis of reason. Even the decisions of an assembly composed of individuals of distinction "are not sensibly superior to the decisions that would be adopted by a gathering of imbeciles." The explanation of this is that men "can only bring to bear in common on the work in hand those mediocre qualities which are the birthright of every average individual. In crowds it is stupidity and not mother-wit that is accumulated." [9] What he seems to have meant is that when a number of persons of varying backgrounds come together, the principal element each has in common with the rest is ignorance of everything outside of his own special interest. Ignorance thus comes to be the dominant factor shaping group decisions. So serious did Le Bon consider the irrationality of crowds that he almost despaired of the future of civilization. Civilization, he argued, has always been the work of a small intellectual aristocracy. "Crowds are only powerful for destruction." They act like microbes which hasten the dissolution of enfeebled bodies. The moment a civilization begins to decay, "it is always the masses that bring about its downfall." [10]

Le Bon discovered in the psychology of crowds the answer to numerous political and social questions. It informed him why so much of history was a tale told by an idiot—why fantasy, delusion, and superstition bulked so large in shaping the course of human affairs. It accounted for the fanaticism, irrationality, and intolerance of religions, for such "revolting insanities," for example, as the doctrine of predestination. It conveyed to his mind a clear picture of revolutions as outbursts of mob frenzy, with restraints thrown to the winds, and with leaders obsessed by fear attempting to cover their weakness by inciting the masses to violence. Revolutions, he taught, are wholly irrational movements. They swing from one extreme to another, and in the end accomplish nothing. The gains apparently produced by the French Revolution were really accomplished by the progress of civilization. Governments are not overthrown; instead, they "commit suicide." "The more we study the history of revolutions the more we discover that they change practically nothing but

[9] *The Crowd.* London, Ernest Benn, 1896, p. 29.
[10] *Ibid.,* p. 18.

the label." [11] Kings and ministers have more symbolic than genuine significance, and their downfall means little. The real rulers of a country, according to Le Bon, are its administrators, its heads of departments and government clerks. These officials, though anonymous, are perennial and constitute a kind of secret power in the state. Because of their knowledge and experience, everyone must defer to them. Without their efficiency and their stabilizing influence, government could not exist.

Le Bon had a low opinion of things political, expecially when controlled by the masses. He placed reform movements like socialism in the same category with Buddhism, Islam, Protestantism, and Jacobinism. All are the progeny of fanaticism, and they obey a logic which has no affinity with reason. Should socialism triumph tomorrow, he said, it would soon prove as intolerant as the Inquisition and the Reign of Terror. The explanation, he maintained, lies in the fact that the masses cannot think. They respond to animal instincts which commonly find expression in acts of cruelty and vengeance. The leaders of the crowd are no better. In fact, they emerge from the mass chiefly because they are more strongly charged with mystic frenzy. Many of them are criminal types, the dregs of civilization. Eager to kill and to plunder, they ally themselves with any movement which seems to offer them opportunities for action. "All the revolutionaries, all the founders of religious or political leagues, have constantly counted on their support." [12]

In addition to the criminal types, the waste products of civilization, every society contains restless and discontented spirits, always ready to rebel against the established order. They are driven by nothing more altruistic than the mere love of revolt; and if, by some miracle, all of their objectives could be realized, they would simply revolt again. Many of them are madmen who turn their frenzy upon themselves when they cannot express it in other ways. But leaders do not make the mob; instead, they are made by it. And the divine right of the mob is rapidly taking the place of the divine right of kings. Le Bon saw with increasing

[11] *The Psychology of Revolution,* trans. Bernard Miall. New York, Putnam, 1913, p. 54.
[12] *Ibid.,* p. 100.

dismay the assertion by the masses of more and more claims to
privilege and power. He thought they would be satisfied with
nothing less than plunging society back into primitive communism. He accused them of demanding the nationalization of
factories, railways, mines, and the soil and "the equal distribution of all products." [13] He overlooked entirely the fact that the
masses, even in his own country, were about as firmly attached
to private ownership as were any of their rulers. Even among
the Jacobins and other radicals of the French Revolution, few
indeed clamored for socialization. What most of them wanted
was not the abolition of private ownership but an extension of
it, so that every adult male might become the proprietor of a
little farm or place of business. In Le Bon's own time the
tendency of French Socialists ran strongly in the direction of
Revisionism, with objectives not markedly different from those
of many bourgeois reformers.

Equally contemptuous and fearful of the masses was Le Bon's
German contemporary Oswald Spengler (1880–1936). Born at
Blankenburg in Saxony, Spengler attended the Latin school at
Halle and the universities of Halle, Munich, and Berlin. After
several unsuccessful attempts at writing poetry, he became a
teacher in the gymnasia of Düsseldorf, Hamburg, and Munich,
and eventually rose to be an *Oberlehrer* or principal. At the age
of thirty-four he completed his monumental *Decline of the West*,
but was unable to find a publisher. When finally issued in 1918,
it won loud acclaim from the futilitarian and pessimistic generation of postwar Germans. There was enough cynicism in
many other countries, also, to give the work an international
appeal, and it was translated into numerous languages. Though
punctuated with smug assumptions of Nordic superiority, it contained a wealth of erudition, to say nothing of original theories
and interpretations. Its author conceived of history as a succession of cultures, each with its stages of birth, development,
decay, and death resembling the morphology of living creatures.
He discovered Western civilization to be undergoing a slow decline which had set in about 1100. This decline, in his opinion,
was comparable to that which had overtaken Rome after the

[13] *The Crowd*, p. 16.

time of Augustus and reflected the same influences of urbanization, skepticism, expansionism, and the rise of the masses under
the leadership of demagogues and eventually of tyrants. Though
Spengler agreed with many of the basic tenets of National Socialism, he did not become a Nazi. He despised Hitler and his
colleagues as vulgar upstarts, and he regarded fascism and democracy with about equal contempt. If there was one system he
hated more than others, it was Soviet Communism, which he
considered the supreme embodiment of mass ignorance and
demagogic despotism.

The political and social philosophy of Spengler awakens
memories of the teachings of Burke and of Nietzsche. Like the
former he worshiped ancestry and tradition, hated individualism
and humanism, and venerated property and inheritance. In common with Nietzsche he glorified war and the will to power, acclaimed man as a beast of prey, and demanded a transvaluation
of values. Unlike Nietzsche, however, he had no use for romanticism. He condemned it as "just as much an expression of rationalist arrogance as are Idealism and Materialism." [14] In his
view, romanticists were sentimentalists and weaklings impelled
by morbid ideas of reforming society, which they considered too
masculine and healthy. He would have no truck with anything
so soft and womanish. Life is war, he taught, and the race which
survives is one which obeys its instincts to fight and conquer.

Except for his worship of tradition, certain refinements of
aristocracy, and a kind of *Bushido*, or code of honor among war-
riors, Spengler revered the law of the jungle. He justified slaughter and subjugation of weaker peoples as convenient avenues to
power, dismissing moralists and pacifists as simply beasts of
prey with broken teeth. He stressed the importance of fecundity
for both nations and individuals. He deplored extinction of the
desire for permanence of the family and described an abundance
of children as the chief sign of a healthy race. The test of the
greatness of a nation, he declared, is the speed with which it can
replace itself. An expanding population is the true foundation of
national glory and epitomizes the Nordic yearning for collec-

[14] *The Hour of Decision,* trans. C. F. Atkinson. New York, Knopf, 1934,
p. 11.

tive immortality. But such expansion, he argued, should not be
accomplished by an increase in the span of life. A severe selection process is needed to weed out the unfit. For this reason
further advances in medical science should not be encouraged,
lest disease as nature's instrument of natural selection be rendered impotent. He deliberately equated barbarism with strength
of race.

That a philosopher with such strong convictions of ruthlessness
and of crude animalism should have despised rationalism is not
surprising. He really went farther and denounced all forms of
intellectualism. He could have agreed with the dictum of
Rousseau that "a thinking man is a depraved animal"; [15] or
with the cynicism of Justice Holmes when he wondered "if
cosmically an idea is any more important than the bowels." [16]
Spengler denounced rationalism as, at bottom, nothing but criticism, "and the critic is the reverse of a creator . . . his work is
artificial and lifeless, and when brought into contact with real
life, it *kills*." Modern intellectualism he described as a "weed
of the pavements," a spurious, ephemeral thing, generated by
rootless mobs.[17] It has nothing in common with the deep wisdom
of old peasant families, who obey their instincts, honor their
traditions, and respect their superiors. Upon the latter foundations exclusively must culture rest; for, Spengler insisted, culture
is a growth, reflecting the slow accumulation of racial experience. It is never the hothouse product of urban intellectuals
excogitating artificial theories from a shallow background of
devitalized knowledge. "Ever in History it is life and life only—
race-quality, the triumph of the will-to-power—and not the victory of truths, discoveries, or money that signifies." History has
always sacrificed truth and justice to might and race, "and passed
the doom of death" upon peoples who regarded truth as more
important than deeds, justice more important than power.[18]
These frank avowals of an anti-intellectual viewpoint appearing

[15] *A Discourse on the Origin of Inequality.* Everyman Library edition, New
York, Dutton, 1913, p. 181.
[16] Mark DeWolfe Howe, ed., *The Holmes-Pollock Letters.* Cambridge,
Mass., Harvard University Press, 1941, II, 22.
[17] *The Hour of Decision,* pp. 10–11, 88.
[18] *The Decline of the West.* New York, Knopf, 1934, II, 507.

at the very end of Spengler's most erudite work, *The Decline of the West*, seem especially significant.

The revolt against intellect invariably sweeps its adherents into the mainstream of anti-democratic thought. Such was the case with Spengler. He had no sympathy either for the wisdom of the majority or for the rights of the individual. He defined "liberal" constitutions as "nothing but anarchy become a habit," and democracy, parliamentarism, and national self-government as "the non-existence of a true State." Even a republic was nothing but the "ruin" of a monarchy that had given itself up. In place of popular sovereignty he called for submission of the many to leaders "who feel themselves born and called to be masters." He declared that a nation "can no more govern itself than an army can lead itself." Both have to be governed, and as long as their members possess healthy instincts, "they will desire to be governed." [19] Spengler was especially caustic in his references to democracy in the United States, which he regarded as the quintessence of the forces of anarchy. In America, he affirmed, there is neither a nation nor a state, but simply a population of "trappers" wandering from town to town in an unscrupulous dollar-hunt. No American obeys a law unless he is too stupid or weak to defy it. In spite of superficial differences, the United States and Soviet Russia are almost identical twins. Both have their dictatorships, which prescribe and regulate every detail of the citizens' lives, what they shall wear and what they shall think as well as what they shall read and what amusements they shall be permitted to enjoy. It mattered little in Spengler's view that the dictator in one case was the Party, and in the other, society. Both countries are alike also, he contended, in their economic organization. In one as in the other great trusts standardize and control every detail of production and marketing. He completely ignored the fact that the trust in the United States is a private institution and may on occasion be a power behind the government, instead of being an agent of the government or of the Party, as in the land of the Soviets.

One of the great obsessions of Spengler's life was the threat of world revolution. He envisaged this threat in two forms—the

[19] *The Hour of Decision,* pp. 34, 36, 59.

menace of a white world-revolution and the danger of a colored world-revolution. With respect to the white revolution, he followed quite closely the conclusions of Le Bon when the latter referred to the dregs of society as constituting a seething reservoir of envy and discontent. Spengler described the white revolutionaries as "abortions, ship-wrecked academicians, criminals and prostitutes, loiterers and the feeble-minded" uniting in opposition to the "great and noble world" of their betters.[20] But he did not stop with such billingsgate. He went on to denounce labor leaders, advocates of the forty-hour week, proponents of social insurance, and reformers who encourage the masses to expect luxury wages with as little work as possible. He distorted Marxism by representing its followers as interested exclusively in the welfare of manual laborers.

Though Spengler professed a dislike for industrial and financial capitalism, he defended property as a necessity of a ripe culture. Wealth, he said, is not the cause or basis of superiority but the *result* and *expression* of it. But the kind of wealth he had in mind was not the paper wealth of the stockmarket speculator, but property in the sense of old and permanent possessions, inherited from ancestors or accumulated by hard and devoted work and cherished and increased to be passed on to descendants. This idea, a favorite among arch-conservatives, enabled Spengler to attack both the proletariat and the finance capitalists as conspirators in a revolution against the men of modest possessions and pride in ancestry, whom he regarded as the real conservators of social values.

In Spengler's eyes the white world-revolution was essentially *class war;* the colored revolution was, of course, *race war.* But he had a peculiar conception of race. In the "colored" population of the world he included not only Negroes, Malays, and Mongolians but the Islamic nations, the peoples of India, and the Russians. Russia, he argued, has degenerated into an Asiatic, "Mongolian" state. The colored revolution, he taught, has been in progress for a long time. It began in the eighteenth century when the British recruited American Indians to attack, burn, and scalp rebellious white colonists, and when the Jacobins mobilized

[20] *Ibid.,* p. 93.

Haitian Negroes in the crusade for the Rights of Man. It reached a climax in World War I when colored men from all over the world were marshaled on European soil to fight for whites against whites. They went home convinced of their strength and of the weakness of the Caucasians. It was not Germany that lost World War I; "the West lost it when it lost the respect of the coloured races." [21] The great danger henceforth, he asserted, is that the two revolutions may be merged, that class war and race war may be joined. The result would be the devastation of everything of value in white civilization. To prevent such a catastrophe nothing less than a belligerent stand by the finest representatives of Nordic vitality will suffice. Spengler believed that Germany was the nation best cast for this role. For history had used Germany sparingly in the great wars and overseas adventures since 1500. She had therefore been able to conserve her precious blood and energy. Had Spengler lived to see the defeat of Germany at the end of World War II, he would probably have sunk completely into a slough of despond.

2. Existentialism

Among the most meaningful and arresting philosophical attitudes of modern times are those classified under the name Existentialism. Germinating early in the nineteenth century, Existentialism attracted little notice until the 1930's and gained no wide acceptance until World War II. Since then it has become especially popular in France and in Germany. The philosophy derives major significance from the fact that it epitomizes many of the dominant intellectual trends of the modern age. It brings together the romanticism, the nihilism, the skepticism, the pragmatism, and even something of the utopianism of the past hundred years. It is a salvationist philosophy in the sense that it places primary emphasis on the need of man to find an escape from a world that has become unendurable. It is a nihilist philosophy to the extent that it denies all values except those created by the individual for his own satisfaction. It is a relativist and skeptical philosophy for the reason that it rejects

[21] *Ibid.*, p. 210.

all absolutes, in the realm of truth as well as in the realm of morality. Its exponents seem almost determined to reduce the cosmos to a vacuum, to make a god out of Nothing. They conceive of man as utterly alone in a vast and indifferent universe. Modern science has completely divested him of the hopes and consolations that sustained his forebears. Yet he is not helpless. He need not succumb to despair. He can save himself by "involvement," or participation in human affairs, by scorning defeatism and resignation to fate, and by making as much as he can out of a miserable and meaningless life. Notwithstanding their rejection of eternal values, the Existentialists, like Bertrand Russell, recognize a kind of Promethean defiance and refusal to surrender to fear and despair as the supreme values of all.

It is not difficult to accord Existentialism a prominent place in the revolt against reason. Few philosophies except those of a strongly mystical or romantic character have been so thoroughly anti-intellectual. Man, according to the Existentialists, is a "passionate," not a thinking animal. Truth, therefore, rests entirely on a subjective basis. One's so-called rational conclusions are the product almost exclusively of his feelings, prejudices, emotions, and experiences. There is no absolute truth; indeed there is not even any truth common to two or more individuals. The emotions, prejudices, and experiences of A will be quite different from those of B. As a consequence, A's truth will be the summation of the life feelings of A, which can never duplicate the life feelings of B.

But in referring to life feelings and experiences, the Existentialist by no means implies that life has meaning or significance. The life of a human being has no more inherent significance than the life of a snake or a toad. It has only that meaning which the individual himself chooses to give it. No principles of right and wrong, truth and error, exist independently of individuals or apart from their life experiences. Values are created by the particular men who choose to live by them and have no significance for anyone else. Some writers have assumed that Existentialists exalt freedom as a goal and ideal of human endeavor. Actually, most of them regard freedom as an essential characteristic of life, a source not of benefit or happiness but of anguish. True, some of them distinguished themselves as leaders of one of the most notable crusades for freedom in modern times, the Resistance of the 1940's against German tyranny in France. But such activities may be regarded as examples of "involvement" reflecting the individual's determination to vindicate his self-respect.

The origins of Existentialism are commonly traced to a Danish theologian of the early nineteenth century, Sören Kierkegaard (1813–1855). The son of a father of stern religious temperament, Kierkegaard was sent to the University of Copenhagen to be educated for the clergy. Though he preferred the study of literature and philosophy, he was finally graduated in theology. But he never took orders, preferring to remain a perpetual student. His inheritance of an ample fortune obviated the necessity of his earning a living. Throughout his life he was obsessed with a sense of the guilt of his father, in which he believed that he shared. The nature of the guilt is unknown, but it hung like an albatross around his neck. Undoubtedly it was at least partly responsible for the qualities of gloom and despair that permeated his philosophy. Though he continued in love with an estimable young lady for many years, he finally broke the engagement, partly because of his sense of guilt, but also because he feared she would never understand the unique role he conceived for himself as the exemplar of a transcendental morality. His chief work, which he entitled *Either-Or,* was published in 1843.

Though Kierkegaard may not have had a primary interest in theology, he had a profound concern for the fate of the Christian religion. He considered the Christianity of his time degenerate; it had become formalized and mechanical and too closely dependent upon the support of the state. But more deplorable in his viewpoint, it had become excessively intellectual. Its leaders were wasting their time threshing over the dead straw of dogmatics and attempting to prove the Christian mysteries by reason. Nothing could be more vain and worthless. Neither Christian truth nor any other, according to Kierkegaard, is a product of reason. Truth is subjective and grows out of the deepest longings of the human heart. It is not learned objectively like a lesson in geography. The existence of God can neither be proved nor disproved. The belief in Christ as a God-man who died on the Cross for the redemption of the sins of the human race is an absurdity, from the logical standpoint. Why then do men believe it? According to the Danish philosopher, it is because of "despair." It is only because they have exhausted every other resource, and have nothing else to cling to, that they really come to believe, truly and sincerely, in Christ as their Savior. Deep in their hearts they know that such a belief alone can give meaning to their lives. Science and logic have nothing to do with it.

Like mystics and romantics in general, Kierkegaard had a weak appreciation of the intellectual progress of his time. The advancement of knowledge was making more headway than he realized. As it gained dominion over the minds of men it did not increase their despair, but brought them confidence. Even when the dolorous events of the twentieth century blighted men's hopes, their despair did not turn them necessarily to a belief in Christ. On the contrary, many of them seemed to prefer the tribal deities of nationalism, of race, and of class. It is perhaps significant that one of Kierkegaard's own followers of a later generation, Martin Heidegger, found the siren appeal of the Nazis too enticing to resist.

Though most of the leading Existentialists of the present day are atheists, the debt they owe to their Danish precursor is immense. They reject, of course, the imperious necessity of a belief in Christ, but they accept *in toto* Kierkegaard's theory of the subjectivity of truth. His doctrines were revived in Germany after World War I and were carefully cultivated by Edmund Husserl and Martin Heidegger. By these men they were passed on to Jean-Paul Sartre, who studied in Germany in 1933–1934. Destined to become the leading apostle of contemporary Existentialism, Sartre was born in Paris in 1905. Graduating from the École Normale Supérieur with highest honors, he became a teacher of philosophy in a lycée in Le Havre and later at the Lycée Condorcet in Paris. His first novel, *Nausea,* represented a synthesis of the ideas of Husserl and Heidegger. Sartre rose to fame in 1943 when he wrote a play entitled *The Flies.* Published under the very noses of the German conquerors, it was an eloquent defense of rebellion in the cause of freedom. In the same year he also published *Being and Not Being,* his major work on

Existentialism. Though the name of the philosophy was invented by Kierkegaard, Sartre, perhaps, has contributed the most succinct definition. What all Existentialists have in common, he says, "is simply the fact that they believe that existence comes before essence—or, if you will, that we must begin from the subjective." [22]

It should be evident from the discussion thus far that Sartre and his colleagues in the Existentialist movement do not seek to explain the world or to solve any of the abstruse problems of metaphysics. They strive rather to explain man and to help him find ways of facing his world and of making his life endurable. Sartre says that "By existentialism we mean a doctrine which makes human life possible, and in addition, declares that every truth and every action implies a human setting and a human subjectivity." [23] Existentialists are deeply perturbed by the increasing depersonalization of man. They see him degraded into an object among objects, a mere speck of dust in a cosmic machine. For this degradation they hold not only science and technology responsible, but the whole complex of modern industrialism, to say nothing of mechanist and rationalist philosophies. As one of their distinguished interpreters expresses it, Existentialism is "a reaction of the philosophy of man against the excesses of the philosophy of ideas and the philosophy of things." [24] The Existentialists propose to rescue man from his status as a puppet of Fate to which the determinist philosophies of the modern world have condemned him, and restore him to the level of a free and responsible human being. They do not believe that man's nature is made for him; instead, they go back to the more primitive doctrine that man makes himself. He is not a fungus or a cauliflower, rigidly determined by the conditions of his environment. He can *choose* and make of himself what he purposes to be.

In stressing the freedom and responsibility of the individual, the Existentialists do not claim they can make man happy. The most they can promise is that they will give him dignity. By rais-

[22] "Existentialism: Jean-Paul Sartre," in Morton White, *The Age of Analysis.* New York, Houghton Mifflin, 1955, p. 122.

[23] *Existentialism.* New York, Philosophical Library, 1947, p. 12.

[24] Emmanuel Mounier, *Existentialist Philosophies.* London, Rockliff, 1948, p. 2.

ing him from the level of a plaything of Fate, they hope to endow him with pride and self-respect. They recognize, however, that freedom brings with it penalties of forlornness and anguish. Man is forlorn because he is alone in the universe. According to Sartre, God does not exist; and even such Christian Existentialists as Karl Jaspers and Gabriel Marcel apparently do not believe in a providential, intervening God. Man is therefore entirely on his own. He was not created by God, and he has no God to instruct his conscience or to provide him with a moral law. The individual is completely free to make his own choices, and he cannot blame anyone but himself for his sins and his failures. The anguish which accompanies freedom grows out of the fact that the individual, in every decision he makes, realizes that he is deciding not merely for himself but is setting an example for others. He knows that he must act as if the whole human race had its eyes fixed upon what he is doing and regulated its conduct accordingly. It is interesting that Sartre, who criticizes Kant for teaching that man must be treated as an end and not as a means, should nevertheless adopt what practically amounts to the Kantian imperative of always acting "as if the maxim of thy action were to become by thy will a universal law of nature." [25]

Sartre occasionally writes as if he regards freedom as an objective value worthy of and for itself, but it seems more probable that he regards freedom as a quality inherent in human nature. It is an instinct which should be released and asserted. It is what distinguishes man from a rooted vegetable or from a sponge incapable of separating itself from the bottom of the sea. As Sartre has asserted, "man is condemned to be free. Condemned, because he did not create himself, yet is nevertheless at liberty, and from the moment that he is thrown into this world he is responsible for everything he does." [26] Why then should the individual be concerned for anyone's freedom but his own? Because he discovers, according to Sartre, that his own freedom depends on the freedom of others, and that the freedom of others depends on his freedom. He therefore mounts barricades or fights battles to

[25] Immanuel Kant, *Critique of Practical Reason*. New York, Longmans, 1909, p. 39.
[26] "Existentialism," *op. cit.*, p. 128.

gain freedom for all. But freedom, in Sartre's judgment, is physical and social and is synonymous with action. There is no such thing as a pure intellectual or moral freedom. He despises the so-called freedom of Buddhists and Stoics, which expresses itself in quietism. True liberty requires "involvement," participation in the affairs of the world. Only in this way can the individual realize his own nature and attain that dignity which belongs to him as a man.

The political theory of Existentialism was deeply influenced, if not actually created, by the conditions of the German conquest and Occupation of France. During the long night from 1940 to 1945 the French people suffered from deprivation and humiliation. Young intellectuals who joined the Resistance began to probe deeply into the meaning of life and to ask themselves questions as to how they could justify the roles they were playing. They rebelled against the apparent futility of existence and groped for some formula or principle that would enable them to meet suffering and danger bravely and nobly and with respect for their comrades. They became increasingly preoccupied with torture and death. The very cruelty of the enemy, Sartre wrote, forced them to ask themselves questions which one never considers in time of peace. And the foremost question of all was: "If they torture me, shall I be able to keep silent?" They were thus brought to a realization of the most basic of all issues—liberty, and solidarity with one's fellows. These issues, they maintained, are the epitome of the deepest knowledge a man can have of himself. "For the secret of a man is not his Oedipus complex or his inferiority complex: it is the limit of his own liberty, his capacity for resisting suffering and death." [27]

Sartre's emphasis upon liberty and solidarity made him a socialist and brought him at one time very close to Communism. He tended to equate liberty with equality, with a leveling-down of all men to the status of the proletariat. He recognized that to achieve such a goal it would be necessary to destroy all privileges; but he did not shrink from this conclusion, for he regarded privileges as having been imposed by force and custom. Even

[27] Marjorie Grene, *Dreadful Freedom*. Chicago, University of Chicago Press, 1948, p. 98.

most of the so-called rights, especially those related to property, are really privileges in disguise. For Sartre the only tenable objective is to merge all of humanity into a single mass, to permit the oppressed classes to absorb and assimilate their oppressors. Only in this way can a real solidarity of the human race be accomplished, with all men united in a single species. But Sartre is perhaps the most curious socialist who ever lived. He could not help admiring the Marxists for their zeal in the cause of Resistance, but he repudiates several of their most basic assumptions. He is a humanist who teaches that the universe is nothing apart from man himself, and he has no tolerance for the Marxist subjection of the individual to an omnipotent party or proletarian state. He rejects the materialism of Marx on the ground that it is destructive of liberty. It robs man of his right to free criticism, the right to facts, the right to pursue truth in his own way. In its dialectical form it provides a mechanical type of social evolution in which individual will and action count for almost nothing.

Equally significant is the fact that Sartre rejects the utopianism of the Marxists. He has no belief in progress or utopian dreams of some future millennium. He has said that he does not know what will come out of the Russian revolution. He thinks that the proletariat plays a more significant role in the land of the Soviets than it does in any other, but he refuses to admit that a classless society is inevitable. He does not agree that the triumph of socialism anywhere is bound to occur. He says merely that he will do all in his power to make it occur. Beyond that he can count on nothing. At the same time, he professes a philosophy of *transcendence* which seems at least faintly reminiscent of Trotsky's doctrine of permanent revolution. Sartre conceives the individual as perpetually dissatisfied with his current situation and as constantly striving to triumph over it and rise above it. One of Sartre's critics sees his revolutionary as a pitiable creature whose essential nature demands that he destroy the values he has created, and "that he go beyond the very liberty for which he has lived his life and risked his death to something beyond liberty itself—and beyond that again, and so forever." [28] Sartre, however, apparently does not believe that an all-encompassing free-

[28] Grene, *op. cit.*, p. 115.

dom can ever be achieved. Given the complexity of society and of the nature of men, there will always be some situations requiring transcendence. Moreover, he points out that "it is not true that a free man cannot hope to be liberated. For he is not free and bound in respect to the same things." [29]

Sartre did not finally break with the Communists until after their suppression of the Hungarian revolt in November 1956. That none of their previous examples of tyranny had impressed him greatly is surprising indeed. Perhaps he believed that the brutality inflicted by Russians upon other Russians was a special case. At any rate, it did not keep him from expressing his sympathy for Soviet Communism and acclaiming it as the chief liberating force in the modern world. As late as 1954 he was one of the speakers at the Soviet-sponsored World Peace Council in East Berlin. He seems to have been only dimly aware of the fundamental conflict between his own philosophical assumptions and Marxist-Leninist doctrine. For he was an arch-individualist, and he continued to preach that Existentialism and humanism are practically synonymous. It would be difficult to imagine any two conceptions more diametrically opposed than Sartre's contention that "man makes himself" and the Marxist doctrine that man is made by his environment. Since Sartre's doctrine implies that human nature is fixed, it leaves little room for progress or improvement. Salvation can consist only in learning to face bravely and with dignity the anguish and tragedy of life. By contrast, the Marxist conception implies that all of man's troubles can be made to disappear with the proper transformation of his environment. How it would be possible to bridge the gulf between such contradictions, Sartre has never told us. Perhaps he feels that his gratitude to the Communists for their loyalty to the Resistance was a sufficient answer. Or possibly in his pro-Communist period he was really more interested in depriving the upper classes of their privileges than he was in crusading for the freedom and dignity of the individual.

That philosophies expressing a revolt against intellect should be propagated widely in the twentieth century is a startling fact.

[29] *Literary and Philosophical Essays.* London, Rider, 1955, p. 229.

It is not, however, a unique phenomenon. Cynicism attracted its first converts during the Golden Age of Athens, and Romanticism germinated in the midst of the Enlightenment. Mystical and anti-rationalist philosophies commonly make their appearance after a considerable period of confidence in the powers of intellect. Sooner or later some people get the idea that such confidence has been carried too far, and a reaction sets in. Besides, certain powerful forces are always at work bolstering this kind of reaction. The supporters of organized religion become easily alarmed over too much dependence upon intellect. Rulers, especially those interested in maintaining authoritarian government, are bound to see in intellectual supremacy a threat to their own power. Individuals and groups concerned with preserving the economic *status quo* regard an unrestricted development of reason and science as likely to call into question their privileged position and their right to collect profits from the labor of others.

Still another conception plays its part in advancing the cause of the anti-intellectuals. This is the notion that reason and science are feeble instruments upon which to rely. They give an inadequate or distorted picture of reality and provide no sufficient means of solving life's problems. Only our instincts and emotions can give us true guidance on matters of vital importance. It is a philosophy summed up in the popular saying, "The heart hath its reasons which the mind can never fathom." Almost an identical creed can be traced to Nietzsche, to Spengler, and, if the truth be known, to some of the Nazis.

Our own age seems virtually unique in its philosophies of revolt against both reason and science. The late Middle Ages produced Nominalism as a reaction against the full-blown rationalism of the Schoolmen; but the Nominalists justified and welcomed science. The romanticists of the late eighteenth and early nineteenth centuries were not openly hostile to empirical methods of knowing. A few, in fact, were deeply interested in science and made contributions to its advancement. Goethe, for example, added much to our knowledge of comparative morphology. Long before Darwin and even before Lamarck, he convinced himself by his own researches of the truth of organic evolution.

It has been left for some in our own era to despise with equal venom all forms of intellectual activity. Such was notably the attitude of Spengler, of Le Bon, of Sorel, and even to a considerable degree of Pareto. It has been implicit also in the philosophy of the Existentialists. For them the all-important truth is the fact of man's *existence*. "Being is prior to essence." Man can accomplish little or nothing by any form of intellectual activity. He can neither probe the mysteries of knowledge nor add to his own happiness. Only by *action*, or "involvement," can he give meaning and dignity to his life. No doubt, most Existentialists would repudiate the assertion that they are anti-intellectual. They claim to be rebelling primarily against the depersonalization of man. They see man treated as a slave of destiny or as a mere instrument of historical forces by mechanistic and deterministic philosophies. Yet by repudiating logic and exalting subjective feelings above everything else, Sartre and his followers added themselves, perhaps unwittingly, to the ranks of the anti-intellectuals.

ADDITIONAL READINGS

Auden, W. H., ed. *The Living Thoughts of Kierkegaard.* New York, McKay, 1952.

Barrett, William. *Irrational Man; a Study in Existential Philosophy.* Garden City, Doubleday, 1959.

Blackham, Harold J. *Six Existentialist Thinkers.* New York, Macmillan, 1952.

Copleston, Frederick C. *Contemporary Philosophy: Studies of Logical Positivism and Existentialism.* London, Burns and Oates, 1956.

Desan, Wilfred. *The Tragic Finale; an Essay on the Philosophy of Jean-Paul Sartre.* Cambridge, Mass., Harvard University Press, 1954.

Durkheim, Émile. *The Division of Labor in Society.* New York, Macmillan, 1933.

Heidegger, Martin. *Existence and Being.* Chicago, Regnery, 1949.

Heinemann, F. H. *Existentialism and the Modern Predicament.* New York, Harper, 1953.

Humphrey, Richard D. *Georges Sorel: Prophet without Honor.* Cambridge, Mass., Harvard University Press, 1951.

Jaspers, Karl. *Reason and Existence.* New York, Noonday Press, 1955.

Kierkegaard, Sören. *Fear and Trembling*. Princeton, Princeton University Press, 1941.

——. *The Sickness unto Death*. Princeton, Princeton University Press, 1941.

Le Bon, Gustave. *The Psychology of Peoples*. New York, Macmillan, 1896.

——. *The Psychology of Socialism*. New York, Macmillan, 1899.

——. *The World in Revolt*. London, T. F. Unwin, 1921.

Sartre, Jean-Paul. *Portrait of the Anti-Semite*. New York, Partisan Review, 1946.

Shklar, Judith. *After Utopia*. Princeton, Princeton University Press, 1957.

Spengler, Oswald. *Man and Technics*. New York, Knopf, 1932.

Wild, John D. *The Challenge of Existentialism*. Bloomington, Ind., Indiana University Press, 1955.

X

Twentieth-Century Conservatism

The majority of political philosophers have been, in some sense, iconoclasts or rebels. They have not been interested in preserving the existing order but in modifying it and, in some cases, dismantling it or tearing it out by the roots. To a large extent, they are forced into these attitudes by the nature of their subject. It is difficult to *be* a political philosopher without being critical of the established pattern or developing blueprints for something better. The most fruitful periods in the history of political thought have been periods of anxiety and conflict. The great systems of Plato and Aristotle were products of the intellectual revolution generated by the Sophists and of the conditions of turbulence accompanying the decline of the city states. The philosophies of Coke and Milton, of Hobbes, Harrington, and Locke grew out of the conflicts between Anglicans and Puritans, Royalists and Roundheads, Whigs and Tories, and the actual revolutions of the seventeenth century. The theories of the classical period in American political thought also had their connections with a time of troubles. Hamilton, Madison, Paine, and Jefferson did not write in isolation. Instead, they produced their essays and pamphlets as weapons in a war of ideas involving such issues as the Leviathan state *vs.* the diminishing state; coercive government; centralized power; democracy *vs.* aristocracy; the need for a bill of rights; and many others. Intellectual warfare, however, produces conservatives as well as radicals, and both must receive attention from the student of political thought.

1. Conservatism, Old Style

Conservatism as a political philosophy cannot be reduced to a single pattern. Like socialism, liberalism, idealism, and democracy, it has several variations. Some conservatives venerate the political economy of the nineteenth century that grew out of the teachings of Malthus, Ricardo, and the members of the Manchester School. They would change this system only slightly for the purpose of adapting it to modern conditions. Other conservatives worship the ghost of Edmund Burke and plead for a return to his reverence for property and respect for the traditions of a landed aristocracy. Though they call themselves *New* Conservatives, no one shows a higher regard for things that are old—old families, old houses, old manners, and especially the old structure of classes. Still other conservatives recognize that the new wine of the twentieth century cannot be poured into the old bottles of the nineteenth. Their solution, in effect, is to reverse the process: to preserve the essential ingredients of the old potation, but to provide new vessels to contain them. They admit, for example, that governmental planning is perfectly legitimate when its purpose is to preserve competition and not to prevent it.

Logic would seem to dictate that those theorists who wish to continue the conservatism of the nineteenth century essentially without change should be considered first. The most facile and sophisticated member of this group is probably Friedrich A. Hayek. Hayek was born in Austria in 1899. He received the degrees of Doctor of Law and Doctor of Political Science from the University of Vienna and soon afterward entered the civil service. In 1923 he came to the United States and worked for a year as a research assistant at New York University. In 1927 he was appointed Director of the Austrian Institute for Economic Research, and, four years later, Tooke Professor of Economic Science and Statistics at the University of London. He became a British subject in 1938. Although he wrote several treatises on technical aspects of economics, his fame depends primarily on *The Road to Serfdom,* which he published in 1944. It was translated into a number of languages and distributed widely, especially in the United States. For some time it remained a kind of Bible for American and British capitalists.

In common with many other conservatives of the twentieth century, Hayek regards Marxian socialism as the principal source of the world's woes. It is a great mistake, he argues, to think of such evils as Fascism and Nazism as mere revolts against reason or reversions to tribalism. Instead, they are products of a long period of cultural evolution. The influences which spawned them were many and various. The élitist and anti-intellectual doctrines of Thomas Carlyle, Houston Stewart Chamberlain, Auguste Comte, and Georges Sorel played some part. The major influence, however, was the collectivism of Marx. In one form or another his teachings were adopted as Holy Writ by eloquent writers who believed that capitalism had outlived its usefulness and ought to be supplanted by a new order. Though many were not socialists, they drew from Marx theories of economic determinism, the increasing misery of the workers, and the need for planning and regimentation to prevent depressions and unemployment. The year 1870, according to Hayek, constituted a watershed in the intellectual history of the Western world. Before that date the great source of ideas for civilized man had been England. After it, the chief center of intellectual stimulation was Germany. "Whether it was Hegel or Marx, List or Schmoller, Sombart or Mannheim, whether it was socialism in its more radical form or merely 'organization' or 'planning' of a less radical kind, German ideas were everywhere readily imported and German institutions imitated." [1] Few of the people who adopted these ideas, according to Hayek, really understood their import. They were mostly men of good will intent upon making life easier for the less fortunate classes. Little did they realize that they were preparing the way for the triumph of a primitive lawlessness that would drag in the mire every humane ideal that had marked the progress of man for centuries.

Hayek also, like other conservatives, insists upon the identity of capitalism with democracy. And by capitalism he means a free,

[1] *The Road to Serfdom.* Chicago, University of Chicago Press, 1944, p. 21.

competitive capitalism. Socialism, in his viewpoint, has always been authoritarian. One of the earliest of its prophets, Henri de Saint-Simon, asserted that those who would not obey his proposed planning boards would be "treated like cattle." [2] Hayek goes on to argue that only under the influence of the strong democratic currents of 1848 did socialism begin to associate itself with the forces of freedom. Marxists came out against war and imperialism, championed, on occasions, freedom of speech, and proclaimed the democratic institutions of the Paris Commune as their model for the proletarian state. It was not long, however, until Marxists and their Leftist allies discovered that if they were to succeed in establishing their system, they must resort to repression and regimentation. The result was a blurring of distinctions between radicals and reactionaries. English and American students returned from Central and Southern Europe uncertain to which camp they belonged and convinced only that they hated the Western liberal tradition. In more recent years it was quite easy for socialists like Mussolini, Pierre Laval, and Vikdun Quisling to become fascists, and for Nazis to become Communists and vice versa.

The antithesis of collectivism and democracy, according to Hayek, lies in the inability of collectivism to operate under a regime of law and within a sphere of respect for the rights of the individual. It is clear that by democracy he does not mean the sovereignty of the majority, which might well be virtually as authoritarian as an autocracy or oligarchy. He thinks of democracy as, first of all, a *Rechtstaat*, a state in which the laws are supreme. The content of these laws is not so important as the fact that they exist, and that they will always be applied without exceptions. For example, it makes little difference whether motorists drive on the right side of the road or on the left so long as they all do the same. Established, formal rules are necessary in order that everyone may know what procedures the state will follow and what actions it is legally permissible for him to take.

[2] This example was a bit unfortunate, for Saint-Simon was much more of a social engineer and a technocrat than a socialist. He advocated planning and the scientific organization of society, but he would apparently have made little change in the system of ownership.

Collectivism, however, makes adherence to such formal rules practically impossible. When the government must decide how many pigs are to be raised, how many acres are to be planted in cotton, which coal mines are to be closed down, and what price is to be charged for pressing a suit, formal principles cannot be followed. Decisions must be made on the basis of circumstances and by balancing interests against one another. In the end some bureaucrat will have to decide which interests are more important or more deserving of the government's favor. Not legal principle but personal views will be the determining factor.

In addition, as Hayek views the problem, collectivism is a deadly menace to democratic procedures. Parliamentary action is too slow and cumbersome to meet the needs of a planning society. The feeling grows that, to get things done, administrators must be freed from legislative fetters. Hayek conceives this development as a primary cause of the triumph of Hitler. Germany was so highly collectivized by 1933 that parliamentary government was out of the question. Hitler did not need to destroy the Weimar Republic; he had merely to take advantage of the decay of democracy and, at the critical moment, obtain the support of the misguided citizens who regarded him as the only leader strong enough to get things done. To anyone familiar with the history of Germany during the interwar period, and especially with the failure of Nazism to gain much headway until after the beginning of the depression, this explanation seems rather superficial.

Though he thinks of himself as a classical liberal, Hayek professes no allegiance to the gospel of *laissez faire*. He emphatically doubts that anything "has done so much harm to the liberal cause as the wooden insistence of some liberals on certain rough rules of thumb, above all the principle of laissez faire." [3] He not only rejects but deplores the concept of a do-nothing state. The state, he believes, may appropriately undertake quite a number of regulatory, restrictive, and even positive functions. It may prevent fraud and deception, limit working hours, render assistance to victims of earthquakes and floods, and assure to everybody a minimum of food, shelter, and clothing to preserve health and the

[3] *Ibid.*, p. 17.

capacity to work. Not even all forms of planning come under
Hayek's ban. He expressly authorizes planning "*for* competition"
but frowns upon planning "*against* competition." [4] He maintains
that the only alternative is submission to the impersonal forces of
the market or to the arbitrary power of other men. In spite of his
concern for a limited social security, he posits the need for a
reservoir of jobless men to which workers can be banished for
indiscipline or incompetence and from which others can be drawn
to take their places. What he apparently means by his approved
forms of planning is not planning by the state at all but utilization
by individual entrepreneurs of the mechanism of the price system
for their own advantage. In so doing, they "adjust their activities
to those of their fellows." [5] This seems like permitting *laissez faire*
to come back through the window.

Hayek rests his case for conservatism on broad philosophical
bases. He sees in the growth of collectivism a progressive abandonment of one of the most valuable elements of Western civilization. It is not merely the liberalism of the eighteenth and nineteenth centuries that is being liquidated, he maintains, but the
basic individualism inherited from Erasmus and Montaigne, from
Cicero and Tacitus, and from Pericles and Thucydides. This basic
individualism he finds summed up in "respect for the individual
man *qua* man"; in other words, the recognition of man's own
views and tastes as supreme in his own sphere, and the belief
that each man should have the fullest opportunity to develop his
own talents and inclinations.[6] True individualism, as Hayek conceives it, began its modern development with John Locke, "and
particularly with Bernard Mandeville and David Hume, and
achieved full stature for the first time in the work of Josiah
Tucker, Adam Ferguson, and Adam Smith and in that of their
great contemporary, Edmund Burke." [7] This line of development
does not include the classical economists of the nineteenth cen-

---

[4] It is difficult, though, to take this distinction seriously, for he speaks
elsewhere of planning as an unmitigated evil and implies that any degree
of it will lead to its universal application.

[5] *Ibid.*, p. 49.

[6] *Ibid.*, pp. 13–14.

[7] *Individualism and Economic Order*. Chicago, University of Chicago
Press, 1948, p. 4.

tury, the Physiocrats, and the Encyclopedists. These writers, according to Hayek, came under the influence of Cartesian rationalism, "which always tends to develop into the opposite of individualism, namely, socialism or collectivism." [8] Why Edmund Burke, who despised the individual, should be included in the category of true individualists, and why such staunch defenders of freedom as the Encyclopedists should be classed as forerunners of collectivism is not readily apparent.

One might suppose that a philosophy dedicated to the preservation of the individualist tradition in Western culture would place a high premium on the competence and worth of the human species. But such is only partly the case. While Hayek professes to exalt freedom, he thinks of the individual as an irrational and fallible being, whose errors must be corrected by a social process with functions analogous to those of a providential God. Indeed, Hayek bases his case against planning largely upon the thesis that the knowledge possessed by any one individual or group of individuals is so tiny a fraction of the whole as to make their efforts to coordinate an entire social structure ridiculous. It is much better, he thinks, that each individual should pursue his own interests, altruistically or selfishly, within the little sphere with which he is familiar. The free market and the price system will then accomplish, in an almost mystical and benevolent way, the greatest good of society. By accommodating themselves to these forces "men will often achieve more than individual human reason could design or foresee." [9] Any serious interference with this process is certain to produce more harm than good. A flagrant example is the graduated income tax for egalitarian purposes. The effect of such taxes, according to Hayek, is to foster social immobility by preventing the successful man from rising by accumulating a fortune. Worse still, they tend to eliminate "that most important element in any free society—the man of independent means." [10] But Hayek does not deride all taxation. He recognizes the virtue of inheritance taxes, provided they are not carried to the confiscatory extremes of those in Great Britain.

[8] *Id.*
[9] *Ibid.*, p. 11.
[10] *Ibid.*, p. 118.

He conceives for them a valuable place as instruments for greater social mobility and dispersion of property.

No account of old-style conservatism would be complete without some attention to two erstwhile chiefs of government noted for their views on political economy. The first is Herbert Hoover; the second, Winston Churchill. Both were born in the same year, and neither would go far toward modifying the economic principles regnant during the days of their youth. Hoover was born in 1874, the son of Iowa Quakers; he was left an orphan at an early age. From the time he was sixteen he was a skillful promoter of business ventures, and he retains his sense of pride in these accomplishments to this day. Graduating from Stanford in 1895, he became a mining engineer in Australia. But he soon moved up to managerial and promotional activities, and by 1908 was accepting commissions all over the world to reorganize and rehabilitate sick enterprises. He invested in some of them and by the age of forty had accumulated enough wealth to retire. After the outbreak of World War I, Hoover was almost continually in public service. He was Chairman of the Commission for Relief in Belgium from 1915 to 1919. He became United States Food Administrator in 1917, a member of the Council of Economic Advisers at the Peace Conference in 1919, and Secretary of Commerce two years later. In 1928 he was elected President of the United States by the largest majority ever given a candidate up to that time. He left office in 1933 the most universally execrated American Executive since the days of Buchanan. His constructive achievements were forgotten amid the storms of wrath that accompanied his denunciation of direct relief and his predictions that "grass would grow in the streets" if the opposition party should win the elections. Hoover returned to public service in 1949 as chairman of a commission to reorganize government agencies.

Like most other old-style conservatives, Hoover carefully avoids the use of that term. The label he prefers to designate his philosophy is "individualism." As long ago as 1922 he defined this philosophy as holding "an abiding faith in the intelligence, the initiative, the character, the courage, and the divine touch in the individual." [11] He practically identified individualism with equality of opportunity and standing up "to the emery wheel of competition." By adhering to such ideals, he maintained, America could be assured of progress and the achievement of as much perfection as her civilization merits. Nor is there much evidence that he has ever abandoned or seriously modified these premises. In 1943 in a counterblast against President Roosevelt's Four Freedoms he postulated the existence of a Fifth Freedom, without which none of the other four would ever be realized. This Fifth Freedom he defined as freedom of men to "choose their jobs and callings, bargain for their own wages and salaries, save and provide by private property for their families and old age." It must also include freedom of men "to engage in enterprise so long as each does not injure his fellowmen." [12] Curiously, however, the Fifth Freedom was not synonymous with *laissez faire*. Its author held it to be perfectly consistent with regulation of railroads, old-age pensions, health and unemployment insurance, and care for widows and orphans and "those upon whom disaster falls." These, he contended, are safeguards for equality of opportunity. He also included protective tariffs among these essential safeguards, on the ground that American labor and American business must be protected against the lower standards of living and cheaper production methods of foreign nations. How tariffs would compel American industrialists to "stand up to the emery wheel of competition," he did not make clear.

Consistency has not been a crowning virtue for Herbert Hoover, any more than it is generally for political leaders. In 1930 he described the Hawley-Smoot Tariff Bill as "vicious, extortionate, and obnoxious"—and then signed it. After the beginning of the depression he sponsored the RFC as an agency to rescue floundering corporations, a five-million-dollar extra subsidy to the Merchant Marine to stimulate shipbuilding, the Grain and Cotton Stabilization Corporation to take surplus wheat and cotton off the market, and the Commodity Credit Corporation to make loans

[11] *American Individualism.* Garden City, Doubleday, 1922, p. 72.
[12] *Addresses upon the American Road.* New York, Van Nostrand, 1946, p. 222.

to farmers for the purpose of pegging prices; but he opposed
direct relief to the unemployed as a form of dole. He urged that
America should support every sane international effort to advance
the economic and social welfare of other nations; but he insisted
upon high protective tariffs to shut out their goods, thereby hindering them from achieving economic recovery. In his address
accepting the Presidential nomination in 1928 he announced as
an important function of government the prevention of "those
fluctuations from boom to slump which bring on the one hand
periods of unemployment and bankruptcy and, on the other,
speculation and waste." Two years later when a group of businessmen implored him to do something effective to relieve unemployment, he replied: "Gentlemen, you are six weeks too late.
The crisis is over." [13]

With regard to both statesmanship and intellectual acumen
most people would probably rank Winston Churchill as superior
to Herbert Hoover. Even one of Churchill's sharpest critics suggested at the time of his elevation to knighthood that he ought
rather to be made a duke—Duke of the Sea, perhaps, "for nothing less would be wholly appropriate." [14] The chief hero of
Britain's war for survival against Nazi aggression was born in
Blenheim Castle in 1874. His mother was an American, his father
a leading Tory politician who later became Chancellor of the
Exchequer under Lord Salisbury. The future Prime Minister's
early scholastic record was scarcely distinguished. He required
three full terms to get out of the lowest "form" at Harrow. Three
times he failed the examinations for admission to Sandhurst (the
British "West Point"), though, once admitted, he completed the
course with honors. After three years of army service in India, he
went to South Africa as a correspondent in the Boer War. He
returned in 1900 and was elected to Parliament as a Conservative.
Four years later increasing dissatisfaction with the protectionist
policies of Joseph Chamberlain led him to cross the floor of the
House of Commons and join the Liberals. In 1908 he was made

[13] *Current Biography*, 1943, p. 309.
[14] Vincent Sheean, "Valediction for Churchill," *New Republic*, CXIII
Aug. 13, 1945, 182–83.

President of the Board of Trade, in 1911 First Lord of the Admiralty, in 1916 Minister of Munitions, and two years later Secretary of State for War. In 1924 he rejoined the Conservatives and became Chancellor of the Exchequer under Stanley Baldwin. From 1935 to 1940 he was out of the Cabinet, partly because he supported the cause of Edward VIII against the Prime Minister in the famous divorce controversy. In 1940 he displaced Neville Chamberlain as head of the Cabinet in order to lead the British nation in a "never surrender" struggle with Nazi Germany. Though the British continued to revere him as a war leader, once victory was achieved in 1945 they replaced his Government with a Labour Cabinet headed by Clement Attlee. With the return of the Conservatives to power in 1951, Churchill resumed his place as the King's Chief Minister. Five years later he retired to devote the remainder of his life to painting and to the completion of his history of the British people in the great crises of recent times.

With his grandiloquent speeches and stalwart pride in ancient traditions, Churchill is regarded by many people as a kind of throwback to the eighteenth century. But the accuracy of this is doubtful. Churchill's theories would seem to have a closer affinity with the doctrines and prejudices of the nineteenth century than with those of any earlier period. He apparently still harbors the notion that the time-honored policies of Palmerston, Disraeli, and Gladstone are the ones which can contribute the most to the fulfillment of Britain's destiny. As late as 1936 he praised "the wonderful unconscious tradition" of splendid isolation and maintenance of the balance of power. By opposing the strongest, most aggressive, most dominating nation on the Continent, he declared, Britain "preserved the liberties of Europe" and extended her fame and her Empire. "I know of nothing," he continued, "which has occurred to alter or weaken the justice, wisdom, valour, and prudence upon which our ancestors acted." [15] His conception of international relations is dominated by a high regard for balance of power and a willingness to employ whatever expedient may be necessary to safeguard or enhance Britain's position. Thus he

[15] Quoted by Virginia Cowles, *Winston Churchill—The Era and the Man.* New York, Harper, 1953, p. 295.

was ready, in the 1930's, to approve of Mussolini and his Fascists as "the necessary antidote to the Russian poison." [16] By the same token, he did not hesitate to embrace the Soviet Union as an ally in the war against Nazi Germany, despite the fact that one year earlier he had described the Soviet system as one which "rots the soul of a nation" and makes it "abject and hungry in peace" and "base and abominable in war." [17] Throughout the War and afterward he acclaimed the old-style imperialism, protested the liquidation of His Majesty's Empire, and expressed revulsion at the very thought of that "half-naked fakir," Mahatma Gandhi, striding up the steps of the Viceregal Palace in India.

Not only with respect to international relations but in the area of domestic affairs as well, Churchill's sympathies reside with his conservative forebears of the nineteenth century. Like them, he believes in free trade and *laissez faire,* though he accepts a modest amount of welfare legislation and interfered only to a limited extent, upon his return to the Government in 1951, with the nationalization measures of the preceding Labour Cabinet. On the other hand, he vehemently opposed the General Strike of 1926, sponsored severe anti-labor legislation, condemned increases in income taxes, and taught that the price mechanism should be the chief reliance for the maintenance of general prosperity. Whether intentionally or not, he has always linked socialism with Communism, contending that both are inseparable from totalitarianism and abject worship of the state. "No Socialist system," he argues, "can be established without a political police. . . . They would have to fall back on some sort of Gestapo—no doubt very humanely directed in the first instance." [18]

With respect to forms of government, Churchill's preference seems to fall upon an aristocracy of ability. He has criticized working-class citizens for demanding power and responsibility beyond their deserts. If they want these prizes, he says, they should climb the ladder of achievement, not remain at the bottom and set up a clamor on the basis of mere numbers. He has a warm

[16] *Ibid.,* p. 272.

[17] *Into Battle, Speeches by the Right Honourable Winston S. Churchill.* London, Cassell, 1941, p. 160.

[18] Colin R. Coote, ed., *A Churchill Reader.* Boston, Houghton Mifflin, 1954, p. 263.

spot in his heart, also, for monarchy as the appropriate form of government for all but the most politically advanced peoples. He said that Germany, for example, should never have been required to establish a republic after World War I. What she needed was a constitutional monarchy in the form of a council of regency for the infant grandson of Wilhelm II. Such a plan would have been much better than a host of elective offices to be filled with "nonentities." [19]

2. The New Conservatism

Since the 1930's conservatism has flourished in a new and distinctive form, especially in the United States. Most of its prophets are comparatively young men who seem to be expressing some deep disillusion with the dominant ideals of the interwar period. They emphatically believe that socialism, pacifism, empiricism, relativism, materialism, and egoism are powerful corrosive agents eating their way toward the very heart of civilization. According to this view, such factors were the major causes of the spread of fascism, World War II, and the threat presented by Soviet Communism to the actual survival of the Western world. As ideals, these factors were personified by a long line of philosophers and critics extending from John Locke, Thomas Paine, Jean-Jacques Rousseau, and Jeremy Bentham to John Stuart Mill, Herbert Spencer, Karl Marx, and John Dewey. These philosophers, their opponents argue, were responsible for the alienation of modern man from the great traditions of his past and for degrading him into an ill-mannered, self-seeking barbarian. Since he is bereft of what Edmund Burke called "the unbought grace of life," he is prone to put his feet in the trough and to trample in the mire the most precious legacies of civilized restraint bequeathed by his ancestors. He becomes an atheist, an anarchist, and a nihilist, ready to destroy everything if only he can gratify his own appetites and elevate himself to the place of his superiors.

The philosophy of the so-called New Conservatives is by no means entirely new. Their approach is definitely backward-looking to an admiration for the ways of the past. They prac-

[19] *The Gathering Storm.* Boston, Houghton Mifflin, 1948, pp. 10–11.

tically refuse to recognize any merit in a single thinker of the twentieth century, with the exception of Winston Churchill, Irving Babbitt, and Paul Elmer More. This attitude is especially characteristic of Russell Kirk, who exalts as his ideological forebears Edmund Burke, John Adams, John Randolph, and Cardinal Newman. Kirk was born in Plymouth, Michigan, in 1918. He received a B.A. degree from Michigan State in 1940, an M.A. from Duke in 1941, and a D.Litt. in Modern History from St. Andrews University in Scotland in 1952. He was an assistant professor of civilization at Michigan State from 1946 to 1953 and is currently Research Professor of Political Science at Post College, Long Island University. He has been an editor of the *National Review*, an ultraconservative journal, since 1956.

On occasions Russell Kirk expounds a philosophy which appears to conform to the true ideals of intellectual liberalism. He pays deference to the proposition that "the unexamined life is not worth living." [20] He defends academic freedom, at least to the extent of opposing inclusive loyalty oaths. He would require of the teacher a pledge to adhere to the truth, to conserve the wisdom of our ancestors, to extend the empire of knowledge, to "guide and awaken the student but not to indoctrinate," to abide by the principles of social order as expressed in the country's constitution, and "always to put freedom of the mind above material advantage and the passions of the hour." [21] His oath for teachers would set forth a code of ethics and responsibilities after the model of the Hippocratic oath for physicians. But this is as far as his liberalism extends. He asserts that theology is the "queen of the sciences" and that religion is the most important subject in the university. If the choice must be made, he declares, it is nobler to believe all things than to doubt all things. Human beings have dignity and rights, he maintains, only because divine wisdom has ordained it so. More and more it becomes evident as one reads his books that much of his philosophy is a compound of three negative attitudes: belief in inequality, contempt for the masses, and opposition to intellect as the key to knowledge. Each of these attitudes requires explanation.

[20] *Academic Freedom*. Chicago, Regnery, 1955, p. 191.
[21] *Ibid.*, pp. 152–53.

No principle is more strongly affirmed by Russell Kirk than the doctrine that men are unequal, and that they have the duty to accept the station in which God has called them to live and labor. They should resign themselves to this system with humility and consecration; for "without inequality, there is no opportunity for charity, or for gratitude." [22] A divine tactic in history has decreed that civilized society be constructed of orders and classes, with little fluidity between them. Order in society is the harmonious arrangement of classes and functions which provides the moral sanction for law and justice. When no one feels settled into an order, then man has no fear of censure but is restrained only by the threat of punishment. The proletarian, who belongs to nothing, is a flagrant example. He is a social atom, enslaved by his appetites, and often shameless. He stands in bold contrast to the "gentleman," who subjects his character and intelligence to enlightened discipline and realizes the value of duty and continuity. No civilized nation, according to Kirk, can endure without a large number of such choice spirits. They are not simply the salt of the earth but its natural and essential rulers, and should be recognized as entitled to an influence far greater than that of the average citizen. For they alone can be depended upon to conserve that which is best and most stable in the social structure and to oppose the revolutionary and innovating tendencies of the masses. They realize that "Providence is the proper instrument for change," and that the mark of a statesman is refusal to interfere with divinely guided social forces.[23]

The class of "gentlemen" is also entitled to its economic stake in society. Its members ought to have property, especially inherited property in land; for nothing can add more to the honor and dignity of men who feel and know themselves to be superior. In fact, property is the most important thing on earth, dearer to the civilized man than life itself. Property and freedom are inseparably linked, since the only persons interested in defending liberty as a priceless possession are the men of considerable wealth who know what it means to live their own lives. They realize that socialism means dreary uniformity, and they will

[22] A Program for Conservatives. Chicago, Regnery, 1954, p. 177.
[23] The Conservative Mind. Chicago, Regnery, 1953, p. 8.

have none of it—not even "creeping socialism," for socialism in any degree ultimately evolves into fascism. The masses, therefore, must be kept in their place lest they destroy the economic sinews which make for elevation of mind and temper in the superior beings. Kirk believes that the United States erred in adopting universal suffrage, direct primaries, popular election of United States Senators, "and other measures calculated to substitute direct democracy for representative government."[24] He agrees with Lord Macaulay that institutions purely democratic must, sooner or later, destroy either liberty or civilization, and possibly both. The great danger is that a Bonaparte will ride into power after a period of rampant democracy. The masses demand to be led. Having humbled or liquidated their natural superiors, they will turn to demagogues or dictators.

Russell Kirk's New Conservatism is not only aristocratic and backward looking but anti-intellectual. He maintains that "a true understanding of liberty" conceives it as "freedom to live within the compass of God's ordinances, not freedom to doubt and demolish."[25] He apparently rejects the intellectualist's adage that "By doubting we are led to inquiry, and by inquiry we perceive the truth." He seems to assume that all men, regardless of faith, will hold a common view of God's ordinances, even though Negro slavery, for example, has been considered divinely ordained in some quarters. He quotes Disraeli to the effect that man is truly great only when he acts from the passions, and that none of the great landmarks of human history—the siege of Troy, the expansion of Islam, the Crusades, the rise of the Jesuits, the French Revolution—was a product of human reason. Even the wisest of men, Kirk avers, cannot live by reason alone. "Pure arrogant reason" leads to a desert of blasted hopes and desperate loneliness, "empty of God and man." Better as guides to conduct and conscience than books and philosophy for most men, and sometimes for all men, are "tradition, prejudice, and prescription."[26] Perhaps this contempt for intellect has some relationship to the fact that the author's books are rife with contradic-

[24] A Program for Conservatives, p. 247.
[25] The Conservative Mind, p. 252.
[26] Ibid., p. 36.

tions. He introduced *The Conservative Mind,* for example, with the doleful statement that radical thinkers had won the day, and that the conservatives had yielded ground in a manner which could only be described as a rout. One year later, in *A Program for Conservatives,* he exulted that the liberal and the radical had failed and "the enormity of their failure" was stamped on the face of Europe and Asia. The "terrible events of our time," he declared, "have buried John Dewey and his generation deeper than any Pharaoh."

A slightly different brand of New Conservatism emerges from the writings of Peter Viereck, who has labored in a variety of intellectual vineyards in both Europe and America. Born in New York in 1916, he was graduated from Harvard *summa cum laude* in 1937 and went on for both master's and doctor's degrees during the next five years. He has taught at Harvard and at Smith College, and is currently Professor of Modern European and Russian History at Mount Holyoke College. He was a Guggenheim Fellow in Rome in 1949–1950, Visiting Lecturer on American Culture at Oxford in 1953, Whittul Lecturer in Poetry, Library of Congress, in 1954, and Fulbright Professor in American Poetry and Civilization at the University of Florence in 1955. He was awarded the Pulitzer prize for poetry in 1949. In addition to numerous poetic works and a novelette, he has written *Conservatism Revisited* (1949), *The Shame and Glory of the Intellectuals* (1953), and *Conservatism: from John Adams to Churchill* (1956).

Viereck's conservatism varies from that of Kirk, first of all, in being founded upon a slightly different collection of deities. Whereas Kirk venerates Burke, John Adams, John Randolph, and Cardinal Newman, Viereck's praise is more lavish for Gouverneur Morris, Alexander Hamilton (whom Kirk repudiates as a radical innovator and the founder of modern industrialism), Rufus Choate, John C. Calhoun, and John Stuart Mill. He has kind words, even, for Joseph de Maistre and Louis Bonald. More important is the fact that Viereck's philosophy has a stronger component of militancy. Though he is not a revolutionist, he is definitely a crusader and would carry the torch for a variety of causes. In his *Shame and Glory of the In-*

tellectuals, written during the Korean War, he becomes highly
dramatic about the Communist menace. Membership in the
Communist party he describes as "morally an act comparable to
murder." Every card-carrying Communist, he says, who joined
the party voluntarily is "up to his knees in the blood of his
party's victims." [27] He seems actually to take pride in his un-
restraint, for he conjures up the specter of 40,000 Russian tanks
"straining at the leash to race westward and pound European
civilization into pulp" the very moment Americans desist from
being "hysterical" about the Soviet menace. No policy of "containment" seems to him adequate to protect the "Christian-
Judaic moral basis of American freedom." He prefers, rather,
what used to be the "roll-back," or liberation, policy. Anything
less, he believes, is the equivalent of tolerating the "incompara-
ble horrors of the Soviet slave camps." [28]

In contrast with Kirk, Viereck has no passion for orders and
classes. He claims not to be interested in aristocracy, but in what
he calls "the aristocratic spirit," which is open to all, regardless
of class. He defines this spirit as "dutiful public service, insistence on quality and standards, the decorum and ethical inner check of noblesse oblige." [29] He goes so far as to say that
democracy is the best government on earth—provided it dedi-
cates itself to making all of its citizens aristocrats. What this
means, apparently, is educating them to be respectful of traditions and obedient to "ethical traffic lights" established to curb
their instincts. But democracy, for Viereck, has no conformity
with popular sovereignty. Every stable society, he says, has devised institutions to prevent majority rule from becoming oppressive. In England there is the House of Lords and in America
the separation of powers, especially the authority of the Supreme
Court as guardian of the Constitution. Democracy, as Viereck
conceives it, is not inconsistent with monarchy—except in America, where the republican tradition is too strongly entrenched.
Anyway, the Supreme Court is a good substitute for royalty. In

[27] *The Shame and Glory of the Intellectuals.* Boston, Beacon Press, 1953.
p. 298.
[28] *Ibid.,* p. 185.
[29] *Conservatism Revisited.* New York, Scribner, 1949, p. 15.

all other countries, Viereck believes, limited monarchy, as opposed to republicanism or dictatorship, "is the normal framework for human politics." Nothing else can be a sufficient stabilizing influence, or provide the happy balance between authority and liberty. A republic, in Freudian metaphor, is "the rebellious son unrestrained." It symbolizes revolt against legitimate rule, and therefore is doomed to perish eventually in violence and anarchy. The overthrow of monarchy in Central and Eastern Europe in 1917–1918 was a grievous mistake, since it fostered confusion and instability and thereby helped to prepare the way for monstrous tyrannies. The countries that preserved their monarchies, Viereck believes, were able to progress peacefully toward social reform. He seems to overlook the serious threats of disorder in Britain at the time of the General Strike, to say nothing of the resistance to reform in Spain under Alphonso XIII or the confusion and breakdown in Italy under Victor Emmanuel III.

In most other respects the theory of Peter Viereck resembles that of Russell Kirk. He is every inch a New Conservative in his defense of the free market as the economy best suited to democracy and in his attitude toward human nature. He believes in Original Sin, affirming that human beings are by nature barbarous, "capable of every insanity and atrocity." [30] One might imagine some conflict between this conception and the Christian idea of "man created in the image of God," but it apparently escapes Viereck entirely. He seems to be nothing if not Christian. He excoriates the liberals of Eastern and Central Europe for abandoning religion and thereby opening the dikes to a flood of pagan totalitarianism. A great problem of the future, he believes, is how to persuade the liberals of the West to avoid a similar tactic of committing suicide.

Viereck is an unswerving champion of British imperialism, which he conceives as a kind of latter-day Roman Empire holding together the entire globe. The weakening of this imperialism, he maintains, has paved the way for Axis and Communist conquests. The unindustrialized colonial peoples constitute a power vacuum. If not ruled by some enlightened empire with traditions

[30] *Ibid.*, p. 29.

of law and humanity, they will be drawn into the orbit of aggressors and tyrants. In rebelling against their former masters, they achieve not liberation but a reduction of their freedom to a much lower level. The people of India, according to Viereck, were less free in the years after independence than they had been before, and were victims of greater barbarity. Such pre-Independence events as the Amritsar Massacre and the beatings and imprisonments inflicted upon followers of Gandhi and Nehru appear not to have required any modification of this view.

Before concluding this section, it seems desirable to consider the relationship of Walter Lippmann to the New Conservatism. During a long career that has covered the Progressive movement, two World Wars, the New Deal, and the Depression, Lippmann's ideas have boxed the compass from free-market individualism to moderate collectivism. He has already been considered in a previous chapter as a critic of democracy; but his philosophy is much broader than that of an interpreter of the ideas of others. He conceives of democracy not simply as a method of governing but as a conception of life in political society. The old problems of how to reconcile order and liberty, security and enterprise, have long disturbed his intellectual equanimity. In *A Preface to Politics,* written in 1913, he referred to the state as "the supreme instrument of civilization." In *The Method of Freedom,* published when the bloom was still on the New Deal, he declared that only by making its people economically secure could a modern state preserve its influence in the world and maintain order, law, and liberty. By 1937, however, he had become thoroughly disillusioned. He was now ready to argue that economic collectivism and liberal democracy were incompatible. He thought it no accident that wherever planned collectivism had been instituted, after World War I, weapons of censorship, espionage, and terrorism had been required to maintain it.

Lippmann's disillusionment extended also to popular participation in government and to the right of the people to determine their own destinies. In his Progressive days he could write of democracy as an indispensable safeguard "against ignorant tyrants." The people would educate their rulers, he thought, and "compel the law to approximate human needs." [31] By 1922, however, when he wrote *Public Opinion*, he had begun to cast aspersions on the common man as the victim of "stereotypes," of mental pictures grotesquely distorted by advertisers, journalists, and demagogues. This conception was reaffirmed and elaborated about fifteen years later in *The Good Society*, with its references to "the sovereign but incompetent people." But the most emphatic assertion of such doctrine is to be found in one of Lippmann's recent books, *The Public Philosophy*. In this work he deplores the triumph of majoritarian democracy based upon the Jacobin heresy that the people are completely sovereign, that they are competent to solve the most difficult problems of public policy, and that what the majority of them want is the only measure of political right. He maintains that a revolution has brought into power in the Western world a class of irresponsible men recognizing no standards or traditions and motivated only by a desire to get as much as they can for themselves. They are resentful of authority and in rebellion against all restraints. Like Toynbee's "internal proletarians," they live in the community but are not a part of it. They are a faceless, anonymous mass, without roots or heritage. For government to continue to be dominated by such people is, in Lippmann's opinion, a prelude to ruin. Emotional, unreasoning men make demands upon society the fulfillment of which brings disaster. In time of peace they demand appeasement of aggressors to avoid the risks and inconveniences of war. In time of war they clamor for unconditional surrender and for the imposition of crushing penalties upon the vanquished. As a consequence, each crisis of recent times has constituted a rehearsal for other and graver crises that followed.

Lippmann's prescription for averting still greater catastrophes in the future is what he calls the "public philosophy." By this he means a body of law and tradition embodied in Magna Charta, the Bill of Rights of 1689, the Declaration of Independence, the first Ten Amendments of the United States Constitution, and certain "traditions of civility" that have guided men of

[31] *A Preface to Politics*, p. 116.

reason and integrity since the time of the Stoics. The public philosophy, according to Lippmann, should really govern, as a higher law restraining rulers, protecting the rights of free individuals, and conserving the values that have come down through the ages. Neither the people directly nor their elected representatives are competent for these tasks. They are too intimately concerned with the needs of the hour and with the placation of selfish interests. Moreover, they lack both the knowledge and the seasoned judgment. Their learning and skills have been derived from glancing at newspapers, listening to radio comment, attending occasional lectures, and perhaps reading a few books. Such fragmentary knowledge would not make a man competent to decide whether to amputate a leg; neither should it qualify him "to choose war or peace, to arm or not to arm, to intervene or to withdraw, to fight on or to negotiate." [32] The functions of the people should be limited to electing and removing the government and to approving or disapproving its performance. They can neither administer the government nor, under normal circumstances, initiate or propose legislation.

But someone must apply the public philosophy. This function, in Lippmann's opinion, belongs to the executive. He alone has the wisdom and patriotism to discern the welfare of the entire state. He embodies, as in Burke's conception, the interests, not simply of the people now living, but of those who lived in the past and of those yet unborn. He is "honor bound not to consider himself as the agent of his electors." [33] Thus, Lippmann implicitly rejects the Jacksonian concept of the President as the representative of the people with an obligation to reflect the popular view.

By only a few standards of measurement does Walter Lippmann deserve a place among the New Conservatives. He is less militant and dogmatic, and he does not indulge in sweeping condemnations. He is a proponent neither of hereditary aristocracy nor of monarchy, though he does believe in a strong, independent executive. His advocacy of a free economy has never included a defense of inherited wealth or of private property as a sacred

[32] *The Public Philosophy.* Boston, Little, Brown, 1955, pp. 24–25.
[33] *Ibid.,* p. 53.

right. Though he has a low opinion of the average man's ability, he does not deride intellect nor uphold a doctrine of Original Sin or innate depravity. On the other hand, he shares with the New Conservatives their respect for tradition and their admiration for Burke and other great pillars of authority and stability. He deplores philosophical relativism, and fears that if philosophers teach that religion is a purely psychological phenomenon, "they will give educated men a bad intellectual conscience if they have religious experiences." [34] Though he describes himself as "a liberal democrat," he seems just about as anxious as Kirk or Viereck to restrict civil liberties when their exercise appears to involve some threat to order or some trouble for the rulers. It is a sophistry to pretend, he says, that in a free country every man has some sort of constitutional or natural right to deceive his neighbor. "There is no more right to deceive than there is a right to swindle, to cheat, or to pick pockets." [35]

More significant are Lippmann's arguments that the right to enjoy free institutions belongs only to those who adhere to them and recognize a duty to maintain them, that freedom of speech has a proper use only as a procedure of truth, and that liberty of expression should be limited to arenas that permit confrontation in debate. In such arguments, Lippmann seems to allow precious little room for nonconformity. One wonders how many of the great movers and shakers in American history could have continued their agitation within a framework of such restrictions. Should William Lloyd Garrison have been punished for denouncing the Constitution of the United States as "a covenant with Hell"? Should Thoreau have been jailed for preaching that men should cultivate respect for the right rather than respect for the law?

3. The Conservative Revolution

When the sun of prosperity spreads its glow over the Western world, there is a common tendency of people to forget their past woes and hardships and to believe that their worries are

[34] *Ibid.*, p. 179.
[35] *Ibid.*, p. 128.

permanently finished. Writers and public leaders come forward with persuasive arguments that a New Era has been slowly embracing us, unnoticed by any but themselves. The late 1920's, with their popular dreams of "a chicken in every pot and a car in every garage," were a classical period in New Era thinking. In accepting the nomination for President in 1928 Herbert Hoover declared that "We in America today are nearer to the final triumph over poverty than ever before in the history of any land." [36] It has been left, however, for the 1940's and 1950's to discover that a major revolution has been silently encompassing us in such a way as to make socialism obsolete and undesirable, to give capitalism an indefinite lease on the future, and to challenge the validity of most of the great reform proposals of the past.

The keynote for the idea that the contemporary world is in the throes of a conservative revolution was sounded in 1941 by the publication of James Burnham's *The Managerial Revolution*. True, a great deal of the substance in this book had been delineated in Adolf A. Berle and Gardiner C. Means, *The Modern Corporation and Private Property* (1932), but Burnham infused it with drama and political significance that gave it a wider appeal. Burnham was born in Chicago in 1905. Educated at Princeton and at Oxford, he became a member of the faculty of philosophy at New York University in 1929 and continued to teach there until 1953. In addition to *The Managerial Revolution*, he has also written *The Machiavellians* (1943) and *Struggle for the World* (1947). A former Trotskyite, he is the author of several books purporting to reveal Communist plots for subversion and world conquest. Since 1955 he has been an editor of the *National Review*.

By the managerial revolution Burnham means the rise to a position of dominance in both industry and government of a new class of ambitious and aggressive leaders who have almost completely displaced the old ruling class of bourgeois capitalists. This new class he calls the "managers." They include production engineers, technologists, industrial chemists, personnel managers, and experts of many descriptions. They differ from the bourgeoisie, as conceived by the Marxists at least, in not being in-

---

[36] *The New York Times*, August 12, 1928.

vestors primarily or even entrepreneurs. They are interested in profits chiefly as a symbol of efficiency; their basic concern is with production. They are not the owners of industry, and they are seldom occupied in launching new ventures. In the main, they are content to operate the establishments already in existence, to improve their efficiency and to increase their output. As Berle and Means pointed out years ago, ownership of large corporations has become separated from management. The owners are the tens of thousands or hundreds of thousands of absentee shareholders, who know little or nothing about the enterprises whose stock they have purchased. They show concern almost solely with their dividend checks and with the fluctuations in value of their shares. Management is in the hands of the officers of the company and their expert subordinates. Though these officials are frequently made the beneficiaries of bonuses and stock option plans, they do not differ greatly from other salaried employees, except in the size of their incomes and their sovereign independence. Nominally chosen by the board of directors, which technically represents the stockholders, they are in fact responsible to nobody. Because of the complexity of modern industrial production, men who have attained the higher reaches of specialized knowledge occupy a position of power and importance scarcely anyone can challenge.

But the class of "managers" is not confined to industrial production. Burnham discovers their counterparts in government and even in the armed services. The modern state has undergone changes in character every bit as drastic as those which have inundated modern industry. It is folly, therefore, according to Burnham, to suppose that the state can be run by the same kind of persons who operated it successfully when its functions were limited to collecting a few taxes, conducting a leisurely diplomacy, and prosecuting offenders against the law. The modern state is the biggest of all bankers; its construction projects surpass those of any private builder; it is deeply involved in the support of agriculture and in research for military, industrial, and welfare purposes. No rudimentary system of rule by politicians or "people's representatives" will any longer suffice. Modern government requires experts just as urgently as does modern industry. And, unrecognized by most observers, the professional administrator has been gradually displacing the homespun lawyer and old-fashioned politician. The process has gone farthest in the totalitarian countries. Soviet Russia, for example, has reduced her parliament to insignificance and exalted her bureaucrats and professional planners.[37] But a similar tendency, Burnham maintains, is developing in the United States. Most "laws" are no longer made by Congress, but by the NLRB, SEC, ICC, FTC, FCC, and the other leading administrative agencies. "Indeed, most of the important laws passed by Congress in recent years have been laws to give up some more of its sovereign powers to one or another agency largely outside of its control." [38]

That Burnham should envisage profound political consequences for the managerial revolution goes almost without saying. He prophesies not only a shift from parliamentary to administrative government but the eventual disappearance of democracy itself. Self-government, he thinks, is impossible in the face of the complexities of the modern world. He does not foresee a universal adoption of totalitarianism, but he does envision a marked extension of the role of the managers. Authority will pass increasingly into the hands of commissioners, bureau chiefs, directors of special agencies, and professional administrators. To be sure, an old-line politocrat like the Secretary of State may continue to hold the theoretically ultimate power, but he is bound to become more and more dependent upon the expert knowledge of his professional subordinates. Although socialism of the Marxist variety is not in the cards for any of the great Western nations, government intervention and control will increase until almost no scope is left for private enterprise and initiative. In Burnham's judgment, both capitalism and democracy as basic institutions of Western society are dead. Periods of social crisis

[37] Burnham had some difficulty, back in 1941, in fitting Stalin and Molotov into the category of managers. Perhaps he feels vindicated, recently, by the disappearance of the old revolutionists and party wheelhorses and the larger role coming to be occupied by professional administrators. Khrushchev, though commonly thought of as a party boss, made his reputation as an administrator. His recent criticism of the Chinese communes on the ground that they leave no room for what Communists are chiefly interested in—production—probably indicates where his real interests lie.

[38] *The Managerial Revolution.* New York, John Day, 1941, p. 148.

and major transition almost invariably give rise to dictatorships. Perhaps, when the transition is completed and the managerial class has consolidated its power, some degree of democracy will again be permitted, but not in the form of popular sovereignty with freedom of the voters to choose between loyalty to the government and support of the opposition. The managers will not tolerate a serious threat to their monopoly of power. Therefore, the ordinary citizen who wishes to play a political role in the society of the future will have to confine his activities to the sphere of local government and to labor unions, vocational and professional associations, and cooperatives.

Not all contemporary theorists interpret the conservative revolution in terms of the rise of a class of technocrats and the displacement of democracy by a rigid authoritarianism. A number of American authors have attempted to portray the situation in a more favorable light. They maintain that the capitalist system, in recent years, has been undergoing a radical transformation which gives it an almost benevolent character. The popular criticisms of it, emanating from socialists and liberal reformers, are no longer valid. They are based upon assumptions made by the classical economists, who may have understood the capitalism of the nineteenth century but certainly had no vision of what was to develop in the twentieth. Pre-eminent among the prophets of this latter-day capitalism is the Harvard economist, John Kenneth Galbraith. A native of Canada, born in 1908, he received his B.A. degree at the University of Toronto and his Ph.D. at the University of California. From 1934 to 1939 he was an instructor in economics at Harvard and from 1939 to 1942 an assistant professor at Princeton. During World War II he served as Deputy Administrator of the Office of Price Administration. After five years as a member of the board of editors of *Fortune,* he returned to Harvard as Professor of Economics in 1949. He is the author of *American Capitalism: The Concept of Countervailing Power* (1952), *A Theory of Price Control* (1952), *The Great Crash* (1955), and *The Affluent Society* (1958).

Galbraith makes plain beyond doubt, especially in *The Affluent Society,* his profound belief that capitalism, and not socialism, is the real measure of human progress. Instead of being a higher

stage of economic life destined to succeed capitalism, as the
Marxists contend, socialism is the product of a low and simple
standard of living. Not a single advanced industrial nation has
put into effect the Marxist gospel, even where socialist political
support was comparatively strong. But the capitalism Galbraith
acclaims is not that celebrated in the lore of the classical economists. Economic developments of the twentieth century have
passed far beyond the conception made famous by Adam Smith
and his disciples. The new capitalism is dominated by the principle of "countervailing power." The old doctrine that competition is the life of trade, and that anything which interferes with
price-cutting to undersell one's rivals is detrimental to society
has gone into oblivion. Leading corporations no longer attempt
to expand their markets by price competition. Instead, they seek
to attract consumers by offering (or claiming to offer) better
quality or extra features, or by diverse subtle schemes for
awakening a desire for their products. The place of price competition as an automatic regulator has been taken by the polarity of
producer and consumer, buyer and seller, employer and worker.
Each of these pairs of opposites constitutes an example of
countervailing power. In Scandinavia consumers band together
into cooperatives to extort concessions from producers. In the
United States this function is performed by supermarkets and
chain stores. To illustrate: Sears, Roebuck and Company forced
the Goodyear Tire and Rubber Company to supply it with tires
at a discount of 30% to 40%, which the mail-order house then
sells under its own brand name at a substantial saving to its
customers.

But gigantic mercantile establishments are not the only wield-
ers of countervailing power. Big labor unions, encouraged and
assisted by the government, also balance and restrict the ambitions of industrial corporations. Likewise, the farmers, with
their unparalleled advantage of price supports, exercise an
enormous market power. Even the investors, with the backing
of the SEC, have better protection than ever before against vic-
timization by financial interests. More significant still, as an instance of countervailing power, has been the emergence of big
business into the stage of "oligopoly" in place of the monopoly

stage so widely predicted by liberals and Marxists. Nearly every industry of any consequence has come to be dominated by three or more leading corporations—petroleum, steel, electrical equipment, chemicals, automobiles, aircraft, to mention but a few. Each of these major producers becomes a competitor for the consumer's dollar within a particular field. More important, the buyers themselves are able to play one producer off against another for their own advantage. This regime of oligopoly, according to Galbraith, is much to be preferred to the classical economists' ideal of unlimited competition; for it means the existence of a small number of strong, progressive companies, capable of surviving through depressions and of paying good wages to their workers, instead of a large number of savage competitors hovering on the verge of bankruptcy. The author contrasts the oil industry, divided into a half-dozen or more prosperous and progressive companies, with the bituminous coal industry, beaten into desperation and poverty by cutthroat competition.

Galbraith contends that the emergence of the new capitalism requires a fundamental change in political policy. He believes that the government should abandon attempts to enforce unlimited competition under the Sherman Act and similar anti-monopoly measures. The most effective instrument for safeguarding the public interest is not mutually destructive rivalry among sellers, but restraints which strong buyers, with abundant purchasing power, are able to exercise. Concentration of industry into a small number of flourishing companies should therefore be permitted and even encouraged. They alone have the resources to promote the research and scientific advancement so essential to improvement of the standard of living. "A benign Providence who, so far, has loved us for our worries, has made the modern industry of a few large firms an almost perfect instrument for inducing technical change." [39] At the same time, Galbraith acknowledges that his principle of countervailing power will remain effective only when there is a relatively low demand. If buyers are plentiful, the seller will yield nothing to

[39] *American Capitalism: The Concept of Countervailing Power.* Boston, Houghton Mifflin, 1952, p. 91.

the bargaining power of any customer. In other words, counter-vailing power has little effect under conditions of inflation. Sig-nificantly, Galbraith fears inflation as a graver threat to the modern economy than depression. Keynesian theory, he says, has provided a remedy for depression but not for inflation. Therefore, he fervently hopes for the continuance of peace and for the absence of excessive pressures for competition in arma-ments.

A few other Americans go even farther than does Galbraith in extolling the virtues of the new capitalism. For example, David E. Lilienthal (1899–), former New Dealer, one-time Direc-tor of TVA and Chairman of the Atomic Energy Commission, frankly avows his faith in Big Business as the hope of the modern world. He is not interested in countervailing power or any other restraints on capitalist ambitions. He seems to think that the merits of our highly developed business structure are so over-whelming that criticism of it would be the act of an ingrate. He recognizes all the economic advantages pointed out by Galbraith —the higher wages and lower costs, the invulnerability to de-pressions, the resources for scientific and technical advancement —and some others besides. But he is not satisfied to stop with economic arguments. He sees in modern capitalism the lone chance for survival of Western ideals of democracy and freedom. No other system could provide the prodigious flow of armament and scientific weapons to defend the free nations against Com-munist aggression. No other system could produce the great surplus of wealth to make possible a shoring-up of the economies of weaker allies. Internal security is also important; and capital-ism is the one system to provide the high standard of living so essential to maintaining the vigor and health of a population. For these reasons Lilienthal considers anti-trust prosecutions and other actions against mass production and mass distribution as ill-advised and harmful. He has no prejudice against govern-ment; he believes that it must continue to play vital roles. But he contends that, for end results in protecting and preserving our free way of life, "we must, in the main, rely upon Big Business." [40]

Equally vigorous in espousing the cause of what he considers

[40] *Big Business: A New Era.* New York, Harper, 1953, p. 113.

a new and enlightened capitalism is another former New Dealer, Adolf A. Berle, Jr. (1895–   ). Trained as a lawyer at Harvard, he practiced in Boston and New York for more than ten years. In 1927 he became Professor of Corporation Law at Columbia. From 1933 to 1938 he was special counsel to the RFC; from 1938 to 1944, Assistant Secretary of State; and from 1945 to 1946, Ambassador to Brazil. He is commonly regarded as a member of the original Brain Trust under Franklin D. Roosevelt. Though the author of several books on corporate organization and finance, his one connection with the world of business is the chairmanship of the board of directors of the American Molasses Company, which he has held since 1946. His chief writings of a political character are *New Directions in the New World* (1940), *The Natural Selection of Political Forces* (1950), and *The Twentieth Century Capitalist Revolution* (1954).

Berle conceives of the twentieth century as an era distinguished by two great revolutions: a socialist revolution in the Eastern world and a capitalist revolution in the West. The latter he regards as the more significant. Western nations, including the United States, have not been the victims of a "creeping socialism"; instead, they have been the beneficiaries of a "galloping capitalism," which has brought in its train a standard of material well-being exceeding the wildest dreams of preceding generations. The capitalist revolution has been marked by a number of significant features: first, a concentration of economic power so vast that 135 companies in the United States have gained possession of nearly half of the country's industrial assets; second, the reduction of poverty to minimal proportions; third, the diffusion of ownership of large corporations among hundreds of thousands of stockholders, so that each corporation becomes virtually a public entity, and a kind of "people's capitalism" results; fourth, the growth of internal production of capital (the creation of "new money" out of profits) and the consequent obsolescence of the old-time investment capitalist; and fifth, the establishment of an international economic framework creating bonds of unity throughout the Western world, in a more effective fashion than has yet been accomplished by any political organization.

Berle acclaims nearly all of the foregoing developments as instances of progress. Like Galbraith, whom he often quotes, he sheds no tears over the passing of small enterprise, with its unlimited and often disastrous forms of price-cutting competition. He doubts that it ever functioned in quite the balanced and self-regulating way described by its proponents. In any case, he denies the validity of appraising the economy of 1954 in terms of the conceptions of a hundred years earlier. He construes the capitalism of the middle twentieth century as a new organism shaped by a multitude of technological, political, and social developments never having previously existed. The idea that it is a system of exploitation operated by bloated malefactors with an insatiable greed for profits is a relic of Marxist propaganda; it may have been partly true in the past but today is wholly inaccurate. Berle goes so far as to suggest that the famous statement of a president of General Motors that "what is good for General Motors is good for the country" was not without justification. It may have been "naive public relations," but its author "could have adduced an impressive array of statistical fact to back up his statement." [41]

To assume that modern corporations are irresponsible exponents of a "public-be-damned" attitude, Berle believes, is to fly in the face of facts. Even if they were determined to adopt such an attitude, they could not persist in it long, he maintains, for they have a "constituency" in the form of the public, whose opinion they dare not defy. He cites the pressure of public disapproval, on the eve of World War II, that forced American oil companies to abandon their cartel arrangements with I. G. Farbenindustrie for an exchange of patents on synthetic rubber and for the apportionment of world markets. In this instance powerful considerations of patriotism and opposition to Nazism gave force to public feeling. In most cases such elements would not be present. As a consequence, it would not be public opinion primarily that would restrain irresponsible actions of corporations but fear of loss of customers.

As a lawyer Berle is deeply impressed by indications in history

[41] *The 20th Century Capitalist Revolution*. New York, Harcourt, 1954, p. 166.

of the development of "conscience" among rulers and others who would ordinarily have unlimited power to oppress and exploit. He sees profound significance in the acceptance by feudal kings and princes of "conscience" as a restriction upon their power and as a protection for the rights of their subjects. In England this "conscience" came to be embodied in the principles of equity as a kind of supplement to the common law. Ultimately, in both England and the United States, it achieved a status equal to that of the law itself. Obviously, Berle anticipates some such development in relation to modern corporations. At present they occupy a position roughly analogous to that of "fiefdoms." But he discovers signs of the growth of a corporation "conscience," which may radically alter their character and transform them into vehicles of public benefaction. Among such signs are corporation grants to higher education, research, hospitals, and foundations. He considers it not inconceivable that in some future day, enlightened corporations may perform a function comparable to that of the Medici, wielding their power and disbursing a portion of their wealth for the general advancement of learning and the enrichment of culture.

4. Liberal Conservatism

Thus far we have observed three types of conservatives adorning the thought of the twentieth century: those who accept the doctrines of the classical economists, with slight modernization, as fundamental tenets; those who hark back to the traditionalism of Edmund Burke or to the pre-industrial conservatism of Gouverneur Morris and Alexander Hamilton; and those who believe that the capitalist leopard of the twentieth century has really changed his spots and has become a gentle and even generous creature instead of the voracious, predatory beast of Marxist folklore. There is also a fourth school whose members acclaim the ways of the past as definitely preferable but advocate modest adaptations to improve their effectiveness or to bring them into line with the newer demands of civilization. Thus they may recommend government intervention for educational or cultural purposes or to satisfy pressure from below and avert revolution; but always under sufficient restraint to prevent the destruction of liberty. As for political organization, they tend to prefer intellectual aristocracy, not primarily because they regard the mass of men as stupid and depraved but because they consider intelligence, training, and a sense of responsibility necessary qualities in a class of governors. But like most aristocrats of this type, they set their standards so high that they can scarcely hope to see them realized. As a consequence, their thinking has often been characterized by frustration and by a sense of weariness and disillusionment.

The designation which seems most appropriate for this fourth school is liberal conservatism. Its representatives have sprung from a variety of backgrounds. The one most exclusively concerned with political economy was Joseph A. Schumpeter. Born in what is now Czechoslovakia in 1883, he obtained doctors' degrees from the universities of Vienna, Sofia, and Columbia. After teaching in various Austrian universities, he became Minister of Finance of the Austrian Republic in 1919. From 1925 to 1932 he was Professor of Economics at the University of Bonn, and from 1932 till his death in 1950 he held the same position at Harvard. His chief works include *The Theory of Economic Development* (1912) and *Capitalism, Socialism and Democracy* (1942). He is commonly recognized as one of the foremost political economists of the twentieth century.

Schumpeter wrote in what appeared to be a lugubrious vein of pessimism. He predicted the breakdown of capitalism and its inevitable supersession by some form of collectivism scarcely distinguishable from socialism. His aristocratic predilections were revealed in his definition of capitalism, which he conceived not simply in economic terms but as "a scheme of values, an attitude toward life, a civilization—the civilization of inequality and of the family fortune." [42] His conception of socialism was almost equally broad. He defined it as "that organization of society in which the means of production are controlled, and the decisions on how and what to produce and on who is to get what, are made by public authority instead of by privately-owned and

[42] "The March into Socialism," *American Economic Review*, XL (May, 1950), p. 450.

privately-managed firms." [43] Since no reference is made to the character of "public authority," this definition is so comprehensive that it might cover fascism, communism, and even some forms of the welfare state.

According to Schumpeter, nearly all the characteristic developments of recent times have been hastening the dissolution of capitalism and promoting an inexorable progression in the direction of socialism. The first development is total war. During World War I every belligerent nation in Europe adopted radical measures of collectivized control which could not be entirely abandoned when the conflict ended. During World War II the United States, as well as Europe, did the same. A second cause is the success of capitalism in raising the standard of living for all and thereby creating a kind of classless society. A third factor is the emergence of a group of intellectuals independent of the business community and highly critical of capitalist methods and institutions. Because business men are forced to concentrate on management and production, they lose their capacity to defend their system against the onslaughts of its intelligent critics. But the major cause of all, in Schumpeter's opinion, is inflation. This factor is also the consequence of the success of the capitalist system, though it may result from war. Any development contributing to full employment inevitably means pressure for higher wages and therefore involves increased costs of production followed by higher prices. With labor unions as powerful as they are, and with the popular belief in high wages as an index of prosperity, inflation is "a perennial pressure" in the capitalist system of today and is a constant threat to its survival in anything like its classical form.

Though Schumpeter professed not to be "disapproving" but only *describing* the prevailing tendencies of recent times, he clearly betrayed a poignant regret that they ever developed. Nevertheless, he was no King Canute commanding the tides to recede. He recognized that change is inevitable. He acknowledged that "Marx was wrong in his diagnoses of the manner in which capitalist society would break down." But he declared "he was not wrong in the prediction that it would break down

[43] *Ibid.*, p. 446.

eventually." [44] For delaying the breakdown, he considered only
one remedy worthy of adoption. This would consist of government decrees for controlling inflation by fixing prices and wages.
But even such direct controls would increase the size and importance of the bureaucracy and might ultimately lead to a comprehensive system of national planning. For Schumpeter, the
march to what he considered the equivalent of socialism was inexorable. Nothing could stop it. The most to be hoped for was a
few years of postponement.

Less fatalistic than Schumpeter but also tormented by frustration and disillusionment with the state of contemporary society
was the German-British sociologist Karl Mannheim (1893–
1947). Born of German parents in Budapest, he completed his
education at the universities of Berlin, Freiburg, and Heidelberg.
Appointed Professor of Sociology at the University of Frankfurt,
he was deprived of his position when the Nazis came into power,
and he became a voluntary exile in Great Britain. From 1933 to
1945 he lectured on sociology at the University of London. In
1947, the year of his death, he was made Professor of Sociology
and Education at the Institute of Education in London. The
book which brought him his chief claim to fame was written
during World War II and published under the title, *Diagnosis
of Our Time*.

Mannheim was as firmly convinced as Schumpeter that the
contemporary world is moving with alarming speed toward collectivization. He saw all around him, not simply in the totalitarian states but in the democracies as well, an increasing concentration and centralization. All the new techniques of industry,
he maintained, were aiding and abetting control by the few. Add
to these, he said, the mass production of ideas through the press
and the possibilities of manipulating minds through broadcasting and the control of education, and it is easy to see how
dictatorship or some other form of minority rule could be the
wave of the future. He recognized, also, the danger that planning
might be used as an entering wedge for a thoroughgoing system
of regimentation. He did not dream for a minute, however, of
turning the clock backward to the risks and uncertainties of

[44] *Ibid.*, p. 456.

laissez faire. Though he recognized the evils in planned societies of the fascist and communist varieties, he denied that these were the only alternatives. There is a Third Way, he asserted, "a new pattern of society which, although using the techniques of planning, maintains its democratic control, and keeps those spheres of freedom and free initiative which are the genuine safeguards of culture and humanity." That the degree of "free initiative" in the economic sphere would be kept down to a minimum was made clear by the author when he said that ownership of capital and profits would be controlled in the public interest, and that the right of the individual to invest his money "must fit in with a comprehensive plan." [45]

But economic freedom was not Mannheim's major interest. He regarded it as important but largely incidental to other objectives. His primary concern was the preservation of the free society and the values of intellectual freedom and respect for personality which he considered inseparable from democracy. The methods he prescribed, however, for achieving those objectives seem difficult to reconcile with the objectives themselves. He insisted, first of all, that democracy must become militant: no more of the flabby neutralism of the past which permitted a man to advocate anarchism, polygamy, free love, tyrannicide, or revolution. Such well-known liberals as Thomas Jefferson, John Stuart Mill, and William James apparently were wrong when they taught that civilization benefits from the clash of divergent doctrines, and that no expression of opinion, no matter how seemingly dangerous, should be prohibited. But the new militant democracy "will have the courage to agree on some basic values which are acceptable to everybody who shares the traditions of Western civilization." [46] Mannheim refers to such virtues as brotherly love, mutual help, decency, social justice, freedom, respect for the person—but he fails to relate them to the Western tradition that he reveres, or to apply them to specific issues. Does brotherly love, for example, imply pacifism? Does respect for the person necessitate exemption for conscientious objectors? Does freedom mean

[45] *Diagnosis of Our Time.* London, Kegan Paul, Trench, Trubner, 1947, p 38.
[46] *Ibid.*, p. 7.

liberty to follow one's conscience or simply an Aristotelian freedom in obedience to the law?

Despite Mannheim's professions of devotion to the virtues and values of the free society, there is evidence that he really envisaged a world almost as completely regimented as Plato's Republic. For one thing, he advocated "democratic tolerance," which he defined as the right "to hate and to exclude those who wish to misuse the methods of freedom to abolish freedom." It would be a tolerance extended to all but the intolerant, after the fashion of Rousseau's "civil religion." Mannheim urged, in the second place, what he called education for "basic conformity." He deplored the policy of non-interference with valuations and indifference to common aims which he thought characterized most democracies. Such a policy, he maintained, leads to drifting and prepares the way for submission and dictatorship. What he meant was that if human beings are left in complete uncertainty with unlimited freedom of choice, they will rebel and embrace authoritarianism in sheer desperation. The appropriate remedy, he thought, was to give them a moderate amount of authoritarianism from the start. He conceived of education on two levels: on the lower level, training in group conformity, habit-formation, and obedience; and on the higher level, a gradual emergence of those qualities "which make for individualization and the creation of independent personalities." [47] He apparently believed that all, or most, members of society could be conducted through both of these stages of education without warping or confusing their minds.

It is perhaps not strange that Mannheim should have considered religion a valuable ally in his plan for achieving basic conformity in democratic societies. No fundamental change in social habits can be accomplished, he believed, without enthusiasm and emotionalization of the new principles men are to adopt. To provide these driving forces is the function of religion. Moreover, "only a generation which has been educated through religion, or at least on the religious level, to discriminate between immediate advantage and the lasting issues of life" will be willing to accept the sacrifice which a "properly planned democratic order" must

[47] *Ibid.*, p. 52.

continually demand from every individual.[48] What he actually visualized was a body of doctrines and codes of behavior similar to the *Summa Theologica* of St. Thomas Aquinas. It would set forth principles couched in religious and moral terms, concrete patterns of conduct, an image of satisfactory social institutions, and "a whole world view as a connecting link between them." Mannheim assured his readers that the proposed doctrines and codes were not meant to be dictatorial rules but a body of ideals "put at the disposal of those who crave for a consistent way of life." [49] As such, they would fulfill a function indispensable to the survival of modern society.

Liberal conservatism concerned almost exclusively with cultural and social values is exemplified by the philosophy of José Ortega y Gasset (1883–1955). Ortega was born in Madrid, the son of the editor of a conservative but influential newspaper. He received his doctorate in philosophy and literature at the University of Madrid in 1904. He continued there as an instructor and lecturer and in 1908 was made Professor of Metaphysics. He took an active part in the opposition to Alfonso XIII, but was dissatisfied when the Revolution of 1931 went too far for his conservative sympathies. Though he accepted a seat in the new Parliament, he did not rally to the support of the Republic when civil war broke out in 1936. Instead, he fled to France. After the victory of the Insurgents in 1939, Franco attempted to induce him to return to Spain. He offered to make him the "official philosopher" of the nation if he would agree to delete certain passages from his writings. Ortega indignantly refused. He became an exile in South America, but eight years later he returned to Spain to found a Free Institute of Philosophy and Cultural Science in Madrid.

Ortega agrees with much in the philosophy of Mannheim. Like Mannheim, he sees the people of the Western world deep in a morass of nihilism. They have rebelled against being ordered and commanded and have become a law unto themselves. They have neither convictions nor standards. They honor no principles and respect no superiors. They have demanded and obtained absolute freedom. But their lives are empty, and they are bored with their

[48] *Ibid.*, p. 103.
[49] *Ibid.*, p. 111.

meaningless existence. As a consequence, they will rebel again and demand a leader, a party, a religion to order their lives and command their loyalties. Ortega predicted, in 1930, that "Before long there will be heard throughout the planet a formidable cry, rising like the howl of innumerable dogs to the stars, asking for someone or something to take command, to impose an occupation, a duty." [50]

According to Ortega, the loftiest ideal of social life ever devised by human beings is liberal democracy. But he seemed to consider it too exalted for ordinary mortals. For it involves a willingness on the part of the majority to limit its power for the benefit of the minority. It suggests generosity and consideration for the weak. It requires a discipline too difficult and demanding for any but the noblest spirits to impose upon themselves. Above all, it is government in accordance with reason, of discussion before action, and of education and persuasion continued to the furthest potential before any resort to force. Such are the attributes of liberal democracy. But as a government where the multitude holds the reins of power, it is out of the question. For the nature of every society is aristocratic. There is always a minority of superior men and a vast majority made up of the inferior and the average. This majority is what Ortega meant by "the masses." The mass man differs from his superiors in making no demands upon himself, in being contented with what he is. He is devoid of standards and of sense of duty and responsibility. He takes all of the achievements of civilization for granted in disregard of the fact that he himself has contributed nothing. When anything goes wrong, he acts like a spoiled child, wrecking and destroying the work of others. Possessing no knowledge or particular skill, he is inherently a barbarian, but he considers himself as good as anyone else.

Since the late nineteenth century the masses, as Ortega defined them, have been in rebellion. In only a few countries have they overturned governments or perpetrated any drastic social upheaval. In most nations their revolt has taken the form of a gradual rise to dominance as a consequence of increasing num-

[50] *The Revolt of the Masses*. New York, Norton, 1932 (22d printing), p. 136.

bers, their burgeoning incomes, and the expansion of economic opportunities as a result of industrialization. But their power is none the less real. They have brought into existence a "hyper-democracy" which recognizes no law but the will of the majority and no right but the interest of the strong. In some places they have fathered such movements as syndicalism and fascism, characterized by contempt for reason and by glorification of violence and "direct action."

The old liberalism gave primacy to reason as an essential element of civilized government. Force was recognized only as a last resort, for, in Ortega's own words, "Civilization is nothing else than the attempt to reduce force to being the *ultima ratio*." [51] But the revolt of the masses, as expressed in syndicalism and fascism, has reversed the order of things. A cult of unreason has been adopted as a kind of final appeal, and force has been exalted as the *prima ratio*. The emergence of this cult is the climax and culmination of a long trend toward barbarism. A man is uncivilized to the extent that he is oblivious of the rights of others and is ready to use violence to gain his ends. The revolt of the masses must be regarded as identical with what has been called "the vertical invasion of the barbarians." If men of such type continue to be masters in Europe, Ortega maintained that thirty years would suffice to send that continent back to the Dark Ages.

In comparison with many of his contemporaries, Ortega had few remedies to propose for the ills of the world. He did, of course, clearly imply that control of political society should be entrusted to men of talent, nobility, and intelligence; for when a society is no longer aristocratic, it ceases to be a society. At the same time, he would have reduced the powers of the government to a low minimum. The greatest danger that threatens civilization today, he said, is state intervention. He feared the bureaucratization of life and the destruction of initiative and spontaneity. Increase the functions of the police, he warned, and you will eventually find them defining the standards and deciding on the principles they are going to impose. If Ortega could have perceived a greater supply of talented overseers, perhaps he would have tempered his opposition to the enlargement of the province of

[51] *Ibid.*, p. 75.

government, but in the back of his mind was the constant dread that it would always be the masses who would control the state.

Like Mannheim, Ortega attached major importance to the shaping and ordering of social opinion. Never has anyone ruled on this earth, he said, except on the basis of public opinion. But the majority of men have no opinions, except what are pumped into them from the outside. The most appropriate agency for performing this function is organized religion. ". . . without a spiritual power, *without someone to command,* and in proportion as this is lacking, chaos reigns over mankind." [52] That the commands of this spiritual power might interfere with the life of reason he esteemed so highly did not seem to enter his mind. Finally, Ortega considered it imperative that Europe should regain the position of dominance that once was hers. By Europe he meant France, Great Britain, and Germany. In these countries alone were to be found the breadth and originality that qualify for leadership of civilization. Moreover, the building-up of these nations into a consolidated union or United States of Europe would be the one enterprise that could counterbalance the victories of the Communist East. The necessary steps to the forging of such a union he left to the ingenuity of others to propose.

Conservatism is undoubtedly a valuable force in contemporary society. It deserves recognition for its part in calling attention to the importance of those qualities which distinguish the civilized from the barbarian existence—such qualities as refinement, civility, respect for personality, reason, and justice. Belief in these qualities is, of course, no man's monopoly. Liberals esteem them highly, and so do some radicals. But the tendency of the conservative is to exalt them above all else and to add to them the more negative virtue of restraint and a reactionary concern with the past and tradition. Most of the conservatives of the twentieth century can also be credited with a desire to promote aristocracy, in the original sense of the rule of the best. But again this is nothing on which they can claim a patent. Thomas Jefferson advocated an aristocracy of virtue and talent, with the proviso merely that the *aristoi* should derive their offices and power from the

[52] *Ibid.,* p. 129.

people. John Stuart Mill proposed to achieve a similar object by plural voting for the educated classes and by the Hare system of proportional representation, which would enable intellectuals to form constituencies and elect representatives to the House of Commons.

The ingredient which seems to differentiate most clearly the conservatives of our century is a body of doctrines which most of them hold in common regarding the nature of man and his capacities for life in society. Briefly stated, these doctrines are: the weakness and vileness of human nature; the incapacity of the average man to use reason in solving his problems; the futility and even harmfulness of most positive forms of social action; the impossibility of democracy and therefore the necessity for a strong executive or for some form of élitism or minority rule; the need for religion as a source of social commandments and as a sanction for basic conformity; the danger that individualism and freedom to experiment with ideas and institutions will lead to fascism or some other form of totalitarianism. Such is the pattern of ideas which seems to possess the minds of most of our modern conservatives, with the notable exception of those who have been described as prophets of the conservative revolution.

Ascribing the evils of our time to ideas one does not like is a common practice, and is by no means confined to a particular school of political thinkers. If one abhors the teachings of Pragmatism, for example, it is tempting to conclude that Pragmatism must bear a major responsibility for the strife and disorders of the present age. But to draw such conclusions is to credit too much to the influence of ideas. It is to ignore such monumental factors as nationalism, the rivalry of empires, the maladjustments of the economic system, the pressure of population upon natural resources, and the breakdown resulting from World War I. The triumph of Bolshevism in Russia can scarcely be explained as an intellectual phenomenon. It occurred rather as a consequence of disorganization produced by the War and of an intense longing for peace. It was the Bolsheviks' slogan of "Peace, Land and Bread" that put them into power, not their Marxist philosophy. The surging mobs that heiled Hitler were not partisans of relativism, empiricism, pacifism, or humanism. They were men of more primitive interests

—peasants, small businessmen, and white-collar workers hounded by fears for their economic future. To the extent that they dwelt at all in the world of ideas, it was in the murky realm of racism, anti-Semitism, and romantic longing to restore the past.

ADDITIONAL READINGS

Berle, Adolf A. *Economic Power and the Free Society*. New York, Fund for the Republic, 1957.

Churchill, Sir Winston. *Blood, Sweat and Tears*. New York, Putnam, 1941.

———. *The Sinews of Peace*. Boston, Houghton Mifflin, 1949.

———. *The Second World War*. Boston, Houghton Mifflin, 1948–1953. Six vols.

———. *While England Slept*. New York, Putnam, 1938.

Galbraith, J. Kenneth. *The Affluent Society*. Boston, Houghton Mifflin, 1958.

Hayek, Friedrich A. *Collectivist Economic Planning*. London, Routledge, 1935.

———. *Individualism and Economic Order*. Chicago, University of Chicago Press, 1948.

Hoover, Herbert. *American Individualism*. Garden City, Doubleday, 1922.

———. *The Challenge to Liberty*. New York, Scribner, 1934.

———. *The New Day*. Stanford, Calif., Stanford University Press, 1928.

Mannheim, Karl. *Ideology and Utopia*. New York, Harcourt, 1946.

Mises, Ludwig von. *The Anti-Capitalistic Mentality*. Princeton, Van Nostrand, 1956.

———. *Planned Chaos*. Irvington-on-Hudson, N. Y., Foundation for Economic Education, 1947.

———. *Socialism: an Economic and Sociological Analysis*. New Haven, Yale University Press, 1951.

Ortega y Gasset, José. *Concord and Liberty*. New York, Norton, 1946.

———. *Man and Crisis*. New York, Norton, 1958.

———. *Man and People*. New York, Norton, 1957.

Rauschning, Hermann. *The Conservative Revolution*. New York, Putnam, 1941.

Rossiter, Clinton L. *Conservatism in America*. New York, Knopf, 1955.

Salomon, Albert. *The Tyranny of Progress*. New York, Noonday Press, 1955.

Viereck, Peter. *Conservatism: From John Adams to Churchill*. Princeton, Van Nostrand, 1956.

————. *Conservatism Revisited*. New York, Scribner, 1949.

Voegelin, Eric A. *The New Science of Politics*. Chicago, University of Chicago Press, 1952.

Wilson, Francis G. *The Case for Conservatism*. Seattle, University of Washington Press, 1951.

CHAPTER
XI

Religious Foundations of
Political Theory

Closely related to conservatism are those theories of modern times which insist that the problems of politics lend themselves to a religious interpretation. Exponents of these theories maintain, in fact, that religion is the ground and substance of civilization, and that without such support it would speedily collapse. The popularity of these views goes back to the reaction that followed the French Revolution. The violence of that movement instilled horror into the minds of conservative people all over Europe. It seemed destructive of every institution and tradition they had long regarded as sacred. Neither the family, the state, nor Christian morality was immune from its baneful influence. But conservatives knew just as well as liberals that the Revolution was the result of anterior causes. They attributed it to the rationalism, materialism, secularism, and humanism of the eighteenth-century Enlightenment. Man, they believed, had set himself up in the place of God, exaggerating his own intellectual powers, denying spiritual values, and repudiating the guidance of priests and kings whom God had appointed. The horrors and wickedness of the Reign of Terror were the natural consequences of such brazen effrontery.

The leaders of the reaction drew still other conclusions. They came to interpret the Enlightenment and the upheaval which followed as a kind of second Fall of Man. Philosophers like Louis

Bonald and Joseph de Maistre immersed themselves in deep pessimism and mourned the end of civilization. Such prophets of doom have had their descendants down through the ages ever since. In fact, it might appear that the world of ideas has never fully recovered from the French Revolution and its after-effects. The lamentations of its opponents have echoed to the present day. Such influential figures as Cardinal Newman, Sören Kierkegaard, Pobedonostsev, Dostoievski, and Nicholas Berdyaev, during the nineteenth century, bewailed the decline of religion and the triumph of secularism as sure indications of the end of the world. They have worthy successors in those poets and philosophers of the twentieth century who believe that religion is the key to culture and that a return to Christianity is the last best hope of saving civilization. These latter-day religionists look upon Lenin and Khrushchev with the same forebodings that were once aroused by Robespierre and Saint-Just. Perhaps they do not reckon with the fact that the home of the Bolshevik Revolution had been perhaps the most devout, "Christian" nation in Europe —in the sense of allegiance to a formal, organized faith. While present in some intellectual circles, free-thinking had made no such progress in Russia as it had in France or Great Britain. Instead, mysticism, the veneration of saints, confession, self-humiliation, and purification by punishment had been the ruling ideas. Western science and liberalism, commonly regarded as the two chief instruments of secularism, had scarcely dented the great wall of orthodoxy in "holy" Russia that was to crumble under the swift attacks of Lenin and his followers.

1. Neo-Orthodoxy

The most virile of the politico-religious movements of the twentieth century is that which has been given the name of Neo-Orthodoxy. It is essentially a Protestant movement, confined primarily to the Reformed and Evangelical churches. It has produced, however, some of the greatest theologians of modern times. Their doctrines revolve around the sinfulness of human nature, the supremacy of faith over reason, the predominance of evil in the world, and the necessity of submission to the will of

God. Leaders of the movement disagree as to the attitude which they believe the individual should take toward the state. Some regard the princes of this world as veritable tools of the Prince of Darkness. The pious Christian should therefore shun them and all their works. He should strive to perfect himself in holiness and overcome the evil in the world by the force of his own example. The majority of Neo-Orthodox theologians, however, consider it a religious duty for the Christian to participate in political and social affairs. He should oppose tyranny and oppression, support democracy, and crusade for freedom and social justice. Though they do not demand an official religion or the subordination of the state to the church, they do contend that secularism has gone too far, and they generally accept the Calvinist (and the Catholic) position that it is the function of Christian ministers to call governments to account.

Neo-Orthodoxy had a dual paternity. Its fathers were two Swiss theologians whose activities and influence extended beyond their native land. The older, Karl Barth, was born in Basel in 1886, the son of a Reformed theologian. Educated at the universities of Bern, Berlin, Tübingen, and Marburg, he entered the clergy in 1909 in Geneva. After 1925 he was Professor of Theology, successively, at the universities of Göttingen, Münster, and Bonn. In 1934 he was deprived of his position and banned from Germany for refusing to take an oath of loyalty to the Hitler government. Returning to Switzerland to teach at Basel, he became an outspoken critic of Nazism, meanwhile aiding refugees from Germany and serving in the Swiss army as a sentry on the German frontier. After the war he visited Hungary and endorsed the position of the Reformed church of that country in refusing to fight the Communist government. As a result, he was accused in some quarters of having been converted to Communism. He has also been condemned for centering his attention on the Kingdom of God and ignoring the practical and often tragic decisions men must make on earth. Both of these criticisms appear unjust. He has vigorously repudiated any sympathy with Communism, maintaining, however, that that movement can be stopped only by a "better justice" in capitalist countries, not by belligerent opposition. He thinks that the Church should remain "above the battle" in the conflict between East and West. As for religion itself, he sees it in confusion and chaos as a result of the "flexible liberalism" of the nineteenth century and the "God-forgetting humanism" this liberalism produced.

Barth's early theological development occurred during the critical years of World War I. In this period he was largely under the influence of Kierkegaard. During most of his life, however, he has walked in the shadow of John Calvin. The system of the Genevan Reformer is reflected in the great majority of his teachings. Barth accepts Calvin's view of the absolute sovereignty of God. The divine ruler of the universe holds everything in the hollow of his hand. Not a sparrow falls to the ground except in accordance with His inscrutable decree. The divine will controls and dominates everything in the universe, including man himself. Man has no means of accomplishing his salvation, of justifying himself before God, or even of performing, by his own efforts, a virtuous act. "Man is a being that has to be overcome by the Word and the Spirit of God, that has to be reconciled to God, justified and sanctified, comforted and ruled and finally saved by God." [1] There is no such thing as righteousness apart from God; apparently, as St. Augustine said, the pagan virtues are simply "splendid vices." Only the grace of God can endow man with the capacity to live a good life. In like manner, the fate of the individual in the afterlife depends entirely upon predestination. For unfathomable reasons of His own, God has elected, from the beginning of the world, certain men to be saved and has consigned all the others to eternal damnation. It should be recognized, however, that Barth is not always an uncompromising Calvinist. He does not share Calvin's legalism or accept unquestioningly his dogma of total depravity. He confesses his attraction to the "thesis of humanism that even fallen man is the bearer of the divine spark." [2] Finally, and perhaps most important, he admits the conception of a God of love. Beneath the awful majesty and terror of a deity of justice and vengeance lies the

---

[1] "Brunner's Aim," in Emil Brunner and Karl Barth, *Natural Theology*. London, The Centenary Press, 1946, p. 126.

[2] *The Word of God and the Word of Man*. Boston, Pilgrim Press, 1928, p. 310.

tender nature of a divine father who loves his creatures.

The key to most of the political philosophy of Karl Barth is his theological doctrine, "God alone can save the world." [3] Through the greater part of his life he has clung to the principle that men can do little of consequence to change their fate. In fact, he has seemed to think that they should not even try. He interprets the advice of Ecclesiastes, "Be not righteous overmuch; neither make thyself over wise," as meaning that God is the architect of change, and that in the perspective of eternity the puny deeds of men are insignificant. In 1946 he urged the nations of Europe to forget their dreams of a new order on earth and to adopt as their prayer, "Thy Kingdom Come." In 1949 he proclaimed love of the poor to be a cardinal message of the Christian gospel. But he proposed no measures for the abolition of poverty. Rather, he appeared to assume the division into rich and poor to be part of a divine plan to enhance the significance of Christ's mission to the down-trodden. Besides, the spiritual riches of the Christian religion would more than compensate for economic privation. Barth did state, however, that the Church should stand for social justice and for equality before the law in order that the weak may not be unduly restricted and the strong unduly protected.

Barth's conception of the relations that should obtain between Church and state resembles closely the Calvinist pattern. He vigorously repudiates the Lutheran model of a Church subordinate to the civil authority. The Pauline injunction that every soul should be subject to the "higher powers" [4] he interprets as a requirement that the Christian should perform his duty in preserving and maintaining the civil community and in assisting the execution of its tasks, at the same time fulfilling his higher obligations as a follower of Christ. He must remember that the civil cause as well as the Christian cause is the cause of God. But this does not mean that Barth regards the two authorities as of equal importance. The world over which the civil authority presides is a world of sin, and therefore its officers are more subject to temptation and are more likely to be contaminated by the evil around them. The Church, according to Barth, has a special

[3] *Ibid.*, p. 281.
[4] Romans 13:1.

mission to call secular rulers to account when they commit injustice or oppress their subjects. He does not go to the same length as did John Knox in authorizing the Church to rebuke rulers for impiety, or for failure to maintain the true religion; but he certainly believes that the spiritual power should hold the ascendancy. For him, it would be a great calamity if the Church were to be absorbed by the state. For the state "has no message to deliver; it is dependent upon a message being delivered to it. It is not in a position to appeal to the authority and grace of God; it is dependent on this happening elsewhere. It does not pray; it depends on others praying for it." [5]

Although the Church has no authority to enforce any particular conception of the just state, it must not be indifferent, in Barth's opinion, to political realities. It has full warrant for conferring its blessing upon whichever seems to be the better political system in any given situation. This authority, however, does not extend to insistence upon concrete forms or ideological patterns. A monarchy may be just as good, under some conditions, as a republic. Any one of the several ideological systems of social-liberalism, cooperativism, syndicalism, or radical Marxism may meet the requirements of social justice in particular settings. It is not even necessary that, in all circumstances, the Church must "withdraw from and oppose what may be practically a dictatorship," provided it has a temporary character and is not a totalitarian state.[6] Under ordinary conditions, though, the government should be a government of laws. A constitution should reign supreme, with equal rights for all and special privileges for none.

The Church should also support, according to Barth, the principle of the separation of powers, as an extra safeguard against tyranny. On the other hand, the Church should avoid the encouragement of political parties, especially of a separate Christian party. Parties are among the most questionable phenomena in political life. To encourage them is to exert a divisive influence in society. The Church must stand unconditionally for all men, for the common cause of the whole community. Indeed, its concern is even broader; it extends to all of humanity. Since God Himself

[5] *Against the Stream*. London, SCM Press, 1954, pp. 22–23.
[6] *Ibid.*, p. 37.

became man, the cause of humanity is of supreme Christian importance. For this reason, the Church must be committed to peace, though not to absolute peace, or peace at any price. In "exceptional cases" violence "must be approved, supported, and if necessary even suggested by the Christian community." [7] As examples, Barth mentions police measures to enforce law-court decisions, revolutions to overthrow incompetent or unworthy rulers, and "defensive war against an external threat to the lawful State." [8] To anyone familiar with the political history of modern times, Barth's "exceptional cases" would virtually appear to constitute the norm.

No state, according to Barth, is wholly good or wholly bad. There are simply better and worse states. But since government was instituted by God, even the most imperfect state reveals something of the divine wisdom and the divine patience. It must not be forgotten that the government to which Paul referred as divinely ordained was the government of the Emperor Nero. The principle that no state is absolutely good or absolutely evil applies with equal force, in Barth's judgment, to political systems and "isms." He does not share the common fear that any one ideology is likely to conquer the entire earth. The Kingdom of God, he believes, has made enough progress that "the devil has already lost his ancient right to the whole human race." [9] Though in the 1930's and 1940's Barth did condemn the Hitler movement, he subsequently made it known that his action was motivated by the conviction that the dangers within Nazism were not clearly recognized. Too many people, including the great Churchill, thought of it as a wholesome antidote to anarchic tendencies and to Communism. Not a few Christians were persuaded that it had elements of social justice in it which would be a healthy corrective for the ills of the depression. Moreover, in contrast with Western democracy, it was black against white. It was not simply the lesser of two evils, but evil itself. "It was a mixture of madness and crime in which there was no trace of reason." [10]

[7] *Ibid.*, p. 41.
[8] *Id.*
[9] *Ibid.*, p. 81.
[10] *Ibid.*, p. 136.

As to the other chief form of totalitarianism, Barth's attitude is radically different. In fact, he will hardly admit that Soviet Communism *is* totalitarian. In drawing a contrast with Nazism, he stresses the element of underlying purpose. The goals of the Soviets are constructive; they incorporate objectives of social justice. The means they employ, though deplorable, are not to be classed with the bloody savagery of the Nazis. They are more like the atrocities of the French Revolution; misguided, perhaps, but animated by nobility of purpose. "It would be quite absurd," he says, "to mention in the same breath the philosophy of Marxism and the 'ideology' of the Third Reich, to mention a man of the stature of Joseph Stalin in the same breath as such charlatans as Hitler, Goering, Hess, Goebbels, Himmler, Ribbentrop, Rosenberg, Streicher, etc." [11] Apparently, for Barth, Soviet Communism is simply a logical extension and fulfillment of the system of Marx. Its leaders, therefore, must be the same self-sacrificing and devoted apostles of social idealism as were the original prophets of Marxism themselves. As late as 1951 he could write that the Soviets had never committed the crime of anti-Semitism or emulated the Nazis in removing and replacing "the real Christ by a national Jesus."

With respect to the great conflict which has raged between East and West since 1947, Barth has had only one answer. He conceives of this conflict as a power-struggle between rival empires and therefore as something with which Christians should have nothing to do. It is not a struggle for civilization, the dignity of the individual, or the free society. Moral issues have been completely overshadowed by competition for political and economic advantage. Barth denies that the Western powers have ever really been interested in opposing tyranny or condemning oppression. If they were they would not be conferring their blessings upon Franco or acquiescing by silence in the atrocities committed by some of their allies in suppressing revolts in their subject territories. The crusade of the West is a crusade merely against *Eastern* totalitarianism and is therefore "not quite honest." [12] The Christian Church should lend no support to such hypocrisy. In-

[11] *Ibid.*, p. 139.
[12] *Ibid.*, p. 138.

stead, it should be a lamp to guide men's feet toward a "third way." It should not succumb to the wiles and prejudices of either the Eastern or the Western colossus but should walk between them and summon them both to put away evil. Its supreme obligation is to preach to all men "the forgotten cause of God and man" and thereby hasten the coming of the Kingdom in all parts of the earth.[13] Such would be its greatest contribution toward a better world.

Before World War II Barth had a zealous co-worker in his compatriot, Emil Brunner. Together they founded a reform movement in Protestantism known as the "Theology of Crisis." It was based upon the doctrine that revelation is the only source of knowledge of God, and that reason and science have no value in the field of religion. Since 1945, however, the two theologians have drifted apart, largely over issues of a political character. Brunner was born in Switzerland in 1889. He received a doctorate in theology at the University of Zürich and soon afterward began his career as a minister of the Reformed church. From 1914 to 1952 he was Professor of Theology at the University of Zürich. In 1952 he became Professor of Christian Ethics and Philosophy at the International Christian University in Japan.

Although Brunner and Barth have been engaged in heated controversy for some time, the differences in their theological beliefs do not seem monumental. Both recognize the unlimited sovereignty of God. Brunner describes Him as an absolute monarch and avows that any concept of democratic equality in relations between man and the Eternal would mean "the end of true religion." [14] Both stress the omnipresence of sin in the world and postulate the corruption of human nature. Sin, they believe, takes the form primarily of rebellion against God. Man takes advantage of his intelligence to deny the Being who created him, to set himself up as lord of his own life. Ultimately, this treason against God completely destroys human dignity, whose only secure basis is the brotherhood of all men under a common Father. Both Barth and Brunner emphasize the bondage of the will and deny that man, by his own efforts, can achieve any knowledge of the

[13] *Ibid.*, p. 131.
[14] *The Scandal of Christianity*. London, SCM Press, 1951, p. 27.

divine or contribute one iota to his soul's redemption. Only by the freely given grace of God can the individual conquer his own corruption, comprehend the mysteries of the Christian revelation, and save himself from the flames of hell.

The chief disagreements between the two men on the theological issues revolve around the conception of man as the image of God and the literal inerrancy of the Scriptures. Barth maintains that the image of God in man was destroyed by the Fall. Brunner contends that in every creation the spirit of the creator somehow persists, and that the ability of man to receive the Word of God and the Holy Spirit provides "a point of contact for the divine grace of redemption." Brunner seems less interested than Barth in upholding the inerrancy of the Scriptures. He admits that "historical criticism has transformed the gospels into a field of ruins." [15] He becomes almost mystical, however, in his sublime faith that, despite the depredations of the critics, God will imbue His followers with absolute certainty that His revelation is true.

The disagreements between the two theological giants over political issues are more fundamental. Indeed, they scarcely stop short of accusing each other of political blindness and indifference to ethical values. For example, Barth accuses Brunner of sympathizing with the so-called "German Christians," who made their peace with Hitler. By way of retaliation, Brunner indicts Barth for underestimating the wickedness of the Soviets and for failing to perceive that the real danger to Christian civilization is secularism. Both men assume that the primary function of the Church is to advance the coming of the Kingdom of God, and they deny that this Kingdom can be identified with any social order that ever has been or ever will be established on earth. Yet Barth seems to think that the Soviet regime has been a powerful agent in doing what is humanly possible to promote social justice. Brunner, on the other hand, denounces Soviet Communism and bestows what limited affection he can give to any political system on democratic socialism. In an address delivered in Cardiff, Wales, in 1952, he praised the great British Labour leaders—Keir Hardie, Philip Snowden, and Ramsay MacDonald—for "fighting for

[15] *Ibid.*, p. 25.

socialism against capitalism in the name of Jesus Christ." He declared that he had long considered it "to be the task of the Church to work for that new social order which has now become a reality in your country." [16] At the same time, he made it clear that crusading for a new social order, while exceedingly important, is not the main task of the Church. Moreover, he warned his British hearers that they must not carry socialism much further, lest it lead to the destruction of democracy. Collectivization, he argued, is unavoidably accompanied by a degree of depersonalization. The individual's sense of responsibility is reduced, and he is encouraged to look to the state as the custodian of his welfare. He thus tends to forget his dependence upon God. How dependence upon God is reconcilable with individual responsibility in the first place is a question which Brunner and other Calvinists have not satisfactorily answered.

In attempting to summarize the political disagreements between Brunner and Barth, we encounter the paradox that Brunner, despite his humanism, is actually more pessimistic than Barth. While his humanism is not boundless, Brunner does argue that, in spite of the Fall, man retains a capacity for virtue and a power to receive the divine Word. He accepts the idea of a natural law impelling man toward his own perfection. The individual can thereby struggle toward limited goals of social welfare and political justice. His actual accomplishments, however, will be small indeed. Should he succeed in creating a Garden of Eden, he would soon find it invaded by the serpent of secularism; for any considerable improvement resulting from man's own efforts causes him to think of himself as his own savior and therefore to forget God. Secularization will ultimately mean the downfall of civilization, since all the great values and ideals that have made possible man's emergence from barbarism have grown out of the Christian ethos.

By contrast, Barth says that all political and social systems, democratic and authoritarian alike, are evil. While he has appeared to lean over backwards to give the Soviets their due, his attitude has been mainly a reaction against the alleged hypocrisy of the West. Actually, Barth denies that anything produced or

[16] *The Church in the New Social Order.* London, SCM Press, 1952, p. 14.

controlled by man, whether pagan or Christian, can be good. This conception, though, is not so pessimistic as it seems. For Barth simply excludes from philosophical consideration all of the events of human history. Nothing has real significance, in his judgment, except the operations of God's will in the world which hasten the advent of His Kingdom. And he seems to have faith that progress toward this goal has already been so great that its final attainment cannot long be delayed. The rise of totalitarianism and the imperialisms of East and West will be nothing but memories in that last great day which will bring freedom and joy to all.

Much more socially and politically conscious than either Barth or Brunner is their American confrere, Reinhold Niebuhr. Born in 1892 in the little town of Wright City, Missouri, Niebuhr was the son of an Evangelical pastor. He obtained his education at Elmhurst College, Eden Theological Seminary in St. Louis, and Yale Divinity School. In 1915 he became pastor of a struggling church in Detroit and gained fame for his interest in problems of industrial justice and as a radical friend of the workingman. In 1928 he joined the faculty of Union Theological Seminary, where he continued his preoccupation with the relation of religion to political and social issues. A pacifist and a socialist, he was chosen as editor of *The World Tomorrow*, a radical Christian journal. About 1940, however, he resigned the editorship and also renounced both his pacifism and his socialism. He became a vehement opponent of fascism and one of the earliest advocates of American participation in World War II. He took the stand that war would be a lesser evil than the triumph of anti-Christian tyranny. In 1944 he was elected Vice-chairman of the Liberal Party in New York. In recent years he has been prominently associated with the liberal, anti-Communist movement in the United States.

Karl Barth and Emil Brunner are theologians first and foremost, with political theory occupying hardly more than an incidental place in their systems. With Niebuhr it is almost the reverse. His interest in civic and international issues is so intense that his theology becomes practically the handmaiden of his political and social theory. Nevertheless, he *is* a theologian and the most vigorous American spokesman of Neo-Orthodoxy, though he dislikes to be classified under that heading. He regards the Christian dogma of an all-powerful but merciful God, who became incarnate in the body of Christ and suffered death on the Cross in expiation of the sins of mankind, as the only doctrine which can give meaning to life and conserve the values of our civilization. Secularism, when carried to its logical extreme, produces skepticism, nihilism, and ultimately despair. But since no one can live in despair, "demonic religions" like Nazism and fanatical nationalism rush in to fill the spiritual vacuum. In addition, according to Niebuhr, Christianity is and always has been the most effective source of opposition to tyranny. The great enemies of tyrants have been men who could say, "We must obey God rather than man." But even this is not all. Democracy requires an attitude of humility in the individual epitomized by the Christian conception of the sinful and tragic nature of man. Only to the extent that the individual recognizes his own unworthiness and the tragedy of life in this world is he capable of tolerance and understanding of the problems of his neighbor. But no utopia of peace and good will can ever be established on earth by the efforts of man; for Niebuhr believes in original sin. He considers this belief absolutely essential to an explanation of the problem of evil. No environmentalist, he argues, has ever answered the question how corrupt and tyrannical institutions could have come into existence if all men are basically good. The doctrine of original sin simply corroborates "a fact which every page of human history attests." [17]

A depreciatory view of human nature provides the heart and core of Niebuhr's political philosophy. True, he does say that men are endowed with both selfish and unselfish impulses. He admits that human beings have a sense of obligation toward the good, "as their minds conceive it," and that they have impulses of pity which bid them fly to the aid of victims of tragedy; but he dwells very briefly on these aspects of human character. His reasoning, which seems to resemble some of the views of Nietzsche, compares man with the beasts of the jungle, virtually to the dis-

[17] *The Children of Light and the Children of Darkness.* New York, Scribner, 1947, pp. 16, 133–34.

credit of man. "The beast of prey," he says, "ceases from its conquests when its maw is crammed; but man's lusts are fed by his imagination, and he will not be satisfied until the universal objectives which the imagination envisages are attained." In his saner moments man sees his life fulfilled as a part of a harmonious whole; "but he has few sane moments; for he is governed more by imagination than by reason and imagination is compounded of mind and impulse." [18]

To Niebuhr it seems axiomatic that man is a predominantly selfish creature. The individual human being is motivated primarily by factors of pride, the will-to-live, and the will-to-power. These influences enter even into the most idealistic enterprises and make "hypocrisy an inevitable by-product of all virtuous endeavor." [19] The will-to-live has altruistic possibilities, since man can realize his true self only in the fulfillment of obligations to others. But men are not interested merely in the realization of self; they strive also for domination and prestige. The will-to-live is therefore almost automatically transmuted into the will-to-power.

Niebuhr's views on man in society bear similarities to those of Le Bon. Like Le Bon, he believes that the behavior of crowds or groups proceeds from lower impulses than characterize the behavior of their individual members when acting alone. In every human group there is more prejudice and passion, less conscience, and less ability to appreciate the needs and rights of others than individuals reveal in their interpersonal relations. As individuals, men know they ought to love and respect each other, though they seldom do so. As racial, economic, and political groups, men "take for themselves, whatever their power can command." [20] Niebuhr seems to think that it is almost impossible to exaggerate the brutality and selfishness of men in the mass. He finds these characteristics especially prevalent in intergroup relations. Classes, racial majorities, powerful interest-groups tyrannize over opposition elements without even the barest acknowledgment of the demands of reason or conscience. No restraint or preventive of

[18] *Moral Man and Immoral Society.* New York, Scribner, 1936, pp. 44, 45.
[19] *Ibid.,* p. 45.
[20] *Ibid.,* p. 9.

this tyranny, he contends, has the remotest chance of success except force. Collective power can never be dislodged unless power is raised against it. To provide such a counterbalance of coercion is a prime obligation of the state. Although no state can maintain unity by coercion alone, it cannot preserve itself without coercion. Either the selfish, exploitative force of some dominant interest or class will prevail, or else it will be the public power expressed through the authority of the state.

Niebuhr has long been interested in the conflict between nations as a special form of intergroup antagonism. This conflict he regards from a viewpoint that is highly colored by his concept of man. Every nation, he avers, has "expansive desires which are rooted in the instinct of survival and soon extend beyond it. The will-to-live becomes the will-to-power." [21] International warfare is one of the oldest of human institutions. Since it long antedates the capitalist economic regime, it cannot be ascribed solely to capitalists. Nor is it true that only kings make war. Though the common people of nearly every nation sentimentally desire peace, they nevertheless harbor feelings of envy, jealousy, bigotry, and greed which foster conflict between communities. Niebuhr wonders whether there is any possibility of escape from "the endless round of force avenging ancient wrongs and creating new ones; of victorious Germany creating a vindictive France and victorious France poisoning Germany with a sense of outraged justice." [22] If there is such an escape, he considers it much more difficult and elusive than sentimental idealists have imagined. Though he recognizes the injustices of the economic order, he denies that wars could be eliminated by abolishing capitalism. Capitalism has simply sharpened, but not created, the imperialism of nations. The trouble is that imperialism provides opportunities for the indulgence of greed by the average citizen, and he does not scruple to take advantage of them. Nor can wars be prevented by pacifist non-violence. In fact, Niebuhr rejects the argument that violence is always evil and non-violence intrinsically good. He seems, here, to accept frankly the Machiavellian principle that

[21] *Ibid.*, p. 18.
[22] *Ibid.*, p. 110.

the end justifies the means. A rational society, he contends, will justify violence when it is employed for a good purpose. The achievement of equal justice, for example, is a nobler social objective than peace. Obviously, therefore, the outlawry of all wars would be a mistake. A war for the liberation of a nation, a race, or a class belongs in a quite different category from a war for the perpetuation of imperialism or class dominance. But Niebuhr provides no method for accurately determining the purposes of wars. Rare indeed have been the conflicts whose instigators have admitted that their objectives were imperialism or class dominance. Practically every war is alleged to be a struggle for liberation or for protection of some nation or class against oppression.

Niebuhr recognizes the desirability of establishing a world community to abate the evils of international conflict. But he sees this problem in essentially the same way that he views the maintenance of order and peace within the state. Both areas involve the organization of power to restrain and prevent the abuse of power. "No community," he says, "whether national or international, can maintain its order if it cannot finally limit expansive impulses by coercion." [23] Niebuhr differs with those who would call a constitutional convention in the immediate future to establish a world republic. No such dream could be realized except on the basis of a sense of world community, which could hardly develop in less than a century. Meanwhile, order and law should be enforced by the preponderant power of the great nations. Again, as in the case of the individual state, appropriate checks must be devised to prevent abuse of this preponderant power. The distinguished theologian hopes for both moral and constitutional checks, but he offers no suggestions for giving them concrete form or for putting them into effect. If he were to follow the pattern of his individual state, he would set up a world government as a counterweight to the power of contending nations. But he rejects this idea as an international solution. He thinks of world government as practically an impossibility, in the foreseeable future, at least. If it does become possible, it will be only because "desperate necessity makes it so." Even then, "ages of tragic

[23] *The Children of Light and the Children of Darkness*, p. 67.

history" will have to elapse to demonstrate that desperate necessity.[24]

2. Secular Exponents of Religious Orthodoxy

Theologians have not been the only champions in the twentieth century of religious orthodoxy as a groundwork for political theory. An important group of philosophers of history and literary men also insists that the teachings of religion provide the only hope of saving mankind from the evils of totalitarianism, depersonalization, and anomie. They see modern nations rushing as heedlessly as the Gadarene swine toward certain destruction. But such a fate does not greatly disturb them. They conceive of history as a rational process, directed by God in accordance with His plan for the redemption of the world. In their apocalyptic vision, the collapse of any particular civilization is not a night but a dawn. God, in His infinite wisdom, permits the downfall of Babylons and Romes in order to clear the way for the triumph of more virtuous nations. Unlike some of their clerical brethren, the secular prophets of religious orthodoxy tend toward conservatism on political and social issues. They incline toward a Burkean admiration for tradition and stability and see specters of personality-destroying collectivism behind almost every shadow. Even the New Deal haunted some of them, lest it turn into totalitarianism.

The best-known of the secular high priests of religious orthodoxy is probably the British historian Arnold Toynbee. Born in 1889, he was educated at Winchester and at Balliol, Oxford. In 1912 he became a fellow and tutor at Balliol and six years later joined the staff of the British Foreign Office. In 1919 he was a member of the British Delegation to the Peace Conference and later in the same year was appointed Professor of Byzantine and Modern Greek Language, Literature, and History at the University of London. Since 1925 he has been Director of Studies in the Royal Institute of International Affairs and Research Professor of International History at the University of London. From 1934 to 1954 he was engaged in writing *A Study of History*, a monu-

[24] *Ibid.*, p. 168.

mental account in ten volumes of the succession of world civilizations. In its majestic sweep of the centuries, it is considered by some as worthy to rank with Edward Gibbon's *Decline and Fall of the Roman Empire,* though the philosophy which pervades it is entirely different. Toynbee defines history as "a vision of God revealing Himself in action to souls that are sincerely seeking Him." [25] This conception bears more of the hallmarks of German Idealism than it does of English rationalism and empiricism.

Much of Toynbee's philosophy of history carries only an incidental significance for political theory. He discovers a succession of about twenty civilizations making up the history of the globe from the earliest times to the present. All of them come into existence and proceed to develop by successfully responding to repeated challenges. Usually the challenge takes the form of a condition of adversity. It must be rigorous enough to stimulate men to try to overcome it, but not so severe as to defeat their efforts or to imbue them with a feeling of hopelessness. Civilizations decline when a challenge confronts them which they fail to meet. The failure may result from militarism and war, barbarization from within, or the growth of an "internal proletariat." By the last term Toynbee means a class like the city mob of ancient Rome who are "in" but not "of" a given society. Despised and disinherited, they nurse grievances against the society and gradually undermine it.

Western civilization of the present day, Toynbee maintains, is in danger of collapse from a variety of causes. For one thing, we are failing to find a successful response for one of the principal conditions which spelled the early demise of Greek civilization—the condition of disunity. The Greek city-states fought each other to the point of exhaustion. The nations of the West are risking the same fate, or a fate of total annihilation, by their snarling and squabbling over power and self-interest. The West is also inviting destruction by its exacerbation of class conflict. Improvements in technology have brought to the masses fabulous material advantages, but they have also given them a keener awareness of social injustice. In due time the West must abolish

[25] *Twentieth Century Authors,* First Supplement. New York, H. W. Wilson, 1955, p. 1003.

both War and Class, or see them win a victory over man which, this time, will be "conclusive and definitive." [26]

Solutions to problems of political organization are imperative, according to Toynbee, if Western nations are to be saved from the downward path that was taken by the Aztecs and the Incas, the Sumerians and the Hittites. On the domestic plane the state must be reconstituted in such a way as to ensure the preservation of liberty and at the same time to make available the benefits of civilization to the whole people. Of even greater urgency is the need for effective international organization. No Behemoth of a world empire bestriding the earth and dictating to the lesser nations will suffice. The *Pax Romana* of the Caesars provided no good precedent for a *Pax Americana* or a *Pax Sovietica*. The *Pax Romana* was a peace of exhaustion. It had no quality of creativeness and was therefore not permanent. It was a foretaste, however, of what the contemporary world is likely to get unless systematic efforts are made to establish a constitutional cooperative world government. Today Soviet Russia and the United States face one another in the center of an arena of power politics. If either should throw down the gage of battle, perhaps one would survive as master of the world, or, more probably, some third power would be able to organize the helpless inhabitants of a ruined planet under a conqueror's fiat. The alternatives, as Toynbee sees them, are not unity and non-unity but what methods of unification are going to prevail. For his part, he would like to see the United Nations transformed into a world government. Writing in 1948, he described the UN as in a stage comparable to that of the United States after the War for Independence. It was a loose federation, which must sooner or later "break up or be transformed into a genuine and effective federation." Achievement of this transformation, he thought, was a goal toward which "we ought to strive with all our might, without allowing ourselves to be dismayed or deterred by difficulties, however baffling." [27]

But with all of his concern about political organization, Toynbee seems to betray an underlying feeling that it is not really of

[26] *Civilization on Trial.* New York, Oxford University Press, 1948, pp. 24–25.
[27] *Ibid.*, pp. 136, 149.

crucial importance. He appears to think that civilizations are doomed to die anyway, and the fact that they do is of little consequence. What really matters is the life of the spirit, which is capable of flourishing in the midst of cultural ruins just as well as at the peak of a civilization's advance. In fact, a great world religion, born in a time of disintegration, "may live on to become the chrysalis from which a new civilization emerges." [28] Nations must learn that religion is their most serious business and the chief instrument of human progress. For the sake of the all-important life of the spirit, they should put their "secular superstructures" back onto religious foundations. Religious foundations mean to Toynbee any of the four "higher religions" that have appeared within the last 4000 years—Christianity, Islam, Hinduism, and the Mahayana form of Buddhism. Why he considers Islam a higher religion with more of a worldwide mission than Judaism he does not make clear. But he does make obvious his preference for Christianity over the other religions. Christianity has played the most effective role, he says, in regenerating decadent cultures. It is invested with a loftier ethical purpose and a more genuine spirituality than any of the others. Their saviors were mere men, or else they were gods dwelling in some distant realm remote from the affairs of the world. The Christian Savior "was a man who believed himself to be the Son of God." The gods of other religions who died for the benefit of man did so by compulsion. The Christian God suffered and died from motives of love.[29] Toynbee's Christianity is, of course, no modernized version of theological rationalism. On the contrary, it is as mystical and otherworldly as the religion of the Fathers. Indeed, it seems to be derived primarily from the Apostle Paul. Nevertheless, Toynbee remains convinced that this ancient faith will not only survive the death of Western culture but will preside over the birth of its successor.

Toynbee's contemporary, Christopher Dawson, also saturates his philosophy of history with a heavy infusion of Christian beliefs. Dawson was born in 1889, as was Toynbee, and was the

[28] *Ibid.*, p. 13.
[29] D. C. Somervell, ed., *A Study of History.* New York, Oxford University Press, 1947, I, 544–47.

son of an army officer stationed in Wales. He obtained his education at Winchester and at Trinity College, Oxford. For a year thereafter he studied economics in Sweden under Gustav Cassel. In 1930 he became Lecturer in the History of Culture at University College, Exeter, and subsequently Lecturer in the Philosophy of Religion at the University of Liverpool. Since 1940 he has been editor of *The Dublin Review*. Among his chief works are *Religion and the Modern State* (1935), *Beyond Politics* (1939), and *Religion and Politics* (1948). In 1914 he became a convert to Catholicism, convinced that the Roman Church is the outstanding "representative in a changing world of an unchanging spiritual order."

Despite the range and intensity of his historical interests, Dawson seems to bear a closer affinity to Barth and Brunner than he does to Toynbee. Like the two Swiss theologians, he discovers the roots of modern political evil in the Enlightenment and indicts the secularism which grew out of that movement as the primary cause of totalitarianism. He describes secularism as "the last of the great European heresies." [30] Protestantism, liberalism, and communism, he argues, have also had pernicious effects on our Christian civilization. "The first eliminated the Church, the second eliminated Christianity, and the third eliminates the human soul." [31] It is worth noting, in addition, that Dawson is considerably more pessimistic than Toynbee. Although both believe that history is a rational process guided and directed by divine intent, Dawson has no vision of Christianity as an instrument of love to bring peace and harmony to the world. "Christ came not to bring peace, but a sword," he asserts, "and the Kingdom of God comes not by the elimination of conflict, but through the increasing opposition and tension between the Church and the world. The conflict between the two cities is as old as humanity and must endure to the end of time." [32]

Moderate conservatism seems to be the underlying theme of Dawson's political theory. He has little or no sympathy for radi-

[30] *Progress and Religion.* London, Sheed and Ward, 1929, p. 193.

[31] *Religion and the Modern State.* New York, Sheed and Ward, 1937, p. 148.

[32] Quoted by Judith N. Shklar, *After Utopia.* Princeton, Princeton University Press, 1957, p. 178.

cal democracy, parliamentary socialism, or any of the popular reform movements that seek to transform the world into an Elysium of comfort and pleasure. But this does not mean whole-hearted approval of the *status quo*. In so far as the existing order is synonymous with individualistic capitalism, he condemns it. He believes that modern industrialism, as sanctified by the classical economists, dehumanized man, desecrated the face of the earth, and brought civilization to the verge of chaos. In addition, capitalism created the paradox of poverty in the midst of plenty and such disheartening conditions as slums, depressions, trade rivalries between nations, and wars for the conquest of empires. At the same time, he expresses views reminiscent of the Hayek thesis that if we abandon the system of free competition, "we shall also have to abandon political individualism and the right to criticize and oppose the government." [33] Perhaps in the final analysis he does not really care very much whether political individualism survives or not. What he seems to think most desirable is some kind of "holy community" which would constitute a successful rival of secular totalitarianism. Neither socialism nor democratic reformism can qualify for this purpose. They are based upon the delusion that this earth can be made into a New Jerusalem. They ignore original sin and the primal curse that was placed upon man when Adam was expelled from the Garden of Eden. They propagate a gospel of materialism and teach that nothing matters except the enjoyment of comfort and the pursuit of pleasure. According to Dawson, God has decreed otherwise. He has ordained that, as a consequence of Adam's sin, all of his descendants shall live out their lives in hardship and pain. To the end of time, no effort or scheme of reformers will be sufficient to change this universal law.

Though Dawson refuses to endorse any particular form of totalitarianism, he does maintain that liberal democracy is a relic of the past, and that the society of the future will bear many of the hallmarks of the fascist system. He thinks of fascism as an inevitable reaction against the secularism, nihilism, and materialism bequeathed by the nineteenth century. Life had been divested of meaning; man had been deprived of significance and

[33] *Religion and the Modern State*, p. 24.

reduced to the level of a pig in a sty. The result was to create a deep spiritual hunger which had to be satisfied. Nationalism represented one attempt to fill the void; socialism, another. Fascism combined elements from both and made the broadest appeal for popular support. Indeed, Dawson discovers authoritarianism to be an almost universal phenomenon in Western countries. Even the New Deal in the United States was a "constitutional dictatorship" with an "obvious analogy" to the "new dictatorships in Europe." [34] For Christians to take a negative attitude toward such movements, and to attack and repudiate them, may be tantamount to "fighting against God and standing in the path of the march of God through history." [35] Of course, Dawson does not mean that all forms of fascism or semi-fascism will be identical. Totalitarianism in the West will be humanitarian and probably pacific. It will include among its features the distribution of free milk and the operation of birth-control clinics, instead of government by secret police and concentration camps. The state, nonetheless, will be authoritarian, universal, and omnicompetent. It will shape the minds and control the lives of its citizens from the cradle to the grave. The schools, the newspapers, and all other instruments for creating and molding public opinion will be its servants and will do its bidding. Compared with the liberal democratic regimes of the nineteenth century, the state that will ride the wave of the future will be almost unrecognizable.

As has been indicated already, Dawson does not welcome the growth of secular totalitarianism. But he considers it inevitable unless humane and rational men develop a satisfactory substitute. The kind words he has to say about fascism, especially the Italian variety, stem from his belief that it was a necessary antidote for the chaotic individualism of the capitalist era. What he really hopes to see develop is a Christian totalitarianism which would provide all the benefits of secular totalitarianism without its excrescences of sadism and tyranny. Christians should emulate fascists in seeking to unify life and in tolerating no division of allegiance. Their allegiance, however, must be rendered to "Christ the King," not to an allegedly superior race or to some

[34] *Ibid.*, p. 23.
[35] *Beyond Politics.* London, Sheed and Ward, 1939, p. 132.

gospel of nationalist frenzy or imperial grandeur. The model Christian state should be founded upon entirely different premises from those of liberal democracy. It should not rest upon the will of the majority or upon the right of the individual to unlimited self-expression. No state has any authority to absorb the whole of human life or to treat the individual as a mere pawn for its purposes. Yet the fact remains, Dawson points out, that under the Catholic conception, the state is authoritarian and hierarchical. The ruler is not simply representative of the people but is an independent sovereign with direct responsibility to God. So long as he rules justly and well, rebellion against him is a cardinal sin.

Dawson extends Christian totalitarianism to include the corporate state. The problem of just relations between capital and labor will not be solved by socialism, with its exaltation of class warfare, but by organizing society in such a way as to promote cooperation between workers and employers in the same division of the productive system. This concern over class warfare seems strangely at variance with Dawson's indifference to conflict in a larger sphere. The establishment of a Catholic state, he reminds us, with power to require a single allegiance to Christ the King will involve conflict. "But conflict is not a bad thing: it is the condition of life." [36]

Significant also as a secular exponent of religious orthodoxy is T. S. Eliot (1888–   ), regarded by many literary critics as the world's most distinguished living poet. Though a native of St. Louis and a descendant of a line of merchants and divines extending back to colonial New England, Eliot has been described as "English in everything but accent and origin." He received his preparatory education at Smith Academy in St. Louis, and completed the requirements for the bachelor's degree at Harvard in three years, taking an M.A. in the fourth. Later he studied at the Sorbonne and at Merton College, Oxford. After some years as a struggling poet and editor of small literary magazines, he won fame in 1922 as the author of *The Waste Land*. One of the most influential works of contemporary literature, it epitomizes the disillusionment and futility that followed in the wake of

[36] *Religion and the Modern State*, pp. 113–14.

World War I. In 1927 Eliot became a British subject, and a year later announced himself "an Anglo-Catholic in religion, a classicist in literature, and a royalist in politics." He emerged as an outstanding playwright in 1935 with the publication of *Murder in the Cathedral*. Since then he has published, among others, two celebrated dramas, *The Cocktail Party* and *The Confidential Clerk*. His literary achievements won high recognition in 1948, when he received the Nobel prize in literature.

In a number of ways Eliot contrasts sharply with Christopher Dawson. To begin with, he has no interest in the merits or deficiencies of capitalism and socialism. Economics, he declares, is "more incomprehensible" to him "than mathematics." [37] Schemes for authoritarianism of any kind also leave him cold. In fact, to his way of thinking, the principal cleavage in modern society is that between secular totalitarianism and Christianity. He does not even approve of nation-states, preferring to see the world reorganized on a basis of regionalism. He has no hope for the future of the United States "until that country falls apart into its natural components," the nature of which he does not explain, except that they would not be the same as the old North and South. [38] He renounces, in theory at least, all interest in conservatism, and also in its opposites, liberalism and radicalism. Conservatism, he says, is "too often conservation of the wrong things; liberalism a relaxation of discipline;" and radicalism "a denial of the permanent things." [39]

Nothing could be more obvious than that the frame of reference for T. S. Eliot's thinking about political and social issues is the Christian religion itself. By this he means an old-time orthodoxy founded upon creeds, dogmas, celibacy, monasticism, otherworldliness, and most of the remaining elements of medieval Catholicism. He urges men to accept as the basis of society a Christianity standing at the farthest pole from paganism. The acid test of every system and every institution is its conformity with the Christian religion. By way of illustration, he concedes that fascism may be condemned on grounds of its violence and cruelty, but he considers these defects as largely incidental. The

[37] *Essays, Ancient and Modern*. New York, Harcourt, 1936, p. 118.
[38] *Ibid.*, p. 133.
[39] *The Idea of a Christian Society*. New York, Harcourt, 1940, p. 102.

real objection, he maintains, is its "paganism." For Eliot, the Christian character of society is of such paramount importance that he comes close to Dawson's advocacy of a *Christian* totalitarianism. He stops short, however, of demanding a single allegiance or of recommending the corporate state. Nevertheless, he insists that education must not be "mere instruction" but must be informed by Christian purpose. The rulers must accept Christianity, not simply as a guide to their personal conduct, "but as the system under which they are to govern." [40] Social customs will be controlled by religious sanctions, and the whole community will be expected to abide by a religio-social code of behavior. Anything less than these requirements is regarded by Eliot as paganism. Even humanitarianism and the pursuit of wisdom come under his criticism. "Wisdom," he declares, "is no substitute for faith"; and the goal of abolishing suffering disregards the "spiritual goods" that may flow therefrom.[41]

Eliot's prescription for the Christian society includes little that would appeal to the interest of the political economist or the political scientist. This, of course, is not surprising, since he contends that the Kingdom of Christ will never be realized on earth, and that "whatever reform or revolution we carry out, the result will always be a sordid travesty of what human society should be." [42] Moreover, he is largely indifferent to forms of government. Democracy, he complains, is deficient in "positive content." What really matters is that the state should be Christian. Reject God, he says, and you might as well pay your respects to Hitler or Stalin. Strong convictions on economic policy seem almost foreign to Eliot's thinking. He has vague preferences for an agricultural society, and he pillories modern industrialism for undermining tradition and separating men from religion. He expresses qualms about the propriety of his being a money-lender, that is, a holder of bonds and debentures, and he doubts that it is moral for him to improve his income by investing in the stock of corporations in the control of which he has no effective voice. He thinks of himself as a kind of "petty usurer in a world manipu-

[40] *Ibid.*, p. 34.
[41] "The Christian Concept of Education," *Malvern, 1941: The Life of the Church and the Order of Society.* London, Longmans, 1941, p. 201; *Essays, Ancient and Modern*, p. 139.
[42] *The Idea of a Christian Society*, p. 60.

lated largely by big usurers." [43] Though he realizes that the
Church once condemned such practices, he makes no specific
proposals for doing anything about them.

The one explicit reform recommended by Eliot is the establishment of what he calls "the Christian Community." What he
envisages is a kind of religious élite, composed of both clergy
and laity, of superior intellectual or spiritual gifts. It would be a
body of "indefinite outline" united by an identity of beliefs and
aspirations. In function it would be somewhat like a spiritual
Ministry of Propaganda and Popular Enlightenment, for it
would "collectively form the conscious mind and the conscience
of the nation." [44] Only by such means can modern societies,
"worm-eaten with liberalism," stand up to the challenge of pagan
totalitarianism. They must be able to match conviction with conviction and show fanatical enemies that they, too, have values
worth defending. Obviously, the Church must occupy a high
place in a society dominated by the Christian Community. According to Eliot, such a society cannot be realized until the "great
majority of the sheep belong to one fold." He urges that the
Church have a direct and official connection with the state,
though it must not sink into a mere department of government.
Like the Christian Community itself, it should possess a high
degree of independence. At times it should be in conflict with the
state, rebuking immoral aberrations, resisting the encroachments
of secular power, or defending the community against tyranny.
What he seems to have in mind is something akin to the Jesuit-
Calvinist theory of a close relationship between Church and
state, but with the Church wielding the ultimate authority in
matters of religion and morality and in protection of the citizens
against oppression.

3. Contemporary Catholic Political Theory

One of the most comprehensive bodies of political thought of
modern times, and of past centuries as well, is the theory of
the Catholic Church. This theory is set forth in encyclicals of
the Popes, and also in the writings of certain philosophers whose

[43] *Ibid.*, p. 103.
[44] *Ibid.*, p. 43.

teachings are accepted so generally in Catholic circles as almost to give them an official status. Contemporary papal theory may be said to have originated with Pope Leo XIII (1810–1903), who occupied the "fisherman's throne" from 1878 to 1903. His predecessor, Pius IX, deeply troubled by the attacks of militant nationalists upon the power of the Church, had condemned nearly all the principal political tendencies of modern times. Liberalism, the separation of church and state, religious liberty, civil marriage, and public education were only a few of the targets of his anathemas. The election of Leo XIII to the See of Peter seemed to bring a more genial climate to the ecclesiastical world. A scholar, man of letters, and former papal nuncio in Brussels, Leo was sympathetically acquainted with the operations of democratic government in modern Euorpe. As a consequence, alliances with monarchists were no longer encouraged; experimental science was patronized; the philosophy of the great rationalist of the thirteenth century, St. Thomas Aquinas, was commended to the faithful as an intellectual guide; and Leo issued so many pronouncements favorable to labor that he was given the title, the "Workingman's Pope."

Leo XIII began his pontificate with a series of encyclicals which seemed to reaffirm many of the assertions of his troubled predecessor. He emphatically stated that all power comes from God, that rulers are divinely appointed, and that subjects are bound to obey them unless they command actions repugnant to natural or divine law. He denounced popular sovereignty, the contract theory of government, and the assumption that rulers have only those powers expressly given them by the people. In opposing liberalism he was almost as uncompromising as Pius IX, for he denounced liberty of worship, unlimited freedom of expression, and the supremacy of human reason. He left no doubt whatever that, in the Catholic view, there is one true religion, and that the Church is the custodian of absolute truth. Nevertheless, he conceded that the Church does not insist upon the sacrosanctity of any particular form of government. It is not wrong, he said, to prefer democracy, "if only the Catholic doctrine be maintained as to the origin and exercise of power." [45]

[45] *Diuturnum Illud*, June 29, 1881; *Libertas Praestantissimum*, June 20, 1888.

He also admitted that various things which the Church regards as evil may be tolerated by rulers for the sake of expediency. God Himself, he pointed out, "permits evil to exist in the world, partly that greater good may not be impeded, and partly that greater evil may not ensue." Thus, in the extraordinary conditions of the modern age, the Church "acquiesces in certain modern liberties, not because she prefers them, but because she judges it expedient to permit them." When "happier times" shall come she will not tolerate them but will insist upon her own absolute standards in fulfilling her God-given duty of providing for the salvation of mankind.[46]

The most generous expression of Pope Leo's political and social philosophy was the encyclical *Rerum Novarum*, which he issued in 1891, the thirteenth year of his reign. In this pronouncement he was concerned primarily with the condition of labor and with conveying a message to workingmen that would draw them away from the siren appeal of Marxian socialism. He began with a vigorous defense of the right of property, in both land and personal possessions. But he soon made clear that he was not conferring his blessings upon the few who had been fortunate enough or shrewd enough to accumulate for themselves wealth in excess of reasonable needs. He approved inheritance and he admitted that everyone has a natural right "to live becomingly"; but he insisted that when necessity has been supplied, and one's position in life fairly considered, it is a Christian duty to give at least a portion of the surplus to the poor. He quoted St. Thomas Aquinas to the effect that "Man should not consider his outward possessions as his own, but as common to all, so as to share them without difficulty when others are in need." Though he deplored attempts to substitute public relief for Christian charity, he was nevertheless ready to accord to the state a large responsibility for the welfare of the indigent and unfortunate. A paramount duty of rulers, he said, should be to make sure that the laws and institutions and general purposes of the commonwealth are such "as to produce of themselves public well-being and private prosperity." Of equal importance is the responsibility of the government in promoting a wide distribution of property. While

[46] *Libertas Praestantissimum*, June 20, 1888.

never admitting the pre-eminence of material over spiritual needs, he repeatedly asserted that everyone has the right to live in dignity and comfort. He argued also that a diffusion of ownership would add to the total amount of wealth produced, on the assumption that men always work harder and more readily on that which is their own.

The assurance of a new dignity and status to Catholic labor was certainly a primary purpose of *Rerum Novarum*. Though Pope Leo clung to the ancient doctrine that earning one's bread by the sweat of one's brow was part of the curse visited upon Adam and all his posterity, he still insisted that labor is nothing to be ashamed of, and that employers must respect in their workers their dignity as men and as Christians. It is "shameful and inhuman," he said, to treat men like slaves or to look upon them as mere human tools. The poor and helpless, he went on to assert, have a special claim to the protection of the state. The well-to-do have many ways of protecting themselves and have less need of public help. But those who lack resources of their own "must rely chiefly upon the assistance of the state." For this reason it is proper to invoke the help and authority of the law if workers are oppressed or degraded or subjected to undue hazards to their health or good morals. Though the Pope recognized the desirability of free negotiation between workers and employers, he argued that the requirement of a living wage takes pre-eminence over any bargain between man and man. He did not believe that this requirement justified state interference to prescribe minimum wages, but he did recommend that the state should lend its approval and protection to workmen's associations. Precisely what he had in mind by these associations is not clear. Probably he was thinking of something akin to the craft guilds of the Middle Ages. At any rate, he was not advocating organizations of workers to exert combined pressure upon employers. Rather, he contemplated benevolent and cooperative associations that would draw the two classes more closely together. As in the case of the medieval guilds, many of their functions would be social and religious.

In 1931 another papal encyclical of major importance to political theory was issued, under the title, *Quadragesimo Anno*.

Its author, Pius XI (1857–1939), was motivated by increasing concern over the depression, the spread of unemployment, the increasing acerbity of class conflict, and the fear of revolution. Evidently believing that *Rerum Novarum* was inadequate for a period of economic crisis, he advocated not simply a wage sufficient for the support of the worker and his family but state assistance in the maintenance of such a wage.[47] He argued that wages either too high or too low cause unemployment and thereby ruin the prosperity of nations and lead to wars and domestic upheavals. He also condemned child labor and, almost without exception, the employment of women. Of perhaps greater historical significance, he drew from Pope Leo's advocacy of workingmen's associations justification for a corporative society. Social life, he complained, had entirely lost its organic character. Whereas, at one time, numerous associations of a semi-independent nature had flourished and had conducted business of vital importance to various trades and professions, in more recent years society had come to comprise nothing but the state and individuals. Pius therefore recommended the reestablishment of vocational groups of such a nature as to bring to an end the existing hostility of employers and workers. The new groups would be organized according to the functions or services rendered to society and would include both workers and employers among their members. Harmony and collaboration would thus take the place of class conflict. Although Pius seemed anxious to reduce the burdens of the state and to deconcentrate its authority, he was widely assumed to have been conferring a benediction upon the corporate state as it then existed in Italy. Within a few years Catholics in Austria, Portugal, and Spain transplanted the corporative idea in the political structures of those countries.[48]

Pius XI's successor, Pius XII (1876–1958), was elected Pope

[47] Six years later, in *Divini Redemptoris,* he enunciated the even more unprecedented doctrine that "the State must take every measure necessary to supply employment."

[48] Since the outbreak of World War II, the corporative idea, for obvious reasons, has found disfavor among many Catholics. See Paul Vignaux, "Corporativism in Europe," *The Review of Politics,* IV (1942), 194–205, 303–14.

on March 2, 1939. Almost exactly six months later Europe was plunged into the maelstrom of war when Hitler invaded Poland, and Britain and France declared war upon Germany. It was perhaps inevitable that the new Pontiff's pronouncements should be concerned primarily with war and peace. A few weeks after the conflict began, he issued the encyclical *Summi Pontificatus*. In it he attributed the coming of the war to the rejection by modern society of the universal norm of morality decreed by God and vouchsafed to mankind through the Roman Church. The denial of the fundamentals of morality, he affirmed, had its origin in the Reformation when a large part of Europe abandoned "that Christian teaching of which the Chair of Peter is the depository and exponent." The effect, he maintained, was to prepare the way for the repudiation of all standards and restraints, and for the assertion of the doctrine of the absolute supremacy of the state. Ultimately the state became a substitute for the Almighty Himself. It usurped control over education and mastery of the family. International law was thrown into the discard, for there could be no appeal to any authority superior to that of the state. Though Pius XII admitted that the war was in part attributable to economic maladjustment, he insisted that the real causes were spiritual and moral. He contended, therefore, that the restoration of peace must wait upon the re-education of mankind, a task that should be assigned to the Church. Critical though he was of the omnipotent state, he never saw fit to recommend the destruction of national sovereignty and the merging of the nations into a world federation. Instead, in his Christmas message of 1944, he proposed merely the outlawing of aggressive war under the threat of combined action of peace-loving nations to punish the aggressor. In common with most of his secular contemporaries, he assumed that new life could be breathed into the outworn system of maintaining peace through collective security.

Like nationalism in the nineteenth century, totalitarianism in the twentieth has had a profoundly disturbing effect upon Catholic thought. It not only offends Christian principles but in any of its militant forms it gravely jeopardizes the position of the Church. For these reasons, a number of philosophers have recognized the need for a broader and more challenging defense of Catholic principles than is to be found in the encyclicals of recent popes. With the aid of certain non-Catholic thinkers like Robert Maynard Hutchins, former Chancellor of the University of Chicago, and Mortimer J. Adler, now Director of the Institute for Philosophical Research in San Francisco, they have launched a Neo-Thomist movement dedicated to a revival of the teachings of St. Thomas Aquinas. The foremost leader of the movement and probably the outstanding Catholic philosopher of the contemporary world is Jacques Maritain. He was born in Paris in 1892 and educated at the Sorbonne. Brought up in an atmosphere of liberal Protestantism, he became dissatisfied with what he considered pale negations and devitalized theology and sought refuge in the philosophy of Bergson. Bergson restored his faith in metaphysics but gave him no answer to his need for an Absolute. His quest for an anchorage of certainty led him to embrace Catholicism in 1906. After years of studying Thomism, he was appointed, in 1913, Professor of Modern History and Philosophy at the Institut Catholique in Paris. His first book, an attack on Bergsonism, was written at the behest of the bishops in charge of the Institut. He has since produced about twenty volumes, including *Freedom in the Modern World* (1935), *True Humanism* (1938), *Scholasticism and Politics* (1940), *The Rights of Man and Natural Law* (1943), and *Man and the State* (1951). After the fall of France, Maritain came to the Western Hemisphere. He became a professor at the Institute of Medieval Studies in Toronto and subsequently at Princeton. In 1945 General De Gaulle appointed him Ambassador to the Vatican. He returned to Princeton in 1948 and retired three years later.

Though Maritain calls himself an "anti-modernist," he actually comes closer to the modern temper than do many of his coreligionists. In certain respects he is a liberal, perhaps for the reason that the philosophy of his thirteenth-century mentor, St. Thomas Aquinas, was also definitely liberal. For example, he rejects the doctrine that rulers are divinely appointed, or that their power comes from God. The authority of secular rulers, he maintains, is conferred upon them by the body politic, that is, by the people or the political society. "The people are the very substance, the living and free substance, of the body politic. The people are above the State, the people are not for the State, the State is for the people." [49] He deprecates the idea of state sovereignty and holds that the concept as well as the word should be eliminated from political philosophy. He regards it as a vestige of the age of tyrants, which was bootlegged, as it were, into modern theory by Hobbes and Rousseau and identified with the will of the people.

Maritain's own concept of political authority is pluralistic. He considers the state as only one of a number of agencies for the control and improvement of man. The state, he concedes, has exclusive jurisdiction over the sphere of public order, but not over religion, education, or morality. It must not mistake itself for the whole of political society or take upon itself the functions which normally appertain to other organs of the body politic. Even the management of economic functions does not properly belong to the state. They should spring from the free initiative of working communities, unions, cooperatives, and federated bodies of producers and consumers. On a large scale they may take the form of public corporations like the TVA. Maritain admits that the state may have to sponsor some group undertakings, but it should decentralize and "destatize" itself, instead of moving in the direction of socialism or nationalization.

More significant, perhaps, than Maritain's pluralism is the element of *personalism* he introduces into his philosophy. By personalism he has in mind the dignity and nobility of the human individual. The human person, he affirms, "is the image of God." Man has nobility and worth because he is endowed with an immortal soul, and "there is nothing above the human soul except God." [50] He therefore argues in defense of a considerable —but not unlimited—measure of individual freedom. Man has inalienable rights, under natural law, to life, liberty, and property. But he does not have an absolute claim to the exercise of these rights. The exercise of a right, according to Maritain, is

[49] *Man and the State.* Chicago, University of Chicago Press, 1951, p. 26.
[50] *The Rights of Man and Natural Law.* New York, Scribner, 1949, pp. 4, 13.

subject to conditions and limitations imposed in each case by
the requirements of justice. For example, a murderer can be justly
condemned to die because, by depriving another of the right
to live, he has forfeited any claim he might justly have had to
the same right. Maritain's liberalism also includes a large measure of religious freedom. He rejects the idea of a state religion
or a universal faith imposed by law. In the Middle Ages, he
admits, dictated beliefs were perfectly feasible and perhaps
justifiable. But the medieval "sacral" age has been superseded
by a modern secular age. In the new age, under democratic
government, nothing short of full toleration of every sect and
variety of approach to God makes sense. Even skepticism and
complete disbelief must be legally permitted. "A genuine democracy cannot impose on its citizens or demand from them,
as a condition for their belonging to the city, any philosophic
or any religious creed." To attempt to do so is simply to encourage totalitarians to inflict their own nefarious creed on the
mind of the masses "by the power of propaganda, lies, and the
police." [51]

The fact cannot be overlooked, however, that Maritain is fully
committed to an absolutist religious philosophy. His liberalism,
therefore, is modified by the deference he feels he must pay to
a body of final truth. While he opposes an established or imposed religion, he insists at the same time that Christianity is an
essential foundation of democracy. The world has had enough
of neutrality, he writes. "Willingly or unwillingly, States will be
obliged to make a choice for or against the Gospel. They will be
shaped either by the totalitarian spirit or by the Christian
spirit." [52] He declares also that "the true religion" should be
aided in its spiritual mission of redeeming and re-educating
mankind. In other words, the state should assist the Church
by asking her priests to spread the Gospel among the masses;
by requesting her monks and nuns to cooperate with social and
educational agencies; and by inviting her more zealous laymen
and her youth organizations to help with the moral uplift of the
nation.

[51] *Man and the State*, pp. 110–11.
[52] *The Rights of Man and Natural Law*, p. 23.

Maritain's liberalism is diluted further by the various restrictions he places on freedom of expression. The political community, he says, "has the right to resist the propagation of lies or calumnies," and, especially, to defend itself against those who disseminate ideas destructive of liberty and of the principles of cooperation and mutual respect upon which society must rest. He does not welcome the use of censorship or police methods, but he argues that "a democratic society is not necessarily an unarmed society." [53] He hopes that the spontaneous pressure of public opinion, at least in peacetime, may be a sufficient instrument of repression against those who would abuse their freedom. At the same time, he approves state interference with freedom of expression on what he calls "practical" as distinct from "ideological" grounds. In the main, the distinction involves the commission of acts as opposed to the expression of ideas, but in some cases it is so subtle as to defy understanding. For instance, he argues that it is improper for the state to judge whether a work of art possesses a quality of immorality, but entirely proper for the same authority to determine whether an author or publisher "plans to make money in selling obscenities." [54]

Religion as a foundation for political theory will probably always have its devoted adherents. Not a few of the problems of political theory have religious or moral significance. The nature of man and his relation to society, the problems of crime and war, the extent of liberty that can be safely granted, the relations of church and state, the possibilities of progress, and the connection between ends and means are some of the more typical and often baffling examples. Even the question of forms of government may provoke religious controversy, and often did so in the past. The early New England Puritans, for example, committed to the doctrine of total depravity, rejected democracy as incompatible with the vileness of human nature and drew the conclusion that only an oligarchy of the elect should rule. Extremists in otherworldliness, like the Jehovah's Witnesses,

[53] *Ibid.*, p. 90.
[54] *Man and the State*, p. 118.

repudiate all forms of earthly governments and recognize only divine authority.

No doubt the exponents of a religious philosophy of the state have made notable contributions in accenting the evils of tyrannical power, in rebuking fanatical nationalists, in exposing the dangers of statism, and in emphasizing the value of a higher law. But some of them have also generated considerable confusion. They have made the individual a citizen of two realms, with a divided loyalty and a double allegiance. Under ordinary conditions he is subject to the laws of the state, but in extraordinary situations, as defined by his church, he must "obey God rather than men." Though religious philosophers accept the admonition to "render unto Caesar the things that are Caesar's, and unto God the things that are God's," they appear generally to assume that the things that are God's are of a higher order. What often follows, as in the teachings of Barth, Toynbee, and Dawson, is a kind of indifferentism or even contempt for the state. Otherworldliness seems almost to be the essence of many religious philosophies, and the inevitable consequence to their followers is the assumption that, in the long run, nothing matters except the things of the spirit.

Lastly, religious philosophers have added to the confusion of modern times by their attitudes toward war and totalitarianism. For the most part, they have vigorously condemned the secular totalitarianism of the Nazis and Communists, but several of them have advocated forms of Christian totalitarianism which would accomplish similar purposes in less repugnant ways. The "holy community" and the corporate state of Christopher Dawson and the "Christian Community" of T. S. Eliot stand out as astonishing examples. With respect to war, the attitude of many of the religious philosophers reflects the Machiavellian doctrine that the end justifies the means. Many of them preach that war is a "lesser evil," and that violence may be used to resist oppression or in defense against an aggressor. According to Karl Barth, the Christian community may even *suggest* violence, if necessary to overthrow oppressive rulers or to defend the state against the threat of attack. Reinhold Niebuhr justifies war for almost any "good" purpose, such as the achievement of equal justice or the liberation of a nation, class, or race. The possibility that the choice of an evil means may pervert or destroy a noble end seems not to be evident to these philosophers.

ADDITIONAL READINGS

Barker, Ernest. *Reflections on Government*. London, Oxford University Press, 1948.

Barth, Karl. *Church and State*. London, Student Christian Movement Press, 1939.

Bennett, John C. *Christian Ethics and Social Policy*. New York, Scribner, 1956.

Berdyaev, Nicholas, *The Fate of Man in the Modern World*. London, Morehouse-Gorham, 1935.

Brunner, Emil. *The Divine Imperative*. Philadelphia, Westminster Press, 1947.

Chesterton, G. K. *Orthodoxy*. New York, Dodd, Mead, 1908.

Dawson, Christopher. *Religion and the Modern State*. London, Sheed and Ward, 1935.

Eliot, T. S. *Notes Towards the Definition of Culture*. New York, Harcourt, 1949.

Gollancz, Victor. *Our Threatened Values*. London, V. Gollancz, 1946.

Hughes, E. J. *The Church and the Liberal Society*. Princeton, Princeton University Press, 1944.

Hughes, Philip. *The Pope's New Order: A Systematic Summary of the Social Encyclicals and Addresses, from Leo XIII to Pius XII*. New York, Macmillan, 1944.

Lewis, C. S. *The Case for Christianity*. New York, Macmillan, 1944.

Maritain, Jacques. *Christianity and Democracy*. New York, Scribner, 1944.

———. *The Person and the Common Good*. New York, Scribner, 1947.

———. *Scholasticism and Politics*. London, Centenary Press, 1945.

———. *True Humanism*. New York, Scribner, 1954.

Niebuhr, Reinhold. *Christianity and Power Politics*. New York, Scribner, 1948.

———. *Faith and History*. New York, Scribner, 1949.

————. *The Nature and Destiny of Man.* New York, Scribner, 1943. Two vols.

Rauschenbusch, Walter. *Christianity and the Social Crisis.* New York, Macmillan, 1913.

————. *Christianizing the Social Order.* New York, Macmillan, 1912.

Ryan, J. A., and Boland, F. J. *Catholic Principles of Politics.* New York, Macmillan, 1947.

Sorokin, Pitirim A. *The Crisis of Our Age.* New York, Dutton, 1941.

Temple, William. *Christianity and the Social Order.* Middlesex, England, Penguin, 1942.

Tillich, Paul. *The Religious Situation.* New York, Meridian, 1956.

Toynbee, Arnold. *Christianity among the Religions of the World.* New York, Scribner, 1957.

————. *Civilization on Trial.* New York, Oxford University Press, 1948.

————. *An Historian's Approach to Religion.* New York, Oxford University Press, 1956.

————. *The World and the West.* New York, Oxford University Press, 1953.

CHAPTER
XII

Psychological Foundations of Political Theory

At first thought it may seem strange that political theories founded upon psychology should be discussed under the general heading of Theories of Conservatism. As scientists, the psychologists have little in common with Idealists, Romanticists, Existentialists, New Conservatives, or exponents of religion as the basis of politics. Yet most psychologists, except those who adhere rigidly to experimental methods, are philosophers as well as scientists. They are profoundly concerned with the nature of man, with the aberrations of his personal conduct, with his potential for adjustment to life in society, with the prevention of delinquency and crime, and with the relative importance of heredity and environment. In pursuance of these interests, many of them express positive convictions regarding the solution of social problems. It is noteworthy, however, that the prevailing tendency is to look for the source of these problems in the individual himself rather than in the institutional structure of society. For this reason the majority of psychologists have little faith in governmental reforms or in the remaking of society to achieve a utopia. They urge, instead, a reorientation of the individual to enable him to accept his environment. They believe that personal unhappiness and delinquency result from frustration and feelings of resentment against some family situation or social condition. They therefore recommend individual adjustment instead of group rebellion or social reform. Except for a small number who advocate specific patterns of political reorganization, they contend that the individual should put his own mental and emotional house in order before attempting to change the world.

1. The Freudian System

Probably no body of thought of modern times has exceeded in influence and significance the psychology of Sigmund Freud. It must be ranked in importance with the hypotheses of Darwin, the doctrines of Marx, and the philosophies of Bentham and J. S. Mill. Freudian psychology has enriched literature and the arts, fostered new approaches to delinquency and crime, revolutionized mental hygiene, and laid the foundations for a better understanding of such political phenomena as dictatorship, hero-worship, collective hysteria, and war. As we shall see, the original Freudian system has undergone numerous modifications at the hands of the founder himself, his followers, and especially his later critics; but no one can deny the tremendous importance of Freud's own contributions.

Sigmund Freud was born in 1856 in Freiburg, Moravia, the son of a merchant. He obtained his M.D. degree at the University of Vienna and soon afterward was appointed a lecturer there in neuropathology. In 1885 he went to Paris to study under Jean Charcot, a neurologist famous for his work on hypnotism and hysteria. Returning to the University of Vienna the following year, he was finally made a professor in 1900 and continued to serve in that capacity until 1938, when the *Anschluss* brought a tragic end to his career as a teacher. The Nazis forced him into seclusion in his home and threatened to send him to a concentration camp, though he was desperately ill with cancer of the jaw. Only the persistent efforts of his non-Jewish disciples saved him from arrest. Even so, his books were burned, and nearly all his property was confiscated. He was offered a refuge in Palestine, but he declined on the ground that he was too deeply immersed in European culture to begin a new life in a strange environment. Besides, he had severed all connection with the Jewish faith many years before. His application for a visa to Holland was politely refused. Finally, he was allowed to go to England, where he was received with honor. He enjoyed the peace and security of his new home for only a year. The spread of the cancer in his jaw necessitated a new operation, from which he never recovered. He died in September, 1939, a short time after the beginning of World War II.

Freud laid the foundations of his psychology, commonly known as psychoanalysis, in 1900 with the publication of *An Interpretation of Dreams*. Thereafter he wrote more than a dozen other books, amplifying and sometimes modifying his earlier theories. By 1914 his achievements were recognized by many as a science and by 1920 were world-famous. The basic premise of psychoanalysis is and always has been the contention that the source of most of human behavior, both mental and physical, is unconscious. Freud considered the human being as essentially a bundle of instincts, primal urges, and drives. In his original theory he designated these drives as hunger and sex, or the ego-instinct and the erotic-instinct. The ego-instinct was concerned with self-preservation, the erotic-instinct with the perpetuation of the species. The ego-instinct comprehended the traits of assertiveness, combativeness, competition, ruthlessness. The erotic-instinct included not merely genital gratification but all that Plato had meant by "love" in the *Symposium:* love of self, of family, of friends, of humanity in general, and even of abstract ideas. Freud saw these two instincts in perpetual conflict. For one reason, grim economic need forced the individual to subordinate erotic gratification to the business of gaining a living. Society, moreover, compelled the individual to renounce pleasure in order to ensure the performance of social responsibilities. As a consequence, the erotic-instinct, and even some aspects of the ego-instinct, were driven inward and assumed the form, to a large extent, of suppressed desires. But they were never completely suppressed or extinguished. They continued to manifest themselves in dreams, in slips of the tongue, in lapses of memory, in losing and mislaying objects, in phobias and compulsions, in obsessions, and in other forms of "abnormal" behavior.

In order to explain more fully the mechanism of suppression, Freud hypothesized a threefold division of human nature. The three "layers" or aspects of the psyche he designated as the *id*, the *ego*, and the *superego*. By the id he meant the instincts, the raw and unmodified urges and basic drives. These he assumed to be as much a part of man's biological nature as the color of his eyes or the shape of his skull. They are the organism's primary inheritance and express the body's innate needs. They are completely within the subconscious. The ego is a higher function of the human psyche which controls the id and protects the organism. Without the ego the organism would be doomed to destruction by the blind strivings of the id for gratification. As Freud expressed it, "The ego represents what we call reason and sanity, in contrast to the id which contains the passions." [1] By the superego Freud meant something like a conscience. He did not regard this as an original function of the human psyche, like the ego and the id, but as an element implanted in the mind by social influences. As he conceived it, the superego was nothing more than the sum total of parental, educational, religious, national, racial, customary, and traditional influences. But in no sense did he minimize its importance. For he described it as the censor, as the source of guilt, and therefore as the primary agency in forcing desires and urges deep into the unconscious. It functioned within the individual as society's policeman for enforcing taboos and moral restrictions. In so doing, it sometimes ran counter to the drives of the id, and burdened the individual with feelings of anxiety, frustration, and guilt which left him neurotic and maladjusted. But such were the natural consequences of a basic conflict which could only be relieved by the insight and understanding made possible for the individual by psychoanalytic therapy.

During the last twenty years of his life Freud revised his original dualism regarding the bases of instinctual behavior. In *Beyond the Pleasure Principle* (1920) and in *Civilization and Its Discontents* (1930), he suggested Eros and Death, in place of hunger and sex, as the two prepotent forces motivating hu-

---

[1] "The Ego and the Id," *Great Books of the Western World*. Chicago, Britannica, 1952, LIV, 702.

man reactions. By Eros he meant the instinct of life, the constructive and unifying instinct, which aims at binding together single individuals, then families, tribes, races, and nations. Eros is the builder of civilization, the source not only of harmony and peace but of creativity. Its vital energy is the *libido* which, as Freud conceived it, includes much more than sex desire. It embraces all those forms of energy which impel human beings toward unity and harmonious relationships with one another. The Death instinct, by contrast, is the instinct of destruction and divisiveness. It propels civilization toward dissolution and disintegration. It expresses itself in aggression, in hostility, and in hatred. Its ultimate purpose is not merely to destroy society but to reduce living things to an inorganic death. Freud did not think of Eros and Death as disjunct forces, operating in complete independence. Instead, he envisaged the aggressive instinct as in considerable measure the consequence of Eros. The trouble, he said, is that civilization demands too much of the unifying instinct. It sets up the ideal, for instance, of loving one's neighbor as oneself. It requires, in addition, the suppression of eroticism in obedience to moral conventions and as a means of diverting energy into "useful" channels. The result is to produce tensions and frustrations which sometimes manifest themselves in aggressions.

According to his most reliable biographer, Freud "had no more than the average interest in politics and modes of government." [2] Except for his opposition to conventional sex morality, he was not a reformer—especially not during his early career. For the most part, he emphasized adaptation, adjustment to established norms, and sublimation or redirection of instinctual urges. His attitude toward human nature was far from benevolent. "Men," he wrote, "are not gentle, friendly creatures wishing for love, who simply defend themselves if they are attacked, but a powerful measure of desire for aggression has to be reckoned as part of their instinctual endowment." As a result, a man's neighbor is not merely a possible helper or object of love but also a possible object of exploitation, of humiliation, thievery,

[2] Ernest Jones, *The Life and Works of Sigmund Freud*. New York, Basic Books, 1953–1957, I, 5.

torture, and murder. *"Homo homini lupus;* who has the courage
to dispute it in the face of all the evidence in his own life and
in history?" [3]

Neither the refinements of culture nor the influence of religion
can be counted on, according to Freud, to curb the savage beast
that lurks in the human breast. Culture has called up in vain
every reinforcement of idealism and appeal to sweet reasonable-
ness; yet the problems of society are as thorny as ever. Religions
succeed in establishing bonds of affection among their own
followers but only by encouraging hostility toward those outside the fold. No better example of this attitude can be found,
according to Freud, than Christianity. Instituted as a religion
of universal love, it was fiercely intolerant of all other cults. Nor
did the father of psychoanalysis credit the Marxists with superior wisdom in claiming that the abolition of private property
would provide the remedy for man's inhumanity. The instinct
of aggression, he pointed out, did not arise as the result of
property. It reigned supreme in primitive times when possessions were extremely scanty. It shows itself in the nursery when
concepts of ownership are not even rudimentary. It lies at the
bottom of all the relations of love and affection between human
beings—"possibly with the single exception of that of a mother
to her male child." [4]

Freud has been accused of being an anti-intellectual who regarded man as a slave of his emotions, incapable of rational
thinking, and seldom rising above the level of the instincts and
complexes. The accusation does not rest, however, on solid
foundations. Freud firmly believed that man is capable of intelligent action. He recognized that it is difficult, and that it
rarely happens, mainly because of the persistence into adult
life of infantile behavior patterns. If these could be eliminated
or redirected, the individual would be freed for rational responses. The process will never be wholly successful, for the
power of the instincts is too strong. But the sustaining faith of
Freud's life was his belief that the advancement of culture will

[3] *Civilization and Its Discontents*. London, Hogarth, 1951, p. 85.
[4] *Ibid.*, p. 89.

gradually but surely mitigate the barbaric tendencies of man's original nature. This is illustrated by his views on war. In an exchange of letters with Albert Einstein, in 1932, he reiterated his earlier conviction that lust for aggression is a powerful factor in man's biological inheritance. He ascribed the origin of the earliest political communities to nothing but violence and brutal conquest. In time, law took the place of a direct resort to brute force, but law itself was nothing but the combined force of the strongest elements in the community banded together to repress the weak. As strong combinations were formed in adjoining areas, they took to fighting one another, and an unending series of international wars was the result.

Freud surmised that war might be abolished if some world authority could be established with overwhelming military force at its command. But he thought the chances very dismal indeed that the nations of the earth would ever permit such an agency to come into existence. He saw almost no hope except in the gradual progress of enlightenment. War, he said, "runs most emphatically counter to the psychic disposition imposed on us by the growth of culture; we are therefore bound to resent war, to find it utterly intolerable." He thought it quite possible that the growth of enlightenment, combined with a dread of new and more horrible weapons, might bring an end to war in the near future. In any case he considered it justifiable to "rest on the assurance that whatever makes for cultural development is working also against war." [5]

In an earlier work, *The Future of an Illusion*, first published in 1927, Freud had also expressed optimism and sublime confidence in the intellect. His subject of discussion was religion, and he compared the individual's quest for supernatural security against terrors of the universe with the child's dependence upon the protection of its parents. Despising religion as a form of infantile regression, he called upon men to recognize that the hardships of civilization are largely of their own making and to strive to conquer them by an exercise of their rational abilities. He avowed that, in the long run, nothing can withstand

[5] William Ebenstein, *Great Political Thinkers*, p. 846.

reason and knowledge. "The voice of the intellect is a soft one," he declared, "but it does not rest until it has gained a hearing." [6] How, then, has Freud come to be regarded as an enemy of intellect and an evangel of hopelessness and dark animality? The explanation stems largely from his theory of the Oedipus complex and the implications he deduced from it. The Oedipus complex is practically the trunk of the tree of Freudian theory. Based on the ancient Greek myth of the individual who unwittingly slew his father and married his own mother, it provided Freud with a central device for explaining almost the whole aggregate of unconscious behavior. Through the interpretation of dreams he claimed to have found universal tendencies in human beings toward parricide and incest. Inherited from previous generations and further developed in infancy, these tendencies toward fondness for one parent and bitter hatred for the other linger with the individual into his life as an adult. They come to be closely connected with the two great instincts of Eros and Death.

But Freud's political and social deductions from the Oedipus complex were even more responsible for his identification with pessimism and contempt for intellect. In *Totem and Taboo* (1913) he undertook to apply the Oedipus myth to some of the deepest mysteries of social organization and to the origin of religion and the god-king. He posited, in the beginning, a primal horde under the leadership of an elder male, who attempted to monopolize all the females of the group. Denied access to these women, the younger men rebelled, killed the old man, and ate his body to acquire his strength. But they were soon overcome by a sense of guilt, and consequently repented of their crime and renounced the women whom they had taken as spoils. The dead chieftain was exalted into a kind of god, in the form of an animal whose flesh must never be eaten; and thenceforth all males must go outside the horde for their sexual partners. Thus came into existence the two most famous taboos of primitive man, the taboo against eating the totem animal (parricide) and the taboo against marriage within the tribe (incest). The prohibition of incest Freud described as "perhaps the most maim-

---

[6] *The Future of an Illusion.* London, Hogarth, 1949, p. 93.

ing wound ever inflicted throughout the ages on the erotic life of man." [7]

In the last book of his life, *Moses and Monotheism*, Freud developed a theory that what holds groups together is veneration of the leader as a father-substitute. He concluded, therefore, that the political process must generally conform to the infantile pattern. The relationship of subjects to the leader has all the characteristics of dependency and helplessness that mark the relationship between the child and his father. Group behavior may consequently be compared with that of infants *en masse*. The qualities which enable the leader to rule are the same as those which assure to the father his dominant position as head of the family. He is an anchor of strength, of decisiveness, of moral certitude, of firm conviction. Freud maintained that the members of the group wish to be dominated by such a figure. It must be remembered, however, that this conclusion reflected a conception of what actually existed, not of what might be possible under different conditions. For there seems always to have been latent in Freud's mind the assumption that men need not be permanently bound by their childhood illusions. Either they can overcome them by their own growth in experience and knowledge or they can be rescued from them by psychoanalysis.

The most faithful disciple of Freud so far as concerns the political uses of psychoanalysis is undoubtedly Harold D. Lasswell. However, he considers himself a political scientist and employs the resources of Freudian psychology merely for analysis of political phenomena. Lasswell was born in Donnellson, Illinois, in 1902, and earned both a bachelor's and a doctor's degree at the University of Chicago. He taught political science at his alma mater from 1924 to 1938, meanwhile devoting several summers to the study of psychoanalysis in various universities of Europe. After a year as political scientist at the Washington School of Psychiatry, he was appointed visiting lecturer at the Yale School of Law, and in 1946 Sterling Professor of Law. Since 1954 he has been a fellow at the Center for Advanced Study in the Behavioral Sciences, and in 1955 he was elected President of the American Political Science Association.

[7] *Civilization and Its Discontents*, p. 74.

The central theme of Lasswell's psychologically grounded political theory would seem to be the doctrine that "political movements derive their vitality from the displacement of private affects upon public objects." [8] By this he means that political movements grow and develop as a consequence of the diversion by their followers of deeply imbedded personal feelings into public channels. To illustrate, men who in childhood or adolescence acquire a bitter hatred of their fathers may direct that hatred later into rebellion against all authority. They thus become anarchists, or possibly political assassins. In his *Psychopathology and Politics,* Lasswell attempted to analyze various types of political leaders in terms of psychopathic traits. He found agitators to be victims of insecurity, often growing out of brother-hostility and fear of loss of parental affection. Their crusading activities are usually prompted by feelings of guilt and a need to do penance for real or imaginary sins of the past. Hard-driving administrators, with a passion for efficiency and scrupulous attention to details, he discovered to be sufferers from feelings of inferiority and often from fears of sexual impotence. Their zeal for achievement is an attempt to cover up a sense of inadequacy. He pointed out, also, that many eminent leaders in history had psychic and/or physical abnormalities which almost certainly influenced their public careers. For instance, Rousseau suffered from paranoia; Alexander the Great was an alcoholic; Napoleon had partly atrophied genitalia; Bismarck was subject to hysteria.

But Lasswell is not interested primarily in description and diagnosis. He recognizes their value for purposes of understanding human motivation, but he does not believe they go far enough. His real objective is what he calls the "politics of prevention." He regards nearly all psychological aberrations as politically dangerous. The inferiority complex, father-hatred, homosexuality, narcissism (exaggerated self-love), guilt-obsessions are only a few of them. Such are the stuff of which fanatics, dictators, and tyrants are formed. The politics of prevention must, of course, be based on accurate diagnosis. It is necessary

[8] "Psychopathology and Politics," *The Political Writings of Harold D. Lasswell.* Glencoe, Illinois, Free Press, 1951, p. 173.

to understand the nature of the tensions that torment men's souls, but it is even more important to relieve those tensions and prevent them from finding an outlet in violence, persecution, and conflict. The politics of prevention does not consist in public discussions and debates, in enacting legislation, or in extensive changes in governmental organization. Nor can it take the form of popular participation in government or an increase in the power of the masses. The task of ruling must be founded upon accurate knowledge, and the discovery of knowledge is a function of specialized research. There will be no solution to the problem of tensions and conflicts until it is recognized that "it takes longer to train a good social scientist than it takes to train a good physical scientist." [9] For the essential task of the former is the difficult process of reorienting people's minds and thereby of reducing strains and maladaptations. [10]

During the 1930's Lasswell attempted to show a persistent relationship between international conflict and personal insecurity. Assuming that the researches of social scientists prove that war is practically universal among all cultures, he sought to discover the sources of such conflict in the fears and anxieties of individuals. By studying the findings of psychoanalysts he came to the conclusion that nearly every child develops phobias regarding himself and his relations with others. For the most part, these phobias take the form of fears of maiming or mutilation, especially fears of castration. In time these fears come to be associated with some person or thing already suspect because of strangeness or unpopularity. As an example, Lasswell cited the case of an American army officer who suffered from a series of nightmares in which he was pursued by a hideous Japanese officer with a huge knife in his hand. Analysis brought out the fact that the American officer had been threatened in

---

[9] Ibid., p. 201.
[10] It is pertinent to add that much of Lasswell's political psychiatry departs widely from that of Freud, who regarded nearly all the foundations of human behavior as instinctual. Lasswell thinks of the fears and obsessions constituting personal insecurity as socially acquired. They are implanted in the mind of the child by ignorant elders who threaten mutilation as a punishment for childhood habits. It is significant that Lasswell hardly ever refers to the Oedipus complex.

childhood with severance of his sex organs if he did not desist from masturbation. Though buried in the subconscious, the fear persisted and was later projected onto the Japanese in a period when they were unpopular because of disturbance of the balance of power in the Far East.

Lasswell seems to believe that the so-called "castration complex" has a large role to play in nearly all examples of international conflict. He recognizes the importance of such conventional factors as trade rivalry, competition in armaments, and threats to the balance of power. But he believes that these factors would seldom result in open conflict were it not for the psychological tensions dominating the minds of the masses on both sides. He takes no stock in the theory that the common people are overwhelmingly pacific, and that it is the ruling classes who involve them in wars. He admits that the masses appear to be unwarlike and that they are often "shocked" by the outbreak of hostilities, but he denies that "a slumbering giant of carnage" ever springs "fully panoplied among a lamblike population." [11] The desire for hostilities may be suppressed, but it is as deeply latent in the minds of the rank and file as it is in the minds of their rulers. The source of it is the morbid fear of mutilation buried in man's unconscious. On occasions this fear becomes so intense that, for large numbers of individuals, there seems no way of escape except to attack. But to make an attack possible one must have enemies. At times they can be found on the domestic scene, in the person of the monopolists, the capitalists, or the Wall Street speculators. More often it is some foreign menace which the unconscious mind singles out as the target for attack. The whole process is irrational and the hostility it generates goes far beyond reasonable bounds.

Lasswell's "politics of prevention" has little to offer, of a remedial character, in the area of international conflict. He concedes that personal insecurity may sometimes find relief in non-political channels—in turning one's aggressions back upon one's self, for example, but such action would ultimately result in suicide. Various forms of sublimation may also provide outlets—crusad-

[11] *World Politics and Personal Insecurity.* New York, Whittlesey House, 1935, p. 76.

ing against moral evils, hunting big game, or perhaps ridding an area of some pest or nuisance. But Lasswell has no endorsement to give to any of these. He fears that crusading against moral evils, for instance, may generate so much intolerance as to make the cure as bad as the disease. He apparently has no interest in any kind of "moral equivalent of war" such as that recommended by William James. Nor does he place much confidence in any of the conventional anti-war remedies. Pacifism he seems to regard as just another yearning for the "quietness of the womb," for the comfort and security of the prenatal condition. Emphasizing the horrors of war as a means of preventing conflict he thinks of as worse than useless; for it is a form of sadism in which the individual relieves his unconscious pleasure in contemplating slaughter and suffering by professing feelings of revulsion. There remains, then, almost nothing but a reliance upon education to purge men's minds of superstitions and false doctrines. With an adequate number of psychiatrically trained social scientists to guide and instruct the masses, perhaps phobias and complexes would never be implanted in the first place. But the specific measures for implementing such a vast program are never mentioned by Lasswell. Nor does he seem to realize the revolutionary character of the social and moral changes that would be required. Freud gave a suggestion of these in *Civilization and Its Discontents* when he argued that civilization grows by restricting the sexual impulses of the individual, though he admitted that these restrictions are carried beyond all reasonable justification.

2. The Neo-Freudians

The Freudian system had scarcely been launched on the sea of psychological theory when conflicts developed between Freud himself and some of his disciples. In Vienna, Alfred Adler repudiated what he considered his master's overemphasis on sex impulses and substituted the inferiority complex as the basic force in unconscious behavior. In Switzerland, Carl Jung introduced the idea of a "collective unconscious," common to all peoples, as a motivating influence in the life of the individual and magnified the importance of religion as an element in psychotherapy. More far-reaching has been the work of a group of younger revisionists who are generally called the Neo-Freudians. Though they pay tribute to Freud's monumental contributions in uncovering the *terra incognita* of the human psyche, they reject a large number of his basic assumptions. Denying that man's nature is moulded primarily by instinctual factors, they accord a much greater role to environment than they do to heredity. As a consequence, they emphasize more heavily the functions of education and emotional conditioning in liberating the individual from his psychic tensions. Finally, and in accordance with the same logic, they are more hopeful than Freud, and they look with disfavor upon the darker strains of mechanism and fatalism that characterized much of his outlook.

Three of the most distinguished and original of the Neo-Freudians—Karen Horney, Harry Stack Sullivan, and Erich Fromm—may be chosen to represent the group. Karen Horney was born in Hamburg, Germany, in 1885, and obtained medical degrees at the universities of Freiburg and Berlin. She came to the United States in 1932 and was naturalized six years later. From 1920 to 1932 she was an instructor at the Institute for Psychoanalysis in Berlin. From 1932 to 1934 she was Associate Director of the Chicago Institute for Psychoanalysis, and from 1935 to 1941 lecturer at the New School for Social Research in New York and also at the New York Psychoanalytic Institute. Her increasing heterodoxy resulted in her disqualification by the New York Institute as both analyst and instructor. As a result, she severed her ties completely with the orthodox Freudian movement and, with a few kindred spirits, founded the Association for the Advancement of Psychoanalysis. She was made Dean of a new school sponsored by the Association, the American Institute for Psychoanalysis, and served in that position until her death in 1952.

Though Karen Horney had nothing that could be called a philosophy of politics or of man's relation to organized society, her psychological conclusions have profound significance for political theory. Her deviation from Freud was summed up in her conception of human nature. A year before she died she spelled out this conception in terms which left no doubt as to her optimistic environmentalist position. Man, she wrote, is "no longer an instinct-ridden creature, but a being capable of choice and responsibility." His destructive and anti-social cravings are not innate "but reactive." "Growing up under favorable conditions," he would develop "his inherent constructive forces, and like every other living organism, would want to realize his potentialities." Human nature is not unalterable, she concluded, but is subject to change.[12]

It is sometimes said that Adler and Jung did not simply modify Freudian theory but left it practically unrecognizable. The same might almost be said of some of the Neo-Freudians. Karen Horney virtually relegated to the discard Freud's physiological-biological determinism and substituted for it a sociological interpretation. She conceived of nearly all of man's urges and drives as reactions to some influence in his social environment. To regard them as instincts, she maintained, was to leave the individual with the sorry alternative of bottling them up within himself and increasing his own misery, or turning them outward and making others miserable. She preferred to think of them as consequences rather than as causes. The craving for destruction, she argued, is not an inborn relic of savagery but a defense reaction against some fancied wrong or danger. She repudiated, therefore, the Freudian thesis of an instinct of Death expressing itself in insatiable cravings to smash and destroy and to kill or maim. She drastically modified, also, the Oedipus theory of Freud. Agreeing with Freud that infancy is of tremendous importance in shaping the personality of the individual, she nevertheless could find no basis for an inborn urge in the male child to murder his father and marry his mother. Such fantasies, she argued, are simply the expressions of fears and anxieties created in the mind of the child by the behavior of his parents. Murderous impulses, for instance, are the child's defense against what he conceives as parental tyranny. Incestuous cravings reflect an anxious dread of being deprived of love. The whole pattern of infantile sexuality she regarded as an expression of the child's feelings of insecurity in what seems to him a hostile world.

[12] "Tenth Anniversary," *American Journal of Psychoanalysis*, XI (1951), 3.

Dr. Horney's vision of a reconstructed society rests partly upon implications contained in her psychological theory. Not a single form of anti-social behavior did she consider to be instinctive or inherited. Selfishness, greed, aggression, destructiveness were all simply means of defense against anxieties generated by disturbed interpersonal relations in the child's environment. Though she did not argue that man is inherently good, she did maintain that the human personality is potentially healthy, and that the proper environmental conditions will ensure its development as a normal entity. At some points she came close to an explicit social philosophy. She denied that the individual, because of compulsive drives for vengeance, gratification, and power, must sooner or later collide with the outside world, making crime, delinquency, and war inevitable. "If there is such a collision," she said, it is not because of man's instincts "but because the environment inspires fears and hostilities." [13]

In one of her chief books, Dr. Horney found a main source of neuroses in conflicts generated by society. An example is the conflict between success in life and the individual's need for affection. Success depends upon selfishness, assertiveness, and fighting for a place in the sun. The person who engages in such efforts, even if he wins the goal, feels himself alienated and surrounded by enemies. Hence an exaggerated need for love which, because of the regulations of society, cannot be fulfilled. Another of the basic conflicts is the conflict between competition and the Christian ideal of brotherly love. Modern society glorifies competition as the avenue to success. But modern society is also a Christian society which exalts the ideals of charity, humility, and love of one's neighbor. The clash of such opposites is bound to produce emotional tension which may result in a neurosis. "The person who is likely to become neurotic is one who has experienced the culturally determined difficulties in an accentuated form, mostly through the medium of childhood experiences, and who has consequently been unable to solve them, or has solved them only at great cost to his personality." [14]

Though Karen Horney never essayed the role of social re-

[13] *New Ways in Psychoanalysis.* New York, Norton, 1939, p. 191.
[14] *The Neurotic Personality of Our Time.* New York, Norton, 1937, p. 290.

former, there can be no doubt that she recognized a definite need for social improvement. She did not agree at all with Freud's thesis that nothing can be done to control man's libidinal drives except to divert them into harmless channels or to wait for the enlightenment which comes from the accretion of culture. As we have seen, she considered neuroses as effects rather than causes of social maladjustments; and she found in fiercely competitive society the real matrix of such maladjustments. Competition generates hostility and ruthlessness and often results in fear of failure. Though success is frequently the consequence of fortuitous circumstances, modern ideology presents it as the fruit of intrinsic merits and glorifies it as a visible sign of the grace of God. Under the pressure of this ideology, the person who achieves success is made to feel that he amounts to something, while the person who fails is made to feel humiliated and defeated. Since Dr. Horney regarded such pressure as a cause of both personal unhappiness and social pathology, she must have fervently hoped for a means of eliminating it. Whether she believed that the means could ever be devised is impossible to determine, for she never advanced any specific proposals. There was perhaps even an element of fatalism in her statement that "competitiveness, and the potential hostility that accompanies it, pervades all human relationships." [15] Possibly we are forced to conclude that, despite her concern over the defects of society, she remained a psychoanalyst devoted to straightening the quirks of individuals so as to enable them to adjust to an unhealthy environment. Believing as she did in the malignance of society, she must have been oppressed at times with the magnitude of her task.

Similar to Karen Horney in his preoccupation with the environmental aspects of psychoanalysis was Harry Stack Sullivan. Sullivan was born in Norwich, N. Y., in 1892 and obtained his medical training at the Chicago College of Medicine and Surgery. His first position was Veterans Bureau Liaison Officer at St. Elizabeth's Hospital in Washington, then under the direction of the eminent Dr. William Alanson White. In 1923 Sullivan was appointed Assistant Physician at Sheppard and Enoch Pratt

[15] *Ibid.*, p. 284.

Hospital and was quickly promoted to Director of Clinical Research. Meanwhile, he served as an instructor and then as Associate Professor at the University of Maryland School of Medicine. In 1936 he became President of the Washington School of Psychiatry and added to his duties three years later the headship of the Georgetown University Department of Psychiatry. In 1945 he became editor of *Psychiatry*, a journal he had helped to found, but death overtook him four years later at the height of his career.

The heart of Sullivan's system was his theory of *interpersonal relations*. He took the emphatic position that no person can live in complete isolation for any considerable period of time. Communion with other persons is as vital to the individual as air and water. The study of such interrelations, according to Sullivan, is the only legitimate province of psychoanalysis. His approach bore a superficial resemblance to that of the physical scientist, when he insisted that psychiatry should restrict itself to observable phenomena, "the processes that involve or go on between people." The strictly private, he asserted, is beyond its jurisdiction. It does not study the individual in mental turmoil; it studies "disordered interpersonal relations nucleating more or less clearly in a particular person." [16] But to obviate the impression that he was interested only in a behaviorist approach toward psychology, it should be pointed out that he defined "person" in such a way as to include imaginary "persons," mentally dissociated from their real embodiments, as in split-personality or schizophrenia. He was actually very deeply concerned with unconscious processes and had developed his theories largely in connection with his work on a therapy for schizophrenia.

Dr. Sullivan's psychoanalysis was socially oriented. Perhaps it was even more so than Karen Horney's, especially with regard to recommendations for social change. Though he recognized the importance of constitutional factors in determining human behavior, he seems to have thought of them as providing little

[16] Dorothy R. Blitsen, "The Significance of Harry Stack Sullivan's Theories for Social Science." Columbia University: unpublished dissertation, 1952, p. 58.

more than a predisposition toward mental illness. In his view, afflictions of the mind are inconceivable apart from the social environment. Psychopathology, therefore, is not so much a medical or biological science as it is a social science. The basic cause of neurotic and psychotic behavior he held to be a craving for security. So vital is this craving that it frequently overrides in importance the satisfaction of physical desires. "A person who suffers insecurity," he said, "is driven by a whip—anxiety—that hurts more than any of the individual whips of biological needs. You will not find anyone pursuing anxiety for pleasure," he concluded.[17] Though he accorded to anxiety an important role as the source of all learning, he could conceive it in no other mode than as an exceedingly unpleasant and frustrating experience. He described anxiety in regard to one's relations with others as "responsible for a great part of the inadequate, inefficient, unduly rigid, or otherwise unfortunate performances of people." It is the source, he wrote, "of a great deal of what comes to a psychiatrist for attention." [18]

It was inevitable so far as his social outlook was concerned that Sullivan should have emphasized the importance of eliminating causes of anxiety. As for methods of achieving this result, however, his mind was no more fertile than that of Dr. Horney. He deplored the dearth in American society of good prescriptions for intimacy with and accommodation to other people, but he had little to suggest for the purpose of making up the deficiency. He had little or no confidence in crusades for reform, in programs for legislation, or in political campaigns to win elections. He thought that any major effort to change institutions overnight would be likely to produce psychic damage far out of proportion to the probable benefits. Crusades to eradicate evil, he contended, merely succeed in magnifying anxieties without appreciably diminishing their causes. Even argumentation, except of the mildest kind, involves so much of a challenge to the participants' self-esteem that the psychiatrist can expect

[17] H. S. Perry, M. L. Gawel and M. Gibbons, eds., *Clinical Studies in Psychiatry*. New York, Norton, 1956, p. 365.
[18] H. S. Perry and M. L. Gawel, eds., *The Interpersonal Theory of Psychiatry*. New York, Norton, 1953, p. 160.

nothing valuable to come of it. With respect to the use of political methods, Sullivan's views were even more pessimistic. He considered the emotional orgies characterizing political campaigns to be particularly conducive to heightening tensions. Moreover, in challenging deeply rooted convictions they contribute to insecurity; for, according to Sullivan, cherished beliefs have a definite utility in buttressing self-esteem and therefore in preventing anxiety. About all that can be credited to Dr. Sullivan in the form of positive contributions to political and social theory, aside from his recognition of the social character of man's behavior, is his willingness to concede the necessity of a better society, together with his profound assurance that social improvement is actually attainable.

The social psychologies of Drs. Sullivan and Horney pale into insignificance when compared with that of Erich Fromm. In fact, it may be argued that Fromm is scarcely a psychologist at all in the sense of concern with individual drives as causes of human behavior. He is essentially a dissecter of society and a propounder of remedies for society's ailments. Fromm was born in Frankfurt, Germany, in 1900. He received a Ph.D. at the University of Heidelberg and studied also at the University of Munich and at the Psychoanalytic Institute in Berlin. For a number of years he lectured at the Psychoanalytic Institute in Frankfurt, at the Institute for Social Research at the University of Frankfurt, and at the International Institute for Social Research in New York. Later he held faculty appointments at Bennington College and the National University of Mexico. Both his training and experience were such as to incline him toward a sociological view of psychoanalysis. His work for the doctorate was based upon sociology as well as psychology. After coming to the United States he became a member of Karen Horney's American Institute for Psychoanalysis and later served on the staffs of the Washington School of Psychiatry and the William Alanson White Institute of Psychiatry in New York. Both of the latter institutions operated under the guiding influence of Harry Stack Sullivan.

The work which first brought fame to Erich Fromm was his book, *Escape from Freedom,* which he published in 1941. In it he attempted to trace the political and social maladies of the contemporary world to the centuries which marked the transition from medieval to modern culture. During the Middle Ages, he claimed, the individual enjoyed security rather than freedom. Nearly everybody was chained to his role in the social order. No matter what his abilities, a man had little chance to move from one class to another. If he were a craftsman or a merchant, his identity was submerged in the guild, and the work he performed and the methods of selling his wares were strictly controlled by the group. His beliefs were dictated and his conduct prescribed by a vast ecclesiastical system which exerted a rigid conformity. But although the individual was not free, neither was he isolated nor abandoned. No one could turn him out to starve when he was too old or too sick to work. He would be cared for by the guild, by the lord of the manor, or by the Church. His little world always afforded him security and protection, and he felt at home and comfortable in it. Since the social order was considered divinely established and sanctioned by natural law, each person was inclined to accept his place in it without questioning or protest. He did not feel called upon to strive or scramble for a higher position by excelling his neighbors. There was little competition for profit or privilege. Suffering, of course, existed, but the Church helped to make it bearable by explaining that man's sojourn on earth was a mere prelude to eternal bliss. Medieval Christianity gave meaning to the life of the humble toiler and preserved him from fears and gnawing doubts.

But this life of security was rudely demolished during the centuries that followed the Middle Ages. The Italian Renaissance gave birth to individuality. Initiative, self-assertion, aggressiveness, the pursuit of power and wealth usurped the place formerly occupied by conformism, self-abnegation, and subordination to the group. Grasping bankers, merchant princes, *condottieri* rode roughshod over rivals and common people alike in efforts to enrich themselves or to maximize their power. Far from regarding conceit and aggrandizement as cardinal sins, the new lords of creation acclaimed these qualities as virtues of the true leader and as justifiable adjuncts of his right to rule. But the influence of the Renaissance in destroying the medieval social pattern was relatively minor in comparison with that of the Reformation. In the judgment of Fromm, Protestantism did more to undermine the feeling of security and oneness with society than any other single factor. The reason, he contends, was its debasement of man, its overemphasis on the wickedness of human nature. It revived the doctrine of original sin and taught that no human action, in and of itself, could have ethical merit. The result, he believes, was to cause the individual to hate and despise himself and therefore to strive to bolster his ego by acquiring possessions and dominating others. Though Protestantism liberated its followers from ecclesiastical regimentation, it enslaved them to a despotic deity who ruled over the universe like a wrathful judge and determined the fate of every inhabitant. Even the faith by which man could justify himself and be saved was implanted in him by divine action. The consequence was to instill in the individual a feeling of helplessness and alienation. He was isolated and alone, much like the unloved child of a tyrannical father. In fact, his condition was similar to that of Luther himself. As Fromm describes him, Luther "was filled with an extreme feeling of aloneness, powerlessness, wickedness. . . . He was tortured by doubts. . . . He hated others, especially the 'rabble,' he hated himself, he hated life; and out of all this hatred came a passionate and desperate striving to be loved." [19]

From this historical setting of alienation and isolation Fromm deduces not only psychological consequences but political and social ones also. Though he refers rather carelessly to an *instinct* of submission, he actually posits historical and environmental causes for both *masochism* and *sadism*. Both traits quite commonly exist in the same individual, and their causes are virtually identical. Both spring from feelings of inferiority and self-hatred. Masochism results when such feelings are turned inward into a sense of guilt, which must be atoned for by torturing oneself. Sadism is an attempt to conquer unbearable notions of helplessness and inferiority by torturing others. Infliction of pain gives some persons a sense of power which they must have in order to

[19] *Escape from Freedom.* New York, Rinehart, 1941, p. 66.

compensate for insignificance. Whereas the masochist gains security by "being swallowed," the sadist gains it "by swallowing somebody else." [20] Fromm found these characteristics well exemplified in the person of Hitler—his love of inflicting cruelty, especially on the weak, his fanaticism and savage denunciations, but also his longing for submission to some outside power, manifested by his reverence for Fate.

Fromm also discovered in the revolt against insecurity and alienation a much broader significance. He held it to be the source of the restless striving and frenetic activity in the modern world. Oppressed by loneliness and hatred of self, modern man seeks to conquer his insignificance by expenditure of energy in unrelenting competition, in compulsive work, and in reckless depletion of natural resources. Such processes have created industrial and political aggregations so enormous and complex that the individuals who serve them have been depressed still further into insignificance. What can they do but fall in step like marching soldiers or adjust themselves to the status of robots at a conveyor belt? What is more, their preparation for fascism is virtually complete. The emptiness of their lives and their sense of humiliation make them eager to merge their identities with some movement which gives them the illusion of power and an escape from their intolerable "freedom."

In his second most important book, *The Sane Society*, Fromm carried his studies of social pathology still farther and accented especially what he regarded as appropriate remedies. He presented the hypothesis that whole societies may be mentally sick and supported it on the basis of World Health Organization statistics on alcoholism, suicide, and homicide in the United States and most nations of northern and western Europe. He introduced also the idea of a cleavage between the mother principle and the father principle, both in the psychology of the individual and in the evolution of the race. He accepted as a starting point Freud's theory of the conscience as an outgrowth of the commands and prohibitions of the father frightening his son into obedience and into recognition of a sense of duty. But in addition to the voice of the father, there is also the voice of the mother,

[20] *Ibid.*, p. 158.

which is the voice of love and forgiveness. In effect, she says: "Your father is quite right in scolding you, but do not take him too seriously; whatever you have done, you are my child, I love you, and I forgive you."[21] These same principles, according to Fromm, characterize all of human existence. The mother principle is the older of the two, and for many centuries society was matriarchal. Religion at first was based on the worship of a Great Mother, symbolizing the earth and the life-giving powers of nature. Male deities, if they existed, were secondary and subordinate beings. But in time the father principle gained dominance; society became patriarchal; and an all-powerful god took the place of the goddess and her son. The change was reflected by the religious revolution of Ikhnaton in Egypt and the establishment of the worship of Yahweh in Palestine. The mother principle did not die out, however. It was revived in medieval Christianity, with the Virgin Mary personifying tenderness and forgiveness as a counter-influence to the stern, avenging, omnipotent Father.[22] To the discredit of Protestantism, its leaders rejected this female principle in religion and went back to the implacable father deity of the ancient Hebrews.

Fromm seems to feel that a proper balance between the mother and father principles is a condition prerequisite to the sanity of a nation. Some peoples have exaggerated the father principle and have become belligerent, intolerant, and domineering. By contrast, a slavish devotion to the mother principle renders a people isolationist, provincial, and excessively "patriotic." They become rooted in the soil on which they live and, like an individual in love with himself, develop narcissistic tendencies. A ridiculous nationalism, manifesting itself in ethnocentrism and xenophobia, is the result. The "blood and soil" chauvinism of the Nazis was a typical example. In fact, Fromm designates nationalism as the "incest fixation" of the modern world. He appears to forget that in *Escape from Freedom* he had interpreted Nazism as a product of feelings of alienation and

[21] *The Sane Society*. New York, Rinehart, 1955, p. 48.
[22] Henry Adams, of course, had idealized the worship of the Virgin in almost these identical terms in his *Mont-Saint-Michel and Chartres*. New York, Houghton Mifflin, 1904.

insignificance evoked originally by Reformation doctrines of the vileness of man and the omnipotence of a wrathful God. He is nonetheless sure that there are positive values in both the mother and father principles. The mother principle, he believes, can be extended to symbolize love and tolerance for all humanity, and the father principle to stand for duty, law, and reason. Not until man succeeds in blending these principles in their higher forms of love and reason, justice and universal brotherliness "will he have found a new, human form of rootedness, will he have transformed his world into a truly human home." [23]

The specific form of this "truly human home" is given by Fromm in his prescriptions for a better society. It must consist, first of all, of sane individuals. The mentally healthy person, he says, "is the productive and unalienated person; the person who relates himself to the world lovingly, and who uses his reason to grasp reality objectively; who experiences himself as a unique individual entity, and at the same time feels one with his fellow man; who is not subject to irrational authority, and accepts willingly the rational authority of conscience and reason." [24] Society itself must also have qualities distinctly recognizable as healthy. Fromm defines a sane society as one in which every individual is treated as an end in himself, and in which no man is an instrument of any other person's greed, narcissism, or exploitation. It is a society also in which man is the center, and in which all political and economic activities are subordinated to his growth and development. It is a society, finally, which fosters creativity in work, stimulates the unfolding of reason, fosters human solidarity, and not only permits but encourages its members to live in relationships of warmth and respect for their fellows. [25]

The organizational pattern which Fromm recommends for his better society is what he calls "communitarian socialism." By this he means something akin to the utopian movements of the early nineteenth century, but with due regard for incorporat-

[23] *The Sane Society,* p. 60.
[24] *Ibid.,* p. 275.
[25] Fromm elaborates these ideas further in *The Art of Loving.* New York, Harper, 1956.

ing as many as possible of the advantages of twentieth-century industrialization. In its economic aspect, communitarian socialism would involve a blending of centralization and decentralization in such a way as to provide for a synthesis of decision-making from "above to below, and from below to above." Despite his use of the term "socialism," Fromm is not interested in ownership by the workers of the means of production, but in participation by the workers in management. He recommends a system of profit-sharing by employees, though he would still leave to the capitalist owners a "reasonable rate of interest" on their investment. Contending that transfer of ownership of industry to the state has only a negligible effect on the status of the worker, he urges instead a change in the work situation. As means to this end, he proposes the democratization of trade unions, the organization of workers into groups small enough to enable the members to relate themselves to one another, the encouragement of stock-ownership plans by employees so as to give them a sense of participation in the enterprises for which they work, and the enlargement of social security so as to provide for a *universal subsistence minimum,* even for the man who quits his job to prepare himself for another.

Communitarian socialism would also have its political and social aspects. For the solution of political problems Fromm suggests the division of society into small units of about five hundred people each in order that they may function as a town meeting. In such small groups political issues could be discussed thoroughly, and minds would be sharpened by conflicting arguments. The same groups, perhaps organized in accordance with vocational interests, might serve as social and recreational units. Fromm has a vision of a happy communitarian life in which people of like interests would "sing together, walk together, dance together, admire together." He goes so far as to argue that the inhabitants of "a relatively primitive village in which there are still real feasts, common artistic shared expressions, and no literacy at all—is more advanced culturally and more healthy mentally than our educated, newspaper-reading, radio-listening culture." [26] Though he may seem to have been

[26] *The Sane Society,* pp. 348–49.

expressing an anti-intellectual viewpoint, his assertions in other contexts appear to indicate that he has no desire to glorify the irrational or to justify ignorance or superstition. Rather, he seeks to overcome the inhuman character of modern civilization and to find a remedy for the alienation of individuals, which prevents them from either exercising or following reason.

3. The Implications of Behaviorism

Psychoanalysis is not the only brand of psychology from which startling inferences can be drawn for political theory. About 1905 a new school of psychological interpretation appeared which repudiated both consciousness and the unconscious as bases for understanding human reactions. The name commonly assigned to this school is behaviorism. The behaviorist attempts to give to psychology the status of a natural science. For this reason he reduces the whole subject of human behavior to a matter of stimuli and responses, which can be observed, tested, and measured just like the production of heat or electricity or the merging of two fluids in a chemical reaction. Every stimulus, he maintains, generates a response, and every response is preceded by a stimulus. This is the sum total of human behavior, or at least it is all that lends itself to scientific analysis. The extreme behaviorist dismisses from consideration everything representing the thoughts, ideas, images, and rationalizations purporting to come from the human mind. He is not even sure that there *is* such a thing as a "mind," for he denies that it can be made the subject of objective study. For the behaviorist, man is essentially an animal, whose responses are susceptible to an almost infinite conditioning or modification, but originally are just as mechanical as those of a monkey or a kangaroo.

The most noted pioneer in the development of psychology as an objective science was Ivan Pavlov. Although his training and experience were those of a physiologist, his discoveries laid the foundations for a new approach to psychology. Previous to his time, psychology had been concerned primarily with states of mind, with sensations, perceptions, remembering, and reasoning. Under the new influence, it was gradually coming to be thought of as an experimental science, studying objective behavior, instead of attempting subjectively to find out what goes on in the "mind." Pavlov was born in 1849, in Ryazan, in central Russia. Though he was the son of a priest whose mode of living was not much different from that of the peasants, he managed to obtain a good education. He completed a course at the University of St. Petersburg and then enrolled in the Medico-Chirurgical Academy, from which he earned an M.D. degree in 1883. Eight years later he became Professor of Pharmacology at the Academy and in 1895 Director of the Department of Physiology at the Institute of Experimental Medicine. By 1904 he had gained international fame for his discoveries and was awarded the Nobel Prize in physiology. His chief contributions resulted from his studies of the nervous systems of animals and of the mechanisms of digestion and secretion. He proved that reflexes can be modified or conditioned, and demonstrated that a large proportion of the behavior of an animal is learned through experience with its environment. He found the center of reflex activity to be located in the cerebral cortex, and showed that a "decorticated" animal is almost incapable of learning anything.

Pavlov's influence on psychology stems primarily from his discovery of the *conditioned reflex,* which occurs when the original stimulus that caused a reflex has been modified or even supplanted by an altogether different stimulus. For example, Pavlov demonstrated that a dog fed repeatedly by the same attendant will secrete gastric juice at the mere sight of the attendant even when he appears without food. He showed also that the salivary glands could be made to function at the sound of a bell if an animal had previously been fed a large number of times to the accompaniment of such sounds. Though Pavlov did not extend these experiments to the human species, he quite clearly believed such a procedure to be feasible. He regarded the human body as a machine, a highly complicated one, but a machine nevertheless. This view is confirmed by the attitude he took toward an operation for gallstones which he underwent at the age of seventy-eight. The removal of the stones and his subsequent recovery impressed him as "one more proof of the law that the organism should be treated like a machine." "Exactly like a speck of dust in a watch," he exclaimed, "the stone was removed and the machine resumed its normal functions!" [27]

Pavlov also had an abiding faith in the efficacy of science to remake human beings and to point the way to a "full, true, and permanent happiness." Only exact science about human nature "and the most sincere approach to it by the aid of the omnipotent scientific method," he declared, "will deliver man from his present gloom, and will purge him of his contemporary shame in the sphere of interhuman relations." [28] He did not deny that inquiry into subjective feelings and states of mind might have some value for understanding the inner world of man, but he looked forward to the time when the subjective might be fused with the objective. Study of the conditioned reflex, he thought, might open the way for study of the entire human organism in an experimental, objective manner.

Pavlov had only a limited interest in political theory. Several times in his life he was deeply troubled by incompetence and corruption in the Russian government. Such was the attitude he took during the Russo-Japanese War and the revolutionary disturbances that followed it. But his radicalism was confined to sympathy with the Octobrists, who were satisfied with a modest extension of the suffrage and the establishment of a *Duma* to give approval to the Tsar's decrees. He was especially critical of the "dreamers" who wished to leap at once to a constitutional monarchy or even to a republic. During the agonizing years of World War I, Pavlov was equally disturbed by the weakness and incompetence of the Imperial Government, but he opposed the idea of another revolution. Even after the Communists came to power, he spoke out so sharply against the Bolsheviks and their program that his friends feared for his personal safety. He continued to disparage the Soviet regime and its policies until about 1932 (four years before his death), when he apparently decided that the threat of a Nazi invasion re-

---

[27] B. P. Babkin, *Pavlov: a Biography*. Chicago, University of Chicago Press, 1949, p. 176.

[28] *Ibid.*, p. 86.

quired patriotic support of the government of his homeland. The Soviet rulers, however, attempted to court Pavlov's favor throughout. They published editions of his works, provided him with comforts and conveniences, and did not even rebuke him for his criticisms. They obviously recognized the tremendous significance for the Soviet experiment of his teachings in regard to conditioned reflexes. For did not these teachings strongly suggest that the nature of every organism, including the human organism, is almost completely malleable? Since nearly all behavior is learned, there can be no such thing as a fixed human nature. Human beings can be made over, by a process of conditioning, in virtually any manner desired. The prospects for a new Soviet society, completely divested of all moral, religious, and economic prejudices acquired under the aegis of capitalism, seemed almost limitless.

The firmest adherent of Pavlov's physiological-psychological theories was John B. Watson, commonly regarded as the founder of behaviorism. He was born in Greenville, South Carolina, in 1878, and received his education at Furman University and the University of Chicago. He obtained a Ph.D. at the latter institution in 1903, supporting himself by working as an assistant janitor, waiter, and nursemaid to a cageful of white rats. After four years as an instructor at the University of Chicago, he was appointed, at the age of thirty, to a professorship at Johns Hopkins. He conducted extensive researches into both human and animal behavior, and for some time was allowed to examine all the infants born in the Johns Hopkins and Harriet Lane Hospitals. His academic career came to an abrupt end, however, in 1920, when he was discharged by the Johns Hopkins trustees as the result of a sensational divorce suit which involved some unfortunate publicity. Watson returned to Chicago and, after months of discouragement, obtained a job with an advertising agency investigating the market for rubber boots from Cairo to New Orleans. Later he sold groceries for R. H. Macy and Company as a means of studying consumer psychology. By 1924 he had become vice-president of a leading advertising firm in New York. Though he continued to write books and articles expounding his theories, he never regained his academic prestige. The tendency of academicians was to condemn him for selling his talents to industry, but it does not seem that the academic world had left him with much of an alternative. His reputation was still sullied at the time of his death in 1958.

Watson adopted the mechanistic implications of Pavlov's psychology with the ardor of a zealot. In fact, he reduced psychology to a kind of muscular, glandular, and visceral physiology. All human behavior, as well as all animal behavior, he argued, consists of physiological responses. Of these, there are two kinds: learned and unlearned responses. The latter include all that the individual is born with: the physiological reactions of hunger and feeding, struggling, withdrawing, breathing, coughing, crying, sneezing, digesting, etc.; and the basic emotions of fear, rage, and love. Practically everything else that the individual does must be classified as learned behavior: the habits; most of the so-called instincts, such as jealousy, envy, curiosity, pugnacity, acquisitiveness; the attitudes; and, of course, the skills, abilities, talents, and tendencies.

Watson dispensed with all such phenomena as consciousness and states of mind as incapable of objective study and therefore as unworthy of the time and attention of the scientific psychologist. In general, his attitude was that anything which cannot be tested and measured should not be assumed to exist. He tended to think of actions or physiological effects as the entire substance of behavior. For example, he regarded the emotion of fear as summed up by recession of blood from the face, trembling of the lips, palpitation of the heart, shortness of breath, reduced secretion of the salivary glands, and similar responses. These reactions, he insisted, are not manifestations of the emotion; they *are* the emotion. In like manner, he argued that thinking is not some mysterious process taking place in the so-called "mind." Instead, it is a form of talking to oneself. No one can think apart from the use of words or other symbols representing ideas. Learning to reason, therefore, is a matter of acquiring a physiological skill, in much the same way that one learns to ride a bicycle. The chief difference lies in the structures involved. Riding a bicycle brings into operation the muscles and nerves of the arms, back, and legs. Reasoning involves primarily the vocal cords and the muscles and nerves of the throat and chest regions. The function of the brain in both processes is essentially the same. It acts as a central coordinating agency for nerve activity.

Absorbed as he was in experimental activity, Watson had few theories of a social or political nature. Much was implied, however, in his strict environmentalism. He insisted that human beings inherit absolutely nothing except anatomical structures, physical characteristics, and unlearned responses. Such qualities as temperament, tendencies, talent, and intelligence are not inherited, except in so far as they may be dependent on bodily structures. Watson went so far as to contend that if he were given a dozen healthy infants, well-formed, and his own specified world to bring them up in, he would "guarantee to take any one at random and train him to become any type of specialist [he] might select—doctor, lawyer, artist, merchant-chief and, yes, even beggar-man and thief, regardless of the talents, penchants, tendencies, abilities, vocations, and race of his ancestors." [29] In making this assertion, he was espousing an equalitarianism far beyond the wildest dreams of Rousseau or Jefferson. He was saying, in effect, that, intellectually, all individuals at birth have an even start. What happens to them afterward depends entirely upon the environment. The significance of this theory for education, morality, crime, and social progress is easy to perceive. Watson maintained that all problems of social order could be solved by training and psychological conditioning. No one commits crimes, he declared, except the insane and the socially untrained. Therefore, he proposed to do away completely with criminal law and with punishment as such, though not with restraint. As a means of controlling and rehabilitating deviants, he recommended the adoption of a scientific procedure based upon what we know of the establishing and breaking-down of conditioned responses.

Most modern psychologists who have followed the tradition initiated by Pavlov have fought shy of a doctrinaire interpreta-

[29] *Behaviorism.* New York, The People's Institute Publishing Co., 1925, p. 82.

tion. Typical of this more moderate position were the views of Edward L. Thorndike. Born in Williamsburg, Massachusetts, in 1874, he earned B.A.'s at Wesleyan and Harvard, an M.A. at Harvard, and a Ph.D. at Columbia. He taught for a period of forty-one years, first at Western Reserve and then at Teachers College, Columbia. For a long period he was perhaps the leading experimental psychologist in the United States. He gained world-wide renown for his studies of the behavior of monkeys, fish, and baby chicks. He won fame also as an ardent exponent of psychological testing, and was primarily responsible for devising the tests for the United States Army during World War I. His views touching on political and social subjects are contained in a massive volume of a thousand pages, *Human Nature and the Social Order*, which he completed in 1939, ten years before his death.

As a psychologist, Thorndike was as rigorous an adherent of the experimental method as were Pavlov and Watson. He had no interest in theorizing about innate ideas, unconscious wishes, or anything else which could not be verified by objective research. Like his Russian and American confreres, he considered the nature of man to differ from that of the other mammals merely in degree of complexity. The individual human being, he asserted, is a product of his genes and of the infinite mixture of environmental factors which exert their influence upon him. The genes are carriers of anatomical characteristics and physical traits, but there is no evidence that they carry ideas, religious beliefs, or social habits. On the other hand, Thorndike did not limit the influence of heredity so strictly as did Watson. He believed that certain tendencies and predispositions are transmissible; for example, a tendency of submission, and even a predisposition toward "kindness and mutual aid in the form of liking to see people rejoicing and smiling rather than complaining and in tears." [30] He thought it possible also to demonstrate in most humans an inborn tendency to give bits of food to children, to rescue them from attacks by animals or from being run over by automobiles, and to comfort and protect the

---

[30] *Human Nature and the Social Order*. New York, Macmillan, 1940, p. 297.

weak. Though he was not sure that human nature contains enough benevolence to justify the hopes of pacifists and utopians, he repudiated the assumption that man, simply because he is a higher animal, must therefore have a beastly nature. He pointed out that chimpanzees, for instance, are rather decent creatures, and that their life in their native habitat is more like a family picnic than an orgy of demons. Significantly, also, he held that humans are capable of improvement. Even their inborn ability to learn, he argued, is not static but is capable of being augmented by favorable environmental conditions. An orphan, transferred from an institution to the care of enlightened foster parents, may undergo an improvement in intelligence quotient of as much as seven points.

When it came to expressing his views on political and social issues, Thorndike was less modest than most of his brethren. He believed that the findings of psychology could be made to illuminate nearly all of man's problems. Political science, he affirmed, is especially in need of this illumination. Its pundits have been dominated too long by theological prejudice about human depravity and have therefore exaggerated the role of force and the effectiveness of punishment in maintaining society. They have ignored the humane tendencies in the human genes and have neglected "the strong correlation between intelligence and morality which has been so potent in protecting civilization and in resurrecting it." [31] Thorndike considered it absurd that, in an age of science, government should be run by lawyers, businessmen, and farmers, who have no conception of the experimental method as a basis for political action. Instead of waiting for the results of research, they act in response to group pressures or in accordance with unproved dogmas about natural law or natural rights. He proposed, therefore, that boards of trustees be established for cities, states, and nations with authority to choose experts for the actual work of governing. The obvious pattern he took as his model was the organization of an American college or university. He did not care particularly how the boards would be chosen. Let them be self-constituted, he said, or chosen by lot from among two hundred

[31] *Ibid.*, p. 741.

"men of good sense." The important thing, he maintained, is that public policies be determined and executed by men with a knowledge of human nature and an appreciation of the value of the scientific method in the solution of social problems—by men who *know*, for instance, that there is no such characteristic as a fighting instinct bred into the marrow of the human species. He admitted that scientists make mistakes, but he thought it "surely better on the average to take *their* medicine than that of ignoramuses." [32]

Every new science or new scientific theory, developed through the ages, has met with fierce opposition, partly from individuals of timorous or conservative natures, but mostly from people who sense a threat to their interests. The Copernican theory was one cardinal example. By repudiating the medieval world view, it swept man out of his majestic position at the center of the universe and reduced him to a particle of dust in an endless cosmic machine. To accept such a mechanistic doctrine seemed to leaders of the Church and to many Renaissance humanists like an insult to God and an affront to the dignity of the human race. Even more upsetting was the Darwinian hypothesis of natural selection. Darwin challenged not only the Biblical theory of special creation but laid the basis for a naturalistic explanation of both animal and human biology. All that remained was the inner life of man, which might still be subject to spiritual or supernatural interpretation. In proposing to compress this realm within the limits of scientific analysis, the leaders of the new schools of psychology have tempted the wrath of almost everyone committed to a belief in the uniqueness of the human species.

Much of the criticism of the psychologists is merited, though perhaps for reasons different from the ones that inspire it. Neither psychoanalysts nor behaviorists appear to recognize the full implications of their findings for political and social theory. The conclusions of psychoanalysts seem to imply that the ideals of selflessness, love, and universal brotherhood taught by the great religions and by philosophers, both Christian and pagan,

[32] *Ibid.*, p. 958.

contradict the realities of human nature and are therefore impossible of attainment. They apparently believe that so long as such exalted ideals are dangled before feeble humanity, countless individuals will strive to achieve them and then succumb to neuroses as a consequence of failure. The logic of the situation would seem to dictate a morality of compromise, reverting perhaps to the Greek ideal of moderation and repudiating the perfectionism and the stern prohibitions of both Judaism and Christianity. But the psychoanalysts shrink from explicitly stating this. Nor are they more specific with regard to education. If it is true that phobias, anxieties, and resentments implanted in the minds of children by thoughtless and ignorant parents manifest themselves later in rebellious, aggressive, and delinquent behavior, why should not the correction of these faults be one of the chief functions of the schools? Liberation of the minds of great numbers of children might well be impracticable, but there seems to be no apparent reason why future parents should not be educated to avoid the infliction of psychological scars on the next generation. Finally, psychoanalysts have contributed little toward a "politics of prevention." They may say that it is desirable to eliminate tensions and conflicts, but they offer few practical suggestions as to how to proceed. They make almost no efforts to educate the public as to how they might recognize the Hitlers of the future, or other psychotics who mask their perversions and aggressions under a cloak of patriotism or of help for the oppressed. Psychoanalysis has scarcely more than scratched the surface of such problems as the elimination of war or the prevention of crime or delinquency. It remains fundamentally a therapy for disturbed individuals rather than for disturbed societies.

As a target for criticism, the behaviorists and other environmentalist schools of psychology have been somewhat less vulnerable than the psychoanalysts. Because of their experimental approach, they have appeared to be more in harmony with the scientific spirit of the age. Yet the implications of their studies are quite revolutionary. They present a picture of man as almost wholly a product of his environment. The elements of human nature transmissible through the genes are a tiny percentage of the total. It would seem obvious, therefore, that man's nature is highly plastic. He can be changed from a sinner into a saint and back again by favorable or unfavorable conditions of his environment. As a consequence, the most important business in the world should be education. Under proper instruction and guidance, teachers and parents could remake society into a peaceful, harmonious, and cooperative unit. Crime and delinquency could be practically eradicated, and so could the insecurities and inner aggressions which lead to conflict and the urge to attack. But something else would be important also. In a behaviorist world political and social policies would be judged in accordance with their actual results, as measured by scientific experiment. No one would be permitted to assume, as did a prominent citizen lately, that the remedy for juvenile delinquency is judges with a "capacity for old-fashioned indignation." Nor would foreign affairs be conducted in accordance with childish notions of bluff, of black and white, or of loss of face. Such gains would be counterbalanced in part by the tendency of behaviorism to encourage a relativist morality, that is, to emphasize the socially expedient at the possible expense of the idealistic or personally ennobling.

ADDITIONAL READINGS

Adorno, Theodore W., and Others. *The Authoritarian Personality*. New York, Harper, 1950.

Alexander, Franz. *Fundamentals of Psychoanalysis*. New York, Norton, 1948.

———. *Our Age of Unreason*. Philadelphia, Lippincott, 1942.

Arnold, Thurman W. *The Folklore of Capitalism*. New Haven, Yale University Press, 1937.

Dollard, John, and Others. *Frustration and Aggression*. New Haven, Yale University Press, 1939.

Doob, Leonard W. *Social Psychology*. New York, Holt, 1952.

Eulau, Heinz, ed. *Political Behavior*. Glencoe, Ill., Free Press, 1956.

Eysenck, Hans J. *The Psychology of Politics*. London, Routledge and Paul, 1954.

Flügel, J. C. *Man, Morals and Society*. London, Duckworth, 1945.

Freud, Sigmund. *A General Introduction to Psychoanalysis*. New York, Liveright, 1935.

Fromm, Erich. *The Fear of Freedom*. London, Routledge and Paul, 1950.

Hoffer, Eric. *The True Believer*. New York, Harper, 1951.

Hyman, Herbert H. *Political Socialization; a Study in the Psychology of Political Behavior*. Glencoe, Ill., Free Press, 1959.

Kardiner, Abram. *The Psychological Frontiers of Society*. New York, Columbia University Press, 1946.

———. *The Individual and His Society*. New York, Columbia University Press, 1939.

Klineberg, Otto. *Social Psychology*. New York, Holt, 1954.

Kluckhohn, Clyde. *Mirror for Man*. New York, McGraw-Hill, 1949.

Lasswell, Harold D. *The Analysis of Political Behavior*. New York, Oxford University Press, 1948.

———. *World Politics and Personal Insecurity*. New York, McGraw-Hill, 1935.

McDougall, William. *The Group Mind*. New York, Putnam, 1920.

———. *Psychoanalysis and Social Psychology*. London, Methuen, 1936.

Marcuse, Herbert. *Eros and Civilization*. Boston, Beacon Press, 1955.

Menninger, Karl A. *Love against Hate*. New York, Harcourt, 1942.

———. *Man against Himself*. New York, Harcourt, 1938.

Money-Kyrle, Roger E. *Psychoanalysis and Politics*. New York, Norton, 1951.

Munroe, Ruth L. *Schools of Psychoanalytic Thought*. New York, Dryden, 1955.

Reik, Theodor. *Myth and Guilt: the Crime and Punishment of Mankind*. New York, Braziller, 1957.

Scheidlinger, Saul. *Psychoanalysis and Group Behavior*. New York, Norton, 1952.

Schilder, Paul. *Psychoanalysis, Man, and Society*. New York, Norton, 1951.

Sullivan, Harry Stack. *Conceptions of Modern Psychiatry*. New York, Norton, 1953.

Tolman, Edward C. *Drives toward War.* New York, Appleton-Century, 1942.

Wallas, Graham. *The Great Society.* New York, Macmillan, 1920.

————. *Human Nature in Politics.* New York, Knopf, 1921.

Watson, John B. *Psychology from the Standpoint of a Behaviorist.* Philadelphia, Lippincott, 1929.

Young, Kimball. *Social Psychology.* New York, Appleton-Century-Crofts, 1956.

CHAPTER
XIII

The Social Environment and Political Theory

According to Aristotle's famous definition, man is a political animal. He also regarded him as a social animal. In fact, he sometimes used the words "society" and "state" as if he considered them synonymous. But he did not really mean them to be such, for he distinguished between bees, who are social animals in the sense that they are not self-sufficient when isolated, and man, who is endowed by nature with the powers of speech and reason, which enable him to "set forth the expedient and inexpedient, and likewise the just and the unjust." Moreover, Aristotle's state ranks prior to and higher than society, since it provides the means whereby man may perfect himself through law and justice; and separated from these, man is the worst of animals. Politics for Aristotle, therefore, includes ethics; and the state is the sole agency deserving the allegiance of human beings. Religion should be made an integral part of it, and so should all other social institutions; for the man who could live outside of the state "must be either a beast or a God." [1]

Few modern social scientists would agree that the state is as all-embracing and all-important as Aristotle supposed it to be. Most of them conceive of political organization as merely one aspect of organized society. The family, religion, and economic

[1] M. F. Egan, ed., *The Politics*. New York, Colonial Press, 1899, pp. 3–4.

institutions are also important. Undoubtedly, this conception is traceable to the intellectual revolution of 300 B.C. when the Stoics, with assistance from the Epicureans, overthrew the supremacy of politics, introduced a division of loyalties, and made man an individual instead of a mere citizen. The influence of these pagan philosophers permeated the Christian religion and thus was transmitted to modern times. The natural-rights individualism of John Locke, which provided the foundation for the political theory of the Enlightenment, had its roots in medieval Christianity. Since Enlightenment individualism was strengthened, in turn, by the economic doctrines of the Physiocrats and Adam Smith, it is not strange that sociologists of the nineteenth century should have been strongly biased against the state. Herbert Spencer and William Graham Sumner, for instance, conceived it essentially as an obstacle to human progress. In more recent decades, the pendulum has swung in the opposite direction. Contemporary sociologists magnify the importance of the state, consider it almost ubiquitous, and take for granted its value in civilizing *homo sapiens*. Such attitudes are even more characteristic of the anthropologists.

1. The Contributions of Anthropology

As one of the youngest of the social sciences, anthropology has had the task of exploding some hoary assumptions regarding man and the state. For centuries it was assumed that all men spent the infancy of the race in a condition of beneficent anarchy, and that the state as a politically organized society appeared only with the dawn of civilization. Anthropological research has demonstrated that the state is one of the oldest of institutions, and that it exists, even in highly complicated form, among many preliterate peoples. Some anthropologists have pointed out that the supposition of custom as the universal antecedent of law is no longer valid, that there are numerous forms of coercion just as effective as physical force, and that forms of government, even among primitive peoples, are infinitely varied and complex.[2]

[2] See, for example, M. J. Herskovits, *Cultural Anthropology*. New York,

During the first four decades of the twentieth century, one of the most highly regarded and influential of anthropologists was Franz Boas (1858–1942). A native of Germany, he studied at the universities of Heidelberg and Bonn and obtained a Ph.D. at the University of Kiel. A keen interest in geography led him to join an expedition to the Arctic in 1883 and brought him into contact with primitive customs. He thereupon decided to make anthropology his profession and spent a year in a small Eskimo settlement in Baffin Land. Upon his return he was appointed an assistant at the Royal Ethnological Museum in Berlin and Docent of Geography at the University. In 1886 he left Germany to conduct research among the Indians of British Columbia. After a period as lecturer at Clark University and anthropologist of the Chicago Exposition, he was appointed to the faculty of Columbia University. He served there as Professor of Anthropology from 1899 to his retirement in 1938. His special field of interest was the race question, and he devoted much energy to exposing what he called "Nordic nonsense." As a consequence, his books were among the first to be burned in Germany after 1933. He also dedicated a large portion of his life to furthering cultural understanding between the United States and the Far East and between the United States and Latin America. His retirement intensified his activity on behalf of intellectual and political freedom. He was a militant crusader against all restrictions on civil liberties.

Boas' studies in mathematics and physics convinced him of the importance of the scientific method in the social sciences. He held that most problems required new, first-hand investigation and could not be solved by depending on existing knowledge. This thesis he applied particularly to the problem of race. On the basis of anatomical data obtained from hospitals, prisons, and charitable institutions, he proved that there is no positive correlation between bodily structures and intelligence or ability. Though the brain measurements of Caucasians and of modern civilized people are larger than those of Negroes and of prehistoric men, respectively, these facts prove nothing.

Knopf, 1955; R. H. Lowie, *Primitive Society*. New York, Boni and Liveright, 1925.

Several individuals of eminence have had small brains, and, by contrast, some criminals have had comparatively large brains. Nor do other anatomical structures bear much significance. In some respects Caucasians appear to have evolved farther from ape-like ancestors than have the members of the colored races; but in other respects the indications are quite opposite—the greater hairiness of body of the Caucasians, for example, and the longer legs of the Negro. In the light of such evidence Boas arrived at the conclusion that "in the main the mental characteristics of man are the same all over the world." [3]

Boas, of course, adopted the position of an environmentalist. He credited very little to heredity beyond anatomical characteristics and bodily structures; and these he almost divested of significance as factors in the progress of species and races. Though he rejected the extreme behaviorist view that the mental activities of man are solely the result of external conditioning, he insisted nevertheless that the environment may profoundly affect mental achievements. Its influence may even be strong enough to overcome physical characteristics. He cited the example of a dialect, spoken with virtually the same enunciation, by all the inhabitants of a particular region, despite considerable differences in size and shape of mouth, thickness of tongue, and formation of larynx. He pointed also to the marked improvement in intelligence scores of Negroes resident for some years in Northern cities compared with their scores before their migration from the rural South. He took the position that nearly all of what we call culture is a matter of timing and of geographic, social, and economic influence. Primitive man was no less intelligent than modern man. He was just as capable of logical thinking and of reasoning in abstractions as is the American or Englishman of the twentieth century. He did not have the same skill in solving problems, simply because his cultural background was not nearly so rich in accumulated knowledge passed down through the centuries. Primitive man thinks differently, in many respects, from his modern descendants, because of his more limited experience and interests, but the fundamental traits of his mind are the same.

[3] *The Mind of Primitive Man.* New York, Macmillan, 1927, p. 104.

Boas held a similar view regarding the achievements of contemporary races. The failure of Negroes, even under superficially favorable conditions, to make as much progress as Caucasians, he attributed to such factors as the lack of resistance of the Negro to white men's diseases and to the stigma of inferiority which still clings to him despite an apparent equality of condition. But Boas denied that there is any warrant for regarding human beings as other than a single family, with the same inherent potential for cultural achievement regardless of racial differences.

In line with his belief in the essential homogeneity of the human species, Boas took a skeptical view of the eugenists' schemes of selective breeding to obtain a superior race or to eliminate the unfit. He doubted that it would ever be possible to decide on a satisfactory formula for what constitutes a superior race, and he argued that geniuses—Beethoven, for example—are sometimes born of defective parents. He also condemned all forms of nationalism designed to further the self-aggrandizement of allegedly superior groups at the expense of other peoples. He criticized especially such movements as Pan-Slavism, Pan-Germanism, and Pan-Americanism. Every individual, he maintained, "needs the widest possible field in which to live and act according to his modes of thought and inner feeling." [4] He came finally to the conclusion that nothing less than a federation of mankind, a world federal republic, would be compatible with the needs and interests of the human race. Such a republic could be patterned after the model of the United States, in such a way as to leave plenty of scope for the development of the special characters of the local units. He thought that the evidence of history supported the view that a progressive enlargement of human association is almost a universal rule. Beginning with the tribe, he traced this enlargement, through the city-state, the counties, duchies, and principalities of feudalism, to the nation-states and consolidated empires of modern times. He found the propelling force behind this movement to be increasing economic complexity. As communities gained control over their food supply, they experienced

[4] *Anthropology and Modern Life.* New York, Norton, 1932, p. 93.

a growth in confidence and in a sense of power. They accordingly absorbed weaker and less highly developed peoples and pre-empted their lands. Thus the total number of groups potentially in conflict with one another was gradually lessened. Though this process was occasionally interrupted, notably after World War I, Boas felt sure that the tendency toward unification was stronger than that of disintegration, and that the forward march would be resumed, with a "federation of nations as the next necessary step in the evolution of mankind." [5]

Second only to Boas as a discoverer of anthropological truths of special significance for political theory was Bronislaw Malinowski (1884–1942). Malinowski was born in Austrian Poland of a long line of nobility and landowners. He earned a Ph.D. at the University of Cracow, with the highest honors of the Austro-Hungarian Empire. In 1910 he became a member of the faculty of the University of London. When World War I broke out, he was interned as an enemy alien—on the Trobriand Islands, off the coast of New Guinea. He was thereby endowed with a magnificent opportunity to continue anthropological research among one of the most primitive peoples on the face of the earth. After the war he became a reader in social anthropology at the University of London, and in 1927 a professor. He also did research among the Pueblo Indians of Mexico and the United States and among the Bantu tribes of South and East Africa. When World War II began, he was on sabbatical leave in the United States. Advised to remain here for the duration, he obtained an appointment as visiting professor at Yale. He died, in 1942, of a heart attack at the age of fifty-eight.

Malinowski was a principal founder of the so-called functional school of anthropology. The members of this school study human culture as a pragmatically connected whole, and examine institutions in the light of their functioning as parts of that whole. He applied this guiding principle with special cogency to political institutions. For example, he insisted that law and custom are always organically connected. There never was a time when custom gave way to law. In like manner, he repudiated completely the old theory of a primitive condition

[5] *Ibid.*, pp. 97, 100.

of anarchy; government in some form, he implied, is as old as the human race. He rejected also many other time-honored assumptions: the notion of a primitive communism which preceded the origin of private property; the assumption that the individual member of a savage tribe is completely submerged in the group and enslaved to customs which he must always obey; and, perhaps most significant of all, the notion that primitive man is to his fellowmen a wolf, and that all that restrains him is physical force and fear of the magic of sorcerers and priests.[6]

Malinowski presented a picture of primitive political institutions astonishingly similar to those of civilized men. He described the primitive state as closely interwoven with the other elements of tribal culture. He found nothing to indicate any general origin through force or conquest; and nothing to suggest surrender, by the people themselves, to a strong ruler as a way of escape from anarchy. Instead, he discovered that the primitive state, at least among the Melanesians, rested upon foundations of reciprocity, exchange of services, and convenience as a means of getting things done. It served also as an agency for maintaining certain observances, such as the rule of exogamy, considered of vital concern to the tribe. Divided as they were between coastal and inland elements, the Melanesians needed a considerable measure of cooperation to facilitate exchange of vegetable products from the interior for products of the sea. It was the function of their state to provide this cooperation. Every individual had his task to fulfill in order to ensure that the system would operate smoothly. Even the chief must obey the rules and perform the obligations required of his office. Crime was comparatively rare and punishments usually mild. Malinowski testified that, during his long stay on the Trobriand Islands, he knew of only one case of murder. The chief might use violence to punish a flagrant insult or adultery with one of his wives; but the penalty he normally applied against an of-

---

[6] He went so far as to assert that "systematic or tyrannical abuse of authority is not to be found under primitive conditions," because of the ties of love, kinship, friendship, and respect usually characterizing primitive societies. *Freedom and Civilization.* New York, Roy, 1944, pp. 118–19, 121, 266–67.

fender was sorcery. The whole concept of punishment was exceedingly vague, and defiance of the laws and outright violations were by no means unknown. When they occurred, they rarely caused much concern. Even incest could be absolved by the proper forms of magic. Many offenses were dealt with by the victim himself or by members of his family. The common procedure was either an invocation of black magic or an attempt to humiliate the offender publicly, which might drive him to suicide.

In describing the political life of primitive man, Malinowski was making no attempt to portray a golden age of bliss and innocence. He was merely trying to get away from the unscientific assumptions of Sir Henry Sumner Maine, W. H. R. Rivers, and others, which were based upon inadequate testimony obtained from missionaries and travelers or by questioning of natives through an interpreter. Malinowski insisted upon the necessity of merging one's life with that of a people for a considerable period in order to study their culture as a whole. Such study would reveal, he asserted, that "the commandments of law and custom are always organically connected and not isolated . . . and that they only exist in the chain of social transactions in which they are but a link." [7] His findings have been corroborated by the researches of other anthropologists, by those of R. H. Lowie among the Eskimos and of R. S. Rattray among the Ashanti on the west coast of Africa. The implications for political theory deserve thoughtful consideration. They indicate that Rousseau was wrong in idealizing the "noble savage," but that he was closer to the truth than Hobbes with his justification of despotic government as an antidote for universal strife, terror, and misery. They demonstrate the falsity of the early Christian conception of the state as a punishment for sin, as well as the Marxist conception of an executive committee of the dominant economic class to hold the masses in subjection. While they fall far short of proving the inherent goodness of human nature, they seem clearly to suggest that men, under normal conditions, at least, realize the utility of cooperation for the

[7] *Crime and Custom in Savage Society.* London, Routledge and Paul, 1926, p. 125.

common welfare. They do not account for the origins of autocracy and tyranny, but they suggest that authoritarian rule results from war and the threat of attack. Pressure of population upon the margin of subsistence impels nations to become invaders and to build up strong governments to facilitate their purposes. Fear of invasion on the part of their neighbors has similar results.

The contemporary anthropologist who raised the most provocative issues connected with political theory was probably Ruth Benedict (1887–1948). The victim of an unhappy childhood, she was the daughter of a New York physician who died when she was two years old. Devoted to his memory and deeply resentful of an overbearing mother, she suffered from feelings of inadequacy and injustice through most of her life. She was subject to violent tantrums till the age of eleven and thereafter to moodiness and fits of despondency. She had a secret "grave" in which she would lie as dead for hours. Though she was graduated from Vassar and achieved some success as a poet and a teacher of English, her marriage was a failure. Chiefly to occupy her mind, she began the study of anthropology at Columbia, in 1919, under Franz Boas. After receiving her Ph.D., she was appointed to a position in the Department and rose to the rank of professor in 1948. Next to Boas himself, she was probably the most distinguished anthropologist at Columbia. She departed widely from her master's influence, however, especially with regard to the use of psychological data. In pursuance of suggestions from Edward Sapir of the University of Chicago, she concluded that the probings of psychoanalysis into the darker recesses of individuals' minds could be used to illuminate many of the more baffling problems of tribal usage and custom. Though she excelled in interpretation, she did not neglect the field research which modern anthropologists consider indispensable. She spent years in intimate contact with Pueblo, Apache, Pima, and Blackfoot tribes. Death overtook her in her sixty-first year as a consequence of a coronary thrombosis.

Ruth Benedict's reputation as an anthropologist rests chiefly upon two books. In *Race: Science and Politics*, published in

1940, she demonstrated even more emphatically than Boas had done the essential similarity of all members of the human species. All have the same structures and organs, though with enormous differences in functioning. These differences, however, are chiefly the result of variations in the environment producing variations in experience and in habits. Some primitive men, for instance, have trained their eyes to observe minutiae in their surroundings with a skill that to the white man seems miraculous. But to primitive people the white man's ability to distinguish letters on a printed page seems just as miraculous. Dr. Benedict was concerned also with puncturing the myth that some races are by nature superior to others in intelligence and talent. She showed that the median intelligence scores of Negroes in such states as New York, Illinois, and Ohio were considerably superior to those of whites in some of the states of the South. In addition, she pointed out that the scores of Negro boys tested in Nashville fell far below those of white boys; that in Chicago they fell somewhat below; and that in New York they were virtually equal. She could not avoid the conclusion that tests designed to measure inborn intelligence were actually measuring educational opportunity. In fact, she became quite skeptical that there is such a thing as inborn intelligence which can be separated from the effects of environmental influences. If it does exist, she was sure it was not a monopoly of any one race.

If there was one theme that occupied a central place in Ruth Benedict's anthropology, it was the idea that human nature is thoroughly plastic. She expounded this idea in the most famous of her writings, *Patterns of Culture*, published in 1934. Emphasizing the part that tradition plays in molding the outlook and attitudes of a people, she drew upon Nietzsche's celebrated dichotomy of Dionysian and Apollonian philosophies of life. The Dionysian believes that in order to solve the riddle of existence he must escape the confines of his five senses and break through to another order of experience. He becomes a mystic, seeking divine illumination through contemplation or self-torture. He believes that the path to wisdom lies in excess, and he cultivates the values of frenzy and ecstasy. He flees from life, covets translation to another world, and longs for union with the divine. By contrast, the Apollonian seeks the fulfillment of life through moderation. His motto is "nothing in excess," and he avoids efforts to transcend sensory experience. He is "of the earth earthy" and distrusts the methods of the mystic.

On the basis of her researches, Dr. Benedict classified various peoples of the world as Dionysian or Apollonian. Perhaps she believed that all peoples could be thus classified. Apparently she considered the Dionysian cultures as by far the more prevalent. The only examples she described of Apollonian peoples were the Pueblo Indians of southwestern United States. As she portrayed them, they stand out as a remarkably sensible and practical people. They know nothing of sin and do not understand why anyone should practice self-torture. Their marriage customs are simple, divorce is easy, and crime is rare. They do punish witchcraft, but theft seldom occurs and is dealt with as a private matter. The only cases of homicide that are remembered were settled quickly by payments between the two families. Though much of the property is individually owned, it is often cared for cooperatively. For example, sheep are privately owned but herded cooperatively by groups of male kindred. The men work jointly in building houses, which then become the property of the women. The same is true of the corn, which is grown and harvested for the common storehouse.

Contrasting sharply with this idyllic pattern is the culture of the Dionysian peoples, whom Benedict found to include the Plains Indians, most of the other Indian tribes of the United States and Mexico, and such natives as the Dobuans of northwestern Melanesia. The dominating traits of these peoples are fear, suspicion, treachery, and violence. They have a morbid sense of sin and of the need for atonement through suffering. They conceive of their deities as malevolent beings who constantly require appeasement. To discover the will of these deities is the function of *shamans*, who torture themselves or consume drugs to induce trances or ecstatic frenzy as means of communicating with the supernatural. Dionysian peoples are stern individualists; they assume that men's motives are invariably evil; and lawlessness is common among them.

It seems possible that Ruth Benedict exaggerated somewhat the contrast between patterns of culture in order to heighten the effect of some of the criticisms she wished to make of our own civilization. Indeed, a leading anthropologist has described her work as better poetry than science.[8] She was obviously perturbed by what she regarded as paranoid features of modern society. By these she meant an inordinate suspicion of human motives, a tendency to regard unintentional injury as a personal affront, megalomania and persecutory delusions, an eagerness for vengeance and a chip-on-the-shoulder belligerence. She saw these traits as especially characteristic of modern nations in their dealings with one another. The chauvinism and saber-rattling of the Great Powers of the twentieth century she thought of as remarkably similar to the sense of humiliation and the head-hunting to wipe out the shame indulged in by Kwiakutl Indians when some neighboring tribe or clan trespassed upon their "rights." She also indicted the egomania, the guilt complexes, the passion to enforce conformity, the waste and the greed, and the competitive ruthlessness which she regarded as the principal elements in the psychoneurotic heritage from Puritanism.

2. Sociology and Political Theory

Morris Ginsberg, one of the leading sociologists of the contemporary world, describes his discipline as "the study of society, that is, of the web or tissue of human interactions and inter-relations."[9] This definition is broad enough to include nearly every achievement, belief, idea, custom, institution, and tradition that has made up the pattern of culture since the beginning of human history. In fact, Ginsberg declares his science to be concerned "with all that happens to human beings in virtue of their relations to each other."[10] The connection of sociology, thus conceived, with political theory seems unescapa-

[8] Cited by Donald Cook, "Ruth Benedict: Culture as Personality," *The New Republic*, CXL (March 2, 1950), 17.

[9] *Reason and Unreason in Society*. Cambridge, Mass., Harvard University Press, 1948, p. 1.

[10] *Id.*

ble. It is significant that most of the great founders of sociology in the nineteenth century—Auguste Comte, Herbert
Spencer, Lester F. Ward, William Graham Sumner—were as
deeply interested in the nature and purposes of the state as
they were in the problems of society in general.

The most incisive contributor to sociological theory in the
early twentieth century was probably the German Max Weber.
Born in 1864, he was the son of a leader of the National Liberal
party and member of the Reichstag. He was educated in the
law and received an appointment as *Privatdocent* at the University of Berlin. Later he became Professor of Law at the
University of Freiburg and then at the University of Heidelberg. After a brief tenure at Heidelberg, his health broke down
and for four years he was a semi-invalid. By 1916 he was able
to take some part in public affairs, and he became one of the
first to oppose vigorously the rule of Wilhelm II. In 1918 he
was given a temporary professorship at the University of
Vienna, and a year later a regular appointment at the University of Munich. During the same years he served on the
commission which drafted the Weimar Constitution, and he is
credited with having originated the provision for popular election of the President. He never identified himself, however,
with any of the revolutionary parties. He rejected Marxism because of his conviction of the importance of ideas in the historical process. His legal studies under the influence of the historical school led him into researches on the nature of institutions
and the social and economic background of the law. He died
of pneumonia, in 1920, at the height of his intellectual career.

Though Max Weber developed no systematic theory, his
contributions to an understanding of modern political problems were shrewd and perceptive. The most provocative were
contained in a volume entitled *The Protestant Ethic and the
Spirit of Capitalism.* In this study Weber presented a thesis
which was elaborated later by R. H. Tawney in *Religion and
the Rise of Capitalism* and by Erich Fromm in *Escape from
Freedom.* The religious revolution of the sixteenth century,
Weber contended, accomplished a spectacular change in individual attitudes and in the fabric of society, especially in Ger-

manic countries. Previous to this time the relaxed system of the Catholic Church had provided solace and security for most of the inhabitants of Christian Europe. Though it prescribed asceticism for monks and nuns, it imposed no such rigors upon ordinary mortals. Under its system of "good works" as means of penance, and the intercession of saints and the Virgin, it enabled the multitude of Christians to pass through this vale of tears with comparative ease and serenity and to indulge rather confident hopes of salvation in a life to come. But the advent of Protestantism made a shambles of this system. Monasticism was abolished, and the rules of asceticism were made universal. The Virgin and the saints were dethroned, and man was brought face to face with a stern Hebraic God. In the presence of this implacable deity, the individual was a worm, degraded and worthless, hating himself and his fellows, unless he could receive some divine illumination that would assure him that he was among the elect. His only reason for existence, it seemed, was to glorify God, and this he could do by worship, prayer, tithing, and Sabbath observance; and also by hard work, frugality, and abstinence from all pleasures in order that he might succeed in the "calling" in which God had placed him. Life was real, life was earnest, and though the grave was not its goal, a fate much worse than death was all that awaited the great mass of mankind. Gone was "the very human Catholic cycle of sin, repentance, atonement, release, followed by renewed sin." [11]

Weber did not place all of the blame for the trends of modern life on the shoulders of the Protestant reformers. He admitted that elements of pessimistic individualism and ruthless competition can be traced far back into history; and he recognized that Luther's economic attitudes were definitely medieval. It was Calvinism rather than Lutheranism, according to Weber, which provided the impetus for the egoism and the capitalist aggressiveness of the modern age. Calvinists lauded activity as a means of glorifying God. He who was diligent in business served the Lord. Among the worst of all vices were those which resulted in a waste of time—idle talk, tippling, gaming, inactive

[11] Talcott Parsons, trans., *The Protestant Ethic and the Spirit of Capitalism.* London, Allen and Unwin, 1930, p. 117.

contemplation. Pursuit of the pleasures of sense was also condemned, at least partly because it interfered with industry and thrift. The good Christian was supposed to work assiduously in some particular vocation, not because of satisfaction from a sense of accomplishment, but because it was a task set by God. The greater his success in business as measured by the wealth he piled up, the more certainty he would have that he had fulfilled his divine assignment. If ruthless methods were required for success, he need not worry, for human beings were really degenerate beasts with no rights that commanded respect. Weber made clear his conviction that the growth of a brutally competitive capitalism contributed enormously to the discontents and estrangements of modern man. It made man richer, but it increased his insecurity. Henceforth, it was either "eat well or sleep well." Medieval Catholicism had provided the latter alternative; Calvinists and their Pietist, Methodist, and Baptist allies chose the former.

In the other of his major works, *The Theory of Social and Economic Organization,* Weber discussed the subject of authority. He wrote an unconventional defense of bureaucracy, praising it for its efficiency and for its "leveling" effects. What he obviously had in mind was government by experts, since he defined bureaucracy as the "exercise of control on the basis of knowledge." He described three types of what he called "pure authority"—rational, traditional, and charismatic. By the first he meant authority resting upon established beliefs in the sanctity of immemorial traditions. By charismatic authority he meant that which stems from some allegedly divine source, or rests upon prodigious heroism, supernatural powers, or exemplary character. The origin of the word he traced to the vocabulary of early Christianity—*charisma*, "gift of grace." Charismatic authority, according to Weber, involves no skill or knowledge and recognizes no rules, customs, or traditions. It has no basis in economics. The true charismatic leader must not work for a living. He must take no more thought for the morrow than do the fowls of the air. His followers will support him with voluntary gifts, or bread will be provided from Heaven. The leader with the benefit of *charisma* is never a reactionary nor even a conservative. Instead, he is a prophet, a revolutionary. He repudiates the past and calls for a new dispensation. His demands may take the form of a new religion, an ascetic moral ideal, a crusade against the infidel, or a program of national rejuvenation. Among the leaders whom Weber considered to be endowed with *charisma* were Jesus, Mohammed, the Popes, and the two Napoleons.[12] Had he lived long enough, he would undoubtedly have added such a venerated leader as Gandhi to the list.

Significant for a theory of the origin of the state was Max Weber's compatriot, Franz Oppenheimer (1864–1943). In contrast with most other sociologists, Oppenheimer was trained as a physician. He held a degree of Doctor of Medicine from the University of Freiburg. He soon became convinced, in the practice of his profession, of the importance of social and economic conditions for the health and well-being of his working-class patients. Accordingly, he abandoned medicine and took a doctorate in philosophy at the University of Berlin, specializing in economics and sociology. In 1908 he published his most noted work, *The State*, which has been translated into all the important languages of the world. In the same year he became an instructor at the University of Berlin, and in 1917 a professor. After the establishment of the Weimar Republic, a chair was created for him at the University of Frankfurt. During the inter-war period, as a leader of the *Bodenreform* movement, he carried on a crusade for the breaking up of Junker estates. He urged the establishment of cooperative agricultural communities as a remedy for the unemployment and poverty of the working class. In 1940 when the Nazis seized his property and abolished his pension, he fled to the United States and settled in Los Angeles, where he died three years later.

Oppenheimer's theory of the origin of the state was similar to that of many other writers who consider themselves political realists. He contended that the state had its genesis in force, and that its original founders were nomads. They swept down from the hills that bordered the fertile valleys and imposed their will

¹² A. M. Hamilton and Talcott Parsons, trans., *The Theory of Social and Economic Organization*. New York, Oxford University Press, 1947, pp. 328–330, 339.

upon the peaceful farmers. Exploiting the labor of their victims and confiscating their property, they lived in fear of acts of vengeance or of outright rebellion. To protect themselves, they provided drastic penalties for acts of violence or revolt, eventually codifying these into a "law of the land." They made one of their own number king and elevated his chief henchmen into a nobility. For the achievement of these ends they had notable advantages. They were mounted on horseback and were therefore better equipped for offensive warfare. Their diet, moreover, consisting as it did of meat and milk, was highly nourishing. Nomads, consequently, had boundless energy. They infused new life into stagnant peoples wherever they went. Brutal and domineering though they might be, they nevertheless built the organization, imposed the discipline, and created the inequalities of rank and class which, according to Oppenheimer, seemed to be necessary as foundations of the state. Finally, nomadic tribes increased rapidly in population. The nomadic form of marriage was commonly polygamous, and a plentiful supply of the milk of animals shortened "the period of nursing for mothers, and consequently [permitted] a greater number of children to be born and to grow into maturity." [13] The result was that nomads periodically burst the confines of their relatively barren homelands and invaded and conquered the territories of more settled peoples.

Oppenheimer was able to marshal a considerable body of historical evidence to support his theory. Quite a few of the great empires of the past appear to have been founded by conquering nomads. Three reservoirs of humanity, time after time, seem to have let loose inundations of peoples that poured into the more fertile valleys of the Old World. From the grasslands north of the Arabian Desert came the Babylonians, the Assyrians, and the Chaldeans successively to conquer the Tigris-Euphrates Valley. From the steppes of Central Asia issued the Medes, the Persians, the Indians, and a few centuries later, the Mongols. The Arabian Desert itself was the starting point of the Hebrew migrations into the Land of Canaan and of the

[13] J. M. Gitterman, trans. *The State, Its History and Development Viewed Sociologically*. New York, Vanguard, 1928, pp. 42–43.

conquests of the Moslems. All of these focal areas were unsuited to agriculture; to this day they are inhabited by nomads. It follows that the peoples mentioned must originally have lived under a pastoral economy and to have begun their conquests under pressure of nomad conditions.

But Oppenheimer overlooked other important areas, such as the Nile Valley, where nomad invasion does not seem to have occurred until the time of the Hyksos, about 1750 B.C. Yet a powerful state had been established in Egypt as early as 3200 B.C. He never recognized, either, the previously cited discoveries of anthropologists which seem to show that the state originates in much the same way as does primitive religious organization— that is, it grows out of the dependence of man upon agencies outside himself for an assured food supply. To cause the rain to fall, for example, he offers sacrifices or performs ceremonies as part of a bargain or contract with the gods. The same sort of reciprocal or contractual arrangement develops among members of the tribe themselves to assure the success of a fishing or hunting expedition or the planting and harvesting of crops. Efficient operation requires leadership and the issuance of rules. Force and punishment may also be introduced, but cooperation, resulting from interdependence, seems to come first.

Two American sociologists who have made impressive additions to political theory are David Riesman and C. Wright Mills. Riesman was born in Philadelphia, in 1909, the son of a German physician. He obtained his education at Harvard, with an A.B. degree in 1931 and an LL.B. in 1934. He met the requirements for admission to the bar in Massachusetts, New York, and the District of Columbia. In 1935–1936 he served as a clerk to Associate Justice Brandeis, of the United States Supreme Court. From 1937 to 1941 he was Professor of Law at the University of Buffalo, and then for a year was Deputy Assistant District Attorney of New York County. Meanwhile, he began taking courses at the Washington School of Psychiatry. He worked with Erich Fromm and read widely in psychoanalytic and sociological materials. Three more years elapsed, which he spent as Assistant Treasurer of the Sperry Gyroscope Company, before he found his real vocation, that of a teacher. In 1946 he became Visiting

Associate Professor and in 1949, Professor, of the Social Sciences at the University of Chicago. In 1958 he was called to the Henry Ford II Chair of the Social Sciences at Harvard.

In the book which first won him fame, *The Lonely Crowd*, Riesman developed a theory of society which had almost the breadth of a philosophy of history. He described two revolutions which he claimed have overtaken Western man since the end of the Middle Ages. The first included the Renaissance, the Reformation, the Commercial and Industrial Revolutions, and the political upheavals of the seventeenth, eighteenth, and nineteenth centuries. The effect of this revolution was to tear man away from the collective, tradition-bound existence of medieval society and to make him an individual. The great object of human beings became one of increasing production, of conquering their physical environment. Recently, however, in the most advanced countries, particularly in the United States, this revolution has been giving way to another, a revolution associated with consumption. It is the ability to consume which now sets the standard instead of the ability to produce. The figures we idolize are no longer the tycoons of industry but the heroes and heroines of sport, entertainment, and amusement. Even our statesmen are likely to be distinguished more for glamour and charm than for forthrightness and intelligence.

Riesman evolved his theory of social development in accordance with a somewhat dubious population hypothesis suggested by the researches of the noted demographer, Frank W. Notestein. According to this hypothesis, population trends in the Western world have passed through three stages. The first was a stage of "high growth potential" when birth rates and death rates were both at their peak. As a consequence, the turnover of generations was extremely rapid, and the bulk of the population was young. The social character-type predominating during this stage was *tradition-directed*. Riesman offered no explanation of this, but probably he meant that the submerging of the individual in society virtually guaranteed a subservience to tradition. The second stage began with the seventeenth century and continued to the end of the nineteenth. This stage, known as the stage of "transitional growth," was marked by falling death rates, precipitated by advances in medicine and improvements in hospitalization and public sanitation. Since birth rates continued high, a "population explosion" resulted. Individualism ran riot, and the character-type that now developed was *inner-directed*. About the beginning of the twentieth century, the most advanced countries of the West showed signs of entering a third stage, the stage of "incipient population decline." As a result of increasing industrialization and urbanization, birth rates began to fall, and Riesman apparently believed that they would eventually sink so low that they would not even balance the death rates. Perhaps there was evidence of such a development at the time he wrote the book, but it is not easy to find. In the United States from 1940–1954, for example, birth rates per thousand rose from 17.9 to 24.6, while death rates per thousand declined only from 10.8 to 9.2. Assuming incipient population decline, Riesman contended that the resulting character-type would be *other-directed*, that is, the typical member of society would become more and more conformist, attuning his thoughts and desires to the expectations and preferences of the people around him. The increasing proportion of middle-aged and aged in the population would be one factor, and perhaps the major one, in producing such attitudes.

Scarcely anything could be more obvious than the fact that Riesman does not welcome the trend toward a society of other-direction. Indeed, he wrote his second most famous book, *Individualism Reconsidered*, largely to combat what he calls "groupism." He ridiculed the idea that unless we achieve "a consensus on values," our democratic society will collapse. He feared the aggrandizement of power much more than he did the aggrandizement of wealth, and he thought "unbridled individualism" a lesser menace than "the all-too-evident danger of the 'garrison state.'"[14] His own choice of a remedy was "ideological pluralism," under which every faction, sect, and cult would be free to follow its own idiosyncrasies; and society would rely upon natural selection to weed out the freakish and socially harmful. Some procedural requirements, such as due process,

[14] *Selected Essays from Individualism Reconsidered.* Garden City, Doubleday, 1955, p. 26.

might have to be enforced, but these would have nothing to do with a general agreement on values.

At the same time that Riesman deplores the tendency toward other-directedness, he thinks this may be canceled in part by another trend in modern society. He believes that the dangers of oligarchy and personal despotism are fast disappearing in the developed nations. Mosca, Michels, Pareto, and Burnham, he argues, were all wrong, with their iron laws of oligarchy and their omnipotent élites and "managers." The old-time leaders, with their "public-be-damned" attitude, have passed from the scene. Though an occasional Ernest T. Weir or Sewell Avery rules like a feudal baron over a corporate domain, they are really relics of the past. Military and naval officers and politicians, too, have become timid and cautious and more concerned with public relations than with the exercise of authority or power. The real rulers in complex societies like that of America are currently "veto groups," whose members rarely initiate proposals but have the capacity to negate the proposals of others. "The only leaders of national scope left in the United States today are those who can placate the veto groups. The only followers left in the United States today are those unorganized and sometimes disorganized unfortunates who have not yet invented their group." [15] If this description were accurate, one would have difficulty imagining how business and government could ever get out of a standstill. Yet the years since 1945 have probably witnessed the initiation by corporations of more new policies than any period of comparable length in American history. The era of the New Deal, presided over by a man whom Riesman thinks of as an exponent of "charm" rather than power, was certainly as rich in positive accomplishments as the administrations of such dominant figures as Woodrow Wilson and Theodore Roosevelt.

A vastly different theory of leadership and power in modern society is presented by the Columbia sociologist, C. Wright Mills (1916–   ). Born and raised in Texas, he obtained his B.A. and M.A. at the University of Texas and a Ph.D. at the

[15] *The Lonely Crowd, a Study of the Changing American Character,* with Nathan Glazer and Reuel Denney. Garden City, Doubleday, 1956, p. 247.

University of Wisconsin, with sociology and anthropology as special fields. In 1941 he was made Associate Professor of Sociology at the University of Maryland. Five years later he accepted an assistant professorship at Columbia. He became an Associate Professor in 1950 and Professor in 1956. He has also served as a lecturer at the William Alanson White Institute of Psychiatry, Fulbright Professor at the University of Copenhagen, and Visiting Professor at Brandeis University and the University of Chicago. The book which first brought him attention was *White Collar*, an analysis of the mores, manners, and morals of the American middle class. He is the author also of *The New Man of Power*, *Character and Social Structures*, and *The Power Elite*.

For C. Wright Mills there is no question of power slipping from the hands of decadent oligarchs into the possession of veto groups. On the contrary, he sees the moguls of modern society as a determined and ruthless élite. Their power exceeds that of the most exalted potentates of the past. "What," he asks, "was Caesar's power at its peak compared with the power of the changing inner circle of Soviet Russia or of America's temporary administrations? The men of either circle can cause great cities to be wiped out in a single night, and in a few nights turn continents into thermonuclear wastelands." [16] The power élite of contemporary America he describes as an intricate set of overlapping cliques. At the top of the economy there are the chief corporation executives; at the top of the political system, the chief policy-determining officials; at the top of the defense establishment, a clique of "soldier-statesmen" hovering among and around the Joint Chiefs of Staff. The character of the oligarchy in other countries is much the same, especially where capitalism is firmly entrenched. Nearly everywhere there is an increasing interlocking of power structures. Government intervention in the economic system is paralleled by corporate intervention in the functions of government.

Mills does not consider the several segments of the ruling élite as equal in power. At times he indicates that it is the corporate rich who wield the scepter. Money, he asserts, is the lord of all and the king of all. It can gain for its possessors the

[16] *The Power Elite.* New York, Oxford University Press, 1957, p. 22.

entrée into any circle of American society. As a consequence, the
social walls are always crumbling. They are being breached and
rebuilt from below. In addition, the corporate chieftains now
dominate the political directorate and push politicians into the
background. But at other times Mills seems desirous of inform-
ing us that it is the military who are at the top of the hierarchy.
He contends that violence is the ultimate basis of power and
the final resort of those who would challenge it. All over the
world the warlords are climbing into the saddle. Before 1941
they had limited influence in the United States. But now with
the crucial policy decisions hinging upon questions of strategy,
the soldier-statesmen and soldier-diplomats have taken their
place in the top echelon of the power structure. They are consulted on issues that go far beyond the military domain. Their
agencies provide about 85 per cent of all money to subsidize research and more than half of the total expenditures of the national government. So strategic is the position they occupy in
the public councils that corporations have adopted the slogan,
"Get yourself a general." Not a few large companies have proceeded to implement the idea, as attested by the number of
MacArthurs, Clays, Doolittles, and Bradleys in positions of
corporate power. But all such developments are inevitable,
according to Mills, in an America for which "war, either hot or
cold, is felt to be the normal and permanent condition." [17]

The one segment of the ruling class in the United States
which seems clearly in Mills' opinion to be losing power is the
political segment. He sees the legislative branch shrinking
virtually into insignificance. Measures which formerly would
have been enacted into laws are not even submitted now to Congress, but issued in the form of decrees from some bureau or
divisional office. But while Mills recognizes a gravitation of
power to the executive branch, he maintains that it, too, is
changing in character. The oldtime politician and even the professional bureaucrat are being shunted into the background.
Executive leadership is passing to "outsiders," mostly to corporation lawyers, investment bankers, iron and steel and automobile
magnates, and soap manufacturers. Curiously, he does not say

[17] *Ibid.*, p. 184.

whether the judiciary is also undergoing a transformation or a loss of power. He might well have considered the historical evidence that, in the United States, the three branches of government are rarely evenly matched. In periods when the legislative and executive are weak, the judiciary quite commonly asserts its pre-eminence. Perhaps Mills mistakes a rotation of power for a decline of power. He has much evidence on his side, however, for the diminution of certain kinds of authority. Diplomats, he points out, have lost ground steadily since the 1940's. When negotiation aimed at peaceful settlement is likely to be regarded as appeasement, the role of diplomacy is meaningless. It has not been diplomats but military men who have arranged the most significant of recent agreements between nations. The defense agreements between the United States and Spain; the establishment of NATO; the disposition of the islands captured from Japan; and even the organization of the Japanese government and the Japanese economy are cardinal examples. The end of the Korean War in 1953 was negotiated by a general "in open collar and without a necktie." [18]

3. The Counter-Utopians

No one would argue that every utopian, either present or past, has been a learned sociologist or anthropologist. Yet everyone familiar with the utopians' theories would agree that, with few exceptions, they have ascribed an overwhelming role to the environment in shaping man's destiny and determining his possibilities. From Sir Thomas More in the sixteenth century to the Owenites and Fourierists of the nineteenth, it has been a basic premise of utopian thought that man is created by his environment, and that if he desires a better world, he has only to correct the false beliefs and inequitable institutions that stand in his way. Doctrines of the goodness of human nature and the possibility of unlimited social progress were given such an impetus by the eighteenth-century Enlightenment that they carried through to 1850, and even in some forms to the end of the century. But a serpent in various guises made its way into the

[18] *Ibid.*, p. 210.

Garden of Eden. Malthusianism was one aspect it took. Malthus saw in the voracity of the sexual appetite a factor that would defeat every plan and scheme for abolishing poverty or reducing the misery that seemed to be the divinely appointed lot of human beings. Darwinism, also, with its suggestion of animal origin for a multitude of human traits, added momentum to the increasing pessimism. Nor is it possible to ignore the influence of Freud, with his emphasis on selfish instincts and his contention that the child at birth inherits racial memories of murder and incest that warp his personality throughout his life. As we have seen, the astringent doctrines of Freud were partly compensated by his hope that the growth of enlightenment would eventually modify man's egoistic heritage; but the public largely overlooked this brighter view.

But the major influence fostering the development of acidulous conceptions of human nature may well have been the revival of doctrines of original sin and general depravity by leading philosophers and theologians after 1800. Eminent among them were Joseph de Maistre, Sören Kierkegaard, Friedrich Nietzsche, and Nicholas Berdyaev. They have had worthy successors in the twentieth century in Christopher Dawson, Karl Barth, Emil Brunner, and Reinhold Niebuhr. With one accord they look upon human beings as sin-infested creatures. Nothing but the grace of God can save them from committing the most loathsome crimes. Maistre, for example, taught that "men cannot help killing each other." They kill not merely for justifiable reasons but even for amusement. Christopher Dawson maintains that "man has no choice except between two roads: the road to Calvary and the road to the slaughter-house." [19] Such doctrines provided an exceedingly inhospitable climate for faith in human progress. Utopianism languished and died with the growth of pessimism and disillusionment. By our own time attitudes of despair were so prevalent that almost every form of idealism became suspect. In particular, socialist utopias began to be singled out as subjects of satire. But dreams of a new world of science and efficiency aroused equal distrust. The French political novelist André Malraux declared that to him "science

[19] Quoted by Judith N. Shklar, *After Utopia*, pp. 19–20, 200.

meant Bikini"—referring, of course, to the atom-bomb test of 1946. Other writers—notably Aldous Huxley, George Orwell, and Arthur Koestler—have sought to vent their disillusionment with the dreams of the past in mordant satire, often in the form of mock utopias. They do not necessarily reject all idealism, but they repudiate those forms which have substituted brutality and cold efficiency for the freedom and humanity originally promised. For this reason it seems better to label them counter-utopians than anti-utopians.

Aldous Huxley, a grandson of the great biologist and agnostic, was born in Surrey, England, in 1894. He prepared for the university at Eton, intending to study medicine, but he contracted keratitis and became, in a few months, almost completely blind. After two years he had recovered enough vision in one eye to read with a magnifying glass. He entered Oxford, specialized in English literature and philology, and received his degree in 1915. He eventually obtained a position on the editorial staff of *The Athenaeum* and, after accumulating a small financial reserve, turned to the writing of novels. By the 1920's he had become a leading prophet of the age of cynicism and sophistication. His *Point Counter Point* and *Antic Hay* were almost romantic idealizations of skepticism regarding absolutes. Later, he somewhat abruptly turned to mysticism, seeking increasingly for depth of understanding in Vedanta and other Oriental religions. He came to the conclusion that the anti-materialist and mystical cults of the East provided the best remedies for freeing the individual from the fundamental disability of egotism. In his later novels, such as *After Many a Summer Dies the Swan* and *Time Must Have a Stop,* he has been intensely occupied with problems of personal, psychological freedom. He has also adopted as a major assumption the mystical doctrine that man's true and final end is "knowledge of the immanent and transcendent Ground of all being."

Huxley's satire, *Brave New World,* published in 1932, marked the transition from his hard and glittering novels of the jazz age to the sentimental and anti-intellectual writings of his later career. The brave new world he described was a communistic type of world society which was to come into existence around

2600 A.D. Everything was owned and controlled by the state, and the lives of the inhabitants were regimented with marvelous efficiency. The principal techniques used for the latter purpose were eugenics, the conditioned reflex, *hypnopaedia* (or mind training during sleep), *soma* (a tranquilizing drug which had all the pleasant consequences of alcohol without the "hangover"), violent-passion surrogates, pregnancy substitutes, and contraceptive training. Christianity was abolished; Our Lord became "Our Ford"; A.D. became A.F.; and the cross was changed to a T. The family also was eliminated; human beings were no longer viviparous; ova were fertilized in test tubes and the embryos developed in incubators. The abolition of motherhood and fatherhood made possible prenatal conditioning. Embryos were treated with chemical solutions so as to produce progeny of varying characteristics, from Alphas, the most superior, down to Epsilons, who were semi-morons. The purpose was to ensure a suitable proportion of different intellectual types for the separate functions of the economy.

The brave new world had a number of appealing features, superficially at least. War was a relic of the past. There was no crime or violence of any kind and no brutality. Disease had been almost eliminated, and the aging process was so completely annihilated that everyone retained his youth and vigor until he was about sixty, when he suddenly died. The whole emphasis was on comfort, well-being, and happiness. Yet Huxley portrayed this society in order to condemn it. Making people contented, he implied, did not make them creative or sane. They needed to suffer pain, to feel passion, to experience dangers. They needed to plumb love's emotional depths, not simply to enjoy its physical pleasures. Perhaps above all, they needed to worship, to sin and repent, to listen to the voice of conscience, and to seek knowledge and understanding above and beyond the realm of sensation.

Since *Brave New World* was published in an age of relative peace and serenity, anterior to the monstrosities of Nazism, the brutal repressions of Stalinism, and the insanity of fission and fusion weapons, one might think that its author would look back upon it as a description of a quite tolerable condition. But, in

1958, when he completed *Brave New World Revisited,* he still regarded the society described in the original work as a chamber of horrors. The chief difference was that he was now much less optimistic as to the period of grace allowed to man before the horrors would overtake him. Then the anticipated date of disaster was the seventh century after Ford. By 1958 the horrible event was "just around the corner." Its imminence, Huxley asserted, had been hastened by three factors: overpopulation, overorganization, and overdevelopment of mass-hypnosis and other forms of psychological manipulation. By the year 2000, he predicted, the population of the world will be practically double the present total. It will increase most rapidly in the countries already overcrowded and frightfully impoverished. Their problems will attain such magnitude that some form of totalitarianism, probably Communism, will seem to be the only solution. The factor of over-organization will affect more seriously the advanced countries. In nearly all of them concentration of ownership and control is proceeding at an alarming rate. Big Business will necessitate Big Government, and the two in combination will stifle freedom and strangle individuality. In some ways the most menacing of all factors, in Huxley's judgment, is overdevelopment of the means of manipulating and exploiting people's minds. He sees as an unmixed evil the progress that has been made with mental conditioning, subliminal projection, *hypnopaedia,* and subconscious persuasion. Dictators, he fears, will make use of these techniques for extorting confessions, brainwashing, indoctrination, and mass conversions to all sorts of prejudices and fallacious dogmas. In fact, he cites many evidences of their use already for these and similar purposes.

The remedies for these ills, as Huxley saw them, grow naturally out of the character of the disease. For overpopulation, birth-control, combined with conservation of agricultural resources and increased production of food. For overorganization, redistribution of property as widely as possible. Apparently he saw no contradiction between this solution and the need for increased production of food. A parceling-out of large holdings of property would be accompanied by increased emphasis upon the importance of the individual. Huxley decried all efforts to minimize the inherited uniqueness of individual persons. He relegated environmental influence to the background and taught a Great Man theory of history reminiscent of that of William James.

For the overdevelopment of means of psychological manipulation, Huxley advocated some prohibitory laws, but above all he stressed education for freedom. This would include training in critical analysis of propaganda—though not too much, lest religion be destroyed and the inculcation of "values" be rendered too difficult. Youth must be taught to prize charity and compassion, love and intelligence, but, most of all, freedom itself; for, without it, human beings can never be fully human. He was not sanguine of success, for he saw no available solution to the problems of overpopulation and overorganization, and he thought the great mass of mankind too easily gulled by bread and circuses into abandoning all interest in freedom. It still did not seem to occur to him that the advantages of security, well-being, and happiness, even under the conditions described in *Brave New World,* might look rather inviting to people living in today's world of international tensions, under the constant threat of a hydrogen holocaust.

A much different idea of counter-utopia issued from the imaginative genius of George Orwell. His real name was Eric Blair, and he was born in Bengal, in 1903, of an Anglo-Indian family. Sent to Eton for schooling, he wasted his time and learned very little, according to his own account. For five years he served with the Indian Imperial Police in Burma. He resigned, partly because the climate had ruined his health, but mainly because he could not endure any longer serving an imperialism which he regarded as a racket. Returning to Europe, he spent a year and a half in Paris writing novels and short stories which no one would publish. When his money ran out, he worked as a dishwasher and a teacher in cheap private schools. Not until he was thirty-two was he able to live on what he earned by writing. In 1936 he went to Spain to fight for the Loyalists in the civil war. He served four months on the Aragon front with the P.O.U.M. (Trotskyites) and was badly wounded. He returned to England to devote himself to writing books and raising vegetables and chickens. What he saw in Spain and afterward of the inner operations of left-wing parties gave him a revulsion against politics. For a time he was a member of the Independent Labour Party but resigned at the beginning of World War II. He died of tuberculosis in London, in 1950, at the age of forty-six.

Orwell's most celebrated book, *Nineteen Eighty-Four*, was a counter-utopia in the most literal sense of the word. It described a world which was the exact opposite of the hedonistic utopias of the past. Their founders dreamed of a paradise of love and peace in which everyone would be happy and just to his neighbors. The world of 1984, as Orwell foresaw it, was grounded upon hatred. The only emotions tolerated were fear, rage, triumph, and self-abasement. No progress was possible except progress toward agony and strife. The states of the world had been reduced to three—Oceania, Eurasia, and Eastasia— and they were constantly at war. All had the same ideologies, though they were known by different names. Their doctrines represented elements taken from Nazism and Soviet Communism, with the addition of various perversions and refinements. Each society also had doubtless the same structure, though Orwell confined his description to that of Oceania. At the apex of the pyramid was Big Brother, who was omnipotent and infallible, but whom no one had ever seen. Immediately below him was the Inner Party, including about two per cent of the population. Then came the Outer Party, corresponding to the hands of the state as the Inner Party corresponded to the brain. At the bottom were the "proles," or the dumb masses, comprising about eighty-five per cent of the population. The system had been born of revolution, followed by purges and counter-purges. By 1970 all of the leaders, with the exception of Big Brother himself, had killed each other off. Thereafter he had consolidated his power and had made himself the focusing point for all the adulation, fear, and loyalty of the citizens.

Orwell's world of 1984 bore only a few resemblances to Huxley's Brave New World. Both were founded upon the same assumption of the malleability of human nature. The rulers of Oceania boasted that they continuously created human nature.

completely transforming it from its pre-Revolutionary patterns. Both systems included control of reproduction so as to abolish the family and eliminate all loyalties except loyalty to the state. The differences, however, were more fundamental. The objective of Brave New World was to promote efficiency which, in turn, would maximize comfort and a kind of bovine happiness. The goal of Oceania was to foster hatred, to set every man's hand against his neighbor, and to obliterate every humane emotion to make room for adulation of Big Brother. The rulers were obsessed by a mania for power, and they saw no way to achieve this except by making men suffer. For them, power was a form of sadism and consisted in inflicting torture and humiliation. Whereas Huxley's new world was a world of peace and contentment, the "utopia" of Orwell was a world of strife, of treachery, of fiendish cruelty, of forced degradation, and of wholesale executions as public spectacles. Finally, the moral climate of the two worlds was vastly different. The world of the seventh century A.F., as Huxley portrayed it, was almost amoral. No limits were set on indulgence or the pursuit of pleasure. Indeed, such things were encouraged as means of keeping the masses contented. In Oceania, by contrast, sensuality was regarded as a crime against the state. Systematic efforts were therefore made to stamp out eroticism. But in spite of Puritanical preachments, violations were rampant. Crime, promiscuity, prostitution, racketeering, and drug-peddling appeared to large numbers of citizens as logical methods of flaunting their contempt for the system. Even the morality of the opponents themselves had been corrupted by the prevailing brutality and degeneracy. Their leader admitted that, if necessary to accomplish his purposes, he would cheat, forge, blackmail, disseminate disease, or throw sulphuric acid into the face of a child.

The third writer we need to consider under the heading of counter-utopians is Arthur Koestler, though he comes close to the category of an anti-utopian. Koestler was born in Budapest in 1905. After completing his education at the University of Vienna, he became a newspaper correspondent in the Middle East. In 1930 he was appointed foreign editor of the Berlin newspaper *B.Z. am Mittag*. The following year he joined the

Communist Party but resigned after the Moscow trials of 1936. When the Spanish Civil War broke out, he went to the fighting front as correspondent for the London *News Chronicle*. He was captured by the Insurgents and condemned to death as a spy. For a hundred days he languished in jail, expecting at any moment to be shot. Protests from England delayed his execution, and he was finally exchanged for another prisoner. The outbreak of World War II found him in France, where he was arrested and interned as an enemy alien. Released after five months, he proceeded to finish his outstanding novel, and subsequently enlisted in the British army. The novel, entitled *Darkness at Noon*, was a narrative of the Moscow trials. It recounts the destruction of a sincere and dedicated Soviet commissar by the brutal dictatorship he has helped to create. Under ingenious psychological tortures his whole personality is transformed, and he not only confesses specific crimes he never committed, but betrays his associates and arraigns himself as a blackguard and a traitor. He tells himself, finally, that nothing matters except loyalty to the Party, and he justifies his self-sacrifice as a necessity for the deterrence of others. Though widely applauded as an explanation of the abject behavior of the defendants in the Moscow trials, Koestler's interpretation would have rested on solider ground had he taken into account the achievements of Pavlov in producing neuroses and complete disorientation by psychological experiments on healthy animals.[20] It seems not unreasonable to suppose that the Soviet prosecutors had knowledge of these experiments.

Koestler developed his counter-utopian views in connection with his famous contrast of the philosophy of the Yogi with that of the Commissar. The Yogi believes, he pointed out, that a better world can never result from changing the organization or institutions of society. Instead, all progress depends on the redemption and purification of individuals. Not until human beings completely purge themselves of selfishness, envy, and hatred can they hope to make the world around them peaceful and

[20] See Ivan Pavlov, "Conditioned Reflexes and Psychiatry," *Lectures on Conditioned Reflexes,* trans. W. H. Grant. New York, International Publishers, 1941, Vol. II.

harmonious. The Yogi philosophy is popular, of course, in Oriental thought, especially in India. It also finds characteristic expression in the Moral Rearmament Movement of Frank Buchman.

At the opposite pole from the Yogi viewpoint is that of the Commissar. As Koestler conceives it, the philosophy of the Commissar is based upon the principle of change from without. The Commissar believes in grasping the "sorry scheme of things entire" and shattering it to bits as a condition prerequisite to a new society. He is interested only in ends, not in means, and is therefore ready to make use of treachery, confiscation, the blood purge, or revolution. Since he attaches supreme importance to the environment and scoffs at the need for changing individuals, he belongs in the camp of the utopians. Yet all attempts to establish the New Jerusalem by Commissar methods have failed, according to Koestler. Either they degenerate into reigns of terror or they lose their momentum and terminate in disastrous compromise. But efforts to change the world from within on a mass scale have also proved unavailing. Excessive concentration on means leads to quietism, passivity, and acceptance of evil. Indifference to the environment spells villages without sewerage and helpless denizens of urban slums living like rats pell-mell in the straw. Though definitely preferring the methods of the Yogi to those of the Commissar, Koestler concludes that "neither the saint nor the revolutionary can save us; only the synthesis of the two." [21] He is not optimistic, however, that the synthesis can be achieved.[22]

An examination of the writings of those who deal with the environmental conditioning of political theory leaves an ineradicable impression of the miasma of pessimism that seems to have enshrouded the modern world. Large numbers appear

[21] *The Yogi and the Commissar.* New York, Macmillan, 1946, p. 247.
[22] In a later book, *Thieves in the Night,* he expresses the view that primitive instincts are so strong that violence is inevitable. He appears to justify and even glorify it as a means of escape from humiliation and intolerable oppression. He makes one of his characters exclaim, "What a luxury to press one's finger on a hard metal trigger and get hanged for it singing the national anthem."

to consider it axiomatic that man's nature is vile, and that therefore it is fatuous to hope for any genuine progress on this sullen earth. Fanaticism, violence, tyranny, and war are alleged to be about all one can expect from such swinish creatures as human beings. Unless men turn aside from self-dependence and pride in their own intellects and adopt some mystical abasement or self-surrender, they can look forward to new Belsens and Dachaus or, at the least, to totalitarian enslavement. We appear to be in danger of falling into the same trap that caught many Darwinists in the last century. Their attention was so completely absorbed by the idea of a competitive, and even violent, struggle for existence that they were unable to appreciate the positive elements in the evolutionary process. Prince Kropotkin pointed these out in his *Mutual Aid, A Factor in Evolution,* but the work aroused only a modest response. Now we have the parallel of philosophers and sociologists so blinded by Calvinist, Hobbesian, Kierkegaardian, or Freudian prejudice against human nature that they can see nothing but remote possibilities of social advancement.

Significantly, the social scientists who hold the most benevolent view of man's prospects are the anthropologists. And it is they who have probed most deeply into the facts of social origins. They find nothing to justify the assumption of a universal condition of strife and violence in primitive society. They discover no inborn tendencies toward sadism, pugnacity, conquest, or domination. On the contrary, they find evidences of cooperation, mutual assistance, and reciprocal bargaining. They do not insist that these tendencies grow out of an essentially angelic human nature; but they do find evidence that even the most primitive of men have intelligence enough to realize the advantages of working together as compared to the risks and dangers of bloodletting and violence. Political philosophers and others who conceive of the state as simply organized force grounded on conquest may profitably ponder the anthropological data.

ADDITIONAL READINGS

Barnett, Homer G. *Anthropology in Administration*. Evanston, Ill., Row, Peterson, 1956.

Benedict, Ruth. *The Chrysanthemum and the Sword*. Boston, Houghton Mifflin, 1946.

Boas, Franz. *Anthropology and Modern Life*. New York, Norton, 1932.

Case, Clarence M. *Non-Violent Coercion*. New York, Century, 1923.

Gerth, H. H., and Mills, C. W. *From Max Weber: Essays in Sociology*. New York, Oxford University Press, 1946.

Ginsberg, Morris. *The Idea of Progress; a Revaluation*. Boston, Beacon Press, 1953.

————. *On the Diversity of Morals*. Melbourne, Heinemann, 1956.

————. *Reason and Unreason in Society*. London, Longmans, 1948.

Goldenweiser, A. A. *Early Civilization*. New York, Knopf, 1922.

Hobhouse, L. T. *Morals in Evolution*. London, Chapman and Hall, 1951.

Lewin, Kurt. *Resolving Social Conflicts*. New York, Harper, 1948.

Lowie, Robert H. *The Origin of the State*. New York, Harcourt, 1927.

————. *Social Organization*. New York, Rinehart, 1953.

————. *Toward Understanding Germany*. Chicago, University of Chicago Press, 1954.

Mannheim, Karl. *Man and Society in an Age of Reconstruction*. New York, Harcourt, 1941.

Michels, Robert. *First Lectures in Political Sociology*. Minneapolis, University of Minnesota Press, 1949.

Mills, C. Wright. *The New Men of Power: America's Labor Leaders*. New York, Harcourt, 1948.

————. *The Sociological Imagination*. New York, Oxford University Press, 1959.

Orwell, George. *Animal Farm*. New York, Harcourt, 1946.

Packard, Vance. *The Status Seekers*. New York, McKay, 1959.

Riesman, David. *Faces in the Crowd*. New Haven, Yale University Press, 1953.

Shapiro, Harry L. *Man, Culture and Society*. New York, Oxford University Press, 1956.

Sorokin, Pitirim A. *Man and Society in Calamity*. New York, Dutton, 1942.

―――. *The Reconstruction of Humanity*. Boston, Beacon Press, 1948.

―――. *Social and Cultural Dynamics*. Boston, Extending Horizons Books, 1957.

―――. *Social Philosophies of an Age of Crisis*. Boston, Beacon Press, 1950.

Tarde, Gabriel. *Social Laws*. New York, Macmillan, 1899.

Trotter, Wilfred. *Instincts of the Herd in Peace and War*. London, Unwin, 1916.

Wallas, Graham. *Our Social Heritage*. New Haven, Yale University Press, 1921.

Whyte, William H. *The Organization Man*. Garden City, Doubleday, 1957.

Woolf, Leonard S. *After the Deluge*. New York, Harcourt, 1931.

PART FOUR

Theories of World Conflict and World Order

CHAPTER
XIV

Nationalism and Its Opponents

Though nationalism is not new, it is certainly one of the most distinctive phenomena of contemporary culture. It has been described as modern man's religion. It has also been described as his "incest," his "insanity." [1] The devout Christian who takes his religion seriously must often be shocked by the idolatry associated with the worship of national glory—the flag-kissing ceremonies, the deification of military heroes, and the deliberate courting of martyrdom in the cause of national "honor." The humane philosopher must find a basis for sad reflection in the fact that, throughout the so-called civilized world, men think of themselves as citizens of particular nations, and almost never as members of the human race. Patriotism, for millions of people, has become synonymous with fanatical attachment to one's own country, and is commonly combined with emotions of hatred and suspicion toward the outside world. Though such terms as xenophobia and chauvinism have been invented to describe what are commonly thought of as perversions of nationalism, actually the outstanding examples of contemporary nationalism have included both of these alleged perversions as basic characteristics.

Nationalism is commonly defined as a program or ideal based on a consciousness of nationhood. This feeling or consciousness

[1] Erich Fromm, *The Sane Society*, p. 58.

may depend on a number of factors. A people may consider themselves a nation because of peculiarities of race, language, religion, or culture. In most cases, however, the factors which weld diverse groups together are a common history and common aspirations for the future or a belief in a common destiny. Only such elements as these can explain the fact that Belgium, Switzerland, and Canada are nations, since in all three there are major differences in language, in religion, or both—to say nothing of different ethnic backgrounds.

Nurtured by the French Revolutionary ideal of Fraternity, nationalism in the modern world has evolved through two stages. From 1800 to about 1848 it was little more than an emotional loyalty to a cultural and linguistic group and a yearning for deliverance from foreign oppression. Since 1848 it has developed into an aggressive movement for national greatness and for the right of each people to extend its rule over similar or related peoples with or without their consent. Occasionally, in our own time, nationalism of the original, liberating type makes its appearance; but all too frequently it deteriorates into the aggressive, xenophobic pattern.

1. The Legacy from the Nineteenth Century

Like every other movement, nationalism has had its advocates and prophets who have excogitated theories not only to defend it but to enlarge its meaning in the minds of its followers. Among these prophets during the nineteenth century, three stand out—a Frenchman, an Italian, and a German. The Frenchman was the noted historian and man of letters, Ernest Renan (1823–1892). He began an education for the priesthood, but abandoned it for science and philology before taking orders. Later he obtained a doctor's degree in philosophy. In 1864 he was appointed Professor of Hebrew and Chaldaic Languages at the College de France. He was transferred soon afterward, however, under ecclesiastical pressure, to a subordinate position in the National Library. He wrote voluminously on various subjects, from race and religion to art and war. The most disturbing experience of his life was probably the Franco-Prussian War.

Before it he had admired the Germans as leaders of thought and culture. After their invasion and conquest of his beloved France, he was profoundly disillusioned. He seemed not to understand that the nationalism he himself preached was one of the potent causes of such disasters.

Renan conceived the nation in a highly idealized fashion. No mundane factors of economics or geography contaminated his thinking. Even history was of secondary consideration. A people, he said, who aspire to be a nation should forget a large part of their history, just as the French have had to forget the massacre of St. Bartholomew's Day and the slaughter of the Albigenses by Count Raymond of Toulouse. What, then, is a nation? According to Renan "a nation is a soul, a spiritual principle." Two things, one in the past and one in the present, combine to make up this soul or spiritual principle. The first is the possession of a rich heritage of memories; and the second is a desire to live together and to make the most of the joint inheritance. By memories Renan obviously did not mean history but a national mythology, or *mystique,* which would celebrate the glories and consecrate the hardships of the past. "To have suffered, rejoiced, and hoped together"—these are the things which make a nation. Of course, nations are not eternal. They have had their beginnings and they will have their ends. Ultimately, in a much different world, they may be replaced by confederations. But given the world in its present condition, their disappearance would be a calamity. "Their existence is the guarantee of liberty, which would be lost, if the world had but one law and one master." True, a multiplicity of laws and masters might result in conflicts; but this did not worry Renan. He justified war as a condition of progress, "the sting which prevents a country from going to sleep." [2]

No less extreme than Renan was the Italian nationalist Giuseppe Mazzini (1805–1872). The son of a physician, he became a student in the University of Genoa with the intention of following his father's profession; but a revulsion against the practice of dissection forced him to graduate in law. His real

[2] Alfred Zimmern, ed., "What Is a Nation?" *Modern Political Doctrines.* London, Oxford University Press, 1939, pp. 202–4.

interest, however, was in literature, and he soon turned to writing as a means of livelihood. He was an ardent romanticist, suffusing his essays and articles with passionate zeal for patriotic causes. About 1828 he joined the *Carbonari* and thereafter dedicated himself to the liberation of Italy and its unification under a republican government. He participated in one dangerous mission after another and was imprisoned several times and sentenced to death at least twice. The best years of his life he spent in captivity or in exile, enduring poverty and loneliness. After unification was achieved, he was elected to Parliament as a deputy from Messina; but he refused to serve because the government of the new Italy was a monarchy.

Mazzini's conception of nationalism differed markedly from that of Renan. Unlike the Frenchman, the Italian liberator gave prominence to both geography and language as foundations of nationhood. The Alps and the Mediterranean, he affirmed, defined the limits of the Italian nation. But so also did language. Wherever Italian was spoken, there was the home of the Italian people. This premise made possible the inclusion of Corsica, Sardinia, and Sicily in the Italian homeland. But Mazzini was also interested in spiritual foundations, and he set forth the claim that the very perfection of Italy's geographic frontiers evidenced divine intent in the founding of the nation. He contended, moreover, that God had chosen Italy for a mission to all humanity. He had appointed her to assume the leadership of the civilized world, as she had done in the time of the Romans and during the great Renaissance. He ignored completely the point that, during the latter period, Italy had maintained her leadership without even a trace of unity.

But for Mazzini, national unification was merely the prelude to a greater destiny. Apart from the nation, the individual was nothing. He had "neither name, token, voice nor rights," and no membership as a brother in the "fellowship of the Peoples." [3] He was a soldier without a banner and no capacity to discharge his duties to the rest of humanity. But as a member of a virile Italian nation, with its proud traditions and consciousness of

[3] Thomas Okey, trans., *The Duties of Man and Other Essays*, New York, Dutton, 1915, p. 53.

greatness, he would be able to fulfill a noble role in shaping the destinies of Europe. Since Mazzini conceded to other nations similar, though less resplendent, missions, what he envisaged as a final end was a republican confederation of humanity united by a common agreement for the moral betterment of mankind. Though he voiced many fiery appeals to the young men of Italy to fight and die, if necessary, for the glory of their country, he remained a passionate defender of liberty and opponent of tyranny. His idealism, like that of many other nationalists of the nineteenth century, stands out in bold contrast to the authoritarianism and chauvinism of their twentieth-century successors.

The German historian and philosopher Heinrich von Treitschke (1834–1896) is more commonly thought of as an imperialist and exponent of power politics than as a nationalist. Under the influence of the Hegelian tradition, he deified the state; but what he meant was the nation-state, and he was one of the most rabid of the racists and anti-Semites in Imperial Germany. He was born in Dresden, the son of an officer in the Saxon army. In his early career he was so well known for his liberal convictions that he was unable to realize his ambition of becoming a professor, though he had distinguished himself as a student at Leipzig and Bonn. He finally succeeded in realizing his objective by becoming a Prussian subject and proclaiming the view that the destiny of all the German states was bound up with that of Prussia. He had his reward in being appointed to professorships successively at Kiel, Heidelberg, and Berlin. He discarded his liberalism completely and put on the mantle of chief eulogist of the Hohenzollern dynasty. Though he supported Bismarck in warring against Socialists and Catholics, he parted company with the Iron Chancellor in advocating colonial expansion. He also contributed enormously to the strong anti-British feeling in Germany toward the end of the century.

In Treitschke's political theory the terms "nation" and "state" were often used interchangeably. He considered the state to be as old as the human race itself, but he did not see how a modern state could exist except on the basis of nationality. He scoffed at the idea of a world state, and taught that every man of his day felt himself a German, a Frenchman, an Englishman, instead of a member of a common humanity. That a nation should cultivate myths of greatness and magnify or even falsify achievements he considered both natural and justifiable. "Every people," he said, "has a right to believe that certain attributes of the Divine reason are exhibited in it to their fullest perfection." Nations, he maintained, can prosper and flourish only under intense competition, comparable to that of the Darwinian struggle for existence. For Treitschke this meant the permanence and inevitability of war. Without war no state could exist. All originated through war, and the protection of their citizens through armed might remained the primary and essential task of a nation. Conquest by the sword was the principal method by which civilization could overcome "barbarism and unreason." War, moreover, provided the means for rescuing humanity from selfishness, effeminacy, and materialism. For these reasons, God would see to it that war should return again and again, as "a terrible medicine for mankind diseased." [4]

The nationalism of Treitschke was overwhelmingly conservative. Not only did he justify the methods of *Machtpolitik*, but he insisted upon the urgency of acquiring colonies "by any possible means." He considered all races except the Caucasian as incapable of civilization. The yellow peoples, he maintained, had no artistic talent and no genius for political liberty. "Their States have always been despotic and unfree." The black races, he contended, had never been good for anything but hewers of wood and drawers of water. Their destiny was to serve the white man and to be the targets of his disgust forever. "The Mulatto is a nigger in all but his paler skin; that he is aware of it is shown by his consorting with other blacks." [5] Such logic, of course, was overpowering! National cohesiveness also required, according to Treitschke, a class structure of society. The very nature of the social organism, he claimed, implied differences of social standing and economic condition among its members. Though it is the duty of government to mitigate distress, the abolition of poverty is neither possible nor desirable.

[4] Blanche Dugdale and Torben de Bille, trans., *Politics*. New York, Macmillan, 1916, I, 15, 19, 65, 69.

[5] *Ibid.*, I, 275, 276.

The masses must forever remain the masses, and there can "be no culture without kitchenmaids." [6]

2. From Mahan and Theodore Roosevelt to Nasser and Nkrumah

Nationalism in the twentieth century has followed with close resemblance the patterns established in the eighteen-hundreds. As in the earlier period, it has taken the form, in some cases, of struggles for national independence or of liberation from foreign rule. Characteristic examples have been the nationalist movements in India, in Indonesia, in various British and French dependencies in Africa, among the Slavic peoples formerly subject to the Austro-Hungarian and Russian empires, and in Israel and the Arab dependencies of the Middle East. In addition, certain countries already independent have passed through unrestrained periods of national regeneration. Notable among them have been Egypt, Turkey, Persia, and China. Regardless of its objectives, the movement has waxed in ferocity. It would be almost impossible to duplicate, from the earlier period, the fanaticism and savagery of an F. T. Marinetti or a Charles Maurras, to say nothing of a Hitler or a Goebbels. Even so gentle a soul as Cardinal Mercier, primate of Belgium during World War I, could assert that "Christ crowns military valor," and that death in defense of the honor of his country assures to the soldier "the salvation of his soul." The distinguished Prince of the Church could not classify the dying soldier as a martyr because of his armed resistance to evil, but he did declare that death on the battlefield "wipes out a whole life of sin." [7]

Of the numerous writers who set the standard for the uncritical nationalism of the twentieth century, perhaps none were more typical than the two Americans Admiral Mahan and Theodore Roosevelt. Alfred Thayer Mahan was born in 1840, the son of a professor of engineering at West Point. He was graduated from the Naval Academy and, after some years of ship

[6] *Ibid.*, I, 42.
[7] Quoted by Ernst Kantorowicz, "Pro Patria Mori in Medieval Political Thought," *American Historical Review*, LVI (1951), 472.

duty, was assigned to give lectures at the War College in New-port, eventually becoming President of the institution. His two books, *The Influence of Sea Power upon History, 1660–1783* and *The Influence of Sea Power upon the French Revolution and Empire*, brought him world-wide attention and provided the basis for the naval doctrines of Theodore Roosevelt and the German Kaiser. Until his death in 1914 Mahan probably exerted more influence on the national policies of his time than did al-most any other individual.

The nationalist theory of Mahan was a mixture of ideas de-rived from *laissez-faire* individualism and Puritan moralism. He conceived of nations as sovereign units engaged in a com-petitive struggle for survival and power. This struggle made possible the health and soundness of the international com-munity. Just as the greatest good of the greatest number was supposed to result from competition among rival entrepreneurs in the business world, the same result could be expected from competition among nations. To establish any kind of world gov-ernment would violate this principle. The decay of nationalism, Mahan warned, would destroy the best antidote "to what is bad in socialism." [8] Moreover, it would undermine the ability of Western peoples to deal successfully with the threat imposed by "the teeming multitudes of central and northern Asia." [9] Mahan opposed not only world government but compulsory arbitration as well. He feared that any requirement that nations arbitrate or conciliate their differences would lead to compromises with un-righteousness. Men would be tempted to tamper with equity and to tolerate injustice, "soothing their consciences with the belief that war is so entirely wrong that beside it no tolerated evil is wrong." [10] Finally, it should be noted that Mahan considered isolationism inconsistent with true nationalism. He believed that America had a mission to be strong and great and to wield a positive influence in international affairs. After the fashion of Great Britain in the nineteenth century, she should throw

[8] *The Interest of America in Sea Power, Present and Future.* Boston, Little, Brown, 1898, p. 122.

[9] *Ibid.*, p. 123.

[10] "The Peace Conference and the Moral Aspects of War," *North American Review*, CLXIX (October, 1899), 447.

her weight into the scales and maintain a balance of power in both Europe and the Far East. To bear her share of the burdens of the world was merely "to assume an inevitable task, an appointed lot, in the work of upholding the common interests of civilization." [11]

No master ever had a more faithful disciple than Mahan found in the young and ebullient Theodore Roosevelt (1858–1919). In 1897 President McKinley appointed Roosevelt Assistant Secretary of the Navy. In this office he took advantage of every opportunity to promote a vigorous foreign and imperial policy by the United States. He is generally said to have been responsible for maneuvering the government into approving an attack on the Philippine Islands, during the temporary absence of the Secretary of the Navy. But he found a desk job too unexciting in the midst of "a glorious little war," and he soon left for the fighting front in Cuba as Lieutenant-Colonel of the Rough Riders. After the Battle of San Juan Hill he proudly reported that he had killed a Spaniard with his own hands, "like a jackrabbit." Returning as a war hero, he was elected Governor of New York in 1898, and two years later Vice President of the United States. But regardless of the position he occupied, he never gave up his quest for "derring-do." In 1917, at the age of fifty-nine, he clamored for the privilege of leading an expeditionary force against the Germans and was deeply hurt when his plea was denied. His personal beliefs were in harmony with the events of his life. "All the great masterful races have been fighting races," he told the Naval War College in 1897.

For Theodore Roosevelt, devotion to the solidarity and greatness of one's nation was the highest purpose of human existence. It was a purpose as sacred and demanding as the worship of one God. "The man who loves other nations as much as he does his own," he asserted, "stands on a par with the man who loves other women as much as he does his own wife." [12] The woman who approved the song, "I Did Not Raise My Boy to Be a Soldier," belonged in an Oriental harem, he said, not in

[11] *The Interest of America in Sea Power*, p. 123.
[12] *Fear God and Take Your Own Part.* New York, George H. Doran, 1916, p. 18.

the United States. Roosevelt skirted the edges of fascism about as closely as did any other leading figure in American history. His major objective as President was to subordinate every class and special interest to the authority of the state. He crusaded against radicals, monopolists, and leaders of organized labor with about equal vehemence. To be sure, he sponsored reforms, but usually with a view to putting some class or group "in its place." He glorified power and physical strength and justified the use of the mailed fist. When the Germans invaded Belgium in 1914, he adopted the attitude that necessity knows no law, and that disaster would have been Germany's portion if she had not acted ruthlessly. The Kaiser's minions proved themselves, he said, "a stern, virile, and masterful people." [13] Roosevelt championed also the fascist-Machiavellian conception of the "dynamic" nation. "When great nations fear to expand," he shouted, "it is because their greatness is coming to an end. Are we still in the prime of our lusty youth, still at the beginning of our glorious manhood, to sit down among the outworn peoples, to take our place with the weak and craven? A thousand times no!" [14]

Great Britain, also, had her outspoken nationalists, especially in the earlier part of the twentieth century, before it became evident that the sun of her glory was beginning to set. Her most popular poet, Rudyard Kipling, could piously describe Britain's "dominion over palm and pine" as sanctioned by no less an authority than God Himself. For a philosophical defense of her national greatness, however, it is necessary to consult the writings of a prominent historian, J. A. Cramb, of Queens College, London. John Adam Cramb was born in 1862 and died on the eve of World War I. Educated at Glasgow and Bonn universities, he was appointed, in 1893, Professor of Modern History at Queens College. His importance as a political thinker rests chiefly on two books, *Reflections on the Origins and Destiny of Imperial Britain* and *Germany and England*. He was not only

[13] "The World War: Its Tragedies and Its Lessons," *The Outlook*, CVIII (September 23, 1914), 170.
[14] Quoted by Richard Hofstadter, *The American Political Tradition and the Men Who Made It.* New York, Knopf, 1948, p. 209.

a nationalist and an imperialist but a militarist of so extreme a persuasion that even the most violent outpourings of Treitschke and Bernhardi seemed to him fair and just. In fact, he had a curious admiration for Imperial Germany as the supreme embodiment of the Teutonic spirit. It is remarkable, therefore, that his writings should have become a chief weapon of anti-German propaganda, both in England and the United States, before and during World War I.

Cramb venerated British nationhood with a fervor almost religious. Indeed, he practically equated the nation with God. He described the death of a British soldier on the battlefield as a sacrifice for "this mysterious, deathless, onward-striving force, call it God, call it Destiny—but name it England. For England it is." [15] He despised pacifists and votaries of pleasure and soft living, and called for dedication to heroism, idealism, and sacrifice. There is a glory in suffering and self-abnegation, he contended, which transcends reason. Man does not live by bread alone but by deeds and sentiments which lift him above the cares and interests of this mundane life. For example, "in war and the right of war man has a possession which he values above religion, above industry, and above social comforts; that in war man values the power which it affords to life of rising above life, the power which the spirit of man possesses to pursue the Ideal." [16] For Cramb the normal and natural relationship among nations was conflict. Peace he regarded as simply a truce on the battlefield of Time. In his view nothing was more axiomatic than the inevitability of an Anglo-German war. Both nations were dowered with a genius for empire, and it was unthinkable that Germany should continue to tolerate a monopoly of one-fourth of the earth by her greedy rival. Such a war would be a tragedy but a sublime tragedy; for the same heroic blood flowed in the veins of both peoples. And the mighty god of all the Teutons would look down upon that conflict, and smile serenely "upon his favorite children, the English and the Germans," locked in mortal combat.[17]

[15] *Germany and England.* New York, Dutton, 1914, p. 141.
[16] *Ibid.,* p. 67.
[17] *Ibid.,* p. 152.

That Germany in the first part of the twentieth century should have been a center of blatant nationalism scarcely needs emphasis. Bordered by potential enemies on both east and west, she developed a kind of fear psychosis. Her romanticists for over a hundred years, from Fichte and Herder to Wagner and Stöcker, had been nurturing a cult of deification of the German spirit. The long struggle for a united Empire made the goal of unity seem vastly important and instilled into the German mind a fanatical devotion to the national interest. Envy and greed contributed also to the mania for greatness. Propagandists for empire portrayed their nation as a victim of injustice and economic impoverishment. Because unification had come so late, Germany, they claimed, had not had a fair opportunity to share in the spoils of colonial acquisition in Asia and Africa. As a result, she found herself after 1900 with a burgeoning industry and a growing population, but with nothing but a few scraggly patches of sand in Africa and the South Pacific to support the homeland. The conclusion seemed obvious that she must either despoil the imperial powers of some of their colonies or conquer territory in Europe or Asia from her own neighbors.

Probably the best-known of German jingoists before and during World War I was Friedrich von Bernhardi (1849–1930). In Britain and the United States his fire-eating militarism was regarded as truly representative of German thinking and therefore as conclusive proof of German villainy. Bernhardi was born in St. Petersburg, the son of a diplomat. He entered the Prussian Army in time to participate in the Franco-Prussian War. Though only a lieutenant, in command of six Hussars, he virtually took credit for the capture of Paris. In 1907 he was made commander of the Seventh Army Corps, but retired two years later to devote his time to military writing. His *Germany and the Next War,* published in 1912, produced a sensation as soon as it became available in English translation. The theme of the book was *Weltmacht oder Niedergang,* which was usually rendered "world domination or downfall," though its author insisted that all he meant was that Germany must become *a* world power or suffer the penalty of downfall.

The political theory of Bernhardi was largely an echo of that of Treitschke, except that he outdid his predecessor in justifying war as an instrument of national policy. He conceived of Germany as surrounded by a ring of enemies, beset on all sides by jealous and hostile nations. This enmity was partly the consequence of her geographic position in the center of a continent; but it was also the result of her need, as the last of the great empires to be consolidated, to assert her rights in vigorous fashion. She had thus stepped on a score of toes and aroused the hostility of a dozen neighbors. Her position, accordingly, was gravely perilous, and she must be prepared to fight her way out. He complained that Germans were too deeply saturated with love of peace. For too long they had been content with the intellectual leadership of Europe. Pacifism had rotted their souls and made their bodies anemic. They must now change their attitude, and instead of regarding war as a curse, they must recognize it as "an indispensable factor of culture, in which a true civilized nation finds the highest expression of strength and vitality." [18] War, he contended, is an ennobling instrument, the chief means of inculcating national ideals and strengthening moral fiber. Far from being anti-Christian, it is entirely compatible with the teachings of Jesus. For did He not say, "I am not come to bring peace on earth, but a sword"? The world has never known a religion more combative than Christianity. "Combat, moral combat, is its very essence." [19] Therefore, according to Bernhardi, if we would preserve Christianity, we must also preserve the law of struggle and the right to appeal to the sword.

Bernhardi was brash in affirming his belief in a grandiose destiny for Germany. No nation had contributed more, he contended, or even as much to the entire development of the human race. Germany was the home of true freedom. She had always been the standard-bearer of free thought, and at the same time a strong bulwark against anarchy and license, which destroy freedom. Bernhardi saw in the Protestant Reformation and Kant's *Critique of Pure Reason* the two chief landmarks in the liberation of mankind; and Germany was the source of both.

[18] *Germany and the Next War*. Longmans, 1914, p. 14.
[19] *Ibid.*, p. 29.

The Reformation broke the intellectual tyranny imposed by the Church, "which checked all free progress." *The Critique of Pure Reason* exposed the fallacies of undisciplined philosophic speculation and defined for the human mind "the limitations of its capacity for knowledge, and at the same time pointed out in what way knowledge is really possible." [20] What he meant was that man was thereby enabled to enjoy the benefits of free inquiry and at the same time to keep his religion. They would never conflict, for each would be on a different level. Such achievements would have been impossible, he claimed, without the advantages of German genius. No nation on earth was so capable of grasping and appropriating the elements of culture and enriching them by its own spiritual endowments. A nation so generously favored must not be required, Bernhardi maintained, to hide her light under a bushel. She has the right to a colonial empire and to an adequate share in the sovereignty of the world. She must be accorded the privilege of making her position in Europe so secure that it can never again be challenged. This means taking measures to curb the onrush of the Slavs and crushing France so completely that she can never again cross Germany's path. Nothing less will suffice to enable the Reich to achieve success in the coming struggle with Great Britain. Britain is the real source of anti-German jealousy. It is she who stands in the way as the chief obstacle to making the German spirit prevail over a large part of the earth.

As every student of history knows, World War I marked a climax in the evolution of nationalism. Fires which had hitherto burned slowly now flamed with a furious intensity. Prejudice, fanaticism, and hatred dominated the writings and speeches of leaders of opinion almost everywhere. Liberals and representatives of humane letters were frequently the most outspoken. Early in the struggle H. G. Wells boasted that "we would end the reign of brutal and artful internationalism forever." The British and their allies, he declared, would fight the war to a finish and would conquer, even though it meant that all their children would die of famine and every ship would be at the bottom of the sea. Then the victors would redraw the map of

[20] *Ibid.*, p. 73.

Europe and give freedom to Poland and all the subject nationalities of the Austro-Hungarian Empire. G. K. Chesterton denounced the Germans as worse savages than the Turks, as "veneered vandals" willfully at war with the very principles which make human society possible.[21] Needless to say, the Germans reciprocated with similar vilifications of *their* enemies. The atmosphere was so poisoned with venom and bitterness that Europeans lost all sense of balance for years to come in appraising peoples whom they feared or distrusted.

The psychopathic extremes of Fascism and Nazism were directly related to the frustrations, hatreds, and desires for revenge generated by the war. And it is probably not inaccurate to regard the furnaces and gas chambers of Buchenwald and Dachau as mere technical variations in the system of wholesale killing of one's enemies. If it was legitimate to exterminate a hated nation by the methods of total war, why was it not also legitimate to exterminate Poles and Jews in concentration camps?

References were made in a previous chapter to the nationalist doctrines which entered into the substance of totalitarian ideologies. In Italy these doctrines emanated from a number of sources—from the Hegelians, from fire-eating Irredentists like Gabriele d'Annunzio, but most of all from the Futurists, who excoriated everything connected with the internationalism and liberalism of the nineteenth century. They denounced pacifism, democracy, humanitarianism, socialism, and libertarianism. They preached the "beauty and necessity of violence" and the inexhaustible vigor of Italian blood. They sang hymns to war as "the world's only hygiene, the noble bath of heroism," without which a people falls asleep in idle egoism or in gluttonous delights in the pleasures of the belly.[22] Upon coming into power, Mussolini adopted this wild-eyed philosophy, modifying it only by an accommodation with Catholicism as a substitute for the anti-clericalism of the Futurists.

The nationalism of the German Nazis was almost inseparable from racism. They conceived of the nation as a kind of tribal brotherhood only vaguely restricted to a definite territory. Hitler

[21] I. C. Willis, *England's Holy War,* pp. 90–91, 118–19.
[22] H. W. Schneider, *Making the Fascist State,* pp. 260–65.

regarded the state as simply a means to an end, an instrument for preserving and perpetuating the superior race. On the one hand, it was a propaganda agency for inculcating and spreading the *mystique* of Aryan supremacy. On the other hand, it was a mechanism of conquest, to be used whenever necessary for the fulfillment of the Aryan myth. The Nazis, of course, despised pacifism, scoffed at the possibility of harmony between nations, and hailed the military virtues as essential to the survival and health of the nation. They took into their household all the intellectual rubbish of Treitschke and Bernhardi regarding war as a necessary medicine for humanity, the permanence and inevitability of conflict, and the value of force as an indispensable instrument of culture. They revived the old dogmas that Germany was encircled by a ring of enemies, that she was a have-not nation desperately in need of *Lebensraum,* and that she was in deadly peril of barbarization by hordes from the East.

World War I and its aftermath also witnessed the growth of passionate nationalism in France. A movement known as Integral Nationalism developed dogmas of traditionalism, authoritarianism, sentimental piety, and dedication to national glory. The most prominent leaders of the movement were Maurice Barrès (1862–1923) and Charles Maurras (1868–1952). Barrès was educated as a lawyer but devoted most of his time to journalism and to the writing of political essays. As a child he had been deeply hurt by the wresting of his native province of Lorraine from France by the Germans. Later he had been humiliated by the Panama scandals and by the treason and disloyalty charged against the Jews during the Dreyfus affair. He became an advocate of Caesarism and a champion of a strong union of Church and state. Believing that in the "soil" and the "dead" he had discovered mystic forces directing the life of the individual, he fathered a cult in which tradition, order, the family, the region, and the nation all became objects of worship. In fairness it should be added that in his later years he broadened his nationalism to include a common Franco-German tradition. Though his influence on this score had some impact on the movement for a *rapprochement* between the two nations, it came too late to undo the effects of his uncritical devotion to nation-worship.

Barrès originally professed an individualism so extreme that it bordered on nihilism. He was soon converted, however, under the reactionary pressures of his time, to what he called "collective egotism." By this he meant that the nature of the individual is predetermined by his social surroundings both past and present and by his racial inheritance. Man finds his true self, he seemed to believe, when he consents to be merely an episode in the evolution of his fatherland and his race. A curious fascination with death, with cemeteries, and with martyrdom bulked large in Barrès' philosophy. Men who died in the name of their country, he said, experienced "a magnificent sweetness." A Frenchman, "who became conscious of his formation," knew that his ancestors in "terrible wrath" looked down upon him.[23] Barrès defined a nation as "a territory where men possess common memories, common habits, a hereditary ideal—a nation is the common possession of an ancient cemetery, and the will to continue to make valid this undivided heritage." [24] But a mystical preoccupation with cemeteries and death was not the only element in Barrès' nationalism. He condemned the parliamentary system, proposing to substitute for it a plebiscitary republic of the sort planned by General Boulanger, whom he supported. It would be a Caesarist dictatorship based upon the votes of the people. Barrès was a racist and an anti-Semite, branding the Jews as capable of treason solely because of their ethnic extraction. His veneration of authority, fatherland, solidarity, and martyrdom led him to justify militarism, though, unlike some of his contemporaries, he did not eulogize violence as a good in itself.

Closely associated with Barrès in the Integral Nationalist movement was Charles Maurras, who traveled the road to reaction even farther. Maurras was born in Provence and studied philosophy in Paris. He was influenced not only by the nationalism of Barrès but by the anti-individualist elements in the philoso-

[23] Quoted by Boyd C. Shafer, *Nationalism: Myth and Reality*. New York, Harcourt, 1955, pp. 27, 181.

[24] Quoted by J. P. Mayer, *Political Thought in France from the Revolution to the Fourth Republic*. London, Routledge and Paul, 1943, p. 87.

phy of Auguste Comte. He also adopted doctrines from Henri Bergson, Georges Sorel, and Édouard Drumont, the anti-Semitic journalist. As in the case of Barrès, it was the Dreyfus affair which brought his ideas to crystallization. From then on he rapidly gained notoriety as a fiery apostle of authority, hierarchy, monarchism, and xenophobia. Though he was an avowed atheist, he wrote eloquently in defense of Catholicism and a close alliance of Church and state. He repudiated both mysticism and materialism, and based his admiration for the Catholic religion upon an aesthetic appreciation of the unity, power, and organization of the Church. He also saw in Catholicism a strong bulwark for his ideas of order, discipline, stability, and reaction. Besides, the majority of the monarchists and authoritarians of that time were Catholics. About 1899 Maurras assisted in the founding of Action française, an organization dedicated to the overthrow of the Republic and the establishment of a conservative, Catholic monarchy. The organization was especially active during the 1930's, and Maurras was imprisoned twice for plotting against the government. After the fall of France in 1940 he supported the regime of Marshal Pétain. Convicted as a fascist collaborator in 1945, he was released for medical reasons seven years later. He renounced his atheism and was received into the Church shortly before his death in 1952.

The nationalism of Maurras was founded primarily on contempt for the individual. He rejected the whole concept of the person as an end in himself, as a being endowed with indefeasible rights. In Maurras' view, the individual existed to fulfill the destiny of the nation and the state. The state was a sublime and noble organism with a life and purpose of its own. It was not bound either by the law or the morality binding upon private persons. Reasons of state entitled the government to act with no other considerations in view but necessity and political interest. The state, he insisted, must have the strength and authority to assure it at all times an absolute mastery. This power, he contended, could not be secured without a king. Despite the fact that those who agreed with him were derided as "a mere handful of nuts rattling in a bag," he held out to the end for monarchy as the ideal government for France. Nothing less, he argued, could defend the nation against the perils of Jacobin democracy. Republics, born of revolution, exalted individualism to the point of anarchy, trampled the glory of France in the mud, and opened the country to German conquest. To save the nation there must be a king. He did not hesitate to advocate the use of force to overthrow the Republic. Its use is always legitimate, he maintained, when the good of the nation is at stake. A small band of resolute leaders would suffice to initiate the movement. History has usually been made by energetic minorities, and the masses provide the followers. "France loves authority and a strong arm." [25] It should be added that Maurras venerated the family, idealized peasant communities, and crusaded for a hierarchy of privileged orders. But in his mind each of these demands had the same essential purpose: to reduce the importance of the individual and to exalt the collectivity represented by the state and the nation. Like most nationalists, he was not satisfied merely with strength from within. A nation declines, he taught, when it ceases to grow. For this reason he advocated forceful expansion in Europe and an extension of the empire overseas.

Among the most vocal representatives of national resurgence movements in countries that have recently gained their independence are the two Africans Gamal Abdel Nasser and Kwame Nkrumah. Nasser was born in 1918, the son of an Egyptian postal clerk. His education was almost exclusively military. He graduated from the Royal Military Academy at the age of twenty-one and later from the Army Staff College. Among his earliest recollections are memories of rebellion—against his father, his superiors in the army, and the agents of the British protectorate. As a schoolboy in Alexandria he was thrown into jail "for political reasons." Released after a few days, he led a demonstration against the British and was wounded in the head by a police bullet. In 1948 he was sent into battle against the Israelis. Four years later he took the primary role in a movement to overthrow the Egyptian monarchy of Farouk I and to replace it eventually with a republic. General Naguib was made head of the new government, with Colonel Nasser as

[25] Quoted by Charlotte T. Muret, *French Royalist Doctrines since the Revolution.* New York, Columbia University Press, 1933, p. 275.

the power behind the scenes. Dissension between the two officers led to the deposition of Naguib in 1954. In 1956 Nasser was elected President of the Egyptian Republic on a ballot which included his name as the only candidate. Meanwhile he continued his efforts to achieve what he considered the two main objectives of the Egyptian revolution: a redistribution of large landholdings among the peasants and the termination of British and French control of the Suez Canal. By 1956 he claimed to have distributed about 500,000 acres of land, and in July of that year he nationalized the Canal. In 1958 he was proclaimed President of the United Arab Republic, consisting of Egypt and Syria. His autobiography, *Egypt's Liberation*, is reported to be one of the best-read books in foreign ministries the world over.

Nasser's conception of nationalism is much broader than the regeneration and glorification of Egypt. He certainly has had the goal of liberating his country from foreign domination and enhancing her strength and capacity for leadership. But his vision has been fixed on larger objectives. He thinks of the whole Arab world, and especially that portion of it that lies in the Middle East, as a racial and cultural unit. The interests of Egypt, he says, are inextricably linked with this region, and its interests with those of Egypt. Here are the crossroads of the world and the vast wealth in petroleum that will enable the area "to rise up to a level of dignity and undertake a positive part in building the future of mankind." [26]

Nasser dreams not merely of Pan-Arab unity but of a Pan-Islamic world under Egyptian leadership. Though he would not follow the example of the Moslem leaders of the Middle Ages and submerge the state in the cult, he clearly believes that Egypt has a mission beyond the borders of the Middle East. If she could unite in friendly cooperation the "80 million Moslems in Indonesia, the 50 million in China, the 40 million in the Soviet Union [!], the 100 million in the Middle East, and the millions in Malaya, Siam, Pakistan, and Burma," the combination would be able "to wield power wisely and without limit." [27]

[26] *Egypt's Liberation: The Philosophy of the Revolution.* Washington, Public Affairs Press, 1955, p. 88.
[27] *Ibid.*, p. 114.

The chief obstacle which looms in Nasser's mind as the barrier to his hopes is "Imperialism." He does not give it a national label, but it is clear that he means British imperialism. It was British imperialism, he says, which gave to the Jews the populated land of Palestine, "tyrannously wresting it from its rightful owners." Britain suppressed the nationalist yearnings of Moslems in Asia and of the 200 millions in darkest Africa who look to Egypt for leadership. Indeed, the anti-British orientation of Nasser's nationalism is so violent as to make one wonder whether, in the event of the liquidation of Britain's empire, he would be able to project his wrath onto a new enemy.[28]

If Nasser has dreams of dominating the black population of Africa, he will have to reckon with the ambitions of Kwame Nkrumah, Prime Minister of Ghana. Nkrumah was born in 1909, the son of a poor and illiterate goldsmith. He attended Catholic missionary schools and, with the help of relatives, was sent to school in America at Lincoln University in Pennsylvania. Here he worked at menial tasks and almost starved until he finally obtained his B.A. degree in 1939. Subsequently he studied at the University of Pennsylvania and at the London School of Economics. He became a candidate for the Ph.D. at the latter institution, but was drawn into the politics of his homeland and never finished his thesis. By 1948 he was recognized as the principal leader of the independence movement in the Gold Coast. Discontent was rife among the natives. Prices of imports were high, as a result of war-time inflation. Veterans who had returned from fighting Britain's battles demanded better housing and opportunities for employment. The repressive activities of the British police were bitterly resented. Nationalist parties and newspapers clamored for dominion status and for a union of all the British West African colonies under the ancient name of Ghana. As the climax of a series of demonstrations in 1950, Nkrumah was arrested and sentenced to a year's imprisonment at hard labor. Undaunted, he continued his agitation against the

[28] Imperialism has also served Nasser as an excuse for establishing a dictatorship. Britain, he claims, played off Egyptian parties against one another, keeping the country in turmoil. Therefore it was necessary to abolish the party system and to set up "a socialist society in which differences will be narrowed." Speech of Nasser on The Future Government of Egypt, May 19, 1955, *Middle Eastern Affairs*, VI (1955), 274–275.

British from behind the bars, using sheets of toilet paper to write editorials for his newspaper. While he was still in prison, his party won control of the Legislative Assembly. He was soon afterward released and, in 1951, was chosen Prime Minister. Six years later the united dominion of Ghana was made an independent state within the British Commonwealth.

Nkrumah is a baffling and contradictory person. He classifies himself as a Marxian Socialist and an undenominational Christian. According to his own statement, the influences most effective in shaping his mind were those of Mahatma Gandhi and Marcus Garvey. How he reconciles the two is almost beyond understanding. Garvey was a West Indian Negro journalist who came to New York in 1917 and whipped up great enthusiasm for the idea of an African Empire to which Negroes from all over the world would emigrate. After collecting $500,000 for a Black Star Steamship Line which never materialized, he was convicted of using the mails to defraud and spent two years in the Atlanta Penitentiary. Upon his release he was deported to Jamaica. His doctrines stood at the opposite pole from those of Gandhi. With his slogan of "Africa for the Africans," he preached hatred of Caucasians and envisioned an empire built on the principle of racial exclusiveness. Apparently Nkrumah admires him for imbuing the Negroes with pride in their race.

Though Nkrumah disavows any intention of driving the white men from Africa, he contends that the Negroes have a heritage of which they can be proud. He speaks of a Golden Age of the Ghana Empire, when great civilizations flourished before the beginning of the slave trade. He refers to a sometime glorious University of Timbuctoo, where eminent scholars translated their works into Hebrew and Greek and exchanged professorships with the University of Cordoba in Spain. It is not lack of brains, he argues, which has kept Africa in darkness, but the white man's oppression.

On the surface, the nationalism of Nkrumah is limited to opposition to foreign subjection. That Negroes should not have the right to govern—or even to misgovern—themselves is a condition he cannot tolerate. He abhors imperialism and quotes the old saying that "He who restricts the freedom of others can never be free himself." He denies that he is or ever has been a Communist, declares that he has no hatred for the British, and professes his opposition to revolution and violence. His program of Positive Action, on which he crusaded for independence, comprised: (1) political agitation; (2) newspaper and educational campaigns; and (3) strikes, boycotts, and noncooperation, "based on the principle of absolute nonviolence." [29] Yet there are elements in both his preaching and his practice that are hard to reconcile with these modest professions. At one time he included among his ambitions a Union of African Socialist Republics. He speaks of Five Year Plans, the mechanization of agriculture, and a program of industrialization. With respect to foreign policy, he is a "neutralist." More serious are the suspicions of totalitarianism which attach to his record. Punishments without trial, deportations, preventive arrests, and disregard for the courts give the period of his rule a number of the characteristics of a police state. Like most revolutionaries, Nkrumah has a haunting fear of counter-revolt. This insecurity, combined with his ambitions for pan-African leadership, make him excessively intolerant of opposition.

3. Racism

Political theories based on concepts of racial inequality and justifying the domination of one race by another are closely related to nationalism. In fact, it may be argued that nationalism is the principal driving force back of racism. From the ancient Hebrews to the descendants of the Boers in South Africa, exponents of the doctrine of a master race have sought to bolster their rights to conquer and rule by claiming for themselves an inherent superiority over their victims. Strong in-group feelings, arising from fear and anxiety, tempt people to exaggerate the merits of those within their own circle and to despise and degrade outsiders. An in-group may, of course, be a family, a clan, or a class; but in modern times, because of the increasing importance of the political and the military, it is more likely

[29] Bankole Timothy, *Kwame Nkrumah: His Rise to Power.* London, Allen and Unwin, 1955, p. 99.

to be a nation. Even such forms of tribalism as anti-Semitism and pan-Arabism are really species of nationalism. The foregoing explanation may seem inapplicable to white supremacy in the United States, which, of course, is a carry-over from slavery. But the enslavement of the Negro was originally a kind of external conquest, followed by abduction. In time, the conquered multiplied in their new home to outnumber their conquerors. Initially, the purpose of the enslavement was economic. But as the years passed, the position of the masters and their families came to be justified on the same grounds of inherent superiority, responsibility to civilization, and God-given right to rule which have been used by nationalists for centuries.

The modern theory of racism was largely the invention of a disgruntled French aristocrat of the nineteenth century, Count Joseph Arthur de Gobineau (1816–1882). Though born in France, he claimed to be descended from a mythical Norwegian pirate by the name of Otto Jarl. In 1853–1855, Gobineau published a four-volume *Essay on the Inequality of the Human Races*. He attempted to prove that "everything great, noble, and fruitful in the works of man on this earth" was produced by a single race whose branches had reigned in all the civilized countries of the globe. This race, he averred, was the Aryan race, which included the Greeks and the Romans, the ancient Persians, and most of the peoples of Northern and Western Europe. Its highest representatives were the modern Teutons. His theory was an amazing *potpourri* of false premises and contradictory conclusions. He assumed a multiple origin of the human species: the white man had originated in the Hindu Kush Mountains, the black man in Africa, and the yellow man in America. Each of the great races and every one of their branches, had a genius of its own, which neither climate, geography, nor economic conditions could erase. The Negroes were anarchistic individualists; the yellow men had a penchant for communism; but the white race had inborn preferences for liberalism, feudalism, parliamentarism, and benevolent imperialism.

Gobineau had difficulty making up his mind as to the effects of race mixture. On the one hand, he argued that a fusion of racial elements was essential to the development of the highest civilization. The ancient Greeks, for example, would never have achieved such excellence in the arts had they not been infiltrated with some of the aesthetic genius of the Negro. At the same time, according to Gobineau, civilizations decline because of dilution of the blood of the conquering race through intermarriage with the conquered. Mongrelization, he contended, is the chief cause of national degeneracy. And the degeneration "corresponds exactly to the quantity and quality of the new blood." [30]

The Aryanism of Gobineau was refined into a gospel of Teutonism by an Englishman who lived in Germany, Houston Stewart Chamberlain (1855–1927). Born in Southhampton, he was the son of a British admiral. Prevented by ill health from entering upon a military or naval career, he turned to the study of art, music, and philosophy, at Geneva, Dresden, and Versailles. He became a devoted admirer of Richard Wagner, settled in Bayreuth, and married Wagner's daughter. Wagner himself had made the acquaintance of Gobineau, and had been deeply impressed by the Frenchman's idolization of the blond Aryan and with his pessimistic outlook on Western civilization. A *Gobineau Vereinigung* was formed as a kind of inner group of the Wagnerian circle, and Chamberlain became its president. In 1899 he published an elaborate exposition of his theories under the title, *Foundations of the Nineteenth Century*. He supported the cause of Germany during World War I, and in 1916 was naturalized as a German citizen.

Chamberlain gave to the word *Teuton* almost as broad a meaning as Gobineau had assigned to the term *Aryan*. The ancient Persians and the people of India were not included, but nearly all the strains of modern Europe as well as the classical Greeks and Romans were alleged to have had Teutonic ancestry. Furthermore, practically every individual of genius or originality during the past 2000 years was claimed by Chamberlain for the Teutonic race. Thus the Apostle Paul was too great a man to have been a Jew. His mother, according to Chamberlain, was a Hellene (that is, a Teuton), and it is well known that great

[30] *The Inequality of the Human Races,* trans. Adrian Collins. New York, G. P. Putnam's Sons, 1915, p. 209.

men inherit their intellects from their mothers. In like manner, Dante could be proved to have been Teutonic because he had a very "expressive countenance and a cupola-like forehead." Though Chamberlain conceded that "the most genuine sons of the Teutonic race may be black-haired," his poetic imagination could describe the ideal Teuton as having "great, radiant, heavenly eyes" and lengthened skulls which active brains, "tortured by longing, had changed from the round lines of animal contentedness and extended towards the front." [31]

The influence of Chamberlain's ideas on later developments in Germany is difficult to estimate, but it must have been considerable. His *Foundations of the Nineteenth Century* made such a favorable impression on Kaiser Wilhelm II that he ordered a special appropriation to promote its distribution. Undoubtedly, Chamberlain's ideas contributed also to the growth of Nazi racism. Hitler doted on the music of Wagner, and there was much in the doleful romanticism of the Wagnerian Circle that harmonized with Nazi doctrine. It has been noted previously, however, that the Nazi racial ideology was supplied primarily by Alfred Rosenberg rather than by Chamberlain. Its flavor was East European more than it was German. Chamberlain had strong reservations against the use of the word *Aryan*. He argued that the supposed Aryans of ancient times had been a mixture of many strains, and he doubted the existence of an Aryan race. More important, Chamberlain was a Christian and accorded the world-redeeming "revelation of Christ" a place among the five foundations of the modern world. The revival of ancient German paganism, which gained the approval of most Nazi leaders, was instituted by Rosenberg, not by Chamberlain.

Racist ideas have not been confined to Europeans. The United States has also had its share of propagandists for Caucasian, and even for Nordic or Aryan, supremacy. And mountebanks and demagogues have not been its sole representatives. In his *Notes on the State of Virginia*, Thomas Jefferson characterized the Negroes as a race with "a strong and disagreeable odor," lacking the capacity for affection, and much inferior to Cau-

[31] *Foundations of the Nineteenth Century.* New York, John Lane, 1912, I, 535.

casians in reasoning. He doubted that any Negro existed with an ability to trace and comprehend the "investigations of Euclid," or to utter a thought "above the level of plain narration." In his famous debates with Stephen A. Douglas as a candidate for United States Senator, Abraham Lincoln referred to "a natural disgust in the minds of nearly all white people at the idea of an indiscriminate amalgamation of the white and black races." He admitted that he did not know what should be done with the institution of slavery. His first impulse was to free all its victims and send them to Liberia, but reflection convinced him that this was impracticable. He then asked himself in consternation, "What next? Free them and make them politically and socially our equals?" His innermost feelings revolted against this. He contended that nature had fixed a gulf between the two races which would probably prevent forever their living together in perfect equality.[32] After the outbreak of the Civil War he said nothing further on the incompatibility of the two races, but he continued to regard the preservation of the Union as more important than the abolition of slavery.

Among leading Americans of the twentieth century who have written elaborate defenses of racial superiority, the names of three stand out. They are William Allen White (1868–1944), Albert J. Beveridge (1862–1927), and David Starr Jordan (1851–1931). White was born in Emporia, Kansas, and never lived more than a few thousand feet from his birthplace. He attended the College of Emporia and Kansas State University but did not graduate from either. After some years as managing editor of another paper, he bought the Emporia *Gazette* and soon made it one of the best-known newspapers in the United States. At first a conservative, he won notice in 1895 for his editorial, "What's the Matter with Kansas?" a caustic diatribe against Populism. Later he went over to the Progressives and, in 1912, supported Theodore Roosevelt. In 1924 he ran for Governor as an independent and, though defeated, polled nearly 150,000 votes. After the beginning of World War II he became a strong advocate of an interventionist policy "short of war," and in 1940 accepted

[32] John Nicolay and John Hay, eds., *Complete Works*, II, 207, 329; III, 229.

the chairmanship of the Committee to Defend America by Aiding the Allies.

Both as a conservative and after he became a Progressive, White held forth on the subject of race superiority with an emotionalism worthy of a Gobineau or a Chamberlain. In 1899, when the United States was having its troubles with the pacification of Cuba, he declared that the Cubans would need a despotic government for many years. "Only Anglo-Saxons," he pontificated, "can govern themselves." It is their Manifest Destiny to go forth in the world as world conquerors. They are the chosen people, appointed by fate to "take possession of all the islands of the sea" and to "exterminate" the peoples they cannot subjugate.[33] Ten years later he was still convinced that Americans of Anglo-Saxon stock were the hope of the world. "The best blood of the earth," he avowed, "is here." This blood would remain "a clean, Aryan blood," because there were no hordes of inferior men gathered about to debase the stock. Anglo-Saxons in the United States were separated by two oceans from the lower races, and by "that instinctive race revulsion to cross breeding that marks the American wherever he is found." [34]

An even more vainglorious racial chauvinism was contained in the writings and speeches of Albert J. Beveridge, Progressive Senator from Indiana. Born on a farm, he devoted his boyhood and youth to rugged toil as a plowboy and to cutting and hauling lumber for the building of railroads. Despite these austerities, he found time for reading Emerson's essays, Gibbon's *Decline and Fall of the Roman Empire*, and the novels of Dickens, Scott, and George Eliot. He also managed to save nearly all his hardearned wages with a view to obtaining a college education. At the age of nineteen he entered DePauw University with total assets of fifty dollars. He carried his trunk on his back through the streets of the town to his lodging-place. In 1885 he was graduated, laden with all the honors and prizes that a small university afforded. Fourteen years later he was elected to the United States Senate, one of the youngest members ever to sit in that body. He was re-elected in 1905 and again in 1922. He

[33] Editorial, Emporia *Gazette*, March 20, 1899.
[34] *The Old Order Changeth*. New York, Macmillan, 1910, p. 252.

took part in the Insurgents' Revolt of 1910, and in 1912 supported the Progressive candidate for President. Though on the domestic scene he advocated liberal economic and social policies, he was a fanatical nationalist and imperialist.

The racism of Beveridge was slightly broader than that of White. The Hoosier Progressive at least included all the Teutons among the chosen people. Moreover, Beveridge gave to his racial chauvinism a religious flavor. It was no mere fate that had done the choosing, but God Himself. God had made the Teutonic peoples "the master organizers of this world to establish system where chaos reigns." He had given them the spirit of progress "to overwhelm the forces of reaction throughout the earth." He had made them adepts in government in order that they might rule efficiently over "savage and senile peoples." And of all the Teutonic race, He had marked the American people as the chosen nation "to finally lead in the regeneration of the world." This was America's exalted mission. God had appointed her people "trustees of the world's progress, guardians of its righteous peace." The words of the divine Master were a judgment upon the anointed nation: "Ye have been faithful over a few things; I will make you ruler over many things." [35]

The American who gave to racist theory its greatest intellectual prestige was the noted scientist and educator, David Starr Jordan. Born on a farm in western New York State, he taught in rural schools to obtain enough money to enroll in Cornell University. Majoring in botany, he did so much extra work that he was awarded the degree of Master of Science instead of the usual bachelor's degree. While still a junior, he was appointed to the faculty with the rank of instructor. After graduation he taught in a succession of small colleges and also found time to obtain the degree of Doctor of Medicine at Indiana Medical College. In 1879 he was made Professor of Natural History at Indiana University, and five years later President of that institution. He had already gained distinction as an ichthyologist, and in 1880 was appointed a member of a United States commission to study the fishes of the Pacific Coast region. In

[35] *The Meaning of the Times.* Indianapolis, Bobbs-Merrill, 1908, pp. 84–85.

1891, when Leland Stanford, mogul of Pacific railroads, decided to found a university as a memorial to his dead son, he determined to offer the presidency to the hard-driving Indiana educator. Jordan accepted and served as President of Stanford University until 1913 and as Chancellor for three years longer. Following his retirement in 1916, he devoted his energies to public affairs. As chairman of the Emergency Peace Federation, he worked desperately to keep the United States from entering World War I. In 1924 he won the Ralph Herman prize of $25,000 for the best practicable plan for preserving international peace. He was an opponent of imperialism and a stalwart champion of world federation.

As a racist Jordan had the unusual faculty of utilizing his scientific acumen to castigate other racists for their ridiculous assumptions, and then proceeding with assumptions of his own that were equally far-fetched. He pilloried attempts to prove that Jesus and Dante were Teutonic, but claimed that he had found evidence that "the present aristocratic strains of Japan" were "Aryans allied to the Greeks." [36] He considered the blood of a nation the cardinal factor determining its history. In the life of any people, he wrote, the vital differences are not matters of education but of "hereditary potentialities." He was firmly convinced that mental characteristics are as truly inheritable as texture of hair or color of skin. He recognized an almost infinite variety of ethnic types. For him, races included not merely Caucasians, Mongolians, and Negroes, but Saxons, Jews, Greeks, Serbians, Montenegrins, Italians, and many others. Each race had traits that marked it off as a separate breed. Knowing its nature would make possible a forecast of its achievements. The Saxon would make Saxon history wherever he went, the Jew would make Jewish history, and the Italian in whatever clime he might settle would "do deeds after his kind." The similarity between this gospel and some of the doctrines of the Nazis is almost embarrassingly evident.

Jordan had a sublime faith that the peoples of the world could be divided into superior and inferior types, and he naively assumed that the problem of distinguishing them was a simple

[36] *The Days of a Man.* Yonkers-on-Hudson, World, 1922, II, 58–59.

one. In general, he considered the best stocks to be those which most closely approximated the blond, Nordic type and the worst to be those at the opposite end of the scale. He could not escape the conclusion that the southern and eastern European "races" were distinctly below the cultural and moral level of such peoples as the British, the Scandinavians, and the Dutch. He despised the French as dissolute and slovenly, and the Spaniards and southern Italians as mentally backward. Even lower in the scale were the Mexicans, whom he described as "ignorant, superstitious, ill-nurtured, with little self-control and no conception of industry or thrift." [37] It seems worthy of note that, in his attitude toward peoples, Jordan was similar to Theodore Roosevelt. Neither was primarily interested in race as such but in certain attributes of character which each considered essential to national greatness. Roosevelt glorified the hairy-chested virtues of courage, manliness, and pugnacity, and admired any nation possessing these qualities regardless of its color or biological antecedents. The qualities which Jordan looked for as evidence of race superiority were the Puritan traits of stability, restraint, efficiency, initiative, and frugality. It was a curious coincidence that Jordan the pacifist and Roosevelt the militarist could bestow their admiration on much the same groups of people.

4. *Internationalism versus Cosmopolitanism*

Accurately conceived, internationalism means a system of relationships among nations or states regarded as sovereign and independent units. If we think of each state as free to conduct its relations with neighboring states as it sees fit, subject only to the restraints it imposes upon itself or to the chastisement of world opinion, we then have a clear conception of what *international* society is like. For the most part, it is a condition of anarchy. From time to time rules have been adopted or institutions created which limit the powers of individual states. But these are mere concessions granted by treaty and are subject to abrogation by any of the granting parties. Moreover, enforce-

[37] *Ibid.*, I, 638.

ment of such rules has always been difficult, and attempts to apply penalties have involved the risk and often the reality of international war.

Internationalism in its constructive and cooperative aspects has been exemplified by the Concert of Europe in the nineteenth century, the Hague arbitration tribunal, the League of Nations, and the United Nations. Among its major prophets have been Woodrow Wilson, Viscount Robert Cecil, James T. Shotwell, Aristide Briand, Winston Churchill, and Franklin D. Roosevelt. But various leaders of thought and opinion have been dissatisfied with a program of world order based on national sovereignty. Instead of a league of states, they have advocated a world political society with a central government capable of acting upon individuals rather than upon nations or states. The world, or at least the major portion of it, would become a federal republic, with agencies of law and justice in place of congresses, treaties, and alliances. Internationalism as defined above would be supplanted by cosmopolitanism or universalism, based upon the premise that the world is a unit, and that its essential components are people, not governments or states.

Numerous writers and thinkers of eminence in the twentieth century have developed theories of cosmopolitanism postulating some form of world republic. In the final chapter of his *Outline of History*, H. G. Wells criticized the League of Nations as a mere league of governments and declared that what the world needed was a "league of men." He called for the establishment of a United States of the World, with a World Constitution providing for a transfer of sovereignty from the separate states to a central authority. David Starr Jordan rang the changes on world citizenship and urged the reduction of nations to "jurisdictions," with only a limited sovereignty comparable to that of the States in the American Union. The world of the future, he insisted, should exemplify the ideal of Goethe that "Above all nations is humanity." [38] The philosopher John Dewey was also sharply critical of the accepted procedures for averting conflict. He condemned the League of Nations, mainly because of its power to invoke military and naval sanctions. The nation against which

[38] *War and Waste*. Garden City, Doubleday, 1914, p. 7.

sanctions are used, he argued, "would feel that it had yielded not to the claims of justice but to superior force, quite as much as if it had been defeated in war."[39] In fact, he contended, the employment of sanctions *is* war, no matter by what name it may be called. He proposed, therefore, an altogether different solution: the adoption of a universal agreement by which every nation would outlaw war, and the establishment of a world court to try to sentence violators. The violators, of course, would be individuals, since, under the agreement, war-making activities would be crimes, the same as any other preparations for violence.

Political and military events of recent years have given a new and stronger impetus to the movement for supra-national organization. The gathering clouds of World War II hastened the publication of Clarence Streit's *Union Now* and the launching of his plan for a federal union of the democracies. Streit was born in the town of California, Missouri, in 1896, and obtained his A.B. degree at Montana State University. He studied later at the Sorbonne and then went to Oxford as a Rhodes scholar. For nearly twenty years he was a newspaper correspondent. Since 1939 he has been president of Federal Union, Inc., and since 1946 editor of *Freedom and Union.*

Streit's plan for world government bore some resemblance to an old-fashioned alliance, since in the beginning it was to include only the democracies. But its founder had enough faith in the spread of democracy to hope that the union he advocated would become truly universal. His plan called for an organization in which individual human beings rather than states would be the units. A central government would have authority to enact laws of common importance to all the citizens of the union. Its officials would be chosen by those citizens; it would derive its authority and its revenue from them; and its coercive powers would be exercised against them exclusively. In short, it would be a union of all the democratic nations on a basis essentially the same as the federal system of the United States. Indeed, its organization was almost a duplicate of that provided by the Constitution of the American republic.

The development of atomic weapons in 1945 and the years

[39] *Characters and Events.* New York, Holt, 1929, pp. 653–54, 658.

following led a number of thoughtful individuals to conclude that nothing less than the immediate establishment of a universal republic could avert the destruction of civilization and, possibly, of man himself. Included among those who advanced this view were Albert Einstein, William O. Douglas, Robert M. Hutchins, Rexford G. Tugwell, and Norman Cousins. The most persuasive exponent of the idea, however, was probably Emery Reves. His book, *The Anatomy of Peace*, was a best-seller for many months. Reves was born in 1904, in a small village in Hungary. He studied at the universities of Berlin and Paris and received the degree of Doctor of Political Economy at the University of Zürich in 1926. After unsuccessful efforts to establish himself in journalism, he went into the publishing business in Paris and London. He founded the Cooperation Publishing Company, of which he is still president and director. He also established the Cooperation Press Service for the syndication of articles and speeches by European statesmen. In 1940 he became a British citizen, but in less than a year he emigrated to the United States and set up his publishing firm in New York City.

In the opinion of Reves, modern man is facing one of the direst tragedies that has ever overtaken the human race. Each of the most progressive and beneficent movements history has produced has gone down in failure, and every inhabitant of the earth seems destined, sooner or later, to cower in the shadows of barbarism and tyranny. Christianity has failed to accomplish even its most basic objective, that of achieving a goal of brotherly love among men of all races and nations. " 'Thou shalt not kill' cannot mean that it is a crime to kill a man of one's own nationality, but that it is a virtue—to be blessed by all Christian churches—to kill a man of the same faith, who happens to be technically the citizen or subject of another nation-state. Such an interpretation of universal moral principles is revolting." [40] But progressive movements of a secular character have failed just as dismally. Socialism would have had little appeal to the ordinary man, according to Reves, apart from its promises of freedom and equality. But its chances of redeeming those promises faded into oblivion when the one great

[40] *The Anatomy of Peace*. New York, Harper, 1945, p. 81.

nation that adopted the socialist program went over the hill to totalitarianism. It was not the state, with its instruments of coercion, that withered away in Russia; it was socialism. Lest anyone consider pinning his hopes on capitalism, Reves asserts that that system also has succumbed to disaster. By capitalism he means the nineteenth-century model, whose basic feature was a free economy. But this capitalism which glorified initiative, free enterprise, and free competition has been supplanted even in Britain and the United States by a regime of government ownership and regulation; tariffs, trusts, and cartels; and laws to prevent both prices and wages from falling to their natural levels.

What is the chief cause of these tragic failures? According to Reves, it is national sovereignty. Christianity has failed, not because men are beasts by nature, but because they live under a condition of international anarchy in which every independent people's security seems to spell insecurity for its neighbors. Socialism has degenerated into totalitarian Communism, not because the Russians have always been steeped in traditions of despotism, but because Russia has sovereign neighbors who fear her, arm themselves against her, and compel her to adopt an authoritarian government as the price of survival. That this course of action was necessary, from the Russian viewpoint, was demonstrated by the invasion of June 22, 1941. But the capitalist nations themselves are only a short distance from a similar concentration of power. Communism and fascism are sisters under the skin. Whereas Communism is the end product of socialism in our existing world of international lawlessness, fascism is the destiny of capitalism. In the judgment of Reves, no nation can avoid such a fate under the pressure of insecurity and the mad scramble to keep up with potential enemies in armaments expansion. Fear will breed hysteria and repression, and $70-billion budgets will necessitate control and regulation which can only eventuate in fascism, though it may not be given that label.

Reves admits that the situation is not totally hopeless. While there is yet time, the statesmen of the world must agree to the calling of a constitutional convention which would arrange for the transfer of sovereignty from the national units to a federal authority, comparable on a world scale to the federal republic of the United States. Relative to each other, the nations of the world are now in the same deplorable position that the thirteen American states were in following their war for independence. The United Nations of today corresponds to the American Confederation of the 1780's. Both had their origin in multilateral treaties, the parties to which were independent states. Under neither was there any transfer of sovereignty or any provision for a regime of law. Both were given the character of mere leagues of governments, whose central congresses were little different from assemblages of diplomats. As Alexander Hamilton pointed out, the "great and radical vice" of the Confederation was the principle of legislation for states or governments in their collective or corporate capacities as distinguished from legislation for individuals. The former could be enforced only by the coercion of arms, which meant war. The latter could be enforced by courts and ministers of justice.

In such comparisons, Reves believes, the statesmen of the present must read lessons for the future. They have little time, for the development of nuclear weapons has magnified the urgency of the problem. It is folly to suppose, he maintains, that the use of such weapons can be limited or controlled; nations fighting for their very existence will use everything they have. He concludes with the lugubrious suggestion that it might be better to precipitate a war between East and West over the issue of world government than to wait for such a struggle to break out over bases, prestige, or boundaries. If a horrible war must be fought, he says, let it be war "for an ideal." The end of such a struggle, he submits, would automatically terminate international wars "and bring victory for world federation." [41] He does not stop to consider, apparently, the many other things it would terminate.

The control and abatement of nationalism, and the substitution for it of an effective world organization, is undoubtedly one of the most critical problems of modern times. In a sense, it overshadows the control of nuclear weapons, since tech-

[41] *Ibid.*, p. 287.

nologically advanced nations could readily devise other instruments for destroying one another if they had the will to do so. Despite the fact that nationalism has been a danger to the world for many centuries, its nature has been only partially understood. Many people have thought of it as a beneficent force, worthy of being equated with liberalism, humanitarianism, and democracy. Statesmen as intelligent as Woodrow Wilson and Thomas G. Masaryk could believe that a world war, involving the slaughter of millions, was justifiable in order to achieve "self-determination" for Poles, Czechs, Slovaks, and Serbians. By contrast, the English liberal Catholic Lord Acton considered nationalism a blessing so long as it was not combined with political independence. Just why he considered it desirable to have any barriers separating particular groups from the rest of humanity, he did not explain.

An understanding of nationalism is complicated by the fact that the patriots of each country, while execrating the nationalism of other countries, consider their own particular brand as exalted and noble. Even psychiatrically oriented efforts to account for the irrational behavior of nations have frequently been clouded by ethnocentric bias. Usually allegations of national insanity have been confined to some enemy or potential enemy; and the results have approached the ludicrous. During World War II, a New York psychiatrist, Richard Brickner, classified the German nation as "paranoid" and recommended a course of therapy similar to that which would be applied to a psychotic individual. The British anthropologist Geoffrey Gorer traced the "compulsive and obsessive" nature of the Japanese nation to the exceedingly strict toilet training of Japanese children. In a similar manner, he has discovered the "aggressiveness" of the Russians to be the consequence of the fact that, as babies, they are swaddled so tightly as almost to preclude movement. When they become adults, they, of course, remember these restrictions, revolt against them, and seek to expand at the expense of their neighbors.

In the past, nationalism has brought benefits to some peoples in the form of enlightened self-rule and relief from oppression. We cannot overlook the cases of the United States, Switzerland, Belgium, and some of the republics of Latin America. India,

Ireland, and Israel might be cited as more recent examples. In the main, however, nationalism since the middle of the nineteenth century has been a reactionary, obscurantist movement. It has been associated with racism, parochialism, bigotry, intolerance, persecution, and fanaticism. Probably because its adherents have been obsessed with power and exaggerated pride as compensations for insecurity and anxiety, it has commonly borne fruit in aggression and sometimes in imperialism. To control or eliminate it by any means short of education in human brotherhood will be difficult so long as we have a world increasingly beset with hatreds and fears.

ADDITIONAL READINGS

Angell, Norman. *From Chaos to Control*. New York, Century, 1933.

————. *The Fruits of Victory*. New York, Century, 1921.

————. *The Unseen Assassins*. New York, Harper, 1932.

Barzun, Jacques. *Race: A Study in Modern Superstition*. New York, Harcourt, 1937.

Boas, Franz. *Race and Democratic Society*. New York, J. J. Augustin, 1945.

Burns, E. M. *The American Idea of Mission*. New Brunswick, Rutgers University Press, 1957.

————. *David Starr Jordan: Prophet of Freedom*. Stanford, Calif., Stanford University Press, 1953.

Buthman, William C. *The Rise of Integral Nationalism in France*. New York, Columbia University Press, 1939.

Byrnes, Robert F. *Anti-Semitism in Modern France*. New Brunswick, Rutgers University Press, 1950.

Cousins, Norman. *Modern Man Is Obsolete*. New York, Viking, 1946.

————. *Who Speaks for Man?* New York, Macmillan, 1953.

Grant, Madison. *The Passing of the Great Race*. New York, Scribner, 1916.

Hankins, F. H. *The Racial Basis of Civilization*. New York, Knopf, 1926.

Hayes, C. J. H. *Essays on Nationalism*. New York, Macmillan, 1926.

————. *France, a Nation of Patriots*. New York, Columbia University Press, 1930.

————. *The Historical Evolution of Modern Nationalism*. New York, R. R. Smith, 1931.

Kohn, Hans. *The Idea of Nationalism*. New York, Macmillan, 1944.

————. *Nationalism: Its Meaning and History*. Princeton, Van Nostrand, 1955.

————. *Prophets and Peoples: Studies in Nineteenth Century Nationalism*. New York, Macmillan, 1946.

Meyer, Cord, Jr. *Peace or Anarchy*. Boston, Little, Brown, 1947.

Montagu, Ashley. *Man's Most Dangerous Myth: The Fallacy of Race*. New York, Harper, 1952.

Myrdal, Gunnar. *An American Dilemma: The Negro Problem and Modern Democracy*. New York, Harper, 1944. Two vols.

Russell, Bertrand. *Why Men Fight*. New York, Century, 1917.

Russell, F. M. *Theories of International Relations*. New York, Appleton-Century-Crofts, 1936.

Schuman, Frederick L. *The Commonwealth of Man*. New York, Knopf, 1952.

Snyder, Louis L. *The Meaning of Nationalism*. New Brunswick, Rutgers University Press, 1954.

Wiggam, A. E. *The Fruit of the Family Tree*. Indianapolis, Ind., Bobbs-Merrill, 1924.

XV

The Gospel of Force
and Its Critics

In the contemporary world, nationalism, force, and conquest seem almost an indissoluble trinity. But this has not always been the case. Aristotle was a nationalist to the extent that he upheld the superiority of Greeks over barbarians; yet he opposed militarism and conquest and insisted upon drastic limitation of the size of the state. Fichte idolized the Prussian nation but advocated a *closed* state as the best means of conserving the national strength and avoiding dangerous involvements. Few would deny that the nationalism of Gandhi equaled in intensity that of any contemporary leader, yet no one would accuse him of advocating physical force or imperialism. Such figures, though, must be stacked up against the multitude of drum-beating prophets of national glory in modern times who have believed in expansion, force, and aggression as the justifiable means for achieving their aims. Since these militant nationalists are usually fanatics, they are impatient with the gradual methods of education, persuasion, and compromise. They demand short cuts which usually can be achieved only by force. In many cases they have mingled idealism with economic greed and ambition for power. In other instances they have been driven by inner compulsions of which they themselves have known little.

1. Imperialism

Historians recognize that imperialism underwent a revival and a change of character in the final quarter of the nineteenth century. The new imperialism was a product of the Industrial Revolution and was largely confined to quests for new markets and opportunities for investment in Asia and Africa. Unlike the imperialism of the sixteenth, seventeenth, and eighteenth centuries, it had no purpose of acquiring bullion to enrich the treasury of the mother country. The lands it coveted were territories rich in iron, copper, petroleum, manganese, and wheat, with opportunities for investment of surplus capital. But the objects of the new imperialism were not exclusively economic. National pride played a part in it also; and so did the desire of zealous Christians to convert the heathen. Military and naval chieftains demanded bases, coaling stations, and new sources of able-bodied recruits. Politicians argued the need for territories where surplus inhabitants of the mother country could settle without being "lost to the flag." Few ever migrated, but the argument continued to be used that colonies were necessary to provide relief for population congestion in the developed nations.

Justifications of imperialism in the twentieth century have been almost as numerous as apologias for nationalism. Curiously, some of the most vocal of the prophets of empire were Americans. One explanation was undoubtedly the newness of American imperialism. It was a fresh adventure which opened up vistas of power and grandeur to a youthful nation. But this was not the sole motivation. Among American expansionists at the beginning of the century were some of the world's most confirmed racists. They preached more luridly even than the British the right of the Anglo-Saxon, or the Teuton, to conquer and rule inferior peoples. Six days after the declaration of war on Spain, Albert J. Beveridge pronounced the American people "a conquering race," who must obey their blood and occupy new lands. God had ordained it so; He had made it a part of His infinite plan that "debased civilizations and decaying races" should disappear "before the higher civilization of the nobler and more virile types of man." [1]

The distinguished constitutional lawyer John W. Burgess (1844–1931), who taught at Columbia University for more than thirty years, also trumpeted the rights of the chosen nations. The Teutonic peoples, he argued, have a mission to carry political civilization into those parts of the world inhabited by "unpolitical and barbaric races," and to insist that they become civilized. If such races cannot achieve this goal by their own efforts, "they must submit to the powers that can do it for them." If they remain recalcitrant in their barbarism, the civilized state "may clear the territory of their presence and make it the abode of civilized man." The latter need not worry about the morality of such a policy "when it becomes manifestly necessary." No rights are thereby violated which are not petty and trivial in comparison with the "transcendent right and duty" of the civilized state "to establish political and legal order everywhere." The civilized states should, of course, refrain from hasty and irresponsible action in seizing power, but they have no obligation to await an invitation from misgoverned or incompetent states. They themselves are the best judges of the proper time and occasion for intervening "for the execution of their great world duty." To shirk their responsibility in this matter would be disloyalty to their mission as the uplifters and guardians of the human race.[2]

Not all American imperialists grounded their theories on dogmas of race superiority. Brooks Adams, youngest son of Lincoln's ambassador to Great Britain, envisioned a gigantic economic struggle among the powers of the world for control of markets and vital resources. All were caught as in a maelstrom, and to resist moving with the current spelled destruction. The explanation stemmed from the fact that every industrialized nation was glutted with products. Its prosperity and even survival depended upon finding markets to absorb the surplus. Adams urged that America join in this competition, even at the risk of war with

[1] *The Meaning of the Times*, p. 42.
[2] *Political Science and Comparative Constitutional Law*. Boston, Ginn, 1890, I, pp. 44–48.

Germany, Japan, Russia, and possibly Britain.

Admiral Mahan also found justification for imperialism, for the most part, on non-racist grounds. But instead of seeing in it a danger of war, he regarded it as an instrument of peace, for his own country, at least. America should make herself strong by acquiring strategic possessions to give her command of the sea. A preparedness to fight and a warlike spirit were the safest insurance against attack. Like John W. Burgess, he made political capacity and the interests of civilization the tests of a people's claims to independence. The right of any people to independence is not an indefeasible right, he contended, but is subordinate to "the natural right of the world at large that resources should not be left idle, but be utilized for the general good." Failure to contribute to this larger result justifies, he asserted, "compulsion from outside." Nor need any tenderness be shown to corrupt or incompetent governments. They should be "discontinued" as unworthy institutions by the bearers of the higher civilization.[3]

It is commonly assumed that German imperialism, in our century, was derived from the teachings of Treitschke. The assumption is correct, in part. The noted German historian was almost morbidly envious of the success of the British in extending their dominion over a fourth of the globe. This achievement had given them an inestimable advantage, for a common language is the basis of a prosperous trade. A nation never quite loses a colony which is bound to her by speech and culture, he argued, "even if the political bond be snapped." Moreover, the acquisition of colonies is an evidence of national growth, and only states of impressive size and power hold any promise for the future. The small state is an absurdity in an age of ferocious power struggles for domination of the earth. Therefore, Germany must see to it that the outcome of her next major war will be "the acquisition of colonies by any possible means." At times Treitschke wrote as if he disparaged overseas possessions and preferred the acquisition of territories contiguous to the motherland. But there is evidence that he had doubts about the value

[3] *The Interest of America in Sea Power, Present and Future*, pp. 52–53, 307–8.

of neighboring territories. At least, he was critical of German expansion into such provinces as Livonia and Kurland, on the border of East Prussia. Here the Teutonic immigrants formed only a thin crust over the mass of the inhabitants, who remained "ungermanized." The only way to prevent them from becoming a danger to their conquerors was to keep them "in as uncivilized a condition as possible." [4]

The imperialist theory of the *enfant terrible* of pre-Nazi Germany, Friedrich von Bernhardi, was quite similar to that of Treitschke, whom he often quoted. Both insisted upon the absolute necessity of a colonial empire, to be obtained, if necessary, by a war in which Germany would defeat her enemies. But Bernhardi was more jealous of France than he was of Britain, and he exaggerated to a greater degree the Slavic menace. His proposals with respect to expansion in Europe were almost entirely defensive. He thought that Germany should have full control over the mouth of the Rhine, but he referred to no other European annexations. The real keys to German greatness, he contended, were to be found in Africa and, to a lesser extent, in Asia and Oceania. A vast colonial empire, carved out of the fertile lands of these areas, would secure "to German nationality and the German spirit throughout the globe that high esteem which is due them." [5] What is more, it would provide homes under the German flag for the million new inhabitants added each year to the German population. It would guarantee to the fatherland ample markets and abundant sources of foodstuffs and raw materials. It would thereby assure a livelihood to the working classes and new opportunities for employment to German engineers, merchants, public-health experts, and technicians. In the future, as Bernhardi saw it, the importance of Germany would depend on two factors: "firstly, how many millions of men in the world speak German? secondly, how many of them are politically members of the German Empire?" [6]

The imperialism of Hitler bore only a remote relationship to the theories of Treitschke and Bernhardi. Like them, he stressed

[4] *Politics*, I, 119, 122.
[5] *Germany and the Next War*, p. 81.
[6] *Ibid.*, p. 83.

the imperious necessity of more territory for Germany to supply the needs of her growing population. In common with them, also, he justified the seizure of territory by force. Nations that shrank from bloodletting, for reasons of cowardice or humanity, were doomed to decay and perish. But, paradoxical as it may seem, Hitler was no bold adventurer eager to strike out for distant conquests that would provide the foundation of a world empire. He was an anxious, frightened man with feelings of uncertainty that bound him close to the motherland. He could experience a sense of security only by pushing the boundaries of his own country farther outward. As a militarist, he longed for the safety of defense in depth. Finally, it is necessary to take into account his special concern for the economic and social organization of Germany. He abhorred both urbanization and industrialization. He had no interest in a flourishing international trade or in colonies as sources of vital materials. What he wanted was *Lebensraum* on Germany's frontiers where more and more peasants could find homes for themselves. He considered trade and manufacturing unhealthy, and the existing disproportion between urban and rural population a prime cause of Germany's woes. The Nazi concept of "blood and soil" reflected a primitivism which did not harmonize with the conventional pattern of imperialism.

It seems almost indisputable that Hitler's expansionism was not derived from the familiar sources. Instead, it was a product mainly of the peculiar lucubrations of Alfred Rosenberg, who also inspired Hitler's racism. Rosenberg believed that Soviet Russia was a ramshackle state, that, in a crisis, the Russian people would not support their government, and that vast expanses of Soviet territory could easily be conquered by Germany. Moreover, if Germany moved boldly she could obtain the support of Great Britain. The territory which Rosenberg thought especially desirable was the Ukraine. Here was a rich granary where millions of good German peasants could find lands to cultivate. As Hitler said later, Germany in possession of the Ukraine would "swim in plenty." With such a vista before him, the Fuehrer spoke scornfully of the Cameroons and other African colonies. European states possessing such empires, he said, were "comparable to pyramids standing on their points." How much better, he exclaimed, to conquer land at Russia's expense and thus give, "with the help of the German sword, the soil to the plow and the daily bread to the nation." [7]

A survey of modern imperialist thought would not be complete without consideration of the most popular critic of imperialism, J. A. Hobson (1858–1940). By a strange quirk of history, his reasoned arguments against imperialism provided the base for the accepted Communist theory of empire and, at the same time, became a virtual gospel for anti-imperialist liberals. Hobson was born in Derby, England, and graduated from Lincoln College, Oxford. For ten years he taught English literature and economics for the extension divisions of Oxford and London Universities. After 1897 he devoted his energies exclusively to research and writing, producing more than a dozen volumes on economics and related subjects. Though a confirmed socialist, he was influenced more by Ruskin than by Marx, and consequently advocated nationalization only of "standardized" industries, leaving those involving personal taste and skill to private initiative. As an economist, he anticipated some of the theories later made famous by Lord Keynes. In other words, he taught that "underconsumption" is the principal cause of depressions. Because of gross inequality in the distribution of income, a tendency toward over-saving results on the part of a wealthy minority. The remainder of the national income is distributed in the form of wages and salaries to the great multitude of workers, farmers, and clerical employees. For the vast majority it constitutes nothing more than a bare subsistence. As a consequence, their consuming power remains so low that there is seldom a sufficient market within a country for the goods its factories produce. Production therefore outruns consumption, and shutdowns are the inevitable result. Hobson's teachings on this subject found little favor with the academic economists of his time, and he was never offered a professorship in any British university. Recognition of his economic insight did not come until Keynes paid him handsome tribute in the 1930's.

Hobson conceived of imperialism as an unmitigated evil. Its

[7] *Mein Kampf*, pp. 182–83.

practitioners were "parasites" and "harpies" who sucked the blood of their own compatriots and of the colonial natives as well. Its fruits were not simply exploitation but militarism, corruption, despotism, and war. It was the surest road to the destruction of democracy and of all that is good in nationalism. In explaining the origin of imperialism, Hobson adhered to a rigid economic determinism. He rejected all theories of the White Man's Burden, Manifest Destiny, and missions to civilize and Christianize as mere window-dressing. He agreed with James Mill that imperialism is nothing but "a vast system of outdoor relief for the upper classes." They covet new markets as dumping grounds for surplus manufactured products. They desire monopolistic control of rich sources of raw materials. But most of all, according to Hobson, they demand opportunities for investment at more profitable returns than they can obtain on their capital in their own country. Completely oblivious of the cost to the nation in guaranteeing and protecting their holdings, they plunge into reckless adventures in unstable areas from motives of sheer greed. Pierpont Morgan, for example, made several million dollars for himself and his friends through handling "the public financial arrangements for the Philippine war." [8]

Hobson deprecated imperialism all the more because he considered it so unnecessary. As Sir Norman Angell was also to prove several years later,[9] he demonstrated that a nation does not need to annex a territory in order to trade with it, or to gain access to its resources. In fact, he showed that there is no correlation whatever between political sovereignty and economic transactions. The trade between France and Germany, for instance, far exceeded that between either country and its colonies. The same was true of Britain and the United States, and the United States and Canada. The distinctive feature of the new imperialism, from the commercial standpoint, is that it adds to modern empires tropical and subtropical territories with which the total trade is "small, precarious, and unprogressive." [10] Nor

[8] *Imperialism: A Study.* London, Allen and Unwin, 1902, p. 57.
[9] *The Great Illusion.* New York, Putnam, 1910.
[10] *Imperialism: A Study,* p. 38.

would he concede the necessity of imperialism as an outlet for surplus population. He denied, to begin with, that the great industrial nations were overcrowded. He admitted that they were densely populated, but he contended that specialization of industry enabled them to support large numbers of inhabitants. He asserted, moreover, that their standard of living was higher than that of countries more sparsely settled. He foresaw, in addition, a leveling-off of their rate of growth, and predicted that by midcentury their populations would be stationary. Finally, he showed the lack of historical support for the acquisition of colonies as a safety-valve for population congestion. Of the total emigrants who went out from Great Britain in the nineteenth century, more than half settled in non-British territories, and only an infinitesimal fraction in colonies acquired under the new imperialism.

In place of imperialism, Hobson advocated alternatives which he considered much more salutary and less dangerous. He would have each nation reorganize its economy in such a way as to reduce inequality within the country and to destroy the opportunities to profit and plunder at the expense of foreigners. "The only safety of nations," he wrote, "lies in removing the unearned increments of income from the possessing classes, and adding them to the wage-income of the working classes or to the public income, in order that they may be spent in raising the standard of consumption." [11] He considered over-saving by the wealthy minority the economic taproot of imperialism. Because they were collecting much more income than they could conveniently spend, capital was a drug on the market. Its possessors therefore sought to invest it in underdeveloped areas and urged that their own government annex such territories to facilitate their schemes. It was time to call a halt, Hobson maintained, to this system under which the welfare of a whole nation was subordinated to the interests of a grasping few who would stop at nothing, not even war, to enhance their profits. What he proposed as a remedy fell little short of economic nationalism. Though he recognized the value of foreign trade, he was not willing to purchase it at the price of war or of exploitation, either at home or abroad. Let

[11] *Ibid.*, p. 89.

each nation, he suggested, cultivate its own garden scientifically and intensively, utilizing all its resources, and allowing no land to be idle because of some dream of greener pastures in distant regions. Let the government confiscate unearned income and add it to the consuming power of the masses. Factories will then hum with activity to meet the increased demand, and there will be work and prosperity for all. The modest amount of capital produced can be absorbed domestically, and foreign trade can be limited to those articles which cannot be produced at home. Neither trade nor investment will operate as causes of international rivalry or foreign conquest.

In 1916 Vladimir Lenin made use of Hobson's teachings in building the foundations of a Bolshevist theory of imperialism. He described the growth of capitalism as an evolution through four stages: from entrepreneurial capitalism, to monopoly capitalism, to finance capitalism, to imperialism. Though he differed from Hobson in regarding imperialism as the ultimate stage of capitalism, he agreed with him in considering the conquest of colonies as the direct result of the possession of excess capital by a wealthy and greedy minority. Imperialism was therefore the consequence of an unfair distribution of income, and the logical remedy for it was the abolition of the profit system and the establishment of socialism. This explanation is still the accepted one in Marxist-Leninist circles, according to available evidence. That the Communist nations and the Soviet Union, in particular, have pursued policies of aggrandizement and expansion since World War II apparently does not strike the Marxist-Leninist theorists as inconsistent with their professions of "anti-imperialist" beliefs.

The doctrines of Hobson and Lenin have been called into question by the events of recent times. For example, imperialism is now practiced by countries with a deficiency of capital, whose economies are just beginning to emerge from a primitive agricultural stage. Characteristic specimens can be found among the Arab nations of the Middle East. Perhaps more significant is an important non-economic factor in present-day imperialism which both Hobson and Lenin failed to foresee. Soviet imperialism in the Balkans and in East Central Europe is not prompted by a demand by Russian citizens for opportunities to invest surplus capital, nor does the United States keep possession of Okinawa and Guam for any similar reason. The motivation in all such cases is strategic. The territories mentioned have military value for either offensive or defensive purposes or both. They will therefore doubtless continue to be held for the advantages they confer in a power struggle between two worlds.

2. Power Politics

The phrase power politics generally conveys a number of ideas. It suggests, first of all, the approach of the realist toward international affairs. The student of international politics, it is assumed, should eschew idealism, sentimentality, and utopian dreams of a perfect world. He should leave morality to theologians and philosophers and center his attention upon the hard facts of struggles for survival, power, and aggrandizement. The only principle governing these struggles that has any meaning is the principle that the end justifies the means. Power politics also involves the idea that the world of nations or independent states is a pack of wolves. Each is intent upon gaining advantages at the expense of the rest. No law controls them, for there is no semblance of an international sovereign who alone could make such a law. There is no restraint whatever except mutual fear of each other's weapons. The traditional concept of power politics seems to suggest that war and preparation for war are the normal patterns of behavior among nations, that combat is a healing and regenerating influence, and that when fighting breaks out, "there is no substitute for victory." Even devastation, if it leads to a speedy triumph, is commonly considered justifiable.

The gospel of power politics is generally regarded as of German origin. Students in England and America have long been familiar with the teaching of Karl von Clausewitz that war is a continuation of diplomacy by other means; with the ponderous piety of Field Marshal von Moltke that "War is an element in the order of the world ordained by God"; with the warning of Treitschke that "Weakness must always be condemned as the most disastrous and despicable of crimes, the unforgivable sin of politics"; [12] and with the gentle admonition of Kaiser Wilhelm II to a regiment of his soldiers departing for China at the time of the Boxer Rebellion: "Use your weapons in such a way that for a thousand years no Chinese shall dare to look upon a German askance."

But Britains and Americans have not been so familiar perhaps with similar preachments by their own countrymen. Theodore Roosevelt wrote that "By war alone can we acquire those virile qualities necessary to win in the stern strife of actual life." John Ruskin declared that he had found that all great nations "were nourished in war, and wasted by peace; taught by war, and deceived by peace; trained by war, and betrayed by peace." [13] One of Britain's most noted military writers, Colonel F. N. Maude, avowed that unless "war is the divinely appointed means by which environment may be readjusted until ethically 'fittest' and 'best' become synonymous, the outlook for the human race is too pitiable for words." Sir John Fisher, First Sea Lord of the Admiralty, provided an equally interesting gem: "The Essence of War is Violence. Moderation in War is imbecility. . . . You hit first, you hit hard, and keep on hitting. You have to be Ruthless, Relentless, and Remorseless." It is noteworthy that this lovable old sea-dog was an idol of the British nation and the recipient of many honors. By a supreme irony, he participated as a delegate in the First Hague Peace Conference. [14]

One of the doughtiest champions of power politics in our own time is Sir Winston Churchill. He not only preaches it, but, as the exigencies of national politics have provided the opportunity, he has practiced it. Though one of the most venomous haters of Communism, he did not hesitate for a moment to embrace Russia as an ally, on June 22, 1941, when Hitler invaded the Soviet Union. With the same alacrity, five years later, he traveled to the United States to urge, in effect, the formation of an Anglo-

[12] *Politics*, I, 95.
[13] "War," *The Crown of Wild Olives*. New York, John Wiley & Sons, 1886, pp. 89–90.
[14] The quotations in this paragraph, except where otherwise indicated, are taken from Kirby Page, *National Defense: A Study of the Origin, Results and Prevention of War*. New York, Farrar and Rinehart, 1931.

American alliance to curb the growing menace of Soviet power. He regards force as the basic element in relations among states, and he thinks of counter-force as its only corrective. He has long believed that the nineteenth-century balance of power, based on the strategic and economic might of the British Empire, was the ideal system for maintaining peace. Undoubtedly, this belief was a potent factor in strengthening his resistance to grants of self-government to British dependencies.

Although Churchill venerates power and considers force the appropriate instrument to keep nations from running amok, he is no Theodore Roosevelt or Heinrich von Treitschke, glorifying war as a good in itself. Instead, he thinks of it as a means to be used when everything else fails. But, when necessary, he would employ it relentlessly. He believes that an enemy should first be reduced to utter helplessness and then treated generously. Ireland should have been conquered before being granted Home Rule. The General Strike should have been smashed as a prerequisite to liberal concessions to the workers. Germany should have been starved in 1918 before being restored to strength as a counterweight against Russia. Such preachments reflect Churchill's addiction to the gospel of force as the remedy for disorder and the preventive of rebellion. Though he condemns pacifism as a "base and perverted conception," in reality he is condemning passivity. Far from objecting to the pursuit of peace as an end in itself, he approves of it. But he denies that a "do-nothing" policy is the way to achieve it. On the contrary, he insists upon positive, constructive procedures of diplomacy, negotiation, alliances, and counter-alliances as alternatives to an appeal to the sword. He would not even rule out appeasement. "Appeasement in itself," he says, "may be good or bad according to the circumstances. Appeasement from weakness and fear is alike futile and fatal. Appeasement from strength is magnanimous and noble and might be the surest and perhaps the only path to world peace." [15] Despite his bitterness toward Communism, he is not horrified by the idea of entering into agreements with the Soviet government. He believes that in a world dominated by two snarling giants, each threatening to destroy

[15] Colin R. Coote, ed., *A Churchill Reader*, p. 156.

the other, negotiation is the sole alternative to war. And he thinks it safe to assume that the Soviets will keep their bargains as long as it is in their interest to do so.

To find numerous expositors of power politics, in these days when its doctrines appear to be so vividly portrayed in events, is not difficult. Edward Hallett Carr, onetime Assistant Editor of the London *Times* and, since 1955, fellow of Trinity College, Cambridge, is a conspicuous example. In *The Twenty Years' Crisis*, written on the eve of World War II, he admitted the existence of an international morality, but he allotted it a distinctly inferior place as a regulator of the conduct of states. Since there is no sovereign to enforce it, he pointed out, no one expects it to be really effective. He concluded, therefore, that the real foundation of peace and order in the international community is the power relationships that happen to exist at a particular time. For example, the Locarno Treaty operated successfully for ten years, not because of the idealism behind it, but because it corresponded to the power situation then obtaining in western Europe.

A better-known expounder of similar ideas is Walter Lippmann. In various writings, beginning as far back as 1915, Lippmann has defended the thesis that plans for national security and world order must always be consonant with the realities of power. He criticizes most of the formulators of policy in American history for neglecting this principle, for extending American obligations far beyond the ability of the nation to enforce them. He considers Theodore Roosevelt almost the only exception. Roosevelt recognized the need for a Panama Canal and acted accordingly; he enlarged the navy and used it as a weapon of diplomacy; he intervened in the First Moroccan Crisis to prevent Germany from gaining a foothold in North Africa. But Lippmann includes other elements in his concept of power politics. Nations interested in world peace must "take the precaution to become members of an indisputably powerful combination." He admonishes the United States especially to abandon its traditional dislike of entangling alliances and to take the initiative in forming alliances of its own. To be a member of an alliance "which can be depended upon to act together, and, when challenged, to fight together," he says, is to achieve the highest degree of security attainable in a world composed of sovereign states.[16] He defends the importance of a balance of power, but not the conventional version of two evenly matched alliances. What he really desires is a balance in favor of our own aggregation of power.

Since World War II the most influential purveyor of power-politics doctrine has been Hans J. Morgenthau. Born in Coburg, Germany, in 1904, he was educated for the law, graduating *magna cum laude* from the University of Munich and *summa cum laude* from the University of Frankfurt. After practicing law for three years, he joined the faculty of the University of Frankfurt. In 1932 he became Instructor in Political Science at the University of Geneva, and three years later Professor of International Law at the International Institute in Madrid. In 1936 he came to the United States and was admitted to citizenship in 1943. Meanwhile, he taught political science at Brooklyn College and at the University of Kansas City. Since 1949 he has been Professor of Political Science and Director of the Center for the Study of American Foreign Policy at the University of Chicago. He has also taught at Harvard, Northwestern, and at the University of California.

Whereas Lippmann maintains that the true interest of the United States lies in preventing any nation *in* Europe from gaining a preponderance of power *outside* of Europe, Morgenthau identifies American security with *balanced* power in Europe itself. He would obviously welcome a restoration of the equilibrium maintained by the *Pax Britannica,* but he recognizes that any such reversal of history would be impossible. For a political revolution has transformed the world. Instead of a multitude of states, which Britain could manipulate to preserve a balance in her own interest, there are now two giants, each of them so strong that no third force can exert a decisive influence. The only alternative, therefore, for the nations interested in peace and stability is to follow the leadership of the United States and to insist that she become strong enough to deter aggression but not so strong as to tempt her to be arrogant and unwilling to negotiate with her opponent. As Morgenthau sees it, negotiation will eventually

[16] *U. S. Foreign Policy: Shield of the Republic.* New York, Pocket Books, 1943, pp. 73, 76.

become necessary. Competition in armaments and the mutual recriminations of the cold war cannot continue indefinitely. The anxiety and tension will become intolerable. The threat of ever more potent weapons will tend to make people desperate. In addition, many areas of both Europe and Asia are unstable, and sooner or later in one of them an explosion will occur comparable in effect to the assassination at Sarajevo. As a consequence, according to Morgenthau, the choice is between negotiation and war. In reality, the latter is no choice at all, for war has become completely irrational, a synonym for the destruction of mankind. Morgenthau would therefore have the Western Allies begin to bargain on a broad front with the Soviet government as soon as possible. Our statesmen would seek to discover what our opponents need and want in order to be secure, and then strive to accommodate such needs and wants to our own security requirements. Like Churchill, he would not rule out appeasement—from strength—or even a division of the world into spheres of influence.

From the foregoing discussion it might appear that Morgenthau is less a theorist of power politics than he is an advocate of peace even at the price of valuable concessions to one's enemy. Without doubt he does place a high premium on peace, but he believes that the methods most likely to succeed in obtaining it are the methods of the political realist. International politics, he maintains, "is an unending struggle for power in which the interests of individual nations must necessarily be defined in terms of power." [17] The international community is a Hobbesian arena of perpetual conflict or threat of conflict, in which the only law is the law of the jungle. There can be no other, for there is no supranational sovereign to create it. The primary cause of the weakness and failure of American foreign policy has been the illusion that nations are bound by the same principles of morality and justice regarded by civilized men as binding upon individuals. The invocation of such principles has been "a magnificent instrument for marshaling public opinion in support of war and warlike policies—and for losing the peace." [18] Its fruits have been such travesties as "making the world safe for democracy," "un-

[17] *In Defense of the National Interest.* New York, Knopf, 1951, p. 13.
[18] *Ibid.*, p. 4.

conditional surrender," and relegation of nations to outer darkness simply because they are Communist. We should recognize that ideologies have no more significance in international relations than moral abstractions. The real enemy of the United States in the contemporary world is not Communism, but Russian imperialism. Communism is simply an instrument for advancing imperialism. Under the conditions obtaining since World War II, Russia would probably be no less dangerous if her government were dominated by Tsarist reactionaries or Milyukov liberals. The real problem confronting us is not atheism or a threat to our democratic liberties, but the same danger to our national security which has always appeared when the balance of power is upset in Europe.[19]

3. Geopolitics

More recent in origin than the theory of power politics is its close relative, geopolitics. Whereas power politics as a clearly defined concept dates back into the nineteenth century, geopolitics did not gain recognition until about the end of World War I. Whether geopolitics grew out of power politics is doubtful; yet the two have so many elements in common that geopolitics might almost be considered a subspecies of power politics. Both fix their attention upon factors of power—in the one case, upon political and military might; in the other, primarily upon size and location of territory. Neither pays any deference to sentiment, ideology, or ideals. The geopolitician is just as much a realist as is the power politician. Finally, both assume the continued existence of international rivalry, struggle, and war. International law and morality are fictions. The community of states is red in tooth and claw, and the only element that really counts is superior strength.

The term "geopolitics," or *Geopolitik*, as the Germans call it,

[19] Ideas quite similar to those of Morgenthau were expressed by Herman Finer in *America's Destiny*. New York, Macmillan, 1947. Dean Acheson, in *Power and Diplomacy*. Cambridge, Mass., Harvard University Press, 1958, also indicates a general adherence to the Morgenthau point of view. The title of his book, however, is a misnomer. He places all of the emphasis on power, with scarcely a hint of negotiation or conciliation.

was invented by a Swede, Rudolf Kjellen (1864–1922). Kjellen belonged to a small group who believed that the destiny of their country lay in a union with a greater Germany as a step toward mastery of Europe and eventually world domination. He conceived of a vastly expanded German empire extending from the Baltic Sea to the Persian Gulf, and from Riga to Dunkerque. The title "father of *Geopolitik*," however, is not commonly assigned to Kjellen, but to his older contemporary, Friedrich Ratzel (1844–1904), a geographer at the University of Munich. His central idea was the doctrine that living-space is the infallible key to national power. He seems to have interpreted his own nation's requirements in this regard quite generously, for he taught that our planet is so small that it really provides adequate space for only one nation.

Scarcely any political theory has been the monopoly of a single nation or region. Geopolitics is not an exception. Almost at the same time that Kjellen and Ratzel were spinning out their doctrines in Central Europe, a few Englishmen were arriving at similar conclusions. Foremost among them was Sir Halford Mackinder (1861–1947). His principal work, *Democratic Ideals and Reality*, was published in 1919, but it did not attract much interest until 1942, when the German armies had deeply penetrated Soviet territory in a desperate struggle for control of Eurasia. Mackinder was born in Gainsborough, England, and educated at Christ Church, Oxford. In 1886 he became a barrister of the Inner Temple. From 1903 to 1908 he was Director of the London School of Economics and Political Science. From 1910 to 1922 he served in Parliament, and in 1926 he became a member of the Privy Council. In his later career he was Vice President of the Royal Geographical Society and a Gold Medalist of the American Geographical Society.

Mackinder's geopolitics was summed up in a famous epigram which he originated early in the twentieth century:

> Who rules East Europe commands the Heartland:
> Who rules the Heartland commands the World-Island:
> Who rules the World-Island commands the World.[20]

[20] *Democratic Ideals and Reality*. New York, Holt, 1942, p. 150.

By the World-Island Mackinder meant the great land mass of Europe, Asia, and Africa which, he argued, constitutes a single continent, not three. The World-Island, he insisted, is the true fulcrum of world power. The Western Hemisphere is simply a lesser island, inferior in proportions, manpower, and resources. By the Heartland he meant that vast lowland plan which extends from the Volga Basin in the west to Lake Baikal in the east, and from the Arctic Ocean on the north to the Himalayas on the south. He thought of it as a virtually impregnable area, inaccessible by sea, and rich enough in resources to be practically self-sufficient. Since East Europe is the gateway to this Heartland, it followed that any European power able to conquer western Russia would control not only the Heartland but ultimately the world. It was undoubtedly this warning which brought Mackinder's book to the attention of Western statesmen and military theorists in 1942. Apparently, they did not consider seriously the dangers to themselves inherent in Russia's position with respect to the Heartland and the World-Island.

Mackinder conceived of world history as a perpetual struggle between the land-based powers and the seafaring powers. For the past four hundred years, he pointed out, a struggle of this character has been going on, resulting in a series of world wars. The land-based powers have been striving to break the barriers imposed upon them by nature and by their political enemies. The seafaring powers have been striving to protect their rich valleys and advantageously located coasts and islands against the hungry hordes from the interior. Until recently, the scales were heavily weighted on the side of the oceanic nations, especially because of their power of blockade. Technological advancement, however, has provided the nations of the interior with weapons just as deadly as those of their opponents, while the spread of industrialization has brought a considerable immunity to the effects of blockade. Mackinder could see no remedy for the constant threat of a renewal of this series of world wars except in a restoration of the balance of power. For this reason he advocated, on the eve of the Peace Settlement of 1919, the erection of a tier of independent states between Germany and Russia. He thought it vital that the territorial division of East Europe "should be into three and not into two state-systems." [21] The architects of the Peace proceeded to establish such a division, with what lamentable results we are only too painfully aware. Perhaps the tier of states was not made strong enough to be an effective weight in the Russo-German balance. Perhaps it was inevitable that Russia and Germany would make a deal for control of the territory between them, and that, sooner or later, one or the other would completely dominate it. Nevertheless, the idea of a balance among three or more states or combinations of states still has a powerful appeal, as is evidenced by contemporary neutralist demands for a "third force" to hold the scales between East and West.

The first man, and for a long time the only man, to appreciate the significance of Mackinder's teachings was the German soldier and geographer Karl Haushofer (1869–1946). The son of an obscure court official, Haushofer entered the army at an early age and became an artillery instructor. He rose to the rank of major-general and retired on a pension in 1924. But while still an officer in the army he had completed the requirements for a doctor's degree in geography at the University of Munich. He visited Hitler while the latter was in prison at Landsberg and poured into his ear a dramatic explanation of the reasons for Germany's defeat in 1918. Hitler was profoundly impressed. After gaining control of the German state, he established the Institut für Geopolitik at the University of Munich and appointed Haushofer to the position of Director. He even went so far as to elevate the general's Jewish wife to the status of "honorary Aryan."

How great was Haushofer's influence upon Hitler is a debatable question. Since the geographer-general was pro-Russian, it is easy to suppose that the Nazi-Soviet Pact of 1939 reflected this influence. Some students have assumed also that large portions of *Mein Kampf*, especially Chapter XIV of Volume II, which expresses an Eastern orientation, were written by Haushofer. But such conclusions overlook the fact that, two years after the Nazi-Soviet Pact, Hitler made war upon Russia, and that Haushofer fell into disfavor with the Nazi chieftains. The truth seems to be that Hitler's thinking was molded by various competing influ-

[21] *Ibid.*, p. 158.

ences. Haushofer's *Geopolitik* was one of them. But it was considerably outweighed by the racism of Alfred Rosenberg. With his background of superstition and prejudice, heavily saturated with anti-Semitism, Hitler was more likely to be convinced by the irrationalism of a racist fanatic than by the environmentalism of a political geographer. The suicide of Haushofer and his wife in 1946 was an appropriate *dénouement* of a tragedy of failure and rejection.

Haushofer defined geopolitics as "the scientific foundation of the art of political action in the life-and-death struggle of state organisms for *Lebensraum*." Except for his emphasis on the state as organism, he might seem to be doing little more than echoing Mackinder. Actually, he followed Mackinder in order to turn him inside out. He recognized the importance of the Heartland and of Russia's relationship to it; but instead of advocating a tier of independent states to keep Russia and Germany apart, he urged their close collaboration. He longed for the revival of the Bismarckian policy of a Russo-German alliance. Germany's destiny lay in the acquisition of land to supply the need of her agriculture, not in becoming another England with urban slums and blighted landscapes. The West, he contended, is decadent, and a new culture is emerging from Asia. Germany should participate in this culture and seek to guide and direct it. Though he recognized certain dangers in flirtation with barbarian hordes from the East, he believed that Germany could educate them and eventually control them. In this way she would gain access to their resources and ultimately absorb their territory. Needless to say, he minimized the importance of ideological conflict. He seemed to think that the Bolshevism of Lenin and Stalin was not much different from the state socialism which Germany had practiced since the 1870's. Above all, he maintained that the old feud between Teuton and Slav, which had contributed to Germany's downfall in 1918, must come to an end. No one can deny that his dreams were magnificent. He gloated over the vision of a transcontinental empire extending from the North Sea to the Pacific Ocean, and eventually incorporating China and India and even Japan. It would replace the aging British Empire and, by virtue of its enormous mass and unassailable power, would command the world.

That the United States should develop an interest in geopolitics may seem strange, in view of the country's insular position, its one-time zeal for colonial empire, and the strength of the Mahan tradition that sea-power is the key to national greatness. But no one should underestimate the role of Manifest Destiny in American history. It would be difficult to conceive of a doctrine more suggestive of the idea that space is the foundation of national importance. Some prophets of the doctrine, at least, identified this "space" as nothing less than the whole continent of North America. It should not be forgotten, either, that the United States still has, or has had in recent years, its Billy Mitchells who taught that "Whoever holds Alaska will hold the world" and its Hanson Baldwins who maintain that the occupation of "space" by land armies remains the secret of victory in war, despite all the progress in air power and "push-button" weapons. But the nation's most prominent expounder of a systematic theory of geopolitics was the late Nicholas J. Spykman, author of *America's Strategy in World Politics* (1942). Spykman was born in Amsterdam in 1893 and was educated at the University of California. From 1913 to 1920 he was a journalist in the Middle East, the Far East, and Australasia. From 1920 to 1923 he taught at the University of California and then went to Yale, where he was eventually appointed Sterling Professor of International Relations and Director of the Institute of International Studies.

The theory of Spykman provides eloquent testimony to the close affinity of geopolitics with power politics. He conceived of competition for power as the very essence of human relations. To deplore man's craving for power, he said, is to flee from the world of reality into a world of dreams. Most emphatically is this true, he argued, of the sphere of international affairs. Here the struggle for power is identical with the struggle for survival. "All else is secondary, because in the last instance only power can achieve the objectives of foreign policy." [22] Like the votaries of *Realpolitik*, he taught that power, in the final analysis, is the

[22] *America's Strategy in World Politics.* New York, Harcourt, 1942, p. 18.

power to wage war. He differed from them mainly in his emphasis upon factors other than military strength as instruments of victory—size of territory, quantity of manpower, nature of frontiers, abundance of raw materials. He regarded these elements as complements to military might. They serve the same purpose of enhancing the strength of the nation in its desperate struggle to survive and to augment its power at the expense of its enemies. This struggle has been a constant phenomenon in international relations, and there is nothing to indicate that it will ever cease. To forget this reality because wars are unpleasant would be to invite disaster. Nations can neither hope to avoid war nor prevent its occurrence, except for brief periods of time. The best they can do is to use war, when necessary, in their own interest and to be as thoroughly prepared as possible to gain a victory.

As a prescription for the success of American foreign policy, Spykman fell back upon the ancient nostrum of a balance of power. He made it clear, however, that he did not mean an equal division of power. Nations are not interested, he pointed out, in an equilibrium. What everyone wants is a generous margin in his own favor. "There is no real security in being just as strong as a potential enemy; there is security only in being a little stronger." [23] What he advocated was the kind of balance which Britain maintained during the nineteenth century. By preventing any state or combination of states on the European Continent from growing too strong, she ensured her own safety. If she had adhered to this policy, she would not have declared war on Germany in 1939. The guarantee to Poland and Rumania "was an erroneous and fatal decision." Conquest and annexation of these countries would have strengthened Germany "but primarily in regard to Russia and not a great deal in regard to the west." [24] For similar reasons, he implied that it was a mistake for the United States to have entered World War II. By so doing, she destroyed the balance of power in both Europe and Asia. The best interests of this country would have been served by a powerful Germany and Russia to checkmate each other in Europe, and a powerful Japan and China to fulfill the same purpose in Asia.

[23] *Ibid.*, p. 21.
[24] *Ibid.*, p. 115.

He denied the feasibility of any such scheme as Charles A. Beard's Continentalism, or defense of the Western Hemisphere in isolation from Europe. Balanced power in both the transatlantic and transpacific zones he considered an absolute prerequisite for the national interests and power position of the United States. What he would say now if he could see the great land mass of Eurasia controlled by two anti-Western colossi, united by at least an ideological alliance, is not difficult to imagine.

Like others of his school, Spykman had no confidence in federations or confederations of nations. World federation he regarded as utopian and doomed to disappoint its advocates. Since it would be accompanied by no change in human nature, it would simply substitute civil wars for international wars. But no confederation or league of states would be successful either. With its membership made up of sovereign states, its actions would of necessity take the form of applications of force by some states against others. But collective action of this sort is rarely effective. It is bound to be slow and uncertain and therefore incapable of dealing with such modern techniques as the blitzkrieg and aerial bombardment. Much more realistic than the League of Nations, he contended, was the Concert of Europe of the nineteenth century, in which force was used by the ruling nations not merely to preserve but also to change the *status quo*. Holland and Turkey, for example, were forced by collective action to acquiesce in Belgian and Greek independence. Statesmen of the modern world, Spykman argued, must resign themselves to the fact that coercion is a reality, that there will be armed conflict as long as the state-system endures, and that sound policy consists in being ready to use whatever means may be necessary to maintain a balance of power for the protection of one's own nation.

4. Non-Violence and Passive Resistance

By no means all writers on international affairs believe in the gospel of force. Many anarchists, for example, have condemned the use of physical coercion under any circumstances, and have argued that the fundamental decency of human beings, with some help from the pressure of public opinion, is sufficient to hold society together. Quakers like Rufus Jones, and some other sincere religionists, have stressed the "power of gentle forces" and have staked their hopes of preventing conflict on education, moral improvement, and organization. Finally, a few extremists and revolutionaries have invented techniques of civil disobedience, noncooperation, and passive resistance as means of defense against tyranny and aggression. Some of the apostles of these methods have been individualists or communistic anarchists; some have been Christian pacifists; and a few have been nationalists who believe in non-violent resistance as the only really effective weapon against a tyrannical ruler or an invader.

Civil disobedience had its origins in the nineteenth century in certain of the teachings of Henry Thoreau (1817–1862). Exalting conscience above law and government, he preached the doctrine of individual nullification. By this doctrine he meant that the individual had the right to disobey and to violate any edict, decree, or statute which offended his conscience. He denied any obligation on the part of citizens to manifest respect for the law. Instead, they should cultivate respect for the right. A single individual, he averred, standing for the right is worth more than the largest of majorities standing for the wrong. Thoreau's civil disobedience, however, was not actually synonymous with passive resistance. Though he despised the state and taught that the best government would be one which governed not at all, he applauded John Brown's attack on Harpers Ferry with its objective of seizing arms to be placed in the hands of slaves for a rebellion against their masters. And when the Civil War broke out two years later, the dying ascetic at Concord rejoiced over the moral regeneration which he thought would accompany the conflict.

Perhaps a better exemplar of both civil disobedience and non-violence was the noted Abolitionist William Lloyd Garrison (1805–1879). To express his opposition to a law in conflict with the higher demands of justice and right, as he interpreted them, Garrison publicly burned the Constitution of the United States. Unlike Thoreau, he would give no sanction to a war for righteousness. "The history of mankind," he said, "is crowded with evidences, proving that physical coercion is not adapted to moral regeneration; that the sinful disposition of man can be subdued only by love; that evil can be exterminated from the earth only by goodness." [25]

The great philosopher of non-violence who bridged the nineteenth and twentieth centuries was the Russian Count Leo Tolstoi (1828–1910). He was the son of a landed proprietor of German extraction who had rebuilt the family fortunes through marriage. As a child, the future novelist was sensitive and moody. The death of his parents before he was six years old placed responsibility for his upbringing in the hands of relatives. They appear to have been gay and pleasure-loving and steeped in French influences. As a result, Tolstoi became interested in Rousseau at an early age and continued under the impact of the great romanticist till the end of his life. Perhaps partly on account of this influence, his university education was a failure. He devoted so much time to frivolity and to the pursuit of his own whims and fancies that he was unable to settle down to concentrated effort in any field. He finally withdrew from the university entirely "on account of ill-health and private reasons." For some time he devoted himself to the movement for emancipation of the serfs and then entered the army, where, strangely, he discovered his talents as a writer. His *Tales from Sebastopol* gained for him such literary celebrity that the Tsar issued special orders that he be removed from posts of danger. As his life advanced, he became more and more preoccupied with religious and philosophical problems and with social reconstruction. He reached the conclusion that pleasure, luxury, and power are evil, and that even intellectual achievements are vain and worthless. Nothing can save humanity, he contended, but the simple teachings of Jesus in the Sermon on the Mount. He called upon all men, therefore, to renounce their strivings for self-aggrandizement, to earn their living by manual toil, and to cultivate the virtues of poverty, humility, and love of humanity. He set the example by deeding his property to his wife and by adopting the dress and humble fare of the peasant.

[25] *Selections from the Writings and Speeches of William Lloyd Garrison.* Boston, R. F. Wallcut, 1852, p. 75.

Apart from selfishness, which he considered ingrained in every human being, Tolstoi placed all the blame for social injustice upon the employment of force. It is force, he maintained, which supports exploitation. It is the bullets in the guns of soldiers and police which enable the rich to live in palaces and fare sumptuously every day while the poor shiver in their wretched hovels and starve for lack of a crust of bread. The state itself, he argued, is a mere instrument of coercion. It is the worst of all criminals, for it conceals oppression under a cloak of law and conscripts young men for wholesale murder. He believed, above all, that violence is immoral. It brutalizes man and reduces him to the level of a savage beast. Moreover, as long as violence is available as a weapon, reliance upon civilized methods is practically impossible. On grounds of expediency also he condemned the use of physical force. It places its user in the hands of his enemies, and both sides then try to outdo each other in fiendish cruelty. When a government, for instance, is overthrown by violence, and a new class or party gains control, the new ruling authority will not be likely to be less oppressive than the old. "On the contrary, obliged to defend itself from its exasperated and overthrown enemies, it will be even more cruel and despotic than its predecessor." In order to introduce and maintain its own system, it will be forced "not only to avail itself of all former methods of violence but to invent new ones as well." [26]

Tolstoi was not interested in ingenious stratagems for implementing his philosophy of nonresistance. The foundation of his idealism was the simple ethical gospel of Jesus, together with a few special interpretations of it provided by the Quakers and by William Lloyd Garrison. The essence of this gospel was love of humanity and a striving for perfection in the image of God. To achieve these goals the individual must purge his mind of envy, selfishness, and hatred. He must cultivate the virtues of humility, long-suffering, and self-denial. He must take and really observe vows of poverty and chastity, renouncing all interest in pleasure and wealth. But the keystone of the whole ethical system, as Tolstoi saw it, was the abandonment of revenge and retaliation. No

[26] *The Kingdom of God Is Within You.* New York, Crowell, 1899, p. 183.

one could love God or become like unto Him who did not love his fellow men. And love of man was utterly incompatible with thoughts and deeds of vengeance. It followed, therefore, that the sincere Christian must scrupulously refrain from recompensing evil with evil. When injured or offended, he must turn to his enemy the other check and bless his revilers and persecutors. Instead of resisting an evil-doer by violence, he should submit to a repetition of the offense if necessary. He should not kill or wound another human being even in self-defense. He should sue no person at the law and make no complaint to a magistrate against anyone who had done him an injury. He should take part in no war or preparation for war and pay no taxes to support such activities. Tolstoi did not mean, however, that the Christian idealist should pursue a policy of complete passivity in the face of evil. His obligation was to refrain merely from repaying evil with evil. Seeking to overcome evil with good was strongly recommended, not forbidden. So also were such non-violent methods as education, persuasion, and conversion.

The techniques of non-violent resistance were invented by men who were influenced by Tolstoi. Pre-eminent among them was the Indian nationalist and mystic Mohandas K. Gandhi. Born in 1869, he was the son of middle-class parents, who endeavored to instill in him loyalty to the traditions of their caste. For his professional education they sent him to England to study law. Upon completing the course he obtained a position with a prosperous Indian firm in South Africa. He built up a successful practice over a period of twenty years, but he soon became chiefly interested in defending his own countrymen against the injustices to which they were subjected by the dominant racial element in South Africa. At the risk of his life and in the face of insults, he campaigned against social and economic discrimination, encouraging the Indian laborers to organize and calling upon the government to remove injustices. In 1914 he returned to India and worked zealously in support of Britain's cause in what he believed to be a war against militarism and autocracy. But disillusionment set in with the renewal of British oppression in 1919. The event which shocked him most deeply was the Amritsar massacre, in which 400 Indians were killed and more than 1000 wounded by a regiment of British soldiers. For nearly thirty years thereafter, Gandhi was occupied almost entirely with a crusade to free India from British rule. His methods were refusal to cooperate with oppressors, attempting to change the evil-doer by force of example, and developing in himself and his followers the attitudes and disciplines necessary to an improved social order. At times he went on hunger strikes, knowing that the British did not dare to make him a martyr. He encouraged his followers to boycott foreign goods, to refuse to pay taxes, and to lie down in vast numbers on highways and railroad tracks. In their totality, Gandhi referred to these techniques as *satyagraha,* which may be loosely translated as "non-violent resistance," but which means literally "soul force" or "the power of truth." With the achievement of self-government for India in 1947, Gandhi turned his attention to moderating the bitter quarrels between Moslems and Hindus. He succeeded, but at the cost of his life. On January 30, 1948, on his way to evening prayers, he was assassinated by a member of a reactionary, chauvinistic Hindu society. His death had at least a temporary sobering effect on the warring factions.

Gandhi was undoubtedly one of the most significant figures of our age. Despite his primitivism, he was almost universally admired as the Mahatma or "Great Soul." Though he remained a Hindu and a supporter of the caste system (but not of discrimination or untouchability), he derived a large part of his philosophy from Jesus of Nazareth, Thoreau, and Tolstoi. But he gave to their doctrines special interpretations designed to render them applicable to the needs of his own country. He had no faith in material progress, and taught that the only hope for India lay in cultivation of her spiritual resources. At one time he repudiated the Industrial Revolution and even Western science and Western medicine. In his *Confession of Faith* (1909) he described medical science as "the concentrated essence of black magic" and hospitals as instruments of the devil. He avowed that "If there were no hospitals for venereal diseases, or even for consumptives, we should have less consumption and less sexual vice amongst us." [27] Later,

[27] C. F. Andrews, *Mahatma Gandhi's Ideas.* New York, Macmillan, 1930, p. 187.

under Nehru's influence, he came to recognize that industrialization was inevitable, but he continued to regard a self-sufficing village economy as the ideal. He thought that a more equitable distribution of land and the encouragement of such handicrafts as spinning and weaving would enable India to feed and to provide employment for all her citizens. But no reform should ever be attempted by force or violence. He stood at the opposite pole from Machiavelli, Lenin, and many others in denying that the end justifies the means. He believed, instead, that the means largely determine or condition the end. He declared openly that he would prefer that India should continue indefinitely in bondage to Britain than that she should gain freedom through violent revolution. Though many of his economic and social ideas were reactionary, his philosophy of passive resistance seems to gain increasing acceptance among victims of oppression.

The most important latter-day prophet of non-violence in the West is the noted Alsatian Albert Schweitzer. Physician, musicologist, Biblical scholar, and philosopher, he is a rare and outstanding example of versatility in an age when most men find difficulty in mastering a single field. Schweitzer was born in 1875, the son of a Lutheran minister. He was educated at the universities of Strasbourg, Paris, and Berlin. He had earned doctorates in theology and philosophy by the time he was twenty-five. Later he completed the requirements for an M.D. After a career as a teacher and organist, he founded the hospital at Lambaréné in French Equatorial Africa in 1913, and has been its director and chief physician ever since. He conceives the project first of all as a humanitarian venture, but also as an expression of his personal need to affirm the sanctity of life in an age when it is too commonly ignored. He has also found time to write numerous books, on the lives and teachings of Jesus and Paul, on music, on the philosophy of civilization, on ethics, and on the quest for peace. His efforts on behalf of international understanding won for him the Nobel Peace Prize in 1952. Though a sincere idealist, Schweitzer professes no political or economic creed and adheres to no school or movement. He considers himself a Christian but belongs to no denomination and is impatient with theological distinctions.

The cardinal influences molding the thinking of Albert Schweitzer have been many and various. He harks back, in the first place, to the pacifism and nonresistance of Lao-Tsze (*ca*. 604–531 B.C.). He venerates also the charity and benevolence of Jesus, the "rationalism" of Paul, the universalism and libertarianism of the Stoics, and the humanitarianism of St. Francis of Assisi. He does not subscribe to everything contained in these sources. For example, he rejects the otherworldliness of Jesus and the dogmatism and fatalism of Paul. Perhaps most of all he is indebted to the Enlightenment—is almost its last survivor. He admires the Enlightenment for its rationalism and for its faith in the possibility of progress. He believes that it was not until Christianity came under this influence that it was stirred into entering the struggle for the welfare of humanity. He does not, however, accept the unqualified optimism of the Enlightenment. He sees the drama of life as replete with pain and death. Not only human beings but the whole creation is born to suffering as the sparks fly upward. All forms of life subsist at the expense of other forms. The will-to-live of one species is almost a sentence of death for another. "Life attracts with a thousand expectations, and fulfills hardly one of them." Unrest, disappointment, and tragedy are the lot of human beings "in the short span of time which lies between our entrance on life and our departure from it." [28]

Yet Schweitzer refuses to commit himself to an abysmal pessimism. Contending that the power of thought is a distinctive element in human nature, he retains his confidence in the capacity of reason to find solutions to at least some of our problems. He believes that, through the achievement of thinking, each lowly individual has a chance to rid mankind of some portion of the misery that afflicts it. He deplores the skepticism, anti-intellectualism, and fatalism that have come to characterize modern civilization. Our contemporaries have adopted the view that there is no final truth, and that if there were, man would be incapable of discovering it, for he is so blinded by superstition and error that he has lost all capacity for accurate thinking. As a consequence, everything is predetermined by instinct, habit, ideolog-

[28] *Civilization and Ethics*. London, Adam and Charles Black, 1946, pp. 209–10.

ical fixation, or economic condition. The primary responsibility for this development Schweitzer places at the door of Hegel. It was a sad day in 1820, Schweitzer says, when the German dialectician wrote the sentence: "The real is the rational, and the rational is the real." When that sentence was written, "our age began, the age which moved on to the World War—and which perhaps some day will end civilization." [29] Schweitzer interprets Hegel to have meant that the process of history is mechanical, and that the idealist is wasting his time in attempting to use his intellectual and moral powers in accomplishing reform.

As Schweitzer himself conceives it, "reverence for life" is the keynote of his philosophy. It would be more accurate to say that "world- and life-affirmation" is the central doctrine of his system. By this principle he means the opposite of the Indian doctrine that all life and effort are evil, and that the highest good is to approach as closely as possible to death without actually dying. World- and life-affirmation conveys the idea that this world has possibilities for good, that man by his own efforts can make it better, and that the individual has the duty to live constructively and to help others to do likewise. Reverence for life is primarily an ethical principle, though it also has philosophical meaning. It involves, first of all, an obligation of sympathy and pity for all living creatures as members of a fraternity of suffering and pain. It is not enough, according to Schweitzer, that one should do good to his fellowmen. He must include in his benevolence the whole animal and plant creation, at least to the extent of avoiding unnecessary and thoughtless killing. Schweitzer recognizes perfectly well the need for exterminating germs, noxious insects, and venomous snakes, but he deplores killing for sport and even the idle plucking of leaves and flowers merely to discard them moments later. Unless all life is considered sacred, he argues, there will be no respect for human life. "The ethic of Reverence for Life is the ethic of Love widened into universality." And "it is only through love that we can attain to communion with God." [30] Schweitzer therefore classifies as evil everything that

[29] Charles R. Joy, ed., *Albert Schweitzer, an Anthology.* New York, Harper, 1947, pp. 215–16.
[30] *Out of My Life and Thought.* New York, Holt, 1933, pp. 232, 238.

annihilates, hampers, or hinders life. Good he defines as anything which saves or enhances life and helps it in every way possible to attain its highest development. He regards reverence for life as the key to peace. Because Western nations do not practice it, they fear and hate one another, and wars become inevitable.

It is tempting to compare Schweitzer and Gandhi. Their philosophies are alike in their pacifism, in their hatred of violence, in their opposition to materialism and mechanization, in their insistence upon altruism and self-sacrifice, and in their conceptions of the dignity and worth of humanity. There is even a resemblance between Gandhi's respect for cow-worship and Schweitzer's reverence for life. Both see in regard for lower creatures an exemplification of universal love. But whereas for Gandhi all killing was evil, Schweitzer condemns only that which is thoughtless and avoidable. Other differences are more fundamental. Though Schweitzer recognizes the dangers to humanism in an overemphasis on science, he shares none of the Indian's suspicion of modern medicine. Though he believes in the general validity of the self-determination of nations, he has no interest in Gandhi's militant nationalism or his zeal for self-sufficiency, for boycotts, and for protective tariffs. Finally, and most important from the political standpoint, Schweitzer's views on passive resistance do not coincide with those of Gandhi. For the Alsatian, all resistance is open to objection. Whether violent or non-violent, it is an application of force to gain an end. And there is a danger that a concealed application may produce more bitterness than an open attack by violence. Only positive acts of sacrifice and benevolence growing out of pity for the tragic plight of all creatures can heal the wounds of a frustrated and frightened humanity. Schweitzer's identification of love with pity may seem a strange equation, but it is the conclusion he reached after years of pondering the phenomena of life in the teeming jungles of Equatorial Africa.

The development of means for massive destruction since World War II has thinned the ranks of those who embrace the gospel of force. There are still advocates of the use of violence who consider it a necessary means for the prevention of greater evils.

But it would be difficult to find a contemporary Treitschke or Marinetti who would justify wholesale slaughter as a remedy for moral weakness or a hygiene for the human race. In his *Thieves in the Night*, Arthur Koestler comes close to this viewpoint when he suggests that fighting back against villainy with all the ferocity at one's command is necessary for a recovery of self-respect, but he is referring to a small-scale war between Jews and Arabs, not to a conflict between super-states with enough power at their disposal to destroy the world. It is now almost universally recognized that international war is the road to complete disaster. No nation could win such a struggle, and none could gain enough from it to compensate for the frightful losses. Recognition of these truths has brought a widespread conviction that some way must be found of preventing World War III. A small number of utopians argue that the only solution is the destruction of national sovereignty and the organization of a world federation. A few die-hard international moralists seem to think that it would be better to go down to destruction holding fast to our principles than to make a single important concession to the enemy whose system we hate. They doubtless want peace—but only on their own terms. An increasing proportion of responsible citizens in nearly all countries, however, appear to believe that some common basis of agreement must be found which will prevent the deadly signal from being given to unloose the horrors of nuclear war.

It is an ironical fact that some of the leading advocates of adjustments and concessions to avoid war are members of the power-politics school. For instance, George F. Kennan, originator of the containment policy and former ambassador to Moscow, proposes the "disengagement" or withdrawal by mutual agreement of forces of the two sides in Central Europe.[31] Hans Morgenthau and Winston Churchill, with their insistence upon negotiation as an alternative to conflict, are even more conspicuous examples. None of these leaders attaches much importance to ideologies or ideals in international relations. None of them recognizes an international law or an international morality. Whether these are major deficiencies or not may depend very largely upon

[31] See his *Russia, the Atom and the West*. New York, Harper, 1958.

whether their proposals yield practical results. A more serious indictment that can be brought against the political realists is that they leave little room for progress. They would patch up agreements to take care of the immediate future, but they offer no permanent solution. They assume that the system of sovereign states will continue indefinitely, and that as long as it lasts it will be dominated by the law of the jungle. They have no confidence in either a moral revolution among men or a transformation of human institutions. The world federationists and the advocates of non-violence may be much more naive, but they can at least be credited with setting their sights on higher objectives.

ADDITIONAL READINGS

Clark, Grover. *The Balance Sheets of Imperialism*. New York, Columbia University Press, 1936.

Clausewitz, Karl von. *Principles of War*. Harrisburg, Pa., Military Service Publishing Co., 1942.

Cramb, J. A. *Reflections on the Origin and Destiny of Imperial Britain*. London, Macmillan, 1900.

Dorpalen, Andreas. *The World of General Haushofer*. New York, Farrar and Rinehart, 1942.

Giddings, F. H. *Democracy and Empire*. New York, Macmillan, 1901.

Halle, Louis J. *Civilization and Foreign Policy*. New York, Harper, 1955.

Jordan, David Starr. *Imperial Democracy*. New York, D. Appleton, 1899.

Kennan, George F. *Realities of American Foreign Policy*. Princeton, Princeton University Press, 1954.

Kissinger, Henry A. *Nuclear Weapons and Foreign Policy*. New York, Harper, 1957.

Lea, Homer. *The Day of the Saxon*. New York, Harper, 1912.

———. *The Valor of Ignorance*. New York, Harper, 1942.

Morgenthau, Hans J. *Politics among Nations*. New York, Knopf, 1948.

———. *Scientific Man vs. Power Politics*. Chicago, University of Chicago Press, 1946.

Muste, A. J. *Not by Might*. New York, Harper, 1947.

Nef, John U. *War and Human Progress.* Cambridge, Mass., Harvard University Press, 1950.

Russell, Bertrand. *Why Men Fight.* New York, Century, 1920.

Schumpeter, Joseph. *Imperialism and Social Classes.* New York, A. M. Kelley, 1951.

Schwarzenberger, George. *Power Politics.* New York, Praeger, 1952.

Sprout, Harold and Margaret, eds. *Foundations of National Power.* Princeton, Van Nostrand, 1946.

Strausz-Hupé, Robert. *Geopolitics: The Struggle for Space and Power.* New York, Putnam, 1942.

———. *Protracted Conflict.* New York, Harper, 1959.

Weigert, Hans W. *Geopolitics; Myth and Reality.* New York, Oxford University Press, 1942.

———. *Generals and Geographers.* New York, Oxford University Press, 1942.

Woolf, Leonard S. *Imperialism and Civilization.* New York, Harcourt, 1928.

Wright, Quincy. *A Study of War.* Chicago, University of Chicago Press, 1943. Two vols.

PART
FIVE

Conclusion

X V I

The Challenge to Political Theory

As an academic discipline, political theory in recent years has been fraught with uncertainty and turmoil. It has been criticized by various interpreters as a dull and sterile exercise in intellectual history. They contend that for fifty years it has been devoid of originality, and that it has contributed little or nothing to the growth and development of a science of politics. Broadly speaking, these interpreters can be grouped into three schools: the systematic school, the analytical school, and the behavioralist school. They adhere to a common premise that the study of political theory as an aspect of history is worthless, but they disagree as to methods and conclusions.

The foremost leader of the systematic school is David Easton of the University of Chicago. He sees as the chief cause of the decline of modern political theory the triumph of historicism. By historicism he means the conception that all ideas are historically determined, and that the nature, causation, and influence of ideas as they appear in history are the sum and substance of political theory. He indicts as the chief exponents of historicism William A. Dunning, Charles H. McIlwain, and George H. Sabine. For Dunning, political theory was simply a form of intellectual history. His almost exclusive concern was to reveal the cultural and political background of innumerable ideas and to demonstrate their subsequent influence. The historicism of Mc-

Ilwain, as Easton conceives it, was even more rigorously deterministic. The Harvard medievalist thought of ideas as mere consequences of historical conditions. They were epiphenomena, mere froth on the ocean, with no influence or effects of their own, except possibly on other ideas. Sabine departed farther than either of his two predecessors from the viewpoint of the pure historicist. He showed zeal for testing the logical validity of the theories of the philosophers he discussed, and he concerned himself with their ethical judgments. But his approach was still similar to that of the majority of political theorists who assume that, "aside from historical description, their major task in moral matters is to clarify, like extreme semanticists, and not to reconstruct, like imaginative moral architects." [1]

Easton's prime objective is to put an end to political theory as an exercise in intellectual history and to substitute for it a search for values and the development of great principles which will give life and meaning to political science. He deplores the fact that political science has lagged behind sociology and economics in the achievement of systematic or general theory. He would like to see the study of politics brought under the sway of some great integrating idea like the marginal utility principle in economics, the Darwinian hypothesis in biology, or the Einstein theory in physics. The nearest approach to any of these in politics is such theories as Michel's Iron Law of Oligarchy. But, according to Easton, formulations like these are too narrow and limited to provide the conceptual framework for a whole discipline. What he seeks is a broad-gauge theoretical scheme to guide, measure, and stimulate study and research in political science. He desires no rigid, mechanical pattern but one that would be flexible and in constant flux. It would be "a system of working hypotheses, adopted and used only as long as it helps to orient empirical research in such a way that socially significant problems are better understood." [2] Despite his reference to empirical research, he would go far toward giving to political science a deductive character. His basic theoretical pattern, or general theory, would consist of "postulates," from which would be deduced "narrower

---

[1] The Political System. New York, Knopf, 1953, p. 254.
[2] Ibid., p. 57.

generalizations." From these in turn would stem specific generalizations "capable of empirical proof." [3] The resemblance between this system and the familiar syllogism of deductive logic seems fairly close.

One of the chief advantages of the deductive approach to political theory, as Easton conceives it, is that it will make possible the development and conservation of values. He deprecates the "hyperfactualism" insisted on by Lord Bryce and his followers, which required the social scientist to avoid any kind of moral judgments as he would the plague. Easton sees the adoption and defense of such judgments as a prime function of the political theorist. What merit, he asks in effect, does a theory have if it does not provide a constellation of judgments which can be used as criteria for appraising a political system and the policies it makes and follows? Since moral judgments are firmly rooted in the emotional life of the individual, they are bound to affect the researcher's investigations. It is imperative, therefore, that he understand them and realize their effects in terms of the kind of system or policies he regards as desirable. Values are not mere axioms which everyone can take for granted. They need to be examined and tested against a background of empirical data but also in relation to the body of hypotheses or principles which the researcher sets up as a model or pattern to govern his studies. The substance of this model or pattern is general theory. Examples of such theory in the past were the natural-rights theory of John Locke, the greatest-happiness principle of Jeremy Bentham, and perhaps the Marxist theory of the class struggle.

The most radical exponent of deductive or systematic political theory is Anatol Rapoport, who has been influenced by Easton. Rapoport is not a political scientist but a mathematician and biologist. He is deeply interested, however, in all the social sciences and especially in efforts to make them exact sciences. Since 1955 he has been connected with the Mental Health Research Institute at the University of Michigan. As an advocate of deductive theory, Rapoport goes farther than Easton. In fact, he almost divorces theory from data. Empirical observation, he holds, may contribute almost nothing to an accurate understand-

[3] *Ibid.*, p. 58.

ing of phenomena. The physicist may spend dozens of years meticulously examining the behavior of ocean waves, and in the end be no wiser than before with regard to an understanding of wave motion. The scientific world was fortunate, in the seventeenth century, that Galileo Galilei flourished as well as Sir Francis Bacon. The latter was an empiricist who insisted that theories must fit the facts. The former did not take facts so seriously, but believed in formulating theories of what *ought* to be true under idealized conditions. Had he not acted on this belief we should not have had the law of falling bodies, which, actually, does not conform to much of the falling that takes place on our planet. The law is, therefore, factually false. "But it is true nevertheless, in a deeper sense. Without such ideally true and factually false laws, mathematical physics would have never left the ground." [4]

Rapoport refuses to concede that an unbridgeable gulf separates the physical from the social sciences. Their aims, he says, are not, or should not be, fundamentally different, and their methods can be exactly the same. For the time being, however, they have different problems. For the physical scientist, the problems of definition, recognition, and accurate classification have been largely or completely solved. By contrast, for the social scientist, such problems are still crucial. He cannot assume that even the majority of his colleagues know what he means when he refers to "democracy," "liberty," or "sovereignty," or that they would recognize the validity of his classification of states or governments. But if these problems could be solved, he could pursue the aims of his science along substantially the same lines as does the physicist. The essence of these aims is to discover "theories" which can be used to explain and to predict events. For the physicist a theory is a collection of theorems. A theorem, in turn, is a proposition which is a strictly logical consequent of other propositions or definitions. To be valid, then, a theorem depends on the validity of antecedent theorems. This process of tracing back continues until some original postulate, assumed to be self-evident, is reached. In this manner, a *pure* theory, log-

---

[4] "Various Meanings of Theory," *American Political Science Review*, LII (1958), 983.

ically consistent but not necessarily in harmony with all of the facts, is evolved. Better than any findings of induction, it will give meaning and direction to the science and provide true "understanding" of phenomena.

Strange as it may seem, Rapoport does not rule out the normative function of pure theory. He rejects the contention that scientists should concern themselves only with "what is," never with "what ought to be." No more than Professor Easton does he shrink from the idea of "value-laden" theory. The quintessence of pure theory, he maintains, is that it should show what ought to be under certain (usually idealized) conditions. Such a theory may not have "practical value," since the idealized conditions may never materialize; but it will probably have great "heuristic" value. In other words, it will reveal or suggest fundamental truths in a situation which would never be disclosed by uninspired or undirected research. Ultimately, pure theory should provide a basis for accurate prediction in politics just as it does in the physical sciences. But to expect this too soon is not wise. Theory is like a system of credit. "One has a right to demand that *somewhere* there are assets to back up the transactions. But, as often as not, these assets may be in the future, and the very act of questioning their existence may set in motion a chain reaction which will preclude their existence." [5] Adhering to this counsel might seem to inhibit criticism of the future potential of almost any theory—spiritualism, for example, or phrenology.

The second of the schools embodying the spirit of revolt against political theory as a species of intellectual history is the analytical school. The members of this school are critical rather than constructive. They do not consider it the function of political theorists to develop an integrating principle to unify and orient political science after the manner of the law of gravitation in seventeenth-century physics. They are, of course, not opposed to theories, but they believe in multiplicity rather than in unity. At the same time, they protest against the assumption of many of the historicists that one political theory is as good as another, or that the only significant difference among them is the difference in their influence. By contrast, the analytical school demands

[5] *Ibid.*, LII, 988.

that every theory be subjected to tests of either logical analysis or empirical inquiry or both. They ignore entirely the evolution of political ideas and pay little attention to their influence. Their concern is rather with the validity of the ideas, especially those of the present day and the more celebrated ones of the past, regardless of their time of development. In common with the systematic school, they make extensive use of the deductive method. They employ quite generally as weapons the processes of logic, especially of that type of logic which is often considered a branch of mathematics. Many of their writings fairly bristle with co-efficients, statistical indexes, and algebraic formulas.

The development of analytical political theory seems to have been inspired by a new movement in philosophy, commonly known as Logical Positivism or Neo-Positivism. Logical Positivism was founded about 1920 by the so-called Vienna Circle, whose members included Rudolf Carnap, Otto Neurath, and Hans Reichenbach. With the threat of Nazification of Austria, most of them became refugees. Neurath settled in England, and Carnap and Reichenbach in the United States. The new movement drew much of its impetus, also, from the work of Ludwig Wittgenstein, who had migrated from Austria to England before World War I. His central doctrine was the argument that the sole task of philosophy is the analysis and clarification of language.

Logical Positivism is one of the most radical and uncompromising philosophies of modern times. It extends considerably beyond the anti-metaphysical doctrines of Auguste Comte. While Comte taught that the only knowledge of value is that which comes from the sciences, the Logical Positivists reject as "meaningless" everything which cannot be reduced to a "one-to-one correspondence" with something in the physical universe. Comte and his successors were content with the scientific method, believing that it could be applied as effectively in the realms of ethics and sociology as in the fields of astronomy and chemistry. The Logical Positivists take the sciences themselves as the exclusive foundations of knowledge and repudiate everything which is not translatable into a framework of physics or mathematical logic. They reduce philosophy to a mere instrument for the discovery of truth in harmony with the facts of the physical world. They almost divest it of content and concern themselves with "syntax," or the structure and interrelations of language, and with attempts to discover new media of expression. These media often take mathematical form.

Pre-eminent among leaders of the analytical school is Robert A. Dahl of Yale. A good example of his work is his dissection of Madisonian democracy in his *Preface to Democratic Theory*.[6] He is not interested in discovering why Madison wrote as he did or in the sources or influence of his teachings. He divides the Madisonian theory into ten hypotheses, with, in some cases, further subdivisions, which he labels "definitions" and "conditions." The method is not only deductive but has an almost Thomistic flavor. He shows, in the first place, that the Madisonian system had two incompatible goals. On the one hand, it was dedicated to the proposition that all the adult citizens should have equal rights, including the right to determine the general direction of governmental policy. On the other hand, it had the objective of giving to minorities, made up of the educated and wealthier classes, certain powers and privileges not to be accorded to the masses. These powers and privileges would have to be protected by constitutional safeguards. But the Madisonian system had other weaknesses, according to Dahl. Its definitions were ambiguous; it assumed propositions to be self-evident which were far from being so; it made deductions that were "dubious and probably false"; and, most serious of all, it was replete with internal contradictions. Several of its hypotheses were dependent upon antecedent hypotheses or definitions which were merely assumed to be valid. With the destruction of the validity of the antecedents, the consequents also fell to the ground. In short, the Madisonian system was "not logically explicable."

[6] University of Chicago Press, 1956. Professor Dahl does not confine his attention exclusively to analysis. In the book referred to he develops a theory of his own, which he calls "polyarchal democracy." It is a doctrine of rule by minorities, which compete with and check each other more effectively than is ever likely to be accomplished by constitutional restraints. This theory falls into the classification of "narrow-gauge" or "synthetic" theories, as Professor Easton calls them, in contradistinction to "systematic" theory.

In an earlier book, which he wrote with Charles E. Lindblom, Professor Dahl displayed a deeper interest in the traditional content of political philosophy. Though he and his collaborator devoted the greater portion of the book to analysis of processes and techniques, they also discussed some of the basic problems which have tried the political genius of man for centuries. What is more, they showed concern for values—or goals, as they preferred to call them. They specified these as the Renaissance-liberal-socialist goals of freedom, rationality, democracy, equality, security, and progress. While they took a dim view of "grand alternatives," they did not hesitate to express a preference for the liberal-democratic type of society as opposed to the totalitarian. At the same time, they rejected utopianism. They conceived of modern society as undergoing a revolution of techniques. These consisted of changes in the *methods* of social action but without the adoption of a comprehensive pattern of social and political reorganization. Such over-all schemes were no longer necessary, since many of their basic aims had already been achieved through the revolution of techniques. For example, the authors maintained that "both socialism and capitalism are dead." Socialism died, not because of its deficiencies, but because of its successes. Western economies have moved closer to "the Fabians than to Gladstone and his Liberals" and perhaps closer "to Marx than to Herbert Spencer." [7] But these results have been in no sense the fruits of a deliberate choice of grandiose ideals. Instead, they represent piecemeal changes introduced for the achievement of specific ends. Their cumulative effect, however, is just as revolutionary as if they were the ingredients of a utopian program.

To discover other exponents of the analytical approach to political theory is not difficult. One of the most prolific writers of articles on the subject is Felix E. Oppenheim, recently of Stanford and the University of Delaware. Dr. Oppenheim is intensely preoccupied with methodology and with definitions and classifications. His interest is not primarily in developing new theories but in devising criteria for testing the validity of theories already formulated. He considers it extremely important that po-

[7] *Politics, Economics and Welfare.* New York, Harper, 1953, pp. 16, 515.

litical theories not be assumed to have equal value, that only those which meet rigorous analytical tests should be taken seriously. His system of analysis is chiefly deductive and is often embellished with mathematical formulas. One example, concerning the problem of "control and unfreedom," will suffice: Senator B wishes to support a UMT-bill, that is, to do x. But since letters from his constituents indicate that the majority (A) oppose UMT, he decides to switch his vote, that is, not to do x. Because he is afraid of losing the next election if he does not switch his vote, B is, with respect to A, unfree. If such fear dissuades B from voting for the bill, his voting against is controlled by A. If B votes for the bill and consequently loses the election, A obviously had no control over B's voting *against* the bill. "Thus, if it is the case that, were B to do x, A would punish B for having done x, then Unfree (A, B, x) and possibly Control (A, B, x̄) by means of dissuasion. On the other hand, if B does x, and A punishes B for having done x, then Unfree (A, B, x) but not Control (A, B, x̄)."[8]

Dr. Oppenheim comes closest to the formulation of new theory in connection with his defense of relativism. And here he is much less abstruse. He denies that there is any fundamental conflict between absolutists and relativists pertaining to values. It is meaningless to pretend, he argues, that absolutists are bulwarks of all that is noble and good because they believe in eternal standards of right and justice; and that relativists are likely to be lewd fellows of the baser sort because they do not believe in enduring standards. It is just as fallacious, he contends, to think of absolutism as the only secure foundation of democracy, and of relativism as a breeding ground for irresponsibility, cynicism, and nihilism. The fundamental difference, he maintains, between absolutism and relativism is a matter of epistemology. Absolutists believe that Justice, Beauty, and Goodness are supreme realities, either because they conform to a divine pattern of natural laws or self-evident ideas, or because they have emerged as the end products of social evolution. "Relativism is an epistemological theory which denies that anything can be shown to be intrinsically good or bad—or indiffer-

[8] "Control and Unfreedom," *Philosophy of Science*, XXII (1955), 286–87.

ent." [9] The relativist argues that it would be just as absurd to discuss the goodness or badness of nuclear science as to debate, in epistemological terms, the goodness or badness of democracy. It is possible for the human mind to recognize the *facts* of nuclear science and also the facts of democracy. But goodness and badness are moral qualities.

Oppenheim's conclusion, therefore, is that moral values have nothing to do with epistemology. Ethical preferences spring from the emotions, not from objective knowledge or views of truth. "A relativist may, without inconsistency, favor discrimination or equality, and practice intolerance, tolerance, or over-tolerance." [10] Absolutists, also, can be found in abundance on either side of nearly every great issue. Some have been liberals, others conservatives; some have upheld democracy, others have condemned it; some have extolled individualism and the dignity of man, others have preached the virtues of reverence, obedience, and conformity. The explanation lies in the fact that these qualities are ethical values, not demonstrable truths. It is possible to make judgments or commitments for or against them; it is not possible to prove or disprove them.

Nevertheless, Oppenheim does contend that relativism provides a more favorable climate for the growth of democratic ideals than does absolutism. The absolutist, he points out, not only professes certain values but believes he can prove their consistency with ideal standards of justice and right. He is therefore likely to assume that *his* values are eternally valid and therefore proper for everyone. The result is intolerance, developing ultimately into suppression and tyranny. By contrast, the relativist recognizes that value-convictions are mere subjective preferences, incapable of objective proof. He makes his own choices, humbly and tolerantly, conceding the right of his neighbor to make different choices. He is consequently able to steer clear of fanaticism and of the self-righteous desire to make everyone over in his own image.

Closely related to the analytical school are those theories

[9] "In Defense of Relativism," *Western Political Quarterly*, VIII (1955), 514.
[10] *Id.*

which attempt to apply the quantification methods of mathematics and physics to the social sciences. These theories are principally three in number: the theory of games, the field theory, and cybernetics. All are concerned with methodology rather than with substantive theory. Cybernetics is the oldest of the three and perhaps the most suggestive of political and social views. It was founded about 1941 by Norbert Wiener, Professor of Mathematical Logic at Massachusetts Institute of Technology. He made up the term "cybernetics" from a Greek word meaning "steersman," and applied it to the entire field of control and communication theory. Cybernetics refers especially to the idea that the human brain and a high-speed electronic computer have many characteristics in common. Both send and receive messages, store and reproduce data, and remember facts and formulas. In the future, computing machines will undoubtedly be developed with at least as much capacity for "learning" and achieving skills as a low-grade moron. Professor Wiener doubts that it will ever be possible to reduce all the problems of social control to mechanical determinism, but he recognizes the danger that the great mass of human beings may someday become robots manipulated by unprincipled leaders who know how to feed the right questions into the machines. He assumes, however, that the machines are here to stay, and that in so far as they promote an orderly solution of critical problems, their results will be good. But he thinks their development should be accompanied by rigorous scientific education of every young person capable of absorbing it.

Noticeably similar to cybernetics is the theory of games originated by John von Neumann, a Hungarian expert on high-speed computers who became a professor of mathematics at the Institute for Advanced Study in Princeton. In 1954 he was appointed by President Eisenhower to the Atomic Energy Commission. The theory of games is based upon the assumption that the process of decision-making in the political and social realms bears marked similarities to the actions of players in such games as chess, poker, and bridge. The objectives involved are objectives of victory, and the methods are methods of strategy, including the specific techniques of calculation, signaling, bluff, and deception. The founders of the theory contend that these factors are especially relevant to the areas of war and diplomacy. They have worked out elaborate mathematical formulas to predict, for example, what will happen if Nation A chooses Action B and at the same time deceives Nation B into believing that Nation A is about to adopt Action B'. Nations and individuals alike are assumed to be completely self-seeking, intent upon gaining the maximum advantage at the expense of their rivals. The exponents of the theory of games are as un-compromising as the Social Darwinists in acclaiming competition as a universal law.

Field theory was originally a conception taken over from physics. Physicists speak of a gravitational field and a magnetic field. By the former they mean the region of force exerted by a planetary body. A magnetic field includes the area of force and the forces themselves exerted by a magnet upon bodies sensitive to it. Both theories imply interaction and interdependence, so that each field constitutes an integral pattern or unit. Field theory in the social sciences is less dependent upon mathematics and more closely related to psychology than is either cybernetics or the theory of games. The original prophet of social-science field theory was Kurt Lewin, who at the time of his death in 1947 was Director of the Research Center for Group Dynamics at M.I.T. Lewin's teachings evolved from his basic contention that the "life space" of the individual or group under study is the field with which the social scientist must deal. By "life space" he meant all of those facts at a given time which are perceived as significant by the group or individual. The test of significance was a pragmatic one: those elements which produced results for the group or individual were significant. The others were not. Lewin maintained that the "life space," on the one hand, and the group or individual, on the other, are interdependent. The individual and his environment thus constitute an indis-soluble unit. Neither can be understood apart from the other. The same holds true for the group and its environment. But only the properties of the field at a given time are actual determinants. History may perpetuate and modify the environment, but only the factors present at a particular moment have definite effects.

The field theorists would therefore argue that what Jefferson said as the founder of the Democratic party is completely irrelevant in the twentieth century. All that really matters is the complex of ideas and economic, social, and political factors of the present day.

No account of the revolt against political theory as a species of intellectual history would be complete without a discussion of the contributions of the behavioralists. As their name implies, the behavioralists focus their attention not on the organization and legal powers of governments but on the politically oriented behavior of active individuals and groups. Like the members of the analytical school, the behavioralists are deeply concerned with methodology. But their approach is not chiefly deductive. What they seek are concepts or formulas which will serve as master-keys to unlock the secrets of political activity. They are empiricists, with a passion for factual research. But they recognize the need for principles or formulas to orient and give meaning to their observations. Though they sometimes extol the virtues of what they call systematic theory, they are not interested in formulations or patterns of any such scope as would be necessary to integrate or unify the whole subject of political science. With their essentially positivist approach, they could scarcely give more than scant recognition to such principles. They believe there is too much mythology in political science already, and, in their view, general theory designed as a conceptual framework would increase the amount.

The great pioneer and inspirer of behavioral political theory was Arthur F. Bentley. Though long neglected and misunderstood, he is now frequently acclaimed as one of the really seminal thinkers of the twentieth century. Bentley was born in 1870, in Freeport, Illinois. After attending York College for one year and the University of Denver for part of another, he left college on account of ill health and worked for a period in his father's bank. In 1890 he entered Johns Hopkins University to study economics. He completed the three-year curriculum in two years and ranked fourth in the graduating class. Soon afterward he went to Germany to pursue graduate study in the universities of Berlin and Freiburg. But the failure of his father's bank forced him to return to the United States, and he took his Ph.D. at Johns Hopkins in 1895. Bentley had only a limited career in the academic profession. After a year as a lecturer at the University of Chicago he became a journalist. He worked as a reporter and later as an editorial writer for Chicago newspapers. Fortunately, these jobs left him much time to visit libraries and to ponder the wealth of political material that came to his attention. By taking advantage of such opportunities, he was able to produce his most celebrated work, *The Process of Government*, in 1908. Virtually ignored for twenty years, it was rediscovered in the 1930's and has since been regarded as a classic. In 1941 Bentley was invited to Columbia University to become Visiting Professor of Philosophy. Except for the brief period in this position, he spent most of the remainder of his mature years as a prosperous fruit-grower in Indiana. In 1924, however, he took an active part in the La Follette Progressive movement. He was made a member of the National Progressive Committee and was placed in charge of the campaign in Indiana. He died in 1957.[11]

Although Arthur F. Bentley's ideas have profound significance for political theory, he was far from a political philosopher in the traditional meaning of that term. He had nothing but contempt for generalities and what he called "mind-stuff" as motivators of human action. "The mind as actor," he said, "is still the old self-action soul with its immortality stripped off. . . . *Mind, faculty, I.Q.*, or what not as an actor in charge of behavior is a charlatan, and *brain* as a substitute for such *Mind* is worse. Such words insert a name in place of a problem." [12] Bentley was almost as much of a positivist as was Auguste Comte or Pareto. He tended to think of general ideas as nothing more than rationalizations or reflections of group-interests. This conception can be illustrated by his attitudes toward the state and toward sovereignty. He ridiculed the notion of the state as a metaphysical entity standing behind the government. All that exists is the government itself, and the government consists of the

---

[11] The biographical data in this paragraph are taken mostly from Sidney Ratner, "A. F. Bentley's Inquiries into the Behavioural Sciences," *British Journal of Sociology*, VIII (1957).

[12] *Knowing and the Known*. Boston, Beacon Press, 1949, pp. 131–32.

activities of the groups and interests expressed within it. The term "sovereignty" is equally meaningless. It may serve some purpose as a weapon of argument in defense of an existing government or as a legal rationalization of policies and procedures, "but as soon as it gets out of the pages of the law-book or the political pamphlet, it is a piteous threadbare joke." [13]

Two elements may be said to constitute the essential ingredients of Bentley's political theory. The first was his reduction of the process of government to the pressures, conflicts, rivalries, and successes of groups and interests. A group he defined as a "way of action in which many men participate." An interest he conceived as a group activity viewed from the standpoint of its objective. Since the two were but different ways of looking at the same thing, he often combined them and spoke of group-interests. In one of his later works he supplanted them entirely with the term "cross-sections." [14] He conceived of all government as a phenomenon of group-interests forming, combining, pressing one another, pushing, competing, and working out adjustments to mediate their conflicts. Expressed in another way, he thought of all government as a process of logrolling and practical compromise. There never was a time, he pointed out, in the history of the American Congress when legislation was enacted in any other way. The record was replete with "deals" and bargains, such as the arrangement for locating the Federal capital on the Potomac by trading votes with the Hamiltonian forces on the assumption of the state debts. Tariff legislation and rivers and harbors appropriations he cited as other examples of plain barter. To condemn such methods, he thought, was to fly in the face of reality. It was to assume the existence of some "pure public spirit" which would enable legislators to pass judgment "in Jovian calm on that which is best 'for the whole people.'" [15] Such assumptions Bentley regarded as pure fictions. He viewed the judicial functions in exactly the same way as he did the legislative. All are reflections of group-interests. Cut through the

[13] *The Process of Government*. Evanston, Illinois, The Principia Press, 1953, p. 264.
[14] *Relativity in Man and Society*. New York, Putnam, 1926.
[15] *The Process of Government*, p. 370.

fine-spun dialectic of a Supreme Court justice, he said, and you will find the actual groups of men underlying and producing the decisions. "Law is activity just as government is. It is a group process, just as government is. It is a forming, a systematization, a struggle, an adaptation of group interests, just as government is." [16]

As suggested above, the second major element in Bentley's political theory was his conception of government as *activity*. It was this conception which made him the real founder of the behavioralist school of political theory. Government, he argued, does not consist of officeholders or of a constitutional structure of chief magistrate, courts, and parliament; instead, it is a vast network of activities. And it is the range and character of these activities which determine the government's power. No dictator, for example, has absolute power by virtue of his office or of his dominant personality. But it is always the dictator plus the army, or the dictator plus the landholding class or some other class that actually rules. The dictator emerges merely as a class leader; it is the class itself that really dominates. One might think of this argument as virtually the equivalent of the Marxist theory of class rule. Bentley, however, criticized Marx for making his class structure too rigid, for setting up classes as abstractions, and for a crude overemphasis on economic motivation. Bentley would have repudiated the Marxist contention that enthroning the working class in place of the owning class will bring a new dawn of equality and freedom. He seemed to believe that a considerable degree of despotism is inevitable under any system of class supremacy and regardless of the form of the government. The government of Great Britain, he wrote, is no less despotic now than it was in the time of the Tudors. The British Cabinet can do things today which the Tudor monarchs would not have dreamed of doing. What really counts, according to Bentley, is the relationship of forces among the contending group-interests represented in the government. When this relationship is balanced and fairly adjusted in the legislature, the executive sinks in prominence. When the adjustment is not perfected in the legislature, which often happens in the American Congress,

[16] *Ibid.*, p. 272.

"then the executive arises in strength to do the work." [17]

When Bentley wrote about behavior or activity, he was not discussing the bodily responses of individuals, after the manner of a behaviorist psychologist. He was not interested in man as an isolated being or even in the interrelations of independent individuals. His method of inquiry arose in opposition to individualist and mechanist explanations of human psychology. He centered his attention upon men in their collective activities, upon cross-sections of humanity, which he regarded as the real stuff of government. He classified activities as either "palpable" or "potential." By *palpable* he meant actual, manifest, or executed activities. By *potential* he meant latent or possible activities, such as the appearance in 1932–1933 of farmers with loaded guns at auctions for the sale of foreclosed mortgages. Although Bentley stressed deeds rather than thoughts or ideas, he was not a crude empiricist ignoring everything but the tangible and material. He recognized that ideas, also, are a part of behavior. True, they are nothing but reflections of group-interests, but no man can be separated from his environment; and the individual apart from his group is a political cipher. Finally, it should be emphasized that Bentley's conception of behavior was "transactional." Others, from Madison to Charles A. Beard, had focused attention on factions, interests, and classes as the catalytic agents in legislation and policy. It was Bentley's achievement to show that the governmental process is made up primarily of "transactions," that is, of barter, bargains, compromises, and adjustments among competing and sometimes overlapping group-interests.

Since the Bentleyan revival of the 1930's, the behavioral approach to political science has flourished apace. A score of thinkers and analysts have described government as a form of activity and the governing process as a resultant of rival pressures and competing interests. Karl W. Deutsch of Yale has related the conflict of interests to international tension and rivalry. E. E. Schattschneider of Wesleyan, V. O. Key of Harvard, and several of their confreres have made studies of political parties as pressure groups and as agents and brokers for competing interests in a struggle for rewards and privileges. Dozens

[17] *Ibid.*, p. 359.

of others have analyzed voting behavior with special attention to the role of associations, political, social, and economic. Stephen K. Bailey of Syracuse has described the making of a law by Congress as a process of jockeying, bargaining, logrolling, and balancing competing pressures from both inside and outside the government. John Chamberlain, in *The American Stakes*, and E. Pendleton Herring, in *The Politics of Democracy*, portray the entire political system as a process of adjusting interrelations. They scoff at the idea that political man can be expected to eschew self-interest and dedicate himself to the pursuit of some will-o'-the-wisp of public welfare or the good of the nation. Chamberlain insists that an absolute prerequisite to the survival of political freedom is unhampered opportunity of interest-groups to compete with one another for the privileges and benefactions at the disposal of government. "Democracy is what results," he writes, "when you have a state of tension in society that permits no one group to dare bid for the total power." [18]

How many recent behavioralists have been directly influenced by Bentley is a problematical issue. Practically all of them agree with him in declining to characterize pressure politics as wicked or immoral. Like him, they consider it a basic reality of modern government, and they regard its results as no more sinister than James Madison's alleged "mischiefs of faction." Few of them, however, have gone to Bentley's extreme of denying the political significance of the individual, and of making group activities the entire substance of politics. For Professor Herring, government is a "process of adjusting the interrelations of individuals, institutions, ideals, and interests." [19] Chamberlain also recognizes the importance of the individual, especially if he is an astute political leader, in balancing and adjusting the clamoring interests. Finally, none of our contemporary behavioralists appears to share Bentley's cynicism in regard to democracy. No one can prove that the Hoosier philosopher was anti-democratic, [20] but his rejection of political ideals as mere rationalizations and his assumption that

[18] *The American Stakes*. New York, Carrick and Evans, 1940, pp. 31–32.
[19] *The Politics of Democracy*. New York, Norton, 1940, p. 27.
[20] R. M. MacIver thinks that he was at least undemocratic. *The Web of Government*, p. 220.

despotism, in one form or another, is a virtual constant in political history seem to indicate that he had little faith in any form of democracy. By contrast, Professor Bailey stresses the vital necessity of "a reasonable political system which will reflect the will of the majority and which will enable the citizens to hold identifiable rulers accountable for policy decisions." [21] Professor Herring admits that, in a world of competing and clamorous interests, the faith of democracy may not prove workable, but he affirms that "it holds the clearest hope for civilization today." [22]

The contemporary behavioralists who may be most accurately described as orthodox followers of Bentley are Bertram M. Gross and David B. Truman. Bertram M. Gross has had wide experience as a staff director and a research consultant to Senatorial committees and to private organizations such as the Public Affairs Institute. From 1946 to 1951 he was executive secretary of the President's Council of Economic Advisers, and in 1952 he was research director of the Democratic National Committee. He agrees with Bentley in almost every particular, stressing the importance of interest-groups and describing their activities as the very essence of government. In common with Bentley, he denies the significance of isolated individuals, contending that any importance they may have "stems from their actual or potential relationship to groups." [23] He seems not, however, to emphasize the bargaining and logrolling elements in the legislative process so heavily as did Bentley. He gave to his book, *The Legislative Struggle*, the subtitle *A Study in Social Combat*. In line with this title, he is more aware than his master of the dangers inherent in the competition of group-interests. He enumerates these as "deadlock, violence, and dictatorship." Though he minimizes the likelihood that any of these dangers will come to pass, he recognizes that all three of them, and especially the first two, are distinct possibilities. Whereas Bentley was content merely to describe and interpret, Gross considers the defects in political systems sufficiently serious to justify at-

[21] *Congress Makes a Law.* New York, Columbia University Press, 1950, p. 239.
[22] *Op. cit.,* p. 35.
[23] *The Legislative Struggle.* New York, McGraw-Hill, 1953, p. 5.

tempts at reform. He remains a good Bentleyan, though, in his insistence that ideas have little chance of success without the support of powerful interests.

A shade less orthodox than Gross is David B. Truman of Columbia University. In his chief work, *The Governmental Process*, he quotes Bentley extensively and admits that the Indiana philosopher's "attempt to fashion a tool" has been "the principal bench mark" for his own thinking.[24] In common with Bentley, he denies the existence of isolated, independent individuals and deplores the tendency to "explain" the policies of the Soviet Union in terms of Stalin, or the New Deal in terms of FDR. Like Bentley also, he rejects the notion of a "public interest" standing apart from and superior to the interests of the various groups composing the nation. He introduces, however, an entirely new element which Bentley scarcely recognized. This is the great mass of unorganized interests, or what Truman calls the "rules of the game." These unorganized interests are really attitudes, or systems of belief, rather than associations or groups. Nevertheless, they are interests, and any serious disturbance of them "will result in organized interaction and the assertion of fairly explicit claims for conformity." [25] The "rules of the game" become a part of the habit patterns of most individuals as a result of early experiences in the family and in the elementary and secondary schools. They embody concepts of justice and fairness similar to those contained in great documents of the national heritage such as the Bill of Rights. Though the "rules of the game" are not always dominant or clearly understood, they are widely enough recognized to exert a restraining influence on organized interest groups and to force them to defer, in considerable measure, to the democratic expectations of the community.

The controversy between those who favor the historical approach to political theory and those who oppose it is not one that can be easily resolved. On the side of the opponents of historicism is the need for more analysis of political theories and

[24] *The Governmental Process.* New York, Knopf, 1951, Preface, ix.
[25] *Ibid.*, p. 512.

the even greater need for accurate methods of testing their validity. Certainly, not all theories are equally valid, but by what methods or standards shall they be measured and tested? That the bench mark should be conformity with some theorem, which in turn is consistent with antecedent theorems, seems questionable. It appears doubtful, also, that much can be gained by the reduction of theories to algebraic equations. Mathematics, after all, is primarily another language, a more convenient and more precise means of communication. The symbols of mathematics usually represent concepts or abstractions; but if the concepts themselves are not equatable, little can be accomplished by reducing them to a formula which may be mathematically sound but factually dubious. Similar questions can be raised regarding the utility of systematic theory as a deductive device for unifying and orienting political science. Nineteenth-century economics was fertilized by a number of such theories. Undoubtedly they had a stimulating and fructifying effect, but most of them have since been discarded, and few people take much stock in the conclusions drawn from them. Perhaps a similar fate would overtake the analogues of such principles in political science.

But the political theorist who is not satisfied merely with historical studies is not necessarily forced to fall back on deduction, mathematical or otherwise. There is a vast array of evidence from psychology and anthropology which has possibilities for political verification that have scarcely been touched. A theorist wishing to test the dogma that force is the foundation of all authority, for example, would find plenty of evidence both for and against its validity in the findings of anthropologists. He would discover that some tribes have managed to operate relatively complex politico-economic systems with little more compulsion than that which derives from habits of obedience and deference to customs. Other societies have considered floggings, mutilations, and executions the indispensable requisites for social order. Despite the work of Harold D. Lasswell, Erich Fromm, Else Frenkel-Brunswik, and others in uncovering the psychological springs of human behavior, little use has been made of psychological data in validating political theory. A good example with which to work would be the *anomie* theory originated by Émile Durkheim and developed by Sebastian de-Grazia. According to this theory, the chief curse of modern times is the loss of political and moral beliefs. With no moorings to cling to, the individual succumbs to a malaise of uneasiness, futility, and despondency. In its acute form this malaise leads to suicide, or to such a desperate longing for solidarity as to result in complete subservience to a dictator. A theory with such enormous psychological implications might well be expected to require the most thorough psychological corroboration.

Notwithstanding the value of data from other sources, evidence from history still has its place in political theory. And history includes the history of ideas. There is as little that is new under the sun of political theory as under any other intellectual sun. For this reason, appraisal of a contemporary political theory may be facilitated by study of the observations of earlier writers on similar subjects. No modern expounder of democratic theory would be wasting his time if he engaged in a comparative study of the views of Rousseau and Locke. Nor would any modern exponent of *Realpolitik* suffer from a perusal of Machiavelli. Political theory is a complicated subject, with complex origins and manifold meanings. To demand that it be fitted to a Procrustean bed of unitary explanation seems less than logical.

ADDITIONAL READINGS

Bentley, Arthur F. *Behavior, Knowledge, Fact.* Bloomington, Ind., Principia Press, 1935.

———. *Relativity in Man and Society.* New York, Putnam, 1926.

Brecht, Arnold. *Political Theory.* Princeton, Princeton University Press, 1959.

DeGrazia, Sebastian. *The Political Community.* Chicago, University of Chicago Press, 1948.

Lewin, Kurt. *Field Theory in Social Science.* New York, Harper, 1951.

Shubik, Martin. *Readings in Game Theory and Political Behavior.* Garden City, Doubleday, 1954.

Von Neumann, John, and Morganstern, Oskar. *Theory of Games and Economic Behavior*. Princeton, Princeton University Press, 1947.

Wiener, Norbert. *Cybernetics*. New York, John Wiley, 1948.

——. *The Human Use of Human Beings*. Boston, Houghton Mifflin, 1950.

Index